CORPORATE ISSUERS, EQUITY VALUATION

CFA® Program Curriculum
2023 • LEVEL 2 • VOLUME 3

WILEY

ISBN 978-1-953337-07-8 (paper)
ISBN 978-1-953337-31-3 (ebook)

2022

Please visit our website at
www.WileyGlobalFinance.com.

CONTENTS

The Financial Statement Modeling learning module should appear in the Financial Statement Analysis topic area, not in the Corporate Issuers topic area. We regret the error in its placement in the print curriculum. It has been placed correctly in the candidate learning ecosystem online.

                           ◙ indicates an optional segment

◙ indicates an optional segment

Equity Valuation

ⓞ indicates an optional segment

How to Use the CFA Program Curriculum

The CFA® Program exams measure your mastery of the core knowledge, skills, and abilities required to succeed as an investment professional. These core competencies are the basis for the Candidate Body of Knowledge (CBOK™). The CBOK consists of four components:

- A broad outline that lists the major CFA Program topic areas (www. cfainstitute.org/programs/cfa/curriculum/cbok)
- Topic area weights that indicate the relative exam weightings of the top-level topic areas (www.cfainstitute.org/programs/cfa/curriculum)
- Learning outcome statements (LOS) that advise candidates about the specific knowledge, skills, and abilities they should acquire from curriculum content covering a topic area: LOS are provided in candidate study sessions and at the beginning of each block of related content and the specific lesson that covers them. We encourage you to review the information about the LOS on our website (www.cfainstitute.org/programs/cfa/curriculum/study-sessions), including the descriptions of LOS "command words" on the candidate resources page at www.cfainstitute.org.
- The CFA Program curriculum that candidates receive upon exam registration

Therefore, the key to your success on the CFA exams is studying and understanding the CBOK. You can learn more about the CBOK on our website: www.cfainstitute.org/programs/cfa/curriculum/cbok.

The entire curriculum, including the practice questions, is the basis for all exam questions and is selected or developed specifically to teach the knowledge, skills, and abilities reflected in the CBOK.

ERRATA

The curriculum development process is rigorous and includes multiple rounds of reviews by content experts. Despite our efforts to produce a curriculum that is free of errors, there are instances where we must make corrections. Curriculum errata are periodically updated and posted by exam level and test date online on the Curriculum Errata webpage (www.cfainstitute.org/en/programs/submit-errata). If you believe you have found an error in the curriculum, you can submit your concerns through our curriculum errata reporting process found at the bottom of the Curriculum Errata webpage.

DESIGNING YOUR PERSONAL STUDY PROGRAM

An orderly, systematic approach to exam preparation is critical. You should dedicate a consistent block of time every week to reading and studying. Review the LOS both before and after you study curriculum content to ensure that you have mastered the applicable content and can demonstrate the knowledge, skills, and abilities described by the LOS and the assigned reading. Use the LOS self-check to track your progress and highlight areas of weakness for later review.

Successful candidates report an average of more than 300 hours preparing for each exam. Your preparation time will vary based on your prior education and experience, and you will likely spend more time on some study sessions than on others.

CFA INSTITUTE LEARNING ECOSYSTEM (LES)

Your exam registration fee includes access to the CFA Program Learning Ecosystem (LES). This digital learning platform provides access, even offline, to all of the curriculum content and practice questions and is organized as a series of short online lessons with associated practice questions. This tool is your one-stop location for all study materials, including practice questions and mock exams, and the primary method by which CFA Institute delivers your curriculum experience. The LES offers candidates additional practice questions to test their knowledge, and some questions in the LES provide a unique interactive experience.

FEEDBACK

Please send any comments or feedback to info@cfainstitute.org, and we will review your suggestions carefully.

Corporate Issuers

LEARNING MODULE

1

Financial Statement Modeling

by Matthew L. Coffina, CFA, Anthony M. Fiore, CFA, and Antonius J. van Ooijen, MSc, CFA.

Matthew L. Coffina, CFA, is at Morningstar Investment Management LLC (USA). Anthony M. Fiore, CFA, is at Silvercrest Asset Management (USA). Antonius J. van Ooijen, MSc, CFA, is at APG Asset Management (Netherlands).

LEARNING OUTCOMES

Mastery	The candidate should be able to:
☐	compare top-down, bottom-up, and hybrid approaches for developing inputs to equity valuation models
☐	compare "growth relative to GDP growth" and "market growth and market share" approaches to forecasting revenue
☐	evaluate whether economies of scale are present in an industry by analyzing operating margins and sales levels
☐	demonstrate methods to forecast cost of goods sold and operating expenses
☐	demonstrate methods to forecast non-operating items, financing costs, and income taxes
☐	describe approaches to balance sheet modeling
☐	demonstrate the development of a sales-based pro forma company model
☐	explain how behavioral factors affect analyst forecasts and recommend remedial actions for analyst biases
☐	explain how competitive factors affect prices and costs
☐	evaluate the competitive position of a company based on a Porter's five forces analysis
☐	explain how to forecast industry and company sales and costs when they are subject to price inflation or deflation
☐	evaluate the effects of technological developments on demand, selling prices, costs, and margins
☐	explain considerations in the choice of an explicit forecast horizon
☐	explain an analyst's choices in developing projections beyond the short-term forecast horizon

The Financial Statement Modeling learning module should appear in the Financial Statement Analysis topic area, not in the Corporate Issuers topic area. We regret the error in its placement in the print curriculum. It has been placed correctly in the candidate learning ecosystem online.

1   INTRODUCTION

- ☐   compare top-down, bottom-up, and hybrid approaches for developing inputs to equity valuation models
- ☐   compare "growth relative to GDP growth" and "market growth and market share" approaches to forecasting revenue

Financial statement modeling is a key step in the process of valuing companies and the securities they have issued. We focus on how analysts use industry information and corporate disclosures to forecast a company's future financial results.

An effective financial statement model must be based on a thorough understanding of a company's business, management, strategy, external environment, and historical results. Thus, an analyst begins with a review of the company and its environment—its industry, key products, strategic position, management, competitors, suppliers, and customers. Using this information, an analyst identifies key revenue and cost drivers and assesses the likely impact of relevant trends, such as economic conditions and technological developments. An analyst's understanding of the fundamental drivers of the business and assessment of future events provide the basis for forecast model inputs. In other words, financial statement modeling is not merely a quantitative or accounting exercise, it is the quantitative expression of an analyst's expectations for a company and its competitive environment.

We begin our discussion with an overview of developing a revenue forecast. We then describe the general approach to forecasting each of the financial statements and demonstrate the construction of a financial statement model, including forecasted revenue, income statements, balance sheets, and statements of cash flows. Then, we describe five key behavioral biases that influence the modeling process and strategies to mitigate them. We then turn to several important topics on the effects of micro- and macroeconomic conditions on financial statement models: the impact of competitive factors on prices and costs, the effects of inflation and deflation, technological developments, and long-term forecasting considerations. The reading concludes with a summary.

Most of the examples and exhibits used throughout the reading can be downloaded as a Microsoft Excel workbook. Each worksheet in the workbook is labeled with the corresponding example or exhibit number in the text.

Financial Statement Modeling: An Overview

Financial statement modeling generally begins with the income statement. The income statement is a logical starting point because most companies derive most of their value from future cash flow generation, determined primarily by the amount of future operating income generated by the business. Exceptions include banks and insurance companies, for which the value of existing assets and liabilities on the balance sheet might be more relevant to the companies' overall value than projected future income. The income statement also provides a useful starting point for modeling a company's balance sheet and cash flow statement.

Income Statement Modeling: Revenue

Companies receive revenue from multiple sources and can be analyzed by geographical source, business segment, or product line. In a geographic analysis, the analyst places a company's revenue into various geographic groupings, which might or might not be the same as the groupings provided by management in company disclosures. These groupings can be narrowly defined, such as by individual countries, or more broadly defined, such as by region of the world. A geographic analysis can be particularly useful for companies operating in multiple countries with different underlying growth rates or competitive dynamics. For example, a company's sales might be experiencing relatively slow growth in one region of the world and relatively fast growth in other regions. By examining each region of the world separately, analysts can enhance their understanding of overall growth.

Segment disclosures in companies' financial reports are often a rich source of information. Both International Financial Reporting Standards (IFRS) and US GAAP require issuers to disclose financial information for any operating segment whose revenue, operating income, or assets account for 10% or more of consolidated revenue, operating income, or assets. Disclosures, typically in the notes to financial statements, include how segments are defined; segment revenues, expenses, assets, and liabilities; and a reconciliation of segment results to consolidated results. In addition to the interim and annual financial reports issued by the company, important information can often be found in other company disclosures, such as press releases, presentations, and conference calls.

In a breakdown by segment, the analyst classifies a company's revenue into various business segments. Many companies operate in more than one industry or market niche with widely differing economics. Although information is often available for the different business segments, analysts should make an independent judgment about whether management's segmentation is relevant and material. Sometimes analysts can regroup reported information in a manner that helps make important points.

Finally, a product line analysis provides the most granular level of detail. A product line analysis is most relevant for a company with a manageably small number of products that behave differently but when combined, account for most of the company's sales.

Example 1 introduces the first of many examples and exhibits that we use. Please note that many numbers have been rounded; so, in replicating results based on the numbers given in the text and exhibits, small apparent discrepancies could reflect the rounding error.

EXAMPLE 1

Analysis of Revenue (1)

Novo Nordisk is a Denmark-based listed biopharmaceutical company. The company provides detailed disclosure of revenue along geographic, business segment, and product lines. All figures are in millions of Danish krone (DKK).

In its 2020 annual report, Novo Nordisk provided the following geographic breakdown of sales for the previous three years. The company also reported revenue in two business segments: Diabetes and Obesity Care and Biopharmaceuticals. Within each segment, disclosure on several individual product lines was also provided. Exhibit 1 and Exhibit 2 are in the Example1 sheet in the downloadable Microsoft Excel workbook.

Exhibit 1: Novo Nordisk's Sales by Geographic Region (DKK millions)

	2020	2019	2018
United States	57,824	57,846	54,488
Other North America	3,293	2,611	2,420
EMEA (Europe, Middle East, Africa)	34,297	32,208	29,226
China	14,084	12,844	11,285
Rest of world	17,448	16,512	14,412
Total net sales	126,946	122,021	111,831

Exhibit 2: Novo Nordisk's Sales by Segment and Product Line (DKK millions)

	2020	2019	2018
Modern insulins	47,677	50,657	50,391
Human insulin	8,873	9,036	9,265
Total insulin	56,550	59,693	59,656
GLP-1 analogs	41,831	33,221	26,129
Other Diabetes Care	4,031	4,247	4,250
Obesity Care	5,608	5,679	3,869
Total Diabetes and Obesity Care	108,020	102,840	93,904
Biopharmaceuticals	18,926	19,181	17,927
Total net sales	126,946	122,021	111,831

1. Modern insulins provide advantages over the more traditional human insulin, such as having a faster or longer-lasting effect on blood sugar. GLP-1 analogs are even newer products that help the human body produce more insulin. Compare Novo Nordisk's recent sales growth rate of its GLP-1 analogs with those of its modern insulins and human insulin products.

Solution

The growth rate of GLP-1 analogs sales was significantly higher than that for modern insulins and human insulin in 2020 and 2019. GLP-1 analogs sales grew 26% and 27% in 2020 and 2019, while modern insulins sales decreased by 6% in 2020 and grew 1% in 2019, and human insulin sales decreased by 2% in both 2020 and 2019.

The full calculations to support this solution are in the Example1 sheet in the downloadable Microsoft Excel workbook.

2. How did Novo Nordisk's sales breakdown by business segment (Diabetes and Obesity Care and Biopharmaceuticals) change from 2018 to 2020?

Solution

In the past two years, Novo Nordisk's sales breakdown by business segment changed slightly: Diabetes and Obesity Care increased from 84% to 85% of total net sales while Biopharmaceuticals decreased from 16% to 15% of total net sales.

> The full calculations to support this solution are in the Example1 sheet in the downloadable Microsoft Excel workbook.

Once the analyst understands the important components of a company's revenue, they must decide whether to use a top-down, bottom-up, or hybrid approach to projecting future revenue. A **top-down approach** usually begins at the level of the overall economy. Forecasts can then be made at lower levels, such as sector, industry, and market for a specific product, to arrive at a revenue projection for the individual company. In contrast, a **bottom-up approach** begins at the level of the individual company or a unit within the company, such as individual product lines, locations, or business segments. Analysts then aggregate their projections for the individual products or segments to arrive at a forecast of total revenue for the company. Moreover, analysts also aggregate their revenue projections for individual companies to develop forecasts for a product market, industry, or the overall economy. A **hybrid approach** combines elements of both top-down and bottom-up analysis and can be useful for uncovering implicit assumptions or errors that could arise from using a single approach.

Top-Down Approaches to Modeling Revenue

Two common top-down approaches to modeling revenue are "growth relative to GDP growth" and "market growth and market share."

Growth relative to GDP growth approach: The analyst first forecasts the growth rate of nominal GDP. The analyst then considers how the growth rate of the specific company being examined will compare with nominal GDP growth. The analyst can use a forecast for real GDP growth to project volumes and a forecast for inflation to project prices. Analysts often think in terms of percentage point premiums or discounts derived from a company's position in the industrial life cycle (e.g., embryonic, growth, shakeout, mature, or decline) or business cycle sensitivity. Thus, an analyst's conclusion might be that a health care company's revenue will grow at a rate of 200 bps above the nominal GDP growth rate. The forecast could also be in relative terms. Thus, if GDP is forecast to grow at 4% and the company's revenue is forecast to grow at a 50% faster rate, the forecast percent change in revenue would be 4% × (1 + 0.50) = 6.0%, or 200 bps higher in absolute terms.

Market growth and market share approach: The analyst first forecasts growth in a particular market. They then consider the company's current market share and how that share is likely to change over time. For example, if a company is expected to maintain an 8% market share of a given product market and the product market is forecast to grow from CNY144 billion to CNY154 billion in annual revenue, the forecast growth in company revenue is from a level of 8% × CNY144 billion = CNY11.5 billion to a level of 8% × CNY154 billion = CNY12.3 billion (considering this product market alone). If the product market revenue has a predictable relationship with GDP, regression analysis might be used to estimate the relationship.

Bottom-Up Approaches to Modeling Revenue

Examples of bottom-up approaches to modeling revenue include the following:

- *Time series*: forecasts based on historical growth rates or time-series analysis.
- *Returns-based measure*: forecasts based on balance sheet accounts. For example, interest revenue for a bank can be calculated as loans multiplied by the average interest rate.
- *Capacity-based measure:* forecasts, for example, in retailing, based on same-store sales growth (for stores that have been open for at least 12 months) and sales related to new stores.

Time-series forecasts are among the simplest. For example, analysts might fit a trend line to historical data and then project sales over the desired time frame (e.g., using Excel's TREND formula). In such a case, analysts would be projecting historical growth rates to continue, but they might also use different assumptions—for example, they might project growth to decline linearly from current rates to some long-run rate. Note that time-series methods can also be used as tools in executing a top-down analysis, such as projecting GDP growth in a growth relative to GDP growth approach.

Hybrid Approaches to Modeling Revenue

Hybrid approaches combine elements of both top-down and bottom-up analysis, and in practice, they are the most common approaches. For example, the analyst could use a market growth and market share approach to model individual product lines or business segments. Then, the analyst can aggregate the individual projections to arrive at a forecast for the overall company because the sum of forecast segment revenue equals the segment market size multiplied by the market share for all segments.

In a volume and price approach, the analyst makes separate projections for volumes (e.g., the number of products sold or the number of customers served) and average selling price. Depending on how these elements are forecast, this approach can be classified as top-down, bottom-up, or hybrid.

EXAMPLE 2

Analysis of Revenue (2)

Use the provided data as well as the data in Example 1 on Novo Nordisk to answer the following questions:

Xiaoping Wu is an equity analyst covering European pharmaceutical companies for his clients in China. Wu projects that global nominal GDP will grow 3% annually over the long run, based on 2% real growth and 1% inflation. The prevalence of diabetes is increasing globally because of increasingly unhealthy diets and sedentary lifestyles. As a result, Wu believes global sales of diabetes drugs will grow 100 bps faster than nominal GDP over the long run. Wu believes the revenue growth rate of Novo Nordisk's Diabetes and Obesity Care segment will decelerate linearly over four years to match the projected long-run growth rate of the diabetes drug market.

1. Is Wu using a top-down, bottom-up, or hybrid approach to modeling Novo Nordisk's revenue?

   Solution

   Wu's long-run revenue projections are based on Novo Nordisk's growth relative to nominal GDP growth, which is a top-down approach. However, his estimated growth rate is applied to only one of Novo Nordisk's segments (Diabetes and Obesity Care), indicating a hybrid approach. Wu's four-year forecasts are also based in part on the historical growth rate of the Diabetes and Obesity Care segment, which is a bottom-up approach. Wu is thus using a hybrid approach.

2. Based on Wu's projections for revenue growth, calculate the estimated revenue growth rate for the Diabetes and Obesity Care segment in 2021. Assume no impact from exchange rate changes.

   Solution

   The data in Example 1 indicate that Novo Nordisk's Diabetes and Obesity Care segment grew by 5% in 2020. Wu projects the long-run growth rate to be in line with the diabetes drug market growth at 4% (100 bps faster than GDP growth of 3%). The difference between the 2020 growth rate and the projected long-run growth rate is 1% (= 5% – 4%), and Wu expects the modest deceleration in growth to occur linearly over four years, implying a reduction of 25 bps per year in the growth rate. The estimated growth rates by year are thus

2021 = 4.75%

2022 = 4.5%

2023 = 4.25%

2024 = 4%

Thereafter, 4%
The estimated revenue growth rate for 2021 is 4.75%.

Helga Hansen is a buy-side analyst in Denmark. In 2021, Hansen was investigating Rybelsus, a Novo Nordisk product launched in 2019, in a class of diabetes drugs called GLP-1 analogs. As of 2021, Rybelsus is one of several GLP-1 analogs on the market, competing with Novo Nordisk's own Victoza and Ozempic, Eli Lilly's Trulicity, and exenatide (brands Byetta and Bydureon) by AstraZeneca. Rybelsus is the same drug compound as Ozempic but is a once-daily pill, unlike Ozempic and all other GLP-1 analogs, which are injectable drugs.

Eli Lilly and AstraZeneca reported global sales of their products in US dollars (USD). Hansen converted the companies' reported figures to Danish krone using annual average USD/DKK exchange rates to compile Exhibit 3, which shows annual sales of the GLP-1 analogs measured in millions of DKK. Exhibit 3 is in the Example2 sheet in the downloadable Microsoft Excel workbook.

Exhibit 3: GLP-1 Analog Sales, Annual (DKK millions)

Product	Company	2020	2019	2018
Victoza	Novo Nordisk	18,747	21,934	24,333
Ozempic	Novo Nordisk	21,211	11,237	1,796
Rybelsus	Novo Nordisk	1,873	50	0
Trulicity	Eli Lilly	33,135	27,533	20,215
Byetta and Bydureon	AstraZeneca	3,374	4,396	4,486

1. What was the growth rate in total GLP-1 analog sales in 2020?

   Solution

   Total GLP-1 analog sales in 2020 and 2019 were DKK78,340 million and DKK65,150 million, respectively. The growth rate of total GLP-1 analog sales in 2020 (78,340 – 65,150/65,150) was 20%.
   The full calculations to support this solution are in the Example2 sheet in the downloadable Microsoft Excel workbook.

2. What percentage of GLP-1 analog sales growth in 2020 can be attributed to Rybelsus?

Solution

Total GLP-1 analog sales increased by DKK13,190 million in 2020. Rybelsus's sales increased by DKK1,823 million, which implies that Rybelsus's growth accounted for (1,823/13,190) ≈ 14% of GLP-1 analog sales growth. The full calculations to support this solution are in the Example2 sheet in the downloadable Microsoft Excel workbook.

3. Hansen previously projected that the growth rate of the GLP-1 analog market would slow to 18% in 2020. She also expected Trulicity market share to fall by 5 percentage points. What was Hansen's estimate of 2020 Trulicity sales? How close was she to the actual result?

Solution

Based on 2019 sales of DKK65,150 million and a projected growth rate of 18%, Hansen projected the total GLP-1 analog sales to be DKK76,877 million in 2020. Trulicity's market share in 2019 was ~42%, which Hansen projected to fall by 5 percentage points, resulting in a ~37% market share in 2020. Hansen thus projected 2020 Trulicity sales to be DKK28,645 million. Actual Trulicity sales in 2020 were DKK33,135 million, so Hansen's estimate was too low by DKK4,490 million or 14%.
The full calculations to support this solution are in the Example2 sheet in the downloadable Microsoft Excel workbook.

4. Is Hansen's approach to modeling sales best described as bottom-up, top-down, or hybrid?

Solution

Hansen bases her estimates on market growth and market share, which would normally imply a top-down approach. The analysis, however, is applied to an individual product line, implying a bottom-up approach. Therefore, Hansen is using a hybrid approach.

2 INCOME STATEMENT MODELING: OPERATING COSTS

☐ evaluate whether economies of scale are present in an industry by analyzing operating margins and sales levels

Disclosure about operating costs is frequently less detailed than disclosure about revenue. If relevant information is available, analysts might consider matching the cost analysis to the revenue analysis. For example, they might model costs separately for different geographic regions, business segments, or product lines. More frequently, analysts will be forced to consider costs at a more aggregated level than the level used to analyze revenue. Analysts should keep in mind their revenue analysis when deriving cost assumptions. For instance, if sales of a relatively low-margin product are expected to grow faster than those of a relatively high-margin product, analysts should project some level of overall margin deterioration, even if they are not certain about the precise margins earned on each product.

Once again, analysts can take a top-down, bottom-up, or hybrid view of costs. In a top-down approach, analysts might consider such factors as the overall level of inflation or industry-specific costs before making assumptions about the individual company. In contrast, in a bottom-up approach analysts would start at the company level, considering such factors as segment-level margins, historical cost growth rates, historical margin levels, or the costs of delivering specific products. A hybrid approach would incorporate both top-down and bottom-up elements.

When estimating costs, analysts should pay particular attention to fixed costs. Variable costs are directly linked to revenue, and they might be best modeled as a percentage of revenue or as projected unit volume multiplied by unit variable costs.

By contrast, fixed costs are not directly related to revenue; rather, they are related to investment in property, plant, and equipment (PP&E) and to total capacity. Practically, fixed costs might be assumed to grow at their own rate, based on an analysis of future PP&E and capacity growth. Analysts should determine whether, at its current level of output, the subject company has **economies of scale**, a situation in which average costs per unit of a good or service produced fall as volume rises. Gross and operating margins tend to be positively correlated with sales levels in an industry that enjoys economies of scale. Factors that can lead to economies of scale include high fixed costs, higher levels of production, greater bargaining power with suppliers, and lower per unit advertising expenses.

Analysts must also be aware of any uncertainty surrounding estimates of costs. For example, banks and insurance companies create reserves against estimated future losses, while companies with large pension plans have long-duration liabilities, the true costs of which might not be known for many years. A review of disclosures about reserving practices related to future obligations and pensions can be helpful in assessing whether cost estimates are reasonable. But most of the time, the external analyst has difficulty anticipating future revisions to cost estimates. Other aspects affecting the uncertainty of cost estimates include competitive factors and technological developments. This impact will be discussed in later sections.

— Gross margins that increase with sales levels provide evidence of economies of scale, assuming that higher levels of sales reflect increased unit sales.

Gross margin more directly reflects the cost of sales than does profit margin.

EXAMPLE 3

Approaches to Modeling Operating Costs

CVS Health Corporation ("CVS"), Walgreens Boots Alliance Inc. ("Walgreens"), and Rite Aid Corporation ("Rite Aid") operate retail drugstores in the United States. There is reason to believe that economies of scale exist in the drugstore business. For example, larger drugstore companies might have the ability to spread fixed costs such as payroll and information technology (IT) across a greater amount of revenue, have greater bargaining leverage with distributors over the cost of pharmaceuticals, and negotiate better payment rates from health insurer customers than smaller drugstore companies. Some financial data from the US retail drugstore segment of CVS, Walgreens, and Rite Aid from fiscal year 2020 are presented in Exhibit 4.

Exhibit 4: 2020 Financial Results for CVS, Walgreens, and Rite Aid (US Retail Drugstore Segments)

FY2020, $ millions	CVS	Walgreens	Rite Aid
Revenues	91,198	107,701	16,365
Cost of goods sold	67,284	85,490	12,109
Selling, general, and administrative expenses	17,768	18,112	4,299

FY2020, $ millions	CVS	Walgreens	Rite Aid
Operating income	6,146	4,099	−44
Same-store sales growth	5.60%	2.80%	3.50%
Number of stores	10,040	9,028	2,510

Customer service could be one driver of revenue for the retail drug business. Retail analysts commonly use a combination of qualitative and quantitative evidence to assess customer service. Qualitative evidence might come from personal store visits or customer surveys. Quantitative evidence might be based on such metrics as selling, general, and administrative (SG&A) expenses per store. Too little spending on SG&A might indicate that stores are under-resourced. Relatedly, same-store sales growth could be an indicator of customer satisfaction. Exhibit 5 shows annual same-store sales growth rates for the three companies from 2011 to 2020.

Exhibit 5: Annual Same-Store Sales Growth Rates: CVS, Walgreens, and Rite Aid

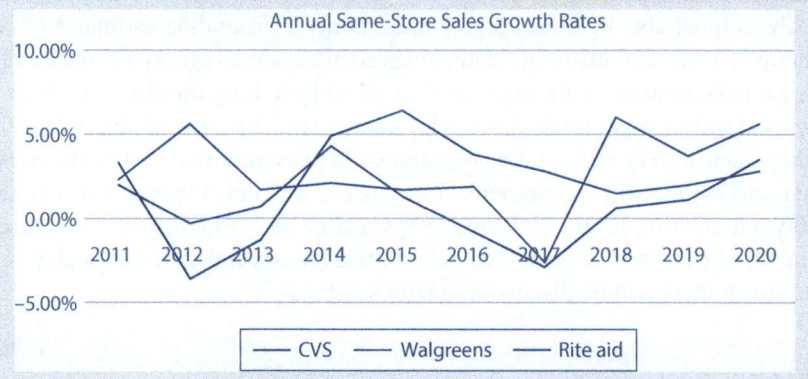

Use the data given to answer the following questions. Exhibits 4 and 5 are in the Example3 sheet in the downloadable Microsoft Excel workbook.

1. Based on the 2020 operating margins, is there evidence suggesting that economies of scale exist in the retail drugstore business? If so, are economies of scale realized in cost of goods sold or SG&A expenses?

   Solution

   Based on operating margins, economies of scale may be present, but whether they are is unclear. CVS and Walgreens are more than five times the size of Rite Aid by annual revenues and reported operating margins of 7% and 4%, respectively, versus less than 0% for Rite Aid. On the other hand, Walgreens is 18% larger by revenues than CVS yet has a significantly lower operating margin (4% versus 7%). Further research is required to uncover whether, for example, Walgreens and CVS have significant differences in prices, the mix of products sold, and so on.

   If anywhere, economies of scale are evident in SG&A expenses. Both CVS and Walgreens have significantly lower SG&A expenses as a percentage of revenues (19% and 17%, respectively) than Rite Aid (26%), while gross margins appear unrelated to scale, given that CVS, Walgreens, and Rite Aid reported gross margins of 26%, 21%, and 26%, respectively.

   The full calculations to support this solution are in the Example3 sheet in the downloadable Microsoft Excel workbook.

Marco Benitez is a United States–based equity analyst with an independent research firm. Benitez is researching service levels in the US drugstore industry.

1. Calculate and interpret the companies' SG&A expenses per store.

   Solution

   SG&A expenses per store for CVS and Rite Aid are similar, at USD1.8 and USD1.7 million, respectively, while Walgreens spent just over USD2 million per store. This comparison might indicate that Walgreens has service levels at its stores that are superior to those of CVS and Rite Aid or that its stores are in higher-cost (payroll and real estate) locations.
   The full calculations to support this solution are in the Example3 sheet in the downloadable Microsoft Excel workbook.

2. Assuming that customer satisfaction is a driver of same-store sales growth, which company appears to have the most satisfied customer base?

   Solution

   Based on recent same-store sales growth rates, CVS appears to have the most satisfied customer base, followed by Walgreens. CVS's same-store sales growth rates have exceeded those of the others in each of the past three years. Over a longer time period, however, both CVS and Walgreens led in same-store sales growth in five of the past 10 years, though CVS's average same-store sales growth rate over the past 10 years is 54 bps higher than Walgreens'.
   The full calculations to support this solution are in the Example3 sheet in the downloadable Microsoft Excel workbook.

3. Benitez projects that Rite Aid will increase its number of stores by 2% annually over the next three years. He believes SG&A expenses per store will increase 1% annually during this time. What is Benitez's projection for total SG&A expense in 2023?

   Solution

   Benitez projects Rite Aid's number of stores will be approximately 2,664 [$= 2{,}510 \times 1.02^3$] by the end of 2023. He projects that SG&A expenses per store will be USD1.76 million [$= 1.71 \times 1.01^3$]. He thus estimates total SG&A expenses to be USD4,701 million in 2023, which is approximately 9% higher than in fiscal 2020.

Jasmine Lewis is another United States–based equity analyst covering the retail drugstore industry. She is considering several approaches to forecasting operating costs for CVS, Walgreens, and Rite Aid. Classify each of the following as a bottom-up, top-down, or hybrid approach.

1. Lewis believes government health care programs in the United States will face budgetary pressures in the future, which will result in lower reimbursements for the retail drugstore industry. Lewis thinks this will lower all drugstores' gross margins.

   Solution

   This case describes a top-down approach because Lewis considers the overall industry environment before individual companies.

2. Lewis projects that Walgreens' historical rate of growth in SG&A expenses will continue for the next five years. But in the long run, he projects SG&A expenses to grow at the rate of inflation.

Solution

In this case, Lewis combines a bottom-up approach (projecting the historical rate of growth to continue) with a top-down approach (basing his long-run assumptions on the overall rate of inflation). Therefore, this is a hybrid approach.

3. To estimate Rite Aid's future lease expense, Lewis makes assumptions about store growth, the mix of owned and leased stores, and average lease expense per store.

Solution

This case describes a bottom-up approach because Lewis bases her forecasts on Rite Aid's historical experience.

3

MODELING OPERATING COSTS: COST OF GOODS SOLD AND SG&A

☐ | demonstrate methods to forecast cost of goods sold and operating expenses

The cost of goods sold (COGS) is typically the single largest cost for companies that make and/or sell products. COGS includes the cost of producing, purchasing, and readying products for sale.

Because sales minus COGS equals gross profit (and gross margin is gross profit as a percentage of sales), COGS and gross profit vary inversely. Forecasting COGS as a percentage of sales and forecasting gross margin percentage are equivalent in that a value for one implies a value for the other.

Because COGS has a direct link with sales, forecasting this item as a percentage of sales is usually a good approach. Historical data on a company's COGS as a percentage of sales usually provide a useful starting point for estimates. For example, if a company is losing market share in a market in which the emergence of new substitute products is also putting the overall sector under pricing pressure, gross margins are likely to decline. But if the company is gaining market share because it has introduced new competitive and innovative products, especially if it has done so in combination with achieving cost advantages, gross margins are likely to improve.

COGS is typically a large cost, and so a small error in this item can have a material impact on the forecasted operating profit. Analysts should consider whether an analysis of these costs (e.g., by segment, by product category, or by volume and price components) is possible and improves forecasting accuracy. For example, some companies face fluctuating input costs that can be passed on to customers only with a time lag. Particularly for companies that have low gross margins, sudden shocks in input costs can affect operating profit significantly. A good example is the sensitivity of airlines' profits to unhedged changes in jet fuel costs. In these cases, a breakdown of both costs and sales into volume and price components is essential for developing short-term forecasts, even if analysts use the overall relationship between sales and input cost for developing longer-term forecasts.

EXAMPLE 4

The Effect of Prices and Costs on Gross Profit and Margin

Assume that a company's COGS as a percentage of sales equals 25%. If input costs double the following period, and the company can pass the entire increase on to its clients through a 25% price increase, COGS as a percentage of sales will increase (to 40%) because an equal absolute amount has been added to the numerator and to the denominator.

	Period 1	Period 2
Sales	100.0	125.0
COGS	25.0	50.0
Gross profit	75.0	75.0
COGS as % of sales	25%	40%
Gross margin %	75%	60%

Thus, although the absolute amount of gross profit will remain constant, the gross margin will decrease (from 75% to 60%).

Analysts should also consider the impact of a company's hedging strategy. For example, commodity-driven companies' gross margins almost automatically decline if input prices increase significantly because of variable costs increasing at a faster rate than revenue growth. Through various hedging strategies, a company can mitigate the impact on profitability. For example, brewers often hedge the cost of barley, a key raw material needed for brewing beer, one year in advance. Although companies usually do not disclose their hedging positions, their general strategy is often revealed in the footnotes of the annual report. Further, the negative impact of increasing sales prices on sales volume can be mitigated by a policy of gradual sales price increases. For example, if the brewer expects higher barley prices because of a bad harvest, the brewer can slowly increase prices to avoid a strong price jump next year.

Competitors' gross margins can also provide a useful cross check for estimating a realistic gross margin. Gross margin differences among companies within a sector should logically relate to differences in their business operations. For example, in the Netherlands, supermarket chain Albert Heijn has a higher gross margin in the very competitive grocery sector because it can leverage its dominant 35% market share to achieve savings in purchases; it also has the ability to make higher-margin private label products. All these competitive advantages contribute to its structurally higher gross margin within the grocery sector. But if a new large competitor emerges (e.g., through consolidation of the fragmented market), Albert Heijn's above-average gross margin could come under pressure.

Note that differences in competitors' gross margins do not always indicate a superior competitive position but could simply reflect differences in business models. For example, some companies in the grocery segment own and operate their own retail stores, whereas other companies operate as wholesalers with franchised retail operations. In the franchised retailing business model, most of the operating costs are incurred by the franchisee; the wholesaler offers products with only a small markup to these franchisees. Compared with a grocer with its own stores, a supermarket wholesaler will have a much lower gross margin. The grocer with its own stores, however, will have much higher operating costs. Even though differences in business models can complicate direct comparisons, competitors' gross margins can nonetheless offer potentially useful insights.

SG&A Expenses

SG&A expenses are the other main type of operating costs. In contrast to COGS, SG&A expenses often have less of a direct relationship with revenues. As an illustration of the profit impact of COGS and SG&A, consider the historical case example of Thai cement and building materials company Siam Cement Group from 2017 to 2018. A summary of the company's key income statement items is shown in Exhibit 6.

Exhibit 6: Siam Cement Group 2017–18 Financials

	2017 (Baht billions)	2018 (Baht billions)	YoY%	Percent of Sales 2017	2018
Net sales	450.92	478.44	6.1	100.0	100.0
COGS	349.31	383.46	9.8	77.5	80.1
Gross profit	101.61	94.98	−6.5	22.5	19.9
SG&A	52.58	55.09	4.8	11.7	11.5
Selected SG&A items:					
Salary and personnel expenses	24.24	23.98	−1.1	5.4	5.0
Freight costs	11.63	11.55	−0.7	2.6	2.4
Research and development	4.18	4.67	11.7	0.9	1.0
Promotion and advertising	2.62	2.58	−1.5	0.6	0.5
Operating income	49.03	39.89	−18.6	10.9	8.3

Note: "YoY%" means year-over-year percentage change.
Sources: Based on information in Siam Cement Group's annual reports.

As shown in the exhibit, Siam Cement was affected in 2018 by higher input costs that could not be fully passed on to customers. Consequently, despite sales growth of 6.1%, gross profit fell by 6.5% and gross margin declined. The company was able to limit its other operating costs; SG&A expenses grew 4.8%, declining slightly as a percentage of revenue. Operating income fell 18.6%. This contrasted with the company's experience in 2016, when lower input costs resulted in widening of the gross margin to 24.7% from 22.3% in 2015 (not shown in Exhibit 7).

Siam Cement's income statement illustrates that companies often disclose the different components of SG&A expenses. Siam Cement, for example, shows separate line items for several distribution cost items, such as freight and rental expenses, and a number of general and administrative expenses, such as depreciation, IT fees, professional fees, and research and development (R&D). Although SG&A expenses overall are generally less closely linked to revenue than COGS, certain expenses within SG&A could be more variable—more closely linked to revenue—than others. Specifically, selling and distribution expenses often have a large variable component and can be estimated, like COGS, as a percentage of sales. The largest component of selling expenses is often wages and salaries linked to sales. Therefore, selling expenses will usually increase with additional salespeople and/or an overall increase in wages and benefits for the sales force.

Other general and administrative expenses are less variable. Overhead costs for employees, for example, are more related to the number of employees at the head office and supporting IT and administrative operations than to short-term changes in the level of sales. R&D expense is another example of an expense that tends to fluctuate less than sales. Consequently, these expenses are more fixed in nature and tend to increase and decrease gradually over time compared with changes in the company's revenue.

In addition to analyzing the historical relationship between a company's operating expenses and sales, benchmarking a company against its competitors can be useful. By analyzing the cost structure of a company's competitors, the efficiency potential and margin potential of a specific company can be estimated. As a final measure, performing certain crosschecks within a forecast model can be useful, too. For example, in the supermarket sector, the projected floor square footage (or metric equivalent) underlying the revenue projections should match the floor space projections underlying the unit selling expense forecasts. Both sales and expense projections can be enhanced if the company provides a breakout of the product and/or geographical segments in the footnotes of its annual report.

EXAMPLE 5

L'Oréal's Operational Cost Structure versus Competitors

As shown in Exhibit 7, L'Oréal reported an EBIT (earnings before interest and taxes) margin of 18.6% in 2019, which makes it the most profitable company among a selection of beauty companies. However, the average EBIT margin of 19.6% for home and personal goods companies operating in mass markets is even greater than that of L'Oréal. Luxury goods companies tend to have higher gross margins, owing to higher prices, than mass market companies, but those margins are offset by higher "go to market" costs such as advertising and promotion (A&P) expenditures. With the exception of Avon, the business model of which is based on direct selling, A&P is substantially greater at the beauty companies than at the mass market producers.

L'Oréal is often considered a pure beauty company. But if the underlying business is examined in detail, the company's operations can be split 50/50 between a luxury beauty high-end business and a general consumer business. In the general consumer business, L'Oréal's products compete with those of such players as Colgate, Procter & Gamble, and Henkel in the mass market. Exhibit 7 presents relevant data and can also be found in the Example4 sheet in the downloadable Microsoft Excel workbook.

Exhibit 7: European and US Home and Personal Care Companies, Beauty vs. Mass Market Companies: Simplified and Common-Size Income Statement (2019)

Company	Sales (mlns)	Gross Margin	A&P %	SG&A/ Other %	EBIT %
Beauty					
L'Oréal	€29,874	73.0%	30.8%	23.6%	18.6%
Estée Lauder	$14,863	77.2%	22.5%	37.1%	17.6%
Beiersdorf	€7,653	57.9%	34.8%	9.6%	13.5%
Avon	$4,763	57.8%	1.5%	53.6%	2.6%
Beauty Average		66.5%	22.4%	31.0%	13.1%

Company	Sales (mlns)	Gross Margin	A&P %	SG&A/ Other %	EBIT %
Mass Market					
Colgate	$15,693	59.4%	10.8%	24.7%	23.9%
Reckitt Group	£12,846	60.5%	14.4%	19.9%	26.2%
Procter & Gamble	$67,684	48.6%	10.0%	18.2%	20.4%
Clorox	$6,214	43.9%	9.8%	16.0%	18.1%
Kimberly-Clark	$18,450	32.7%	4.1%	13.5%	15.1%
Henkel	€20,114	45.9%	N/A	31.9%	14.0%
Mass Market Average		48.5%	9.8%	20.7%	19.6%

Notes: The data for some of the companies listed in Exhibit 7 have been adjusted to reflect differences in accounting choices. For example, some of the consumer product companies include shipping and handling expenses in cost of sales, whereas others include these costs as a component of SG&A expenses.

Sources: Based on information in company reports.

1. Assuming the following information, what will L'Oréal's new operating margin be?

   • L'Oréal's beauty and mass market operations each represent half of revenues.

   • L'Oréal will be able to bring the overall cost structure of its mass market operations in line with the average of mass market companies (EBIT = 19.6%).

   • The cost structure of L'Oréal's beauty operations will remain stable (assumed EBIT = 18%).

   Solution

   Operating margin will increase from 18.6% to 18.8%, which is 50% of 19.6% (mass market EBIT margin) plus 50% of 18% (assumed beauty EBIT margin).

   The full calculations to support this solution are in the Example4 sheet in the downloadable Microsoft Excel workbook.

2. What will happen to L'Oréal's EBIT margin if the company is able to adjust the operating cost structure of its mass market segment (50% of revenues) partly toward the average of its mass market peers but maintain its high gross margin? Assume the following:

   • The cost structure of half of the business, the beauty operations, will remain stable (EBIT margin = 18%).

   • L'Oréal's mass market operations will have a gross margin of 60.75% (the average of the current gross margin of 73% and the 48.5% reported by its mass market peers).

• L'Oréal's mass market A&P costs will fall by half from 30.8% of sales to 15.4% of sales, while other mass market SG&A costs will remain at the corporate average.

Solution

EBIT margin will increase from 18.6% to 19.9%. The projected beauty EBIT is EUR2,689 million, while the projected mass market EBIT is EUR5,937 million, assuming mass market sales of EUR14,937 million, gross margin of 60.75%, A&P % of 15.4%, and SG&A/Other % of 23.6%.

The full calculations to support this solution are in the Example4 sheet in the downloadable Microsoft Excel workbook.END BOX

EXAMPLE 6

Analysis of the Consumer Goods Company Unilever

The consumer goods company Unilever reported an overall underlying operating margin of 18.4% in 2019. As shown in Exhibit 8 (see the Example5 sheet in the downloadable Microsoft Excel workbook), the operating margin is lowest in the fastest growing product category, home care products. The other parts of the business, personal care and foods categories, enjoy higher margins but are growing more slowly.

Exhibit 8: Unilever Revenue and Profit from Product Categories (€ millions, unless noted)

Segment	2019	2018	'19/'18 YoY	Avg Growth Rate 2017–2019
Beauty & Personal Care	21,868	20,624	6%	3%
Foods & Refreshments	19,287	20,227	−5%	−5%
Home Care	10,825	10,131	7%	3%
Total revenues	51,980	50,982	2%	0%
Underlying operating profit				
Beauty & Personal Care	4,960	4,543	9%	
Foods & Refreshments	3,382	3,576	−5%	
Home Care	1,605	1,344	19%	
Total	9,947	9,463	5%	
Underlying operating profit margin				
Beauty & Personal Care	22.7%	22.0%		
Foods & Refreshments	17.5%	17.7%		
Home Care	14.8%	13.3%		
Total	19.1%	18.6%		

Notes: Underlying operating profit is a non-IFRS operating profit measure, equal to IFRS operating profit adjusted for items such as restructuring costs.

Source: Based on Unilever's 2019 full-year and fourth quarter results.

1. Determine the estimated sales, operating profit, and operating profit margin by using the following two approaches: (A) Assume total sales growth of 2.0% and overall underlying operating margin of 19.1% for the next five years, and (B) assume each individual segment's sales growth and underlying operating margin continue at the same rate reported in 2019. Which approach will result in a higher underlying estimated operating profit after five years?

Solution

Exhibit 9 shows that operating profit after five years will be EUR10,962 million under approach A and EUR11,549 million under approach B. The full calculations to support this solution are in the Example5 sheet in the downloadable Microsoft Excel workbook.

Exhibit 9: Sales and Operating Profit for Unilever, 2018–2023E (€ millions, unless noted)

Approach A	2019A	2020E	2021E	2022E	2023E	2024E
Total revenues	51,980	53,020	54,080	55,162	56,265	57,390
Growth rate		2.00%	2.00%	2.00%	2.00%	2.00%
Underlying operating profit	9,947	10,127	10,329	10,536	10,747	10,962
Growth rate		2%	2%	2%	2%	2%
Underlying operating profit margin	19.1%	19.1%	19.1%	19.1%	19.1%	19.1%
Approach B						
Sales	2019A	2020E	2021E	2022E	2023E	2024E
Beauty & Personal Care	21,868	23,187	24,586	26,069	27,641	29,308
Growth rate		6%	6%	6%	6%	6%
Foods & Refreshments	19,287	18,391	17,536	16,721	15,944	15,203
Growth rate		−5%	−5%	−5%	−5%	−5%
Home Care	10,825	11,567	12,359	13,205	14,110	15,077
Growth rate		7%	7%	7%	7%	7%
Total revenues	51,980	53,144	54,481	55,995	57,695	59,588
Margins	2019A	2020E	2021E	2022E	2023E	2024E
Beauty & Personal Care	22.7%	22.7%	22.7%	22.7%	22.7%	22.7%
Foods & Refreshments	17.5%	17.5%	17.5%	17.5%	17.5%	17.5%
Home Care	14.8%	14.8%	14.8%	14.8%	14.8%	14.8%
Underlying operating profit	2019A	2020E	2021E	2022E	2023E	2024E
Beauty & Personal Care	4,960	5,259	5,576	5,913	6,269	6,648

Approach A	2019A	2020E	2021E	2022E	2023E	2024E
Foods & Refreshments	3,382	3,225	3,075	2,932	2,796	2,666
Home Care	1,605	1,715	1,832	1,958	2,092	2,235
Total	9,947	10,199	10,484	10,803	11,157	11,549

2. Compare and explain the results under the two alternative approaches (A and B) in Question 1.

Solution

Approach A assumes a constant 2.0% total sales growth rate and a stable 19.1% underlying operating margin. Therefore, the operating profit growth rate is in line with the revenue growth rate and constant at 2.0%, which therefore assumes no difference in growth rates and profitability of the segments. Approach B assumes growth rates of 6%, –5%, and 7% of sales for the Beauty & Personal Care, Foods & Refreshments, and Home Care segments. This results in a faster overall compounded growth rate than with Approach A (3% versus 2%) and an annual increase, on average, in the total underlying operating profit margin of 6 bps due to the mix effect of different segment margins. In 2024E, Approach A yields an underlying operating profit margin of 19.1% compared with 19.4% for Approach B.

3. Assume Unilever can grow segment revenues over the next five years at the following rates: Beauty & Personal Care 3.0%, Foods & Refreshments 2.0%, and Home Care 4.0%. But underlying operating profit margins in Beauty & Personal Care will fall 20 bps annually for the next five years (because of high competition, limited growth, and costs resulting from the adoption of sustainable packaging), and operating profit margins in the Foods & Refreshments and Home Care segments will increase by 15 and 50 bps, respectively, each year for the next five years (helped by increasing demand for the company's products and better utilization of its factories). Calculate the overall underlying operating profit margin in each of the next five years.

Solution

As shown in Exhibit 10, the overall underlying operating profit margin improves from 19.1% in 2019 to 19.5% in 2024 because the margin decline in Beauty & Personal Care is more than offset by the margin increase in Foods & Refreshments and the faster growing Home Care segment. The full calculations to support this solution are in the Example5 sheet in the downloadable Microsoft Excel workbook.

Exhibit 10: Sales and Operating Profit for Unilever 2019–2024E (€ millions, unless noted)						
Sales	**2019A**	**2020E**	**2021E**	**2022E**	**2023E**	**2024E**
Beauty & Personal Care	21,868	22,524	23,200	23,896	24,613	25,351
Growth rate		3%	3%	3%	3%	3%
Foods & Refreshments	19,287	19,673	20,066	20,468	20,877	21,294
Growth rate		2%	2%	2%	2%	2%
Home Care	10,825	11,258	11,708	12,177	12,664	13,170

Sales	2019A	2020E	2021E	2022E	2023E	2024E
Growth rate		4%	4%	4%	4%	4%
Total revenues	51,980	53,455	54,974	56,540	58,153	59,816
Margins	**2019A**	**2020E**	**2021E**	**2022E**	**2023E**	**2024E**
Beauty & Personal Care	22.7%	22.5%	22.3%	22.1%	21.9%	21.7%
Foods & Refreshments	17.5%	17.7%	17.8%	18.0%	18.1%	18.3%
Home Care	14.8%	15.3%	15.8%	16.3%	16.8%	17.3%
Underlying operating profit	**2019A**	**2020E**	**2021E**	**2022E**	**2023E**	**2024E**
Beauty & Personal Care	4,960	5,064	5,169	5,277	5,386	5,496
Foods & Refreshments	3,382	3,479	3,579	3,681	3,786	3,894
Home Care	1,605	1,725	1,853	1,988	2,131	2,282
Total	9,947	10,268	10,601	10,946	11,303	11,672
Margin	19.1%	19.2%	19.3%	19.4%	19.4%	19.5%

4   MODELING NON-OPERATING COSTS AND OTHER ITEMS

☐ | demonstrate methods to forecast non-operating items, financing costs, and income taxes

Line items on the income statement that appear below operating profit, such as interest income, interest expense, income taxes, noncontrolling interest, income from affiliates, and shares outstanding, also need to be modeled. The two most significant non-operating expenses in income statement modeling are financing expenses (i.e., interest) and taxes.

Financing Expenses

Financing expenses consist of interest income and interest expense, which are typically netted. Interest income depends on the amount of cash and investments on the balance sheet as well as the rates of return earned on investments. Interest income is a key component of revenue for banks and insurance companies, but it is generally less significant to non-financial companies. Interest expense depends on the level of debt on the balance sheet as well as the interest rate associated with the debt. Interest expense is typically presented net of interest income on the income statement, with the individual components disclosed in the notes to financial statements. Analysts should be aware of the effect of changing interest rates on the net interest expense and market value of company's debt.

==When forecasting financing expenses, the capital structure of a company is a key determinant. For practical purposes, the debt level in combination with the interest rate are the main drivers in forecasting debt financing expenses.== Usually, the notes to the financial statements provide detail about the maturity structure of the company's debt and the corresponding interest rates. This information can be used to estimate future financing expenses.

EXAMPLE 7

Interest Expense Calculations

Dutch grocer Ahold Delhaize, operating in several regions, has a debt structure with a relatively high amount of debt, primarily in the form of leases, as shown in Exhibit 12 (see the Example6 worksheet in the downloadable Microsoft Excel workbook).

Exhibit 11: Ahold's Debt, Interest Income, and Expense

€ millions	3 Jan. 2021	29 Dec. 2019	Average
Loans	3,863	3,841	3,852
Other non-current financial liabilities (primarily leases)	8,905	8,716	8,811
Current financial liabilities	2,386	3,257	2,822
Gross debt	15,154	15,814	15,484
Less: cash and cash equivalents	2,933	3,717	3,325
Net debt	12,221	12,097	12,159
Interest income	35	65	
Interest expense	138	175	
Net interest expense	103	110	

Source: Ahold Delhaize 2020 Annual Report

---

1. Calculate the interest rate on the average gross debt and interest rate on the average cash position for the year ended 3 Jan. 2021.

   Solution

   Interest rate on average gross debt is calculated as interest expense divided by average gross debt: (EUR138 million/EUR15,484 million) = 0.89% or 89 bps. The interest rate on average cash position is interest income divided by the average cash position (EUR35 million/EUR3,325 million) = 1.05%.

2. Calculate the interest rate on the average net debt, assuming the other financial income and expenses are not related to the debt or cash balances, for the year ended 3 Jan. 2021.

   Solution

   The interest rate on the average net debt is calculated as net interest expense divided by average net debt (EUR103 million/EUR12,159 million) = 0.85% or 85 bps.

Handwritten margin notes:

- A method of forecasting that recognizes the relationship between the income statement account (interest expense) and the balance sheet account (debt) would be a preferable method for forecasting interest expense when compared with methods that forecast based solely on the income statement account.

Effective interest rate = interest expense ← Income statement / Avg gross debt ← balance sheet

—Operating (EBIT) margin is a pre-tax profitability measure that can be useful in the peer comparison of companies in countries with different tax structures.

Corporate Income Tax

Income taxes are primarily determined by the geographic composition of profits and the tax rates in each geography but can also be influenced by the nature of a business. Some companies benefit from special tax treatment—for example, from R&D tax credits or accelerated depreciation of fixed assets. Analysts should also be aware of any governmental or business changes that can alter tax rates.

Differences in tax rates can be an important driver of value. Generally, there are three types of tax rates:

- The statutory tax rate, which is the corporate tax rate in the country in which the company is domiciled.
- The effective tax rate, which is calculated as the reported income tax expense amount on the income statement divided by the pre-tax income.
- The cash tax rate, which is the tax actually paid (cash tax) divided by pre-tax income.

Differences between cash taxes and reported taxes typically result from differences between financial accounting standards and tax laws and are reflected as a deferred tax asset or a deferred tax liability.

In forecasting tax expense and cash taxes, respectively, the effective tax rate and cash tax rate are key. A good understanding of their operational drivers and the financial structure of a company is useful in forecasting these tax rates.

Differences between the statutory tax rate and the effective tax rate can arise for many reasons. Tax credits, withholding tax on dividends, adjustments to previous years, and expenses not deductible for tax purposes are among the reasons for differences.

Effective tax rates can differ when companies are active outside the country in which they are domiciled. The effective tax rate becomes a blend of the different tax rates of the countries in which the activities take place in relation to the profit generated in each country. If a company reports a high profit in a country with a high tax rate and a low profit in a country with a low tax rate, the effective tax rate will be the weighted average of the rates and higher than the simple average tax rate of both countries.

In some cases, companies have also been able to minimize their taxes by using special purposes entities. For example, some companies create specialized financing and holding companies to minimize the amount of taxable profit reported in high tax rate countries. Although such actions could reduce the effective tax rate substantially, they also create risks if, for example, tax laws change.

In general, an effective tax rate that is consistently lower than statutory rates or the effective tax rates reported by competitors might warrant additional attention when forecasting future tax expenses. The notes on the financial statements should disclose other types of items, some of which could contribute to a temporarily high or low effective tax rate. The cash tax rate is used for forecasting cash flows, and the effective tax rate is relevant for projecting earnings on the income statement.

In developing an estimated tax rate for forecasts, analysts should adjust for any one-time events. If the income from equity-method investees is a substantial part of pre-tax income and also a volatile component of it, the effective tax rate excluding this amount is likely to be a better estimate for the future tax costs for a company. The tax impact from income from participations is disclosed in the notes on the financial statements.

Often, a good starting point for estimating future tax expense is a tax rate based on normalized operating income, before the results from associates and special items. This normalized tax rate should be a good indication of the future tax expense, adjusted for special items, in an analyst's earnings model.

Building a model allows the effective tax amount to be found in the profit and loss projections and the cash tax amount on the cash flow statement (or given as supplemental information). The reconciliation between the profit and loss tax amount and the cash flow tax figures should be the change in the deferred tax asset or liability.

Tax Rate Estimates

ABC, a hypothetical company, operates in Countries A and B. The tax rate in Country A is 40%, and the tax rate in Country B is 10%. In the first year, the company generates an equal amount of profit before tax in each country, as shown in Exhibit 13 (see the Example 7 sheet in the downloadable Microsoft Excel workbook).

Exhibit 12: Tax Rates That Differ by Jurisdiction

	A	B	Total
Profit before tax	100	100	200
Effective tax rate	40%	10%	25%
Tax	40	10	50
Net profit	60	90	150

1. What will happen to the effective tax rate for the next three years if the profit before tax in Country A is stable but the profit before tax in Country B grows 15% annually?

Solution

The effective tax rate will gradually decline because a higher proportion of profit will be generated in the country with the lower tax rate each year. In Exhibit 13, the effective tax rate declines from 25% in the beginning to 22% in the third year.

Exhibit 13: Worksheet for Problem 1

	Year			
	0	1	2	3
Profit before tax, Country A	100	100	100	100
Growth rate		0%	0%	0%
Profit before tax, Country B	100	115	132	152
Growth rate		15%	15%	15%
Total profit before tax	200	215	232	252
Effective tax rate, Country A	40%	40%	40%	40%
Effective tax rate, Country B	10%	10%	10%	10%

	Year			
	0	**1**	**2**	**3**
Total tax	50	52	53	55
Total effective tax rate	25%	24%	23%	22%

2. Evaluate the cash tax and effective tax rates for the next three years if the tax authorities in Country A allow some costs (e.g., accelerated depreciation) to be taken sooner for tax purposes. For Country A, the result will be a 50% reduction in taxes paid in the current year but an increase in taxes paid by the same amount in the following year (this happens each year). Assume stable profit before tax in Country A and 15% annual before-tax-profit growth in Country B.

Solution

The combined cash tax rate (last line in Exhibit 14) will be 15% in the first year and then rebound in subsequent years. Only the rate for the first year will benefit from a tax deferral; in subsequent years, the deferral for a given year will be offset by the addition of the amount postponed from the previous year. The combined effective tax rate will be unaffected by the deferral. As shown in Exhibit 14, beginning with the second year, the combined cash tax and effective tax rates decline over time but remain identical to each other. The full calculations to support this solution are in the Example7 sheet in the downloadable Microsoft Excel workbook.

Exhibit 14: Worksheet for Problem 2

	Year			
	0	**1**	**2**	**3**
Profit before tax, Country A	100	100	100	100
Growth rate		0%	0%	0%
Profit before tax, Country B	100	115	132	152
Growth rate		15%	15%	15%
Total profit before tax	200	215	232	252
Effective tax rate, Country A	40%	40%	40%	40%
Effective tax rate, Country B	10%	10%	10%	10%
Total tax per income statement	50	52	53	55
Total effective tax rate	25%	24%	23%	22%
Cash taxes, Country A	20	40	40	40
Cash taxes, Country B	10	12	13	15
Total cash tax	30	52	53	55

	Year			
	0	**1**	**2**	**3**
Cash tax rate	15%	24%	23%	22%

3. Repeat the exercise of Problem 2, but now assume that Country B, rather than Country A, allows some costs to be taken sooner for tax purposes and that the tax effect described applies to Country B. Continue to assume stable profit before tax in Country A and 15% annual profit growth in Country B.

Solution

The combined effective tax rate unchanged from Exhibit 13 and Exhibit 14. Because of the growth assumed for Country B, however, the annual tax postponement will result in a lower cash tax rate in Country B than the effective tax rate in Country B. Consequently, as shown in Exhibit 15, the combined cash tax rate will be less than the effective tax rate.

Exhibit 15: Worksheet for Problem 3

	Year			
	0	**1**	**2**	**3**
Profit before tax, Country A	100	100	100	100
Growth rate		0%	0%	0%
Profit before tax, Country B	100	115	132	152
Growth rate		15%	15%	15%
Total profit before tax	200	215	232	252
Effective tax rate, Country A	40%	40%	40%	40%
Effective tax rate, Country B	10%	10%	10%	10%
Total tax per income statement	50	52	53	55
Total effective tax rate	25%	24%	23%	22%
Cash taxes, Country A	40	40	40	40
Cash taxes, Country B	5	11	12	14
Total cash tax	45	51	52	54
Cash tax rate	23%	24%	23%	22%

The next section addresses several points to note in modeling dividends, share count, and unusual expenses.

Income Statement Modeling: Other Items

A company's stated dividend policy helps in modeling future dividend growth. Analysts will often assume that dividends grow each year by a certain dollar amount or as a proportion of net income.

If a company shares an ownership interest in a business unit with a third party, the company might report minority interest expense or income from consolidated affiliates on its income statement. If a company owns more than 50% of an affiliate, it will generally consolidate the affiliate's results with its own and report the portion of income that does not belong to the parent company as minority interest. If a company owns less than 50% of an affiliate, it will not consolidate results but will report its share of income from the affiliate under the equity method. If the affiliate is profitable, minority interest would be reported as deduction from net income, whereas if a consolidated affiliate generates losses, minority interest would be reported as an addition to net income to shareholders. In either case, income or expense from these jointly owned businesses can be material.

Share count (shares issued and outstanding) is a key input in the calculation of an intrinsic value estimate and earnings per share. Share count changes for three primary reasons: dilution related to stock options, convertible bonds, and similar securities; issuance of new shares; and share repurchases. The market price of a stock is an important determinant of future share count changes, which can complicate their estimation. Projections for share issuance and repurchases should fit within the analyst's broader analysis of a company's capital structure.

Finally, unusual charges can be almost impossible to predict, particularly past the next couple of years. For this reason, analysts typically exclude unusual charges from their forecasts. But if a company has a habit of frequently classifying certain recurring costs as "unusual," analysts should consider some normalized level of charges in their model.

5   BALANCE SHEET AND CASH FLOW STATEMENT MODELING

| | describe approaches to balance sheet modeling

Income statement modeling is the starting point for balance sheet and cash flow statement modeling. Analysts normally have a choice of whether to focus on the balance sheet or cash flow statement; the third financial statement will naturally result from the construction of the other two. Here, we focus on the balance sheet.

Some balance sheet line items—such as retained earnings—flow directly from the income statement, whereas other lines like working capital accounts—such as accounts receivable, accounts payable, and inventory—are very closely linked to income statement projections.

A common way to model working capital accounts is with efficiency ratios, as in Example 8.

[Handwritten margin note: Forecasting working capital accounts by using the company's historical efficiency ratios to project future performance is a bottom-up approach]

EXAMPLE 9

Working Capital Forecasts with Efficiency Ratios

Exhibit 17 (see the Example8 sheet in the downloadable Microsoft Excel workbook) shows revenues, COGS, and year-end working capital account balances for YY Ltd., a fictional company, for years 1–3. Based on the data in the Exhibit, answer questions 1–3.

Exhibit 16: YY Ltd. Financial Data, millions of CNY

Year	1	2	3
Revenue	174,915	205,839	245,866
COGS	152,723	177,285	209,114
Accounts receivable	5,598	6,949	10,161
Inventory	29,481	32,585	41,671
Accounts payable	46,287	59,528	72,199

1. Calculate days sales outstanding, inventory days on hand, and days payable outstanding for years 1, 2, and 3, using year-end balances and assuming a 365-day fiscal year.

   Solution

   Days sales outstanding is equal to accounts receivable/(revenues/365), inventory days on hand is equal to inventories/(COGS/365), and days payable outstanding is equal to accounts payable/(COGS/365). Using the data in Exhibit 17, the three ratios for years 1–3 are as follows. Full calculations to support this solution are in the Example8 sheet in the downloadable Microsoft Excel workbook.

Year	1	2	3
Days sales outstanding	12	12	15
Inventory days on hand	70	67	73
Days payable outstanding	111	123	126

2. Your colleague Liang forecasts revenue growth of 18%, 16%, and 13% and gross margins of 17%, 17%, and 16% in years 4, 5, and 6, respectively. Using Liang forecasts, calculate expected revenue and COGS in each of year 4, 5, and 6.

   Solution

   Using Liang's forecasts for annual revenue growth and gross margins and the data in Exhibit 17, expected revenue and COGS for years 4–6 are as follows, shown in millions of CNY. Full calculations to support this solution are in the Example8 sheet in the downloadable Microsoft Excel workbook.

Year (millions of CNY)	1	2	3	4	5	6
Revenue	174,915	205,839	245,866	290,122	336,541	380,292
Growth rate		18%	19%	18%	16%	13%

Year (millions of CNY)	1	2	3	4	5	6
COGS	152,723	177,285	209,114	240,801	279,329	319,445
Gross margin	13%	14%	15%	17%	17%	16%

3. Liang forecasts that days sales outstanding, inventory days on hand, and days payable outstanding in years 4, 5, and 6 will remain the same as year 3 amounts. Using Liang's forecasts as well as forecasted revenue and COGS, calculate expected accounts receivable, inventory, and accounts payable year-end balances for each of year 4, 5, and 6.

Solution

Each of the efficiency ratios can be rearranged to yield working capital balances because we have values for two of the three variables in them: the efficiency ratios are assumed to remain constant from year 3 levels and the revenue and COGS variables have already been forecast.

Days sales outstanding is equal to accounts receivable/(revenues/365), thus, accounts receivable is equal to days sales outstanding × (revenues/365). Similarly, inventories is equal to inventory days on hand × (COGS/365) and accounts payable is equal to days payable outstanding × (COGS/365).

Using the data in Exhibit 17 and the revenue and COGS forecasts, year-end working capital account balances are as follows, shown in millions of CNY. Full calculations to support this solution are in the Example8 sheet in the downloadable Microsoft Excel workbook.

Year (millions of CNY)	1	2	3	4	5	6
Revenue	174,915	205,839	245,866	290,122	336,541	380,292
COGS	152,723	177,285	209,114	240,801	279,329	319,445
Accounts receivable	5,598	6,949	10,161	11,990	13,908	15,716
Inventories	29,481	32,585	41,671	47,985	55,663	63,657
Accounts payable	46,287	59,528	72,199	83,139	96,442	110,292
Days sales outstanding	12	12	15	15	15	15
Inventory days on hand	70	67	73	73	73	73
Days payable outstanding	111	123	126	126	126	126

Working capital projections can be modified by both top-down and bottom-up considerations. In the absence of a specific opinion about working capital, analysts can look at historical efficiency ratios and project recent performance or a historical average to persist in the future, as in Example 8, which would be a bottom-up approach. Conversely, analysts might have a specific view of future working capital. For example, if they project economy-wide retail sales to decline unexpectedly, that could result in slower inventory turnover (higher inventory days on hand) across the retail sector. Because the analysts began with a forecast for a large sector of the economy, this would be considered a top-down approach.

Projections for long-term assets—such as PP&E and intangible assets—are less directly tied to the income statement for most companies. Net PP&E and intangible assets primarily change because of capital expenditures and depreciation and amortization, both of which are important components of the cash flow statement. Depreciation and amortization forecasts are usually based on historical depreciation, management's disclosures, and levels of long-term assets. Capital expenditure forecasts depend on the analysts' judgment of the future capacity expansion, which is generally driven by revenue growth and the business model. Capital expenditures can be thought of as including both **maintenance capital expenditures**, which are necessary to sustain the current business, and **growth capital expenditures**, which are needed to expand the business. All else being equal, maintenance capital expenditure forecasts should normally be higher than depreciation because of inflation.

Finally, analysts must make assumptions about a company's future capital structure. Leverage ratios—such as debt-to-capital, debt-to-equity, and debt-to-EBITDA—can be useful for projecting future debt and equity levels. Analysts should consider historical company practice, management's financial strategy, and the capital requirements implied by other model assumptions when projecting the future capital structure.

EXAMPLE 10

Balance Sheet Modeling

Exhibit 18 shows financial data for YY Ltd. related to its PP&E and intangible assets. Based on the data in Exhibit 18 and the data and analysis from Example 8, answer questions 1 and 2 (see the Example 9 sheet in the downloadable Microsoft Excel workbook).

Exhibit 17: YY Ltd. Long-Term Asset Data, millions of CNY			
Year	1	2	3
PP&E, net	5,068	6,992	6,306
Goodwill	282	248	253
Intangible assets, net	1,779	1,424	4,013
Total fixed assets	7,129	8,664	10,572
Capital expenditures – PP&E	3,785	3,405	3,026
Capital expenditures – intangibles	333	142	3,310
Depreciation expense	220	324	518
Amortization expense	529	486	666

Note: PP&E and intangibles asset account balances were also affected each year by changes in exchange rates and by disposals, which are not shown in the exhibit. Assume that such effects are zero in years 4–6.

1. Using the data from Exhibits 17 and 18, calculate the following for years 1–3.

   • Capital expenditures (for both PP&E and intangibles) as a percentage of revenue.

- Depreciation expense as a percentage of beginning of the year PP&E, net (for years 2 and 3).

- Amortization expense as a percentage of beginning of the year intangible assets, net (for years 2 and 3).

Solution

Using the data from Example 8 and Exhibit 18, the following percentages were calculated. Full supporting calculations are in the Example 9 sheet in the downloadable Microsoft Excel workbook.

Year	1	2	3
Revenue	174,915	205,839	245,866
Capital expenditures - PP&E % of revenue	2.2%	1.7%	1.2%
Capital expenditures - intangibles % of revenue	0.2%	0.1%	1.3%
Depreciation % of beginning PP&E		6%	7%
Amortization % of beginning intangibles		27%	47%

2. Given the following assumptions and forecasted revenue from Example 8, calculate expected total fixed assets for years 4–6.

- Capital expenditures for PP&E as a percentage of revenue to remain at the year 3 level

- Capital expenditures for intangibles as a percentage of revenue to remain at the year 1 level

- Goodwill to remain at the year 3 level

- Depreciation and amortization expenses as a percentage of beginning of year PP&E, net, and intangible assets, net, to remain at year 3 levels.

Exhibit 19 shows financial data for YY Ltd. related to its capital structure and profitability. Based on the data in Exhibit 17 and the data and analysis from Example 8, answer question 3 (see the Example 9 sheet in the downloadable Microsoft Excel workbook).

Exhibit 18: YY Ltd. Debt and Profitability Data, millions of CNY

Year	1	2	3
Gross debt	10,931	17,624	17,597
Revenue	174,915	205,839	245,866
EBITDA	9,304	12,343	14,190

Year	1	2	3
EBITDA margin	5.3%	6.0%	5.8%

Solution

Using the data from Example 8 and Exhibit 18, total expected fixed assets for years 4–6 were calculated as CNY12,351 million; CNY15,179 million; and CNY18,662 million, respectively. PP&E, net, each year was calculated as the prior period balance plus capital expenditures minus depreciation expense. Intangible assets, net, each year was calculated in a similar fashion. Goodwill was held constant at CNY253 million. Full supporting calculations are in the Example 9 sheet in the downloadable Microsoft Excel workbook.

Year	1	2	3	4	5	6
Revenue	174,915	205,839	245,866	290,122	336,541	380,292
PP&E, net	5,068	6,992	6,306	9,410	12,854	16,583
Goodwill	282	248	253	253	253	253
Other intangible assets, net	1,779	1,424	4,013	2,688	2,072	1,827
Total fixed assets	7,129	8,664	10,572	12,351	15,179	18,662
Capital expenditures - PP&E	3,785	3,405	3,026	3,571	4,142	4,680
Capital expenditures - PP&E % of revenue	2.2%	1.7%	1.2%	1.2%	1.2%	1.2%
Capital expenditures - intangibles	333	142	3,310	552	641	724
Capital expenditures - intangibles % of revenue	0.2%	0.1%	1.3%	0.2%	0.2%	0.2%
Depreciation expense	220	324	518	467	697	952
Depreciation % of beginning PP&E		6%	7%	7%	7%	7%
Amortization expense	529	486	666	1,877	1,257	969
Amortization % of beginning Intangibles		27%	47%	47%	47%	47%

3. YY Ltd. management has a year 6 gross debt to EBITDA ratio target of 2.0.

- Assuming an EBITDA margin of 6.0%, revenue forecasts from Example 8, and gross debt-to-EBITDA ratios of 1.25, 1.50, and 2.0 for years 4, 5, and 6, respectively, calculate expected gross debt for years 4–6.

- Given the results of part A, how much incremental borrowing does the forecast imply from year 3 to year 6?

Solution

Gross debt of CNY21,579 million; CNY30,289 million; and CNY45,635 million are estimated for years 4–6 for YY Ltd. This forecast is found by first multiplying forecasted revenue by the forecasted EBITDA margin to calculate forecasted EBITDA. Then, the expected gross debt to EBITDA ratio is multiplied by the forecasted EBITDA to calculate forecasted gross debt. Full supporting calculations are in the Example 9 sheet in the downloadable Microsoft Excel workbook.

Year	1	2	3	4	5	6
Gross debt	10,931	17,624	17,597	21,759	30,289	45,635
Revenue	174,915	205,839	245,866	290,122	336,541	380,292
EBITDA	9,304	12,343	14,190	17,407	20,192	22,818
EBITDA margin	5.3%	6.0%	5.8%	6.0%	6.0%	6.0%
Gross debt to EBITDA	1.17	1.43	1.24	1.25	1.50	2.00

Once projected income statements and balance sheets have been constructed, future cash flow statements can be projected. Analysts will normally make assumptions about how a company will use its future cash flows—whether for share repurchases, dividends, additional capital expenditures, acquisitions, and so on.

6   BUILDING A FINANCIAL STATEMENT MODEL

☐ | demonstrate the development of a sales-based pro forma company model

This section provides an example of building a financial statement model. The subject company is the Rémy Cointreau Group (Rémy), a French company that sells primarily spirits. After providing a brief overview of the company, we will focus primarily on the mechanics of constructing pro forma income statements, statements of cash flows, and balance sheets. Data sources for this example include the company's fiscal year ended 31 March 2021 and 2020 annual reports, the company's interim reports, and corresponding investor presentations for additional information on the underlying results of the respective divisions.

Company Overview

Rémy, whose reporting year ends 31 March, operates and reports three business segments:

1. Cognac. This division, composed primarily of Rémy Martin brand cognac, represented approximately 73% of FY2021 (year-end 31 March 2021) revenue and 94% of total current operating profit. Current operating profit is a non-IFRS measure reported by Rémy equal to IFRS operating profit excluding items related to discontinued brands or items deemed infrequent or immaterial, such as impairment or litigation provisions.

2. **Liqueurs & Spirits.** A diverse portfolio of spirits brands, the main brands in this segment are Cointreau, Metaxa, St-Rémy, Mount Gay, Bruichladdich, and The Botanist. The segment represented approximately 25% of FY2021 revenue and 14% of current operating profits.

3. **Partner Brands.** This segment includes other companies' brands that are marketed through Rémy's distribution network. They represented approximately 3% of FY2021 revenue and just under 0% of current operating profit, earning a slight operating loss in FY2021 of –EUR0.8 million. This division's importance has declined significantly over time as the company discontinued distribution ("partner brand") contracts.

Segment financial information is summarized in Exhibit 19. As shown, the company's largest business segment is also its most profitable: The Cognac segment earned a current operating profit margin of approximately 30% (= EUR221 million/EUR735 million) in fiscal year 2021. Exhibits 20–33 are in the downloadable Microsoft Excel workbook in a single worksheet titled Rémy. We strongly recommend following along with the Excel workbook and exploring the model construction in detail.

Exhibit 19: Analysis of Rémy's Turnover and Operating Profit			
Revenue (€ millions)	**FY2019**	**FY2020**	**FY2021**
Cognac	774	736	735
Liqueurs & Spirits	264	262	248
Partner Brands	87	28	27
Total revenues	1,126	1,025	1,010
Current Operating Profit (€ millions)			
Cognac	236	200	221
Liqueurs & Spirits	39	38	33
Partner Brands	5	–2	–1
Holding/Corporate-level costs	–15	–20	–17
Total current operating profit	264	215	236
Current Operating Profit Margins			
Cognac	30.4%	27.1%	30.1%
Liqueurs & Spirits	14.7%	14.3%	13.3%
Partner Brands	5.6%	–6.2%	–3.0%
Holding/Corporate-level costs (% of total revenue)	–1.3%	–2.0%	–1.7%
Total current operating margin	23.5%	21.0%	23.4%

Source: Based on information in consolidated financial statements of Rémy Cointreau Group for year ended 31 March 2021 and 2020.

Construction of pro forma income statements, as Exhibit 20 illustrates, is composed of four forecasting steps: revenue, COGS, other operating expenses, and, finally, non-operating items.

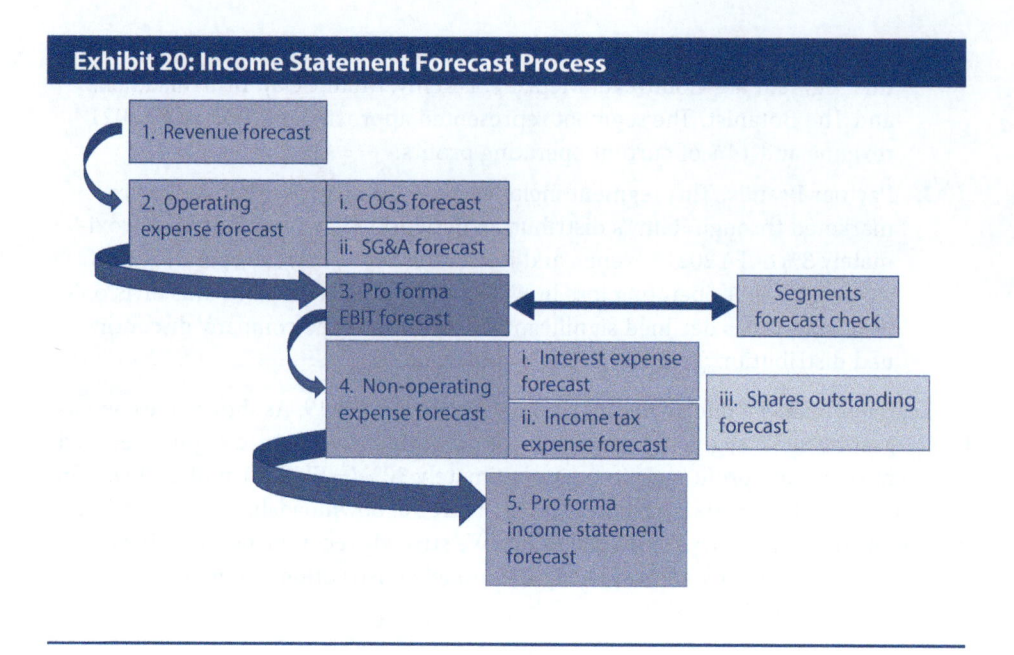

Exhibit 20: Income Statement Forecast Process

Revenue Forecast

The revenue forecasts use primarily a hybrid approach because trends in the individual segments (bottom-up) are combined with the overall cognac and spirits market development (top-down). For each segment, the change in revenue is driven by volume, price, and foreign currency estimates that are based on historical trends as adjusted for expected deviations from trend. Price changes refer not only to price changes for a single product but also to changes in price/mix, which are defined as changes in average prices that result from selling a different mix of higher- and lower-priced products. Changes in revenue attributable to volume or price/mix are organic growth and are shown separately from the impact of acquisitions and divestitures (scope change) and foreign exchange (forex impact in the model).

In the Cognac segment, historical volume growth is usually in the 4%–6% range. For future years, volume growth is expected to remain robust but be slower than the 9.1% achieved in 2021 as the global recovery from the COVID-19 pandemic and associated recession fades (volumes were down 10.1% in FY2020). The growing number of affluent Asian consumers will likely keep demand high, while developed market consumption is likely to be rather flat. In the model, the assumption is for 7% volume growth in 2022, declining to 6% in 2023 and 2024.

Price/mix contributed approximately 6.0%, 2.6%, and −5.4% to the Cognac segment revenue growth in FY2019, FY2020, and FY2021, respectively. Although the impact of price/mix on revenue growth has fluctuated in recent years, price/mix will likely remain a relatively significant contributor to revenue growth in the future given the favorable structure of the industry and the company's efforts to increase the share of revenues accounted for by what it calls "exceptional spirits" (those that cost more than USD50 per bottle and are seeing a 10% annual demand growth). A 4% price/mix contribution to revenue growth is assumed in 2022, with the trend maintained into 2023 and 2024. The combined projections for 2022 of 7% volume growth and 4% price/mix impact results in overall organic revenue growth of 11.3%, calculated as $[(1 + 0.07) \times (1 + 0.04)] - 1$.

In addition to the impact of volume and price/mix, Rémy's revenues are affected by movements in exchange rates. Company disclosures indicate that more than 70% of revenues are realized outside the eurozone, whereas most of Rémy's production occurs within the eurozone. The model forecasts no foreign currency impact on revenue in the 2022–24 forecast period.

Exhibit 21 summarizes historical and projected information for the Cognac segment's revenue.

Exhibit 21: Historical and Projected Information for Cognac Segment Revenue							
	FY2018	FY2019	FY2020	FY2021	FY2022E	FY2023E	FY2024E
Cognac Segment Revenues (€ million)	760	774	736	735	818	902	994
YoY%	7.4%	1.9%	−5.0%	−0.1%	11.3%	10.2%	10.2%
Volume growth %	6.0%	5.9%	−10.1%	9.1%	7.0%	6.0%	6.0%
Price/mix %	7.2%	6.0%	2.6%	−5.4%	4.0%	4.0%	4.0%
Organic growth %	13.6%	12.3%	−7.8%	3.2%	11.3%	10.2%	10.2%
Forex impact and scope change %	−5.8%	−4.0%	2.5%	−3.8%	0.0%	0.0%	0.0%
Effect of IFRS 15 adoption	0.0%	−6.0%	0.0%	0.0%	0.0%	0.0%	0.0%
YoY%	7.8%	2.3%	−5.3%	−0.6%	11.3%	10.2%	10.2%

Sources: Based on data from Rémy Cointreau Group and authors' analysis.

A similar analysis can be performed to project revenue for the other segments. Then, the amounts can be summed to derive projected consolidated revenue.

COGS

Rémy's gross margin has remained roughly flat from FY2018 (67.5%) to FY2021 (67.3%) as total sales have decreased modestly. Going forward, we project gross margin to increase by 100 bps in each of the next three years based on increasing total revenues, particularly from price/mix, which is strongly accretive to gross margin (see the previous section on "Revenue Forecast"). Management has set a FY2030 objective of a 72.0% gross margin, largely in line with our forecasts. Should revenue growth prove more (less) robust than our forecast, we expect more (less) gross margin accretion.

SG&A Expenses and Other Operating Expense

Distribution costs increased significantly over time, from 26.1% of revenue in FY2009 (not shown in the exhibits) to 38% in FY2018, and thereafter decreasing to 33.8% in FY2021. In particular, the setup of Rémy's distribution network in Asia increased the cost base. Rémy is very committed to its brand building and is also diversifying geographically. We estimate modest increases in distribution costs as a percentage of revenue, of 20 bps per year. Administrative costs as a percentage of revenue have increased from 8.1% to 10.1% as revenues have fallen, owing to the COVID-19 pandemic. However, the growth in absolute euro amounts has been modest, with costs of approximately EUR100 million in FY2019–FY2021. We expect 1% growth in administrative costs per year through FY2024E.

Other operating expense (income), composed primarily of provisions for impairments of intangible assets, restructurings, and divestiture gains, has fluctuated from −EUR2 million to EUR20 million from FY2018 to FY2021. Because we do not anticipate any transactions that would result in other operating expenses or income, we forecast zero for this line in the model.

Exhibit 22 provides a consolidated income statement for Rémy through the EBIT and EBIT margin line.

Exhibit 22: Consolidated Historical and Projected Income Statement (Operating) for Rémy Cointreau Group (€ millions, unless noted)

	FY2018	FY2019	FY2020	FY2021	FY2022E	FY2023E	FY2024E
Sales	1,127	1,126	1,025	1,010	1,095	1,181	1,275
Cost of sales	366	415	348	330	347	362	379
Gross profit	761	711	677	680	748	819	897
Gross margin	67.5%	63.1%	66.1%	67.3%	68.3%	69.3%	70.3%
Change in gross margin	0.8%	−4.4%	2.9%	1.3%	1.0%	1.0%	1.0%
Distribution costs	433	346	355	342	373	404	439
Distribution costs as % of sales	38.4%	30.7%	34.6%	33.8%	34.0%	34.2%	34.4%
Administrative expenses	92	101	107	103	104	105	106
Administrative expenses as % of sales	8.1%	8.9%	10.4%	10.1%	9.5%	8.9%	8.3%
Other operating expense (income)	13	−2	20	0	0	0	0
EBIT	223	266	196	236	272	310	352
EBIT margin	19.8%	23.6%	19.1%	23.3%	24.8%	26.2%	27.6%

Sources: Based on information from Rémy Cointreau Group and authors' analysis.

Operating Profit by Segment

In this section, we alternatively estimate operating profit and margin using a segment approach. Rémy discloses current operating profit for each of its segments as well as an operating cost at the corporate or holding company level. Recall that current operating profit is a non-IFRS measure that excludes certain items. These certain items are disclosed on Rémy's income statement as "Other operating expense (income)." Therefore, the sum of the segment current operating profit equals consolidated EBIT before other operating expense (income).

For the Cognac segment, the forecast of higher revenue growth, based partially on strong price/mix growth, assumes an improving product mix that will also result in a higher gross margin. But the benefit to gross margin will be somewhat mitigated by higher distribution costs. Thus, the expectation is that the Cognac segment's operating margin will increase to 33.4% by FY2024. As a benchmark, this forecast can be compared with the financial results reported by Hennessy (part of LVMH), another cognac brand. That company's operating margin in its Wine & Spirits segment in FY2017–2019 was 30%–32%, though that business has a significantly higher mix of lower-priced products with lower gross margins.

For the other segments, there is not much upside. In the Liqueurs & Spirits division, we assume operating margin to increase modestly to 13.6%. In total, Rémy Cointreau Group's consolidated operating margin is forecast to improve from 23.4% in FY2021 to 27.6% in FY2024, largely because of growth and margin improvement in the Cognac segment, the most profitable division, and leverage from that sales growth on corporate-level costs.

While a segment approach like Exhibit 23 can be used instead of a consolidated approach to forecasting revenue and operating profit, it is also commonly used as a "check" on the consolidated forecasts. This analysis revealed, for example, that the model relies significantly on margin improvement in the Cognac segment.

Exhibit 23: Historical and Projected Operating Profit by Segment for Rémy Cointreau Group

Revenue (€ mlns)	FY2018	FY2019	FY2020	FY2021	FY2022E	FY2023E	FY2024E
Cognac	760	774	736	735	818	902	994
Liqueurs & Spirits	267	264	262	248	251	253	256
Partner Brands	100	87	28	27	26	26	26
Total revenues	1,127	1,126	1,025	1,010	1,095	1,181	1,275

Current Operating Profit (€ mlns)	FY2018	FY2019	FY2020	FY2021	FY2022E	FY2023E	FY2024E
Cognac	204	236	200	221	255	291	332
Liqueurs & Spirits	43	39	38	33	34	34	35
Partner Brands	5	5	−2	−1	−1	−1	−1
Holding/ Corporate-level costs	−16	−15	−20	−17	−16	−15	−14
Total current operating profit	237	264	215	236	271	309	352

Current Operating Profit Margins	FY2018	FY2019	FY2020	FY2021	FY2022E	FY2023E	FY2024E
Cognac	26.9%	30.4%	27.1%	30.1%	31.2%	32.3%	33.4%
Liqueurs & Spirits	16.0%	14.7%	14.3%	13.3%	13.4%	13.5%	13.6%
Partner Brands	5.3%	5.6%	−6.2%	−3.0%	−3.0%	−3.0%	−3.0%

Revenue (€ mlns)	FY2018	FY2019	FY2020	FY2021	FY2022E	FY2023E	FY2024E
Holding/ Corporate-level costs	−1.4%	−1.3%	−2.0%	−1.7%	−1.5%	−1.3%	−1.1%
Total current operating profit	21.0%	23.5%	21.0%	23.4%	24.8%	26.2%	27.6%

Sources: Based on information from Rémy Cointreau Group and authors' analysis.

Non-Operating Items

Three types of non-operating line items are included in the model: finance expenses (i.e., interest expenses), income taxes, and shares outstanding.

Net finance cost on Rémy's income statement is interest expense on debt less interest income earned on cash and investments. Forecasting net finance cost, therefore, requires estimating the debt and cash positions and interest rates paid and earned.

Companies pay a fixed or variable interest rate on debt. If the interest rate is variable, the rate is typically determined by a market reference rate plus a credit spread. As shown in Exhibit 24, Rémy's interest expenses are fixed and calculated as 1.7% incurred on gross debt at the beginning of the period (EUR720 million at end of FY2020). Other financial expenses are assumed to be zero. Gross debt and the interest rate paid on it are estimated to remain flat from the year ended FY2021 level

Although interest income is typically forecasted after forecasting the cash position from the forecasted statement of cash flows, in this case we have simply estimated EUR0 in interest income through the model period; in each of FY2018–FY2021, annual interest income was EUR0, EUR0, EUR0.1, and EUR0.2 million, respectively, because Rémy maintains its liquidity in assets with zero or very low yields. For companies that own liquid assets with higher interest rates, or in higher interest rate environments, interest income should be forecast in the same manner as interest expense: forecasted cash and investments multiplied by a forecasted interest rate.

Exhibit 24: Debt Position and Financial Costs and Income for Rémy (€ millions, unless noted)

	FY2018	FY2019	FY2020	FY2021	FY2022E	FY2023E	FY2024E
Long-term financial debt	397	424	452	424	424	424	424
Short-term financial debt and accrued interest	73	98	268	92	92	92	92
Gross debt	470	522	720	515	515	515	515
Interest expense	14.5	13.7	12.9	12.1	8.7	8.7	8.7
Interest rate (on beginning balance)		2.9%	2.5%	1.7%	1.7%	1.7%	1.7%
Interest income	0.0	0.0	0.1	0.2	0.0	0.0	0.0
Net finance cost	14.5	13.7	12.8	11.9	8.7	8.7	8.7

Sources: Based on information from Rémy Cointreau Group and authors' analysis.

Corporate Income Tax Forecast

The French statutory tax rate at the time of analysis is 32%. Rémy Cointreau Group's effective tax rate has, over the longer run, been close to the statutory rate. Therefore, an estimated 32% effective tax rate is used in the forecast period. Rémy has no material minority interests in any of its subsidiaries.

Shares Outstanding

Shares outstanding to compute earnings per share (EPS) on the income statement are disclosed in two ways, both weighted averages throughout the fiscal year: basic and diluted. Basic shares outstanding includes common equity securities outstanding, while diluted shares outstanding is a type of what-if analysis; it is basic shares outstanding plus the number of shares from the exercise or conversion of in-the-money instruments, less an assumed repurchase of those if-issued shares.

Typically, the two major factors that affect shares outstanding over time are share issuance related to equity-based compensation of employees (increases shares outstanding) and share repurchases (decreases shares outstanding). Less common but sometimes significant transactions that also affect shares outstanding include acquisitions financed with stock, secondary issuance, and conversions of preferred stock or other instruments to common stock.

Exhibit 25 shows beginning and ending basic shares outstanding for the past six fiscal years as well as the annual net amount of share repurchases and issuance, which were gathered from the statements of stockholders' equity and notes to financial statements. Additionally, the basic and diluted shares outstanding on the income statement used to calculate basic and diluted EPS (weighted averages) are shown and differed by approximately 2.6 million shares in each of the past five years.

Exhibit 25: Shares Outstanding for Rémy (€ millions, unless noted)						
	FY2016	FY2017	FY2018	FY2019	FY2020	FY2021
Beginning basic shares outstanding	48.6	48.6	49.6	50.0	49.8	49.8
Share repurchases	−0.0	0.0	−0.3	−1.0	−0.0	0.0
Share issuance	0.0	1.0	0.7	0.8	0.1	0.4
Ending basic shares outstanding	48.6	49.6	50.0	49.8	49.8	50.3
Weighted average basic shares	48.6	49.1	49.8	50.1	49.8	50.1
Dilutive securities	0.1	2.7	2.6	2.6	2.6	2.6
Weighted average diluted shares	48.7	51.8	52.4	52.7	52.4	53.1

As evident in Exhibit 26, shares outstanding for Rémy have not changed materially in six years because the company does not pay significant share-based compensation nor has it repurchased shares. Additionally, management has not disclosed an intention to repurchase shares in the near term. Therefore, the model assumes that weighted average basic and diluted shares outstanding on the income statement remain flat at the FY2021 level.

Pro Forma Income Statement

Now with the forecast components in place, a consolidated pro forma income statement can be constructed, as shown in Exhibit 26. Although not presented on the face of the income statement as disclosed by the company, the calculation of EBITDA is shown after EBIT by adding depreciation and amortization expense from the statement of cash flows. It is not linked to other quantities on the income statement but merely shown as a useful profitability measure.

Exhibit 26: Consolidated Historical and Projected Income Statement for Rémy Cointreau Group (€ millions, unless noted)

	FY2018	FY2019	FY2020	FY2021	FY2022E	FY2023E	FY2024E
Sales	1,127	1,126	1,025	1,010	1,095	1,181	1,275
Cost of sales	366	415	348	330	347	362	379
Gross profit	761	711	677	680	748	819	897
Gross margin	67.5%	63.1%	66.1%	67.3%	68.3%	69.3%	70.3%
Change in gross margin	0.8%	−4.4%	2.9%	1.3%	1.0%	1.0%	1.0%
Distribution costs	433	346	355	342	373	404	439
Distribution costs as % of sales	38.4%	30.7%	34.6%	33.8%	34.0%	34.2%	34.4%
Administrative expenses	92	101	107	103	104	105	106
Administrative expenses as % of sales	8.1%	8.9%	10.4%	10.1%	9.5%	8.9%	8.3%
Other operating expense (income)	13	−2	20	0	0	0	0
EBIT	223	266	196	236	272	310	352
EBIT margin	19.8%	23.6%	19.1%	23.3%	24.8%	26.2%	27.6%
Depreciation and amortization (add-back)	22	30	33	34			
Depreciation and amortization as % of sales	1.9%	2.7%	3.3%	3.4%			
EBITDA	245	296	229	270			
EBITDA margin	21.7%	26.3%	22.3%	26.7%			
Net finance costs	15	14	13	12	9	9	9
Other financial expenses	8	19	15	3	0	0	0

	FY2018	FY2019	FY2020	FY2021	FY2022E	FY2023E	FY2024E
Total financial expenses	22	33	28	15	9	9	9
Profit before tax	201	233	167	221	263	301	344
Income tax	54	68	61	78	84	96	110
Effective tax rate	26.6%	29.0%	36.4%	35.1%	32.0%	32.0%	32.0%
Income from associates	1	–7	0	1	0	0	0
Profit from continuing operations	148	159	107	144	179	205	234
Profit from discontinued operations	0	0	6	0	0	0	0
Net profit for the year	148	159	113	144	179	205	234
YoY%		8%	–29%	27%	24%	14%	14%
EPS basic continuing operations	2.97	3.18	2.14	2.88	3.58	4.09	4.67
EPS diluted continuing operations	2.82	3.02	2.04	2.74	3.40	3.89	4.44
EPS basic total	2.97	3.18	2.27	2.88	3.58	4.09	4.67
EPS diluted total	2.82	3.02	2.16	2.74	3.40	3.89	4.44
Average number of shares, basic, mlns	49.8	50.1	49.8	50.1	50.1	50.1	50.1
Average number of shares, diluted, mlns	52.4	52.7	52.4	52.6	52.6	52.6	52.6

Pro Forma Statement of Cash Flows

The forecast statements of cash flows begin with forecasted net income and other amounts from the forecast income statement, and then typically require estimates for capital expenditures, depreciation and amortization, working capital, share-based compensation, dividends, and share repurchases. Once the forecasted income statements and statements of cash flows are completed, forecasting the balance sheet is largely a matter of properly linking the spreadsheet, as illustrated in Exhibit 28.

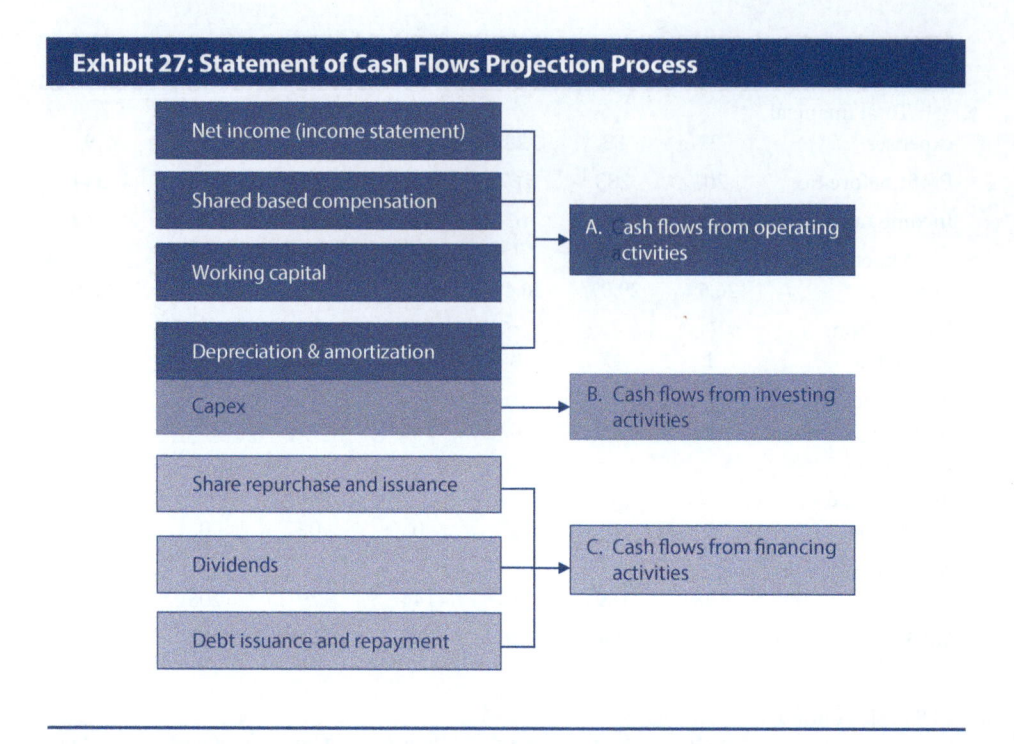

Exhibit 27: Statement of Cash Flows Projection Process

Net income (income statement)

Shared based compensation

Working capital

A. Cash flows from operating activities

Depreciation & amortization

Capex

B. Cash flows from investing activities

Share repurchase and issuance

Dividends

C. Cash flows from financing activities

Debt issuance and repayment

Capital Investments and Depreciation Forecasts

Capital investment, or capex, as a percentage of revenue was 5.3% in FY2021. Given the healthy volume growth prospects, we expect capex to remain at a modestly above historical average level of 5.0% of sales through FY2024. With Rémy's growing fixed asset base, it is logical that depreciation will increase. The model assumes that depreciation and amortization (D&A) is equal to 4.2% of prior year fixed assets, the average of the past three years. The breakdowns of capex and D&A are shown in Exhibit 28.

Exhibit 28: Capex, D&A Breakdowns

	2018	2019	2020	2021	2022E	2023E	2024E
D&A (€ millions)	22	30	33	34	36	36	37
As % of prior year fixed assets		4.0%	4.3%	4.2%	4.2%	4.2%	4.2%
Capex, PP&E and Intangibles (€ millions)	34	45	65	54	55	59	64
Capex as % of sales	3.0%	4.0%	6.3%	5.3%	5.0%	5.0%	5.0%
Capex/D&A ratio	1.6	1.5	1.9	1.6	1.5	1.6	1.7

Sources: Based on information from Rémy Cointreau Group and authors' analysis.

Working Capital Forecasts

We have assumed that working capital ratios will remain similar to what the company experienced in the FY2018–21 period. In Exhibit 29, we include only the relevant balance sheet items related to revenues and costs (i.e., inventories, accounts receivable, and accounts payable) and keep the other items constant. Rémy Cointreau Group had positive net working capital of 105% of its sales in fiscal year 2021. The largest working capital component is inventory because much of Rémy's cognac requires years of aging. Inventory days on hand in FY2021 was 1,493, which reflects an approximate 300-day increase owing to the volume slowdown during the COVID-19 pandemic. Inventory days are partially mitigated by extended payment terms to suppliers; days payable outstanding has averaged around 500 days since FY2018.

We model the working capital accounts by projecting working capital ratios (days of inventory, days sales outstanding, days payable outstanding) which are combined with the sales and cost of sales forecast to produce projected working capital accounts on the balance sheet. We expect inventory days to decline through FY2024 as the inventory increase that occurred during the COVID-19 pandemic is worked through, expect days sales outstanding to remain at FY2021 levels, and model days payable outstanding to decline back to an average level, again reflecting a normalization after the COVID-19 pandemic. As a result of the decrease in inventory days, the model projects a net positive contribution from working capital to the reconciliation of net income to cash flows from operations on the statement of cash flows, which is in stark contrast to prior years' negative contribution.

Exhibit 29: Working Capital Development for Rémy

	FY2018	FY2019	FY2020	FY2021	FY2022E	FY2023E	FY2024E
Inventories (€ millions)	1,170	1,246	1,364	1,493	1,426	1,340	1,245
Accounts receivable	210	271	199	158	171	185	200
Accounts payable	517	544	534	586	597	604	610
Working capital, net	863	973	1,029	1,065	1,000	922	835
% of sales	77%	86%	100%	105%	91%	78%	65%
Change in working capital		−110	−56	−36	64	79	87
Days inventories on hand	1,166	1,095	1,431	1,650	1,500	1,350	1,200
Days sales outstanding	68	88	71	57	57	57	57
Days payable outstanding	515	478	561	648	628	608	588

Sources: Based on information from Rémy Cointreau Group and authors' analysis.

Forecasted Cash Flow Statement

With net income, D&A, change in working capital, capex, and debt estimates already in place, the cash flow statement, shown in Exhibit 31 is almost automatically generated by linking the relevant lines on a spreadsheet. The three significant items left to forecast are share-based compensation, share repurchases or issuance, and dividends. Going forward, the model assumes flat share-based compensation, no share repurchases or issuance, and dividends paid equal to the FY2021 level through FY2024. Lines labeled "other" are aggregated and zeroed out going forward because they are immaterial, difficult to forecast, or both.

Exhibit 30: Projected Statement of Cash Flows for Rémy (€ millions)

	FY2018	FY2019	FY2020	FY2021	FY2022E	FY2023E	FY2024E
Net income (loss)	148	159	113	144	179	205	234
D&A	22	30	33	34	36	36	37
Share-based compensation	3	3	4	2	2	2	2
Investment in working capital	−7	−162	−72	−13	64	79	87
Other non-cash amounts	20	22	3	10	0	0	0
Cash flows from operations	185	53	81	177	281	322	360
Capex (PP&E and intangibles)	−34	−45	−65	−54	−55	−59	−64
Other investing activities	2	92	12	62	0	0	0
Cash flows from investments	−32	47	−53	8	−55	−59	−64
Debt issuance (repayment)	0	11	196	−246	0	0	0
Share issuance (repurchases)	−27	−104	−2	2	0	0	0
Dividends paid	−25	−9	−132	−10	−10	−10	−10
Cash flows from financing	−52	−102	62	−253	−10	−10	−10
FX translation effects	8	−6	1	−1	0	0	0
Net change in cash	109	−8	91	−68	217	254	287
Cash and equivalents, beginning	78	187	179	269	201	418	671
Cash and equivalents, end	187	179	269	201	418	671	958

Note: Apparent small discrepancies in addition reflect the effects of rounding error.
Sources: Based on information from Rémy Cointreau Group and authors' analysis.

Forecasted Balance Sheet

The forecasted balance sheet is given in Exhibit 31 and is based on the combination of the projected income statement (Exhibit 26), the projected statement of cash flows (Exhibit 30), and the historical starting balance sheet. The balance sheet items that were not specifically discussed are held constant, which preserves the accounting identity. For ease of presentation, the stockholders' equity lines (e.g., common stock, additional paid in capital, retained earnings, treasury shares, accumulated other comprehensive income) are aggregated. For each forecast period, common stockholders' equity is the prior year value plus net income and share-based compensation less dividends.

If each of the discussed lines is linked properly—and other lines are held constant from FY2021—the forecasted balance sheet should balance each year. Consult the Rémy worksheet in the downloadable Microsoft Excel workbook for greater detail.

Exhibit 31: Projected Balance Sheet for Rémy (€ millions)

	FY2018	FY2019	FY2020	FY2021	FY2022E	FY2023E	FY2024E
Cash and equivalents	186.8	178.6	269.4	201.0	418	671	958
Accounts receivable	210	271	199	158	171	185	200
Inventories	1,170	1,246	1,364	1,493	1,426	1,340	1,245
Other current assets	16	5	16	10	10	10	10
Total current assets	1,583	1,700	1,848	1,861	2,025	2,206	2,412
PP&E, intangibles, goodwill, net	752	785	808	845	864	887	913
Investment in associates	20	1	1	2	2	2	2
Other non-current assets	186	139	131	73	73	73	73
Total assets	2,542	2,625	2,789	2,781	2,964	3,168	3,400
Short-term/current debt	73	98	268	92	92	92	92
Accounts payable	517	544	534	586	597	604	610
Other current liabilities and accrued expenses	26	31	39	42	42	42	42
Total current liabilities	616	673	842	720	731	737	744
Long-term/non-current debt	397	424	452	424	424	424	424
Other non-current liabilities	121	102	92	88	88	88	88
Total common equity	1,407	1,425	1,403	1,548	1,720	1,918	2,144
NCI	1	1	1	1	1	1	1
Total equity and liabilities	2,542	2,625	2,789	2,781	2,964	3,168	3,400

Sources: Based on information from Rémy Cointreau Group and authors' analysis.

Valuation Model Inputs

In the previous sections, we have built a model that projects the income statement, cash flow statement, and balance sheet for Rémy Cointreau Group. This model is the starting point for most valuation models. Valuation estimates can be made based on a variety of metrics, including free cash flow, EPS, EBITDA, and EBIT. The company-specific inputs needed to build a discounted cash flow (DCF) to the firm model (to estimate enterprise value) are shown in Exhibit 32. All the variables are sourced from the forecasted income statements and statements of cash flows.

Exhibit 32: Calculating Free Cash Flow to the Firm as Basis for a DCF Valuation Model (€ millions)

	FY2021	FY2022E	FY2023E	FY2024E
EBIT	236	272	310	352
Taxes (32% tax rate)	−75	−87	−99	−113
After-tax EBIT	160	185	211	240
D&A	34	36	36	37
Change in working capital	−13	64	79	87
Capital expenditures	−54	−55	−59	−64
Free cash flow to the firm	127	230	267	300

Source: Based on the authors' analysis.

---

7 BEHAVIORAL FINANCE AND ANALYST FORECASTS

> ☐ explain how behavioral factors affect analyst forecasts and recommend remedial actions for analyst biases

Studies have shown that experts in many fields persistently make forecasting errors arising from behavioral biases, and investment analysts' models of financial statements are in no way immune. To improve forecasts and the investment decisions based on them, analysts must be aware of the impact of biases and potential remedies for them. Five key behavioral biases that influence analyst forecasts are overconfidence, illusion of control, conservatism, representativeness, and confirmation bias.

Overconfidence in Forecasting

Overconfidence bias is a bias in which people demonstrate unwarranted faith in their own abilities. Studies have identified that 90 percent *confidence intervals* for forecasts, which should leave only 10% error rates, turn out to be wrong as much as 40% of the time (Russo and Schoemaker 1992). Studies have also suggested that individuals are more confident when making contrarian predictions that counter the consensus. That is, overconfidence arises more frequently when forecasting what others do not expect (Dunning, Griffin, Milojkovic, and Ross 1990).

To mitigate overconfidence bias, analysts should record and share their forecasts and review them regularly, identifying *both* the correct and incorrect forecasts they have made. Given the wide range of outcomes for most financial variables, an analyst will likely find that they have been wrong as much or more often than they have been right. The goal is to recognize that forecast error rates are high, so mitigating actions that widen the confidence interval of forecasts should be taken. One such action is **scenario analysis**. By asking, "Where could I be wrong and by how much?," an analyst can generate different forecast scenarios.

EXAMPLE 11

Mitigating Overconfidence: Scenario Analysis for Rémy

In the earlier sections, a financial statement model was constructed for Rémy Cointreau Group that includes only one set of forecasted numbers, or one scenario. Creating several more scenarios is an important modeling step because the range of outcomes for the most important variable is wider than a single point.

Three important variables in the forecast of free cash flow are organic sales growth in the Cognac segment, EBIT margin, and net working capital as a percentage of sales. A benefit of the spreadsheet-driven model is that the forecasts can be easily modified to calculate different free cash flow estimates. The base case inputs and forecast for 2024E free cash flow to the firm, as well as figures for two different scenarios, are shown in Exhibit 34.

Alternative Scenario 1 assumes that the Cognac segment's organic growth remains the same as its FY2021 rate, an EBIT margin of 23.6%, where it was before the COVID-19 pandemic, and working capital of 86% of sales, also the pre-pandemic level from FY2019. Alternative Scenario 2 assumes the same Cognac segment organic growth rate as the base case but an EBIT margin of 25.0% and working capital of 90% of sales. This scenario reflects strong growth but a high level of reinvestment in sales and marketing costs and aged cognac inventory to support that growth.

As Exhibit 34 demonstrates, there is a wide range of free cash flow estimates for 2022E–2024E because of a wide range of reasonable inputs for key variables.

Exhibit 33: Calculating Free Cash Flow to the Firm as Basis for a DCF Valuation Model (€ millions)

Base Case	2022E	2023E	2024E
Cognac segment organic growth	11.3%	10.2%	10.2%
EBIT margin	24.8%	26.2%	27.6%
Working capital as % of sales	91%	78%	65%
Free cash flow to the firm est.	230	267	300
Alternative Scenario 1	**2022E**	**2023E**	**2024E**
Cognac segment organic growth	4.0%	4.0%	4.0%
EBIT margin	23.6%	23.6%	23.6%
Working capital as % of sales	86%	86%	86%
Free cash flow to the firm est.	318	133	129
Alternative Scenario 2	**2022E**	**2023E**	**2024E**
Cognac segment organic growth	11.3%	10.2%	10.2%
EBIT margin	25.0%	25.0%	25.0%
Working capital as % of sales	90%	90%	90%

Base Case	2022E	2023E	2024E
Free cash flow to the firm est.	240	109	105

Illusion of Control

A bias often linked to overconfidence, illusion of control is a tendency to overestimate the ability to control what cannot be controlled and to take ultimately fruitless actions in pursuit of control. This bias often manifests in analysts' beliefs that forecasts can be rendered more accurate in two ways: by acquiring more information and opinions from experts and by creating more granular and complex models. Although additional information and complexity in model specification can improve forecasting accuracy, there are diminishing marginal returns. The amount of material information available for an investment is finite, and adding immaterial information will mislead. Complex models tend to be overfitted to historical data sets which do not prove robust in a range of environments that include never-before-seen outliers. Excessive breadth of data and model complexity can also conceal assumptions and make updating forecasts upon the receipt of new information difficult. Finally, analysts face significant opportunity costs; additional hours modeling one company could mean that the analyst will examine fewer opportunities in total.

Beyond awareness of the bias and the recognition that uncertainty is an inherent characteristic in investments, illusion of control can be mitigated by restricting modeling variables to those that are regularly disclosed by the company, focusing on the most important or impactful variables, and speaking only with those who are likely to have unique or significant perspectives.

EXAMPLE 12

Illusion of Control: How Much Model Complexity?

Rémy Cointreau Group regularly reports revenues by segment and by geographic region (Europe/Middle East/Africa, the Americas, and Asia Pacific). It does not disclose segment revenue by geographic region (e.g., the Cognac segment revenue in the Asia Pacific region), nor does it disclose revenue by sales channel, such as retailers versus bars and restaurants, travel retail, and so on. In its quarterly earnings calls, however, the company often makes numerous references to segment growth rates in specific regions and growth rates of specific channels, even though the actual numbers are not disclosed. Such a practice is common, especially during the COVID-19 pandemic because large sales channel shifts occurred: travel retail in most regions experienced declines >90%, sales shifted from bars and restaurants to retailers for at-home consumption, and different geographies were affected by the pandemic at different times.

An analyst might be tempted to collect all these growth rates and other anecdotal figures that management discloses on its earnings calls and, perhaps by combining them with third-party estimates of sales, to build an extensive revenue model for Rémy in which each segment is broken out into geographic regions and sales channels.

Although such an endeavor might be useful to set expectations and to monitor over time, building the revenue forecast in this way would introduce several problems and probably not materially improve accuracy. First, because the data used in the model are not regularly disclosed, there is no way to check actuals versus estimates. Second, model construction would take dozens of hours. Finally, and perhaps most importantly, whether the constituent small parts of such a model would be accurate is unclear, which would not make the consolidated revenue forecast any more accurate than a simpler model.

Conservatism Bias

Conservatism bias a bias in which people maintain their prior views or forecasts by inadequately incorporating new information. This often happens in forecasting when an analyst does not update their forecasting after receiving conflicting information, such as disappointing earnings results or a competitor action. Although the most common form of conservatism is the reluctance to incorporate new negative information into a forecast, analysts could also fail to adequately incorporate positive information and thus have estimates that are too low. A different name for conservatism bias in this context is anchoring and adjustment, referring to an analyst using their prior estimates as an "anchor" that is subsequently adjusted. Although nothing is wrong with modifying a previous forecast, the previous forecast or anchor tends to exert significantly influence; in other words, the adjustment is too small, and the updated forecast is too close to the previous forecast.

Conservatism bias can be mitigated by reviews of forecasts and models by an investment team at a regular interval, such as each quarter, and by creating flexible models with fewer variables, to make changing assumptions easier. Because conservatism bias is related to overconfidence and illusion of control, mitigating those biases can also serve to mitigate conservatism.

EXAMPLE 13

Conservatism Bias: Rémy Management Guidance for FY2022

The base case forecasts in the Rémy Cointreau Group model call for organic revenue growth of 11.3% and net income growth of 24% in FY2022E over FY2021. However, during the earnings call for the fourth quarter of FY2021, Rémy management gave the following guidance for FY2022:

- "Fiscal year 2022 will be a strong year of growth and investment, and we are on track to achieve our 2030 [objectives of a 72% gross margin and 33% operating margin]."

- "Being ahead of [our] 2030 strategic plan and given the favorable environment, [we] have decided to revise up [our] strategic investments [in sales and marketing] to support brands through the recovery and boost their medium-term growth potential by developing brand awareness and attractiveness."

- Fiscal year 2022 will have "top-line and bottom-line growth in the mid-teens in organic terms."

Based on these comments, your colleague suggests revising the Rémy model slightly by reducing the operating margin forecast to reduce net income growth from 24% to 20%.

1. What behavioral bias does your colleague's suggestion exhibit, and what research or steps should be taken, if any, with respect to revising the Rémy model? Explain your answer.

Solution

Your colleague is exhibiting conservatism bias, or anchoring and adjustment; they are anchored to the prior forecast of 24% net income growth and not fully considering management's guidance on profitability.

Changing the model to follow the guidance without further consideration is not necessarily appropriate because results can and often do under- or outperform guidance. However, in this case, management guidance differs quite significantly from the FY2022E forecast on both sales growth and net income growth. As a first step, management's credibility should be assessed by examining the company's performance against management guidance in the past. Second, the guidance should be considered as a scenario in the scenario analysis, and the investment implications of that scenario should be examined; for example, if the company will in fact increase sales and profits at a mid-teens rate in FY2022, does that result in an investment decision? Finally, the performance of, and guidance provided by, other alcohol and spirits companies should be compared to these figures as a check for reasonableness.

Representativeness Bias

Representativeness bias refers to the tendency to classify information based on past experiences and known classifications. New information might resemble or seem representative of familiar elements already classified, but can in fact be very different and is better viewed from a different perspective. In these instances, the classification reflex can deceive, producing an incorrect understanding that biases all future thinking about the information. Base-rate neglect is a common form of representativeness bias in forecasting. In base-rate neglect, a phenomenon's rate of incidence in a larger population, or characteristics of a larger class to which a specific member belongs—its base rate—is neglected in favor of situation- or member-specific information. Considering the base rate is sometimes known as the "outside view," while the situation-specific is known as the "inside view."

For example, an analyst is modeling operating costs and margins for a biopharmaceutical company. The "inside view" approach would consider company-specific factors such as the types of drugs the company sells, the number of salespeople needed in each geography for each drug, and so on. The "outside view" approach would view the company as a member of the "biopharmaceuticals" industry, of which there are many others, and use industry or sector averages for gross margin, R&D expense as percentage of sales, and so on in the model.

Neither the outside nor inside view is superior; what makes for a superior forecast is considering both. One way of doing so is by starting with the base rate but determining which factors make the target company different from the base rate or class average and what the implications of those differences are, if any. For example, the analyst modeling the biopharmaceuticals company might start with industry averages in the model but change some of the variables to account for factors such as royalties versus product sales revenues, geographic composition of revenues, and whether the company is likely to face patent expirations on its products over the forecast period.

EXAMPLE 14

Considering Base Rates for Rémy

While constructing the Rémy model in the earlier section, little attention was given to comparable companies or to the broader industry to which Rémy belongs. In other words, the model was constructed primarily with the "inside view." In this example, Rémy is put in the context of six other spirits-focused alcohol companies: Brown-Forman Corporation, Pernod Ricard SA, Davide Campari-Milano N.V., Diageo plc, Becle S.A.B de C.V. (Cuervo), and the Wine & Spirits segment of LVMH (LVMH W&S) for the last five most recently reported fiscal years at the time of analysis. The variable used for the industry comparison is the five-year average of EBIT margin because it is a key model input, and the profitability of an individual company is strongly influenced by industry profitability. Many of these peer companies are significantly larger by revenue than Rémy, which is useful because we have modeled Rémy becoming larger over time. The analysis for Exhibit 35 is included in the Exhibit35 worksheet in the downloadable Microsoft Excel workbook.

Exhibit 34: EBIT Margin Comparison of Spirits Companies, Last Five Reported Fiscal Years (€ millions)

EBIT margin	MRY-4	MRY-3	MRY-2	MRY-1	Most Recent Year (MRY)
Rémy	20%	20%	24%	19%	23%
Brown Forman	34%	32%	34%	32%	34%
Pernod	24%	25%	26%	26%	12%
Campari	22%	26%	25%	25%	17%
Diageo	27%	30%	30%	31%	18%
Cuervo	23%	26%	20%	18%	20%
LVMH W&S	31%	31%	32%	31%	29%
Peer average (ex Rémy)	27%	28%	28%	27%	22%
Peer five-year average (ex Rémy)	26%				

1. Evaluate the base case forecasts in the Rémy model as well as Rémy's management's FY2030 objective of a 33% operating margin considering the analysis in Exhibit 35.

   Solution

   The base case forecasts in the Rémy model are for EBIT margins of 24.8%, 26.2%, and 27.6% in FY2022E, FY2023E, and FY2024E, respectively. The most recently reported fiscal year(s) for most of the peer companies include the effect of deleveraging from sales declines associated with the COVID-19 pandemic. Aside from that, the base case forecasts are close to the peer average and by that measure appear reasonable, though they are substantially higher than the past five years of profitability for Rémy itself.

   Rémy management's objective of 33% operating margin in 2030 appears high relative to those of its peers; only one company, Brown Forman, has achieved that level of profitability, on annual revenues ~3.0x that of Rémy. Industry-leading growth and profitability of Rémy's Cognac segment will be required to meet this objective.

Confirmation Bias

Confirmationbiasis the tendency to look for and notice what confirms prior beliefs and to ignore or undervalue whatever contradicts them. A common manifestation of this bias among investment analysts is to structure the research process in pursuit of only positive news or certain criteria, or with a narrow scope. For example, an analyst might research a particular company but conduct only cursory research on its competitors and companies that offer substitute products. An analyst who has a positive view on a company might speak only to other analysts who share that view and the company's management, all of whom will likely tell the analyst what they want to hear and already know. Confirmation bias is closely related to overconfidence and representativeness biases.

The extent to which company management can be excessively optimistic is shown in Exhibit 35, which analyzes the annual report of a major European bank for 2007, published mere months before it entered bankruptcy and was nationalized.

Speaking with management is valuable given their role and should not be excluded from the research process, but analysts must be aware of management's inherent bias and seek differing perspectives, especially when examining a company with significant controversy. Two approaches to mitigating confirmation bias in the forecasting process are to speak to or read research from analysts with a negative opinion on the security under scrutiny and to seek perspectives from colleagues who are not economically or psychologically invested in the subject security.

Exhibit 35: Management Optimism

Consider this text analysis of the chairman's statement and business review in the 2007 annual report of a major European bank published in 2008, a few months before the bank was rescued by the government.

Occurrences of			
Negative words		**Positive words**	
Disappoint/disappointed	0	Good	55
Bad/badly	0	Excellent	12
Poor	0	Success/successful	35
Weaker/weakening	7	Improvement	23
Slowdown	6	Strong/stronger/strongly	78

Source: Royal Bank of Scotland plc, Annual Report and Accounts 2007, SVM Analysis.

THE IMPACT OF COMPETITIVE FACTORS IN PRICES AND COSTS

8

- ☐ explain how competitive factors affect prices and costs
- ☐ evaluate the competitive position of a company based on a Porter's five forces analysis

One of the tools that analysts can use to think about how competition will affect financial results is Michael Porter's widely used "five forces" framework (see Porter 1980). The framework identifies five forces that affect the intensity of a company's competitive environment and thus cost and price projections. These forces include the following: threat of substitute products, intensity of rivalry among incumbent companies, bargaining power of suppliers, bargaining power of customers, and threat of new entrants.

The first force is the threat of substitute products. If numerous substitutes exist and switching costs are low, companies have limited pricing power. Conversely, if few substitutes exist and/or switching costs are high, companies have greater pricing power.

The second force is the intensity of rivalry among incumbent companies. Pricing power is limited in industries that are fragmented and that have limited growth, high exit barriers, high fixed costs, and basically identical product offerings.

The third force is the bargaining power of suppliers. Companies (and overall industries) whose suppliers have greater ability to increase prices and/or limit the quality and quantity of inputs face downward pressure on profitability. Suppliers' bargaining power is generally a function of relative size, the relative importance the supplier places on a particular product, and the availability of alternatives.

The fourth force is the bargaining power of customers. Companies (and overall industries) whose customers have greater ability to demand lower prices and/or control the quality and quantity of end products face downward pressure on profitability. Buyer power is the reverse of supplier power. Bargaining power of customers is generally lower in markets with a fragmented customer base, a non-standardized product, and high switching costs for the customer.

The fifth force is the threat of new entrants. Companies in industries in which the threat of new entrants is high because of the presence of above-market returns face downward pressure on profitability. In contrast, if there are barriers to entry, it could be costly for new competitors to enter a market. It is easier for incumbents to raise prices and defend their market position when barriers to entry are high.

Cognac Industry Overview

This industry overview will focus on the cognac industry because it is Rémy Cointreau Group's most important business segment, accounting for over 90% of total operating profit. (In practice, an analyst would also perform a similar industry analysis for the company's other major segments.) An important feature of the cognac market is that supply is limited and demand is growing. Supply is limited because the production of cognac, like that of champagne, is highly regulated, in this case through the Bureau National Interprofessionnel du Cognac. By regulation, cognac can be produced only in a limited geographic area, in and around the town of Cognac in southwest France. Furthermore, within the region, production volume is capped each year. Approximately 98% of production is exported. The cognac market is highly concentrated, with the top four players controlling 78% of world volume and 84% of global value. Rémy's market share is approximately 16% and 18% of global volume and value, respectively (*The Spirits Business,* June 2018). Demand for cognac has been growing because of increasing demand from Asia, particularly China and Singapore, more than offsetting a weakening European market. The global spirits market has grown more than 5% annually during the 2000–17 period (*Source:* IWSR drinks market analysis). Simultaneously, Rémy has also seen a product mix improvement because consumers increasingly prefer superior quality and more expensive cognac. Exhibit 36 summarizes Porter's five forces analysis of the cognac industry.

Exhibit 36: Porter's Five Forces Analysis of the Cognac Industry

Force	Degree	Factors to Consider
Threat of substitutes	Low	• Cognac consumers show brand loyalty and do not easily shift to other beverages or high-end spirits.
Rivalry	Low	• The market is consolidated, with four players controlling 78% of the world market in volume and 84% of global value. • Only the European market is fragmented, with less than half of the market controlled by the top four.
Bargaining power of suppliers	Low/medium	• A large number of small independent vineyards supply inputs. • Most of the distillation is carried out by a large body of independent distillers that sell to the big houses.
Bargaining power of buyers	Low	• Premium beverages are sold primarily to wine and spirits retail outlets that do not coordinate purchasing. • Premium beverages are consumed primarily in small and fragmented on-premises outlets (restaurants, etc.).

Threat of new entrants	Low	• Producers have long-term contracts with suppliers in the Cognac area.
		• Barriers to entry are high.
		  ○ Building brands is difficult because they must have heritage/pedigree.
		  ○ A large capital investment is required to build an inventory with "aged" cognac and set up a distribution network.

In summary, the cognac market, Rémy's largest and most profitable operating segment, exhibits a favorable profitability profile. In addition to limited supply and growing demand, the industry faces a generally favorable situation with respect to substitutes, rivalry, suppliers, buyers, and potential new entrants.

ANALYSIS OF ANHEUSER-BUSCH INBEV USING PORTER'S FIVE FORCES

The competitive structure a company faces can vary among countries, with implications for modeling revenue growth, profit margins, capital expenditures, and return on investments. For example, Anheuser-Busch (AB) InBev, the largest global brewer, operates in many countries, two of which are the United Kingdom and Brazil, the world's third largest beer market. AB InBev's competitive position and prospects in the highly consolidated and growing Brazilian market are much more favorable than in the fragmented and declining UK market.

The Brazilian beer market is divided among four players. AmBev (AB InBev's subsidiary in Brazil, of which it owns a 61.9% stake) is the dominant brewer with an estimated 65% market share in 2018 versus 20% for Heineken and 12% for Petropolis, Brazil's largest privately owned brewing group. Helped by its dominant market position and strong distribution network, AmBev was able to report an EBITDA margin of nearly 50.4% in 2018 (ri.ambev.com.br), the highest in the global beer industry. The industry participants focus less on price competition and more on expanding distribution and "premiumization" (i.e., selling more expensive beers.) Although the 2015–18 time period saw challenging trading conditions due to subdued consumer demand, causing years of decline in the market by volume, Brazil is still considered a promising market. In this environment, an analyst would likely forecast solid revenue growth for AmBev. Exhibit 37 presents an analysis of the Brazilian beer market using Porter's five forces framework. Most of the competitive forces represent a low threat to profitability (consistent with AmBev's historical profitability), implying that analysts would most likely forecast continued above-average profitability.

Exhibit 37: Analysis of the Brazilian Beer Market Using Porter's Five Forces

Force	Degree	Factors to Consider
Threat of substitutes	Medium	• Beer consumers do not easily shift to other beverages, but such alternatives as wine and spirits are available. • Unlike in many other countries, the range of beers is relatively limited.
Rivalry	Low	• AmBev dominates the market with a 65% market share. Its economies of scale in production and distribution yield significant cost advantages relative to competition. • Price competition is limited because of AmBev's cost advantages and because of typically increasing beer volumes.
Bargaining power of suppliers	Low	• The primary inputs (water, hops, barley, and packaging) are basically commodities.
Bargaining power of buyers	Low	• Beer is mostly consumed in bars and restaurants. The owners of these outlets represent a large and highly fragmented group of beer buyers. • The supermarket industry in Brazil is relatively fragmented, and supermarkets are less likely to offer alternatives, such as private labels.
Threat of new entrants	Low	• New entrants face relatively high barriers to entry because of the high costs of building a brewery, establishing a national distribution network, and establishing a nationally known brand name.

The UK beer market is also divided among four players, but the competitive structure is totally different than in Brazil. The market is more fragmented, with smaller market shares held by the largest players. Heineken, MolsonCoors, AB InBev, and Carlsberg had market shares of 24% (adbrands.net), 18%, 18% (www.ab-inbev.com), and 11% (carlsberggroup.com), respectively, in 2018. Consequently, the British market has no dominant brewer. Given the high fixed costs of a brewery, declining volumes of UK beer consumption, and the highly consolidated customer base, which provides the clients with substantial purchasing power (particularly in the retail channels), price competition is usually intense. A gradual switch from drinking beer in pubs and restaurants ("on-trade") to consumption at home ("off-trade") is making brewers even more exposed to the bargaining power of the dominant retail supermarket (grocers) chains. Increasing taxes on beer and rents faced by pub landlords add to the burden faced by the industry, leading to a steady decline of Britain's pub industry. Profitability has been lower than the beer industry's global average; operating margins are believed to be less than 10%. In this kind of environment, analysts would most likely forecast only very cautious revenue growth, if any. Exhibit 38 presents an analysis of the UK beer market using Porter's five forces framework.

Exhibit 38: Analysis of the UK Beer Market Using Porter's Five Forces

Force	Degree	Factors to Consider
Threat of substitutes	Medium	• Beer consumers do not easily shift to other beverages, but such alternatives as wine, spirits, and cider are available.
Rivalry	High	• The market is relatively fragmented with no dominant market leader and large numbers of small breweries. • Declining beer volumes make price wars more likely.[a] • Brand loyalty is less developed because of the extensive range of alternative beers.
Bargaining power of suppliers	Low	• The primary inputs (water, hops, barley, and packaging) are basically commodities.
Bargaining power of buyers	High	• The large supermarket chains that dominate the grocery sector have significant bargaining power. • Large pub chains in the "on-trade" business (where beer is sold in pubs and restaurants) also have strong bargaining power.
Threat of new entrants	Low	• Barriers to entry are relatively high because of the high costs of building a brewery, establishing a national distribution network (particularly given the history of brewers owning pubs and bars), and establishing a nationally known brand. • Because the United Kingdom consists of islands, companies with breweries in other countries face higher transportation costs than existing participants.

[a] *In some declining markets, companies focus on increasing prices to offset declining volumes, but in the case of beer, where the market is very fragmented and thus there is no price leadership, price increases are less feasible.*

There is a distinction between Porter's five forces and other factors that can affect profitability, such as government regulation and taxes:

> Industry structure, as manifested in the strength of the five competitive forces, determines the industry's long-run profit potential because it determines how the economic value created by the industry is divided.... Government is not best understood as a sixth force because government involvement is neither inherently good nor bad for industry profitability.

The best way to understand the influence of government on competition is to analyze how specific government policies affect the five competitive forces. (Porter 2008, page 10)

EXAMPLE 15

EuroAlco case

In 20X2, EuroAlco was the beer market leader in Eurolandia (a fictional country) with 35% market share. The other large brewers held 15%, 15%, 10%, and 7% share, respectively. The Eurolandia market is considered a growth market. It historically had high overall alcohol consumption but a relatively low per capita consumption of beer, a product that is attracting interest from the growing, younger population and is further supported by increasing disposable incomes.

At the start of year 20X1, the Eurolandia government, in its fight to curb alcohol consumption, tripled the excise duty (a special tax) on beer from EUR0.3 per liter to EUR0.9 and announced that excise duty will further increase by EUR0.1 per liter.

In the following year, 20X2, EuroAlco made efforts to strengthen the position of the more expensive brands in its portfolio. These efforts led to a 20% increase in selling costs. Similar to most consumer staple companies, EuroAlco experienced higher production costs. Poor grain harvests put price pressure on buyers of almost all feedstocks, and rising oil prices resulted in higher packaging costs. In 20X2, competing companies were much more cautious with A&P spending than EuroAlco.

Two analysts research EuroAlco at the start of year 20X3. In making their EuroAlco forecasts, both analysts use market data and the published annual report from EuroAlco (see Exhibit 39 and/or the Example14 worksheet in the downloadable Microsoft Excel workbook). Based on the published data, they consider a number of scenarios and reach different conclusions.

Exhibit 39: EuroAlco Key Financial and Operational Data

€ millions	20X2	20X1	20X0	% change 20X2/20X1	% change 20X1/20X0
Retailer gross sales	11,504	10,248	9,180	12%	12%
Excise duty	2,900	2,520	900	15%	180%
As % of retail revenues	25%	25%	10%		
Value-Added-Tax, VAT (20%)	1,434	1,288	1,380	11%	−7%
Retailer net sales	7,170	6,440	6,900	11%	−7%
Typical retailer profit[a]	935	840	900	11%	−7%
As % of retailer net sales	13%	13%	13%		
Brewer net sales	6,235	5,600	6,000	11%	−7%

Key Financial Indicators	20X2	20X1	20X0	% change 20X2/20X1	% change 20X1/20X0
Volume (mln hectoliters)	29	28	30	4%	−7%
Net sales	6,235	5,600	6,000	11%	−7%

€ millions	20X2	20X1	20X0	% change 20X2/20X1	% change 20X1/20X0
Cost of sales	3,190	2,800	3,150	14%	−11%
Gross profit	3,045	2,800	2,850	9%	−2%
Selling expenses	2,088	1,680	1,650	24%	2%
Administrative expenses	145	140	150	4%	−7%
Operating profit	812	980	1,050	−17%	−7%
Average invested capital	3,000	3,000	3,100	0%	−3%
Gross margin	48.8%	50.0%	47.5%		
Selling expense %	33.5%	30.0%	27.5%		
Operating margin	13.0%	17.5%	17.5%		
Return on invested capital (pre-tax)	27%	33%	34%		

€ per hectoliter (hl)	20X2	20X1	20X0	% change 20X2/20X1	% change 20X1/20X0
Retail price	397	366	306	8%	20%
Excise duty	100	90	30	11%	200%
VAT	49	46	46	7%	0%
Typical distributor profit	32	30	30	7%	0%
Brewer net sales	215	200	200	8%	0%
Cost of sales	110	100	105	10%	−5%
Gross profit	105	100	95	5%	5%
Selling expenses	72	60	55	20%	9%
Administrative expenses	5	5	5	0%	0%
Operating profit	28	35	35	−20%	0%

Note: Average invested capital includes debt and equity capital.
[a] *This is the gross profit for retailers, companies that buy beer directly from the brewers and sell to end users.*

Both analysts assume that the government will impose a further increase in the excise duty (special tax on beer). They also assume that the excise duty increase will be borne by the consumers, who will face a 10% price increase that will allow the brewers to maintain their net (after-tax) revenues per hectoliter (hl). They assume that half the cost of sales is fixed per hectoliter and half is variable based on volume, that selling expenses will remain unchanged as a percentage of sales, and that administrative expenses are fixed.

1. Analyst A expects price elasticity of 0.8, indicating that volume will fall by 8% given the 10% retail price increase. Calculate the impact on operating profit and operating profit margin in 20X3 using Exhibit 40, which is also in the Example14 sheet in the downloadable Microsoft Excel workbook.

   Solution

   Exhibit 41 (see the Example14 worksheet in the downloadable Microsoft Excel workbook) shows the results for both analysts' projections. Analyst A predicts that operating profit will decrease by 25% to EUR608 in 20X3, resulting in an operating margin decline from 13.0% in 20X2 to 10.6% in 20X3. Analyst A calculates a revenue decline of 8% to EUR5,736 based on volume dropping by 8% and a constant price per hectoliter of EUR215. The decrease in volume reflects the price elasticity of 0.8 and the price increase of 10% as a result of the excise duty increase. COGS sold fell only 4% because part of the costs are fixed. COGS as the sum of fixed and variable costs is EUR1,595 + [26.68 (hl volume) × 55 (hl cost)] = EUR1,595 + 1,467 (ignoring rounding error) or EUR3,062. Analyst A predicts selling expenses will decline in line with sales by 8% and administrative costs will remain unchanged because of their fixed character in the short term.

2. Analyst B expects price elasticity of 0.5, indicating that volume will fall by 5% given the 10% retail price increase. Calculate the impact on operating profit and operating profit margin in 20X3 using Exhibit 40, which is also in the Example14 sheet in the downloadable Microsoft Excel workbook.

Exhibit 40: EuroAlco's Costs Structure for 20X2–20X3E (€ millions, unless noted)

		Analyst A		Analyst B	
	20X2	20X3E	YoY%	20X3E	YoY%
Volume (millions of hl)	29	26.7	−8.0%	27.6	−5.0%
Brewer net sales(€ per hl)	215				
Net sales	6,235				
Cost of sales	3,190				
Gross profit	3,045				
Gross margin	48.8%				
Selling expenses	2,088				
Administrative expenses	145	145		145	
Operating profit	812				
Operating profit margin	13.0%				
Cost of sales (fixed)	1,595	1,595		1,595	
Cost of sales (variable)	1,595				
Cost of sales (variable) per hl	55	55		55	
Selling expenses as % of sales	33.5%	33.5%		33.5%	

Solution

Analyst B forecasts that operating profit will decline by 16% to EUR684. Analyst B's calculations follow the same pattern as those of Analyst A, but Analyst B predicts a smaller, 5%, decline in volume. Analyst A's estimates are more pessimistic than those of Analyst B. Note that the net price per hectoliter for the brewer is held constant while the price for the consumer increased 10% as a result of the excise duty increase. Because of Analyst B's more optimistic volume forecast, fixed costs are spread over a higher level of sales than is the case for Analyst A. Consequently, Analyst B will have a higher operating margin estimate than Analyst A. However, both analysts are predicting a decline in operating margin in 20X3.

Exhibit 41: Analysts' Results for EuroAlco's Cost Structure and Projection (€ millions, unless noted)

		Analyst A		Analyst B	
	20X2	20X3E	YoY%	20X3E	YoY%
Volume (millions of hl)	29	26.7	−8%	27.6	−5%
Brewer net sales per hl	215	215	0%	215	0%
Net sales	6,235	5,736	−8%	5,923	−5%
Cost of sales	3,190	3,062	−4%	3,110	−3%
Gross profit	3,045	2,674	−12%	2,813	−8%
Gross margin	48.8%	46.6%	−5%	47.5%	−3%
Selling expenses	2,088	1,921	−8%	1,984	−5%
Administrative expenses	145	145	0%	145	0%
Operating profit	812	608	−25%	684	−16%
Operating profit margin	13.0%	10.6%	−19%	11.6%	−11%
Cost of sales (fixed)	1,595	1,595	0%	1,595	0%
Cost of sales (variable)	1,595	1,467	−8%	1,515	−5%
Cost of sales (variable) per hl	55	55	0%	55	0%
Selling expenses as % of net sales	33.5%	33.5%	0%	33.5%	0%

3. Gross margin improved in 20X1 (50.0%) but fell in 20X2 (48.8%). Cost of sales was relatively high in 20X2 because of high barley costs, an important input for brewing beer. Assume that in 20X2, half of the cost of sales is fixed and half is based on volume. Of the variable part of the cost of sales, assume that half the amount is related to the barley price in 20X2. Barley prices increased 25% in 20X2. Consider a scenario where no additional taxes are imposed in 20X3, revenues and volumes remain stable, and barley prices return to their 20X1 level. Calculate EuroAlco's estimated gross **margin** for 20X3.

Solution

If barley prices return to their 20X1 level, they will decline 20% in 20X3. Because volumes are assumed to remain constant, other variable costs will not change. Gross profit in 20X2 was 48.8% of sales, which indicates the cost of sales was 51.2% (100% − 48.8%). Barley is 25% of the cost of sales (because barley represents half of variable costs, and variable cost of sales represents half of total cost of sales). Cost of sales is predicted to decline by 25% × 20% = 5%. New cost of sales will be 51.2% − (5% × 51.2%) or 48.6%. Consequently, gross margin is predicted to be 100% − 48.6% = 51.4% in 20X3. Compared with the gross margin of 48.8% in 20X2, gross margin is predicted to increase by 260 bps.

Exhibit 42: Gross Margin Analysis

	20X3	20X2	YoY%
Volume	29	29	0%

	20X3	20X2	YoY%
Revenue	6,235	6,235	0%
Cost of sales	3,031	3,190	−5%
Variable	1,436	1,595	−10%
Barley related	638	798	−20%
Not barley related	798	798	0%
Fixed	1,595	1,595	0%
Gross profit	3,205	3,045	5%
Gross margin	51.4%	48.8%	

4. EuroAlco's selling expenses increased from 30% of sales in 20X1 to 33.5% of sales in 20X2. Which competitive forces most likely influenced EuroAlco's significant increase in selling expenses?

Solution

Intra-industry rivalry and threat of substitutes most likely influenced EuroAlco's significant increase in selling costs. By spending more on advertising, EuroAlco wanted to enhance the brand loyalty of its products, thus improving its competitive position versus its brewer rivals and makers of other alcoholic beverages. Furthermore, buyers' bargaining power probably also influenced EuroAlco's increased spending to the extent that advertising creates demand by the ultimate consumer. Strong demand at the ultimate consumer level for EuroAlco's specific brands could enhance the company's bargaining position with its direct customers, the distributors who serve as intermediaries.

5. Retailers are the direct customers of brewers. They buy directly from the brewer and sell to the ultimate consumer. Analyst A expects that the increase in mass retailers in Eurolandia will cause brewers' margins to decline. He expects EuroAlco's operating margin will decrease from 13% in 20X2 to 8% in 20X6, with stable sales (EUR6,235 million) and an unchanged amount of average invested capital (EUR3,000 million). Analyst B also sees the increasing importance of the larger food retailers but expects that EuroAlco can offset potential pricing pressure by offering more attractive trade credit (e.g., allowing the retailers longer payment terms). He thinks operating margin can remain stable at 13% with no sales growth. Average invested capital (EUR3,000 million), however, will double because of the extra investments in inventory and receivables. Describe the analysts' expectations about the impact of large retailers on brewers in terms of Porter's five forces and return on invested capital (ROIC; pre-tax). Which of the two scenarios would be better for EuroAlco?

Solution

The increase in mass retailers in EuroAlco is expected to strengthen the bargaining power of buyers relative to brewers. According to Analyst A, this will lead to a lower operating margin of 8%, while Analyst B believes margins can be maintained if the company offers much more favorable credit terms reflected in doubling of invested capital. Analyst A expects operating profit on invested capital to fall from 27.1% (13% × EUR6,235/EUR3,000) to 16.6% (8% × EUR6,235/EUR3,000). Analyst B's assumptions indicate that the ROIC (operating profit divided by invested capital) in 20X2 of 27% will fall by half to 13.5% as the operating profit is earned on double the amount of invested capital (i.e., 13% x EUR6,235/EUR6,000). The scenario envisioned by Analyst A is better for EuroAlco. Full supporting calculations are in the Example14 worksheet in the downloadable Microsoft Excel workbook.

In summary, Porter's five forces framework and similar analytical tools can help analysts assess the relative profit potential of a company by helping them understand the company's industry and its position within that industry. Understanding the industry and competitive contexts of a company helps analysts estimate whether, for example, sales growth is likely to be relatively high or low (relative to history, relative to the overall growth in the economy or a sector, and/or relative to competing companies) and whether profit margins are likely to be relatively high or low (relative to historical profit margins and relative to competing companies). The process of incorporating an industry and competitive analysis into expectations for future financial performance requires judgment. Suppose analysts observe that a given company is the market leader in a moderately competitive industry with limited buyer and supplier power and relatively high barriers to entry. In broad terms, analysts might project that the company's future revenue growth will be in line with that of the overall industry and that its profit margins and ROIC might be somewhat higher than those of other companies in the industry. But there is no mechanical link between the analysts' observations and projecting the company's future sales growth and profit margin. Instead, the link is more subjective and probabilistic.

9 INFLATION AND DEFLATION

☐ | explain how to forecast industry and company sales and costs when they are subject to price inflation or deflation

Inflation and deflation (i.e., the overall increase and decrease in the prices of goods and services) can significantly affect the accuracy of forecasts for a company's future revenue, profit, and cash flow. The impact of inflation or deflation on revenue and expenses differs from company to company. Even within a single company, the impact of inflation or deflation is generally different for revenue and expenses categories.

Some companies are better able to pass on higher input costs by raising the prices at which they sell their output. The ability to pass on price increases can be the result of, for example, strong branding (Coca-Cola) or proprietary technology (Apple). Companies that are well positioned to pass on price increases are, in turn, more likely to have higher and more stable profits and cash flow, relative to competitors.

We first consider the impact of inflation on sales and then on costs.

Sales Projections with Inflation and Deflation

The following analysis addresses the projection of industry sales and company sales in the presence of inflation.

Industry Sales and Inflation or Deflation

Most increases in the cost of inputs, such as commodities or labor, will eventually result in higher prices for end products. Industry structure can be an important factor in determining the relationship between increases in input costs and increases in the price of end products. For example, in the United States, the beer market is an oligopoly, with one player, AB InBev, controlling almost half of the market. Moreover, the three-tier structure of the US beer market, in which the producers (the brewers) must use a third party (the wholesalers) to get their products (beer) to the consumers (bars, restaurants, and retailers) results in a fragmented customer base because brewers are not allowed to deliver directly to the end consumer but rather must use wholesale distributors. These wholesalers often differ state by state. Large nationwide retailers, such as Wal-Mart, still must negotiate with several different wholesalers instead of using their dominant national market position to negotiate directly with the brewers. The industry structure in the United States has likely contributed to increases in beer prices roughly in line with the US Consumer Price Index. In other words, beer prices have generally risen during years of inflation in input costs and decreased when costs have eased (though there have been brief exceptional periods where the opposite has occurred). If necessary, US brewers have been able to increase prices to compensate for costs of inflation. In contrast, European beer companies distribute through a more concentrated customer base—namely, such dominant retail outlets as Carrefour, Tesco, and Ahold—which results in a weaker pricing position for the brewers. Also, the European market lacks an overall dominant brewer. As a result of the industry structure and the lack of underlying volume growth, changes in beer prices in Europe have been on average 100 bps less than customer inflation.

Exhibit 43: US General Inflation and Inflation in Beer Prices

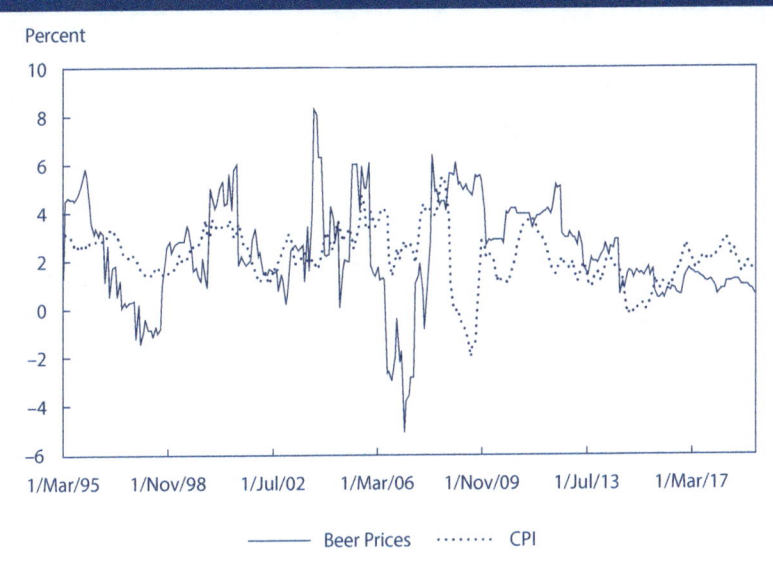

Source: US Bureau of Labor Statistics.

A company's efforts to pass on inflation through higher prices can have a negative impact on volume if the demand is price elastic, which is the case if cheaper substitutes are available. If selling prices could be increased 10% while maintaining unit sales volume to offset an increase of 10% in input costs, gross profit margin percentage would be the same but the absolute amount of gross profit would increase. In the short term, however, volumes will usually decline as result of a price increase. The decline would depend not only on the price elasticity of demand but also on the reaction of competitors and the availability of substitutes. Lower input costs also make lower consumer prices possible. The first competitor to lower prices will usually benefit with an uptick in volume. Competitors react quickly, however, resulting in a short-term benefit. The price–volume trade-off can make accurate revenue projections difficult. In an inflationary environment, raising prices too late will result in a profit margin squeeze but acting too soon could result in volume losses. In a deflationary environment, lowering prices too soon will result in a lower gross margin, but waiting too long will result in volume losses.

In the highly competitive consumer goods market, pricing is strongly influenced by movements in input prices, which can account for half of the COGS. In some time periods, customers' price sensitivity has resulted in a strong inverse relationship between volume and pricing. For example, Exhibit 44 illustrates Unilever's annual underlying volume and price growth from 2001 to 2020. Increased input prices for packaging, wheat, and milk forced Anglo-Dutch consumer staple company Unilever to increase prices for its products significantly in 2008. Consequently, volumes deteriorated. But as raw material prices fell in 2009–2010, the company's prices were lowered and volumes recovered strongly. As the company started to increase prices in 2011, volume growth once again slowed. In 2016, the company faced challenging conditions in several emerging markets as currency-devaluation-led cost increases led to weaker volumes. Both volume and price growth have moderated to low-single digit growth rates, also exhibiting lower volatility.

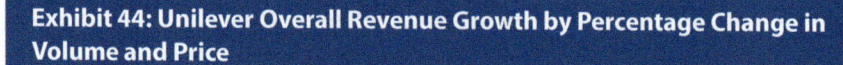

Exhibit 44: Unilever Overall Revenue Growth by Percentage Change in Volume and Price

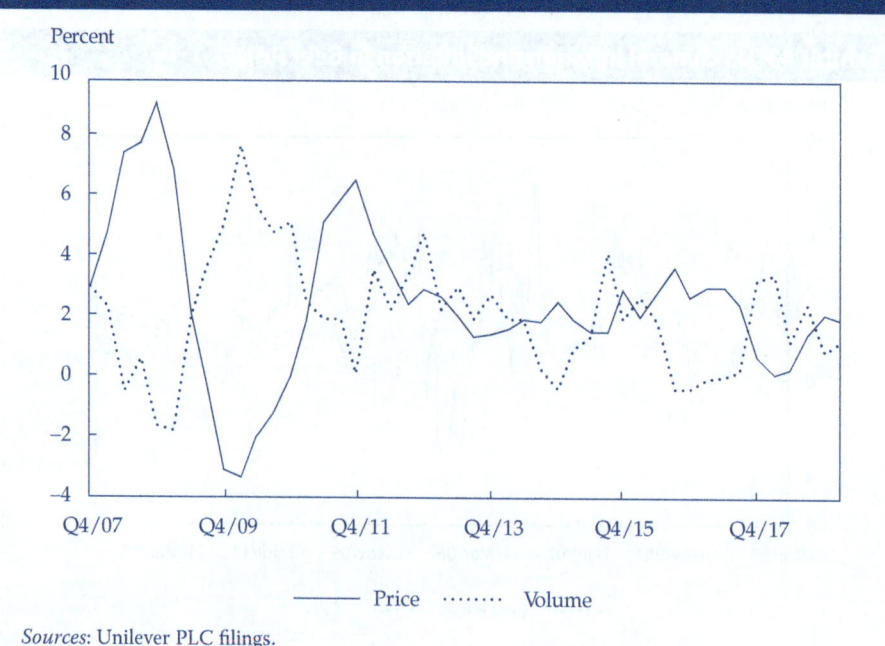

Sources: Unilever PLC filings.

Company Sales and Inflation or Deflation

Revenue projections in a model are based on the expected volume and price development. Forecasting revenue for a company faced with inflation in input costs requires some understanding of the price elasticity of the products, the different rates of cost inflation in the countries where the company is active, and, if possible, the likely inflation in costs relevant to a company's individual product categories. Pricing strategy and market position are also important.

The impact of higher prices on volume depends on the price elasticity of demand (i.e., how the quantity demanded varies with price). If demand is relatively price inelastic, revenues will benefit from inflation. If demand is relatively price elastic (i.e., elasticity is greater than unit price elasticity), revenue can decline even if unit prices are raised. For example, a regression of volume on food inflation in UK food stores from 1989 to 2012 (shown in Exhibit 45) gives a regression slope coefficient of –0.398. (For every increase by 1 percentage point in year-on-year food prices, year-on-year sales decreased by approximately 0.4%.)

An analyst covering UK food retailers can use this information when building forecast profit models. By assuming an expected level of food inflation, volume growth can be estimated and revenue calculated.

Exhibit 45: UK Relationship between Food Inflation and Volume, January 1989–February 2012

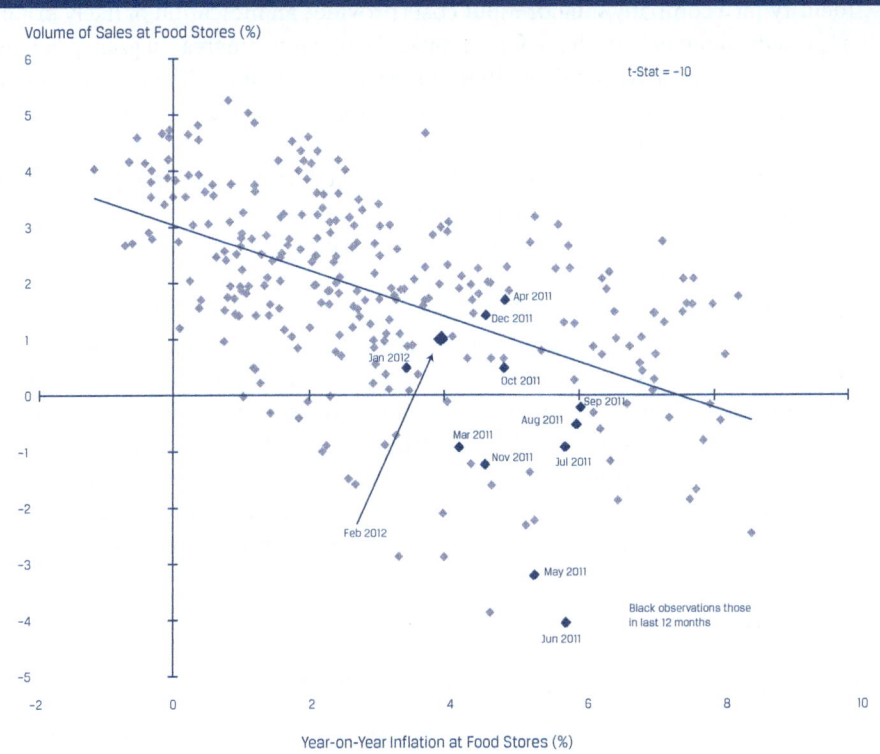

Source: Based on data from Datastream. Analysis is the authors'.

The expected pricing component for an international company should consider the geographic mix of its revenues to reflect different rates of inflation among countries. Of course, strategy and competitive factors, in addition to inflation in input costs, play roles in price setting.

AB InBev's volume growth and pricing have been more robust in emerging markets, for example, thanks to strong demand for its new beer products. The impact of inflation is also an important factor. In its Latin America South division, which then mainly consisted of Argentina, the brewer reported strong 24.7% organic revenue growth in 2011, of which only 2.1% was driven by volume and the remainder by price. As costs increased in line with revenues, operating margin remained more or less stable, and organic operating profit growth was high at 27%. With only a limited negative currency impact, reported operating profit increased 24% in US dollars.

High inflation in a company's export market relative to a company's domestic inflation rate generally implies that the export country's currency will come under pressure and any pricing gain could be wiped out by the currency losses. The strong pricing increases AB InBev reported in its Latin America South division were clearly driven by input price inflation. The absence of a negative currency impact should be seen as a positive surprise but not as a typical outcome. A country's currency will usually come under pressure and depreciate if high rates of inflation persist for an extended period.

Most analysts adjust for recent high inflation in foreign countries by assuming a normalized growth rate for both revenues and costs after one or two years. This constant currency growth rate is based on an underlying growth rate assumption for the business. This approach can understate revenues in the short term. Other analysts reflect in their forecasts the high impact of inflation on revenues and expense and adjust growth rates for the expected currency (interest rate parity) impact. This approach is also imperfect given the difficulty in projecting currency rates.

Identifying a company's major input costs provides an indication of likely pricing. For a specialist retail bakery chain, for example, the impact of increased grain prices will be more significant than for a diversified standard supermarket chain. Consequently, it seems logical that the bakery is likely to increase its prices by a higher percentage than the grocer in response to increased grain prices.

Company strategy is also an important factor. Faced with rising input prices, a company might decide to preserve its margins by passing on the costs to its customers, or it might decide to accept some margin reduction to increase its market share. In other words, the company could try to gain market share by not fully increasing prices to reflect increased costs. On the one hand, Sysco Company (the largest food distributor to restaurants and institutions in North America) has sometimes not passed on food price increases in recessionary conditions out of concern of not financially weakening already recession-affected customers (e.g., restaurants, private clubs, schools, nursing homes). On the other hand, in 2011 and 2012, the large French cognac houses substantially increased the prices of their products in China to reduce strong demand. Because older cognac generates a higher price, it can be more profitable to build an inventory of vintage cognac rather than maximizing short-term volumes.

EXAMPLE 16

Passing on Input Cost Increases or Not

Four food retail analysts are assessing the impact of a potential increase in input costs on the global supermarket chain Carrefour. In this hypothetical scenario, they believe that rising oil prices and packaging prices will affect many of the company's suppliers. They believe that Carrefour is likely to be confronted with 4% inflation in its COGS (with stable volume). The analysts have their own expectations about how the company will react. Exhibit 46 shows Carrefour's 2020 results, and Exhibit 48 shows the four analysts' estimates of input prices, volume growth, and pricing for the following year. Both exhibits are in the Example15 worksheet in the downloadable Microsoft Excel workbook.

Exhibit 46: Carrefour Data (€ millions, unless noted)	
	2020
Total revenue	72,150
COGS	56,705
Gross profit	15,445
Gross margin	21.4%

Source: Based on data from Carrefour's annual report ("Universal Registration Document") for 2020.

Exhibit 47: Four Analysts' Estimates of Carrefour's Reaction to Inflation

	A	B	C	D
Price increase for revenues	0.00%	2.00%	3.00%	4.00%
Volume growth	5.00%	2.00%	1.00%	−4.00%
Total revenue growth	5.00%	4.04%	4.03%	−0.16%
Input costs increase	4.00%	4.00%	4.00%	4.00%

1. What are each analyst's predictions for gross profit and gross margin?

   Solution

   The results for each analyst are shown in Exhibit 48 and the Example15 worksheet in the downloadable Microsoft Excel workbook. For Analyst B, revenues increase 4% [= (1.02 × 1.02) − 1] and COGS 6.1% [= (1.02 × 1.04) − 1]. The difference between the calculated revenue and COGS is the new gross profit and gross margin is gross profit as a percentage of revenue.

Exhibit 48: Results for Analysts' Predictions (€ millions, unless noted)

	2020	Analyst A 2021E	YoY%	Analyst B 2021E	YoY%	Analyst C 2021E	YoY%	Analyst D 2021E	YoY%
Total revenue	72,150	75,758	5.0%	75,065	4%	75,058	4.0%	72,035	−0.2%
COGS	56,705	61,922	9.2%	60,153	6%	59,563	5.0%	56,614	−0.2%
Gross profit	15,445	13,836	−10%	14,912	−3%	15,495	0%	15,420	−0.2%
Gross margin	21.4%	18.3%		19.9%		20.6%		21.4%	

2. Which analyst has the highest forecast for gross margin?

   Solution

   The highest gross margin is projected by Analyst D, who assumes that selling prices would increase by 4% to offset rising input costs and keep gross margin stable from the 2020 level.

3. Which analyst has the highest forecast for gross profit?

   Solution

   The highest gross profit is projected by Analyst D.

Cost Projections with Inflation and Deflation

The following analysis addresses the forecasting of industry and company costs in the presence of inflation and deflation.

Industry Costs and Inflation or Deflation

Familiarity with the specific purchasing characteristics of an industry can also be useful in forecasting costs. For example, long-term price-fixed forward contracts and hedges can delay the impact of price increases. Thus, an analyst forecasting costs for an industry in which companies customarily use such purchasing practices would incorporate any expected input price fluctuations more slowly than they would for an industry in which the participants do not use long-term contracts or hedges.

Monitoring the underlying drivers of input prices can also be useful in forecasting costs. For example, weather conditions can have a dramatic impact on the price of agricultural products and consequently on the cost base of industries that rely on them. An analyst observing a particular weather pattern might thus be able to incorporate this information into forecasts of costs.

How inflation or deflation affects an industry's cost structure depends on its competitive environment. For example, if the participants within the industry have access to alternative inputs or are vertically integrated, the impact of volatility in input costs can be mitigated. Jacobs Douwe Egberts (JDE) is a coffee company that has been facing high and volatile coffee prices. However, its coffee is a blend of different kinds of beans. By shifting the mix slightly, JDE can keep both taste and costs constant by reducing the amount of the more expensive types of coffee beans in the blend. But if all supplier countries significantly increase the price of coffee simultaneously, JDE cannot use blending as an offset and will be confronted with overall higher input costs. To sustain its profitability, JDE will have to increase its prices to its clients. But if competition from other companies, such as Nestlé (Nespresso, Dolce Gusto, Nescafe) makes it difficult to increase prices, JDE will have to look for alternatives if it wants to keep its profit margins stable. An easy solution for the short term could be reducing A&P spending, which usually improves profit. For the longer term, however, it could be harmful for revenues because the company's brand position could be weakened.

For example, in 2010, Russia experienced a heat wave that destroyed large parts of its grain harvest, causing prices for malting barley, a major input for beer, to increase significantly. Carlsberg, as the largest Russian brewer at that time, was particularly hard hit because it had to pay more for its Russian barley and also needed to import grain into the country, incurring additional transportation costs. By increasing imports from Western Europe, Carlsberg also pushed up barley prices in this region, affecting the cost base of other Western European brewers.

Company Costs and Inflation or Deflation

In forecasting a company's costs, it is often helpful to segment the cost structure by category and geography. For each item of cost, an assessment should be made about the impact of potential inflation and deflation on input prices. This assessment should take into account the company's ability to substitute cheaper alternatives for expensive inputs or to increase efficiency to offset the impact of increases in input prices. For example, although a jump in raw material prices in 2011 caused Unilever's and Nestlé's gross margins to fall sharply (by 110–170 bps), increases in operational efficiencies, such as reducing advertising spending, enabled both companies to achieve slightly higher overall operating profit margins that year. Example 17 shows the use of common size (percent-of-sales) analysis of inflation in input costs.

EXAMPLE 17

Inflation in Input Costs

Two fictional consumer staple companies—chocolate and sweets specialist "Choco A" and a food producer "Sweet B"—have costs that are constantly affected by inflation and deflation. Exhibit 49 (see the Example16 worksheet in the downloadable Microsoft Excel workbook) presents a common size analysis.

Exhibit 49: Common Size Analysis for Sweet B and Choco A

	Sweet B	Choco A
Net sales	100%	100%
COGS	50%	36%
Gross margin	50%	64%
SG&A	31%	47%
Depreciation	3%	4%
EBIT	16%	13%
Raw materials	22%	22%
Packaging	12%	10%
Other COGS	16%	4%
Total COGS	50%	36%

Assume inflation of 10% for all costs (except depreciation) and that the companies are not able to pass on this increase through higher prices (total revenues will remain constant).

1. Calculate the gross profit margin for each company. Which company will experience the greater reduction in gross profit margin?

   Solution

   The company with the higher COGS as a percent of net sales—equivalently, the lower gross margin—will experience the greater negative impact. Sweet B has a lower gross margin than Choco A: 50% compared with 64%, as shown in Exhibit 49. After the 10% increase in COGS to $1.10 \times 50\% = 55\%$, Sweet B's gross margin will fall to 45%, as shown in Exhibit 50. Sweet B's resulting gross margin of 45% represents a proportional decline of 10% from the initial value of 50%. In contrast, the proportional decline in Choco A's gross margin is approximately 4%/64% = 6%.

2. Calculate the operating profit margin for each company. Which company will experience the greater reduction in operating profit (EBIT) margin?

   Solution

   Choco A has higher overall costs than Sweet B, primarily as a consequence of its high SG&A expenses. Choco A's operating profit margin will drop to approximately 5%, as shown in Exhibit 50, representing a proportional decline of approximately 62% compared with a proportional decline of approximately 8%/16% = 50% for Sweet B.

3. Assume inflation of 10% only for the raw material costs (reflected in COGS) and that the companies are not able to pass on this increase through higher prices. Which company will be more affected negatively in terms of gross profit margin and operating profit margin?

   Solution

   The company with the higher raw material expense component will experience the more negative effect. In this case, raw materials represent 22% of net sales for both Sweet B and Choco A. Gross margin and operating margin will decline by 220 bps for both. This impact is more severe on gross margin on a relative basis for Sweet B (2.2%/50% = 4.4% decline) than for Choco A (2.2%/64% = 3.4% decline). But the relative effect on operating margin will be more severe for Choco A (2.2%/13% = 16.9% decline) than for Sweet B (2.2%/16% = 13.8%).

Exhibit 50: Effect of Cost Inflation

	All Costs (Except Depreciation) + 10%		Raw Materials + 10%	
	Sweet B	Choco A	Sweet B	Choco A
Net sales	100%	100%	100%	100%
COGS	55%	40%	52%	38%
Gross margin	45%	60%	48%	62%
SG&A	34%	52%	31%	47%
Depreciation	3%	4%	3%	4%
EBIT	8%	5%	14%	11%

10   TECHNOLOGICAL DEVELOPMENTS

☐ | evaluate the effects of technological developments on demand, selling prices, costs, and margins

Technological developments have the potential to change the economics of individual businesses and entire industries. Quantifying the potential impact of such developments on an individual company's earnings involves making certain assumptions about future demand. Such assumptions should be explored through scenario and/or **sensitivity analysis** so that a range of potential earnings outcomes can be considered. When a technological development results in a new product that threatens to cannibalize demand for an existing product, a unit forecast for the new product combined with an expected cannibalization factor can be used to estimate the impact on future demand for the existing product. When developing an estimate of the cannibalization factor, it might be useful to segment the market if the threat of substitution differs across segments.

Technological developments can affect demand for a product, the quantity supplied of a product, or both. When changes in technology lead to lower manufacturing costs, the supply curve will shift to the right as suppliers produce more of the product at the same price. Conversely, if technology results in the development of attractive substitute products, the demand curve will shift to the left. Consider the following historical example.

EXAMPLE 18

(Historical example)

Quantifying the Tablet Market's Potential to Cannibalize Demand for Personal Computers

The worldwide tablet market experienced a major technological development with the introduction of the Apple iPad tablet in April 2010, which was expected to have (and indeed did have) important implications for the manufacturers of desktop and laptop computers. A tablet promised to offer the capabilities of a portable personal computer (PC) with a touchscreen interface instead of a keyboard. Another distinguishing feature of tablets is that, unlike the majority of PCs that run on the Microsoft Windows platform, the then-new tablets would run on a non-Microsoft operating system, namely Apple's iOS and Google's Android. Given the tablet's ability to perform many of the most common tasks of a PC—including emailing, browsing the web, sharing photos, playing music, watching movies, playing games, keeping a calendar, and managing contacts—an analyst at that time might reasonably have wondered to what extent sales of tablets might cannibalize demand for PCs and the potential impact that might have on Microsoft's sales and earnings. Exhibit 51 (the Example17 worksheet in the downloadable Microsoft Excel workbook) presents one approach to answering these questions. It is set at the start of 2012, just over a year after the launch of the iPad. It is presented from the position of an analyst assessing the impact of the tablet on the PC market and Microsoft.

Exhibit 51: Unit and Revenue Projections ($ thousands, unless noted)

PRE-CANNIBALIZATION PC PROJECTIONS	FY2011	FY2012E	FY2013E	FY2014E	3-Year CAGR
Consumer PC shipments	170,022	174,430	184,120	193,811	4.5%
Non-consumer PC shipments	180,881	185,570	195,880	206,189	4.5%
Total global PC shipments	350,903	360,000	380,000	400,000	4.5%
% of which is consumer	48%	48%	48%	48%	
% of which is non-consumer	52%	52%	52%	52%	
Consumer tablet shipments	36,785	82,800	111,250	148,750	59.3%
Non-consumer tablet shipments	1,686	7,200	13,750	26,250	149.7%
Total global tablet shipments	38,471	90,000	125,000	175,000	65.7%
% of which is consumer	96%	92%	89%	85%	
% of which is non-consumer	4%	8%	11%	15%	
Cannibalization factor, consumer	30%	30%	30%	30%	

PRE-CANNIBALIZATION PC PROJECTIONS	FY2011	FY2012E	FY2013E	FY2014E	3-Year CAGR
Cannibalization factor, non-consumer	10%	10%	10%	10%	
# of consumer PCs cannibalized by tablets	11,036	24,840	33,375	44,625	
# of non-consumer PCs cannibalized by tablets	169	720	1,375	2,625	
Total PCs cannibalized by tablets	11,204	25,560	34,750	47,250	
% of total PCs cannibalized by tablets	3.2%	7.1%	9.1%	11.8%	

Handwritten annotations in left margin:
.3 × 36,785 → (pointing to "# of consumer PCs cannibalized by tablets")
.1 × 1,686 → (pointing to "# of non-consumer PCs cannibalized by tablets")

POST-CANNIBALIZATION PC PROJECTIONS					
Consumer PC shipments	158,987	149,590	150,745	149,186	–2.1%
Non-consumer PC shipments	180,712	184,850	194,505	203,564	4.0%
Total global PC shipments	339,699	334,440	345,250	352,750	1.3%
Microsoft implied average selling price					
Consumer	$85	$85	$85	$85	
Non-consumer	$155	$155	$155	$155	
Revenue impact for Microsoft ($ millions)					
Consumer	938	2,111	2,837	3,793	
Non-consumer	26	112	213	407	
Total revenue impact	964	2,223	3,050	4,200	

Notes: CAGR is compound annual growth rate. Non-consumer includes enterprise, education, and government purchasers.

Sources: Based on data from Gartner, JPMorgan, Microsoft, and authors' analysis.

To begin, worldwide market shipments of PCs in FY2011 were 350.9 million units, and worldwide shipments of tablets were 38.5 million units (*Source:* Gartner Personal Computer Quarterly Statistics Worldwide Database). Shipments to consumers represented 96% of total tablet shipments during fiscal year 2011. Next, we estimate the magnitude of the potential substitution effect, or cannibalization factor, that tablets will have on the PC market. Because the cannibalization factor depends on many different variables, including user preferences, end-use application, and whether the purchaser already owns a PC, just to name a few, we use a range of potential estimates. Moreover, we also divide the worldwide PC market into consumer and non-consumer (enterprise, education, and government purchasers) because the degree of substitution is likely to differ between the two. For purposes of illustration, we assume a cannibalization factor of 30% for the consumer market and 10% for the non-consumer market in our base case scenario.

In addition, the base case scenario assumes that non-consumer adoption of tablets increases to 15% of the market from 4% in 2011. Moreover, although the composition of the global PC market is roughly evenly divided between consumers and non-consumers (48% and 52% in fiscal year 2011, respectively), the non-consumer segment is significantly more profitable for Microsoft because approximately 80% of the company's Office products are sold to enterprise, education, and government institutions. The average selling price (ASP) estimates are derived by dividing Microsoft's estimated average revenue for the prior three years by customer type by Microsoft's estimated PC shipments for each type of customer. By multiplying the projected number of PCs cannibalized by tablets by the estimated ASP, we are able to derive an estimate of the revenue impact for Microsoft. For example, in FY2012, it is projected that 24.8 million consumer PCs will be cannibalized by sales of tablets. With an average consumer ASP of USD85, this cannibalization implies a revenue loss for Microsoft of USD2.1 billion (24.8 million units × USD85 ASP per unit = USD2.1 billion).

Once the revenue impact has been projected, the next step is to estimate the impact of lower PC unit volumes on operating costs and margins. We begin by analyzing the cost structure of Microsoft and, more specifically, the breakdown between fixed and variable costs. Most software companies have a cost structure with a relatively high proportion of fixed costs and a low proportion of variable costs because costs related to product development and marketing (mostly fixed) are sunk and unrecoverable, whereas the cost of producing an additional copy of the software (mostly variable) is relatively low. Because very few, if any, companies provide an explicit breakdown of fixed versus variable costs, an estimate almost always needs to be made. One method is to use the formula

%Δ (Cost of revenue + Operating expense)/%Δ revenue, → estimate of variable cost

where %Δ is "percentage change in," used as a proxy for variable cost percentage. Another approach is to assign an estimate of the percentage of fixed and variable costs to the various components of operating expenses. Both approaches are illustrated in Exhibit 52 and Exhibit 53 (see the Example17 worksheet in the downloadable Microsoft Excel workbook).

Exhibit 52: Estimation of Variable Costs for Microsoft, Method 1 ($ millions)

Selected Operating Segments	FY2009	FY2010	FY2011	FY2011/FY2009 Percentage Change
Revenue:				
Windows and Windows Live	15,563	18,792	18,778	
Microsoft business division	19,211	19,345	21,986	
Total segment revenue	34,774	38,137	40,764	17%
Operating expenses:				
Windows and Windows Live	6,191	6,539	6,810	
Microsoft business division	8,058	7,703	8,159	

Selected Operating Segments	FY2009	FY2010	FY2011	FY2011/FY2009 Percentage Change
Total operating expense	14,249	14,242	14,969	5%

*%Variable cost estimate ≈ %Δ (Cost of revenue + Operating expense)/%Δ revenue ≈ 5%/17% ≈ **29%**.*
*%Fixed cost ≈ 1 − %Variable cost ≈ 1 − 29% ≈ **71%**.*

Exhibit 53: Estimation of Variable Costs for Microsoft, Method 2 ($ millions)

Operating Expenses	FY2009	FY2010	FY2011	FY2009– FY2011 Average	% of Total Op Expense	Estimated % of Cost Fixed	Fixed Cost Contribution
Cost of revenue (excl. depreciation)	10,455	10,595	13,577	11,542	29%	20%	6%
Depreciation expense	1,700	1,800	2,000	1,833	5%	100%	5%
Total cost of revenue	12,155	12,395	15,577	13,376	34%		10%
R&D	9,010	8,714	9,043	8,922	22%	100%	22%
Sales and marketing	12,879	13,214	13,940	13,344	34%	80%	27%
General and admin.	4,030	4,063	4,222	4,105	10%	100%	10%
Total operating expenses	38,074	38,386	42,782	39,747	100%		60%
Estimated percentage of Microsoft's total cost structure that is fixed:							70%

Note: Fiscal year ends in June.

Sources: Microsoft 2011 Form 10-K and authors' analysis.

As can be seen, Microsoft's cost structure appears to consist of approximately 70% fixed costs and 30% variable costs. Note, however, that a growing company like Microsoft will typically re-invest in PP&E to support future growth, so even those expenses that appear to be "fixed" will increase over time. To adjust for this expected growth in fixed costs, this example includes an assumption that the change in fixed costs will be half the rate of the change in sales. Variable costs are projected to change at the same rate as sales. As shown in Exhibit 54, after incorporating these assumptions into the projections, an assumed 7.0% compound annual growth rate (CAGR) in revenue through FY2014 would translate into a 10.6% CAGR in operating income [$(36,757/27,161)^{1/3} − 1 = 0.106$, or 10.6%]. In addition, these assumptions would result in an operating margin expansion of 410 bps over the same period (42.9% − 38.8% = 4.1%, or 410 bps) because of the significant amount of operating leverage that exists as a result of a relatively large fixed cost base. With the further assumptions of no change in other income, a constant effective tax rate, and no change in shares outstanding, the pre-cannibalization model, shown in Exhibit 54, results in projected revenue of USD85.7 billion, operating income of USD36.8 billion, an operating margin of 42.9%, and EPS that increases at a CAGR of 10.3% to USD3.62 in FY2014.

Exhibit 54: Microsoft Pre-Cannibalization EPS Projections ($ millions)

	FY2011	FY2012E	FY2013E	FY2014E	3-Year CAGR
Revenue	69,943	74,839	80,078	85,683	7.0%
YoY% change		7.0%	7.0%	7.0%	
Operating Expenses					
Fixed (70%)	29,947	30,996	32,080	33,203	3.5%
Variable (30%)	12,835	13,733	14,694	15,723	7.0%
Total operating expenses	42,782	44,729	46,775	48,926	4.6%
Operating income	27,161	30,110	33,303	36,757	10.6%
Operating margin	38.83%	40.23%	41.59%	42.90%	
Other income (expense)	910	910	910	910	
Pre-tax Income	28,071	31,020	34,213	37,667	
Provision for income taxes	4,921	5,438	5,998	6,603	
Effective tax rate	17.53%	17.53%	17.53%	17.53%	
Net income	23,150	25,582	28,215	31,064	
Weighted average shares outstanding, diluted	8,593	8,593	8,593	8,593	
Estimated EPS pre-cannibalization	$2.69	$2.98	$3.28	$3.62	10.3%

In the post-cannibalization scenario, as shown in Exhibit 55, revenue is reduced each year to reflect the expected impact from cannibalization. The expected impact of cannibalization results in a decrease in the CAGR of revenue over the period to 5.2%, down from 7.0% in the pre-cannibalization scenario. Given the reduction in revenue growth and holding the cost structure constant at 70/30 fixed versus variable costs, operating income growth slows to a CAGR of 8.0%, down from 10.6% in the pre-cannibalization scenario. Operating margin at the end of the period is reduced by approximately 100 bps from 42.9% to 41.9% because the company is unable to leverage its fixed cost base to the same degree as a result of slower revenue growth. Overall, in the post-cannibalization scenario, Microsoft is expected to generate revenue of USD81.5 billion, operating income of USD34.2 billion, an operating margin of 41.9%, and EPS that increase at a CAGR of 7.7% to USD3.37 in FY2014. Thus, the cannibalization of PCs as a result of projected growth in the tablet market is expected to reduce the company's annual revenues in FY2014 by USD4.2 billion, operating income by USD2.6 billion, operating margins by 96 bps, and EPS by USD0.25.

Exhibit 55: Microsoft Post-Cannibalization EPS Projections, Base Case Scenario ($ millions, unless noted)

	FY2011	FY2012E	FY2013E	FY2014E	3-Year CAGR
Revenue	69,943	72,616	77,028	81,483	5.2%
YoY% change		3.8%	6.1%	5.8%	
Operating Expenses					
Fixed (70%)	29,947	30,520	31,447	32,356	2.6%
Variable (30%)	12,835	13,325	14,135	14,952	5.2%
Total operating expenses	42,782	43,845	45,581	47,308	3.4%
Operating income	27,161	28,771	31,446	34,175	8.0%
Operating margin	38.83%	39.62%	40.82%	41.94%	
Other income (expense)	910	910	910	910	
Pre-tax income	28,071	29,681	32,356	35,085	
Provision for income taxes	4,921	5,203	5,672	6,151	
Effective tax rate	17.53%	17.53%	17.53%	17.53%	
Net income	23,150	24,478	26,684	28,934	
Weighted average shares outstanding, diluted	8,593	8,593	8,593	8,593	
Estimated EPS post-cannibalization	$2.69	$2.85	$3.11	$3.37	7.7%
Estimated impact on operating margin		−61 bps	−76 bps	−96 bps	
Estimated impact on EPS		−$0.13	−$0.18	−$0.25	−2.6%

Estimating the Impact of Cannibalization

Answer the following questions using Exhibit 52 through 56 (see the Example17 worksheet in the downloadable Microsoft Excel workbook) on Microsoft:

1. Estimate post-cannibalization global PC shipments in FY2012 assuming a cannibalization factor of 40% for consumers and 15% for non-consumers.

   Solution

   The number of PCs cannibalized by tablets is equal to the product of the expected number of global tablet shipments, the percentage representation of each category, and the cannibalization factor for the category. Exhibit 51 shows that tablet shipments in FY2012 are projected to be 90 million units. (90 million tablets × 92% consumer representation × 40% consumer cannibalization factor = 33.12 million consumer PCs cannibalized by tablets) + (90 million tablets × 8% non-consumer representation × 15% cannibalization = 1.08 million non-consumer PCs cannibalized by tablets) = 34.2 million total PCs cannibalized by tablets. Post-cannibalization shipments are equal to pre-cannibalization shipments minus expected cannibalization, or 360 million – 34.2 million = 325.8 million.

2. Using the results derived in Question 1, estimate the post-cannibalization revenue in FY2012 for Microsoft.

   Solution

   The estimated impact on revenue is equal to the product of the number of PCs cannibalized and the ASP. Using the results obtained in Question 1 and the ASP data contained in Exhibit 51, the expected revenue impact can be calculated as (33.12 million consumer PCs cannibalized by tablets × USD85 ASP = USD2.815 billion) + (1.08 million non-consumer PCs cannibalized by tablets × USD155 ASP = USD167.4 million) = USD2.983 billion total impact on revenue for Microsoft. Post-cannibalization revenue is equal to pre-cannibalization revenue minus the estimated impact on revenue from cannibalization, or USD74.839 billion – USD2.983 billion = USD71.856 billion.

3. Using the estimate for post-cannibalization revenue derived in Question 2 and the cost structure provided, estimate post-cannibalization operating income and operating margin in FY2012 for Microsoft. Assume that fixed costs change at half the rate of the change in sales.

   Solution

Exhibit 56: Solution to Problem 3 ($ millions)

	FY2011	FY2012E	Notes:
Revenue	69,943	71,856	Derived from Question 2
YoY%		2.74%	Rate of change in sales used to estimate operating expenses
Operating Expenses			
Fixed (70%)	29,947	30,357	Fixed costs change at half the rate of the change in sales, or 29,947 × (1 + 2.74%/2)
Variable (30%)	12,835	13,186	Variable costs change at the same rate as the change in sales, or 12,835 × (1 + 2.74%)
Total operating expenses	42,782	43,543	Although not shown, operating expenses include COGS

	FY2011	FY2012E	Notes:
Operating income	27,161	28,314	Revenue minus total operating expense, or 71,856 − 43,543 = 28,313
Operating margin	38.8%	39.4%	Operating income divided by revenue, or 28,313/71,856 = 39.4%

Post-cannibalization operating income and operating margin in FY2012 for Microsoft are USD28,314 million and 39.4%, respectively.

4. Using the estimate for operating income derived in Question 3 and the data in the exhibits, calculate the expected post-cannibalization EPS in FY2012 for Microsoft. Assume that other income (expense), the effective tax rate, and the diluted weighted average shares outstanding provided for FY2011 remain constant in FY2012.

Solution

Exhibit 57: Solution to Problem 4 ($ millions, unless noted)

	FY2011	FY2012E	Notes:
Revenue	69,943	71,856	
YoY%		2.74%	
Operating Expenses			
Fixed (70%)	29,947	30,357	
Variable (30%)	12,835	13,186	
Total operating expenses	42,782	43,543	
Operating income	27,161	28,314	
Operating margin	38.8%	39.4%	
Other income (expense)	910	910	
Pre-tax income	28,071	29,224	Operating income + Other income (expense), or 28,314 + 910 = 29,224
Provision for income taxes	4,921	5,123	Pre-tax Income × Effective tax rate, or 29,224 × 17.53% = 5,123
Effective tax rate	17.53%	17.53%	
Net income	23,150	24,101	Pre-tax income − Provision for income taxes, or 29,224 − 5,123 = 24,101
Weighted average shares outstanding, diluted	8,593	8,593	

	FY2011	FY2012E	Notes:
Estimated EPS post-cannibalization	$2.69	$2.80	Net income/Wtd Avg Shs Out, or 24,101/8,593 = $2.80

Whenever one is estimating something that depends on many different variables that are difficult to measure, we recommend altering some of the assumptions to generate a range of estimates based on various scenarios. Thus, having developed a forecast under a base case cannibalization scenario, we are able to analyze the sensitivity of the results by altering the cannibalization assumptions. The base case scenario corresponds to the assumptions in the boxed center of the table in Exhibit 58. Exhibit 59 summarizes the results of bull and bear case scenarios, showing the estimated FY2014 EPS under alternative estimated cannibalization factors.

Exhibit 58: Estimated 2014 EPS Sensitivity to Changes in Cannibalization Rates

		Non-Consumer Cannibalization				
		0.0%	5.0%	10.0%	15.0%	20.0%
	15%	-$0.11	-$0.12	-$0.14	-$0.15	-$0.16
	20%	-$0.15	-$0.16	-$0.17	-$0.19	-$0.20
	25%	-$0.19	-$0.20	-$0.21	-$0.22	-$0.23
Consumer Cannibalization	30%	-$0.22	-$0.24	-$0.25	-$0.26	-$0.27
	35%	-$0.26	-$0.27	-$0.28	-$0.30	-$0.31
	40%	-$0.30	-$0.31	-$0.32	-$0.33	-$0.35
	45%	-$0.34	-$0.35	-$0.36	-$0.37	-$0.38

Exhibit 59: Post-Cannibalization EPS Projections for Bull and Bear Scenarios ($ millions, unless noted)

Bull Case Scenario (Cannibalization Factor: 15% Consumer/5% Non-Consumer)

	FY2011	FY2012E	FY2013E	FY2014E	3-Year CAGR
Revenue	69,943	73,728	78,553	83,583	6.1%
YoY%		5.4%	6.5%	6.4%	
Operating Expenses					
Fixed (70%)	29,947	30,758	31,764	32,781	3.1%
Variable (30%)	12,835	13,529	14,414	15,338	6.1%
Total operating expenses	42,782	44,287	46,179	48,119	4.0%
Operating income	27,161	29,441	32,374	35,464	9.3%
Operating margin	38.83%	39.93%	41.21%	42.43%	

Bull Case Scenario (Cannibalization Factor: 15% Consumer/5% Non-Consumer)

	FY2011	FY2012E	FY2013E	FY2014E	3-Year CAGR
Other income (expense)	910	910	910	910	
Pre-tax income	28,071	30,351	33,284	36,374	
Provision for income taxes	4,921	5,321	5,835	6,377	
Effective tax rate	17.53%	17.53%	17.53%	17.53%	
Net income	23,150	25,030	27,449	29,998	
Weighted average shares outstanding, diluted	8,593	8,593	8,593	8,593	
Estimated EPS post-cannibalization	**$2.69**	**$2.91**	**$3.19**	**$3.49**	**9.0%**
Estimated impact on operating margin		**−30 bps**	**−38 bps**	**−47 bps**	
Estimated impact on EPS		**−$0.06**	**−$0.09**	**−$0.12**	**−1.3%**

Bear Case Scenario (Cannibalization Factor: 40% Consumer/20% Non-Consumer)

	FY2011	FY2012E	FY2013E	FY2014E	3-Year CAGR
Revenue	69,943	71,801	75,869	79,812	4.5%
YoY%		2.7%	5.7%	5.2%	
Operating Expenses					
Fixed (70%)	29,947	30,345	31,205	32,016	2.3%
Variable (30%)	12,835	13,175	13,922	14,646	4.5%
Total operating expenses	42,782	43,521	45,127	46,661	2.9%
Operating income	27,161	28,280	30,742	33,151	6.9%
Operating margin	38.83%	39.39%	40.52%	41.54%	
Other income (expense)	910	910	910	910	
Pre-tax income	28,071	29,190	31,652	34,061	
Provision for income taxes	4,921	5,117	5,549	5,971	
Effective tax rate	17.53%	17.53%	17.53%	17.53%	
Net income	23,150	24,073	26,103	28,090	
Weighted average shares outstanding, diluted	8,593	8,593	8,593	8,593	
Estimated EPS post-cannibalization	**$2.69**	**$2.80**	**$3.04**	**$3.27**	**6.7%**

Bear Case Scenario (Cannibalization Factor: 40% Consumer/20% Non-Consumer)

	FY2011	FY2012E	FY2013E	FY2014E	3-Year CAGR
Estimated impact on operating margin		–85 bps	–107 bps	–136 bps	
Estimated impact on EPS		–$0.18	–$0.25	–$0.35	–3.6%

LONG-TERM FORECASTING

11

- ☐ explain considerations in the choice of an explicit forecast horizon
- ☐ explain an analyst's choices in developing projections beyond the short-term forecast horizon

The choice of the forecast time horizon can be influenced by certain factors, including the investment strategy for which the security is being considered, the cyclicality of the industry, company-specific factors, and the analyst's employer's preferences. Most professionally managed investment strategies describe the investment time frame, or average holding period, in the stated investment objectives of the strategy; the time frame should ideally correspond with average annual turnover of the portfolio. For example, a stated investment time horizon of three to five years would imply average annual portfolio turnover between 20% and 33% (average holding period is calculated as one/portfolio turnover). The cyclicality of the industry could also influence the analyst's choice of time frame because the forecast period should be long enough to allow the business to reach an expected mid-cycle level of sales and profitability. Similar to cyclicality, various company-specific factors, including recent acquisition or restructuring activity, can influence the selection of the forecast period to allow enough time for the realization of the expected benefits from such activity to be reflected in the financial statements. In other cases, there might be no individual analyst choice in the sense that the analyst's employer has specified more or less fixed parameters. Much of the discussion so far has focused on various methods of forecasting a company's income statement, balance sheet, and cash flow for an explicit short-term forecast period. Although the underlying principles remain the same if one extends the time horizon, certain considerations and choices are available to the analyst when developing longer-term projections.

Longer-term projections often provide a better representation of the normalized earnings potential of a company than a short-term forecast, especially when certain temporary factors are present. **Normalized earnings** are the expected level of mid-cycle earnings for a company in the absence of any unusual or temporary factors that affect profitability (either positively or negatively). For example, at any given point in time, a company's profitability can be influenced by a number of temporary factors, including the stage in the business cycle, recent merger and acquisition activity, and restructuring activity. Similarly, normalized free cash flow can be defined as the expected level of mid-cycle cash flow from operations adjusted for unusual items just described less recurring capital expenditures. By extending the forecast period, an analyst is able to

[handwritten margin note:] –An investment company's turnover is not relevant for forecasting future results.

adjust for these unusual or temporary factors and derive an estimate of earnings that the company is likely to earn in a normal year. We will consider various alternatives for two aspects of long-term forecasting: revenue forecasts and terminal value.

As with most income statement projections, a long-term forecast begins with a revenue projection, with most of the remaining income statement items subsequently derived from the level or change in revenue. Revenue projection methods were covered earlier.

Case Study: Estimating Normalized Revenue

Exhibit 60 contains 10 years of historical revenue data and four years of estimated normalized data for Continental AG, a global automotive supplier. The accompanying bar chart in Exhibit 61 graphically depicts the data and includes a trend line based on a linear regression of the data. The numerical values for each point along the trend line can be found by using the TREND formula in Microsoft Excel. The TREND formula uses observations on the dependent variable (in this case revenue) and observations on the explanatory (time) variable to perform a linear regression by using least squares criterion to find the best fit. After computing the best fit regression model, the TREND formula returns predicted values associated with new points in time. The Exhibit61&62 worksheet in the downloadable Microsoft Excel workbook demonstrates the calculations used in the exhibits.me) variable to perform a linear regression by using least squares criterion to find the best fit. After computing the best fit regression model, the TREND formula returns predicted values associated with new points in time. The Exhibit61&62 worksheet in the downloadable Microsoft Excel workbook demonstrates the calculations used in the exhibits.

Exhibit 60: Historical and Estimated Revenue Data for Continental AG, 2011–2024E (€ billions)													
€ blns	**2011**	**2012**	**2013**	**2014**	**2015**	**2016**	**2017**	**2018**	**2019**	**2020**	**2021**	**2022**	**2023**	**2024**
Revenue	30.5	32.7	33.3	34.5	39.2	40.6	44.0	44.4	44.5	37.7				
Normalized revenue	31.8	33.2	34.6	36.0	37.4	38.9	40.3	41.7	43.1	44.5	45.9	47.3	48.7	50.1
Percent above/ below trend	−4.1%	−1.4%	−3.7%	−4.2%	4.8%	4.4%	9.3%	−6.6%	3.3%	−15.2%				

Sources: Continental AG annual reports.

Exhibit 61: Historical and Estimated Revenue for Continental AG, 2011–2024E

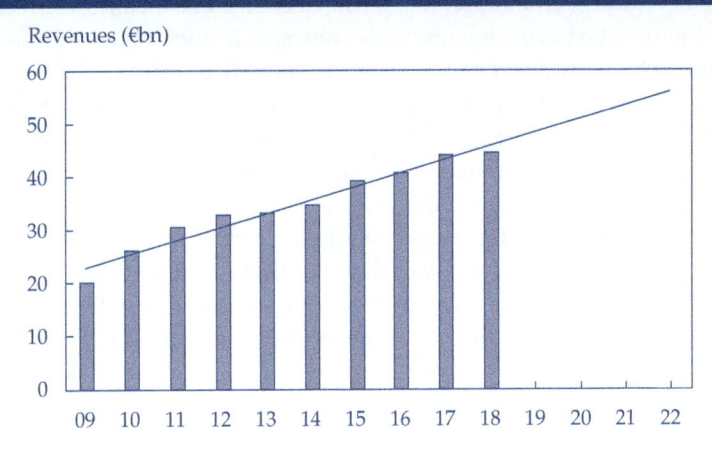

Revenues (€bn)

The "growth relative to GDP growth" and "market growth and market share" methods discussed earlier can also be applied to developing longer-term projections. Once a revenue projection has been established, previously described methods of forecasting costs can be used to complete the income statement, balance sheet, and cash flow statement.

If an analyst is creating a valuation model such as a DCF model, estimating a terminal value is required to capture the going-concern value of the company after the explicit forecast period. Certain considerations should be kept in mind when deriving the terminal value based on long-term projections.

First, an analyst should consider whether the terminal year free cash flow projection should be normalized before that cash flow is incorporated into a long-term projection. For example, if the explicitly forecasted terminal year free cash flow is "low" (e.g., because of business cycle reasons or capital investment projects), an adjustment to normalize the amount might be warranted. Second, an analyst should consider whether and how the future long-term growth rate will differ from the historical growth rate. For example, even some mature companies might be able to accelerate their long-term growth rate through product innovation and/or market expansion (e.g., Apple), whereas other seemingly well-protected "growers" could experience an unanticipated decline in their business as a result of technological change (e.g., Eastman Kodak Company, a global commercial printing and imaging company).

One of the greatest challenges facing the analyst is anticipating inflection points, when the future will look significantly different from the recent past. Most DCF models rely on a perpetuity calculation, which assumes that the cash flows from the last year of an explicit forecast grow at a constant rate forever. Because the perpetuity can account for a relatively large portion of the overall valuation of the company, it is critical that the cash flow used is representative of a "normalized" or "mid-cycle" result. If the analyst is examining a cyclical company, using a boom year as the starting point for the perpetuity could result in a grossly overstated valuation. Similarly, using a trough year could result in a valuation that is much too low.

Another important consideration is economic disruption. The economy can occasionally experience sudden, unprecedented changes that affect a wide variety of companies, such as the 2008 global financial crisis or the COVID-19 pandemic. Even a company with a sound strategy and solid operations can be thrown far off course by a sudden economic disruption, particularly if the company has a high degree of financial leverage.

— If the future growth or profitability of a company is likely to be lower than the historical average, then the target multiple should reflect a discount to the historical multiple to reflect this difference in growth and/or profitability.

If a multiple is used to derive the terminal value of a company, the choice of the multiple should be consistent with the long-run expectations for growth and required return.

Regulation and technology are also potential drivers of inflection points, and it is important for the analyst to keep a close eye on both. Government actions can have extreme, sudden, and unpredictable impacts on some businesses. Technological advances can turn fast-growing innovators obsolete in a matter of months. Both regulation and technology affect some industries more than others. Utilities experience intense regulation but might not see a significant technological change for decades. Semiconductor manufacturers must constantly keep up with new technology but experience relatively light regulation. Pharmaceutical manufacturers are heavily exposed to both regulation and technological advances.

Finally, long-term growth is a key input in the perpetuity calculation. Some companies and industries can grow faster than the overall economy for long periods of time, causing them to account for an increasing share of overall output. Examples include some technology companies, such as Tencent, Amazon, and Google. Other companies, such as those in the print media sector, are likely to grow slower than the overall economy or even shrink over time. Using an unrealistic long-term growth rate can put the analyst's valuation far off the mark.

EXAMPLE 19

Important Considerations When Making Assumptions

1. Turkish Airlines (THYAO.IS) operates in the highly cyclical global airline industry. Operating margins for 2011–2019 are shown in the following table and in the Example18 worksheet in the downloadable Microsoft Excel workbook.

	2011	2012	2013	2014	2015	2016	2017	2018	2019
Operating margin	1.0%	10.8%	6.5%	5.6%	8.6%	−2.9%	9.0%	9.9%	7.9%

On the basis of only the information in the table, which of the following operating margins would *most likely* be appropriate to use in a perpetuity calculation for Turkish Airlines to arrive at a reasonable intrinsic value estimate?

A. 6.0%

B. 9.0%

C. 9.9%

Solution

A is correct. Because the airline industry is cyclical, an estimate of "mid-cycle" or "normalized" operating margin is necessary to estimate a perpetuity value. The nine-year average operating margin was 6.3%.

For each of the companies in the following problems, indicate which of the choices is *least likely* to cause a change in the company's outlook.

2. ABC Diesel (hypothetical company), a manufacturer of diesel-power trucks.

A. Environmental regulations have been getting tighter in most regions, and consistent with past experience, this need to make the engines less polluting is expected to continue over the next several years.

B. Consumers have started switching to trucks with electric engines, threatening ABC's historic strength in diesel engine trucks.

C. ABC Diesel has formed a partnership with Electrico (hypothetical), a company involved in research and innovation in electric engines.

Solution

A is correct. Although it is important that environmental regulations have been getting stricter, this is consistent with past experience and so does not represent a turning point.

3. Abbott Laboratories, a diversified manufacturer of health care products, including medical devices.

A. It has become more difficult for medical device manufacturers to receive regulatory approval for new products because of heightened safety concerns.

B. A competitor has demonstrated favorable efficacy data on a medical device candidate that will compete with an important Abbott product.

C. Management reiterates its long-standing approach to capital deployment.

Solution

C is correct. Management is sticking with its historical approach to capital deployment, so this does not represent a turning point.

4. Grupo Aeroportuario del Sureste, operator of nine airports in Mexico, especially in the tourist-heavy southeast.

A. A technological advance will allow airlines to save 5% on fuel costs, but it is not expected to meaningfully alter passenger volumes. Similar developments in the past have benefited airlines but not airports, whose price per passenger is regulated.

B. Global economic disruption has caused a sharp decline in international travel.

C. Regulators will allow the construction of a new airport by a competitor in Grupo Aeroportuario del Sureste's service territory.

Solution

A is correct. Although the technological advance is good for the airlines, it will not have a meaningful effect on passenger volumes, which will likely prevent the airports from sharing in that benefit. In contrast, both B and C could have a significant impact on the long-run earnings power of Mexican airports.

5. LinkedIn, operator of an online social network for professionals and part of Microsoft Corporation, with limited investment needs and no debt.

A. Facebook, another online social network, announces a plan to enhance its offerings in the professional category.

B. Regulators announce an investigation of LinkedIn's privacy practices, which could result in significant changes to the service.

C. The US Federal Reserve has just increased interest rates. Although this will raise borrowing costs, the rate increase is not expected to have a negative impact on the economy.

Solution

C is correct. Because LinkedIn carries no debt, it is unlikely that higher interest rates will cause a change in the company's outlook.

12   CONCLUSIONS AND SUMMARY

Industry and company analysis are essential tools of fundamental analysis. The key points made include the following:

- Analysts can use a top-down, bottom-up, or hybrid approach to forecasting income and expenses. Top-down approaches usually begin at the level of the overall economy. Bottom-up approaches begin at the level of the individual company or unit within the company (e.g., business segment). Time-series approaches are considered bottom-up, although time-series analysis can be a tool used in top-down approaches. Hybrid approaches include elements of top-down and bottom-up approaches.

- In a "growth relative to GDP growth" approach to forecasting revenue, the analyst forecasts the growth rate of nominal GDP and industry and company growth relative to GDP growth.

- In a "market growth and market share" approach to forecasting revenue, the analyst combines forecasts of growth in particular markets with forecasts of a company's market share in the individual markets.

- Operating margins that are positively correlated with sales provide evidence of economies of scale in an industry.

- Some balance sheet line items, such as retained earnings, flow directly from the income statement, whereas accounts receivable, accounts payable, and inventory are very closely linked to income statement projections.

- A common way to model working capital accounts is to use efficiency ratios.

- ROIC, defined as net operating profit less adjusted taxes divided by the difference between operating assets and operating liabilities, is an after-tax measure of profitability. High and persistent levels of ROIC are often associated with having a competitive advantage.

- Competitive factors affect a company's ability to negotiate lower input prices with suppliers and to raise prices for products and services. Porter's five forces framework can be used as a basis for identifying such factors.

- Inflation (deflation) affects pricing strategy depending on industry structure, competitive forces, and the nature of consumer demand.

- When a technological development results in a new product that threatens to cannibalize demand for an existing product, a unit forecast for the new product combined with an expected cannibalization factor can be used to estimate the impact on future demand for the existing product.

- Factors influencing the choice of the explicit forecast horizon include the projected holding period, an investor's average portfolio turnover, the cyclicality of an industry, company-specific factors, and employer preferences.

- Key behavioral biases that influence analyst forecasts are overconfidence, illusion of control conservatism, representativeness, and confirmation bias.

PRACTICE PROBLEMS

The following information relates to questions 1-7

Angela Green, an investment manager at Horizon Investments, intends to hire a new investment analyst. After conducting initial interviews, Green has narrowed the pool to three candidates. She plans to conduct second interviews to further assess the candidates' knowledge of industry and company analysis.

Prior to the second interviews, Green asks the candidates to analyze Chrome Network Systems, a company that manufactures internet networking products. Each candidate is provided Chrome's financial information presented in Exhibit 1.

Exhibit 1: Chrome Network Systems Selected Financial Information ($ millions)

	Year-End		
	2017	2018	2019
Net sales	46.8	50.5	53.9
Cost of sales	18.2	18.4	18.8
Gross profit	28.6	32.1	35.1
SG&A expenses	19.3	22.5	25.1
Operating income	9.3	9.6	10.0
Interest expense	0.5	0.7	0.6
Income before provision for income tax	8.8	8.9	9.4
Provision for income taxes	2.8	2.8	3.1
Net income	6.0	6.1	6.3

Green asks each candidate to forecast the 2020 income statement for Chrome and to outline the key assumptions used in their analysis. The job candidates are told to include Horizon's economic outlook for 2020 in their analysis, which assumes nominal GDP growth of 3.6%, based on expectations of real GDP growth of 1.6% and inflation of 2.0%.

Green receives the models from each of the candidates and schedules second interviews. To prepare for the interviews, Green compiles a summary of the candidates' key assumptions in Exhibit 2.

Exhibit 2: Summary of Key Assumptions Used in Candidates' Models

Metric	Candidate A	Candidate B	Candidate C
Net sales	Net sales will grow at the average annual growth rate in net sales over the 2017–19 time period.	Industry sales will grow at the same rate as nominal GDP, but Chrome will have a 2 percentage point decline in market share.	Net sales will grow 50 bps slower than nominal GDP.
Cost of sales	The 2020 gross margin will be the same as the average annual gross margin over the 2017–19 time period.	The 2020 gross margin will decline as costs increase by expected inflation.	The 2020 gross margin will increase by 20 bps from 2019.
SG&A expenses	The 2020 SG&A/net sales ratio will be the same as the average ratio over the 2017–19 time period.	The 2020 SG&A will grow at the rate of inflation.	The 2020 SG&A/net sales ratio will be the same as the 2019 ratio.
Interest expense	The 2020 interest expense assumes the effective interest rate will be the same as the 2019 rate.	The 2020 interest expense will be the same as the 2019 interest expense.	The 2020 interest expense will be the same as the average expense over the 2017–19 time period.
Income taxes	The 2020 effective tax rate will be the same as the 2019 rate.	The 2020 effective tax rate will equal the blended statutory rate of 30%.	The 2020 effective tax rate will be the same as the average effective tax rate over the 2017–19 time period.

1. Based on Exhibit 1, which of the following provides the strongest evidence that Chrome displays economies of scale?

   A. Increasing net sales

   B. Profit margins that are increasing with net sales

   C. Gross profit margins that are increasing with net sales

2. Based on Exhibit 2, the job candidate *most likely* using a bottom-up approach to model net sales is:

   A. Candidate A

   B. Candidate B

   C. Candidate C

3. Based on Exhibit 2, the modeling approach used by Candidate B to project future net sales is *most accurately* classified as a:

   A. hybrid approach.

   B. top-down approach.

    C. bottom-up approach.

4. Based on Exhibit 1 and Exhibit 2, Candidate C's forecast for cost of sales in 2020 is *closest* to:

    A. USD18.3 million.

    B. USD18.9 million.

    C. USD19.3 million.

5. Based on Exhibit 1 and Exhibit 2, Candidate A's forecast for SG&A expenses in 2020 is *closest* to:

    A. USD23.8 million.

    B. USD25.5 million.

    C. USD27.4 million.

6. Based on Exhibit 2, forecasted interest expense will reflect changes in Chrome's debt level under the forecast assumptions used by:

    A. Candidate A.

    B. Candidate B.

    C. Candidate C.

7. Candidate B asks Green if she had additional information on Horizon's industry peers and competitors, to put the profitability estimates in a richer context. By asking for this additional information for their analysis, Candidate B is seeking to mitigate which behavioral bias?

    A. Illusion of control

    B. Base rate neglect

    C. Conservatism

The following information relates to questions 8-14

Angela Green, an investment manager at Horizon Investments, intends to hire a new investment analyst. After conducting initial interviews, Green has narrowed the pool to three candidates. She plans to conduct second interviews to further assess the candidates' knowledge of industry and company analysis.

Prior to the second interviews, Green asks the candidates to analyze Chrome Network Systems, a company that manufactures internet networking products. Each candidate is provided Chrome's financial information presented in Exhibit 1.

Exhibit 1: Chrome Network Systems Selected Financial Information ($ millions)

	Year-End		
	2017	**2018**	**2019**
Net sales	46.8	50.5	53.9
Cost of sales	18.2	18.4	18.8
Gross profit	28.6	32.1	35.1
SG&A expenses	19.3	22.5	25.1
Operating income	9.3	9.6	10.0
Interest expense	0.5	0.7	0.6
Income before provision for income tax	8.8	8.9	9.4
Provision for income taxes	2.8	2.8	3.1
Net income	6.0	6.1	6.3

Green asks each candidate to forecast the 2020 income statement for Chrome and to outline the key assumptions used in their analysis. The job candidates are told to include Horizon's economic outlook for 2020 in their analysis, which assumes nominal GDP growth of 3.6%, based on expectations of real GDP growth of 1.6% and inflation of 2.0%.

Green receives the models from each of the candidates and schedules second interviews. To prepare for the interviews, Green compiles a summary of the candidates' key assumptions in Exhibit 2.

Exhibit 2: Summary of Key Assumptions Used in Candidates' Models

Metric	Candidate A	Candidate B	Candidate C
Net sales	Net sales will grow at the average annual growth rate in net sales over the 2017–19 time period.	Industry sales will grow at the same rate as nominal GDP, but Chrome will have a 2 percentage point decline in market share.	Net sales will grow 50 bps slower than nominal GDP.
Cost of sales	The 2020 gross margin will be the same as the average annual gross margin over the 2017–19 time period.	The 2020 gross margin will decline as costs increase by expected inflation.	The 2020 gross margin will increase by 20 bps from 2019.
SG&A expenses	The 2020 SG&A/net sales ratio will be the same as the average ratio over the 2017–19 time period.	The 2020 SG&A will grow at the rate of inflation.	The 2020 SG&A/net sales ratio will be the same as the 2019 ratio.

Metric	Candidate A	Candidate B	Candidate C
Interest expense	The 2020 interest expense assumes the effective interest rate will be the same as the 2019 rate.	The 2020 interest expense will be the same as the 2019 interest expense.	The 2020 interest expense will be the same as the average expense over the 2017–19 time period.
Income taxes	The 2020 effective tax rate will be the same as the 2019 rate.	The 2020 effective tax rate will equal the blended statutory rate of 30%.	The 2020 effective tax rate will be the same as the average effective tax rate over the 2017–19 time period.

8. Based on Exhibit 1, which of the following provides the strongest evidence that Chrome displays economies of scale?

   A. Increasing net sales

   B. Profit margins that are increasing with net sales

   C. Gross profit margins that are increasing with net sales

9. Based on Exhibit 2, the job candidate *most likely* using a bottom-up approach to model net sales is:

   A. Candidate A

   B. Candidate B

   C. Candidate C

10. Based on Exhibit 2, the modeling approach used by Candidate B to project future net sales is *most accurately* classified as a:

    A. hybrid approach.

    B. top-down approach.

    C. bottom-up approach.

11. Based on Exhibit 1 and Exhibit 2, Candidate C's forecast for cost of sales in 2020 is *closest* to:

    A. USD18.3 million.

    B. USD18.9 million.

    C. USD19.3 million.

12. Based on Exhibit 1 and Exhibit 2, Candidate A's forecast for SG&A expenses in 2020 is *closest* to:

    A. USD23.8 million.

    B. USD25.5 million.

    C. USD27.4 million.

13. Based on Exhibit 2, forecasted interest expense will reflect changes in Chrome's

debt level under the forecast assumptions used by:

A. Candidate A.

B. Candidate B.

C. Candidate C.

14. Candidate B asks Green if she had additional information on Horizon's industry peers and competitors, to put the profitability estimates in a richer context. By asking for this additional information for their analysis, Candidate B is seeking to mitigate which behavioral bias?

A. Illusion of control

B. Base rate neglect

C. Conservatism

The following information relates to questions 15-21

Angela Green, an investment manager at Horizon Investments, intends to hire a new investment analyst. After conducting initial interviews, Green has narrowed the pool to three candidates. She plans to conduct second interviews to further assess the candidates' knowledge of industry and company analysis.

Prior to the second interviews, Green asks the candidates to analyze Chrome Network Systems, a company that manufactures internet networking products. Each candidate is provided Chrome's financial information presented in Exhibit 1.

Exhibit 1: Chrome Network Systems Selected Financial Information ($ millions)			
		Year-End	
	2017	**2018**	**2019**
Net sales	46.8	50.5	53.9
Cost of sales	18.2	18.4	18.8
Gross profit	28.6	32.1	35.1
SG&A expenses	19.3	22.5	25.1
Operating income	9.3	9.6	10.0
Interest expense	0.5	0.7	0.6
Income before provision for income tax	8.8	8.9	9.4
Provision for income taxes	2.8	2.8	3.1
Net income	6.0	6.1	6.3

Green asks each candidate to forecast the 2020 income statement for Chrome and to outline the key assumptions used in their analysis. The job candidates are told to include Horizon's economic outlook for 2020 in their analysis, which assumes nominal GDP growth of 3.6%, based on expectations of real GDP growth of 1.6% and inflation of 2.0%.

Green receives the models from each of the candidates and schedules second interviews. To prepare for the interviews, Green compiles a summary of the candidates' key assumptions in Exhibit 2.

Exhibit 2: Summary of Key Assumptions Used in Candidates' Models

Metric	Candidate A	Candidate B	Candidate C
Net sales	Net sales will grow at the average annual growth rate in net sales over the 2017–19 time period.	Industry sales will grow at the same rate as nominal GDP, but Chrome will have a 2 percentage point decline in market share.	Net sales will grow 50 bps slower than nominal GDP.
Cost of sales	The 2020 gross margin will be the same as the average annual gross margin over the 2017–19 time period.	The 2020 gross margin will decline as costs increase by expected inflation.	The 2020 gross margin will increase by 20 bps from 2019.
SG&A expenses	The 2020 SG&A/net sales ratio will be the same as the average ratio over the 2017–19 time period.	The 2020 SG&A will grow at the rate of inflation.	The 2020 SG&A/net sales ratio will be the same as the 2019 ratio.
Interest expense	The 2020 interest expense assumes the effective interest rate will be the same as the 2019 rate.	The 2020 interest expense will be the same as the 2019 interest expense.	The 2020 interest expense will be the same as the average expense over the 2017–19 time period.
Income taxes	The 2020 effective tax rate will be the same as the 2019 rate.	The 2020 effective tax rate will equal the blended statutory rate of 30%.	The 2020 effective tax rate will be the same as the average effective tax rate over the 2017–19 time period.

15. Based on Exhibit 1, which of the following provides the strongest evidence that Chrome displays economies of scale?

    A. Increasing net sales

    B. Profit margins that are increasing with net sales

    C. Gross profit margins that are increasing with net sales

16. Based on Exhibit 2, the job candidate *most likely* using a bottom-up approach to model net sales is:

    A. Candidate A

    B. Candidate B

    C. Candidate C

17. Based on Exhibit 2, the modeling approach used by Candidate B to project future net sales is *most accurately* classified as a:

    A. hybrid approach.

    B. top-down approach.

    C. bottom-up approach.

18. Based on Exhibit 1 and Exhibit 2, Candidate C's forecast for cost of sales in 2020 is *closest* to:

    A. USD18.3 million.

    B. USD18.9 million.

    C. USD19.3 million.

19. Based on Exhibit 1 and Exhibit 2, Candidate A's forecast for SG&A expenses in 2020 is *closest* to:

    A. USD23.8 million.

    B. USD25.5 million.

    C. USD27.4 million.

20. Based on Exhibit 1, forecasted interest expense will reflect changes in Chrome's debt level under the forecast assumptions used by:

    A. Candidate A.

    B. Candidate B.

    C. Candidate C.

21. Candidate B asks Green if she had additional information on Horizon's industry peers and competitors, to put the profitability estimates in a richer context. By asking for this additional information for their analysis, Candidate B is seeking to mitigate which behavioral bias?

    A. Illusion of control

    B. Base rate neglect

    C. Conservatism

The following information relates to questions 22-28

Angela Green, an investment manager at Horizon Investments, intends to hire a new investment analyst. After conducting initial interviews, Green has narrowed the pool to three candidates. She plans to conduct second interviews to further assess the candidates' knowledge of industry and company analysis.

Prior to the second interviews, Green asks the candidates to analyze Chrome Network Systems, a company that manufactures internet networking products. Each candidate is provided Chrome's financial information presented in Exhibit 1.

	Year-End		
	2017	**2018**	**2019**
Net sales	46.8	50.5	53.9
Cost of sales	18.2	18.4	18.8
Gross profit	28.6	32.1	35.1
SG&A expenses	19.3	22.5	25.1
Operating income	9.3	9.6	10.0
Interest expense	0.5	0.7	0.6
Income before provision for income tax	8.8	8.9	9.4
Provision for income taxes	2.8	2.8	3.1
Net income	6.0	6.1	6.3

Green asks each candidate to forecast the 2020 income statement for Chrome and to outline the key assumptions used in their analysis. The job candidates are told to include Horizon's economic outlook for 2020 in their analysis, which assumes nominal GDP growth of 3.6%, based on expectations of real GDP growth of 1.6% and inflation of 2.0%.

Green receives the models from each of the candidates and schedules second interviews. To prepare for the interviews, Green compiles a summary of the candidates' key assumptions in Exhibit 2.

Exhibit 2: Summary of Key Assumptions Used in Candidates' Models

Metric	Candidate A	Candidate B	Candidate C
Net sales	Net sales will grow at the average annual growth rate in net sales over the 2017–19 time period.	Industry sales will grow at the same rate as nominal GDP, but Chrome will have a 2 percentage point decline in market share.	Net sales will grow 50 bps slower than nominal GDP.
Cost of sales	The 2020 gross margin will be the same as the average annual gross margin over the 2017–19 time period.	The 2020 gross margin will decline as costs increase by expected inflation.	The 2020 gross margin will increase by 20 bps from 2019.
SG&A expenses	The 2020 SG&A/net sales ratio will be the same as the average ratio over the 2017–19 time period.	The 2020 SG&A will grow at the rate of inflation.	The 2020 SG&A/net sales ratio will be the same as the 2019 ratio.

Metric	Candidate A	Candidate B	Candidate C
Interest expense	The 2020 interest expense assumes the effective interest rate will be the same as the 2019 rate.	The 2020 interest expense will be the same as the 2019 interest expense.	The 2020 interest expense will be the same as the average expense over the 2017–19 time period.
Income taxes	The 2020 effective tax rate will be the same as the 2019 rate.	The 2020 effective tax rate will equal the blended statutory rate of 30%.	The 2020 effective tax rate will be the same as the average effective tax rate over the 2017–19 time period.

22. Based on Exhibit 1, which of the following provides the strongest evidence that Chrome displays economies of scale?

   A. Increasing net sales

   B. Profit margins that are increasing with net sales

   C. Gross profit margins that are increasing with net sales

23. Based on Exhibit 2, the job candidate *most likely* using a bottom-up approach to model net sales is:

   A. Candidate A

   B. Candidate B

   C. Candidate C

24. Based on Exhibit 2, the modeling approach used by Candidate B to project future net sales is *most accurately* classified as a:

   A. hybrid approach.

   B. top-down approach.

   C. bottom-up approach.

25. Based on Exhibit 1 and Exhibit 2, Candidate C's forecast for cost of sales in 2020 is *closest* to:

   A. USD18.3 million.

   B. USD18.9 million.

   C. USD19.3 million.

26. Based on Exhibit 1 and Exhibit 2, Candidate A's forecast for SG&A expenses in 2020 is *closest* to:

   A. USD23.8 million.

   B. USD25.5 million.

   C. USD27.4 million.

27. Based on Exhibit 2, forecasted interest expense will reflect changes in Chrome's

debt level under the forecast assumptions used by:

A. Candidate A.

B. Candidate B.

C. Candidate C.

28. Candidate B asks Green if she had additional information on Horizon's industry peers and competitors, to put the profitability estimates in a richer context. By asking for this additional information for their analysis, Candidate B is seeking to mitigate which behavioral bias?

A. Illusion of control

B. Base rate neglect

C. Conservatism

The following information relates to questions 29-35

Nigel French, an analyst at Taurus Investment Management, is analyzing Archway Technologies, a manufacturer of luxury electronic auto equipment, at the request of his supervisor, Lukas Wright. French is asked to evaluate Archway's profitability over the past five years relative to its two main competitors, which are located in different countries with significantly different tax structures.

French begins by assessing Archway's competitive position within the luxury electronic auto equipment industry using Porter's five forces framework. A summary of French's industry analysis is presented in Exhibit 1.

Exhibit 1: Analysis of Luxury Electronic Auto Equipment Industry Using Porter's Five Forces Framework

Force	Factors to Consider
Threat of substitutes	Customer switching costs are high
Rivalry	Archway holds 60% of world market share; each of its two main competitors holds 15%
Bargaining power of suppliers	Primary inputs are considered basic commodities, and there are a large number of suppliers
Bargaining power of buyers	Luxury electronic auto equipment is very specialized (non-standardized)
Threat of new entrants	High fixed costs to enter industry

French notes that for the year just ended (2019), Archway's COGS was 30% of sales. To forecast Archway's income statement for 2020, French assumes that all companies in the industry will experience an inflation rate of 8% on the COGS. Exhibit 2 shows French's forecasts relating to Archway's price and volume changes.

Exhibit 2: Archway's 2020 Forecasted Price and Volume Changes	
Average price increase per unit	5.00%
Volume growth	−3.00%

After putting together income statement projections for Archway, French forecasts Archway's balance sheet items. He uses Archway's historical efficiency ratios to forecast the company's working capital accounts.

Based on his financial forecast for Archway, French estimates a terminal value using a valuation multiple based on the company's average price-to-earnings multiple (P/E) over the past five years. Wright discusses with French how the terminal value estimate is sensitive to key assumptions about the company's future prospects. Wright asks French:

"What change in the calculation of the terminal value would you make if a technological development that would adversely affect Archway was forecast to occur sometime beyond your financial forecast horizon?"

29. Which profitability metric should French use to assess Archway's five-year historic performance relative to its competitors?

   A. Current ratio

   B. Operating margin

   C. Return on invested capital

30. Based on the current competitive landscape presented in Exhibit 1, French should conclude that Archway's ability to:

   A. pass along price increases is high.

   B. demand lower input prices from suppliers is low.

   C. generate above-average returns on invested capital is low.

31. Based on the current competitive landscape presented in Exhibit 1, Archway's operating profit margins over the forecast horizon are *least likely* to:

   A. decrease.

   B. remain constant.

   C. increase.

32. Based on Exhibit 2 Archway's forecasted gross profit margin for 2020 is *closest* to:

   A. 62.7%.

   B. 67.0%.

   C. 69.1%.

33. French's approach to forecasting Archway's working capital accounts would be *most likely* classified as a:

   A. hybrid approach.

   B. top-down approach.

C. bottom-up approach.

34. The *most appropriate* response to Wright's question about the technological development is to:

    A. increase the required return.

    B. decrease the price-to-earnings multiple.

    C. decrease the perpetual growth rate.

35. If the luxury electronic auto equipment industry is subject to rapid technological changes and market share shifts, how should French best adapt his approach to modeling?

    A. Examine base rates

    B. Speak to analysts who hold diverse opinions on the stock

    C. Forecast multiple scenarios

The following information relates to questions 36-42

Gertrude Fromm is a transportation sector analyst at Tucana Investments. She is conducting an analysis of Omikroon, N.V., a (hypothetical) European engineering company that manufactures and sells scooters and commercial trucks.

Omikroon's petrol scooter division is the market leader in its sector and has two competitors. Omikroon's petrol scooters have a strong brand name and a well-established distribution network. Given the strong branding established by the market leaders, the cost of entering the industry is high. But Fromm antici-pates that small, inexpensive, imported petrol-fueled motorcycles could become substitutes for Omikroon's petrol scooters.

Fromm uses ROIC as the metric to assess Omikroon's performance.

Omikroon has just introduced the first electric scooter to the market at year-end 2019. The company's expectations are as follows:

- Competing electric scooters will reach the market in 2021.
- Electric scooters will not be a substitute for petrol scooters.
- The important research costs in 2020 and 2021 will lead to more efficient electric scooters.

Fromm decides to use a five-year forecast horizon for Omikroon after consider-ing the following factors:

Factor 1	The annual portfolio turnover at Tucana Investments is 30%.
Factor 2	The electronic scooter industry is expected to grow rapidly over the next 10 years.
Factor 3	Omikroon has announced it would acquire a light truck manufacturer that will be fully integrated into its truck division by 2021 and will add 2% to the company's total revenues.

Fromm uses the base case forecast for 2020 shown in Exhibit 1 to perform the following sensitivity analysis:

- The price of an imported specialty metal used for engine parts increases by 20%.
- This metal constitutes 4% of Omikroon's cost of sales.
- Omikroon will not be able to pass on the higher metal expense to its customers.

Exhibit 1: Omikroon's Selected Financial Forecasts for 2020 Base Case (€ millions)

	Petrol Scooter Division	Commercial Truck Division	Electric Scooter Division	Total
Sales	99.05	45.71	7.62	152.38
Cost of sales				105.38
Gross profit				47.00
Operating profit				9.20

Omikroon will initially outsource its electric scooter parts. But manufacturing these parts in-house beginning in 2021 will imply changes to an existing factory. This factory cost EUR7 million three years ago and had an estimated useful life of 10 years. Fromm is evaluating two scenarios:

Scenario 1   Sell the existing factory for EUR5 million. Build a new factory costing EUR30 million with a useful life of 10 years.

Scenario 2   Refit the existing factory for EUR27 million.

36. Using Porter's five forces analysis, which of the following competitive factors is likely to have the *greatest* impact on Omikroon's petrol scooter pricing power?

   A. Rivalry

   B. Threat of substitutes

   C. Threat of new entrants

37. The metric used by Fromm to assess Omikroon's performance takes into account:

   A. degree of financial leverage.

   B. operating liabilities relative to operating assets.

   C. competitiveness relative to companies in other tax regimes.

38. Based on Omikroon's expectations, the gross profit margin of Omikroon's electric scooter division in 2021 is *mostlikely* to be affected by:

   A. competition.

   B. research costs.

   C. cannibalization by petrol scooters.

39. Which factor *best* justifies the five-year forecast horizon for Omikroon selected by Fromm?

    A. Factor 1

    B. Factor 2

    C. Factor 3

40. Fromm's sensitivity analysis will result in a decrease in the 2020 base case gross profit margin *closest to*:

    A. 0.55 percentage points.

    B. 0.80 percentage points.

    C. 3.32 percentage points.

41. Fromm's estimate of growth capital expenditure included in Omikroon's PP&E under Scenario 2 should be:

    A. lower than under Scenario 1.

    B. the same as under Scenario 1.

    C. higher than under Scenario 1.

42. To validate the forecast for rapid growth in the electronic scooter market over the next 10 years, Fromm speaks to the management of Omikroon and investor relations of ZeroWheel, a competitor. Fromm might be subject to which behavioral bias?

    A. Conservatism

    B. Overconfidence

    C. Confirmation

The following information relates to questions 43-49

Nigel French, an analyst at Taurus Investment Management, is analyzing Archway Technologies, a manufacturer of luxury electronic auto equipment, at the request of his supervisor, Lukas Wright. French is asked to evaluate Archway's profitability over the past five years relative to its two main competitors, which are located in different countries with significantly different tax structures.

French begins by assessing Archway's competitive position within the luxury electronic auto equipment industry using Porter's five forces framework. A summary of French's industry analysis is presented in Exhibit 1.

Exhibit 1: Analysis of Luxury Electronic Auto Equipment Industry Using Porter's Five Forces Framework

Force	Factors to Consider
Threat of substitutes	Customer switching costs are high
Rivalry	Archway holds 60% of world market share; each of its two main competitors holds 15%
Bargaining power of suppliers	Primary inputs are considered basic commodities, and there are a large number of suppliers
Bargaining power of buyers	Luxury electronic auto equipment is very specialized (non-standardized)
Threat of new entrants	High fixed costs to enter industry

French notes that for the year just ended (2019), Archway's COGS was 30% of sales. To forecast Archway's income statement for 2020, French assumes that all companies in the industry will experience an inflation rate of 8% on the COGS. Exhibit 2 shows French's forecasts relating to Archway's price and volume changes.

Exhibit 2: Archway's 2020 Forecasted Price and Volume Changes

Average price increase per unit	5.00%
Volume growth	−3.00%

After putting together income statement projections for Archway, French forecasts Archway's balance sheet items. He uses Archway's historical efficiency ratios to forecast the company's working capital accounts.

Based on his financial forecast for Archway, French estimates a terminal value using a valuation multiple based on the company's average price-to-earnings multiple (P/E) over the past five years. Wright discusses with French how the terminal value estimate is sensitive to key assumptions about the company's future prospects. Wright asks French:

"What change in the calculation of the terminal value would you make if a technological development that would adversely affect Archway was forecast to occur sometime beyond your financial forecast horizon?"

43. Which profitability metric should French use to assess Archway's five-year historic performance relative to its competitors?

    A. Current ratio

    B. Operating margin

    C. Return on invested capital

44. Based on the current competitive landscape presented in Exhibit 1, French should conclude that Archway's ability to:

    A. pass along price increases is high.

    B. demand lower input prices from suppliers is low.

    C. generate above-average returns on invested capital is low.

45. Based on the current competitive landscape presented in Exhibit 73, Archway's operating profit margins over the forecast horizon are *least likely* to:

   A. decrease.

   B. remain constant.

   C. increase.

46. Based on Exhibit 2, Archway's forecasted gross profit margin for 2020 is *closest* to:

   A. 62.7%.

   B. 67.0%.

   C. 69.1%.

47. French's approach to forecasting Archway's working capital accounts would be *most likely* classified as a:

   A. hybrid approach.

   B. top-down approach.

   C. bottom-up approach.

48. The *most appropriate* response to Wright's question about the technological development is to:

   A. increase the required return.

   B. decrease the price-to-earnings multiple.

   C. decrease the perpetual growth rate.

49. If the luxury electronic auto equipment industry is subject to rapid technological changes and market share shifts, how should French best adapt his approach to modeling?

   A. Examine base rates

   B. Speak to analysts who hold diverse opinions on the stock

   C. Forecast multiple scenarios

The following information relates to questions 50-56

Gertrude Fromm is a transportation sector analyst at Tucana Investments. She is conducting an analysis of Omikroon, N.V., a (hypothetical) European engineering company that manufactures and sells scooters and commercial trucks.

Omikroon's petrol scooter division is the market leader in its sector and has two competitors. Omikroon's petrol scooters have a strong brand name and a well-established distribution network. Given the strong branding established by the market leaders, the cost of entering the industry is high. But Fromm antici- pates that small, inexpensive, imported petrol-fueled motorcycles could become substitutes for Omikroon's petrol scooters.

Fromm uses ROIC as the metric to assess Omikroon's performance.

Omikroon has just introduced the first electric scooter to the market at year-end 2019. The company's expectations are as follows:

- Competing electric scooters will reach the market in 2021.
- Electric scooters will not be a substitute for petrol scooters.
- The important research costs in 2020 and 2021 will lead to more efficient electric scooters.

Fromm decides to use a five-year forecast horizon for Omikroon after considering the following factors:

Factor 1   The annual portfolio turnover at Tucana Investments is 30%.

Factor 2   The electronic scooter industry is expected to grow rapidly over the next 10 years.

Factor 3   Omikroon has announced it would acquire a light truck manufacturer that will be fully integrated into its truck division by 2021 and will add 2% to the company's total revenues.

Fromm uses the base case forecast for 2020 shown in Exhibit 1 to perform the following sensitivity analysis:

- The price of an imported specialty metal used for engine parts increases by 20%.
- This metal constitutes 4% of Omikroon's cost of sales.
- Omikroon will not be able to pass on the higher metal expense to its customers.

Exhibit 1: Omikroon's Selected Financial Forecasts for 2020 Base Case (€ millions)

	Petrol Scooter Division	Commercial Truck Division	Electric Scooter Division	Total
Sales	99.05	45.71	7.62	152.38
Cost of sales				105.38
Gross profit				47.00
Operating profit				9.20

Omikroon will initially outsource its electric scooter parts. But manufacturing these parts in-house beginning in 2021 will imply changes to an existing factory. This factory cost EUR7 million three years ago and had an estimated useful life of 10 years. Fromm is evaluating two scenarios:

Scenario 1   Sell the existing factory for EUR5 million. Build a new factory costing EUR30 million with a useful life of 10 years.

Scenario 2   Refit the existing factory for EUR27 million.

50. Using Porter's five forces analysis, which of the following competitive factors is

likely to have the *greatest* impact on Omikroon's petrol scooter pricing power?

A. Rivalry

B. Threat of substitutes

C. Threat of new entrants

51. The metric used by Fromm to assess Omikroon's performance takes into account:

A. degree of financial leverage.

B. operating liabilities relative to operating assets.

C. competitiveness relative to companies in other tax regimes.

52. Based on Omikroon's expectations, the gross profit margin of Omikroon's electric scooter division in 2021 is *mostlikely* to be affected by:

A. competition.

B. research costs.

C. cannibalization by petrol scooters.

53. Which factor *best* justifies the five-year forecast horizon for Omikroon selected by Fromm?

A. Factor 1

B. Factor 2

C. Factor 3

54. Fromm's sensitivity analysis will result in a decrease in the 2020 base case gross profit margin *closest to*:

A. 0.55 percentage points.

B. 0.80 percentage points.

C. 3.32 percentage points.

55. Fromm's estimate of growth capital expenditure included in Omikroon's PP&E under Scenario 2 should be:

A. lower than under Scenario 1.

B. the same as under Scenario 1.

C. higher than under Scenario 1.

56. To validate the forecast for rapid growth in the electronic scooter market over the next 10 years, Fromm speaks to the management of Omikroon and investor relations of ZeroWheel, a competitor. Fromm might be subject to which behavioral bias?

A. Conservatism

B. Overconfidence

C. Confirmation

The following information relates to questions 57-63

Nigel French, an analyst at Taurus Investment Management, is analyzing Archway Technologies, a manufacturer of luxury electronic auto equipment, at the request of his supervisor, Lukas Wright. French is asked to evaluate Archway's profitability over the past five years relative to its two main competitors, which are located in different countries with significantly different tax structures.

French begins by assessing Archway's competitive position within the luxury electronic auto equipment industry using Porter's five forces framework. A summary of French's industry analysis is presented in Exhibit 1.

Exhibit 1: Analysis of Luxury Electronic Auto Equipment Industry Using Porter's Five Forces Framework

Force	Factors to Consider
Threat of substitutes	Customer switching costs are high
Rivalry	Archway holds 60% of world market share; each of its two main competitors holds 15%
Bargaining power of suppliers	Primary inputs are considered basic commodities, and there are a large number of suppliers
Bargaining power of buyers	Luxury electronic auto equipment is very specialized (non-standardized)
Threat of new entrants	High fixed costs to enter industry

French notes that for the year just ended (2019), Archway's COGS was 30% of sales. To forecast Archway's income statement for 2020, French assumes that all companies in the industry will experience an inflation rate of 8% on the COGS. Exhibit 2 shows French's forecasts relating to Archway's price and volume changes.

Exhibit 2: Archway's 2020 Forecasted Price and Volume Changes

Average price increase per unit	5.00%
Volume growth	−3.00%

After putting together income statement projections for Archway, French forecasts Archway's balance sheet items. He uses Archway's historical efficiency ratios to forecast the company's working capital accounts.

Based on his financial forecast for Archway, French estimates a terminal value using a valuation multiple based on the company's average price-to-earnings multiple (P/E) over the past five years. Wright discusses with French how the terminal value estimate is sensitive to key assumptions about the company's future prospects. Wright asks French:

"What change in the calculation of the terminal value would you make if a technological development that would adversely affect Archway was forecast to occur sometime beyond your financial forecast horizon?"

57. Which profitability metric should French use to assess Archway's five-year his-

toric performance relative to its competitors?

A. Current ratio

B. Operating margin

C. Return on invested capital

58. Based on the current competitive landscape presented in Exhibit 1, French should conclude that Archway's ability to:

A. pass along price increases is high.

B. demand lower input prices from suppliers is low.

C. generate above-average returns on invested capital is low.

59. Based on the current competitive landscape presented in Exhibit 1, Archway's operating profit margins over the forecast horizon are *least likely* to:

A. decrease.

B. remain constant.

C. increase.

60. Based on Exhibit 2, Archway's forecasted gross profit margin for 2020 is *closest* to:

A. 62.7%.

B. 67.0%.

C. 69.1%.

61. French's approach to forecasting Archway's working capital accounts would be *most likely* classified as a:

A. hybrid approach.

B. top-down approach.

C. bottom-up approach.

62. The *most appropriate* response to Wright's question about the technological development is to:

A. increase the required return.

B. decrease the price-to-earnings multiple.

C. decrease the perpetual growth rate.

63. If the luxury electronic auto equipment industry is subject to rapid technological changes and market share shifts, how should French best adapt his approach to modeling?

A. Examine base rates

B. Speak to analysts who hold diverse opinions on the stock

C. Forecast multiple scenarios

The following information relates to questions 64-70

Gertrude Fromm is a transportation sector analyst at Tucana Investments. She is conducting an analysis of Omikroon, N.V., a (hypothetical) European engineering company that manufactures and sells scooters and commercial trucks.

Omikroon's petrol scooter division is the market leader in its sector and has two competitors. Omikroon's petrol scooters have a strong brand name and a well-established distribution network. Given the strong branding established by the market leaders, the cost of entering the industry is high. But Fromm anticipates that small, inexpensive, imported petrol-fueled motorcycles could become substitutes for Omikroon's petrol scooters.

Fromm uses ROIC as the metric to assess Omikroon's performance.

Omikroon has just introduced the first electric scooter to the market at year-end 2019. The company's expectations are as follows:

- Competing electric scooters will reach the market in 2021.
- Electric scooters will not be a substitute for petrol scooters.
- The important research costs in 2020 and 2021 will lead to more efficient electric scooters.

Fromm decides to use a five-year forecast horizon for Omikroon after considering the following factors:

Factor 1	The annual portfolio turnover at Tucana Investments is 30%.
Factor 2	The electronic scooter industry is expected to grow rapidly over the next 10 years.
Factor 3	Omikroon has announced it would acquire a light truck manufacturer that will be fully integrated into its truck division by 2021 and will add 2% to the company's total revenues.

Fromm uses the base case forecast for 2020 shown in Exhibit 1 to perform the following sensitivity analysis:

- The price of an imported specialty metal used for engine parts increases by 20%.
- This metal constitutes 4% of Omikroon's cost of sales.
- Omikroon will not be able to pass on the higher metal expense to its customers.

Exhibit 1: Omikroon's Selected Financial Forecasts for 2020 Base Case (€ millions)

	Petrol Scooter Division	Commercial Truck Division	Electric Scooter Division	Total
Sales	99.05	45.71	7.62	152.38
Cost of sales				105.38
Gross profit				47.00

	Petrol Scooter Division	Commercial Truck Division	Electric Scooter Division	Total
Operating profit				9.20

Omikroon will initially outsource its electric scooter parts. But manufacturing these parts in-house beginning in 2021 will imply changes to an existing factory. This factory cost EUR7 million three years ago and had an estimated useful life of 10 years. Fromm is evaluating two scenarios:

Scenario 1   Sell the existing factory for EUR5 million. Build a new factory costing EUR30 million with a useful life of 10 years.

Scenario 2   Refit the existing factory for EUR27 million.

64. Using Porter's five forces analysis, which of the following competitive factors is likely to have the *greatest* impact on Omikroon's petrol scooter pricing power?

A. Rivalry

B. Threat of substitutes

C. Threat of new entrants

65. The metric used by Fromm to assess Omikroon's performance takes into account:

A. degree of financial leverage.

B. operating liabilities relative to operating assets.

C. competitiveness relative to companies in other tax regimes.

66. Based on Omikroon's expectations, the gross profit margin of Omikroon's electric scooter division in 2021 is *mostlikely* to be affected by:

A. competition.

B. research costs.

C. cannibalization by petrol scooters.

67. Which factor *best* justifies the five-year forecast horizon for Omikroon selected by Fromm?

A. Factor 1

B. Factor 2

C. Factor 3

68. Fromm's sensitivity analysis will result in a decrease in the 2020 base case gross profit margin *closest to*:

A. 0.55 percentage points.

B. 0.80 percentage points.

C. 3.32 percentage points.

69. Fromm's estimate of growth capital expenditure included in Omikroon's PP&E under Scenario 2 should be:

A. lower than under Scenario 1.

B. the same as under Scenario 1.

C. higher than under Scenario 1.

70. To validate the forecast for rapid growth in the electronic scooter market over the next 10 years, Fromm speaks to the management of Omikroon and investor relations of ZeroWheel, a competitor. Fromm might be subject to which behavioral bias?

A. Conservatism

B. Overconfidence

C. Confirmation

The following information relates to questions 71-77

Gertrude Fromm is a transportation sector analyst at Tucana Investments. She is conducting an analysis of Omikroon, N.V., a (hypothetical) European engineering company that manufactures and sells scooters and commercial trucks.

Omikroon's petrol scooter division is the market leader in its sector and has two competitors. Omikroon's petrol scooters have a strong brand name and a well-established distribution network. Given the strong branding established by the market leaders, the cost of entering the industry is high. But Fromm anticipates that small, inexpensive, imported petrol-fueled motorcycles could become substitutes for Omikroon's petrol scooters.

Fromm uses ROIC as the metric to assess Omikroon's performance.

Omikroon has just introduced the first electric scooter to the market at year-end 2019. The company's expectations are as follows:

- Competing electric scooters will reach the market in 2021.
- Electric scooters will not be a substitute for petrol scooters.
- The important research costs in 2020 and 2021 will lead to more efficient electric scooters.

Fromm decides to use a five-year forecast horizon for Omikroon after considering the following factors:

Factor 1	The annual portfolio turnover at Tucana Investments is 30%.
Factor 2	The electronic scooter industry is expected to grow rapidly over the next 10 years.
Factor 3	Omikroon has announced it would acquire a light truck manufacturer that will be fully integrated into its truck division by 2021 and will add 2% to the company's total revenues.

Fromm uses the base case forecast for 2020 shown in Exhibit 1 to perform the following sensitivity analysis:

- The price of an imported specialty metal used for engine parts increases by 20%.
- This metal constitutes 4% of Omikroon's cost of sales.
- Omikroon will not be able to pass on the higher metal expense to its customers.

Exhibit 1: Omikroon's Selected Financial Forecasts for 2020 Base Case (€ millions)				
	Petrol Scooter Division	**Commercial Truck Division**	**Electric Scooter Division**	**Total**
Sales	99.05	45.71	7.62	152.38
Cost of sales				105.38
Gross profit				47.00
Operating profit				9.20

Omikroon will initially outsource its electric scooter parts. But manufacturing these parts in-house beginning in 2021 will imply changes to an existing factory. This factory cost EUR7 million three years ago and had an estimated useful life of 10 years. Fromm is evaluating two scenarios:

Scenario 1   Sell the existing factory for EUR5 million. Build a new factory costing EUR30 million with a useful life of 10 years.

Scenario 2   Refit the existing factory for EUR27 million.

71. Using Porter's five forces analysis, which of the following competitive factors is likely to have the *greatest* impact on Omikroon's petrol scooter pricing power?

   A. Rivalry

   B. Threat of substitutes

   C. Threat of new entrants

72. The metric used by Fromm to assess Omikroon's performance takes into account:

   A. degree of financial leverage.

   B. operating liabilities relative to operating assets.

   C. competitiveness relative to companies in other tax regimes.

73. Based on Omikroon's expectations, the gross profit margin of Omikroon's electric scooter division in 2021 is *mostlikely* to be affected by:

   A. competition.

   B. research costs.

   C. cannibalization by petrol scooters.

74. Which factor *best* justifies the five-year forecast horizon for Omikroon selected by Fromm?

    A. Factor 1

    B. Factor 2

    C. Factor 3

75. Fromm's sensitivity analysis will result in a decrease in the 2020 base case gross profit margin *closest to*:

    A. 0.55 percentage points.

    B. 0.80 percentage points.

    C. 3.32 percentage points.

76. Fromm's estimate of growth capital expenditure included in Omikroon's PP&E under Scenario 2 should be:

    A. lower than under Scenario 1.

    B. the same as under Scenario 1.

    C. higher than under Scenario 1.

77. To validate the forecast for rapid growth in the electronic scooter market over the next 10 years, Fromm speaks to the management of Omikroon and investor relations of ZeroWheel, a competitor. Fromm might be subject to which behavioral bias?

    A. Conservatism

    B. Overconfidence

    C. Confirmation

The following information relates to questions 78-84

Nigel French, an analyst at Taurus Investment Management, is analyzing Archway Technologies, a manufacturer of luxury electronic auto equipment, at the request of his supervisor, Lukas Wright. French is asked to evaluate Archway's profitability over the past five years relative to its two main competitors, which are located in different countries with significantly different tax structures.

French begins by assessing Archway's competitive position within the luxury electronic auto equipment industry using Porter's five forces framework. A summary of French's industry analysis is presented in Exhibit 1.

Exhibit 1: Analysis of Luxury Electronic Auto Equipment Industry Using Porter's Five Forces Framework	
Force	**Factors to Consider**
Threat of substitutes	Customer switching costs are high
Rivalry	Archway holds 60% of world market share; each of its two main competitors holds 15%
Bargaining power of suppliers	Primary inputs are considered basic commodities, and there are a large number of suppliers
Bargaining power of buyers	Luxury electronic auto equipment is very specialized (non-standardized)
Threat of new entrants	High fixed costs to enter industry

French notes that for the year just ended (2019), Archway's COGS was 30% of sales. To forecast Archway's income statement for 2020, French assumes that all companies in the industry will experience an inflation rate of 8% on the COGS. Exhibit 2 shows French's forecasts relating to Archway's price and volume changes.

Exhibit 2: Archway's 2020 Forecasted Price and Volume Changes	
Average price increase per unit	5.00%
Volume growth	−3.00%

After putting together income statement projections for Archway, French forecasts Archway's balance sheet items. He uses Archway's historical efficiency ratios to forecast the company's working capital accounts.

Based on his financial forecast for Archway, French estimates a terminal value using a valuation multiple based on the company's average price-to-earnings multiple (P/E) over the past five years. Wright discusses with French how the terminal value estimate is sensitive to key assumptions about the company's future prospects. Wright asks French:

"What change in the calculation of the terminal value would you make if a technological development that would adversely affect Archway was forecast to occur sometime beyond your financial forecast horizon?"

78. Which profitability metric should French use to assess Archway's five-year historic performance relative to its competitors?

    A. Current ratio

    B. Operating margin

    C. Return on invested capital

79. Based on the current competitive landscape presented in Exhibit 1, French should conclude that Archway's ability to:

    A. pass along price increases is high.

    B. demand lower input prices from suppliers is low.

    C. generate above-average returns on invested capital is low.

80. Based on the current competitive landscape presented in Exhibit 1, Archway's operating profit margins over the forecast horizon are *least likely* to:

    A. decrease.

    B. remain constant.

    C. increase.

81. Based on Exhibit 2, Archway's forecasted gross profit margin for 2020 is *closest* to:

    A. 62.7%.

    B. 67.0%.

    C. 69.1%.

82. French's approach to forecasting Archway's working capital accounts would be *most likely* classified as a:

    A. hybrid approach.

    B. top-down approach.

    C. bottom-up approach.

83. The *most appropriate* response to Wright's question about the technological development is to:

    A. increase the required return.

    B. decrease the price-to-earnings multiple.

    C. decrease the perpetual growth rate.

84. If the luxury electronic auto equipment industry is subject to rapid technological changes and market share shifts, how should French best adapt his approach to modeling?

    A. Examine base rates

    B. Speak to analysts who hold diverse opinions on the stock

    C. Forecast multiple scenarios

The following information relates to questions 85-91

Gertrude Fromm is a transportation sector analyst at Tucana Investments. She is conducting an analysis of Omikroon, N.V., a (hypothetical) European engineering company that manufactures and sells scooters and commercial trucks.

Omikroon's petrol scooter division is the market leader in its sector and has two competitors. Omikroon's petrol scooters have a strong brand name and a well-established distribution network. Given the strong branding established by the market leaders, the cost of entering the industry is high. But Fromm anticipates that small, inexpensive, imported petrol-fueled motorcycles could become substitutes for Omikroon's petrol scooters.

Fromm uses ROIC as the metric to assess Omikroon's performance.

Omikroon has just introduced the first electric scooter to the market at year-end 2019. The company's expectations are as follows:

- Competing electric scooters will reach the market in 2021.
- Electric scooters will not be a substitute for petrol scooters.
- The important research costs in 2020 and 2021 will lead to more efficient electric scooters.

Fromm decides to use a five-year forecast horizon for Omikroon after considering the following factors:

Factor 1	The annual portfolio turnover at Tucana Investments is 30%.
Factor 2	The electronic scooter industry is expected to grow rapidly over the next 10 years.
Factor 3	Omikroon has announced it would acquire a light truck manufacturer that will be fully integrated into its truck division by 2021 and will add 2% to the company's total revenues.

Fromm uses the base case forecast for 2020 shown in Exhibit 1 to perform the following sensitivity analysis:

- The price of an imported specialty metal used for engine parts increases by 20%.
- This metal constitutes 4% of Omikroon's cost of sales.
- Omikroon will not be able to pass on the higher metal expense to its customers.

Exhibit 1: Omikroon's Selected Financial Forecasts for 2020 Base Case (€ millions)

	Petrol Scooter Division	Commercial Truck Division	Electric Scooter Division	Total
Sales	99.05	45.71	7.62	152.38
Cost of sales				105.38
Gross profit				47.00
Operating profit				9.20

Omikroon will initially outsource its electric scooter parts. But manufacturing these parts in-house beginning in 2021 will imply changes to an existing factory. This factory cost EUR7 million three years ago and had an estimated useful life of 10 years. Fromm is evaluating two scenarios:

Scenario 1	Sell the existing factory for EUR5 million. Build a new factory costing EUR30 million with a useful life of 10 years.
Scenario 2	Refit the existing factory for EUR27 million.

85. Using Porter's five forces analysis, which of the following competitive factors is

likely to have the *greatest* impact on Omikroon's petrol scooter pricing power?

A. Rivalry

B. Threat of substitutes

C. Threat of new entrants

86. The metric used by Fromm to assess Omikroon's performance takes into account:

A. degree of financial leverage.

B. operating liabilities relative to operating assets.

C. competitiveness relative to companies in other tax regimes.

87. Based on Omikroon's expectations, the gross profit margin of Omikroon's electric scooter division in 2021 is *mostlikely* to be affected by:

A. competition.

B. research costs.

C. cannibalization by petrol scooters.

88. Which factor *best* justifies the five-year forecast horizon for Omikroon selected by Fromm?

A. Factor 1

B. Factor 2

C. Factor 3

89. Fromm's sensitivity analysis will result in a decrease in the 2020 base case gross profit margin *closest to*:

A. 0.55 percentage points.

B. 0.80 percentage points.

C. 3.32 percentage points.

90. Fromm's estimate of growth capital expenditure included in Omikroon's PP&E under Scenario 2 should be:

A. lower than under Scenario 1.

B. the same as under Scenario 1.

C. higher than under Scenario 1.

91. To validate the forecast for rapid growth in the electronic scooter market over the next 10 years, Fromm speaks to the management of Omikroon and investor relations of ZeroWheel, a competitor. Fromm might be subject to which behavioral bias?

A. Conservatism

B. Overconfidence

C. Confirmation

SOLUTIONS

1. C is correct. Economies of scale are a situation in which average costs decrease with increasing sales volume. Chrome's gross margins have been increasing with net sales. Gross margins that increase with sales levels provide evidence of economies of scale, assuming that higher levels of sales reflect increased unit sales. Gross margin more directly reflects the cost of sales than does profit margin.

Metric	2017	2018	2019
Net sales	$46.8	$50.5	$53.9
Gross profit	28.6	32.1	35.1
Gross margin (gross profit/net sales)	61.11%	63.56%	65.12%

2. A is correct. A bottom-up approach for developing inputs to equity valuation models begins at the level of the individual company or a unit within the company. By modeling net sales using the average annual growth rate, Candidate A is using a bottom-up approach. Both Candidate B and Candidate C are using a top-down approach, which begins at the level of the overall economy.

3. B is correct. A top-down approach usually begins at the level of the overall economy. Candidate B assumes industry sales will grow at the same rate as nominal GDP but that Chrome will have a 2 percentage point decline in market share. Candidate B is not using any elements of a bottom-up approach; therefore, a hybrid approach is not being employed.

4. C is correct. Candidate C assumes that the 2020 gross margin will increase by 20 bps from 2019 and that net sales will grow at 50 bps slower than nominal GDP (nominal GDP = Real GDP + Inflation = 1.6% + 2.0% = 3.6%). Accordingly, the 2020 forecasted cost of sales is USD19.27 million, rounded to USD19.3 million.

Metric	Calculation	Result
2020 gross margin = 2019 gm + 20 bps	$35.1/$53.9 = 65.12% + 0.20% =	65.32%
2020 CoS/net sales = 100% − gross margin	100% − 65.32% =	34.68%
2020 net sales = 2019 net sales × (1 + Nominal GDP − 0.50%)	$53.9 million × (1 + 0.036 − 0.005) = $53.9 million × 1.031 =	$55.57 million
2020 cost of sales = 2020 net sales × CoS/net sales	$55.57 × 34.68% =	$19.27 million

5. B is correct. Candidate A assumes that the 2020 SG&A/net sales will be the same as the average SG&A/net sales over the 2017–19 time period and that net sales will grow at the annual average growth rate in net sales over the 2017–19 time period. Accordingly, the 2020 forecasted SG&A expenses are USD25.5 million.

Metric	Calculation	Result
Average SG&A/net sales, 2017–2019*	(41.24% + 44.55% + 46.57%)/3 =	44.12%
Average annual growth sales in net sales, 2017–2019**	(7.91% + 6.73%)/2 =	7.32%
2020 net sales = 2019 net sales × (1 + Average annual growth rate in net sales)	$53.9 million × 1.0732 =	$57.85 million

Metric	Calculation	Result
2020 SG&A = 2020 net sales × Average SG&A/net sales	$57.85 million × 44.12% =	$25.52 million

* SG&A/net sales are calculated as follows:

	2017	2018	2019
Net Sales	$46.8	$50.5	$53.9
SG&A expenses	$19.3	$22.5	$25.1
SG&A-to-sales ratio	41.24%	44.55%	46.57%

** Growth rate in net sales is calculated as follows:

Year	Calculation
2018	($50.5/$46.8) − 1 = 7.91%
2019	($53.9/$50.5) − 1 = 6.73%

6. A is correct. In forecasting financing costs, such as interest expense, the debt/equity structure of a company is a key determinant. Accordingly, a method that recognizes the relationship between the income statement account (interest expense) and the balance sheet account (debt) would be a preferable method for forecasting interest expense when compared with methods that forecast based solely on the income statement account. By using the effective interest rate (interest expense divided by average gross debt), Candidate A is taking the debt/equity structure into account. Candidate B (who forecasts 2020 interest expense to be the same as 2019 interest expense) and Candidate C (who forecasts 2020 interest expense to be the same as the 2017–19 average interest expense) are not taking the balance sheet into consideration.

7. B is correct. Base rates refer to attributes of a reference class and base rate neglect is ignoring such class information in favor of specific information. By incorporating industry data, Candidate B is seeking to mitigate this.

8. C is correct. Economies of scale are a situation in which average costs decrease with increasing sales volume. Chrome's gross margins have been increasing with net sales. Gross margins that increase with sales levels provide evidence of economies of scale, assuming that higher levels of sales reflect increased unit sales. Gross margin more directly reflects the cost of sales than does profit margin.

Metric	2017	2018	2019
Net sales	$46.8	$50.5	$53.9
Gross profit	28.6	32.1	35.1
Gross margin (gross profit/net sales)	61.11%	63.56%	65.12%

9. A is correct. A bottom-up approach for developing inputs to equity valuation models begins at the level of the individual company or a unit within the company. By modeling net sales using the average annual growth rate, Candidate A is using a bottom-up approach. Both Candidate B and Candidate C are using a top-down approach, which begins at the level of the overall economy.

10. B is correct. A top-down approach usually begins at the level of the overall econ-

omy. Candidate B assumes industry sales will grow at the same rate as nominal GDP but that Chrome will have a 2 percentage point decline in market share. Candidate B is not using any elements of a bottom-up approach; therefore, a hybrid approach is not being employed.

11. C is correct. Candidate C assumes that the 2020 gross margin will increase by 20 bps from 2019 and that net sales will grow at 50 bps slower than nominal GDP (nominal GDP = Real GDP + Inflation = 1.6% + 2.0% = 3.6%). Accordingly, the 2020 forecasted cost of sales is USD19.27 million, rounded to USD19.3 million.

Metric	Calculation	Result
2020 gross margin = 2019 gm + 20 bps	$35.1/$53.9 = 65.12% + 0.20% =	65.32%
2020 CoS/net sales = 100% − gross margin	100% − 65.32% =	34.68%
2020 net sales = 2019 net sales × (1 + Nominal GDP − 0.50%)	$53.9 million × (1 + 0.036 − 0.005) = $53.9 million × 1.031 =	$55.57 million
2020 cost of sales = 2020 net sales × CoS/net sales	$55.57 × 34.68% =	$19.27 million

12. B is correct. Candidate A assumes that the 2020 SG&A/net sales will be the same as the average SG&A/net sales over the 2017–19 time period and that net sales will grow at the annual average growth rate in net sales over the 2017–19 time period. Accordingly, the 2020 forecasted SG&A expenses are USD25.5 million.

Metric	Calculation	Result
Average SG&A/net sales, 2017–2019*	(41.24% + 44.55% + 46.57%)/3 =	44.12%
Average annual growth sales in net sales, 2017–2019**	(7.91% + 6.73%)/2 =	7.32%
2020 net sales = 2019 net sales × (1 + Average annual growth rate in net sales)	$53.9 million × 1.0732 =	$57.85 million
2020 SG&A = 2020 net sales × Average SG&A/net sales	$57.85 million × 44.12% =	$25.52 million

*SG&A/net sales are calculated as follows:

	2017	2018	2019
Net Sales	$46.8	$50.5	$53.9
SG&A expenses	$19.3	$22.5	$25.1
SG&A-to-sales ratio	41.24%	44.55%	46.57%

** Growth rate in net sales is calculated as follows:

Year	Calculation
2018	($50.5/$46.8) − 1 = 7.91%
2019	($53.9/$50.5) − 1 = 6.73%

13. A is correct. In forecasting financing costs, such as interest expense, the debt/equity structure of a company is a key determinant. Accordingly, a method that recognizes the relationship between the income statement account (interest expense) and the balance sheet account (debt) would be a preferable method for

forecasting interest expense when compared with methods that forecast based solely on the income statement account. By using the effective interest rate (interest expense divided by average gross debt), Candidate A is taking the debt/equity structure into account. Candidate B (who forecasts 2020 interest expense to be the same as 2019 interest expense) and Candidate C (who forecasts 2020 interest expense to be the same as the 2017–19 average interest expense) are not taking the balance sheet into consideration.

14. B is correct. Base rates refer to attributes of a reference class and base rate neglect is ignoring such class information in favor of specific information. By incorporating industry data, Candidate B is seeking to mitigate this.

15. C is correct. Economies of scale are a situation in which average costs decrease with increasing sales volume. Chrome's gross margins have been increasing with net sales. Gross margins that increase with sales levels provide evidence of economies of scale, assuming that higher levels of sales reflect increased unit sales. Gross margin more directly reflects the cost of sales than does profit margin.

Metric	2017	2018	2019
Net sales	$46.8	$50.5	$53.9
Gross profit	28.6	32.1	35.1
Gross margin (gross profit/net sales)	61.11%	63.56%	65.12%

16. A is correct. A bottom-up approach for developing inputs to equity valuation models begins at the level of the individual company or a unit within the company. By modeling net sales using the average annual growth rate, Candidate A is using a bottom-up approach. Both Candidate B and Candidate C are using a top-down approach, which begins at the level of the overall economy.

17. B is correct. A top-down approach usually begins at the level of the overall economy. Candidate B assumes industry sales will grow at the same rate as nominal GDP but that Chrome will have a 2 percentage point decline in market share. Candidate B is not using any elements of a bottom-up approach; therefore, a hybrid approach is not being employed.

18. C is correct. Candidate C assumes that the 2020 gross margin will increase by 20 bps from 2019 and that net sales will grow at 50 bps slower than nominal GDP (nominal GDP = Real GDP + Inflation = 1.6% + 2.0% = 3.6%). Accordingly, the 2020 forecasted cost of sales is USD19.27 million, rounded to USD19.3 million.

Metric	Calculation	Result
2020 gross margin = 2019 gm + 20 bps	$35.1/$53.9 = 65.12% + 0.20% =	65.32%
2020 CoS/net sales = 100% − gross margin	100% − 65.32% =	34.68%
2020 net sales = 2019 net sales × (1 + Nominal GDP − 0.50%)	$53.9 million × (1 + 0.036 − 0.005) = $53.9 million × 1.031 =	$55.57 million
2020 cost of sales = 2020 net sales × CoS/net sales	$55.57 × 34.68% =	$19.27 million

19. B is correct. Candidate A assumes that the 2020 SG&A/net sales will be the same as the average SG&A/net sales over the 2017–19 time period and that net sales will grow at the annual average growth rate in net sales over the 2017–19 time period. Accordingly, the 2020 forecasted SG&A expenses are USD25.5 million.

Metric	Calculation	Result
Average SG&A/net sales, 2017–2019*	(41.24% + 44.55% + 46.57%)/3 =	44.12%
Average annual growth sales in net sales, 2017–2019**	(7.91% + 6.73%)/2 =	7.32%
2020 net sales = 2019 net sales × (1 + Average annual growth rate in net sales)	$53.9 million × 1.0732 =	$57.85 million
2020 SG&A = 2020 net sales × Average SG&A/net sales	$57.85 million × 44.12% =	$25.52 million

SG&A/net sales are calculated as follows:

	2017	2018	2019
Net Sales	$46.8	$50.5	$53.9
SG&A expenses	$19.3	$22.5	$25.1
SG&A-to-sales ratio	41.24%	44.55%	46.57%

** *Growth rate in net sales is calculated as follows:*

Year	Calculation
2018	($50.5/$46.8) − 1 = 7.91%
2019	($53.9/$50.5) − 1 = 6.73%

20. A is correct. In forecasting financing costs, such as interest expense, the debt/equity structure of a company is a key determinant. Accordingly, a method that recognizes the relationship between the income statement account (interest expense) and the balance sheet account (debt) would be a preferable method for forecasting interest expense when compared with methods that forecast based solely on the income statement account. By using the effective interest rate (interest expense divided by average gross debt), Candidate A is taking the debt/equity structure into account. Candidate B (who forecasts 2020 interest expense to be the same as 2019 interest expense) and Candidate C (who forecasts 2020 interest expense to be the same as the 2017–19 average interest expense) are not taking the balance sheet into consideration.

21. B is correct. Base rates refer to attributes of a reference class and base rate neglect is ignoring such class information in favor of specific information. By incorporating industry data, Candidate B is seeking to mitigate this.

22. C is correct. Economies of scale are a situation in which average costs decrease with increasing sales volume. Chrome's gross margins have been increasing with net sales. Gross margins that increase with sales levels provide evidence of economies of scale, assuming that higher levels of sales reflect increased unit sales. Gross margin more directly reflects the cost of sales than does profit margin.

Metric	2017	2018	2019
Net sales	$46.8	$50.5	$53.9
Gross profit	28.6	32.1	35.1

Metric	2017	2018	2019
Gross margin (gross profit/net sales)	61.11%	63.56%	65.12%

23. A is correct. A bottom-up approach for developing inputs to equity valuation models begins at the level of the individual company or a unit within the company. By modeling net sales using the average annual growth rate, Candidate A is using a bottom-up approach. Both Candidate B and Candidate C are using a top-down approach, which begins at the level of the overall economy.

24. B is correct. A top-down approach usually begins at the level of the overall economy. Candidate B assumes industry sales will grow at the same rate as nominal GDP but that Chrome will have a 2 percentage point decline in market share. Candidate B is not using any elements of a bottom-up approach; therefore, a hybrid approach is not being employed.

25. C is correct. Candidate C assumes that the 2020 gross margin will increase by 20 bps from 2019 and that net sales will grow at 50 bps slower than nominal GDP (nominal GDP = Real GDP + Inflation = 1.6% + 2.0% = 3.6%). Accordingly, the 2020 forecasted cost of sales is USD19.27 million, rounded to USD19.3 million.

Metric	Calculation	Result
2020 gross margin = 2019 gm + 20 bps	$35.1/$53.9 = 65.12% + 0.20% =	65.32%
2020 CoS/net sales = 100% − gross margin	100% − 65.32% =	34.68%
2020 net sales = 2019 net sales × (1 + Nominal GDP − 0.50%)	$53.9 million × (1 + 0.036 − 0.005) = $53.9 million × 1.031 =	$55.57 million
2020 cost of sales = 2020 net sales × CoS/net sales	$55.57 × 34.68% =	$19.27 million

26. B is correct. Candidate A assumes that the 2020 SG&A/net sales will be the same as the average SG&A/net sales over the 2017–19 time period and that net sales will grow at the annual average growth rate in net sales over the 2017–19 time period. Accordingly, the 2020 forecasted SG&A expenses are USD25.5 million.

Metric	Calculation	Result
Average SG&A/net sales, 2017–2019*	(41.24% + 44.55% + 46.57%)/3 =	44.12%
Average annual growth sales in net sales, 2017–2019**	(7.91% + 6.73%)/2 =	7.32%
2020 net sales = 2019 net sales × (1 + Average annual growth rate in net sales)	$53.9 million × 1.0732 =	$57.85 million
2020 SG&A = 2020 net sales × Average SG&A/net sales	$57.85 million × 44.12% =	$25.52 million

* SG&A/net sales are calculated as follows:

	2017	2018	2019
Net Sales	$46.8	$50.5	$53.9
SG&A expenses	$19.3	$22.5	$25.1
SG&A-to-sales ratio	41.24%	44.55%	46.57%

** Growth rate in net sales is calculated as follows:

Year	Calculation
2018	($50.5/$46.8) − 1 = 7.91%
2019	($53.9/$50.5) − 1 = 6.73%

27. A is correct. In forecasting financing costs, such as interest expense, the debt/equity structure of a company is a key determinant. Accordingly, a method that recognizes the relationship between the income statement account (interest expense) and the balance sheet account (debt) would be a preferable method for forecasting interest expense when compared with methods that forecast based solely on the income statement account. By using the effective interest rate (interest expense divided by average gross debt), Candidate A is taking the debt/equity structure into account. Candidate B (who forecasts 2020 interest expense to be the same as 2019 interest expense) and Candidate C (who forecasts 2020 interest expense to be the same as the 2017–19 average interest expense) are not taking the balance sheet into consideration.

28. B is correct. Base rates refer to attributes of a reference class and base rate neglect is ignoring such class information in favor of specific information. By incorporating industry data, Candidate B is seeking to mitigate this.

29. B is correct. Operating (EBIT) margin is a pre-tax profitability measure that can be useful in the peer comparison of companies in countries with different tax structures. Archway's two main competitors are located in different countries with significantly different tax structures; therefore, a pre-tax measure is better than an after-tax measure, such as ROIC. The current ratio is a liquidity measure, not a profitability measure.

30. A is correct. Porter's five forces framework in Exhibit 1 describes an industry with high barriers to entry, high customer switching costs (suggesting a low threat of substitutes), and a specialized product (suggesting low bargaining power of buyers). Furthermore, the primary production inputs from the large group of suppliers are considered basic commodities (suggesting low bargaining power of suppliers). These favorable industry characteristics will likely enable Archway to pass along price increases and generate above-average returns on invested capital.

31. A is correct. The current favorable characteristics of the industry (high barriers to entry, low bargaining power of suppliers and buyers, low threat of substitutes), coupled with Archway's dominant market share position, will likely lead to Archway's profit margins being at least equal to or greater than current levels over the forecast horizon.

32. C is correct. The calculation of Archway's gross profit margin for 2020, which reflects the industry-wide 8% inflation on COGS, is calculated as follows:

Revenue growth	1.85%
COGS increase	4.76%
Forecasted revenue (Base revenue = 100)	101.85
Forecasted COGS (Base COGS = 30)	31.43
Forecasted gross profit	70.42

Forecasted gross profit margin	69.14%

Revenue growth = (1 + Price increase for revenue) × (1 + Volume growth) − 1

= (1.05) × (0.97) − 1

= 1.85%.

COGS increase = (1 + Price increase for COGS) × (1 + Volume growth) − 1

= (1.08) × (0.97) − 1

= 4.76%.

Forecasted revenue = Base revenue × Revenue growth increase

= 100 × 1.0185

= 101.85.

Forecasted COGS = Base COGS × COGS increase

= 30 × 1.0476

= 31.43.

Forecasted gross profit = Forecasted revenue − Forecasted COGS

= 101.85 − 31.43

= 70.42.

Forecasted gross profit margin = Forecasted gross profit/Forecasted revenue

= 70.42/101.85

= 69.14%.

33. C is correct. French is using a bottom-up approach to forecast Archway's working capital accounts by using the company's historical efficiency ratios to project future performance.

34. B is correct. If the future growth or profitability of a company is likely to be lower than the historical average (in this case, because of a potential technological development), then the target multiple should reflect a discount to the historical multiple to reflect this difference in growth and/or profitability. If a multiple is used to derive the terminal value of a company, the choice of the multiple should be consistent with the long-run expectations for growth and required return. French tells Wright he believes that such a technological development could have an adverse impact on Archway beyond the forecast horizon.

35. C is correct. Forecasting a single scenario would not be appropriate given the high degree of uncertainty and range of potential outcomes for companies in this industry.

36. B is correct. Small, inexpensive, imported petrol-fueled motorcycles are substitutes for petrol scooters and could increasingly have an impact on Omikroon's petrol scooter pricing power.

37. B is correct. Return on invested capital is net operating profit minus adjusted taxes divided by invested capital, where invested capital is defined as operating assets minus operating liabilities.

38. A is correct. Competition from other electric scooter manufacturers is expected to begin in one year. After this time, competing electric scooters could lead to lower demand for Omikroon's electric scooters and affect Omikroon's gross profit margin.

39. B is correct. The electric scooter market is expected to grow rapidly, so the contribution of Omrikoon's new electric scooter division is forecast to expand significantly over the next 10 years. A is not correct because the investment company's portfolio turnover is not relevant for forecasting Omnrikoon's future results. C is not correct because the light truck division is expected to add only 2% to total revenues in the future.

40. A is correct. The sensitivity analysis consists of an increase of 20% in the price of an input that constitutes 4% of cost of sales. Change in gross profit margin because of that increase is calculated as the change in cost of sales because of price increase divided by sales:

= (Cost of sales × 0.04 × 0.2)/Sales

= (105.38 × 0.04 × 0.2)/152.38

= 0.0055

41. C is correct. In Scenario 2, growth capital expenditure of EUR27 million for the refit of the existing idle factory is higher than the growth capital expenditure in Scenario 1 of EUR25 million. The EUR25 million is the cost of building a new factory for EUR30 million less the proceeds from the sale of the existing idle factory of EUR5 million.

42. C is correct. The management of Omikroom and investor relations of ZeroWheel are almost certainly biased in favor of expecting strong growth for the markets they participate in. To evaluate the forecast, Fromm should seek more independent sources and balance the biased sources with sources biased in the opposite direction or an analyst who is more skeptical.

43. B is correct. Operating (EBIT) margin is a pre-tax profitability measure that can be useful in the peer comparison of companies in countries with different tax structures. Archway's two main competitors are located in different countries with significantly different tax structures; therefore, a pre-tax measure is better than an after-tax measure, such as ROIC. The current ratio is a liquidity measure, not a profitability measure.

44. A is correct. Porter's five forces framework in Exhibit 1 describes an industry with high barriers to entry, high customer switching costs (suggesting a low threat of substitutes), and a specialized product (suggesting low bargaining power of buyers). Furthermore, the primary production inputs from the large group of suppliers are considered basic commodities (suggesting low bargaining power of suppliers). These favorable industry characteristics will likely enable Archway to pass along price increases and generate above-average returns on invested capital.

45. A is correct. The current favorable characteristics of the industry (high barriers to entry, low bargaining power of suppliers and buyers, low threat of substitutes), coupled with Archway's dominant market share position, will likely lead to Arch-

way's profit margins being at least equal to or greater than current levels over the forecast horizon.

46. C is correct. The calculation of Archway's gross profit margin for 2020, which reflects the industry-wide 8% inflation on COGS, is calculated as follows:

Revenue growth	1.85%
COGS increase	4.76%
Forecasted revenue (Base revenue = 100)	101.85
Forecasted COGS (Base COGS = 30)	31.43
Forecasted gross profit	70.42
Forecasted gross profit margin	69.14%

Revenue growth = (1 + Price increase for revenue) × (1 + Volume growth) − 1

= (1.05) × (0.97) − 1

= 1.85%.

COGS increase = (1 + Price increase for COGS) × (1 + Volume growth) − 1

= (1.08) × (0.97) − 1

= 4.76%.

Forecasted revenue = Base revenue × Revenue growth increase

= 100 × 1.0185

= 101.85.

Forecasted COGS = Base COGS × COGS increase

= 30 × 1.0476

= 31.43.

Forecasted gross profit = Forecasted revenue − Forecasted COGS

= 101.85 − 31.43

= 70.42.

Forecasted gross profit margin = Forecasted gross profit/Forecasted revenue

= 70.42/101.85

= 69.14%.

47. C is correct. French is using a bottom-up approach to forecast Archway's working capital accounts by using the company's historical efficiency ratios to project future performance.

48. B is correct. If the future growth or profitability of a company is likely to be lower than the historical average (in this case, because of a potential technological development), then the target multiple should reflect a discount to the historical

multiple to reflect this difference in growth and/or profitability. If a multiple is used to derive the terminal value of a company, the choice of the multiple should be consistent with the long-run expectations for growth and required return. French tells Wright he believes that such a technological development could have an adverse impact on Archway beyond the forecast horizon.

49. C is correct. Forecasting a single scenario would not be appropriate given the high degree of uncertainty and range of potential outcomes for companies in this industry.

50. B is correct. Small, inexpensive, imported petrol-fueled motorcycles are substitutes for petrol scooters and could increasingly have an impact on Omikroon's petrol scooter pricing power.

51. B is correct. Return on invested capital is net operating profit minus adjusted taxes divided by invested capital, where invested capital is defined as operating assets minus operating liabilities.

52. A is correct. Competition from other electric scooter manufacturers is expected to begin in one year. After this time, competing electric scooters could lead to lower demand for Omikroon's electric scooters and affect Omikroon's gross profit margin.

53. B is correct. The electric scooter market is expected to grow rapidly, so the contribution of Omrikoon's new electric scooter division is forecast to expand significantly over the next 10 years. A is not correct because the investment company's portfolio turnover is not relevant for forecasting Omnrikoon's future results. C is not correct because the light truck division is expected to add only 2% to total revenues in the future.

54. A is correct. The sensitivity analysis consists of an increase of 20% in the price of an input that constitutes 4% of cost of sales. Change in gross profit margin because of that increase is calculated as the change in cost of sales because of price increase divided by sales:

= (Cost of sales × 0.04 × 0.2)/Sales

= (105.38 × 0.04 × 0.2)/152.38

= 0.0055

55. C is correct. In Scenario 2, growth capital expenditure of EUR27 million for the refit of the existing idle factory is higher than the growth capital expenditure in Scenario 1 of EUR25 million. The EUR25 million is the cost of building a new factory for EUR30 million less the proceeds from the sale of the existing idle factory of EUR5 million.

56. C is correct. The management of Omikroom and investor relations of ZeroWheel are almost certainly biased in favor of expecting strong growth for the markets they participate in. To evaluate the forecast, Fromm should seek more independent sources and balance the biased sources with sources biased in the opposite direction or an analyst who is more skeptical.

57. B is correct. Operating (EBIT) margin is a pre-tax profitability measure that can be useful in the peer comparison of companies in countries with different tax structures. Archway's two main competitors are located in different countries with significantly different tax structures; therefore, a pre-tax measure is better than an after-tax measure, such as ROIC. The current ratio is a liquidity measure,

not a profitability measure.

58. A is correct. Porter's five forces framework in Exhibit 1 describes an industry with high barriers to entry, high customer switching costs (suggesting a low threat of substitutes), and a specialized product (suggesting low bargaining power of buyers). Furthermore, the primary production inputs from the large group of suppliers are considered basic commodities (suggesting low bargaining power of suppliers). These favorable industry characteristics will likely enable Archway to pass along price increases and generate above-average returns on invested capital.

59. A is correct. The current favorable characteristics of the industry (high barriers to entry, low bargaining power of suppliers and buyers, low threat of substitutes), coupled with Archway's dominant market share position, will likely lead to Archway's profit margins being at least equal to or greater than current levels over the forecast horizon.

60. C is correct. The calculation of Archway's gross profit margin for 2020, which reflects the industry-wide 8% inflation on COGS, is calculated as follows:

Revenue growth	1.85%
COGS increase	4.76%
Forecasted revenue (Base revenue = 100)	101.85
Forecasted COGS (Base COGS = 30)	31.43
Forecasted gross profit	70.42
Forecasted gross profit margin	69.14%

Revenue growth = (1 + Price increase for revenue) × (1 + Volume growth) − 1

= (1.05) × (0.97) − 1

= 1.85%.

COGS increase = (1 + Price increase for COGS) × (1 + Volume growth) − 1

= (1.08) × (0.97) − 1

= 4.76%.

Forecasted revenue = Base revenue × Revenue growth increase

= 100 × 1.0185

= 101.85.

Forecasted COGS = Base COGS × COGS increase

= 30 × 1.0476

= 31.43.

Forecasted gross profit = Forecasted revenue − Forecasted COGS

= 101.85 − 31.43

= 70.42.

Forecasted gross profit margin = Forecasted gross profit/Forecasted revenue

= 70.42/101.85

= 69.14%.

61. C is correct. French is using a bottom-up approach to forecast Archway's working capital accounts by using the company's historical efficiency ratios to project future performance.

62. B is correct. If the future growth or profitability of a company is likely to be lower than the historical average (in this case, because of a potential technological development), then the target multiple should reflect a discount to the historical multiple to reflect this difference in growth and/or profitability. If a multiple is used to derive the terminal value of a company, the choice of the multiple should be consistent with the long-run expectations for growth and required return. French tells Wright he believes that such a technological development could have an adverse impact on Archway beyond the forecast horizon.

63. C is correct. Forecasting a single scenario would not be appropriate given the high degree of uncertainty and range of potential outcomes for companies in this industry.

64. B is correct. Small, inexpensive, imported petrol-fueled motorcycles are substitutes for petrol scooters and could increasingly have an impact on Omikroon's petrol scooter pricing power.

65. B is correct. Return on invested capital is net operating profit minus adjusted taxes divided by invested capital, where invested capital is defined as operating assets minus operating liabilities.

66. A is correct. Competition from other electric scooter manufacturers is expected to begin in one year. After this time, competing electric scooters could lead to lower demand for Omikroon's electric scooters and affect Omikroon's gross profit margin.

67. B is correct. The electric scooter market is expected to grow rapidly, so the contribution of Omrikoon's new electric scooter division is forecast to expand significantly over the next 10 years. A is not correct because the investment company's portfolio turnover is not relevant for forecasting Omnrikoon's future results. C is not correct because the light truck division is expected to add only 2% to total revenues in the future.

68. A is correct. The sensitivity analysis consists of an increase of 20% in the price of an input that constitutes 4% of cost of sales. Change in gross profit margin because of that increase is calculated as the change in cost of sales because of price increase divided by sales:

= (Cost of sales × 0.04 × 0.2)/Sales

= (105.38 × 0.04 × 0.2)/152.38

= 0.0055

69. C is correct. In Scenario 2, growth capital expenditure of EUR27 million for the refit of the existing idle factory is higher than the growth capital expenditure in Scenario 1 of EUR25 million. The EUR25 million is the cost of building a new factory for EUR30 million less the proceeds from the sale of the existing idle factory

of EUR5 million.

70. C is correct. The management of Omikroom and investor relations of ZeroWheel are almost certainly biased in favor of expecting strong growth for the markets they participate in. To evaluate the forecast, Fromm should seek more independent sources and balance the biased sources with sources biased in the opposite direction or an analyst who is more skeptical.

71. B is correct. Small, inexpensive, imported petrol-fueled motorcycles are substitutes for petrol scooters and could increasingly have an impact on Omikroon's petrol scooter pricing power.

72. B is correct. Return on invested capital is net operating profit minus adjusted taxes divided by invested capital, where invested capital is defined as operating assets minus operating liabilities.

73. A is correct. Competition from other electric scooter manufacturers is expected to begin in one year. After this time, competing electric scooters could lead to lower demand for Omikroon's electric scooters and affect Omikroon's gross profit margin.

74. B is correct. The electric scooter market is expected to grow rapidly, so the contribution of Omrikoon's new electric scooter division is forecast to expand significantly over the next 10 years. A is not correct because the investment company's portfolio turnover is not relevant for forecasting Omnrikoon's future results. C is not correct because the light truck division is expected to add only 2% to total revenues in the future.

75. A is correct. The sensitivity analysis consists of an increase of 20% in the price of an input that constitutes 4% of cost of sales. Change in gross profit margin because of that increase is calculated as the change in cost of sales because of price increase divided by sales:

= (Cost of sales × 0.04 × 0.2)/Sales

= (105.38 × 0.04 × 0.2)/152.38

= 0.0055

76. C is correct. In Scenario 2, growth capital expenditure of EUR27 million for the refit of the existing idle factory is higher than the growth capital expenditure in Scenario 1 of EUR25 million. The EUR25 million is the cost of building a new factory for EUR30 million less the proceeds from the sale of the existing idle factory of EUR5 million.

77. C is correct. The management of Omikroom and investor relations of ZeroWheel are almost certainly biased in favor of expecting strong growth for the markets they participate in. To evaluate the forecast, Fromm should seek more independent sources and balance the biased sources with sources biased in the opposite direction or an analyst who is more skeptical.

78. B is correct. Operating (EBIT) margin is a pre-tax profitability measure that can be useful in the peer comparison of companies in countries with different tax structures. Archway's two main competitors are located in different countries with significantly different tax structures; therefore, a pre-tax measure is better than an after-tax measure, such as ROIC. The current ratio is a liquidity measure, not a profitability measure.

79. A is correct. Porter's five forces framework in Exhibit 1 describes an industry with high barriers to entry, high customer switching costs (suggesting a low threat of substitutes), and a specialized product (suggesting low bargaining power of buyers). Furthermore, the primary production inputs from the large group of suppliers are considered basic commodities (suggesting low bargaining power of suppliers). These favorable industry characteristics will likely enable Archway to pass along price increases and generate above-average returns on invested capital.

80. A is correct. The current favorable characteristics of the industry (high barriers to entry, low bargaining power of suppliers and buyers, low threat of substitutes), coupled with Archway's dominant market share position, will likely lead to Archway's profit margins being at least equal to or greater than current levels over the forecast horizon.

81. C is correct. The calculation of Archway's gross profit margin for 2020, which reflects the industry-wide 8% inflation on COGS, is calculated as follows:

Revenue growth	1.85%
COGS increase	4.76%
Forecasted revenue (Base revenue = 100)	101.85
Forecasted COGS (Base COGS = 30)	31.43
Forecasted gross profit	70.42
Forecasted gross profit margin	69.14%

Revenue growth = (1 + Price increase for revenue) × (1 + Volume growth) − 1

= (1.05) × (0.97) − 1

= 1.85%.

COGS increase = (1 + Price increase for COGS) × (1 + Volume growth) − 1

= (1.08) × (0.97) − 1

= 4.76%.

Forecasted revenue = Base revenue × Revenue growth increase

= 100 × 1.0185

= 101.85.

Forecasted COGS = Base COGS × COGS increase

= 30 × 1.0476

= 31.43.

Forecasted gross profit = Forecasted revenue − Forecasted COGS

= 101.85 − 31.43

= 70.42.

Forecasted gross profit margin = Forecasted gross profit/Forecasted revenue

$$= 70.42/101.85$$

$$= 69.14\%.$$

82. C is correct. French is using a bottom-up approach to forecast Archway's working capital accounts by using the company's historical efficiency ratios to project future performance.

83. B is correct. If the future growth or profitability of a company is likely to be lower than the historical average (in this case, because of a potential technological development), then the target multiple should reflect a discount to the historical multiple to reflect this difference in growth and/or profitability. If a multiple is used to derive the terminal value of a company, the choice of the multiple should be consistent with the long-run expectations for growth and required return. French tells Wright he believes that such a technological development could have an adverse impact on Archway beyond the forecast horizon.

84. C is correct. Forecasting a single scenario would not be appropriate given the high degree of uncertainty and range of potential outcomes for companies in this industry.

85. B is correct. Small, inexpensive, imported petrol-fueled motorcycles are substitutes for petrol scooters and could increasingly have an impact on Omikroon's petrol scooter pricing power.

86. B is correct. Return on invested capital is net operating profit minus adjusted taxes divided by invested capital, where invested capital is defined as operating assets minus operating liabilities.

87. A is correct. Competition from other electric scooter manufacturers is expected to begin in one year. After this time, competing electric scooters could lead to lower demand for Omikroon's electric scooters and affect Omikroon's gross profit margin.

88. B is correct. The electric scooter market is expected to grow rapidly, so the contribution of Omrikoon's new electric scooter division is forecast to expand significantly over the next 10 years. A is not correct because the investment company's portfolio turnover is not relevant for forecasting Omnrikoon's future results. C is not correct because the light truck division is expected to add only 2% to total revenues in the future.

89. A is correct. The sensitivity analysis consists of an increase of 20% in the price of an input that constitutes 4% of cost of sales. Change in gross profit margin because of that increase is calculated as the change in cost of sales because of price increase divided by sales:

$$= (\text{Cost of sales} \times 0.04 \times 0.2)/\text{Sales}$$

$$= (105.38 \times 0.04 \times 0.2)/152.38$$

$$= 0.0055$$

90. C is correct. In Scenario 2, growth capital expenditure of EUR27 million for the refit of the existing idle factory is higher than the growth capital expenditure in Scenario 1 of EUR25 million. The EUR25 million is the cost of building a new factory for EUR30 million less the proceeds from the sale of the existing idle factory of EUR5 million.

91. C is correct. The management of Omikroom and investor relations of ZeroWheel are almost certainly biased in favor of expecting strong growth for the markets they participate in. To evaluate the forecast, Fromm should seek more independent sources and balance the biased sources with sources biased in the opposite direction or an analyst who is more skeptical.

LEARNING MODULE

2

Analysis of Dividends and Share Repurchases

by Gregory Noronha, PhD, CFA, and George H. Troughton, PhD, CFA.

Gregory Noronha, PhD, CFA, is at the University of Washington, Tacoma (USA). George H. Troughton, PhD, CFA (USA).

LEARNING OUTCOMES

Mastery	The candidate should be able to:
☐	describe the expected effect of regular cash dividends, extra dividends, liquidating dividends, stock dividends, stock splits, and reverse stock splits on shareholders' wealth and a company's financial ratios
☐	compare theories of dividend policy and explain implications of each for share value given a description of a corporate dividend action
☐	describe types of information (signals) that dividend initiations, increases, decreases, and omissions may convey
☐	explain how agency costs may affect a company's payout policy
☐	explain factors that affect dividend policy in practice
☐	calculate and interpret the effective tax rate on a given currency unit of corporate earnings under double taxation, dividend imputation, and split-rate tax systems
☐	compare stable dividend with constant dividend payout ratio, and calculate the dividend under each policy
☐	describe broad trends in corporate payout policies
☐	compare share repurchase methods
☐	calculate and compare the effect of a share repurchase on earnings per share when 1) the repurchase is financed with the company's surplus cash and 2) the company uses debt to finance the repurchase
☐	calculate the effect of a share repurchase on book value per share
☐	explain the choice between paying cash dividends and repurchasing shares
☐	calculate and interpret dividend coverage ratios based on 1) net income and 2) free cash flow
☐	identify characteristics of companies that may not be able to sustain their cash dividend

1

DIVIDENDS: FORMS AND EFFECTS ON SHAREHOLDER WEALTH AND FINANCIAL RATIOS

☐ describe the expected effect of regular cash dividends, extra dividends, liquidating dividends, stock dividends, stock splits, and reverse stock splits on shareholders' wealth and a company's financial ratios

This reading covers the features and characteristics of dividends and share repurchases as well as the theory and practice of corporate payout policy. A **dividend** is a distribution paid to shareholders. Dividends are declared (i.e., authorized) by a corporation's board of directors, whose actions may require approval by shareholders (e.g., in most of Europe) or may not require such approval (e.g., in the United States). Shares trading **ex-dividend** refers to shares that no longer carry the right to the next dividend payment. The **ex-dividend date** is the first date that a share trades without (i.e., "ex") this right to receive the declared dividend for the period. All else holding constant, on the ex-dividend date the share price can be expected to drop by the amount of the dividend. In contrast to the payment of interest and principal on a bond by its issuer, the payment of dividends is discretionary rather than a legal obligation and may be limited in amount by legal statutes and debt contract provisions. Dividend payments and interest payments in many jurisdictions are subject to different tax treatment at both the corporate and personal levels.

In this reading, we focus on dividends on common shares (as opposed to preferred shares) paid by publicly traded companies. A company's **payout policy** is the set of principles guiding cash dividends and the value of shares repurchased in any given year. Payout policy (also called distribution policy) is more general than dividend policy because it reflects the fact that companies can return cash to shareholders by means of share repurchases and cash dividends. One of the longest running debates in corporate finance concerns the impact of a company's payout policy on common shareholders' wealth. Payout decisions, along with financing (capital structure) decisions, generally involve the board of directors and senior management and are closely watched by investors and analysts.

Dividends and share repurchases concern analysts because, as distributions to shareholders, they affect investment returns and financial ratios. The contribution of dividends to total return for stocks is formidable. For example, the total compound annual return for the S&P 500 Index with dividends reinvested from the beginning of 1926 to the end of 2018 was 10.0%, as compared with 5.9% on the basis of price alone. Similarly, from 1950 to 2018 the total compound annual return for the Nikkei 225 Index with dividends reinvested was 11.1%, as compared with 8.0% on the basis of price alone. Dividends also may provide important information about future company performance and investment returns. Analysts should strive to become familiar with all investment-relevant aspects of dividends and share repurchases.

This reading is organized as follows. Section 2 reviews the features and characteristics of cash dividends, liquidating dividends, stock dividends, stock splits, and reverse stock splits and describes their expected effect on shareholders' wealth and a company's financial ratios. Section 3 presents theories of the effects of dividend policy on company value. In Section 4, we discuss factors that affect dividend policy in practice. In Section 5, we cover three major types of dividend policies. Section 6 presents share repurchases, including their income statement and balance sheet effects and equivalence to cash dividends (under certain assumptions). Section 7 presents global trends in payout policy. Section 8 covers analysis of dividend safety. The reading concludes with a summary.

Dividends: Forms and Effects on Shareholder Wealth and Issuing Company's Financial Ratios

Companies can pay dividends in a number of ways. Cash dividends can be distributed to shareholders through regular, extra (also called special or irregular), or liquidating dividends. Other forms of dividends include stock dividends and stock splits. In this section, we review the different forms that dividends can take and explain their impact on both the shareholder and the issuing company.

Regular Cash Dividends

Many companies choose to distribute cash to their shareholders on a regular schedule. The customary frequency of payment, however, may vary among markets. In the United States and Canada, most companies that pay dividends choose a quarterly schedule of payments, whereas in Europe and Japan, the most common choice is to pay dividends twice a year (i.e., semiannually). Elsewhere in Asia, companies often favor paying dividends once a year (i.e., annually). Exhibit 1 summarizes typical dividend payment schedules for selected markets.

Exhibit 1: Geographic Differences in Frequency of Payment of Cash Dividends	
Market	**Most Common Frequency**
Canada, United States	Quarterly
Australia, Japan, Saudi Arabia	Semiannually
Egypt, Germany, Thailand	Annually

Most companies that pay cash dividends strive to maintain or increase their dividends. A record of consistent dividends over a long period of time is important to many companies and shareholders because it is widely interpreted as evidence of consistent profitability. At a minimum, most dividend-paying companies strive not to reduce dividends when they are experiencing temporary problems.

Regular dividends, and especially increasing regular dividends, also signal to investors that their company is growing and will share profits with its shareholders. Perhaps more importantly, management can use dividend announcements to communicate confidence in the company's future. Accordingly, an increase in the regular dividend (especially if it is unexpected) often has a positive effect on share price.

Extra or Special (Irregular) Dividends

An **extra dividend** or **special dividend** (also known as an irregular dividend) is either a dividend paid by a company that does not pay dividends on a regular schedule or a dividend that supplements regular cash dividends with an extra payment. These extra dividend payments may be brought about by special circumstances. For example, in December 2018 Hong Kong Stock Exchange (HKEX)-listed Tencent Holdings, a leading provider of internet value-added services, declared a special dividend of HKD250 million to its shareholders after its spin-off Tencent Music went public in New York. This special dividend was approximately 3.5% of Tencent's annual dividend.

Like many high-growth technology companies, Tencent had a history of paying very low dividends—with a yield of just 0.26% for 2018 (compared to an average of 4.6% for all stocks listed on the Hong Kong Stock Exchange).

Companies, particularly in cyclical industries, have sometimes chosen to use special dividends as a means of distributing more earnings only during strong earnings years. During economic downturns, when earnings are low or negative, cash that might otherwise be used for dividends is conserved. For example, a company may choose to declare a small regular dividend, and then when operating results are good, it may declare an extra dividend at the end of the year. In May 2018, Mumbai-listed Ingersoll-Rand (India) Ltd, a diversified industrial manufacturer, declared a special "second interim" dividend of Rs202 in addition to the regular annual Rs6 dividend, whereas for the prior 2 decades, the company had paid only the regular Rs6 dividend (excepting a special 2011 Rs24 dividend). The 2018 second interim dividend was paid out of current year profits and accumulated surpluses from earlier years. At the time, the company's reported year-on-year net profit growth was 25%.

Example 1 concerns a hypothetical company with a stated **dividend policy**—the strategy a company follows to determine the amount and timing of dividend payments—regarding the payment of extra dividends. In the example, the **dividend payout ratio** refers to common share cash dividends divided by net income available to common shares over the same time period.

EXAMPLE 1

AfriSage Technologies' Dividend Policy

AfriSage Technologies (AST), a hypothetical company, is a leading provider of commercial and enterprise software solutions in Southern African Development Community (SADC) countries. AST's financial data are reported in South African Rand (ZAR). In November 2017, AfriSage's board of directors modified its dividend policy, stating:

The company will target an investment-grade, long-term credit rating to secure strategic financial flexibility for investments in future growth. The ordinary dividend shall be at least 35% of net income. Excess capital will be returned to shareholders after the board has taken into consideration the company's cash at hand, projected cash flow, and planned investment from a medium-term perspective as well as capital market conditions.

Selected AfriSage Financial per Share Data		
	2018	**2017**
Shares outstanding	632.5 million	632.5 million
Earnings per share	ZAR14.23	ZAR12.65
Cash dividends per share	ZAR7.61	ZAR10.68

1. Calculate the cash dividend payout ratio for 2018 and 2017.

Solution:

With the same number of shares outstanding, the dividend payout ratio on a per share basis is dividends per share divided by earnings per share.

For 2018: ZAR7.61/ZAR14.23 = 53.5%.

For 2017: ZAR10.68/ZAR12.65 = 84.4%.

> 2. Assuming the board's new dividend policy became effective in 2018, calculate the amount of the annual ordinary dividend on the basis of AfriSage's minimum payout policy in 2018 and the amount that could be considered an extra dividend.
>
> ## Solution:
>
> Under a policy of 35% of earnings, the minimum amount of dividends would be ZAR14.23 × 0.35 = ZAR4.98. The amount of the extra dividend would then be ZAR7.61 – ZAR4.98 = ZAR2.63.

Liquidating Dividends

A dividend may be referred to as a **liquidating dividend** when a company:

- goes out of business and the net assets of the company (after all liabilities have been paid) are distributed to shareholders;
- sells a portion of its business for cash and the proceeds are distributed to shareholders; or
- pays a dividend that exceeds its accumulated retained earnings (impairs stated capital).

These points illustrate that a liquidating dividend is a return of capital rather than a distribution from earnings or retained earnings.

Stock Dividends

Stock dividends are a non-cash form of dividends. With a **stock dividend** (also known as a **bonus issue of shares** or a scrip dividend), the company distributes additional shares (typically 2–10% of the shares then outstanding) of its common stock to shareholders instead of cash. Although the shareholder's total cost basis remains the same, the cost per share held is reduced. For example, if a shareholder owns 100 shares with a purchase price of US$10 per share, the total cost basis would be US$1,000. After a 5% stock dividend, the shareholder would own 105 shares of stock at a total cost of US$1,000. However, the cost per share would decline to US$9.52 (US$1,000/105).

Superficially, the stock dividend might seem an improvement on the cash dividend from both the shareholders' and the company's point of view. Each shareholder ends up with more shares, which did not have to be paid for, and the company did not have to spend any actual money issuing a dividend. Furthermore, stock dividends are generally not taxable to shareholders because a stock dividend merely divides the "pie" (the market value of shareholders' equity) into smaller pieces. The stock dividend, however, does not affect the shareholder's proportionate ownership in the company because other shareholders receive the same proportionate increase in shares. Additionally, the stock dividend does not change the value of each shareholder's ownership position because the increase in the number of shares held is accompanied by an offsetting decrease in earnings per share, and other measures of value per share, resulting from the greater number of shares outstanding.

The second point is illustrated in Exhibit 2, which shows the impact of a 3% stock dividend to a shareholder who owns 10% of a company with a market value of US$20 million. As one can see, the market value of the shareholder's wealth does not change, assuming an unchanged **price-to-earnings ratio** (the ratio of share price, P, to earnings per share, E, or P/E). That assumption is reasonable because a stock dividend does not alter a company's asset base or earning power. (As the reader will see shortly, the same is true of a stock split.) The total market value of the company is unaffected by the stock dividend because the decrease in the share price is exactly offset by the increase in the number of shares outstanding.

Exhibit 2: Illustration of the Effect of a Stock Dividend		
	Before Dividend	**After Dividend**
Shares outstanding	1,000,000	1,030,000
Earnings per share	US$1.00	US$0.97 (1,000,000/1,030,000)
Stock price	US$20.00	US$19.4175 (20 × 0.9709)
P/E	20	20
Total market value	US$20 million	US$20 million (1,030,000 × US$19.4175)
Shares owned	100,000 (10% × 1,000,000)	103,000 (10% × 1,030,000)
Ownership value	US$2,000,000 (100,000 × US$20)	US$2,000,000 (103,000 × US$19.4175)

Note: The exhibit shows intermediate results rounded to four decimal places, but final results are based on carrying intermediate results at full precision.

Companies that regularly pay stock dividends see some advantages to this form of dividend payment. It favors long-term investors, which, in turn, may lower the company's cost of equity financing. The payment of a stock dividend also helps increase the stock's float, which improves the liquidity of the shares and dampens share price volatility.

A traditional belief is that a lower stock price will attract more investors, all else equal. US companies often view the optimal share price range as US$20 to US$80. For a growing company, payment of a regular stock dividend is more likely to help keep the stock in the "optimal" range. In February 2019, for example, Massmart—the second-largest distributor of consumer goods in Africa—changed its established policy of paying interim and final dividends in cash and instead declared a scrip dividend for the 2018 final dividend. When the company pays the same dividend rate on the new shares as it did on the old shares, a shareholder's dividend income increases; however, the company could have accomplished the same result by increasing the cash dividend.

From a company's perspective, the key difference between a stock dividend and a cash dividend is that a cash dividend affects a company's capital structure, whereas a stock dividend has no economic impact on a company. Cash dividends reduce assets (because cash is being paid out) and shareholders' equity (by reducing retained earnings). All else equal, liquidity ratios, such as the cash ratio (cash and short-term marketable securities divided by current liabilities) and current ratio (current assets divided by current liabilities), should decrease, reflecting the reduction in cash. Financial leverage ratios, such as the debt-to-equity ratio (total debt divided by total shareholders' equity) and debt-to-assets ratio (total debt divided by total assets), should also increase. Stock dividends, on the other hand, do not affect assets or shareholders' equity. Although retained earnings are reduced by the value of the stock dividends paid (i.e., by the number of shares issued × price per share), contributed capital increases by the same amount (i.e., the value of the shares issued). As a result, total shareholders' equity does not change. Neither stock dividends nor stock splits (which are discussed in the next section) affect liquidity ratios or financial leverage ratios.

Stock Splits

Stock splits are similar to stock dividends in that they have no economic effect on the company, and the shareholders' total cost basis does not change. For example, if a company announces a two-for-one stock split, each shareholder will be issued an additional share for each share currently owned. Thus, a shareholder will have twice as many shares after the split as before the split. Therefore, earnings per share (and all other per share data) will decline by half, leaving the P/E and equity market value unchanged. Assuming the corporation maintains the same dividend payout ratio as before the split, **dividend yield** (annual dividends per share divided by share price) will also be unchanged. Apart from the effect of any information or benefit that investors perceive a stock split to convey, stock splits (like stock dividends) should be neutral in their effect on shareholders' wealth.

Although two-for-one and three-for-one stock splits are the most common, such unusual splits as five-for-four or seven-for-three sometimes occur. It is important for shareholders to recognize that their wealth is not changed by the stock split (just as it was not changed for a stock dividend, all else equal). Exhibit 3 shows an example of a two-for-one split and its impact on stock price, earnings per share, dividends per share, dividend payout ratio, dividend yield, P/E, and market value.

Exhibit 3: Before and After a Two-for-One Stock Split

	Before Split	After Split
Number of shares outstanding	4 million	8 million
Stock price	€40.00	€20.00 (€40/2)
Earnings per share	€1.50	€0.75 (€1.50/2)
Dividends per share	€0.50	€0.25 (€0.50/2)
Dividend payout ratio	1/3	1/3
Dividend yield	1.25%	1.25% (€0.25/€20.00)
P/E	26.7	26.7 (€20.00/€0.75)
Market value of equity	€160 million	€160 million (€20.00 × 8 million)

As can be seen, a two-for-one stock split is basically the same as a 100% stock dividend because all per share data have been reduced by 50%. The only difference is in the accounting treatment: Although both stock dividends and stock splits have no effect on total shareholders' equity, a stock dividend is accounted for as a transfer of retained earnings to contributed capital. A stock split, however, does not affect any of the balances in shareholder equity accounts.

A company may announce a stock split at any time. Typically, a split is announced after a period in which the stock price has risen. Many investors view the announcement of a stock split as a positive sign pointing to future stock price increases. More often, however, announced stock splits merely recognize that the stock has risen enough to justify a stock split to return the stock price to a lower, more marketable price range.

Several of the largest companies in the world (as measured by market value) had stock splits in the last decade. For example, Schneider Electric SA (France) had a two-for-one split in 2011; Whole Foods Market (United States) had a two-for-one split in 2013. In each case, the stock split came after a significant rise in stock price but was not, in and of itself, a meaningful predictor of future price action. However, data show that stock splits have been on the decline in the United States. Although S&P 500 constituent stock splits averaged 45 per year between 1980 and 2017, they reached the maximum of 114 splits in 1986 and have steadily declined since 2015 (e.g., only 5 splits in 2017). This decline in stock splits has been attributed to greater use of funds and exchange-traded funds (ETFs) by individual investors and to changes in market microstructure that have de-linked such transaction costs as commissions paid to number of shares traded. Thus, the concept of a "marketable price range" of a company's stock has become less important.

Much less common than stock splits are reverse stock splits. A **reverse stock split** increases the share price and reduces the number of shares outstanding—again, with no effect on the market value of a company's equity or on shareholders' total cost basis. Just as a high stock price might lead a company to consider a stock split, so too a low stock price may lead a company to consider a reverse stock split. The objective of a reverse stock split is to increase the price of the stock to a higher, more marketable range. As reported in *Barron's*, companies execute reverse splits "to attract institutional investors and mutual funds that often shy from buying stocks trading below US$5." Reverse stock splits are perhaps most common for companies in, or coming out of, financial distress. Kitov Pharma, an Israeli drug developer, announced a 1-for-20 reverse split in December 2018, reducing its issued shares to 16 million, in order to meet minimum share price listing criteria to begin trading on the Tel Aviv Stock Exchange and to begin the trading of its ADRs on the NASDAQ in January 2019.

Reverse splits, historically less common in Asia, are becoming more popular. For example, reverse stock splits were not permitted in Japan under Corporation Law until 2001, but since 2007, they have been actively encouraged by the Tokyo Stock Exchange to meet the Exchange's objective of standardizing trading lot size to 100 shares for listed companies by 1 October 2018. While most companies were compliant by the deadline, on that date 23 companies reduced their trading lot size to 100 shares by carrying out reverse stock splits. As an example, in May 2018 Fuji Electric Co. Ltd announced that it would conduct a 5-for-1 reverse stock split on 1 October 2018 to adjust the unit of investment in the company to a level deemed desirable by the TSE (between ¥50,000 and ¥500,000).

EXAMPLE 2

Globus Maritime Announces a Reverse Split

In May 2018, Globus Maritime Ltd, a Greek dry bulk shipping company providing worldwide maritime transportation services, was warned by NASDAQ that it no longer met the continuing listing requirements once its share price had traded below the US$1 a share minimum price requirement for 30 consecutive business days. Globus was given until the end of October 2018 to regain compliance. Globus announced a 1 for 10 reverse split to occur on 15 October. On 12 October, shares were trading at US$4.25 before the reverse split had taken place.

1. If the reverse split were to take place when the share price was US$4.25, find the expected stock price after a 1-for-10 reverse split, assuming no other factors affect the split.

Solution:

If the price was US$4.25 before the reverse split, for every 10 shares, a shareholder would have 1 share priced at 10 × US$4.25 = US$42.50.

2. Comment on the following statement: "Shareholder wealth is negatively affected by a reverse stock split."

Solution:

The statement is not generally correct. Considering the reverse split on its own, the market capitalization of the common equity would be unchanged. If the reverse split was interpreted as a good decision (e.g., because the company will be able to retain the advantages of being listed on the NASDAQ), its price and thus market capitalization might increase. But other factors—such as continued limited growth of its operations or continued small share float and turnover—could drive down the stock's value.

DIVIDEND POLICY AND COMPANY VALUE: THEORIES 2

☐ | compare theories of dividend policy and explain implications of each for share value given a description of a corporate dividend action

Since the early 1960s, financial theorists have debated the extent to which dividend policy (decisions about whether, when, and in what amount to pay dividends) should and does matter to a company's shareholders. One group of theorists believes that dividend policy is irrelevant to shareholders. This group typically holds that only the decisions of the company that are directly related to investment in working and fixed capital affect shareholders' wealth. A second group holds that dividend policy does matter to investors, for one or more reasons, and that a company can affect shareholders' wealth through its dividend policy. Typically, dividend relevance is attributed to either the belief that investors value a unit of dividends more highly than an equal amount of uncertain capital gains or to one or more market imperfections. Such imperfections include taxes (because dividends may be taxed differently than capital gains), asymmetric information (corporate insiders are better informed about their company's prospects than outside investors), and agency costs (management has a tendency to squander extra cash). We examine these positions and the assumptions that underlie them in the following subsections.

Dividend Policy Does Not Matter

In a 1961 paper, Miller and Modigliani ("MM") argued that in a world without taxes, transaction costs, and equal ("symmetric") information among all investors—that is, under **perfect capital market** assumptions—a company's dividend policy should have no impact on its cost of capital or on shareholder wealth. Their argument begins by assuming a company has a given capital budget (e.g., it accepts all projects with a positive net present value, or NPV) and that its current capital structure and debt ratio are optimal. Another way of stating this argument is that the dividend decision is independent of a company's investment and financing decisions. For example, suppose that an all-equity financed company decided to pay as a dividend the investment amount it required for its capital budget. To finance capital projects, the company could issue additional common shares in the amount of its capital budget (such financing would leave its capital structure unchanged). The value of the newly issued shares would exactly offset the value of the dividend. Thus, if a company paid out a dividend that represented 5% of equity, its share price would be expected to drop by 5%. If a common stock in Australia is priced at A$20 before an A$1 per share dividend, the implied new price would be A$19. The shareholder has assets worth A$20 if the dividend is not paid or assets worth A$20 if the stock drops to A$19 and an A$1 dividend is paid.

Note that under the MM assumptions, there is no meaningful distinction between dividends and share repurchases (repurchases of outstanding common shares by the issuing company): They are both ways for a company to return cash to shareholders. If a company had few investment opportunities such that its current cash flow was more than that needed for positive NPV projects, it could distribute the excess cash flow via a dividend or a share repurchase. Shareholders selling shares would receive A$20 a share, and shareholders not selling would hold shares whose value continued to be A$20. To see this, suppose the company being discussed has 10,000 shares outstanding, a current free cash flow of A$10,000, and a present value of future cash flows of A$190,000. Thus, the share price is (A$10,000 + A$190,000)/10,000 = A$20. Now if the company uses the free cash flow to repurchase shares, in lieu of paying a dividend of A\$1, it will repurchase 500 shares (A\$10,000/A\$20 = 500). The 9,500 shares left outstanding have a claim on the A\$190,000 future cash flow, which results in a share price of A\$20 (A\$190,000/9,500 = A\$20).

An intuitive understanding of MM dividend irrelevance also follows from the concept of a "homemade dividend." In a world with no taxes or transaction costs, if shareholders wanted or needed income, they could construct their own dividend policy by selling sufficient shares to create their desired cash flow stream. Using the example above, assume the company did not pay the A\$1 dividend and the stock remained at A\$20. A holder of 1,000 shares who desired A\$1,000 in cash could sell 50 shares at A\$20, thus reducing his or her holdings to 950 shares. Note that by reducing share holdings, second-period dividend income is reduced; higher dividend income in one period is at the expense of exactly offsetting lower dividend income in subsequent periods. The irrelevance argument does not state that dividends per se are irrelevant to share value but that dividend *policy* is irrelevant. By taking the earning power of assets as a given and assuming perfect capital markets, policy alternatives merely involve tradeoffs of different dividend streams of equal present value.

In the real world, market imperfections create some problems for MM's dividend policy irrelevance propositions. First, both companies and individuals incur transaction costs. A company issuing new shares incurs **flotation costs** (i.e., costs in selling shares to the public that include underwriters' fees, legal costs, registration expenses, and possible negative price effects) often estimated to be as much as 4% to 10% of the capital raised, depending on the size of the company and the size of the issue. Shareholders selling shares to create a "homemade" dividend would incur transaction costs and, in some countries, capital gains taxes (of course, cash dividends incur taxes in most countries). Furthermore, selling shares on a periodic basis to create an income stream of dividends can be problematic over time if share prices are volatile. If share prices decline, shareholders have to sell more shares to create the same dividend stream.

Dividend Policy Matters: The Bird in the Hand Argument

Financial theorists have argued that, even under perfect capital markets assumptions, investors prefer a dollar of dividends to a dollar of potential capital gains from reinvesting earnings because they view dividends as less risky. A related viewpoint is that "the typical dollar of reinvestment has less economic value to the shareholder than a dollar paid in dividends" (Graham, Dodd, Cottle, and Tatham 1962). These arguments are similar and have sometimes been called the "bird in the hand" argument, a reference to the proverb "a bird in the hand is worth two in the bush." By assuming that a given amount of dividends is less risky than the same amount of capital gains, the argument is that a company that pays dividends will have a lower cost of equity capital than an otherwise similar company that does not pay dividends; the lower cost of equity should result in a higher share price. MM contend that this argument is incorrect because, under their assumptions, paying or increasing the dividend today does not affect the risk of future cash flows. Such actions only lower the ex-dividend price of the share.

Dividend Policy Matters: The Tax Argument

In some countries, dividend income has traditionally been taxed at higher rates than capital gains. In the United States since 2012, for instance, dividends on shares held at least 60 days have been taxed at a maximum rate of 20%, which exceeds the long-term capital gains tax rate of 15%. In mainland China, there is no capital gains tax on shares; however, dividend income is taxed at 20% for shares held less than a month, 10% for shares held between one month and a year, and since 2015 at 0% for shares held longer than a year.

An argument could be made that in a country that taxes dividends at higher rates than capital gains, taxable investors should prefer companies that pay low dividends and reinvest earnings in profitable growth opportunities. Presumably, any growth in earnings in excess of the opportunity cost of funds would translate into a higher share price. If, for any reason, a company lacked growth opportunities sufficient to consume its annual retained earnings, it could distribute such funds through share repurchases (again, the assumption is that capital gains are taxed more lightly than dividends). Taken to its extreme, this argument would advocate a *zero* dividend payout ratio. Real world market considerations may complicate the picture. For example, in some jurisdictions governmental regulation may require companies to distribute excess earnings as dividends or to classify share repurchases as dividends if the repurchases appear to be ongoing in lieu of dividend payments.

OTHER THEORETICAL ISSUES: SIGNALING

3

- ☐ describe types of information (signals) that dividend initiations, increases, decreases, and omissions may convey
- ☐ explain how agency costs may affect a company's payout policy

In the following section, we present additional perspectives related to the theory of dividend policy.

The Information Content of Dividend Actions: Signaling

MM assumed that all investors—including outside investors—have the same information about the company: a situation of symmetric information. In reality, corporate managers typically have access to more detailed and extensive information about the company than do outside investors.

A situation of asymmetric information raises the possibility that dividend increases or decreases may affect share price because they may convey new information about the company. A company's board of directors and management, having more information than outside investors, may use dividends to signal to investors about (i.e., convey information on) the company's prospects. A company's decision to initiate, maintain, increase, or cut a dividend may convey more credible information than positive words from management because cash is involved. For a signal to be effective, it must be difficult or costly to mimic by another entity without the same attributes. Dividend increases are costly to mimic because a company that does not expect its cash flows to increase will not be able to maintain the dividend at increasingly high levels in the long run. (In the short run, a company may be able to borrow to fund dividends.)

Empirical studies broadly support the thesis that dividend initiations or increases convey positive information and are associated with future earnings growth, whereas dividend omissions or reductions convey negative information and are associated with future earnings problems. A dividend declaration can help resolve some of the information asymmetry between insiders and outsiders and help close any gap between the market price of shares and their intrinsic value. Evidence in both developed and emerging market equities suggests the presence of an earnings and return effect following dividend initiation announcements. In general, company earnings increase in the year of dividend initiation and in the following several years, and then the announcement of the initiation of a regular cash dividend is accompanied by an excess return. By looking at two historical examples of signaling, Example 3 provides further support for the idea that dividend initiations contain value-relevant information.

EXAMPLE 3

Historical Examples: Information on Dividend Initiations

Following are two examples of the information content of dividend initiations following the 2008 global financial crisis.

A. Oracle Corporation, a leading business software maker, initiated a US$0.05 quarterly dividend in May 2009. Oracle's annual US$0.20 dividend amounts to about US$1 billion, a relatively small amount compared with operating cash flow of US$8 billion and another US$9 billion in cash and cash-equivalent assets on its balance sheet at the end of fiscal year 2009. An analyst who follows Oracle for institutional investors saw the Oracle announcement as a signal that the company was well positioned to ride out the downturn and also gain market share.

B. In mid-2009, Paris-based Groupe Eurotunnel announced its first ever dividend after it completed a debt restructuring and received insurance proceeds resulting from a fire that had closed the Channel Tunnel. In a 2 June 2009 press release, Eurotunnel's CEO said that this "marked a turning point for the company as its business has returned to the realm of normality"; the company anticipated a return to profitability.

Some researchers have argued that a company's dividend initiation or increase tends to be associated with share price increases because it attracts more attention to the company. Managers have an incentive to increase the company's dividend if they believe the company to be undervalued because the increased scrutiny will lead to a positive price adjustment. In contrast, according to this line of reasoning, managers of overvalued companies have little reason to mimic such a signal because increased scrutiny would presumably result in a downward price adjustment to their shares.

EXAMPLE 4

Signaling with Dividends and the Costs of Mimicking

Suppose that the management of a company with poor future prospects recommends to the board of directors an increase in its dividend. Management explains to the board that investors may then believe that the company has positive future prospects, leading to an increase in share value and shareholder wealth.

---

1. State whether such imitation is likely to achieve the stated objective over the long term.

Solution:

No, such dividend increases are not likely to achieve the stated objective over the long term for the company described.

2. Justify your answer to Question 1.

Solution:

Dividend increases are costly to mimic because a company that does not expect its cash flows to increase will not be able to maintain the increased dividend. The company will have to either cut the dividend in the future or go to the market to obtain new equity or debt funding to pay the dividend. Both these alternatives are costly for the company because they result in downward revisions, on average, to the stock price.

Many companies take pride in their record of consistently increasing dividends over a long period of time. Standard & Poor's, for example, identifies companies in its US-based S&P 500 Index, Europe 350 Index, Pan Asia Index, and S&P/TSX Canadian Index that have increased their dividend for a number of consecutive years (at least 25 years in the case of the S&P 500, at least 10 years in the case of the Europe 350, at least 7 years in the case of Pan Asia Index, and at least 5 years in the case of the S&P/TSX). These companies are in various industries. When a company's earnings and cash flow outlook has been and continues to be positive, it often views a policy of increasing dividends as an important tool to convey that information to existing and potential shareholders. Companies that consistently increase their dividends seem to share certain characteristics:

- Dominant or niche positions in their industry
- Global operations
- Relatively less volatile earnings
- Relatively high returns on assets
- Relatively low debt ratios (dividend payouts unlikely to be affected by restrictions in debt covenants)

Dividend cuts or omissions, in contrast, present powerful and often negative signals. For companies under financial or operating stress, the dividend declaration date may be viewed with more than usual interest. Will they cut the dividend? Will they omit the dividend altogether? In these instances, merely maintaining the dividend or not cutting it as much as expected is usually viewed as good news (i.e., that current difficulties are transitory and manageable), unless investors view managers as trying to convey erroneous information to the market.

In principle, although difficult in practice, management can attempt to send a positive signal by cutting the dividend. Telstra, a major Australian telecoms company with an enviable record of paying close to 90% of profits as dividends, announced in 2017 a 30% cut in its dividend—its first cut in more than 20 years. Telstra's management explained it intended to use the funds conserved to reinvest in the business. It was planning for the longer term and retaining financial flexibility as a priority because the company faced significant challenges from rising competition and competing technologies. Although management's message was met with an initial 12% share price decline as disappointed yield-focused investors exited the stock, it was, in retrospect, a positive signal. Telstra was viewed by institutional investors as successfully using its cash flow to reorganize to meet business challenges, and it was regarded as one of the few cases in which a large Australian dividend payer was not cutting payouts as a result of extreme financial pressure.

Dividend Reductions and Price Increases

In November 2018, BT Group Plc, one of the world's largest providers of communication services and solutions operating in over 170 countries, announced it would cut its interim dividend from 4.85 pence a share to 4.62 pence a share. The company also revealed that net cash flow from operating activities had plunged 71% to £754 million and that revenue had fallen 2% to £11.6 billion, with declines across all divisions.

All this despite the fact that in the first six months of the year, the company reported a pretax profit increase to £1.3 billion from £1.1 billion a year prior and a 2% increase in adjusted earnings (EBITDA) to £3.7 billion from £3.6 billion as the telecoms giant cut costs as part of its restructuring. One analyst commented that while the dividend decrease was an "unwelcome surprise," it was also a "prudent move" given the 71% decline in net cash and thus "should not take too much sheen on a dividend yield, which previously stood at an attractive 6.4%." It was also noted that BT Group was replacing its chief executive in February 2019; thus, future dividends would depend on decisions made by the new leadership. As the market digested this information, the telecoms company's share price rose 6.9% to 257 pence per share.

Source: Renae Dyer, "BT Shares Surge Despite Dividend Cut as It Expects Earnings to Hit Top End of Guidance," Proactive Investors (1 November 2018).

Another example of the signaling content of dividends can be found in the actions of eBay, the e-commerce multinational corporation, and its initial dividend declaration in 2019 (24 years after the online retailer was established in 1995 during the dot-com boom). Technology companies have among the lowest dividend yields and below-average dividend payout ratios. This is because most technology companies have high R&D requirements, and some (e.g., integrated circuit manufacturers) are capital intensive. Those that are profitable often achieve returns on assets and owners' equity that are well above average. In addition, business risk is considerable as discoveries and unforeseen advances change the product landscape. All of these considerations would suggest a policy of low (or no) dividend payments so that internally generated funds are directed toward new product development and capital investment that will maintain high growth and returns. Some companies in the technology sector, however, do mature. Legacy tech companies that initiated dividends as their businesses matured and growth slowed include Apple in 2012, Cisco in 2011, Oracle in 2009, and Microsoft in 2003. At the time of eBay's dividend initiation, such non-dividend-paying tech companies as Alibaba, Weibo, Baidu, and JD.com remained the norm in markets where the technology sector was still growing.

In early 2019, eBay declared its first-ever dividend and announced that it would begin paying quarterly dividends of US$0.14 a share, which represented a yield of 1.6% (for comparison, Microsoft's dividend yield at the time was 1.9% and Cisco's was 2.9%). At the same time, eBay announced an increase in its existing share repurchase program to US$4 billion. Investor reaction was mixed. Some believed that eBay was signaling an interest in broadening its investor focus by attracting a new group of shareholders focused on income over growth while refraining from undertaking unprofitable expansion. Others viewed the dividend declaration as an admission that it was becoming a mature company—that it could no longer deliver high returns from reinvesting its earnings. The future growth prospects for the stock, they would argue, had been diminished. In other words, although the dividend initiation showed confidence in eBay's cash flow generation, investors preferred for management's use of internal investments to regenerate eBay's core business. Regardless, few could argue that eBay's dividend initiation declaration in 2019 was not a corporate event of some importance.

Agency Costs and Dividends as a Mechanism to Control Them

Large, publicly traded corporations typically have a substantial separation between the professional managers who control the corporation's operations and the outside investors who own it. When agents (the managers) and owners (the shareholders) are two separate parties, managers may have an incentive to maximize their own welfare at the company's expense because they own none or relatively small percentages of the company for which they work and thus do not bear all the costs of such actions. This incentive is ultimately also a problem of unequal (asymmetric) information between managers and outside investors because if outside investors could perfectly observe managers, managers would be dissuaded from such actions. One managerial incentive of particular concern is the potential private benefit managers may obtain from investment in negative net present value (NPV) projects. Such projects will generate negative economic returns; but because they may grow the size of the company (measured in sales or assets) and thus enlarge the manager's span of control, the manager may have the incentive to invest in them. This is a particular problem when management's compensation is tied to assets or sales rather than value enhancement, a flaw in the firm's corporate governance. The potential overinvestment agency problem might be alleviated by the payment of dividends. In particular, by paying out all free cash flow to equity in dividends, managers would be constrained in their ability to overinvest by taking on negative NPV projects. This concern or hypothesis that management may create an overinvestment agency cost is known as Jensen's free cash flow hypothesis.

The potential for managers to squander free cash flow by undertaking unprofitable projects is a consideration to be evaluated on a case-by-case basis. Prior to initiating its dividend in 2003, for example, Microsoft accumulated increasingly large cash positions but was not observed to squander monies on unprofitable projects. In some cases, such cash positions may provide financial flexibility to respond quickly to changes in the environment, to grasp unforeseen opportunities, or to survive periods of restricted credit, as in the case of Ford Motor Company's accumulation of cash during profitable years in the 1990s and similarly by Japanese automotive parts manufacturer Denso Corporation in the late 2000s and 2010s. Clearly, there are industry-specific and life-cycle conditions to consider. In general, it makes sense for growing companies in industries characterized by rapid change to hold cash and pay low or no dividends, but it does not make sense for large, mature companies in relatively non-cyclical industries. In general, there is empirical support for the market reaction to dividend change announcements to be stronger for companies with greater potential for overinvestment than for companies with lesser potential for overinvestment.

Another concern when a company is financed by debt as well as equity is that paying dividends can exacerbate the agency conflict between shareholders and bondholders. When a company has debt outstanding, the payment of dividends reduces the cash cushion available to the company for the disbursement of fixed required payments to bondholders. The payment of large dividends, with the intention of transferring wealth from bondholders to shareholders, could lead to underinvestment in profitable projects. All else equal, both dividends and share repurchases increase the default risk of debt. Reflecting bondholders' concern, the bond **indenture** (contract) often includes a covenant restricting distributions to shareholders that might impair the position of bondholders. A typical form of this restriction is to define the maximum allowable amount of distributions to shareholders during the life of the bond. This amount of funds is usually a positive function of the company's current and past earnings and issues of new equity and a negative function of dividends paid since the bonds were issued. Such covenants often do not really restrict the level of dividends as long as those dividends come from new earnings or from new issues of stock. What the covenant attempts to do is prevent the payment of dividends financed by the sale of the company's existing assets or by the issuance of new debt. Covenants that specify minimum levels of EBITDA and/or EBIT coverage of interest charges are frequently used as well. These covenants provide some assurance that operating earnings include a cushion for the payment of fixed charges. Other covenants focus on balance sheet strength—for example, by specifying a maximum value for the ratio of debt to tangible net worth.

EXAMPLE 6

Agency Issues and Dividends

1. Two dividend-paying companies A and B directly compete with each other. Both companies are all-equity financed and have recent dividend payout ratios averaging 35%. The corporate governance practices at Company B are weaker than at Company A. For example, at B but not A, the chief executive officer is also chair of the board of directors. Recently, profitable investment opportunities for B have become fewer, although operating cash flow for both A and B is strong.

   Based only on the information given, investors who own shares in both A and B are *most likely* to press for a dividend increase at:

   A. Company A, because it has better growth prospects than Company B.

   B. Company B, because a dividend increase may mitigate potential over-investment agency problems.

   C. Company B, because a dividend increase may mitigate potential underinvestment agency problems.

Solution:

B is correct. Company B's strong operating cash flow in an environment of fewer profitable growth opportunities may tempt Company B's management to overinvest. The concern is increased because of Company B's relatively weak corporate governance.

The final example in this section illustrates the complex agency considerations that may affect dividend policy.

EXAMPLE 7

Electric Utilities, Agency Costs, and Dividends

Electric utilities often have above average dividend yields. A distinctive characteristic of many utility companies is that they pay a high percentage of earnings as dividends, while periodically issuing new equity to invest in the many projects necessitated by the capital-intensive nature of their business. This practice of financing dividends with new equity appears unwise because new equity is expensive. Researchers examining a set of US-based electric utilities, however, have demonstrated that there may be a good reason for paying dividends and then issuing equity: the mitigation of the agency problems between managers and shareholders and between utility regulators and utility shareholders.

> Because electric utilities are typically monopolies in the sense that they are usually the only providers of electricity in a given area, they are regulated so they are not able to set electricity rates at monopolistically high levels. The regulators are expected to set rates such that the company's operating expenses are met and investors are provided with a fair return. The regulators, however, are usually elected, or are political appointees, and view ratepayers as potential voters. Thus, utility shareholders, in addition to facing potential manager–shareholder agency issues because managers have incentives to consume perquisites or to overinvest, also face a regulator–shareholder conflict in which regulators set rates low to attract the votes of individuals being served by the utility.
>
> In the utility industry, therefore, dividends and the subsequent equity issue are used as mechanisms to monitor managers and regulators. The company pays high dividends and then goes to the capital markets to issue new equity. If the market does not think that shareholders are getting a fair return because regulators are setting rates too low, or because managers are consuming too many perks, the price at which new equity can be sold will fall until the shareholder expectations for returns are met. As a result, the company may not be able to raise sufficient funds to expand its plant to meet increasing electricity demand—the electric utility industry is very capital intensive—and, in the extreme, customer needs may not be met. Faced with this possibility, and potentially angry voters, regulators have incentives to set rates at a fair level. Thus, the equity market serves to monitor and arbitrate conflicts between shareholders and both managers and regulators.

OTHER THEORETICAL ISSUES: SUMMARY | 4

☐ | explain how agency costs may affect a company's payout policy

What can we conclude about the link between dividends and valuation? In theory, in the absence of market imperfections Miller and Modigliani (1961) find that dividend policy is irrelevant to the wealth of a company's investors. But in reality, the existence of market imperfections makes matters more complicated. In addition, some investors are led, by logic or custom, to prefer dividends.

Unfortunately, in the search for the link between dividend policy and value, the evidence is inconclusive. It is difficult to show an exact relationship between dividends and value because so many variables affect value. We have presented factors that would seem to explain why some companies put emphasis on dividends and others do not. Financial theory predicts that reinvestment opportunities should be the dominant factor. Indeed, no matter where they are located in the world, small, fast-growing companies pay out little or none of their earnings. Regardless of jurisdiction, more mature companies with fewer reinvestment opportunities tend to pay dividends. For these mature companies, taxes, regulations/laws, tradition, signaling, ownership structure, and attempts to reconcile agency conflicts all seem to play a role in determining the dividend payout ratio. At a minimum, in looking at a company an analyst should evaluate whether a given company's dividend policy matches its reinvestment opportunities and legal/financial environment.

5

FACTORS AFFECTING DIVIDEND POLICY IN PRACTICE

☐   explain factors that affect dividend policy in practice

☐   calculate and interpret the effective tax rate on a given currency unit of corporate earnings under double taxation, dividend imputation, and split-rate tax systems

In Section 3 we discussed theories of dividend policy and value and concluded that the issue is, at best, unresolved. In this section we explore six factors that affect a company's dividend policy, which we defined earlier as decisions about whether, when, and in what amount to pay dividends:

- Investment opportunities
- The expected volatility of future earnings
- Financial flexibility
- Tax considerations
- Flotation costs
- Contractual and legal restrictions

Boards of directors and managers spend considerable time setting dividend policy despite the lack of clear guidance from theory to inform their deliberations. The factors listed are, however, often mentioned by managers themselves as relevant to dividend policy selection in practice. Some of the factors we explore, such as taxation, are not company-specific, whereas other factors, such as possible contractual restrictions on dividend payments and the expected volatility of future earnings, are more company-specific. The factors may be interrelated, and the presence of one may enhance or diminish the effect of another. Importantly, the independence between the investment, financing, and dividend decisions assumed by MM may no longer hold when such market imperfections as information effects, agency problems, and taxes are recognized.

Investment Opportunities

All else equal, a company with many profitable investment opportunities will tend to pay out less in dividends than a company with fewer opportunities because the former company will have more uses for internally generated cash flows. Internally generated cash flow is generally a cheaper source of equity funding than new equity issuance. Opportunities for new investments, and the speed with which a company needs to respond to them, are influenced by the industry in which the company operates. A company with the ability to delay the initiation of projects without penalty may be willing to pay out more in dividends than a company that needs to act immediately to exploit profitable investment opportunities. Technology companies tend to have much lower average dividend yields than utilities. The chief explanation may be the size and time horizon of profitable investment opportunities in relation to annual operating cash flow generated. For technology companies, the pace of change is rapid, so having internally generated funds available to react to profitable opportunities affords them valuable flexibility. For utility companies, for which there are typically fewer such opportunities and for which change is much slower, higher dividend payouts are indicated.

The Expected Volatility of Future Earnings

Several important factors in the dividend payout decision have been identified as important to managers. Most managers

- had a target payout ratio based on long-run sustainable earnings;
- focused more on dividend changes (increases or decreases) than on dividend levels; and
- were reluctant to increase the dividend if the increase might soon need to be reversed.

Findings in the United States, United Kingdom, and other countries suggest that managers are reluctant to cut dividends—preferring to smooth them over time. Smoothing takes the form of relating dividend increases to the long-term earnings growth rate, even if short-term earnings are volatile. All else equal, the more volatile earnings are, the greater the risk that a given dividend increase may not be covered by earnings in a future time period. Thus, when earnings are volatile, we expect companies to be more cautious in the size and frequency of dividend increases. These findings also hold for other countries, although variation between countries has been noted in managers' willingness to decrease dividends based on available investment opportunities.

Financial Flexibility

Companies may not initiate, or may reduce or omit, dividends to obtain the financial flexibility associated with having substantial cash on hand. A company with substantial cash holdings is in a relatively strong position to meet unforeseen operating needs and to exploit investment opportunities with minimum delay. Having a strong cash position can be particularly valuable during economic contractions when the availability of credit may be reduced. Financial flexibility may be viewed as a tactical consideration that is of greater importance when access to liquidity is critical and when the company's dividend payout is relatively large.

A classic example of explaining a dividend decision in terms of the need to preserve financial flexibility occurred with Skanska AB, based in Sweden. On 8 February 2019, Skanska AB, one of the world's biggest construction and development companies, announced its board's suggestion to cut Skanska's dividend going forward by 30% to SKr6.00. This would allow for continued expansion of its project development business while maintaining its financial ability to deliver sustainable shareholder returns. Skanska's Chief Executive Anders Danielsson stated:

> As we enter 2019, there are political and macroeconomic uncertainties which are likely to increase further. In many of our home geographies and sectors, the markets are levelling out and it is difficult to predict how long this relatively favourable environment will last.
>
> *Source*: "Skanska Warns of 'Increasing Uncertainties' and Proposes Dividend Cut," *Financial Times* (8 February 2019): https://www.ft.com/content/9201486e-2b81-11e9-a5ab-ff8ef2b976c7.

The cut was expected to conserve SKr920 million on an annual basis. With approximately SKr19 billion of cash on hand at the time of the statement and with operating cash flows at least covering the previous dividend, the dividend reduction appeared to be accurately characterized as "precautionary." Although the dividend cut announcement was accompanied by a 9% decline in Skanska's share price, the share price quickly recovered. Within two months, it had risen 7% above its pre-dividend cut announcement value, indicating the market's favorable response to Skanska's decision to cut the dividend arising from uncertainty in its operating environment and the desire to maintain financial flexibility.

When increasing financial flexibility is an important consideration, a company may decide to distribute money to shareholders primarily by means of share repurchases (covered in Section 6) rather than regular dividends. A program to repurchase shares in the open market does not involve a formal requirement that any repurchases be executed, and share repurchases in general do not establish the same expectations for continuation in the future as regular dividends.

Tax Considerations

Taxation is an important factor that affects investment decisions for taxable investors, in particular, because it is the after-tax return that is most relevant to investors. Different jurisdictions tax corporate dividends in a wide variety of ways. Some tax both capital gains and dividend income. Others tax dividends but not capital gains. Even within a given country, taxation can be quite complex. In addition, because taxation is a major fiscal policy tool that is subject to politics, governments have a tendency to "re-address" tax issues, sometimes with great frequency. As with other aspects of taxation, governments use the taxation of dividends to address a variety of goals: to encourage or discourage the retention or distribution of corporate earnings; to redistribute income; or to address other political, social, and/or investment goals.

For the global investor, foreign taxes can be as important as domestic taxes. Foreign tax credits in the investor's home country also may figure importantly into the overall taxation issue. For example, France requires companies domiciled in France to withhold dividends paid to foreign investors at the corporate tax rate (reduced to 25% by 2022), but investors in other countries can usually claim a tax credit on their home country tax return for the amount of that tax, especially where a double tax agreement exists.

Taxation Methods

We look at three main systems of taxation that determine dividends: double taxation, imputation, and split-rate. Other tax systems can be a combination of these.

In a **double taxation system**, corporate pretax earnings are taxed at the corporate level and then taxed again at the shareholder level if they are distributed to taxable shareholders as dividends. Exhibit 4 illustrates double taxation, where the individual tax rate on dividends is an assumed maximum of 15%.

Exhibit 4: Double Taxation of Dividends at 15% Personal Tax Rate (per US$100)	
	15.0%
Net income before taxes	US$100
Corporate tax rate	35%
Net income after tax	US$65
Dividend assuming 100% payout	US$65
Shareholder tax on dividend	US$9.75
Net dividend to shareholder	US$55.25
Double tax rate on dividend distributions*	44.8%

* Based on pretax income.

Investors will clearly prefer a lower tax rate on dividends, but it is not clear whether they prefer a higher or lower payout. Payout preferences will depend on whether there is a tax on long-term capital gains for shareholders in their country and whether the tax rate on capital gains is higher or lower than the tax rate on dividends. Later, we will discuss a company's decision with respect to the dividend payout ratio.

A second major taxation system is the **dividend imputation tax system**, which effectively ensures that corporate profits distributed as dividends are taxed just once, at the shareholder's tax rate. Australia and New Zealand use a dividend imputation tax system. Under this system, a corporation's earnings are first taxed at the corporate level. When those earnings are distributed to shareholders in the form of dividends, however, shareholders receive a tax credit, known as a **franking credit**, for the taxes that the corporation paid on those distributed earnings (i.e., corporate taxes paid are imputed to the individual shareholder). If the shareholder's marginal tax rate is higher than the company's, the shareholder pays the difference between the two rates. Exhibit 5 shows one variation of a tax imputation system in which a shareholder with a lower marginal tax bracket than the company's actually receives a tax credit for the difference between the corporate rate and his own rate.

Exhibit 5: Taxation of Dividends Based on Tax Imputation System (A$)

	Marginal Shareholder Tax Rate	
	15%	47%
Pretax income	A$100	A$100
Taxes at 30% corporate tax rate	30	30
Net income after tax	70	70
Dividend assuming 100% payout	70	70
Shareholder tax on pretax income	15	47
Less tax credit for corporate payment	30	30
Tax due from shareholder	(15) — tax credit	17 — tax paid of A$17
Effective tax rate on dividend	15/100 to shareholder = 15%	47/100 = 47%

A **split-rate tax system** is a third taxation system of greater historical than current importance. Under this system, corporate earnings that are distributed as dividends are taxed at a lower rate at the corporate level than earnings that are retained. At the level of the individual investor, dividends are taxed as ordinary income. Earnings distributed as dividends are still taxed twice, but the relatively low corporate tax rate on earnings mitigates that penalty. Exhibit 6 depicts this split-rate tax system for dividends.

Exhibit 6: Taxation of Dividends Based on Split-Rate System (per €100)

Pretax earnings	€200
Pretax earnings retained	100
35% tax on retained earnings	35
Pretax earnings allocated to dividends	100
20% tax on earnings allocated to dividends	20
Dividends distributed	80
Shareholder tax rate	35%

After tax dividend to shareholder	$[(1 - 0.35) \times 80] = 52$
Effective tax rate on dividend	$[20\% + (80 \times 0.35)\%] = 48\%$

Shareholder Preference for Current Income versus Capital Gains

All other things being equal, one could expect that the lower an investor's tax rate on dividends relative to his or her tax rate on capital gains, the stronger the investor's preference for dividends. But other issues also impinge on this preference. The investor may buy high-payout shares for a tax-exempt retirement account. Even if dividends are taxed at a lower rate than capital gains, it is not clear that shareholders will necessarily prefer higher dividends. After all, capital gains taxes do not have to be paid until the shares are sold, whereas taxes on dividends must be paid in the year received even if reinvested. In addition, in some countries, such as the United States and Australia, shares held at the time of death benefit from a step-up valuation or tax exemption as of the death date. Finally, tax-exempt institutions, such as pension funds and endowment funds, are major shareholders in most industrial countries. Such institutions are typically exempt from both taxes on dividends and taxes on capital gains. Hence, all other things being equal, they are indifferent as to whether their return comes in the form of current dividends or capital gains.

Flotation Costs

Another factor that affects a company's dividend policy is flotation cost. Flotation costs include 1) the fees that the company pays (to investment bankers, attorneys, securities regulators, auditors, and others) to issue shares and 2) the possible adverse market price impact from a rise in the supply of shares outstanding. Aggregate flotation costs are proportionally higher (in terms of percentage of gross proceeds) for smaller companies (which issue fewer shares) than for larger companies. Flotation costs make it more expensive for companies to raise new equity capital than to use their own internally generated funds. As a result, many companies try to avoid establishing a level of dividends that would create the need to raise new equity to finance positive NPV projects.

EXAMPLE 8

A Company That Needs to Reinvest All Internally Generated Funds

1. Boar's Head Spirits Ltd., based in the United Kingdom, currently does not pay a dividend on its common shares. Boar's Head has an estimated operating cash flow of £500 million. The company's financial analyst has calculated its cost of capital as 12%. The same analyst has evaluated modernization and expansion projects with a positive NPV that would require £800 million. The cost of positive NPV projects exceeds estimated operating cash flow by £300 million (£800 million – £500 million). Having an above average debt ratio for its industry, Boar's Head is reluctant to increase its long-term debt

in the next year. Discuss whether you would expect Boar's Head to initiate a dividend based on the above facts.

Solution:

One would expect Boar's Head would not initiate a dividend. As things stand, internally generated funds, as represented by operating cash flow, are not sufficient to fund positive NPV projects. So, payment of a dividend would be at the expense of rejecting positive NPV projects unless the balance of such projects and the dividend were both financed by debt. Given its concern about debt levels, the company would not be expected to pay a dividend that needs to be financed by debt. Because the company has unfunded positive NPV projects, it could consider issuing new shares to fund those projects. The company, however, would not be expected to issue shares solely for the purpose of paying dividends.

Contractual and Legal Restrictions

The payment of dividends is often affected by legal or contractual restrictions or rules. In some countries, such as Brazil, the distribution of dividends is legally mandated (with certain exceptions). In other countries (e.g., Canada and the United States) the payment of a dividend not specifically indicated to be a liquidating dividend may be restricted by an **impairment of capital rule**. Such a rule requires that the net value of the remaining assets as shown on the balance sheet be at least equal to some specified amount (related to the company's capital).

Contractual restrictions on the amount of dividends that can be paid are often imposed by bondholders in bond indentures. These restrictions require that the company maintain certain ratios (interest coverage ratios, current ratio, etc.) or fulfill certain conditions before dividend payments can be made. Debt covenants in a bond indenture are a response to the agency problems that exist between shareholders and bondholders and are put in place to limit the ability of the shareholders to expropriate wealth from bondholders. As an extreme example, in the absence of covenants or legal restrictions management could liquidate the company's assets and pay the proceeds to the shareholders as a liquidating dividend, leaving the bondholders with nothing to settle their claims.

If a company has issued preference shares, dividends on common shares may not be paid until preference share dividends are paid. In addition, if the preference dividends are cumulative, then preference dividends that are in arrears must be paid before any common dividend can be paid.

Factors Affecting Dividend Policy: Summary

Several factors of varying degrees of importance can affect a company's dividend policy. In the following example, we explore how these factors affect the dividend policy of a hypothetical company named Makinasi Appliances Company.

EXAMPLE 9

Makinasi Appliances Company Cuts Its Dividend

1. In September 2018, Makinasi Appliances Company, a hypothetical global home appliances manufacturer, announced it would cut its dividend for the first time in its history. The company, which pays quarterly dividends, said

the dividend would be reduced to US$0.70 a share from the US$1.60 paid a year earlier. The 2017 total dividend was US$6.50 a share. The dividend cut ends a 400% cumulative increase in the dividend over 10 years. Faced with plunging global demand for appliances (Makinasi's sales were forecasted to fall 19%) and ongoing competition in the white goods industry, Makinasi was expecting a loss as high as US$32.5 million (operating loss of US$46 million) for fiscal year ending March 2019, compared with the analyst forecasted loss of US$18.3 million for the same period. The company already had a loss of US$28.6 million in fiscal year 2018 (the operating loss was US$30.4 million). Makinasi's plans are to aggressively cut costs: It plans to cut production-related costs by US$18 million and fixed costs by US$21 million. The company has said that the lower dividend is because of the difficulty in maintaining the dividend at its previous level. Board member bonuses have been eliminated, and manager bonuses have been reduced by 40%. Capital spending will be cut by 30% to US$27 million, and R&D spending will be cut by 13.5% to US$24million.

The company announced plans to raise capital via a bond issue for up to US$50 million. The national credit rating agency has cut Makinasi's bond rating from A to A−.

Discuss Makinasi's decision to cut its dividend in light of the factors affecting dividend policy covered in this section.

Solution:

Of the six factors discussed in this section, the *volatility of future earnings* and preservation of *financial flexibility* are the major factors influencing Makinasi's decision to cut its dividend. Paying the full dividend would have lowered Makinasi's liquidity ratios and forced it to raise even more external capital. In addition, paying the full dividend probably would likely have resulted in a more severe downgrade in its bond rating and an increase in the cost of debt financing. Paying the full dividend when faced with huge, larger than expected operating losses also might have sent a signal to investors that Makinasi was not serious about cutting costs and curtailing losses. *Flotation costs* could also play a role in Makinasi's case. Flotation costs on new equity are typically higher than those on new debt; it is possible that if it paid a dividend of more than US$0.70 a share, it would have to issue new equity in addition to the US$50 million in debt.

6   PAYOUT POLICIES

☐ compare stable dividend with constant dividend payout ratio, and calculate the dividend under each policy

☐ describe broad trends in corporate payout policies

In the following sections we discuss two types of dividend policies: stable dividend and constant dividend payout ratio policies. A **stable dividend policy** is one in which regular dividends are paid that generally do not reflect short-term volatility in earnings.

This type of dividend policy is the most common because managers are very reluctant to cut dividends, as discussed earlier. A **constant dividend payout ratio policy** is the policy of paying out a constant percentage of net income in dividends. In Section 6, we discuss share repurchases as an alternative to the payment of cash dividends.

Stable Dividend Policy

This dividend policy is the most common. Companies that use a stable dividend policy base dividends on a long-term forecast of sustainable earnings and increase dividends when earnings have increased to a sustainably higher level. Thus, if the long-term forecast for sustainable earnings is slow growth, the dividends would be expected to grow slowly over time, more or less independent of cyclical upward or downward spikes in earnings. If sustainable earnings were not expected to grow over time, however, the corresponding dividends would be level (i.e., not growing). Compared with the constant payout ratio policy, a stable dividend policy typically involves less uncertainty for shareholders about the level of future dividends. This is so because the constant payout ratio policy reflects to a higher degree short-term volatility in earnings and/or in investment opportunities.

Many companies pride themselves on a long record of gradually and consistently increasing dividends. Exhibit 7 shows the record of Gruppo Hera (Hera), an Italian multi-utility company that operates in waste management, water, gas, electricity and central heating distribution, and energy trading and electricity generation. Between 2003 and 2018, dividends per share (DPS) show an upward trajectory. Earning declines during this period were accompanied by stable or increasing dividends, underscoring the company's longer-term stated policy of a stable and growing dividend, irrespective of yearly earnings. Consequently, Hera's payout ratio varies widely, between 52% to 125%, over the period shown. For the long term, Hera's management appeared notably optimistic about earnings prospects. In 2019, they committed to a continuing increase in annual dividends per share from €0.10 up to €0.11 by 2022.

Exhibit 7: Gruppo Hera Earnings and Dividends

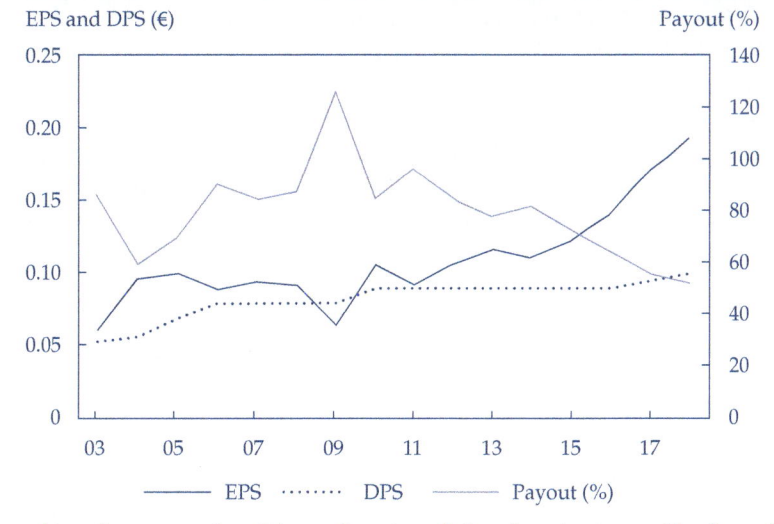

Source: https://eng.gruppohera.it/group/investor_relations/investor_proposition/hera_share/dividends/

As the example shows, dividends over the period were either stable or rising—even while earnings experienced considerable variability.

A stable dividend policy can be modeled as a process of gradual adjustment toward a target payout ratio based on long-term sustainable earnings. A **target payout ratio** is a goal that represents the proportion of earnings that the company intends to distribute (pay out) to shareholders as dividends over the long term.

A model of gradual adjustment (which may be called a "target payout adjustment model") was developed by John Lintner (1956). The model reflects three basic conclusions from his study of dividend policy: 1) Companies have a target payout ratio based on long-term, sustainable earnings; 2) managers are more concerned with dividend changes than with the level of the dividend; and 3) companies will cut or eliminate a dividend only in extreme circumstances or as a last resort.

A simplified version of Lintner's model can be used to show how a company can adjust its dividend. For example, suppose that the payout ratio is below the target payout ratio and earnings are expected to increase. The expected increase in the dividend can be estimated as a function of four variables: expected earnings next year, the target payout ratio, the previous dividend, and the adjustment factor (one divided by the number of years over which the adjustment in dividends should take place). Suppose that the current dividend is US$0.40, the target payout ratio is 50%, the adjustment factor is 0.2 (i.e., the adjustment is to occur over five years), and expected earnings are US$1.50 for the year ahead (an increase from the US$1 value of last year). The expected increase in dividends is US$0.07, as shown here:

Expected increase in dividends

= (Expected earnings × Target payout ratio − Previous dividend) × Adjustment factor

= (US$1.50 × 0.5 − US$0.40) × 0.2

= US$0.07

Therefore, even though earnings increased 50% from US$1.00 to US$1.50, the dividend would only incrementally increase by about 17.5% from US$0.40 to US$0.47.

By using this model, note that if in the following year earnings temporarily fell from US$1.50 to US$1.34, the dividend might well be increased by up to US$0.04 [(US$1.34 × 0.5 − US$0.47) × 0.2 = US$0.04] a share, because the implied new dividend of US$0.51 would still be moving the company toward its target payout ratio of 50%. Even if earnings were to fall further or even experience a loss, the company would be reluctant to cut or eliminate the dividend (unless its estimate of sustainable earnings or target payout ratio were lowered); instead, it would rather opt to maintain the current dividend until future earnings increases justified an increase in the dividend.

EXAMPLE 10

Determining Dividends by Using a Target Payout Adjustment Model

1. Last year Luna Inc. had earnings of US$2.00 a share and paid a regular dividend of US$0.40. For the current year, the company anticipates earnings of US$2.80. It has a 30% target payout ratio and uses a 4-year period to adjust the dividend. Compute the expected dividend for the current year.

Solution:

Expected dividend

> = Previous dividend + [(Expected earnings × Target payout ratio − Previous dividend) × Adjustment factor)]
>
> = US$0.40 + [(US$2.80 × 0.3 − US$0.40) × (1/4)]
>
> = US$0.40 + [(US$0.84 − US$0.40) × (1/4)]
>
> = US$0.51 dividend, an US$0.11 increase
>
> Thus, although earnings are expected to increase by 40%, the increase in the dividend would be 27.5%. Despite the adjustment process, the payout ratio would fall from 20% (US$0.40/US$2.00) to 18.2% (US$0.51/US$2.80). The firm would move toward its target payout ratio if earnings growth were slower and the adjustment time period were shorter (i.e., the adjustment factor higher).

Constant Dividend Payout Ratio Policy

In this type of policy, a dividend payout ratio decided on by the company is applied to current earnings to calculate the dividend. With this type of dividend policy, dividends fluctuate with earnings in the short term. Constant dividend payout ratio policies are infrequently adopted in practice. Example 11 illustrates this type of policy with Pampas Fertilizer, a hypothetical company.

EXAMPLE 11

Pampas Fertilizer Changes from a Stable to a Constant Dividend Payout Ratio Policy

Pampas Fertilizer, a hypothetical company, is the leading fertilizer producer in Argentina. Its earnings tend to be highly volatile. Demand for fertilizer is seasonal, typically being higher in summer than in winter. On the supply side, costs are primarily driven by ammonia prices that are subject to business cycle influences and are thus very volatile. In consideration of earnings volatility, Pampas might have difficulty sustaining a steadily rising dividend level. In view of such considerations, Pampas changed its dividend policy from a stable dividend policy to a constant dividend payout ratio policy (called a "variable dividend policy" by management) in its fiscal year 2018. The following is the explanation by the company:

Pampas has paid cash dividends on our common stock since 2003. The annual dividend rate of ARS0.50 per share of common stock, or ARS1.50 per quarter, was paid each fiscal quarter, as shown in the following table, through the second quarter of fiscal year 2018.

Effective 30 November 2017, the company's board of directors approved the use of a variable dividend policy to replace the company's fixed dividend policy. Beginning with the third quarter of fiscal year 2018, Pampas began to pay a dividend to shareholders of its common stock on a quarterly basis for each quarter for which the company reports net income in an amount equal to 25% of such quarterly income.

The board of Pampas implemented the variable dividend policy to more accurately reflect the results of the company's operations while recognizing and allowing for the cyclicality of the fertilizer industry.

Exhibit 8 shows quarterly data for fiscal years 2019 and 2018 in Argentine pesos (ARS).

> **Exhibit 8: Earnings per Share (EPS) and Dividends per Share (DPS) for Pampas Fertilizer (Fiscal Years Ending 31 March)**
>
> | Fiscal Period | EPS(ARS) | DPS(ARS) |
> |---|---|---|
> | 2019:Q4 | 9.32 | 2.350 |
> | 2019:Q3 | 4.60 | 1.152 |
> | 2019:Q2 | 15.41 | 3.852 |
> | 2019:Q1 | 10.53 | 2.636 |
> | 2018:Q4 | 7.84 | 1.961 |
> | 2018:Q3 | 18.65 | 4.660 |
> | 2018:Q2 | 26.30 | 1.500 |
> | 2018:Q1 | 21.22 | 1.500 |

1. From the table, identify the fiscal quarter when Pampas first applied a constant dividend payout ratio policy.

Solution:

Pampas first used that policy in the third quarter of fiscal year 2018. Until then, a quarterly dividend of ARS1.500 was paid irrespective of quarterly earnings. The payout ratios in all subsequent quarters round to approximately 25%.

2. Demonstrate that the dividend for 2019:Q4 reflects the stated current dividend policy.

Solution:

(EPS ARS9.32)/4 = ARS2.330, which differs only slightly from the reported dividend of ARS2.350 (EPS are rounded to two decimal places, so rounding error is expected).

Global Trends in Payout Policy

An interesting question is whether corporations are changing their dividend policies in response to changes in the economic environment and in investor preferences. Dividend policy practices have international differences and change through time, even within one market, consistent with the idea that companies adapt their dividend policy over time to changing investor tastes. Typically, fewer companies in a given US stock market index have paid dividends than have companies in a comparable European stock market index. In some Asian markets, companies have significantly increased their dividend payouts, albeit from a lower base, as these companies and markets mature. In addition, the following broad trends in dividend policy have been observed:

- The fraction of companies paying cash dividends has been in long-term decline in most developed markets (e.g., the United States, Canada, the European Union overall, the United Kingdom, and Japan). In Asia-Pacific, however, the value paid out in annual dividends tripled from 2009 to 2019. In the rest of the world, the value of annual dividend payouts only doubled over the same period.

- Since the early 1980s in the United States and the early 1990s in the United Kingdom and continental Europe, the fraction of companies engaging in share repurchases has trended upward. Since the late 2010s, share repurchases by major companies in Asia, particularly in mainland China and Japan, have been substantial (following a history of little to no prior share repurchase activity).

Research on dividend behavior globally shows that aggregate dividend amounts as well as payout ratios have generally increased over time, although the fraction of dividend payers has decreased. For example, studies using data from around the world substantiate the proportion of cash dividend paying firms declining over the long term, with aggregate dividend payments concentrated in a relatively small number of firms. Post-global financial crisis, there has been some reversal in the long-term downward trend in the fraction of dividend payers and payout ratios. The dividend payers are, on average, larger, more profitable, have fewer growth opportunities, and spend less on R&D compared to the non-dividend payers.

Moreover, researchers have documented internationally a negative relationship between dividend initiations/increases and enhanced corporate governance and transparency (such as mandatory adoption of IFRS rules and enforcement of new insider trading laws). This is consistent with the notion of the decreasing information content of dividends and their reduced signaling role as governance and transparency of markets improves. Similarly, findings show less generous dividend payout policies in countries requiring detailed corporate disclosures and having strong investor protection. The reduction in both information asymmetry and agency issues resulting from improved corporate governance, along with the flexibility offered by share repurchases, appear to explain the long-term decline in dividend payers.

SHARE REPURCHASES 7

- [ ] compare share repurchase methods
- [ ] calculate and compare the effect of a share repurchase on earnings per share when 1) the repurchase is financed with the company's surplus cash and 2) the company uses debt to finance the repurchase
- [ ] calculate the effect of a share repurchase on book value per share

A **share repurchase** (or **buyback**) is a transaction in which a company buys back its own shares. Unlike stock dividends and stock splits, share repurchases use corporate cash. Hence, share repurchases can be viewed as an alternative to cash dividends. Shares that have been issued and subsequently repurchased are classified as **treasury shares/stock** if they may be reissued or **canceled shares** if they will be retired; in either case, they are not then considered for dividends, voting, or computing earnings per share.

In contrast to the case of cash dividends, usage or growth in usage of share repurchases has historically required enabling regulation. In the United Kingdom, share repurchases became legal in 1981. They were never explicitly illegal in the United States, but usage became substantial only subsequent to US Securities and Exchange Commission rule 10b–18 in 1982. (That rule protected repurchasing companies from charges of share manipulation if repurchases were conducted consistent with the terms of the rule.) Other markets in continental Europe and Asia have also followed with enabling regulation (e.g., 1995 for Japan, 1998 for Germany and Singapore, 1999 for India and Norway, 2000 for Denmark and Sweden). Share repurchases in many markets remain subject to more restrictions than in the United States. Restrictions include requiring shareholder approval of share repurchase programs, limiting the percent of share repurchases to a certain fraction (often 10%) of outstanding shares, allowable repurchase mechanisms, and other restrictions to protect creditors. In many markets, use of share repurchases is becoming increasingly common.

In general, when an amount of share repurchases is authorized, the company is not strictly committed to following through with repurchasing shares. This situation contrasts with the declaration of dividends, where that action does commit the company to pay the dividends. Another contrast with cash dividends is that whereas cash dividends are distributed to shareholders proportionally to their ownership percentage, share repurchases in general do not distribute cash in such a proportionate manner. For example, if repurchases are executed by a company via buy orders in the open market, cash is effectively being received by only those shareholders with concurrent sell orders.

The next section presents the means by which a company may execute a share repurchase program.

Share Repurchase Methods

Following are the four main ways that companies repurchase shares, listed in order of importance.

1. **Buy in the open market.** This method of share repurchase is the most common, with the company buying its own shares as conditions warrant in the open market. The open market share repurchase method gives the company maximum flexibility. Open market repurchases are the most flexible option for a company because there is no legal obligation to undertake or complete the repurchase program; a company may not follow through with an announced program for various reasons, such as unexpected cash needs for liquidity, acquisitions, or capital expenditures. In the United States, open market transactions do not require shareholder approval, whereas in Europe, shareholder approval is required for buybacks. After studying buybacks in 32 countries, findings by Manconi, Peyer, and Vermaelen (2015) suggest that all companies have shareholder authorization in place to allow management the opportunity to buy back undervalued shares in the future. They conclude that the need for shareholder approval does not compensate for poor corporate governance and instead limits management's flexibility to time buybacks to create long-term shareholder value. Authorizations to repurchase stock can last for years. In many shareholders' minds, the announcement of a repurchase policy provides support for the share price. If the share repurchases are competently timed to minimize price impact and to exploit perceived undervaluation in the marketplace, this method is also relatively cost effective.

2. **Buy back a fixed number of shares at a fixed price.** Sometimes a company will make a **fixed price tender offer** to repurchase a specific number of shares at a fixed price that is typically at a premium to the current market price. For example, in Australia, if a stock is selling at A$37 a share, a company might offer to buy back 5 million shares from current shareholders at A$40. If shareholders are willing to sell more than 5 million shares, the company will typically buy back a pro rata amount from each shareholder. By setting a fixed date, such as 30 days in the future, a fixed price tender offer can be accomplished quickly.

3. **Dutch auction.** A Dutch auction is also a tender offer to existing shareholders, but instead of specifying a fixed price for a specific number of shares, the company stipulates a range of acceptable prices. A Dutch auction uncovers the minimum price at which the company can buy back the desired number of shares with the company paying that price to all qualifying bids. For example, if the stock price is A$37 a share, the company would offer to buy back 5 million shares in a range of A$38 to A$40 a share. Each shareholder would then indicate the number of shares and the lowest price at which he or she would be willing to sell. The company would then begin to qualify bids beginning with those shareholders who submitted bids at A$38 and continue to qualify bids at higher prices until 5 million shares had been qualified. In our example, that price might be A$39. Shareholders who bid between A$38 and A$39, inclusive, would then be paid A$39 per share for their shares. Like Method 2, Dutch auctions can be accomplished in a short time period.

4. **Repurchase by direct negotiation.** In some markets, a company may negotiate with a major shareholder to buy back its shares, often at a premium to the market price. The company may do this to keep a large block of shares from overhanging the market (and thus acting to dampen the share price). A company may try to prevent an "activist" shareholder from gaining representation on the board of directors. In some of the more infamous cases, unsuccessful takeover attempts have ended with the company buying back the would-be suitor's shares at a premium to the market price, referred to as a **greenmail** transaction, often to the detriment of remaining shareholders. Private repurchases can also be made at discounts to the market price, reflecting the relatively weaker negotiating position of large investors with liquidity needs.

Outside the United States and Canada, almost all share repurchases occur in the open market (Method 1). Note that not all the methods listed may be permissible according to local regulations.

EXAMPLE 12

BCII Considers Alternative Methods of Share Repurchase

The board of directors of British Columbia Industries, Inc. (BCII) is considering a 5 million common share repurchase program. BCII has a sizable cash and marketable securities portfolio. BCII's current stock price is C$37. The company's chief financial officer wants to accomplish the share repurchases in a cost-effective manner. Some board members want repurchases accomplished as quickly as possible, whereas other board members mention the importance of flexibility. Discuss the relative advantages of each of the following methods with respect to cost, flexibility, and speed:

1. Open market share repurchases.

Solution:

Open market share repurchases give the company the most flexibility. BCII can time repurchases, making repurchases when the market prices its stock below its perceived intrinsic value. BCII can also change amounts repurchased or even not execute the repurchase program. Open market repurchases are typically made opportunistically, with cost a more important consideration than speed. Because open market repurchases can be conducted so as to minimize any effects on price and can be timed to exploit prices that are perceived to be below intrinsic value, this method is also relatively cost effective.

2. A fixed price tender offer.

Solution:

A fixed price tender offer can be accomplished quickly, but the company usually has to offer a premium. Obviously, this raises the cost of the buy-back; however, the premium may provide a positive signal to investors regarding management's view of the value of the stock.

3. Dutch auction tender offer.

Solution:

Dutch auctions generally enable a company to do the buyback at a lower price than with a fixed price tender offer. For example, a fixed price tender offer for 5 million shares at C$40 would cost BCII C$200 million. If the Dutch auction were successful at C$38, the cost would be C$190 million, a savings of C$10 million. Dutch auctions can be accomplished quickly, though usually not as quickly as fixed price tender offers

Financial Statement Effects of Repurchases

Share repurchases affect both the balance sheet and income statement. Both assets and shareholders' equity decline if the repurchase is made with surplus cash. As a result, leverage increases. Debt ratios (leverage) will increase even more if the repurchase is financed with debt.

On the income statement, fewer shares outstanding could increase earnings per share (i.e., by reducing the denominator) depending on how and at what cost the repurchase is financed. We discuss the effects on the income statement and balance sheet in the following sections.

Changes in Earnings per Share

One rationale for share repurchases often cited by corporate financial officers and some investment analysts is that reducing the number of shares outstanding can increase earnings per share (EPS). Assuming a company's net income does not change, a smaller number of shares after the buyback will produce a higher EPS. If a company's share repurchase is financed by high-cost borrowing, the resulting lower net income can offset the effect of the reduced shares outstanding, producing a lower EPS.

Example 13 and Example 14 show changes in EPS resulting from alternative methods of financing a share repurchase.

EXAMPLE 13

Share Repurchase Using Surplus Cash

1. Takemiya Industries, a Japanese company, has been accumulating cash in re-cent years with a plan of expanding in emerging Asian markets. Takemiya's management and directors believe that such expansion is no longer practi-cal, and they are considering a share repurchase using surplus cash. Take-

miya has 10 million shares outstanding, and its net income is ¥100 million. Takemiya's share price is ¥120. Cash not needed for operations totals ¥240 million and is invested in Japanese government short-term securities that earn close to zero interest. For a share repurchase program of the contemplated size, Takemiya's investment bankers think the stock could be bought in the open market at a ¥20 premium to the current market price, or ¥140 a share. Calculate the impact on EPS if Takemiya uses the surplus cash to repurchase shares at ¥140 per share.

Solution:

First, note that current EPS = (¥100 million net income)/(10 million shares) = ¥10.00. If Takemiya repurchases shares, net income is unchanged at ¥100 million. A share repurchase at ¥140 a share reduces share count by approximately 1.7 million shares (¥240,000,000/¥140) so that 8.3 million shares remain outstanding. Thus, after the share repurchase, EPS should be (¥100 million)/(8.3 million shares) = ¥12.00, approximately. EPS would increase by 20% as a result of the share repurchase. Note that EPS would increase even more if the open market purchases were accomplished at the prevailing market price without the premium.

In the absence of surplus cash and equivalents, companies may fund share repurchases by using long-term debt. Example 14 shows that any increase in EPS is dependent on the company's after-tax borrowing rate on the funds used to repurchase stock.

EXAMPLE 14

Share Repurchases Using Borrowed Funds

Selamat Plantations, Inc., plans to borrow Malaysian ringgit (MYR)12 million, which it will use to repurchase shares. The following information is given:

- Share price at time of share repurchase = MYR60
- Earnings after tax = MYR6.6 million
- EPS before share repurchase = MYR3
- Price/Earnings (P/E) = MYR60/MYR3 = 20
- Earnings yield (E/P) = MYR3/MYR60 = 5%
- Shares outstanding = 2.2 million
- Planned share repurchase = 200,000 shares

1. Calculate the EPS after the share repurchase, assuming the after-tax cost of borrowing is 5%.

Solution:

EPS after buyback = (Earnings − After-tax cost of funds)/Shares outstanding after buyback

= [MYR6.6 million − (MYR12 million × 0.05)]/2 million shares

= [MYR6.6 million − (MYR0.6 million)]/2 million shares

= MYR6.0 million/2 million shares

= MYR3.00

With the after-tax cost of borrowing at 5%, the share repurchase has no effect on the company's EPS. Note that the stock's earnings yield, the ratio of earnings per share to share price or E/P, was MYR3/MYR60 = 0.05 or 5%, equal to the after-tax cost of debt.

2. Calculate the EPS after the share repurchase, assuming the company's borrowing rate increases to 6% because of the increased financial risk of borrowing the MYR12 million.

Solution:

EPS after buyback = (Earnings − After-tax cost of funds)/Shares outstanding after buyback

= [MYR6.6 million − (MYR12 million × 0.06)]/2 million shares

= [MYR6.6 million − (MYR0.72 million)]/2 million shares

= MYR5.88 million/2 million shares

= MYR2.94

Note that in this case, the after-tax cost of debt, 6%, is greater than the 5% earnings yield; thus, a reduction in EPS resulted.

In summary, a share repurchase may increase, decrease, or have no effect on EPS. The effect depends on whether the repurchase is financed internally or externally. In the case of internal financing, a repurchase increases EPS only if the funds used for the repurchase would *not* earn their cost of capital if retained by the company. In the case of external financing, the effect on EPS is positive if the earnings yield exceeds the after-tax cost of financing the repurchase. In Example 14, when the after-tax borrowing rate equaled the earnings yield of 5%, EPS was unchanged as a result of the buyback. Any after-tax borrowing rate above the earnings yield would result in a decline in EPS, whereas an after-tax borrowing rate less than the earnings yield would result in an increase in EPS.

These relationships should be viewed with caution so far as any valuation implications are concerned. Notably, to infer that an increase in EPS indicates an increase in shareholders' wealth would be incorrect. For example, the same surplus cash could also be distributed as a cash dividend. Informally, if one views the total return on a stock as the sum of the dividend yield and a capital gains return, any capital gains as a result of the boost to EPS from the share repurchase may be at the expense of an offsetting loss in dividend yield.

Changes in Book Value per Share

Price-to-book value per share is a popular ratio used in equity valuation. The following example shows the impact of a share repurchase on book value per share (BVPS).

EXAMPLE 15

The Effect of a Share Repurchase on Book Value per Share

The market price of both Company A's and Company B's common stock is US$20 a share, and each company has 10 million shares outstanding. Both companies have announced a US$5 million buyback. The only difference is that Company A has a market price per share greater than its book value per share, whereas Company B has a market price per share less than its book value per share:

- Company A has a book value of equity of US$100 million and BVPS of US$100 million/10 million shares = US$10. *The market price per share of US$20 is greater than BVPS of US$10.*

- Company B has a book value of equity of US$300 million and BVPS of US$300 million/10 million shares = US$30. *The market price per share of US$20 is less than BVPS of US$30.*

Both companies:

- buy back 250,000 shares at the market price per share (US$5 million buyback/US$20 per share = 250,000 shares) and

- are left with 9.75 million shares outstanding (10 million pre-buyback shares – 0.25 million repurchased shares = 9.75 million shares).

After the share repurchase:

- Company A's shareholders' equity at book value falls to US$95 million (US$100 million – US$5 million), and its *book value per share decreases* from US$10 to US$9.74 (shareholders' equity/shares outstanding = US$95 million/9.75 million shares = US$9.74).

- Company B's shareholders' equity at book value falls to US$295 million (US$300 million – US$5 million), and its *book value per share increases* from US$30 to US$30.26 (shareholders' equity/shares outstanding = US$295 million/9.75 million = US$30.26).

[handwritten margin note: Book value falls by the size of the buyback]

==This example shows that when the market price per share is greater than its book value per share, BVPS will decrease after the share repurchase. When the market price per share is less than BVPS, however, BVPS will increase after a share repurchase.==

VALUATION EQUIVALENCE OF CASH DIVIDENDS AND SHARE REPURCHASE

8

☐ | explain the choice between paying cash dividends and repurchasing shares

A share repurchase should be viewed as equivalent to the payment of cash dividends of equal amount in terms of the effect on shareholders' wealth, all other things being equal. "All other things being equal" in this context is shorthand for assumptions that the taxation and information content of cash dividends and share repurchases do not differ. Understanding this baseline equivalence result permits more advanced analysis for when taxation and/or information content do differ between cash dividends and share repurchases. Example 16 demonstrates the claim of equivalence in the "all other things being equal" case.

EXAMPLE 16

The Equivalence of Share Repurchases and Cash Dividends

1. Rohit Chemical Industries, Inc. (RCII) has 10 million shares outstanding with a current market value of Rs200 per share. WCII's board of directors is considering two ways of distributing RCII's current Rs500 million free cash flow to equity. The first method involves paying an irregular or special cash dividend of Rs500 million/10 million = Rs50 per share. The second method involves repurchasing Rs500 million worth of shares. For simplicity, we make the assumptions that dividends are received when the shares go ex-dividend and that any quantity of shares can be bought at the market price of Rs200 per share. We also assume that the taxation and information content of cash dividends and share repurchases, if any, do not differ. How would the wealth of a shareholder be affected by RCII's choice of method in distributing the Rs500 million?

Solution:

Cash Dividend

After the shares go ex-dividend, a shareholder of a single share would have Rs50 in cash (the dividend) and a share worth Rs200 − Rs50 = Rs150. The ex-dividend value of Rs150 can be demonstrated as the market value of equity after the distribution of Rs500 million divided by the (unchanged) number of shares outstanding after the dividend payment, or [(10 million) (Rs200) − Rs500 million]/10 million = Rs1,500 million/10 million = Rs150. Total wealth from ownership of one share is, therefore, Rs50 + Rs150 = Rs200.

Share Repurchase

With Rs500 million, RCII could repurchase Rs500 million/Rs200 = 2.5 million shares. The post-repurchase share price would be unchanged at Rs200, which can be calculated as the market value of equity after the Rs500 million share repurchase divided by the shares outstanding after the share repurchase, or [(10 million) (Rs200) − Rs500 million]/(10 million − 2.5 million) = Rs1,500 million/7.5 million = Rs200. Total wealth from ownership of one share is, therefore, Rs200—exactly the same as in the case of a cash dividend. Whether the shareholder actually sold the share back to RCII in the share repurchase is irrelevant for a shareholder's wealth: If the share was sold, Rs200 in cash would be realized; if the share was not sold, its market value of Rs200 would count equally toward the shareholder's wealth.

The theme of Example 16 is that a company should not expect to create or destroy shareholder wealth merely by its method of distributing money to shareholders (i.e., by share repurchases as opposed to cash dividends). Example 17 illustrates that if a company repurchases shares from an individual shareholder at a negotiated price representing a premium over the market price, the remaining shareholders' wealth is reduced.

EXAMPLE 17

Direct Negotiation: A Share Repurchase That Transfers Wealth

1. AfriCitrus (AC) common shares sell at South African rand (ZAR)200, and there are 10 million shares outstanding. Management becomes aware that Kirk Mzazi recently purchased a major position in its outstanding shares with the intention of influencing the business operations of AC in ways the current board does not approve. An adviser to the board has suggested approaching Mzazi privately with an offer to buy back ZAR500 million worth of shares from him at ZAR250 per share, which is a ZAR50 premium over the current market price. The board of AC declines to do so because of the effect of such a repurchase on AC's other shareholders. Determine the effect of the proposed share repurchase on the wealth of shareholders other than Mzazi.

Solution:

With ZAR500 million, AC could repurchase ZAR500 million/ZAR250 = 2 million shares from Mzazi. The post-repurchase share price would be ZAR187.50, which can be calculated as the market value of equity after the ZAR500 million share repurchase divided by the shares outstanding after the share repurchase, or [(10 million)(ZAR200) – ZAR500 million]/(10 million – 2 million) = ZAR1,500 million/8 million = ZAR1875.50. Shareholders other than Mzazi would lose ZAR200 – ZAR187. 50 = ZAR12.50 for each share owned. Although this share repurchase would conserve total wealth (including Mzazi's), it effectively transfers wealth to Mzazi from the other shareholders.

THE DIVIDEND VERSUS SHARE REPURCHASE DECISION

9

☐ | explain the choice between paying cash dividends and repurchasing shares

The question of the valuation implications of share repurchases and dividends is of great interest to investors. Many investors and corporate managers believe that share repurchases have, on average, a net positive effect on shareholder value Studies have found that share repurchase announcements are accompanied by significant positive excess returns both around the announcement date and for the next two years—and in some studies, five years. An explanation consistent with that finding is that managements tend to buy back their stock when it is undervalued in the marketplace and issue stock when it is overvalued.

Theory concerning the dividend–share repurchase decision generally concludes that share repurchases are equivalent to cash dividends of equal amount in their effect on shareholders' wealth, all other things being equal. Further discussion about the choice revolves around what might not "be equal" and what might cause one distribution mechanism to be preferred over the other. The use of share repurchases also may be legally restricted.

In general, share repurchases can be considered part of a company's broad policy on distributing earnings to shareholders. Also, a company may engage in share repurchases for reasons similar to those mentioned in connection with cash dividends—for example, to distribute free cash flow to equity to common shareholders. A number of additional reasons for share repurchases include the following:

- Potential tax advantages
- Share price support/signaling that the company considers its shares a good investment
- Added managerial flexibility
- Offsetting dilution from employee stock options
- Increasing financial leverage

In jurisdictions that tax shareholder dividends at higher rates than capital gains, share repurchases have a tax advantage over cash dividends. Even if the two tax rates are equal, the option to defer capital gains taxes—by deciding not to participate in the share repurchase—will be valuable to many investors.

Management of a company may view its own shares as undervalued in the marketplace and hence a good investment. Although management's stock market judgment can be just as good or bad as that of any other market participant, corporate management typically does have more information about the company's operation and future prospects than does any outside investor or analyst. Furthermore, share repurchases via open market purchase, the dominant repurchase mechanism, allow management to time share repurchases with respect to market price. The announcement of a share repurchase program is often understood as a positive signal about the company's prospects and attractiveness as an investment. An unexpected announcement of a meaningful share repurchase program can often have the same positive impact on share price as would a better-than-expected earnings report or similar positive event. In the days following the global stock market crash of October 1987, a number of prominent companies announced huge buybacks in an effort to halt the slide in the price of their shares and show confidence in the future. It may have been an important aspect in the stock market recovery that followed. Some investment analysts, however, take issue with the notion that initiation of share repurchases is a positive signal, because a repurchase program could mean that the company has no new profitable investment opportunities and is thus returning cash to shareholders.

Unlike regular cash dividends, share repurchase programs appear not to create the expectation among investors of continuance in the future. Furthermore, in contrast to an announced dividend, the announcement of a share repurchase by open market purchase does not typically create an obligation to follow through with repurchases. Additionally, the timing of share repurchases via open market activity is at managers' discretion. Share repurchases also afford shareholders flexibility because participation is optional, which is not the case with the receipt of cash dividends.

For some companies, share repurchases are used to offset the possible dilution of earnings per share that may result from the exercise of employee stock options. Whether stated or not, many companies try to repurchase at least as many shares as were issued in the exercise of stock options—even though the options are typically exercised at lower prices than the repurchase price.

Another reason for repurchasing shares is to modify the company's capital structure because share repurchases can be used to increase leverage. Share buybacks funded by newly issued debt increase leverage more than those funded by surplus cash.

Among other reasons mentioned for share repurchases by corporate managers is the objective of increasing EPS. This objective, however, is problematic for two reasons. First, even when share repurchases result in an EPS increase, the required rate of return will likely increase, reflecting higher leverage. Second, according to finance theory, changing EPS by changing the number of shares outstanding does not affect shareholder wealth given that total free cash flow is unchanged.

EXAMPLE 18

Share Repurchase to Increase Financial Leverage

Deira Oasis Holdings Inc. (DOHI), with debt and a debt ratio of United Arab Emirates durham (AED)30 million and 30%, respectively, plans a share repurchase program involving AED7 million or 10% of the market value of its common shares.

1. Assuming nothing else changes, what debt ratio would result from financing the repurchases using cash on hand?

Solution:

Assuming nothing else changes, if DOHI uses cash on hand to make the share repurchase, the debt ratio would increase to 32% (AED30 million/ AED93million = 0.3226 or 32.3%).

2. Assuming nothing else changes, what debt ratio would result from financing the repurchases using new debt?

Solution:

Assuming nothing else changes, if DOHI uses debt to finance the share repurchase, the debt ratio would increase to 37% (AED37 million/AED100 million = 0.3700 or 37.0%).

3. Discuss the effect on value of equity from financing the repurchases using cash on hand, assuming DOHI's net income and P/E remain the same.

Solution:

After repurchase, DOHI's equity stands at AED63 million. However, with the same net income and fewer shares outstanding, its EPS would increase. Then, with the same P/E, DOHI's market value of equity would be expected to increase above AED63 million.

4. Discuss the effect on value of equity from financing the repurchases using new debt, assuming DOHI's after-tax cost of debt is greater than its E/P, which remains the same.

Solution:

After repurchase, DOHI's equity stands at AED63 million. However, with the after-tax cost of debt exceeding the E/P, its EPS would decrease. Then, with the same P/E, DOHI's market value of equity would be expected to decrease below AED63 million.

5. Discuss the effect on value of debt from financing the repurchases using new debt, assuming the conditions in question 4 and knowing that DOHI is in imminent danger of a credit rating downgrade.

Solution:

After repurchase, DOHI's debt stands at AED37 million. However, with the real threat of a credit rating downgrade, spreads for DOHI's debt versus government treasuries would widen. Then, DOHI's market value of debt would be expected to decrease below AED37 million.

Note that with the assumptions in questions 4 and 5, the post-repurchase market values of both equity and debt would be expected to decrease. Therefore, the proportion of each in DOHI's post-repurchase capital structure is indeterminate based on the information given.

Exhibit 9 shows the results. By either means of financing the share repurchase, financial leverage increases.

Exhibit 9: Estimated Impact on Capital Structure (AED millions)

| | Before Buyback | | After Buyback | | | |
| | | | All Cash | | All Debt | |
	AED	%	AED	%	AED	%
Debt	30	30	30	32	37	37
Equity (at market)	70	70	63	68	63	63
Total Cap	100	100	93	100	100	100

Deira Oasis Holdings' beginning debt ratio was 30%. If Deira Oasis Holdings uses borrowed funds to repurchase equity, the debt ratio at market value will increase to 37%, which is significantly more than if it used excess cash (32%).

EXAMPLE 19

ITOCHU Corporation Announces Share Buyback to Improve ROE

1. In October 2018, ITOCHU Corporation, a leading Japanese *sogo shosha* (general trading company), reported that in order to improve its return on equity (ROE) it would repurchase shares by fiscal year-end March 2019 to achieve a target medium-to-long-term ROE of 13% or higher. Accordingly, ITOCHU said it could repurchase shares in the amount up to ¥30 billion. In February 2019, ITOCHU announced it was increasing its share repurchase target up to ¥100 billion. ITOCHU repurchases in these first two tranches are shown in Exhibit 10.

Exhibit 10: Share Buyback Activities, October 2018 to March 2019

Period	Shares Repurchased	Average Price (¥)	Total Value (¥)
December 2018 – January 2019	15,097,200	1,987	30 billion

Period	Shares Repurchased	Average Price (¥)	Total Value (¥)
February – March 2019	19,024,200	1.997	38 billion
Sum	**34,121,400**	**1,993**	**68 billion**

Source: Annual Report 2019 (online version), ITOCHU Corporation: https://www.itochu.co.jp/en/ir/financial_statements/2020/__icsFiles/afieldfile/2019/08/09/20_1st_03_e.pdf.

ITOCHU was followed by many other large Japanese companies—including SoftBank, Sony, Haseko, Tokyo Tatemono, and Toppan Printing. Also in February 2019, these companies announced large share buyback programs to improve ROE in response to shareholder activist pressure to improve shareholder returns and governance.

A company can use both special cash dividends and share repurchases as a supplement to regular cash dividends. These means of distributing cash are often used in years when there are large and extraordinary increases in cash flow that are not expected to continue in future years. In making these types of payments, the company essentially communicates that the distribution, like the increase in cash flow, should not be expected to continue in the future. In this context, a share repurchase is effectively an alternative to paying a special cash dividend.

Some companies initiate payouts to shareholders using share repurchases rather than cash dividends. As with the case of a share repurchase substituting for a special cash dividend, the use of share repurchases is again with the expectation that it will not be viewed as creating a fixed commitment.

Although all of the preceding can be the stated or unstated reasons for share repurchases, in general, share repurchases increase when the economy is strong and companies have more cash. During recessions, when cash is often short, share repurchases typically fall. From the fourth quarter of 2004 to the fourth quarter of 2008, the 500 companies in the S&P 500 spent US$1.8 trillion on share repurchases as compared with US$2 trillion on capital expenditures and US$1 trillion on cash dividends. In the market crash of 2008–2009, share repurchases plummeted. Major companies (particularly in the global financial sector) that had made large share repurchases encountered challenges to their financial viability in 2008 and 2009. This caused them to abandon their share repurchases and then to drastically curtail, or even eliminate, their dividends. The predominance of large US banks abandoning their share repurchase programs following the 2008 global financial crisis is shown in Exhibit 11.

Exhibit 11: Historical Example: Share Repurchases and Dividends for Several Large US Banks

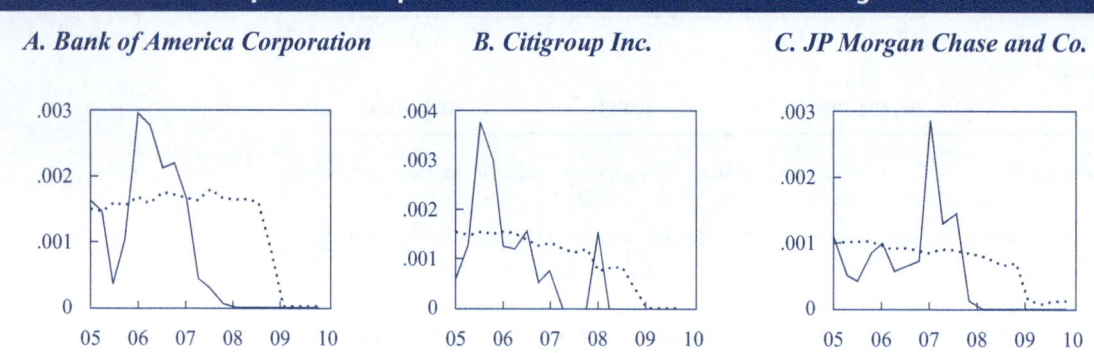

Source: Hirtle (2016).

The curtailing of share repurchases following the 2008 global financial crisis was a general occurrence; it was not restricted to the banking sector. As can be seen in Exhibit 12, data for the companies in the Russell 1000 Index, a broader US stock index than the S&P 500, show that share repurchases grew at almost twice the rate of cash dividends between 2000 and 2007, 25.0% compared to 13.0%. However, during the financial crisis of 2008–2009, companies cut back sharply on their discretionary share repurchases, from US$680 billion to US$223 billion, because many faced shrinking operating cash flows or even financial distress. Although cash dividends were also cut, the decline was much less considerable (US$286 billion to US$262 billion). By 2015, corporate operating cash flows had recovered to the point where total distributions (cash dividends plus share repurchases) reached US$1,102 billion, surpassing their previous peak of US$966 billion in 2007. Share repurchases increased nearly three times from their 2009 levels to reach US$650 billion. However, cash dividends reached US$452 billion, or over 40% of total distributions; this compares to slightly less than 30% of total distributions (US$286 billion/US$966 billion) in 2007. The higher proportion of dividends in total distributions may reflect investors' increased appetite for dividend yield during the extended period of low (or even negative) interest rates on many fixed-income securities that has prevailed in many developed countries since the end of the financial crisis.

Exhibit 12: Historical Example: Share Repurchases and Cash Dividends: Russell 1000 Companies (2000 to 2015)

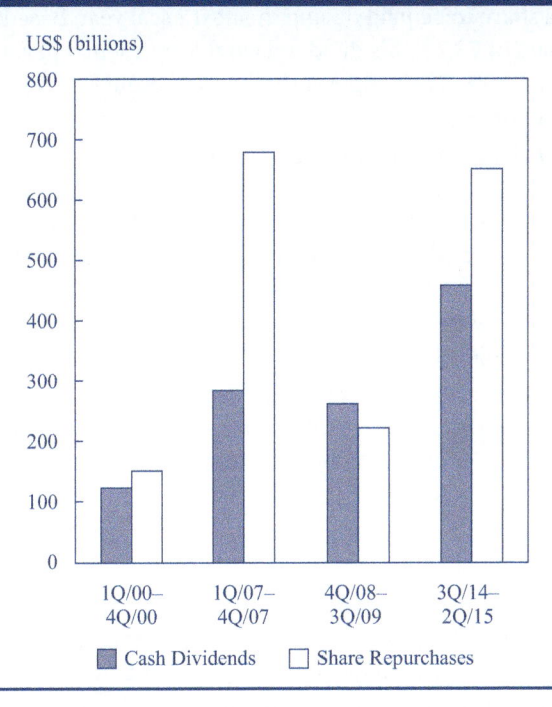

Time Period	Cash Dividends*	Share Repurchases	CAGR Cash Dividends	CAGR Repurchases
	(US$ billions)		(Base Year is 2000)	
1Q2000–4Q2000	126	152	—	—
1Q2007–4Q2007	286	680	13.0%	25.0%
4Q2008–3Q2009	262	223	9.0%	4.0%
3Q2014–2Q2015	452	650	10.0%	11.0%

* Includes special dividends.

Source: JP Morgan, "2015 Distribution Policy" (September 2015).

Example 20, in which a hypothetical company's board of directors initiates a cash dividend, integrates a number of themes related to cash dividends, stock dividends (in which additional shares are distributed to shareholders instead of cash), and share repurchases.

EXAMPLE 20

Shenzhen Medical Devices' Dividend Policy Decision

Shenzhen Medical Devices Ltd. (SMDL) is a hypothetical company based in Shenzhen, China. SMDL is emerging as a leader in providing medical testing equipment to the pharmaceutical and biotechnology industries. SMDL's primary markets are growing, and the company is spending ¥100 million a year on research and development to enhance its competitive position. SMDL is highly profitable and has substantial positive free cash flow after funding positive NPV projects. During the past three years, SMDL has made significant share repurchases. Subsequent to the removal of tax on cash dividends from shares held more than a year in mainland China, SMDL management is proposing the initiation of a cash dividend. The first dividend is proposed to be an annual dividend of ¥0.40 a share to be paid during the next fiscal year. Based on estimated earnings per share of ¥3.20, this dividend would represent a payout ratio (DPS/EPS) of 0.125 or 12.5%. The proposal that will be brought before the board of directors is the following:

"Proposed: Shenzhen Medical Devices Ltd. will institute a program of cash dividends. The first dividend will be an annual dividend of ¥0.40 a share, to be paid at a time to be determined during the next fiscal year. Thereafter, an annual dividend will be paid, equal to or above this amount, consistent with the intention of reaching a target payout ratio of 25% in line with management's expectation for long-term sustainable earnings—thereby retaining funds sufficient to finance profitable capital projects."

The company's board of directors will formally consider the dividend proposal at its next meeting in one month's time. Although some directors favor the dividend initiation proposal, other directors, led by Director Z, are skeptical of it. Director Z has stated:

"The initiation of a cash dividend will suggest to investors that SMDL is no longer a growth company."

As a counterproposal, Director Z has offered his support for the initiation of an annual 2% stock dividend. Director W, a director who is neutral to both the cash dividend and stock dividend ideas, has told Director Z the following:

"A 2% stock dividend will not affect the wealth of our shareholders."

Exhibit 13 presents selected *pro forma* financials of SMDL, if the directors approve the initiation of a cash dividend.

Exhibit 13: Shenzhen Medical Devices Ltd. Pro Forma Financial Data Assuming Cash Dividend (¥ millions)

Income Statement		Statement of Cash Flows	
Sales	1,200	Cash flow from operations	135
Earnings before taxes	155	Cash flow from investing activities	(84)
Taxes	35	Cash flow from financing activities	
Net income	120	Debt repayment	(4)
		Share repurchase	(32)
		Proposed dividend	(15)
		Estimated change in cash	0

Ratios		Five-Year Forecasts	
Current ratio	2.1	Sales growth	8% annually
Debt/Equity (at market)	0.27	Earnings growth	11% annually
Interest coverage	10.8x	Projected cost of capital	10%
ROA	10.0%		
ROE	19.3%		
P/E	20x		
E/P	5.0%		

Using the information provided, address the following:

1. Critique Director Z's statement.

Solution:

The following points argue against the thesis of Director Z's statement:

- As discussed in the text, dividend initiations and increases are on average associated with higher future earnings growth.
- Forecasted sales and earnings growth rates are relatively high.
- SMDL still has considerable positive NPV projects available to it, as shown by the cash flow from investing activities of negative ¥84 million. This fact is consistent with SMDL being a company with substantial current growth opportunities.
- For the past three years, SMDL has been making share repurchases, so investors are already cognizant that management is distributing cash to shareholders. The initiation of a dividend as a continuation of that policy is less likely to be interpreted as an information signaling event.

2. Justify Director W's statement.

Solution:

A stock dividend has no effect on shareholder wealth. A shareholder owns the same percentage of the company and its earnings as it did before the stock dividend. All other things being equal, the price of a stock will decline to reflect the stock dividend, but the decline will be exactly offset by the greater number of shares owned.

3. Identify and explain the dividend policy that the proposed ¥0.40 a share cash dividend reflects.

Solution:

As shown in the statement of cash flows, the ¥0.40 a share annual dividend reflects a total amount of ¥15 million, fully using SMDL's free cash flow after acceptance of positive NPV projects. However, the proposal brought before the board also states a commitment to maintain the annual dividend at ¥0.40 a share (or greater), as a stable dividend policy would typically imply. Further, the proposal refers to a target payout ratio based on long-term sustainable earnings. These facts taken together are most consistent with a stable dividend policy based on a target payout adjustment model. (The relatively low target payout ratio of 25% of long-term sustainable earnings allows for sufficient funding of profitable capital projects, suitable for maintaining growth as a pharmaceutical company.)

10   ANALYSIS OF DIVIDEND SAFETY

☐   calculate and interpret dividend coverage ratios based on 1) net income and 2) free cash flow

☐   identify characteristics of companies that may not be able to sustain their cash dividend

The global recession that began in late 2007 gave rise to the largest number of dividend cuts and suspensions since the Great Depression of the 1930s. By mid-2009, S&P 500 dividends for US companies were down by 25% from the prior year, and, as indicated earlier in Exhibit 13, by 3Q 2009 dividends for companies in the broader Russell 1000 index declined by over 8% from 2007 levels. Other markets experienced similar dividend cuts following the global financial crisis; for example, UK companies reduced dividends by 15% and Australian companies by 9% in 2009. In this section, we discuss how an analyst can form a judgment on the likelihood that a company's cash dividend may be cut.

The traditional way of looking at dividend safety is the dividend payout ratio (dividends/net income) and its inverse, the **dividend coverage ratio** (net income/dividends). A higher dividend payout ratio or a lower dividend coverage ratio tends to indicate, all else equal, higher risk of a dividend cut. The logic is that with a relatively high dividend payout ratio, a relatively small percentage decline in earnings could cause the dividend not to be payable out of earnings.

EXAMPLE 21

Traditional Measures of Dividend Safety

1. Given the following data, calculate the dividend payout and coverage ratios:

Mature European SA	FY2019
Net income available for common stock	€100 million
Dividends paid	€40 million

Solution:

Dividend payout ratio	40/100 = 40%
Dividend coverage ratio	100/40 = 2.5x

In judging these ratios, various generalizations may be stated based on observed practice. In stating these generalizations, we emphasize that they should be confirmed for the particular market and time period being addressed.

Small, young companies generally do not pay dividends, preferring to reinvest internally for growth. However, as such companies grow, they typically initiate dividends and their payout ratios tend to increase over time. Large mature companies often target dividend payout ratios of 40% to 60% so that dividend coverage ratios range from about 1.7x to 2.5x, excluding "extra" payments. Mature companies are expected to be in this range over the course of a 5- to 10-year business cycle. Higher dividend payout ratios (or lower dividend coverage ratios) often constitute a risk factor that a dividend may be cut if earnings decline. High dividend payout ratios in relation to those of peer group companies may also point to dividend safety concerns. When a dividend coverage ratio drops to 1.0, the dividend is considered to be in jeopardy unless non-recurring events, such as an employee strike or a typhoon, are responsible for a temporary decline in earnings. In judging safety, qualitative pluses are awarded for companies that have had stable or increasing dividends, while minuses accrue to companies that have reduced their dividend in the past. Indeed, concerning this issue, Graham et al. (1962) stated that "[t]he absence of rate reduction in the past record is perhaps as important as the presence of numerous rate advances."

Free cash flow to equity represents the cash flow available for distribution as dividends after taking account of working and fixed capital expenditure needs. If those needs are ignored, distribution of dividends may be at cross-purposes with shareholder wealth maximization. Cash flow—specifically, free cash flow to equity (FCFE)—not reported net income, should be viewed as the source of cash dividend payments from that perspective. Thus, analysis of dividend safety can properly include payout and coverage ratios based on FCFE rather than net income. Other cash flow definitions besides FCFE have also been used in such ratios. Examining the correlation of dividends with cash flow measures may also provide insights.

Payouts should be considered in terms of share repurchases as well as dividends because they both represent cash distributions to shareholders. Arguably, a comprehensive measure of dividend safety would relate FCFE to both cash dividends and share repurchases:

FCFE coverage ratio = FCFE/[Dividends + Share repurchases].

[handwritten annotation: FCFE = CFO − FCInv + net borrowing]

If that ratio is 1, the company is returning all available cash to shareholders. If it is significantly greater than 1, the company is improving liquidity by using funds to increase cash and/or marketable securities. A ratio significantly less than 1 is not sustainable because the company is paying out more than it can afford by drawing down existing cash/marketable securities, thereby decreasing liquidity. At some point the company will have to raise new equity or cut back on capital spending.

Fundamental risk factors with regard to dividend safety include above-average financial leverage. Additional issuance of debt, whether to fund projects or to finance the dividend, may be restricted during business downturns.

Example 22 shows an analysis of dividend sustainability for Lygon Resources Ltd. (Lygon), a hypothetical company that is one of the world's largest producers of fertilizer products. The analysis includes the traditional earnings/dividend coverage approach and an alternative FCFE approach that considers total cash payouts to shareholders—dividends and share repurchases.

EXAMPLE 22

Lygon's Coverage Ratios

Lygon Resources Ltd. is a lithium miner and producer with operations in Australia, South America, and South Africa, and export markets worldwide. The company has paid dividends since 1995. Exhibit 14 shows financial information for the company.

Exhibit 14: Lygon Resources

Years Ending 31 December (A$ millions)	2015	2016	2017	2018
Net income (earnings)	540	458	399	341
Cash flow from operations	837	824	679	628

Years Ending 31 December (A$ millions)	2015	2016	2017	2018
FCInv (capital expenditures)	554	417	296	327
Net borrowing	(120)	(39)	79	(7)
Dividends paid	121	256	277	323
Stock repurchases	0	105	277	0

1. Using the above information, calculate the following for 2015, 2016, 2017, and 2018:

   A. Dividend/earnings payout ratio.

   B. Earnings/dividend coverage ratio.

   C. Free cash flow to equity (FCFE).

   D. FCFE/[Dividend + Stock repurchase] coverage ratio.

Solution:

   A. Dividend/earnings payout = A$121/A$540 = 0.224 or 22.4% in 2015; A$256/A$458 = 0.559 or 55.9% in 2016; 0.694 or 69.4% in 2017; and 0.947 or 94.7% in 2018.

   B. Earnings/dividend coverage = A$540/A$121 = 4.46x in 2015; A$458/A$256 = 1.79x in 2016; 1.44x in 2017; and 1.06x in 2018.

   C. FCFE = Cash flow from operations (CFO) – FCInv + Net borrowing = A$837 – A$554 + (A$120) = A$163 in 2015; A$824 – A$417 + (A$39) = A$368 in 2016; A$462 in 2017; and A$294 in 2018.

   D. FCFE coverage of dividends + Share repurchases = FCFE/[Dividends + Stock repurchases] = A$163/(A$121 + 0) = 1.35x in 2015, and A$368/(A$256 + A$105) = 1.02x in 2016. Similar calculations result in 0.83x in 2017 and 0.91x in 2018.

   These results are summarized in Exhibit 15.

Exhibit 15: Lygon Resources Coverage Ratios

Years Ending 31 December	2015	2016	2017	2018
A. Dividend-to-earnings payout ratio	22.4%	55.9%	69.4%	94.7%
B. Earnings-to-dividend coverage ratio (x)	4.46	1.79	1.44	1.06
C. Free cash flow to equity (FCFE) (mil.)	163	368	462	294
D. FCFE/[div. + stock repurch.] cover. (x)	1.35	1.02	0.83	0.91

2. Discuss the trends in earnings/dividend coverage and in FCFE/[Dividend + Stock repurchase] coverage.

Solution:

Although earnings/dividend coverage was nearly 4.5x in 2015, it declined steadily over the four years. By 2018, accounting earnings were just sufficient to pay the dividend (1.06x earnings-to-dividend coverage ratio). An analyst who looked at this metric should have suspected problems.

The FCFE coverage ratio was 1.35x in 2015, a year before the stock repurchase program began. In 2016, the FCFE coverage of dividends and stock repurchases declined to 1.02x. Lower capital expenditures were offset by increased dividends and the new stock repurchase program. Despite declining capital expenditures and positive net borrowings, the FCFE coverage ratio continued to fall substantially to 0.83x in 2017 as the company elected to increase distributions to shareholders. Despite completing the stock repurchase program the previous year, by 2018 FCFE had deteriorated so much that FCFE coverage of dividends was still less than 1.0x (0.91x).

3. Comment on the sustainability of Lygon's dividend and stock repurchase policy after 2017/2018.

Solution:

With the FCFE coverage ratio falling to 0.83x in 2017, management likely realized that it was not prudent to undertake any new discretionary stock repurchases. By 2018, net income was still declining and FCFE coverage of the dividend at less than 1.0x meant that management should probably consider cutting the dividend.

The deterioration over time of Lygon's earnings/dividend coverage and FCFE coverage (of dividends and stock repurchases) was clear. There may be other instances when the earnings-to-dividend coverage ratio declines but still appears healthy. This is why it is important for analysts to closely examine the level and trend of the FCFE coverage ratio and the components of FCFE. Analysts should be particularly alert to companies that support their dividends and stock repurchases by reducing productive capital spending or by adding net debt or by some combination of the two because these neither are sustainable policies.

Whether based on a company's net income or free cash flow, past financial data do not always predict dividend safety. Surprise factors and other unexpected events can confound the most rigorous analysis of past data. Equity and debt markets were shaken in 2008–2009 by the losses taken by almost all US and European banks. These losses led to the cutting and, in some cases, virtual elimination of cash dividends. Not all 21st century investors would agree with Graham et al.'s 1962 assertion that "for the vast majority of common stocks, the dividend record and prospects have always been the most important factor controlling investment quality and value." But most investors would agree that when the market even begins to suspect a decrease or suspension of a company's cash dividend, that expectation is likely to weigh unfavorably on that company's common stock valuation. Therefore, many analysts look for external stock market indicators of market expectations of dividend cuts.

Extremely high dividend yields in comparison with a company's past record and forward-looking earnings is often another warning signal that investors are predicting a dividend cut. For example, the dividend yield on Singapore-listed telecoms company StarHub shares was 9.4% just prior to its fixed-to-variable dividend cut in 2019. After the announced dividend cut to a variable 80% of net profit for 2019 onwards, StarHub shares were still projected to yield about 5.6%, relatively high compared to its yield in recent years prior to the fixed dividend (which were generally about 5%). At the time, shareholder equity value was anticipated to go to zero by 2020 if the fixed dividend continued. In such cases, investors bid down the price of shares such that after the expected cut the expected total return on the shares remains adequate.

The observations of Madden (2008) support an attitude of caution with respect to very high dividend yields. Madden examined yields for the 1,963 stocks in the MSCI World Index. His company classified 865 companies out of the 1,963 companies as a "High Dividend Universe" (HDU). In the early months of the economic decline, Madden found that 78.6% of the companies in the HDU had questionable ability to maintain their dividend payments as compared with 30.7% of all the companies in the MCSI World Index. This point is supported by more recent evidence. Research using data for the S&P 500 Index stocks from 2005 to 2015 shows that the top 5% of dividend-yielding stocks accounted for over 8% of the bottom decile of performance. This over-representation of very high dividend-yielding stocks in the bottom decile of performance is likely attributable to deteriorating corporate fundamentals resulting in non-sustainable dividends. Similarly, in 2016 analysts became concerned that many European companies' dividends were unsustainable because they were paying out the highest proportion of their earnings as dividends in decades (a 60% payout ratio) at a time when their earnings were declining. This caused some companies to change their policies and cut dividends for future reinvestment and balance sheet improvement.

SUMMARY

A company's cash dividend payment and share repurchase policies constitute its payout policy. Both entail the distribution of the company's cash to its shareholders affect the form in which shareholders receive the return on their investment. Among the points this reading has made are the following:

- Dividends can take the form of regular or irregular cash payments, stock dividends, or stock splits. Only cash dividends are payments to shareholders. Stock dividends and splits merely carve equity into smaller pieces and do not create wealth for shareholders. Reverse stock splits usually occur after a stock has dropped to a very low price and do not affect shareholder wealth.

- Regular cash dividends—unlike irregular cash dividends, stock splits, and stock dividends—represent a commitment to pay cash to stockholders on a quarterly, semiannual, or annual basis.

- There are three general theories on investor preference for dividends. The first, MM, argues that given perfect markets dividend policy is irrelevant. The second, "bird in hand" theory, contends that investors value a dollar of dividends today more than uncertain capital gains in the future. The third theory argues that in countries in which dividends are taxed at higher rates than capital gains, taxable investors prefer that companies reinvest earnings in profitable growth opportunities or repurchase shares so they receive more of the return in the form of capital gains.

- An argument for dividend irrelevance given perfect markets is that corporate dividend policy is irrelevant because shareholders can create their preferred cash flow stream by selling the company's shares ("homemade dividends").

- Dividend declarations may provide information to current and prospective shareholders regarding management's confidence in the prospects of the company. Initiating a dividend or increasing a dividend sends a positive signal, whereas cutting a dividend or omitting a dividend typically sends a negative signal. In addition, some institutional and individual shareholders see regular cash dividend payments as a measure of investment quality.

- Payment of dividends can help reduce the agency conflicts between managers and shareholders, but it also can worsen conflicts of interest between shareholders and debtholders.

- Empirically, several factors appear to influence dividend policy, including investment opportunities for the company, the volatility expected in its future earnings, financial flexibility, tax considerations, flotation costs, and contractual and legal restrictions.

- Under double taxation systems, dividends are taxed at both the corporate and shareholder level. Under tax imputation systems, a shareholder receives a tax credit on dividends for the tax paid on corporate profits. Under split-rate taxation systems, corporate profits are taxed at different rates depending on whether the profits are retained or paid out in dividends.

- Companies with outstanding debt often are restricted in the amount of dividends they can pay because of debt covenants and legal restrictions. Some institutions require that a company pay a dividend to be on their "approved" investment list. If a company funds capital expenditures by borrowing while paying earnings out in dividends, it will incur flotation costs on new debt issues.

- Using a stable dividend policy, a company tries to align its dividend growth rate to the company's long-term earnings growth rate. Dividends may increase even in years when earnings decline, and dividends will increase at a lower rate than earnings in boom years.

- A stable dividend policy can be represented by a gradual adjustment process in which the expected dividend is equal to last year's dividend per share plus [(Expected earnings × Target payout ratio – Previous dividend) × Adjustment factor].

- Using a constant dividend payout ratio policy, a company applies a target dividend payout ratio to current earnings; therefore, dividends are more volatile than with a stable dividend policy.

- Share repurchases, or buybacks, most often occur in the open market. Alternatively, tender offers occur at a fixed price or at a price range through a Dutch auction. Shareholders who do not tender increase their relative position in the company. Direct negotiations with major shareholders to get them to sell their positions are less common because they could destroy value for remaining stockholders.

- Share repurchases made with excess cash have the potential to increase earnings per share, whereas share repurchases made with borrowed funds can increase, decrease, or not affect earnings per share depending on the company's after-tax borrowing rate and earnings yield.

- A share repurchase is equivalent to the payment of a cash dividend of equal amount in its effect on total shareholders' wealth, all other things being equal.

- If the buyback market price per share is greater (less) than the book value per share, then the book value per share will decrease (increase).

- Companies can repurchase shares in lieu of increasing cash dividends. Share repurchases usually offer company management more flexibility than cash dividends by not establishing the expectation that a particular level of cash distribution will be maintained.

- Companies can pay regular cash dividends supplemented by share repurchases. In years of extraordinary increases in earnings, share repurchases can substitute for special cash dividends.

- On the one hand, share repurchases can signal that company officials think their shares are undervalued. On the other hand, share repurchases could send a negative signal that the company has few positive NPV opportunities.

- Analysts are interested in how safe a company's dividend is, specifically whether the company's earnings and, more importantly, its cash flow are sufficient to sustain the payment of the dividend.
- Early warning signs of whether a company can sustain its dividend include the dividend coverage ratio, the level of dividend yield, whether the company borrows to pay the dividend, and the company's past dividend record.

REFERENCES

Graham, Benjamin, David Dodd, Sidney Cottle, Charles Tatham. 1962. Security Analysis, 4th edition. New York: McGraw-Hill.

Hirtle, Beverly. 2016. "Bank Holding Company Dividends and Repurchases during the Financial Crisis." Federal Reserve Bank of New York Staff Reports, no. 666.

Lintner, John. 1956. "Distribution of Incomes of Corporations among Dividends, Retained Earnings and Taxes." American Economic Review, vol. 46, no. 2: 97–113.

Madden, Ian. 2008. "High Dividend Stocks: Proceed with Caution."

Miller, Merton H., Franco Modigliani. 1961. "Dividend Policy, Growth, and the Valuation of Shares." Journal of Business, vol. 34, no. 4: 411–433. 10.1086/294442

PRACTICE PROBLEMS

1. The payment of a 10% stock dividend by a company will result in an increase in that company's:

   A. current ratio.

   B. financial leverage.

   C. contributed capital.

2. If a company's common shares trade at very low prices, that company would be *most likely* to consider the use of a:

   A. stock split.

   B. stock dividend.

   C. reverse stock split.

3. In a recent presentation, Doug Pearce made two statements about dividends:

   | Statement 1 | "A stock dividend will increase share price on the ex-dividend date, all other things being equal." |
   | Statement 2 | "One practical concern with a stock split is that it will reduce the company's price-to-earnings ratio." |

   Are Pearce's two statements about the effects of the stock dividend and stock split correct?

   A. No for both statements.

   B. Yes for Statement 1, and no for Statement 2.

   C. No for Statement 1, and yes for Statement 2.

4. All other things being equal, the payment of an internally financed cash dividend is *most likely* to result in:

   A. a lower current ratio.

   B. a higher current ratio.

   C. the same current ratio.

The following information relates to questions 5-9

John Ladan is an analyst in the research department of an international securities firm. Ladan is currently analyzing Yeta Products, a publicly traded global consumer goods company located in the United States. Selected data for Yeta are presented in Exhibit 1.

Exhibit 1: Selected Financial Data for Yeta Products			
Most Recent Fiscal Year		**Current**	
Pretax income	US$280 million	Shares outstanding	100 million
Net income after tax	US$182 million	Book value per share	US$25.60
Cash flow from operations	US$235 million	Share price	US$20.00
Capital expenditures	US$175 million		
Earnings per share	US$1.82		

Yeta currently does not pay a dividend, and the company operates with a target capital structure of 40% debt and 60% equity. However, on a recent conference call, Yeta's management indicated that they are considering four payout proposals:

Proposal #1: Issue a 10% stock dividend.

Proposal #2: Repurchase US$40 million in shares using surplus cash.

Proposal #3: Repurchase US$40 million in shares by borrowing US$40 million at an after-tax cost of borrowing of 8.50%.

Proposal #4: Initiate a regular cash dividend.

5. The implementation of Proposal #1 would generally lead to shareholders:

   A. having to pay tax on the dividend received.

   B. experiencing a decrease in the total cost basis of their shares.

   C. having the same proportionate ownership as before implementation.

6. If Yeta's management implemented Proposal #2 at the current share price shown in Exhibit 1, Yeta's book value per share after implementation would be *closest* to:

   A. US$25.20.

   B. US$25.71.

   C. US$26.12.

7. Based on Exhibit 1, if Yeta's management implemented Proposal #3 at the current share price, earnings per share would:

   A. decrease.

   B. remain unchanged.

   C. increase.

8. Based on Yeta's target capital structure, Proposal #4 will *most likely:*

   A. increase the default risk of Yeta's debt.

   B. increase the agency conflict between Yeta's shareholders and managers.

   C. decrease the agency conflict between Yeta's shareholders and bondholders.

9. The implementation of Proposal #4 would *most likely* signal to Ladan and other

investors that future earnings growth can be expected to:

A. decrease.

B. remain unchanged.

C. increase.

10. Match the phrases in Column A with the corresponding dividend theory in Column B. Note that you may use the answers in Column B more than once.

Column A	Column B
1. Bird in the hand	a) Dividend policy matters
2. Homemade dividends	b) Dividend policy is irrelevant
3. High tax rates on dividends	

11. Which of the following assumptions is *not* required for Miller and Modigliani's (MM) dividend theory?

A. Shareholders have no transaction costs when buying and selling shares.

B. There are no taxes.

C. Investors prefer dividends over uncertain capital gains.

12. Sophie Chan owns 100,000 shares of PAT Company. PAT is selling for €40 per share, so Chan's investment is worth €4,000,000. Chan reinvests the gross amount of all dividends received to purchase additional shares. Assume that the clientele for PAT shares consists of tax-exempt investors. If PAT pays a €1.50 dividend, Chan's new share ownership after reinvesting dividends at the ex-dividend price is *most* likely to be closest to:

A. 103,600.

B. 103,750.

C. 103,900.

13. Which of the following is *most* likely to signal negative information concerning a company?

A. Share repurchase.

B. Decrease in the quarterly dividend rate.

C. A two-for-one stock split.

14. WL Corporation is located in a jurisdiction that has a 40% corporate tax rate on pretax income and a 30% personal tax rate on dividends. WL distributes all its after-tax income to shareholders. What is the effective tax rate on WL pretax income distributed in dividends?

A. 42%.

B. 58%.

C. 70%.

15. Which of the following factors is *least likely* to be associated with a company having a low dividend payout ratio?

    A. High flotation costs on new equity issues.

    B. High tax rates on dividends.

    C. Low growth prospects.

16. The dividend policy of Berkshire Gardens Inc. can be represented by a gradual adjustment to a target dividend payout ratio. Last year Berkshire had earnings per share of US$3.00 and paid a dividend of US$0.60 a share. This year it estimates earnings per share will be US$4.00. Find its dividend per share for this year if it has a 25% target payout ratio and uses a five-year period to adjust its dividend.

    A. US$0.68.

    B. US$0.80.

    C. US$0.85.

17. Beta Corporation is a manufacturer of inflatable furniture. Which of the following scenarios best reflects a stable dividend policy for Beta?

    A. Maintaining a constant dividend payout ratio of 40–50%.

    B. Maintaining the dividend at US$1.00 a share for several years given no change in Beta's long-term prospects.

    C. Increasing the dividend 5% a year over several years to reflect the two years in which Beta recognized mark-to-market gains on derivatives positions.

18. A company has 1 million shares outstanding and earnings are £2 million. The company decides to use £10 million in surplus cash to repurchase shares in the open market. The company's shares are trading at £50 per share. If the company uses the entire £10 million of surplus cash to repurchase shares at the market price, the company's earnings per share will be *closest* to:

    A. £2.00.

    B. £2.30.

    C. £2.50.

19. Devon Ltd. common shares sell at US$40 a share, and their estimated price-to-earnings ratio (P/E) is 32. If Devon borrows funds to repurchase shares at its after-tax cost of debt of 5%, its EPS is *most likely* to:

    A. increase.

    B. decrease.

    C. remain the same.

20. A company can borrow funds at an after-tax cost of 4.5%. The company's stock price is US$40 per share, earnings per share is US$2.00, and the company has 15 million shares outstanding. If the company borrows just enough to repurchase 2 million shares of stock at the prevailing market price, that company's earnings

per share is *most likely* to:

A. increase.

B. decrease.

C. remain the same.

21. Crozet Corporation plans to borrow just enough money to repurchase 100,000 shares. The following information relates to the share repurchase:

Shares outstanding before buyback	3.1 million
Earnings per share before buyback	US$4.00
Share price at time of buyback	US$50
After-tax cost of borrowing	6%

Crozet's earnings per share after the buyback will be *closest* to:

A. US$4.03.

B. US$4.10.

C. US$4.23.

22. A company with 20 million shares outstanding decides to repurchase 2 million shares at the prevailing market price of €30 per share. At the time of the buyback, the company reports total assets of €850 million and total liabilities of €250 million. As a result of the buyback, that company's book value per share will *most likely*:

A. increase.

B. decrease.

C. remain the same.

23. An analyst gathered the following information about a company:

Number of shares outstanding	10 million
Earnings per share	US$2.00
P/E	20
Book value per share	US$30

If the company repurchases 1 million shares at the prevailing market price, the resulting book value per share will be *closest* to:

A. US$26.

B. US$27.

C. US$29.

24. If a company's objective is to support its stock price in the event of a market downturn, it would be advised to authorize:

A. an open market share repurchase plan to be executed over the next five years.

B. a tender offer share repurchase at a fixed price effective in 30 days.

    C.   a Dutch auction tender offer effective in 30 days.

25. A company has positive free cash flow and is considering whether to use the entire amount of that free cash flow to pay a special cash dividend or to repurchase shares at the prevailing market price. Shareholders' wealth under the two options will be equivalent unless the:

    A.   company's book value per share is less than the prevailing market price.

    B.   company's book value per share is greater than the prevailing market price.

    C.   tax consequences and/or information content for each alternative is different.

26. Assume that a company is based in a country that has no taxes on dividends or capital gains. The company is considering either paying a special dividend or repurchasing its own shares. Shareholders of the company would have:

    A.   greater wealth if the company paid a special cash dividend.

    B.   greater wealth if the company repurchased its shares.

    C.   the same wealth under either a cash dividend or share repurchase program.

27. Investors may prefer companies that repurchase their shares instead of paying a cash dividend when:

    A.   capital gains are taxed at lower rates than dividends.

    B.   capital gains are taxed at the same rate as dividends.

    C.   the company needs more equity to finance capital expenditures.

The following information relates to questions 28-29

Janet Wu is treasurer of Wilson Chemical Company, a manufacturer of specialty chemicals used in industrial manufacturing and increasingly in technology applications. Wilson Chemical is selling one of its older divisions for US$70 million cash. Wu is considering whether to recommend a special dividend of US$70 million or a repurchase of 2 million shares of Wilson common stock in the open market. She is reviewing some possible effects of the buyback with the company's financial analyst. Wilson has a long-term record of gradually increasing earnings and dividends.

28. Wilson's share buyback could be a signal that the company:

    A.   is decreasing its financial leverage.

    B.   views its shares as undervalued in the marketplace.

    C.   has more investment opportunities than it could fund internally.

29. The most likely tax environment in which Wilson Chemical's shareholders would prefer that Wilson repurchase its shares (share buybacks) instead of paying divi-

dends is one in which:

A. the tax rate on capital gains and dividends is the same.

B. capital gains tax rates are higher than dividend income tax rates.

C. capital gains tax rates are lower than dividend income tax rates.

SOLUTIONS

1. C is correct. A stock dividend is accounted for as a transfer of retained earnings to contributed capital.

2. C is correct. A reverse stock split would increase the price per share of the stock to a higher, more marketable range that could possibly increase the number of investors who would consider buying the stock.

3. A is correct. Both statements are incorrect. A stock dividend will decrease the price per share, all other things being equal. A stock split will reduce the price and earnings per share proportionately, leaving the price-to-earnings ratio the same.

4. A is correct. By reducing corporate cash, a cash dividend reduces the current ratio, whereas a stock dividend (whatever the size) has no effect on the current ratio.

5. C is correct. The implementation of Proposal #1, a stock dividend, would not affect a shareholder's proportionate ownership because all shareholders would receive the same proportionate increase in shares. Stock dividends, which are generally not taxable to shareholders, do not impact an investor's total cost basis (they merely reduce the cost basis per share).

    A is incorrect because stock dividends are generally not taxable to shareholders. A stock dividend merely divides the "pie" (the market value of shareholders' equity) into smaller pieces.

    B is incorrect because an investor's total cost basis will not be affected by a stock dividend; a stock dividend merely reduces the cost basis per share.

6. B is correct. If Yeta implemented Proposal #2, a repurchase of US$40 million in shares, the resulting book value per share (BVPS) would be US$25.71, calculated as follows:

    1. Yeta has a current BVPS of US$25.60; therefore, total book value of equity is US$2,560 million (= US$25.60 × 100,000,000 shares).

    2. The number of shares Yeta would repurchase is US$40 million/US$20.00 per share = 2 million shares.

    3. Yeta shareholders' book value of equity after the buyback would be US$2,520 million (= US$2,560 million − US$40 million).

    4. The number of shares after the buyback would be 98 million (= 100 million − 2 million).

    5. The BVPS after the buyback would be US$2,520 million/98 million = US$25.71.

    A is incorrect because US$25.20 incorrectly uses 100 million shares instead of 98 million shares in calculating BVPS after the buyback: US$2,520 million/100 million = US$25.20.

    C is incorrect because US$26.12 incorrectly uses US$2,560 million (current book value) instead of US$2,520 million as the book value of equity in calculating BVPS after the buyback. The BVPS after the buyback is incorrectly calculated as US$2,560 million/98 million = US$26.12.

7. C is correct. In the case of external funding, a company's earnings per share will increase if the stock's earnings yield, which is the ratio of earnings per share to

share price, exceeds the after-tax cost of borrowing. Yeta's earnings yield is 9.10% (= US$1.82/US$20.00), which exceeds the after-tax cost of borrowing of 8.50%.

A is incorrect because EPS will increase (not decrease) if the stock's earnings yield (= US$1.82/US$20.00) exceeds the after-tax cost of borrowing. Yeta's earnings yield of 9.10% exceeds the after-tax cost of borrowing of 8.50%.

B is incorrect because EPS will increase (not remain unchanged) if the stock's earnings yield (= US$1.82/US$20.00) exceeds the after-tax cost of borrowing. Yeta's earnings yield of 9.10% exceeds the after-tax cost of borrowing of 8.50%.

8. A is correct. Yeta is financed by both debt and equity; therefore, paying dividends can increase the agency conflict between shareholders and bondholders. The payment of dividends reduces the cash cushion available for the disbursement of fixed required payments to bondholders. All else equal, dividends increase the default risk of debt.

B is incorrect because the agency conflict between shareholders and managers would decrease (not increase) with the payment of dividends. Paying out free cash flow to equity in dividends would constrain managers in their ability to overinvest by taking on negative net present value (NPV) projects.

C is incorrect because paying dividends can increase (not decrease) the agency conflict between shareholders and bondholders. The payment of dividends would reduce the cash cushion available to Yeta for the disbursement of fixed required payments to bondholders. The payment of dividends transfers wealth from bondholders to shareholders and increases the default risk of debt.

9. C is correct. Dividend initiations convey positive information and are associated with future earnings growth, whereas dividend omissions or reductions convey negative information and are associated with future earnings problems.

A is incorrect because dividend initiations convey positive information and are associated with an expected increase (not a decrease) in future earnings growth. Dividend omissions or reductions convey negative information and are associated with future earnings problems.

B is incorrect because dividend initiations convey positive information and are associated with an expectation that future earnings growth will increase (not remain unchanged). In contrast, dividend omissions or reductions convey negative information and are associated with future earnings problems.

10. The appropriate matches are as follows:

Column A	Column B
1. Bird in the hand	a) Dividend policy matters
2. Homemade dividends	b) Dividend policy is irrelevant
3. High tax rates on dividends	a) Dividend policy matters

11. C is correct. The MM dividend theory assumes no taxes or transaction costs, but it does not assume investors have a preference for dividends over capital gains.

12. C is correct. Because the clientele for PAT investors has the same tax rate (zero) for dividends and capital gains, the ex-dividend stock price of PAT should decline by the amount of the dividend to €40 − €1.50 = €38.50. Chan will purchase €150,000/€38.50 = 3,896 additional shares. This increases her total shares owned to 103,896. Chan's new share ownership is closest to 103,900.

13. B is correct. A decrease in the quarterly dividend rate is likely to signal negative information. A decrease is typically understood as signaling poor future business

prospects.

14. B is correct. The effective tax rate can be computed as 1 minus the fraction of 1 unit of earnings that investors retain after all taxes, or $1 - (1 - 0.40)(1 - 0.30) = 0.58$ or 58% effective tax rate. Another way to obtain the solution: Corporate taxes $= 1.00 \times 0.40 = 0.40$ and Personal taxes $= 0.60$ in dividends $\times 0.30 = 0.18$, so Total tax $= 0.40 + 0.18 = 0.58$, or 58% effective rate.

15. C is correct. With low growth prospects, a company would typically have a high payout ratio, returning funds to its shareholders rather than retaining funds.

16. A is correct. The estimated dividend per share is US$0.68.

    Previous DPS = US$0.60

    Expected EPS = US$4

    Target payout ratio = 0.25

    Five-year adjustment factor = 1/5 = 0.2

    Expected dividend = Previous dividend + (Expected earnings × Target payout ratio − Previous dividend) × Adjustment factor

    = US$0.60 + [(US$4.00 × 0.25 − US$0.60) × 0.2]

    = US$0.60 + US$0.08

    = US$0.68

17. B is correct. Choice A is consistent with a constant dividend target payout ratio policy. Choice C is not correct because the earnings increases described are not sustainable long term.

18. C is correct. At the current market price, the company can repurchase 200,000 shares (£10 million/£50 = 200,000 shares). The company would have 800,000 shares outstanding after the repurchase (1 million shares − 200,000 shares = 800,000 shares).

    EPS before the buyback is £2.00 (£2 million/1 million shares = £2.00). Total earnings after the buyback are the same because the company uses surplus (nonearning) cash to purchase the shares, but the number of shares outstanding is reduced to 800,000. EPS increases to £2.50 (£2 million/ 800,000 shares = £2.50).

19. B is correct. If the P/E is 32, the earnings-to-price ratio (earnings yield or E/P) is 1/32 = 3.125%. When the cost of capital is greater than the earnings yield, earnings dilution will result from the buyback.

20. A is correct. The company's earnings yield (E/P) is US$2/US$40 = 0.05. When the earnings yield is greater than the after-tax cost of borrowed funds, EPS will increase if shares are repurchased using borrowed funds.

21. A is correct.

    Total earnings before buyback: US$4.00 × 3,100,000 shares = US$12,400,000

    Total amount of borrowing: US$50 × 100,000 shares = US$5,000,000

    After-tax cost of borrowing the amount of funds needed: US$5,000,000 × 0.06 = US$300,000

Number of shares outstanding after buyback: 3,100,000 – 100,000 = 3,000,000

EPS after buyback: (US$12,400,000 – US$300,000)/3,000,000 shares = US$4.03

The P/E before the buyback is US$50/US$4 = 12.5; thus, the E/P is 8%. The after-tax cost of debt is 6%; therefore, EPS will increase.

22. C is correct. The company's book value before the buyback is €850 million in assets – €250 million in liabilities = €600 million. Book value per share is €600 million/20 million = €30 per share. The buyback will reduce equity by 2 million shares at the prevailing market price of €30 per share. The book value of equity will be reduced to €600 million – €60 million = €540 million, and the number of shares will be reduced to 18 million; €540 million/18 million = €30 book value per share. If the prevailing market price is equal to the book value per share at the time of the buyback, book value per share is unchanged.

23. C is correct. The prevailing market price is US$2.00(20) = US$40.00 per share; thus, the buyback would reduce equity by US$40 million. Book value of equity before the buyback is US$300 million. Book value of equity after the buyback would be US$300 million – US$40 million = US$260 million. The number of shares outstanding after the buyback would be 9 million. Thus, book value per share after the buyback would be US$260 million/9 million = US$28.89 ≈ US$29.

24. A is correct. Of the three methods, only an authorized open market share repurchase plan allows the company the flexibility to time share repurchases to coincide with share price declines.

25. C is correct. For the two options to be equivalent with respect to shareholders' wealth, the amount of cash distributed, the taxation, and the information content must be the same for both options.

26. C is correct. When there are no taxes, there are no tax differences between dividends and capital gains. All other things being equal, the effect on shareholder wealth of a dividend and a share repurchase should be the same.

27. A is correct. When capital gains are taxed at lower rates than dividends, investors may prefer companies that return cash to shareholders through share repurchases rather than dividends.

28. B is correct. Management sometimes undertakes share repurchases when it views shares as being undervalued in the marketplace.

29. C is correct. Shareholders would prefer that the company repurchase its shares instead of paying dividends when the tax rate on capital gains is lower than the tax rate on dividends.

3

Environmental, Social, and Governance (ESG) Considerations in Investment Analysis

by Deborah S. Kidd, CFA, Young Lee, CFA, JD, and Johan Vanderlugt.

Deborah S. Kidd, CFA, is at CFA Institute (USA). Young Lee, CFA, JD, is at MacKay Shields (USA and Europe). Johan Vanderlugt is at NN Investment Partners (Netherlands).

LEARNING OUTCOMES	
Mastery	**The candidate should be able to:**
☐	describe global variations in ownership structures and the possible effects of these variations on corporate governance policies and practices
☐	evaluate the effectiveness of a company's corporate governance policies and practices
☐	describe how ESG-related risk exposures and investment opportunities may be identified and evaluated
☐	evaluate ESG risk exposures and investment opportunities related to a company

INTRODUCTION

1

Environmental, social, and governance (ESG) considerations are increasingly being integrated into investment analysis. Evaluating how ESG factors potentially affect a company may provide analysts with a broader perspective on the risks and investment opportunities of a company's securities. Although corporate governance has long been recognized as having a significant impact on a company's long-term performance, investors have become increasingly concerned with environmental and social factors and how companies manage their resources and risk exposures that relate to such factors. Mismanagement of these resources has led to a number of high-profile corporate events that have negatively affected security prices. Increasingly stringent regulatory environments, potentially finite supplies of natural resources, and global trends toward energy conservation and waste reduction have led many investors to place greater emphasis on the management of environmental risks. Similarly, such issues as worker health and safety policies, community impact, and marketing practices have increased the visibility of how a company manages its social capital.

This reading provides an overview of ESG considerations in investment analysis. Section 2 provides an overview of the global variations in corporate ownership structures, as well as how these ownership structures may affect corporate governance outcomes. In Section 3, we discuss company-specific factors that should be considered when evaluating corporate governance in the investment process. Section 4 discusses the identification of ESG-related risks and opportunities that are relevant to security analysis. Section 5 demonstrates the evaluation of ESG-related risks and opportunities through several examples. The reading concludes with a summary of the key points discussed.

2   OWNERSHIP STRUCTURES AND THEIR EFFECTS ON CORPORATE GOVERNANCE

☐   describe global variations in ownership structures and the possible effects of these variations on corporate governance policies and practices

The global corporate governance landscape comprises a vast range of ownership structures that reflect unique economic, political, social, legal, and other forces in each country and/or region. Within any of these distinct ownership structures, one may find a variety of complex relationships involving shareholders and other stakeholders who have an interest in the company. Those other stakeholders include creditors, managers (executives), employees, directors, customers, suppliers, governments, and regulators. An understanding of the variation of ownership structures, the conflicts that arise within these structures, types of influential shareholders, and the effects of ownership structure on corporate governance are important considerations for analyzing corporate governance in the investment process.

Dispersed vs. Concentrated Ownership

Corporate ownership structures are generally classified as *dispersed*, *concentrated*, or a hybrid of the two. **Dispersed ownership** reflects the existence of many shareholders, none of which has the ability to individually exercise control over the corporation. In contrast, **concentrated ownership** reflects an individual shareholder or a group (called *controlling shareholders*) with the ability to exercise control over the corporation. In this context, a group is typically a family, another company (or companies), or a sovereign entity.

On a global basis, concentrated ownership structures are considerably more common than dispersed ownership structures. A global corporate governance report by the Organisation for Economic Co-operation and Development (OECD)[1] noted that 38 out of 47 jurisdictions analyzed have predominantly concentrated ownership structures. Among the other nine jurisdictions, four were characterized as having dispersed ownership structures (Australia, Ireland, the United Kingdom, and the United States) and five were characterized as having "hybrid" corporate ownership structures (Canada, Germany, Japan, the Netherlands, and Switzerland). The OECD's classification of corporate ownership structure by jurisdiction is shown in Exhibit 1.

---

1 OECD (2017).

Exhibit 1: Corporate Ownership Classifications	
Jurisdictions with Concentrated Ownership	
Austria, Belgium, Brazil, Chile, China, Colombia, Czech Republic, Denmark, Estonia, Finland, France, Greece, Hungary, Iceland, India, Indonesia, Israel, Italy, Latvia, Mexico, New Zealand, Norway, Poland, Portugal, Russia, Singapore, Slovenia, South Africa, South Korea, Spain, Sweden, Turkey, United Arab Emirates	State ownership is characteristic of certain countries, such as China, Norway, and Sweden. In other countries, including Brazil, Mexico, Portugal, and South Korea, families are the predominant shareholders. Company groups are prevalent in a number of additional countries, such as India and Russia.
Jurisdictions with Dispersed Ownership	
Australia, Ireland, United Kingdom, United States	Among the largest companies in Australia, the majority of shares are held (albeit dispersed) by financial institutions. In Ireland, ownership shares tend to be widely dispersed, although there are a few family-controlled companies. Among UK companies, few have major shareholders owning 25% or more of shares. In the United States, ownership of public companies is generally characterized by dispersed shareholdings; listed companies are rarely under the control of a major shareholder.
Hybrid Jurisdictions	
Canada, Germany, Japan, Netherlands, Switzerland	In Canada, among the largest listed firms, a meaningful minority have controlling shareholders. In Germany, a significant number of companies are under "tight control," but in many cases shares are broadly distributed (especially for listed companies). In Japan, a small minority of listed companies have a shareholder that owns a majority of shares. The Netherlands has a more dispersed ownership structure than most continental European countries; however, when accounting for "trust offices," ownership is somewhat more concentrated. In Switzerland, the largest listed companies have more dispersed ownership than medium-sized and smaller companies.

Source: OECD (2017).

The degree of share ownership alone may not necessarily reflect whether the control of a company is dispersed or concentrated. This is true because controlling shareholders may be either **majority shareholders** (i.e., own more than 50% of a corporation's shares) or **minority shareholders** (i.e., own less than 50% of shares). In certain ownership structures, shareholders may have disproportionately high control of a corporation relative to their ownership stakes as a result of horizontal and/or vertical ownership arrangements. **Horizontal ownership** involves companies with mutual business interests (e.g., key customers or suppliers) that have cross-holding share arrangements with each other. This structure can help facilitate strategic alliances and foster long-term relationships among such companies. **Vertical ownership** (or pyramid ownership) involves a company or group that has a controlling interest in two or more holding companies, which in turn have controlling interests in various operating companies.

The existence of *dual-class* (or multiple-class) shares can also serve to disconnect the degree of share ownership from actual control. **Dual-class shares** grant one share class superior or sole voting rights, whereas the other share class has inferior or no voting rights. When used in connection with vertical ownership arrangements, the company or group at the top of the pyramid can issue to itself all or a disproportionately high number of shares with superior voting rights and thus maintain control of the operating companies with relatively fewer total shares of a company owned.

Conflicts within Different Ownership Structures

The type of corporate ownership structure affects corporate governance policies and practices because of the potentially different set of conflicts that may exist between shareholders and managers, as well as among shareholders themselves.

The combination of *dispersed* ownership and *dispersed* voting power is generally associated with shareholders who lack the power to exercise control over managers. These shareholders are referred to as *weak shareholders*, and such managers are referred to as *strong managers*. Under this combination, conflict between the shareholders and managers of a corporation may be significant. Shareholders are interested in maximizing shareholder value. There is a risk, however, that managers will seek to use a company's resources to pursue their own interests. In corporate governance, this conflict is known as a *principal–agent* problem. This problem can be mitigated if controlling shareholders are present because they may be able to control the board of directors (and, in turn, the appointment of managers) and have the incentive to monitor management.

The combination of *concentrated* ownership and *concentrated* voting power often results in controlling shareholders maintaining a position of power over both managers and minority shareholders; these controlling shareholders are referred to as *strong shareholders*, and such managers are referred to as *weak managers*. In this scenario, controlling shareholders can effectively monitor management because they are able to control the board of directors and, in turn, the appointment of managers. With concentrated ownership and concentrated voting power, however, controlling owners may also be able to allocate company resources to their own benefit at the expense of minority owners. This conflict is known as a *principal–principal* problem.

The combination of *dispersed* ownership and *concentrated* voting power generally leads to the principal–principal problem as well. The one difference, however, is that the strong controlling shareholders do not own a majority of the shares of a company. In this scenario, controlling shareholders with less than majority ownership can exert control over other minority owners through certain mechanisms, such as dual-class share structures and pyramid structures, and can also monitor management owing to their outsized voting power.

Finally, the combination of *concentrated* ownership and *dispersed* voting power arises when there are legal restrictions on the voting rights of large share positions, known as **voting caps**. A number of sovereign governments have imposed voting caps to deter foreign investors from obtaining controlling ownership positions in strategically important local companies.

EXAMPLE 1

Conflicts between Shareholders and Managers

1. The managers of Company A, a widely held conglomerate, collectively own approximately 30% of the outstanding shares. No other shareholder owns more than a 1% share. Each ownership share has equivalent voting rights. Describe the potential conflict between the shareholders and managers of Company A given its ownership structure and voting rights.

Solution:

Company A has dispersed ownership and dispersed voting power. In this ownership structure, shareholders do not appear to have the ability to control or monitor managers; that is, there are weak shareholders and strong managers. In this case, a risk exists that managers may seek to use company

> resources to prioritize their own interests rather than to maximize shareholder value. This type of conflict is known as the *principal–agent* problem.

Types of Influential Shareholders

In different parts of the world, the types of corporate shareholders that have a significant influence on corporate governance vary. Each of these shareholder types possesses its own unique set of motivations, interests, and agendas. By identifying these shareholders, an investment analyst is in a position to further assess corporate governance risks.

Banks

In several regions, notably in Europe and Asia, banks often have considerable control over corporations with which they have a lending relationship as well as an equity interest. A conflict of interest could arise if banks have loan exposures to a corporation in addition to their equity investment. For example, if a bank has both a lending relationship with and an equity interest in a corporation, it could seek to influence the corporation to take out large loans, and perhaps on less favorable terms, to the potential detriment of other shareholders. In this situation, appropriate corporate governance controls could ensure that banks that are both creditors and investors appropriately balance their interests as lenders against their interests as shareholders.

Families

Family ownership is the predominant form of corporate structure in some parts of the world, notably Latin America and, to a slightly lesser extent, Asia and Europe. In some cases, also commonly in Latin America, individuals serve on the board of directors of multiple corporations. This situation, known as **interlocking directorates**, typically results in the same family or the same member of a corporate group controlling several corporations. A benefit of family control is lower risks associated with principal–agent problems as a result of families having concentrated ownership and management responsibility. Conversely, drawbacks of family ownership may include poor transparency, lack of management accountability, modest consideration for minority shareholder rights, and difficulty in attracting quality talent for management positions.

State-Owned Enterprises

State-owned enterprises (SOEs) often exist in corporate sectors that are strategically important to a sovereign government, have minimum initial or ongoing capital requirements that are beyond the private sector's funding ability, or provide certain products or services (e.g., power generation or health services) that the state believes should be provided at a certain price or minimum standard. Listed SOEs are partially owned by sovereign governments but also have shares traded on public stock markets. This structure is called a *mixed-ownership model*. This model tends to have lower market scrutiny of management than that of corporate ownership models, which have implicit or explicit state guarantees to prevent corporate bankruptcy. In some cases, SOEs may pursue policies that enhance social or public policy considerations at the expense of maximizing shareholder value.

Institutional Investors

In many countries, institutional investors—typically mutual funds, pension funds, insurance companies, and hedge funds—collectively represent a significant proportion of equity market ownership. Because these investors tend to have considerable resources and market expertise, they can use informed judgment in exercising their shareholder rights. In markets with widely dispersed ownership, institutional investors do not typically control a large enough ownership position to qualify as a controlling shareholder. Institutional investors can promote good corporate governance, however, by holding a company's board and management accountable when the board or management does not appear to be acting in the best interests of shareholders.

Group Companies

Some ownership structures, such as the previously mentioned horizontal and vertical ownership structures, may result in shareholders having disproportionately high control relative to their ownership stakes. Cross-holding share arrangements and long-term relationships between these group companies may restrict the potential for a transfer of share ownership—as well as create a potential obstacle for outsiders to purchase a significant portion of shares in companies. Without appropriate corporate governance policies/procedures or regulatory protections, there is a greater risk that corporations controlled by groups engage in related-party transactions at the expense of minority shareholders. Examples of group companies are Samsung (South Korea), Sanwa (Japan), and Grupo Carso (Mexico).

Private Equity Firms

Private equity firms, notably those involved in venture capital and leveraged buyouts, are strategic owners that invest in privately owned companies or in public companies with the intent to take them private. Venture capital firms invest in the early stages of a company and provide oversight of portfolio companies. Similarly, leveraged buyout (LBO) firms typically have majority control in mature companies. The involvement of venture capital and LBO firms in the management of corporations may bring important changes to companies' corporate governance, such as the development of corporate codes and implementation of performance-based manager compensation.

Foreign Investors

Foreign investors, particularly when investing in emerging market countries, can have a significant influence on local companies when they own more shares than domestic investors own. Foreign investors from countries that have more stringent standards may demand higher levels of transparency and accountability. If a local company chooses to cross-list its shares in another country with greater transparency requirements and investor protections, local minority shareholders may benefit from the arrangement.

Managers and Board Directors

When managers and board directors are also shareholders of a company, they are known as **insiders**. As their ownership positions increase, insiders are more likely to dedicate company resources toward long-term profitability because their economic interests in the company have become more aligned with the interests of external shareholders. Large ownership positions, however, may also provide insiders with increased power and an accompanying desire to protect their own interests at the expense of other shareholders.

Effects of Ownership Structure on Corporate Governance

This subsection highlights the effects of ownership structures on corporate governance policies and practices. Key considerations include board independence; board structure; special voting arrangements; corporate governance codes, laws, and listing requirements; and stewardship codes.

Director Independence

Independent board directors (or independent board members) are defined as those with no material relationship with the company with regard to employment, ownership, or remuneration. The percentage of independent board directors tends to be higher in jurisdictions with generally dispersed ownership structures relative to those countries with generally concentrated ownership structures. Independent directors originated in dispersed ownership jurisdictions as a means to strengthen the board's monitoring role over managers. The proportion of independent directors on boards has increased over time amid regulatory responses to corporate scandals (e.g., the Enron Corporation scandal in the early 2000s).

Independent directors generally serve a narrower role in concentrated ownership structures than in dispersed ownership structures. For example, the United States requires that some committees (such as the audit, nomination, and compensation committees) be composed entirely of independent directors. Conversely, in most jurisdictions with concentrated ownership structures, nomination and remuneration committees are not mandatory; when these committees do exist, jurisdictions typically recommend that the committees be wholly or largely composed of independent directors. In short, the principal–agent problem is generally less of a concern in a concentrated ownership structure than in a dispersed ownership structure.

Almost all OECD countries have introduced a requirement or recommendation for the level of independent directors serving on boards. These requirements and recommendations vary by jurisdiction, however. Some countries impose or recommend a minimum number of independent directors (typically ranging from one to three), whereas others impose or recommend a minimum ratio of independent directors (typically ranging from 20% to 50% or greater).

Board Structures

A corporation's board of directors is typically structured as either one tier or two tier. A **one-tier board** structure consists of a single board of directors, composed of executive (internal) and non-executive (external) directors. A **two-tier board** structure consists of a supervisory board that oversees a management board. A one-tier board is the most common structure, but a number of jurisdictions mandate a two-tier board structure (e.g., Argentina, Germany, and Russia), whereas other jurisdictions offer the choice of a one-tier or two-tier board (e.g., Brazil and France). The supervisory board of a two-tier board can serve as a control function through activities such as inspecting the corporation's books and records, reviewing the annual report, overseeing the work of external auditors, analyzing information provided by the management board, and setting or influencing management compensation. In certain countries, such as Germany, the supervisory boards comprise representatives from key stakeholders, such as banks and labor or other groups.

Special Voting Arrangements

Several jurisdictions have special voting arrangements to improve the position of minority shareholders. For example, Brazil, India, Portugal, Turkey, Italy, Israel, and the United Kingdom have special arrangements that facilitate engagement of minority shareholders in board nomination and election processes. When a UK company has a controlling shareholder, a condition for obtaining a "premium listing" (i.e., meeting the United Kingdom's highest standards of regulation and corporate governance) on the London Stock Exchange is that independent directors must be separately approved by both the entire shareholder base and non-controlling shareholders.

Corporate Governance Codes, Laws, and Listing Requirements

Many countries have adopted national corporate governance codes in which companies disclose their adoption of recommended corporate governance practices or explain why they have not done so. In some jurisdictions, companies are required to go beyond this "comply or explain" approach. In Japan, for example, companies with no outside directors must justify why appointing outside directors is not appropriate. Some jurisdictions do not have national corporate governance codes but make use of company law or regulation (e.g., Chile) or stock exchange listing requirements (e.g., India) to achieve similar objectives.

Stewardship Codes

Many countries have introduced voluntary codes, known as *stewardship codes*, that encourage investors to exercise their legal rights and increase their level of engagement in corporate governance. In some cases, stewardship codes are not entirely voluntary. As an example, the UK Stewardship Code includes a duty for institutional investors to monitor the companies in which they invest and requires that UK asset managers investing in the shares of UK companies publish a "comply or explain" statement of commitment to the UK Stewardship Code.

3　EVALUATING CORPORATE GOVERNANCE POLICIES AND PROCEDURES

☐　evaluate the effectiveness of a company's corporate governance policies and practices

Effective corporate governance is critical for a company's reputation and competitiveness. Benefits of effective corporate governance may include higher profitability, growth in return on equity (or other return metrics), better access to credit, higher and sustainable dividends, favorable long-term share performance, and a lower cost of capital. In contrast, companies with ineffective corporate governance may experience reputational damage, reduced competitiveness, potential share price weakness/volatility, reduced profitability, and a higher cost of capital.

Corporate governance factors are often difficult to quantify. However, an understanding of these factors and their impact on governance policies and procedures can be important for investors to consider. Understanding the disclosed corporate governance policies and procedures is a key starting point for investors. Regular dialogue and engagement efforts with companies can help investors better understand corporate governance policies and procedures. In some situations, shareholder activism can be used to attempt to compel a company to act in a desired manner. **Shareholder activism** refers to strategies used by shareholders to attempt to compel a company to act in a desired manner.

The quality of corporate governance is typically reflected in a company's behavior in the market and toward its stakeholders. To that end, an evaluation of a corporation's board of directors is a starting point for investors. We discuss several of the considerations relating to boards of directors in this section. In addition, a company's policies regarding business ethics, bribery and corruption, whistleblower protection, and related-party transactions can help analysts evaluate a company's corporate governance. In practice, analysts typically adjust the risk premium (cost of capital) or credit spread of a company to reflect their assessment of corporate governance considerations.

Board Policies and Practices

A starting point for evaluating a board's effectiveness is its policies and practices. An oversight role is one aspect of a board's effectiveness—for example, whether the board is high-performing or dysfunctional. Each capital market is subject to different corporate governance issues, depending on its predominant ownership structure, history, legal environment, culture, and industry diversity. For example, boards of companies with concentrated family ownership structures and concentrated voting power may engage in related-party transactions that benefit family members or affiliates at the expense of outside shareholders.

Board of Directors Structure

Generally, when evaluating board structure, investors consider whether the organization and structure of the board—whether it is a one-tier or two-tier structure—provide sufficient oversight, representation, and accountability to shareholders. A related topic is "CEO duality," whereby the chief executive officer (CEO) also serves as chairperson of the board. CEO duality may raise concerns that the monitoring and oversight role of the board may be compromised relative to independent chairperson and CEO roles. When the chairperson is not independent or the role is combined, a company may appoint a lead independent director to help protect investor interests.

Board Independence

The independence of the directors, which we discussed previously, is a relevant consideration for investors. The absence or presence of a minority of independent directors is a negative aspect of corporate governance. Without independent directors, the potential exists for management to act in a self-serving manner. Consequently, a lack of independent directors on a board may increase investors' perception of the corporation's risk.

Board Committees

The number of board committees and how the committees operate are relevant considerations in an investor's analysis of governance. Committees vary by corporation and industry but generally include audit, governance, remuneration (or compensation), nomination, and risk and compliance committees. When evaluating a company's board committees, investors assess whether there are sufficiently independent committees that focus on key governance concerns, such as audit, compensation, and the selection of directors. The presence of non-independent committee members or executive directors may prompt the consideration of potential conflicts of interest or biases, such as those relating to compensation decisions (remuneration committee), management selection (nomination committee), and the integrity of financial reporting (audit committee).

Board Skills and Experience

The underlying skill set and experience of board directors are important investor considerations. A board with concentrated skills and experience may lack sufficient expertise to govern, as may a board with diverse skills and expertise that are not directly related to the company's core operations. In certain sectors/industries that rely on natural resources or face potentially large ESG risks, board members typically have expertise in environmental, climate, or social issues.

An issue related to skills and experience is board tenure. According to many corporate governance codes, a board director's tenure is considered long if it exceeds 10 years. Long tenure of a board member could be viewed positively or negatively. On the positive side, a board member with a long tenure may have a comprehensive understanding of how the corporation's business operates, as well as how effective company management has been during the director's tenure. On the negative side, long tenure may affect the independence of board members (i.e., they could be too closely aligned with management) or may result in directors being less willing to embrace changes in the corporation's business.

Board Composition

Board composition primarily reflects the number and diversity of directors, including their professional, cultural, and geographical background, as well as gender, age, and tenure. Boards with too many members or that lack diversity may govern less effectively than boards that are smaller or more diverse. For example, a board with long-tenured board members could become controlling, self-serving, or resistant to the introduction of new practices or policies that may benefit stakeholders.

Other Considerations in Board Evaluation

Board evaluation is necessary to maintain a company's competitive position and to meet the expectations of investors. Dimensions of the board evaluation process may include who evaluates the board, what should be evaluated, to whom the evaluation is targeted, and how the evaluation will be accomplished.

A board evaluation can be performed by the board itself (self-evaluation) or by an outsider on behalf of the board (external review). Some boards may decide to evaluate their performance on an "as needed" basis, whereas others will prefer to conduct a periodic external review. A board evaluation typically covers how the board performs its duties, its leadership, its structure (including the committees), and the interaction between board members and management (including culture). Apart from internal stakeholders, the evaluation may be targeted to the company's shareholders, regulators, or other external stakeholders.

EXAMPLE 2

Evaluating the Board of Directors

1. A junior analyst is analyzing the board of directors of Style, a fictional global clothing retailer based in Italy. Style was founded by the Donato family and is publicly traded. Style's 11-member board of directors has a chairperson—who is not the CEO—and two independent directors. Among the six non-independent directors, the Donato family accounts for four of them. All these family members have served on the board for at least 20 years. The gender and age characteristics of the board are both diverse, with women representing five of the board's directors—including its chair, Leila Donato—and the directors ranging in age from 35 to 75 years old.

   Describe considerations that the junior analyst would use in evaluating the effectiveness of Style's board of directors.

Solution:

The CEO and chairperson roles are separate for Style (no CEO duality), which can be considered a sign of effective corporate governance. In addition, the board appears to be diverse in terms of age and gender, which is typically considered a positive attribute. Conversely, board independence appears to be substandard: Only two board directors are independent, whereas four Donato family members, including the chairperson (Leila Donato), are board members. The tenure of the family board members is also likely to be considered a negative attribute (it far exceeds the typical 10 years).

Executive Remuneration

Executive remuneration involves such issues as transparency of compensation, performance criteria for incentive plans (both short term and long term), the linkage of remuneration with the company strategy, and the pay differential between the CEO and the average worker. When a corporation has a "say-on-pay" provision, shareholders can vote and/or provide feedback on remuneration issues. A clawback policy allows a company to recover previously paid remuneration if certain events, such as financial restatements, misconduct, breach of the law, or risk management deficiencies, are uncovered.

There is increasing concern among investors regarding "excessive" remuneration, often represented by the ratio of CEO pay to average-worker pay. In evaluating a company's executive remuneration, investors typically consider whether the company's remuneration policies and practices provide appropriate incentives for management to drive the value of a corporation. Company disclosures such as those metrics (also known as key performance indicators, or KPIs) used in executive incentive plans may be useful tools for analysis.

Shareholder Voting Rights

Shareholder voting rights are important investor considerations. Under **straight voting** share structures, shareholders are granted the right of one vote for each share owned. Dual-class share structures differ from straight voting in that company founders and/ or management typically have shares with more voting power than the class of shares available to the general public. That is, dual-class share structures—in contrast to the one share, one vote principle of straight voting—can benefit one group of shareholders over another. Because a potential conflict of interest may exist between minority shareholders and the company's founders and management (some of whom may also serve on the board of directors), it is important for investors to be aware of dual-class share structures when investing.

IDENTIFYING ESG-RELATED RISKS AND OPPORTUNITIES

4

☐ | describe how ESG-related risk exposures and investment opportunities may be identified and evaluated

A primary challenge when integrating ESG factors into investment analysis is identifying and obtaining information that is relevant and decision-useful. In practice, ESG-related data are generally obtained from publicly available corporate filings, documents, and communications such as corporate sustainability reports that may or may not be assured by a third party. Some of the challenges analysts face are related to inconsistent reporting of ESG information and metrics as well as the fact that the level of disclosure varies because most ESG-related disclosures are voluntary. ESG-related disclosure has generally increased over time, however, because of increased stakeholder and shareholder interest in understanding whether a company effectively manages its ESG risks and opportunities.

Materiality and Investment Horizon

When considering ESG factors in investment analysis, analysts need to evaluate the *materiality* of the underlying data. In an ESG context, materiality typically refers to ESG-related issues that are expected to affect a company's operations, its financial performance, and the valuation of its securities. In overall financial reporting, information is considered to be material if omission or misstatement of the information could influence users' decisions. Companies' as well as stakeholders' definitions of materiality in an ESG context may differ. Some companies may use the term "material" in emphasizing positive ESG information, although such information may have little impact on the company's operations or financial performance. In contrast, a company may minimize or not report negative ESG information that investors might consider material.

Analysts also consider their investment horizon and holding period when deciding which ESG factors to consider in their analysis, especially credit analysts, because of the different maturities of bonds. Some ESG issues may affect a company's performance in the short term, whereas other issues may be more long term in nature. It is important to note that the time horizon of ESG factors' impact can move from the long term to the short term and vice versa depending on a wide variety of external factors, such as a sudden change in regulation or an ESG-related controversy such as an oil spill. An investor with a short-term investment horizon may find that longer-term ESG issues can have little effect on a security's market value in the near term. Consider a manufacturing company operating in an industry that is expected to face stricter environmental regulations in the future. An investor with a short-term horizon may expect that the company's profitability will not be affected in the short term. An investor with a long-term horizon, however, may anticipate costly upgrades to plants and equipment or significant regulatory fines that are likely to reduce profitability over the longer term.

Relevant ESG-Related Factors

Corporate governance considerations, such as the structure of the board of directors, are often reasonably consistent across most companies, although best practices vary greatly regionally. In contrast, there is no globally accepted best practice with regard to environmental and social considerations. When identifying a company's specific ESG risks and opportunities, analysts must determine the relevant factors that affect its industry. For example, energy companies are clearly more affected by environmental factors, whereas banking institutions are typically more affected by social factors (e.g., data security and privacy issues or customer satisfaction) than by environmental factors. Meanwhile, both industries are subject to governance factors. Once an analyst has determined which ESG-related factors are relevant to a company's industry, the analyst can identify applicable qualitative and quantitative data.

Approaches used to identify a company's (or industry's) ESG factors include (1) proprietary methods, (2) ratings and analysis from ESG data providers, and (3) not-for-profit industry initiatives and sustainability reporting frameworks. For example, Access to Nutrition Index evaluates the world's largest food and beverage manufacturers' policies and performance related to the most pressing nutrition challenges: obesity and undernutrition. Each of the above approaches can be used independently, or a combination of approaches can be used.

The first way of identifying company and industry ESG factors is the proprietary method approach. In this approach, analysts use their own judgment or their firm's proprietary tools to identify ESG information by researching companies, news reports, industry associations, environmental groups, financial markets, labor organizations, industry experts, and government organizations. Company-specific ESG data are generally publicly available from such sources as annual reports, corporate citizenship or sustainability reports, proxy reports, and regulatory filings (e.g., the annual 10-K report required by the US Securities and Exchange Commission). Company disclosures can generally be found on company websites.

Exhibit 2 illustrates an example of how management of one key ESG-related issue—climate change—is disclosed by City Developments Limited (CDL) in its sustainability report. Note that other real estate companies may report this information differently. In fact, ESG disclosures in general can range from minimal reporting to comprehensive data and information that span several pages, thus potentially creating comparability issues for analysts. As we discuss later in this section, a number of organizations and initiatives are working toward voluntary or mandatory standardization of various ESG-related metrics.

Exhibit 2: Climate Change Scenario Planning for City Developments Limited

Aligned with the recommendations of Task Force on Climate-related Financial Disclosures (TCFD) and Intergovernmental Panel on Climate Change (IPCC), CDL aims to better prepare its business for the potential financial impacts of both physical and transition risks of climate change.

CDL approached the study with two scenarios by 2030: one in which it assumed the world would decarbonize fast enough to meet the Paris Agreement's goal of limiting climate change to a global average surface temperature rise of 2°C; and another scenario that used a more ambitious 1.5°C above pre-industrial level rise. A systematic and cohesive approach was used to holistically assess and quantify all potential impacts on CDL's selected portfolio from material climate-related risks and opportunities.

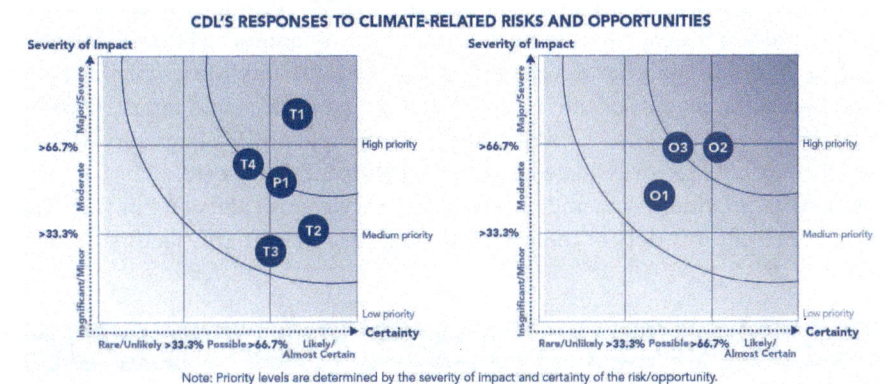

CDL'S RESPONSES TO CLIMATE-RELATED RISKS AND OPPORTUNITIES

Note: Priority levels are determined by the severity of impact and certainty of the risk/opportunity.

Source:

Transition Risks

T1	Climate-related policy risks (e.g., increased carbon taxes and more-stringent building standards) increase operating and construction costs
T2	Water security risks increase operating costs and disrupt business continuity
T3	Call for companies to take greater responsibility of their waste production, leading to increased operating costs

Transition Risks

T4	Climate risks lead to higher insurance premiums, lower coverage, and expose uninsurable assets

Physical Risks

P1	Increased frequency and severity of climate events such as floods and heat-waves increase the risk of stranded assets

Opportunities

O1	Consumer activism is on the rise globally
O2	Global shift to low-carbon growth is gaining steam
O3	Pioneering adoption of green finance in Singapore

Source: CDL, "Integrated Sustainability Report 2020."

The second approach in identifying company/industry ESG factors—ESG data providers—involves the use of information supplied by an ESG data provider (vendor), such as MSCI or Sustainalytics. These vendors obtain publicly available corporate ESG disclosures and translate them into individual ESG analyses, scores, and/or rankings for each company in the vendor's universe, often with subjective assessments by ESG analysts. In addition, vendors may score and/or rank companies within their industries and provide detailed industry analyses relating to ESG considerations.

The third approach in identifying ESG factors involves the consideration of not-for-profit initiatives and sustainability reporting frameworks that provide data and insights on ESG issues. These include the International Integrated Reporting Council (IIRC), the Global Reporting Initiative (GRI), the Sustainable Accounting Standards Board (SASB), and the 2° Investing Initiative (2DII), to name a few. The IIRC is a coalition of industry participants that promotes a standardized framework of ESG disclosures in corporate reporting. The GRI has worked with various stakeholder groups to develop sustainability reporting standards. These standards include a list of business activity groups (industries) with relevant sustainability topics that correspond to each group. A GRI report excerpt relating to the consumer durables and household and personal products sector is shown in Exhibit 3. The exhibit indicates the proposed ESG-related topics for this sector as well as additional specifications on these topics, if available. The SASB seeks to promote uniform accounting standards for sustainability reporting. In doing so, it has developed the SASB Materiality Map, which lists relevant ESG-related, sector-specific factors that the organization and industry working groups deem to be material. Exhibit 4 displays a sample SASB Materiality Map that shows the key ESG factors (shaded boxes) for the health care sector.

As well as providing data and analysis, ESG service providers and not-for-profit initiatives provide a variety of tools to help integrate relevant ESG factors.

Exhibit 3: GRI Sustainability Topics—Consumer Durables and Household and Personal Products Sector

Category	Proposed Topic	Topic Specification (where applicable)
Environmental	Materials sourcing	Rare metals; Sourcing standards for raw materials; Sourcing standards on animal testing; Wood-based products from responsibly managed forests
	Product packaging	Not applicable
	Plastic use	Product and packaging

Category	Proposed Topic	Topic Specification (where applicable)
	Chemicals use	International and national chemical safe use regulations; Personal care products; Phthalates and parabens
	Energy efficiency of end products	Consumer electronics
	Life cycle assessment of products	Not applicable
	Product transport efficiency	Not applicable
Social	Migrant workers	Recruitment and employment
	Product safety	Personal care products—human health and the environment
	Transparent product information and labeling	Not applicable
	Access to products, technologies, and services	Consumers with disabilities
	Electronic waste (e-waste) management	Consumer awareness
	Product design	Eco-friendly personal care products
	Product innovation	Energy consumption, GHG emissions and packaging
Other	Corporate governance	Executive board compensation; Gender participation on governance bodies
	Supplier screening	Environmental and social standards in the supply chain

Source: GRI, "Sustainability Topics for Sectors: What Do Stakeholders Want to Know?" (2013).

Exhibit 4: SASB Materiality Map—Health Care Sector

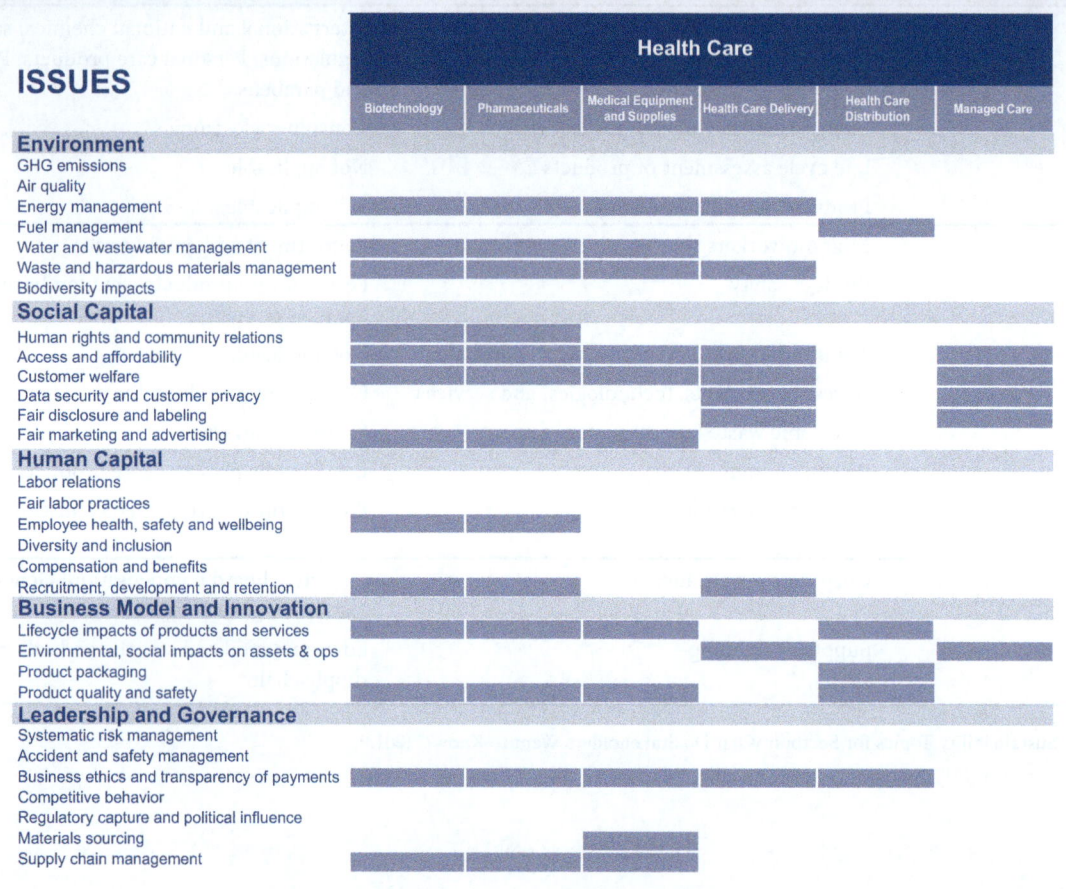

Source: Sustainability Accounting Standards Board.

From a risk/reward perspective, the use of **ESG integration**—the implementation of qualitative and quantitative ESG factors in traditional security and industry analysis as well as portfolio construction—typically differs for equity and fixed-income (debt) analysis. In equity analysis, ESG integration is used to both identify potential opportunities and mitigate downside risk, whereas in fixed-income analysis, ESG integration is generally focused on mitigating downside risk as the bond redeems at par on maturity.

The process of identifying and evaluating relevant ESG-related factors is reasonably similar for both equity and corporate credit analysis, because they share the same above-mentioned proprietary methods although material factors may differ based on relevance to credit. ESG integration techniques are also reasonably similar, such as adjustments to forecasted financial metrics and ratios, although the implication differs in practice.

In equity security analysis, ESG-related factors are often analyzed in the context of forecasting financial metrics and ratios, adjusting valuation model variables (e.g., discount rate), or using sensitivity and/or scenario analysis. For example, an analyst might increase her forecast of a hotel company's operating costs because of the impacts of excessive employee turnover—lost productivity, reduced customer satisfaction, and increased expenses for employee searches, temporary workers, and training programs. As another example, an analyst might choose to lower the discount rate for a snack food company that is expected to gain a competitive advantage by transitioning to a sustainable source of a key ingredient in its products.

In credit analysis, ESG factors may be integrated using internal credit assessments, forecasting financial ratios, and relative credit ranking of companies (or governments). In terms of valuation, relative value, spread, duration, and sensitivity/scenario analysis are often used. For example, an analyst may include the effect of lawsuits on the credit ratios, cash flow, or liquidity of a toy company. The same analyst may also estimate the potential for the credit spreads of the toy company's bonds to widen from these lawsuits. Generally speaking, the effect on the credit spreads of an issuer's debt obligations or its credit default swaps (CDSs) may differ depending on maturity. As a different example, consider an analyst who believes that a coal company faces long-term risk from potential **stranded assets**—that is, assets that are obsolete or not economically viable, often owing to changes in regulatory or government policy and/or shifts in demand. In this case, the analyst may believe that valuation of the coal company's 10-year-maturity notes would be considerably more negatively affected than its 1-year-maturity notes.

One particular type of bond an analyst might encounter is a **green bond**. The sidebar "Green Bonds" provides more detail about these securities and how investors typically analyze them. Increasingly, investors use scenario analysis and stress tests to assess the potential impact of key factors, such as physical risks of climate change.

GREEN BONDS

Green bonds are bonds in which the proceeds are designated by issuers to fund a specific project or portfolio of projects that have environmental or climate benefits. The first green bond, the Climate Awareness Bond, was issued by the European Investment Bank in 2007. Issuers have the primary decision for labeling their bonds "green." This decision is made in close cooperation with the lead underwriter. At a minimum level, issuers provide detail to the investors about the green eligibility criteria for the use of proceeds, in line with the Green Bond Principles (discussed in the next paragraph). Issuers are responsible for providing investors with details on the criteria used to classify the bonds as green and how the bond's proceeds are used. In some cases, issuers may commission independent reviews of the green criteria to provide investors with greater transparency. Issuers of green bonds typically incur additional costs related to the monitoring and reporting of the use of the bond's proceeds. However, these issuers may benefit from a more diversified investor base and potentially a new-issue premium if demand is strong.

The Green Bond Principles, a set of voluntary standards to guide issuers in the determination of labeling a bond as green, were developed in 2014 by a consortium of investment banks. Ongoing monitoring and further development of the Green Bond Principles is the responsibility of the International Capital Market Association, a global securities self-regulatory organization. As the green bond market has evolved, index providers, credit rating agencies, and the not-for-profit Climate Bonds Initiative have developed their own methodologies or standards to assess labeled green bonds. In addition, the European Commission is exploring the feasibility of imposing specific criteria that must be met for a bond to be labeled green.

Green bonds typically resemble an issuer's conventional bonds, with the exception that the bond proceeds are earmarked for green projects. Green bonds normally have the same credit ratings and bondholder recourse as conventional bonds of the same issuer (all else being equal). In addition to conventional or "plain vanilla" corporate bonds, other types of green bonds include project bonds, mortgage-backed and asset-backed securities, and municipal bonds. For example, the state of California's $300 million general obligation 2014 green bond issue is backed by the state's General Fund, just as California's other general obligation bonds are.

Because only the use of proceeds differs, the analysis and valuation of green bonds are essentially the same as those of conventional bonds. Some green bonds, however, may command a premium, or tighter credit spread, versus comparable conventional bonds because of market demand. One unique risk of green bonds is **greenwashing**, which is the risk that the bond's proceeds are not actually used for a beneficial environmental or climate-related project. Greenwashing can result in an investor overpaying for a bond

> (if the investor paid a premium for the bond's green feature) or holding a bond that does not satisfy a prescribed environmental or climate investment mandate. Liquidity risk may also be a consideration for green bonds, given that they are often purchased by buy-and-hold investors.

5   EVALUATING ESG-RELATED RISKS AND OPPORTUNITIES

☐ | evaluate ESG risk exposures and investment opportunities related to a company

By integrating ESG considerations into the investment process, investors can take a broader perspective of company and industry analysis. In this way, the potential effects of ESG factors on a company's financial statements and valuation can be assessed and, in turn, can help drive investment decisions. In this section, we discuss examples of how ESG considerations can be integrated into financial analysis and valuation, from both an equity and a corporate bond perspective.

ESG Integration

A typical starting point for ESG integration is the identification of material qualitative and quantitative ESG factors that pertain to a company or its industry. An analyst may evaluate these factors on both a historical and a forecast basis, as well as relative to a company's peers, and then make relevant adjustments to a company's financial statements or valuation. ESG-related adjustments to a company's income statement and cash flow statement typically relate to projected revenues, operating/non-operating costs, operating margins, earnings, capital expenditures, or other items. ESG-related adjustments to a company's balance sheet often reflect an analyst's estimate of impaired assets. For equities, valuation adjustments often include adjusting a company's cost of capital using the discount rate or a multiple of price or terminal value. For bonds, an analyst may adjust an issuer's credit spread or CDS to reflect anticipated effects from ESG considerations.

The use of qualitative and quantitative research, as well as securities valuation of equities and fixed income, are key elements of the "ESG Integration Framework" (see Exhibit 5). Portfolio construction, asset allocation, scenario analysis, and risk management form the remainder of this framework.

Exhibit 5: The ESG Integration Framework

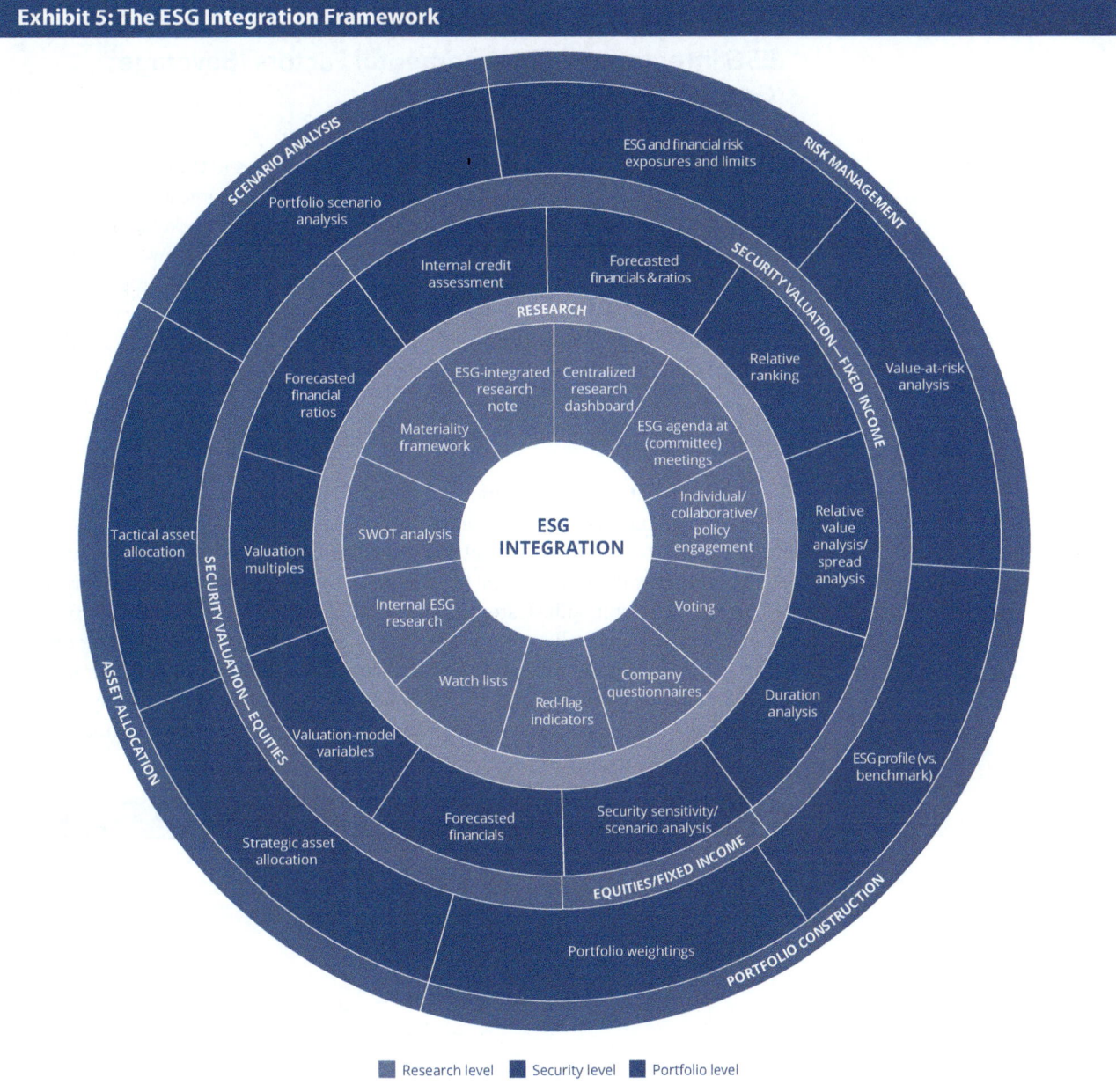

Source: Guidance and Case Studies for ESG Integration: Equities and Fixed Income, 2018

Examples of ESG Integration

This section provides examples of ESG integration for three fictitious companies in different industries: beverages, pharmaceuticals, and banks. For simplicity, each integration example focuses on either environmental, social, or governance factors—largely depending on which is most relevant for that company or its industry. Note that although specific industries are used in the examples, the underlying concepts can be applied to other industries as well. Finally, given the scope of this reading, we focus on the *effects* of ESG integration on financial analysis and valuation rather than the computations involved.

EXAMPLE 3

ESG Integration—Environmental Factors (Beverage Company)

1. Based in the United States, Frizzle Drinks (Frizzle) is a fictitious non-alcoholic beverage company that ranks among the largest in the world. Frizzle operates in both developed and emerging markets, including countries where water is scarce. Frizzle is a significant user of water in its operations. Given that water is a key ingredient in Frizzle's beverages, the continued availability of water is critical to the company's manufacturing process. Because of its extensive use of water, Frizzle faces ongoing regulatory scrutiny for pollution and effects on climate change. Ultimately, how Frizzle conserves and manages its water usage has implications for product pricing and company/brand reputation.

   Sam Smith, CFA, is analyzing the effects of environmental factors on Frizzle's financial statements. Based on his research, Smith considers "water intensity" to be a key ESG metric for the beverage industry. Water intensity is defined as the ratio of total liters of water used per one liter of a beverage product. Exhibit 6 illustrates the trend of Frizzle's water intensity ratio from 2009 to 2021, as well as the consensus forecast ratio for the subsequent four years. Frizzle has steadily decreased its water usage over the past several years. From 2009 to 2021, its water intensity ratio declined by 27%. By the end of 2025(F), the company aims to reduce its water intensity by another 13%.

   Exhibit 6: Water Intensity Ratio (in liters)

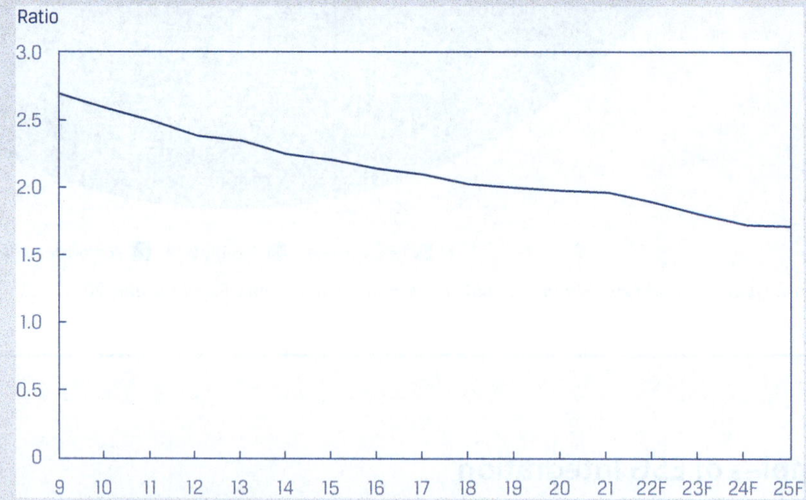

   Note: (F) indicates forecast year.

   Exhibit 7 compares the year-over-year change in Frizzle's water intensity ratio with that of its peer group over the past three years. To facilitate comparison among companies of varying sizes, Smith normalized the reported water intensity ratios by calculating the water intensity ratio per $1 million of revenue. Exhibit 7 illustrates that Frizzle's water intensity has decreased considerably relative to its peers over the past few years, particularly in the last reported year, 2021.

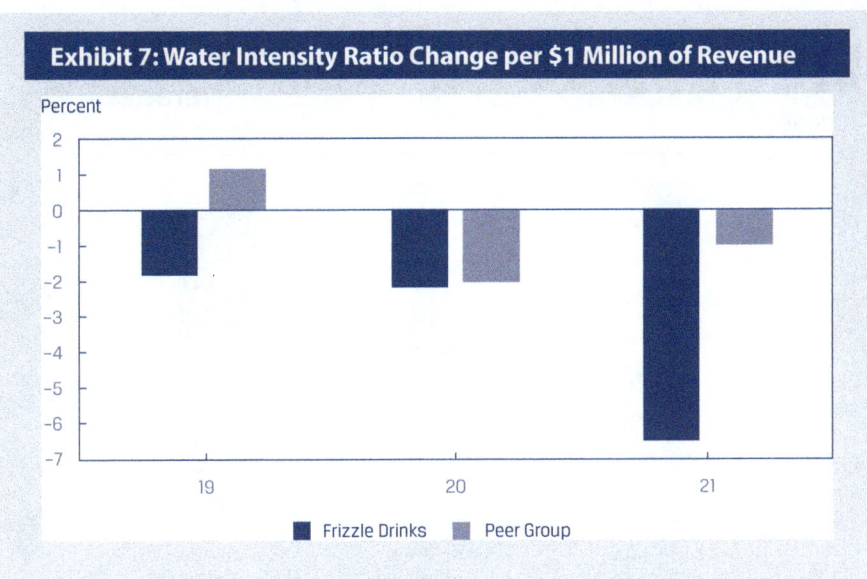

Exhibit 7: Water Intensity Ratio Change per $1 Million of Revenue

Next, Smith analyzes the effects of Frizzle's water intensity on its overall financial performance and compares it with the adjusted financial performance of its peers. As one example, Smith adjusts Frizzle's operating costs to account for the improved effects of water intensity (i.e., reduced usage). For the first projected year, 2022, Smith expects that Frizzle's cost of goods sold as a percentage of revenues (before any ESG adjustment) will be 40% and its peer group average will be 42%. For the same forecast period, Smith assumes that Frizzle's reduction in water intensity will result in a 1% reduction in its cost of goods sold/revenues, whereas the peer group average will remain the same. Exhibit 8 demonstrates this improvement in cost of goods sold/revenues on both an absolute and a relative basis. By extension, Exhibit 9 shows the absolute and relative improvement in Frizzle's gross margin (sales minus cost of goods sold) percentage.

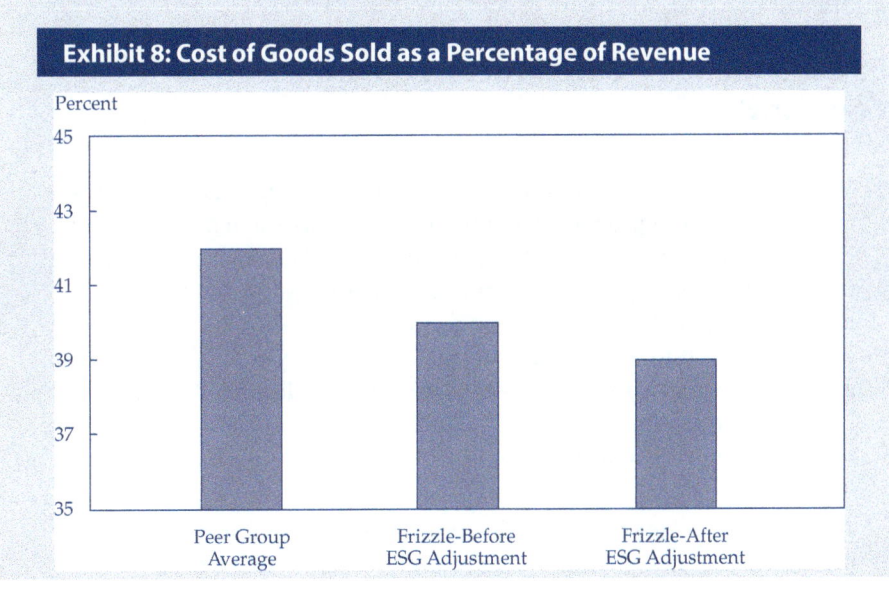

Exhibit 8: Cost of Goods Sold as a Percentage of Revenue

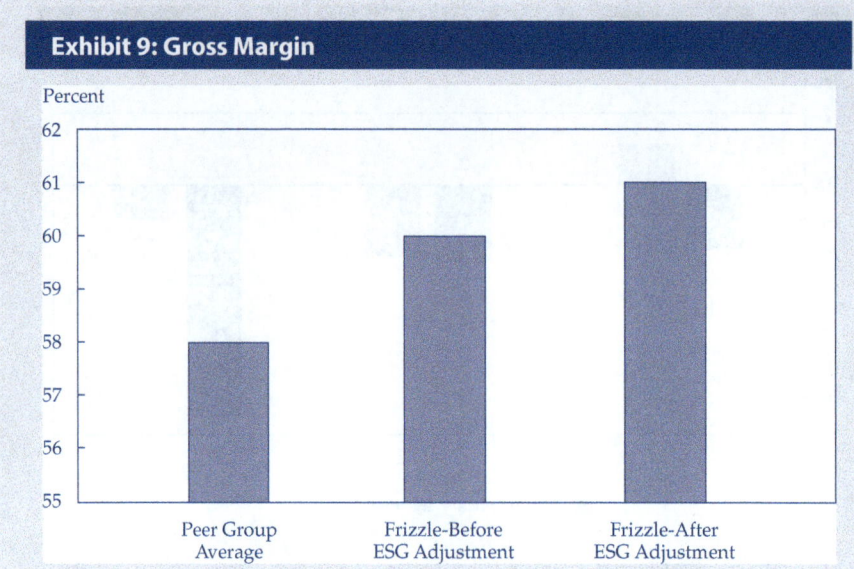

Exhibit 9: Gross Margin

In the last step of the integration analysis, Smith incorporates Frizzle's adjusted financial performance in valuing Frizzle's stock, bonds, and, if applicable, CDSs. In this example, Smith judges that Frizzle's lower cost of goods sold from the adjustment would result in higher forecast earnings and, all else being equal, a theoretically higher fair value for Frizzle's stock. With respect to Frizzle's bonds and CDSs, Frizzle's operating cash flow would improve through a lower cost of goods sold. When assessing the credit spreads of Frizzle's bonds and/or CDSs, Smith will analyze whether the lower relative ESG risk is already reflected in current spread levels and adjust accordingly.

EXAMPLE 4

ESG Integration—Social Factors (Pharmaceutical Company)

1. Well Pharma (Well) is a fictitious European pharmaceutical company that manufactures drug products for autoimmune diseases and immune disorders. Over the last five years, Well has had the weakest track record among its peers in terms of product recalls and regulatory warning letters for manufacturing and marketing-related violations. Specifically, the company has been subject to four major drug quality and safety scandals arising from adverse side effects. These scandals have resulted in lost sales, multiple lawsuits, and significant fines. Business disruptions, lawsuits, and fines have reduced revenues and increased costs for the company.

   As Well's experience shows, product quality is a material social factor for pharmaceutical companies in general. Smith assumes that a drug company's product quality is a combination of the factors shown in Exhibit 10.

Exhibit 10: Social Factors—Pharmaceuticals

Factor	Description
Product Quality Controversies	Have there been any controversies linked to the company's product or service quality and responsibility?
Regulatory Warning Letters	Number of regulatory warning letters received by the company
Product Recalls	Number and severity of product recalls (voluntary and involuntary)
Regulatory Fines	Level of fines imposed by regulator linked to poor product quality and/or irresponsible behavior
Product Quality Certifications Percentage	Percentage of plants certified according to a widely accepted product safety/quality standard (e.g., ISO 9001 or equivalent)

Exhibit 11 shows the number of regulatory warning letters received, as well as product and marketing controversies faced, by Well and several peers. As the graph shows, Well has received significantly more of these letters than its peers have.

Exhibit 11: Regulatory Warning Letters and Product Quality Controversies

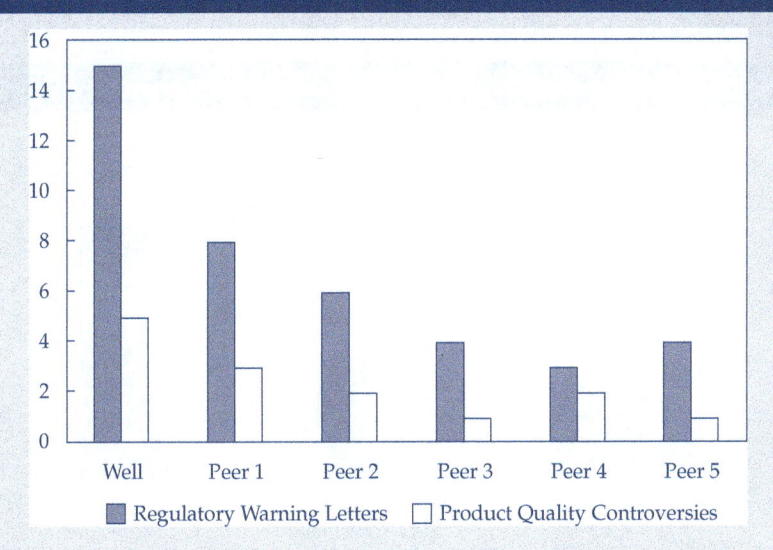

Exhibit 12 demonstrates how the factors listed in Exhibit 10 may affect the financial statements of Well and other pharmaceutical companies.

Exhibit 12: Social Factor Effects on Financial Performance

Factor	Financial Impact
Product Quality Controversies	Damage to brand value resulting in potential decrease in sales
Regulatory Warning Letters	Increased costs to comply with regulatory requirements

Factor	Financial Impact
Product Recalls	Losses in sales revenue; increased costs of implementing product recalls
Regulatory Fines	Provisions for pharmaceutical sales returns and product-related litigation
Product Quality Certifications Percentage	Lower percentage increases risks of product quality issues, leading to product recalls and related costs

Based on these financial effects, Smith adjusts Well's projected revenues, operating expenses, and non-operating expenses. The nature of these financial statement adjustments will likely differ depending on whether Smith expects these product quality issues to be recurring or non-recurring in nature. Smith assumes that revenues will decrease by 2% over the next year because of existing product quality controversies. For operating expenses, Smith assumes that Well's cost of goods sold relative to revenues will increase by 1.3% to reflect product quality and additional investments in its manufacturing process. Exhibit 13 shows that Well's cost of goods sold as a percentage of revenues is in line with that of its peers, but the additional costs will increase this ratio well above that of the peer group. In addition to operating expenses, Smith forecasts that Well's non-operating expenses, such as restructuring charges, and other non-recurring costs will be an additional 4.5% of operating income. Exhibit 14 shows the current non-operating expense ratio for Well versus its peer group average, as well as the forecast amount.

Exhibit 13: Cost of Goods Sold as a Percentage of Revenue

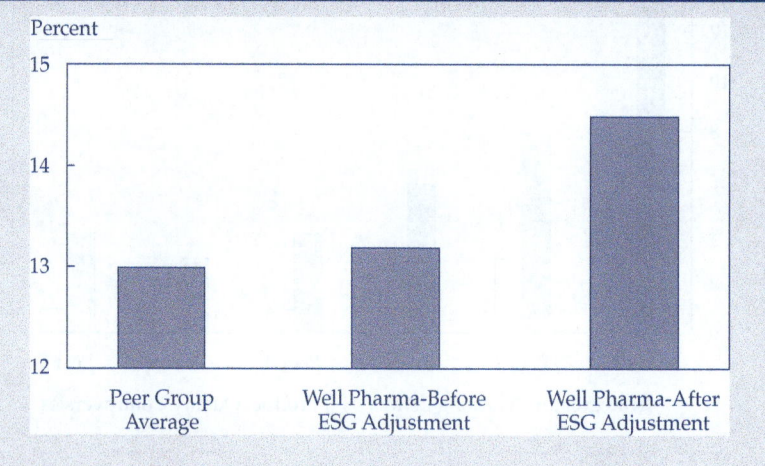

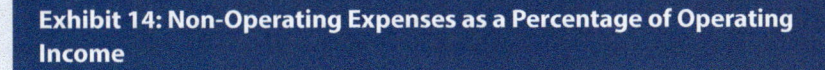

Exhibit 14: Non-Operating Expenses as a Percentage of Operating Income

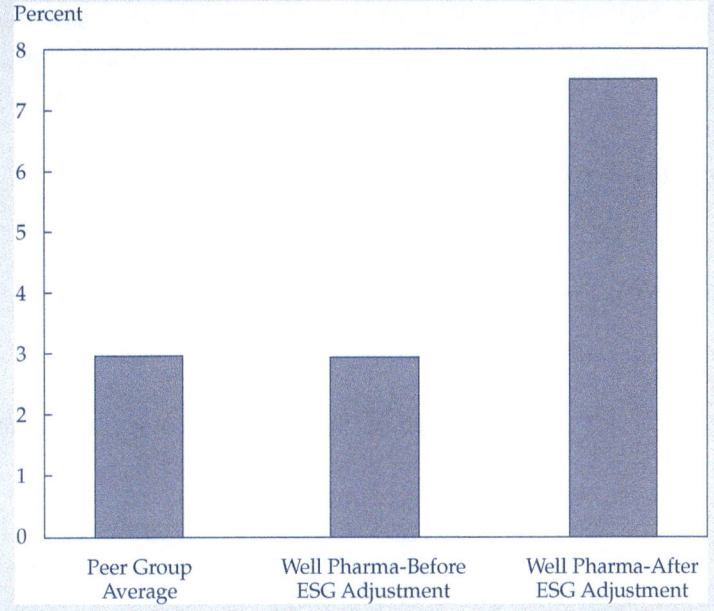

Smith believes that the valuation implications for Well's stock and bonds could be significant based on its poor product quality and safety track record. Expectations of future poor performance could have a direct impact on earnings and cash flow to the detriment of both shareholders and bondholders. In addition, Smith believes there could be adverse valuation implications if investors view Well's brand value and reputation as impaired.

EXAMPLE 5

ESG Integration—Governance Factors (Bank Holding Company)

1. Sumiyoshi Banking Group (Sumiyoshi) is a fictitious Japanese bank holding company, with operations in Japan (80% of revenues), the United States, and Southeast Asia. Sumiyoshi's core businesses are commercial banking, leasing, securities, and consumer finance. As with most global banks, corporate governance reforms have become increasingly prominent for Sumiyoshi.

   Smith has prepared Exhibit 15 to show how Sumiyoshi's board of directors compares with the majority of its domestic peer group, on the basis of governance factors discussed in Section 2 of this reading.

Exhibit 15: Corporate Governance Factors—Banks

	Domestic peer group	Sumiyoshi Bank
Board type	Two tier	Two tier
Board size, no. of directors	13	14
Total assets/director	JPY14.9 million	JPY13.3 million
CEO duality	Yes	Yes

	Domestic peer group	Sumiyoshi Bank
Independent chairperson	Yes	No
Board independence %	47%	36%
Board gender diversity	17% female; 83% male	7% female; 93% male
Directors with long tenure (>10 years)	0%	14%
Number of board committees	5	4
Audit, nomination, remuneration, and risk committees in place?	Yes	Yes
Additional board committees?	Yes, governance committee	No
Non-executive directors with industry executive experience/total independent directors	67%	20%
Short-term and long-term incentive plan metrics disclosed?	No	No
Concentrated ownership	No single large shareholder	No single large shareholder
Say-on-pay provision	Yes	No
Straight voting	Yes	Yes
Dual-class shares	No	No

Smith notes that Sumiyoshi lags its peers in in several elements of board composition, such as the lack of an independent chairperson, a lower level of board independence and diversity, fewer board members with industry executive experience, and a number of board directors with long tenures. In addition to board composition, Smith uses credit risk as a proxy for a bank's corporate governance risk. In particular, Smith reviews one key banking credit measure—non-performing loans (NPLs). NPLs are loans that are not current in paying the contractual amounts that are due (i.e., interest or principal payments).

Smith analyzes Sumiyoshi's credit risk by dividing its NPLs by the amount of its total loans outstanding. Smith estimates that Sumiyoshi's ratio of NPLs to total loans is 50 bps higher than its peer group average, reflecting Sumiyoshi's comparatively weaker credit/governance risk. To account for the effect of higher credit risk than that of its peers, Smith may increase the risk premium embedded in his valuation of Sumiyoshi's stock. When valuing Sumiyoshi's corporate bonds, Smith might increase the credit spread relative to peers embedded in the company's outstanding issues.

SUMMARY

- Shareholder ownership structures are commonly classified as dispersed, concentrated, or a hybrid of the two.

- Dispersed ownership reflects the existence of many shareholders, none of which, either individually or collectively, has the ability to exercise control over the corporation. Concentrated corporate ownership reflects an individual shareholder or a group (controlling shareholders) with the ability to exercise control over the corporation.

- Controlling shareholders may be either majority shareholders or minority shareholders.

- Horizontal ownership involves companies with mutual business interests that have cross-holding share arrangements with each other. Vertical (or pyramid) ownership involves a company or group that has a controlling interest in two or more holding companies, which in turn have controlling interests in various operating companies.

- Dual-class (or multiple-class) shares grant one or more share classes superior or even sole voting rights while other share classes have inferior or no voting rights.

- Types of influential owners include banks, families, sovereign governments, institutional investors, group companies, private equity firms, foreign investors, managers, and board directors.

- A corporation's board of directors is typically structured as either one tier or two tier. A one-tier board consists of a single board of directors, composed of executive (internal) and non-executive (external) directors. A two-tier board consists of a supervisory board that oversees a management board.

- CEO duality exists when the chief executive officer also serves as chairperson of the board.

- A primary challenge of integrating ESG factors into investment analysis is identifying and obtaining information that is relevant, comparable, and decision-useful.

- ESG information and metrics are inconsistently reported by companies, and such disclosure is voluntary, which provides additional challenges for analysts.

- In an ESG context, materiality typically refers to ESG-related issues that are expected to affect a company's operations or financial performance and the valuation of its securities.

- Corporate governance considerations, such as the structure of the board of directors, tend to be reasonably consistent across most companies. In contrast, environmental and social considerations often differ greatly.

- Analysts typically use three main sources of information to identify a company's (or industry's) ESG factors: (1) proprietary research, (2) ratings and analysis from ESG data providers, or (3) research from not-for-profit industry organizations and initiatives.

- In equity analysis, ESG integration is used to both identify potential opportunities and mitigate downside risk, whereas in fixed-income analysis, ESG integration is generally focused on mitigating downside risk.

- A typical starting point for ESG integration is the identification of material qualitative and quantitative ESG factors that pertain to a company or its industry.

PRACTICE PROBLEMS

The following information relates to questions 1-6

Theresa Blass manages the Toptier Balanced Fund (the Fund) and recently hired John Yorkton, a junior analyst, to help her research investment opportunities. Blass plans to integrate environmental, social, and governance (ESG) factors into her analysis. She is researching an equity investment in Titian International, a global steel producer. She asks Yorkton to identify ESG factors impacting Titian and estimate the equity valuation for the company. Yorkton uses proprietary methods to identify the ESG factors.

Yorkton points out that Titian's steel production is energy intensive and relies on coal in producing its main product, stainless steel. The firm's major customers are oil and gas firms using stainless steel in their drilling operations. Most of Titian's steel capacity is located in developing economies, where it currently faces few environmental regulations. Titian has a 10-member board with a chairperson and 5 independent members. The chairperson is not the CEO, and the board is diverse, with 6 women. The company has an excellent record on employee health and safety. In a discussion with Blass about ESG factors in investment analysis, Yorkton makes the following statements:

Statement 1   Material ESG information used in investment analysis is best obtained from the individual companies.

Statement 2   The level of disclosure varies among companies because these disclosures are voluntary.

Statement 3   The time horizon has little effect on the materiality of the underlying ESG factors.

Yorkton integrates ESG factors into the equity valuation of Titian. He believes the company faces significant long-term risk due to regulatory changes regarding greenhouse gas emissions in the developing economies. These changes will have a negative impact on Titian's steel capacity and its production costs. Based on long-term forecasts from the International Energy Agency (IEA), Yorkton expects oil and natural gas demand to decline over the next decade, reducing oil company capital expenditures on exploration and drilling. He uses a discounted cash flow model to value Titian stock.

1. The potential problem with Yorkton's approach to identifying ESG factors is the:

   A. promotion of uniform accounting standards.

   B. subjective assessment of ESG scores and rankings.

   C. inconsistent reporting of ESG information and metrics among firms.

2. The most relevant industry risk factors affecting Titian are:

   A. social.

   B. governance.

   C. environmental.

3. Which of the statements made by Yorkton on ESG factors in investment analysis is correct?

   A. Statement 1

   B. Statement 2

   C. Statement 3

4. Titian faces long-term risk from _____ due to potential regulatory changes in the developing economies.

5. Yorkton's ESG integration approach is likely to impact equity valuation by:

   A. increasing revenues.

   B. raising the discount rate.

   C. reducing operating costs.

6. After integrating the ESG factors into the discounted cash flow model, the equity value of Titian is likely to:

   A. decrease.

   B. remain unchanged.

   C. increase.

The following information relates to questions 7-10

Emily Marker, CFA, is a fixed-income analyst for the Namsan Funds. Her supervisor asks her to identify ESG factors and value the corporate bonds of BR Hotels, a publicly traded boutique hotel company. Marker notes that BR Hotels is a "green hotel" company that prioritizes sustainability and has successfully reduced water and energy usage at its hotels. The founding family owns 55% of the outstanding shares. Each ownership share has equivalent voting rights. The board of directors of BR Hotels consists of 15 members, with independent CEO and chairperson roles. The board includes one independent member and two women, and 20% of the board members have experience in the hotel industry.

BR Hotels has historically had a high labor turnover rate. Most of its workforce are paid at or near the minimum wage, and the company offers no health benefits. Marker and her supervisor discuss how BR Hotels will be affected by the expected passage of legislation raising the minimum wage and growing pressure to offer benefits. Marker integrates ESG factors in the investment valuation of BR Hotels' corporate bonds.

7. The potential conflict between or among shareholders and managers of BR Hotels can best be described as:

   A. voting caps.

   B. a principal-agent problem.

   C. a principal-principal problem.

8. BR Hotels' corporate governance risk is increased by:

    A. CEO duality.

    B. family control.

    C. the low percentage of independent board members.

9. The security analysis of BR Hotels is most *likely* focused on:

    A. mitigating downside risk.

    B. adjusting the discount rate.

    C. identifying potential opportunities.

10. After integrating the ESG factors, the credit spread on BR Hotels' bonds is most likely to:

    A. decrease.

    B. remain unchanged.

    C. increase.

SOLUTIONS

1. C is correct. Yorkton uses the proprietary method to identify company and industry ESG factors. This approach relies on using company-specific ESG data that is publicly available from annual reports, proxy reports, corporate sustainability reports, and regulatory filings such as the 10-K. The problem is inconsistent reporting of ESG information and metrics among firms. The level of disclosure also varies considerably among companies because ESG-related disclosures are voluntary. This creates comparability issues for analysts.

   A is incorrect because the promotion of uniform accounting standards is an alternative approach used to identify ESG reports. This approach involves not-for-profit initiatives and sustainability reporting frameworks that develop a standardized framework of ESG disclosures in corporate reporting. As an example, the Sustainable Accounting Standards Board (SASB) seeks to promote uniform accounting standards.

   B is incorrect because it relates to an alternative approach to identifying company and industry ESG factors. This approach involves using information supplied by ESG data vendors, such MSCI or Sustainalytics. The vendors provide ESG scores and/or rankings for each company. The problem with this approach is the subjective element to the interpretation of ESG scores and rankings.

2. C is correct. In identifying a company's ESG risks and opportunities, an analyst must determine which ESG factors are relevant to its industry. Industries such as energy and steel are typically more impacted by environmental factors. This is clearly the case with Titian. Titian's steel production is energy intensive and relies on coal in producing its main product, stainless steel. Its major customers are oil and natural gas companies, and most of its steel capacity is located in developing economies, where it currently faces few environmental regulations. Changes in such regulations and projected declining demand for its main product are major risk factors for the firm.

   B is incorrect because social factors are typically not the most important industry-related ESG risk factors for steel companies. Employee health and safety is a material social factor for this company. This is not a risk since the company has an excellent record on employee health and safety.

   C is incorrect because governance factors are not a major risk for Titian. Titian's board comprises 10 members, of whom 5 are independent. In addition, the board has gender diversity and no CEO duality, since the chairperson is not the CEO.

3. B is correct. Statement 2 is correct because the level of disclosure varies considerably among companies since ESG-related disclosures are voluntary. This creates a comparability issue for analysts. This is a problem associated with the proprietary methods used to identify company and industry ESG factors.

   A is incorrect because Statement 1 is incorrect. The problems in doing ESG investment analysis based on company information are that the reporting of this information is inconsistent and that disclosures vary among companies.

   C is incorrect because Statement 3 is incorrect. The time horizon is an important factor affecting the materiality of the underlying ESGfactors. Some ESG issues may affect a company's performance in the short term, whereas other issues may be more relevant in the long term. This is especially true in credit analysis because of the different maturities of the bonds.

4. Titian faces long-term risk from *stranded assets* due to potential regulatory

changes in the developing economies.

If regulatory changes on greenhouse gas emissions are enacted in these developing economies, much of Titian's stainless steel capacity will become obsolete or not economically viable. This will result in ESG-related adjustments to Titian's balance sheet. The further reduction in oil demand will make the steel capacity economically unviable.

5. B is correct. Titian faces significant long-term environmental risk factors. The imposition of stricter regulation on greenhouse gas emissions in the developing countries will result in stranded assets, as much of Titian steel capacity becomes obsolete and not economically viable. Shifting away from low-cost coal usage will likely result in higher operating costs, and declining oil and natural gas demand will result in lower revenues for stainless steel. Thus Yorkton should raise the discount rate for Titian to account for the higher environmental risk.

   A is incorrect because Titian's revenues are likely to decline as a result of the projected fall in demand for oil and natural gas. As a result, oil and natural gas companies will cut their exploration and drilling budgets and reduce their purchases of stainless steel.

   C is incorrect since operating costs are likely to rise as Titian shifts away from using low-cost coal to more expensive energy sources.

6. A is correct. The stock price for Titian is likely to decline. Titian faces significant long-term environmental risk as a result of more stringent future regulation on greenhouse gas emissions in the developing economies and a future decline in demand for its main product, stainless steel. Thus in the discount cash flow model, Titian should increase the cost of equity and most likely lower the growth rate in cash flow. Both factors will cause the price to fall.

   B is incorrect since the price of Titian is likely to decline and not remain unchanged.

   C is incorrect since the price of Titian is likely to decline and not increase.

7. C is correct. BR Hotels has concentrated ownership, given that the family owns 55% of the shares. It also has concentrated voting power, since each ownership share has equal voting rights. In this ownership structure, the controlling shareholders have power over both management and minority shareholders. The controlling shareholders are referred to as strong shareholders and the managers as weak managers. The conflict in this structure exists between the controlling shareholders and the minority shareholders. The controlling shareholders can potentially divert resources for their own benefit at the expense of the minority shareholders. This conflict is referred to as a principal-principal problem.

   A is incorrect since the conflict for BR Hotels is a principal-principal problem. Voting caps are legal restrictions on the voting rights of large share positions. They result from an ownership structure of concentrated ownership and dispersed voting rights.

   B is incorrect since the conflict for BR Hotels is a principal-principal problem. The principal-agent problem occurs when the ownership structure has dispersed ownership and dispersed voting rights. In this case, the structure has weak shareholders and strong management, with a potentially significant conflict between the shareholders and the management.

8. C is correct. The corporate governance risk for BR Hotels is high due to a low percentage of independent board members. Of the 15 members on the board, only one is independent. Many OECD countries have introduced a recommendation for the minimum ratio of independent directors serving on the board. They typically set the minimum ratio of independent directors in a range of 20%–50%

or greater. BR Hotels falls below this range.

A is incorrect since CEO duality is not a governance problem for BR Hotels. BR Hotels' CEO and chairperson are separate, so there is no CEO duality. This is typically a sign of effective corporate governance. The independent chairperson and CEO roles help protect investor interests.

B is incorrect because family control is not likely to increase governance risk for BR Hotels. Family control lowers the risks associated with principal-agent problems. This is the result of the family's having concentrated ownership and management responsibility. The lower risk associated with the principal-agent problem is somewhat offset by the drawbacks of family control, which include poor transparency, modest considerations for minority shareholder rights, and difficulty in attracting quality management talent.

9. A is correct. The implementation of ESG factors in security analysis differs for equity analysis and fixed-income analysis. For BK Hotels' corporate bonds, the focus of ESG integration is on mitigating downside risk. In contrast, in equity analysis, ESG integration is used to both identify potential opportunities and mitigate downside risk.

B is incorrect since adjusting the discount rate is typically used in equity analysis and not in fixed-income analysis. In valuing a stock, an analyst may choose to adjust the discount factor to account for the ESG risk. In fixed-income analysis, the credit spread or CDS is adjusted to reflect the ESG risk.

C is incorrect since identifying potential opportunities is used in equity analysis and not in fixed-income analysis. In fixed-income analysis, the focus of ESG integration is on mitigating downside risk. In equity analysis, ESG integration is used to both identify potential opportunities and mitigate downside risk.

10. C is correct. BR Hotels faces significant corporate governance and social risk. Corporate governance risk is high due to a low number of independent board members (1 out of 15 members), lack of gender diversity (2 women out of 15 members), and low percentage of board members with hotel industry experience (20%). These factors are likely to increase investors' perception of the corporation's risk. The social risk for BR Hotels is also high. BR Hotels has a high labor turnover rate, pays most of its workforce at or near the minimum wage, and offers no health benefits. Legislation raising the minimum wage and the growing pressure on BR Hotels to offer benefits would increase operating costs. This could have a negative impact on future cash flows, which would be detrimental to the bond holders. The valuation of BR Hotels' bonds could be adversely affected by the higher ESG risk. To account for the higher ESG risk, the credit spread on BR Hotels' bonds is likely to increase.

A is incorrect since the credit spread on BR Hotels' bonds is likely to increase and not decrease.

B is incorrect since the credit spread on BR Hotels' bonds is likely to increase and not remain unchanged.

Cost of Capital: Advanced Topics

by Lee M. Dunham, PhD, CFA, and Pamela Peterson Drake, PhD, CFA.

Lee M. Dunham, PhD, CFA, is at Creighton University (USA). Pamela Peterson Drake, PhD, CFA, is at James Madison University (USA).

LEARNING OUTCOMES

Mastery	The candidate should be able to:
☐	explain top-down and bottom-up factors that impact the cost of capital
☐	Compare methods used to estimate the cost of debt.
☐	explain historical and forward-looking approaches to estimating an equity risk premium
☐	compare methods used to estimate the required return on equity
☐	estimate the cost of debt or required return on equity for a public company and a private company
☐	evaluate a company's capital structure and cost of capital relative to peers

INTRODUCTION

1

A company's **weighted average cost of capital (WACC)** represents the cost of debt and equity capital used by the company to finance its assets. The **cost of debt** is the after-tax cost to the issuer of debt, based on the return that debt investors require to finance a company. The **cost of equity** represents the return that equity investors require to own a company, also referred to as the **required rate of return on equity** or the required return on equity.

A company's WACC is used by the company's internal decision makers to evaluate capital investments. For analysts and investors, it is a critical input used in company valuation.

Equation 1 reminds us that a company's WACC is driven by the proportions, or weights (the w_i), of the different capital sources used in its capital structure, applied to the costs of each source (the r_i), with d, p, and e subscripts denoting debt, preferred equity, and common equity, respectively:

$$\text{WACC} = w_d r_d (1 - t) + w_p r_p + w_e r_e. \tag{1}$$

(These weights are all non-negative and sum to 1.0.)

Determining a company's WACC is an important, albeit challenging, task for an analyst given the following:

- Many different methods can be used to calculate the costs of each source of capital; there is no single, "right" method.

- Assumptions are needed regarding long-term **target capital structure**, which might or might not be the current capital structure.

- The company's marginal tax rate must be estimated and might be different than its average or effective tax rate.

Estimating the cost of capital for a company thus involves numerous, sometimes complex, assumptions and choices, all of which affect the resulting investment conclusion.

2   COST OF CAPITAL FACTORS

> ☐ explain top-down and bottom-up factors that impact the cost of capital

Financial theory argues that companies should seek the optimal mix of debt and equity that results in the lowest WACC and maximizes shareholder wealth. Given differences in risk and financial risk tolerances across companies, the capital structure, cost of debt, and costs of equity vary across companies.

A company's cost of capital is influenced by the type of capital the company seeks. Because of its lower risk relative to equity, debt capital typically has a lower cost than equity capital. A company's cost of debt, before considering the tax deductibility of interest, can be represented as the sum of the benchmark **risk-free rate** and a **credit spread** that compensates investors for the risk inherent in the company's debt security:

$$r_d = r_f + \text{Credit spread}. \tag{2}$$

The credit spread reflects company-specific factors such as the riskiness of the company's business model, future profitability and growth prospects, applicable tax rates, the protective covenants in the debt securities, the company's policy regarding debt leverage—and possible changes thereto, the maturity and callability of the debt, and the nature and liquidity of the company's assets and operations.

A company's cost of equity can be represented by the sum of the benchmark risk-free rate and an equity risk premium that compensates investors for the risk inherent in the company's equity securities, or

$$r_e = r_f + (\text{ERP} + \text{IRP}), \tag{3}$$

where the **equity risk premium (ERP)** is a market risk premium for bearing the systematic risk of investing in equities in general, and the **idiosyncratic risk premium (IRP)** is a company-specific risk premium for bearing the company-specific risks of investing in the subject company's equity securities.

Because preferred equity typically has a stated dividend rate and a higher claim on assets than common equity, the ERP for a company's preferred equity is likely to be smaller than the ERP for its common equity, resulting in preferred equity having a lower cost than common equity.

Factors influencing a company's cost of capital can either be top-down (i.e., external or systematic) or bottom-up (i.e., company specific or idiosyncratic). Exhibit 1 summarizes these key factors.

Top-Down, External	Bottom-Up, Company Specific
Exhibit 1: Cost of Capital Factors	
• Capital availability	• Revenue, earnings, and cash flow volatility
• Market conditions	• Asset nature and liquidity
• Legal and regulatory considerations/country risk	• Financial strength, profitability, and leverage
• Tax jurisdiction	• Security features

Top-Down External Factors

Top-down factors include macroeconomic factors such as risk-free rates, aggregate credit spreads, and the ERP.

Capital Availability

One cost of capital determinant is the general availability of capital in the company's market, region, or country. Greater capital availability typically leads to more favorable terms for corporate issuers and lower associated costs of capital.

Developed economies typically have more established, liquid capital markets with greater capital availability, more stable currencies, better property protection, and a greater strength in the rule of law than those of developing economies. Consequently, the perceived risk associated with investing in companies in more mature capital markets is lower than for companies in less mature economies. Lower perceived risk translates into lower credit spreads, ERPs, and costs of capital for companies in more mature, or developed, economies.

In regions with less developed capital markets, a lack of corporate debt markets could require companies to rely on other means for funding, such as bank loans or the shadow banking system. **Shadow banking** refers to any type of lending by financial institutions not regulated as banks.

Market Conditions

A company's cost of capital is also highly influenced by **market conditions** such as interest rates, inflation rates, and the macroeconomic environment. The credit spreads and ERPs demanded by debt and equity investors reflect overall credit and equity market conditions in addition to issuer-specific risk factors. Higher credit spreads and ERPs signify higher risk to potential new debt and equity capital providers, respectively, who demand higher returns for supplying capital.

Macroeconomic and country-specific economic factors, such as inflation rates, are reflected in benchmark interest rates and the overall level of credit spreads, which tend to widen during recessions and tighten during expansionary times. When interest rates are relatively low and credit spreads are tight, the costs of debt and equity capital are lower. Higher relative rates of inflation, represented in a higher risk-free rate, increase the cost of capital for companies.

Similarly, the ERP demanded by investors tends to increase during recessions and decrease during expansionary times. In developed economies, more predictable and transparent monetary policy contributes to greater certainty and lower volatility in interest rates and inflation rates, lowering the cost of capital for companies.

Macroeconomic conditions over the longer term—as measured by business cycles—also affect companies' costs of capital. During expansionary times, as credit spreads narrow, or tighten, companies tend to borrow more, to fund growth and expansion or refinance existing debt, as their cost of debt becomes cheaper. Similarly, during recessionary times when credit spreads can widen, companies tend to borrow less. Finally, exchange rates also affect the cost of capital. In countries with greater exchange rate volatility and higher associated currency risk, companies have higher costs of capital.

Legal and Regulatory Considerations, Country Risk

Empirical evidence suggests a strong relationship between capital market conditions in different countries and the legal traditions followed by those countries. Countries with common law–based legal systems tend to be more mature and have stronger legal systems, as measured by greater enforceability of investor rights, than countries with civil law–based legal systems. Legal systems with greater investor protections often support more developed capital markets, providing investors with a greater sense of security with respect to their investments. Investors in mature regulatory environments offering greater investor protections typically demand lower credit spreads and ERPs, leading to lower costs of capital for corporate issuers.

Companies' costs of capital are also influenced by regulatory policies and guidelines set by government or other related entities, which can drive key financial decisions such as those related to capital structure, payout policy, and pricing. Financial institutions and utility companies, for instance, are examples of entities in highly regulated industries.

Tax Jurisdiction

Another factor in cost of capital determination is the company's marginal income tax rate. In many countries and jurisdictions, interest expense is a tax-deductible expense, effectively reducing a company's after-tax cost of debt due to associated tax savings. The higher a company's marginal income tax rate, the greater the tax benefit associated with using debt in the capital structure.

EXAMPLE 1

External Factors and Cost of Capital

GW is a junior analyst researching two companies that are in the same industry but headquartered, and seeking to raise capital, in different countries. GW gathers the following information on each country's capital market:

Feature	Country A	Country B
Credit spreads	Wide	Narrow
Volatility in interest rates	High	Low
Inflation rate	High	Low
Capital availability	Low	High
Corporate tax rate	15%	25%

1. Which country is more likely to have lower costs of capital for corporate issuers, and why?

   Solution

   Country B is more likely to have lower costs of capital for corporate issuers. All else equal, given a higher corporate income tax rate in Country B, corporate issuers in that country would benefit from a lower after-tax cost of debt. The higher the company's marginal income tax rate, the greater the attractiveness of using debt in the company's capital structure because of the associated tax savings benefit, assuming interest expense is tax deductible and the company has taxable income.

   Additionally, corporate issuers in Country B benefit from narrow credit spreads, low volatility in interest rates, and a low inflation rate, all of which contribute to lower costs of capital for corporate issuers. When interest rates and volatility are relatively low and/or credit spreads are narrow, the cost of debt and equity capital is lower than in periods of high interest rates and volatility and wide credit spreads.

   Further, the higher supply of capital available in a given market often leads to more favorable terms for corporate issuers, resulting in a lower cost of capital.

2. Country A is considering tax legislation that, if passed, would raise the corporate income tax rate from 15% to 25%. What effect is this likely to have on the cost of debt for corporate issuers in Country A?

   Solution

   The tax legislation under consideration would raise the corporate income tax rate in Country A from 15% to 25% and have the effect of lowering the after-tax cost of debt for corporate issuers in that country. As long as a company has the taxable income before interest available to offset the interest on debt, there is a benefit to the tax deductibility of interest and, therefore, a lower cost of debt.

3. What assumption are you making in drawing conclusions regarding the effect of tax legislation in Country A?

   Solution

   The assumption necessary for the tax legislation to have an effect on companies' costs of capital depends on whether the interest is deductible for tax purposes. If interest is not deductible, there would be no effect on the WACC; if interest is deductible and the company has taxable earnings, the effect is to reduce the WACC.

Bottom-Up Company Specific Factors

In addition to the external environment, a company's business model influences its cost of capital. Analysts must assess company-specific characteristics such as revenue sensitivity, earnings volatility, the nature and liquidity of assets owned or used, current and anticipated financial leverage, and features embedded in the company's debt and equity securities to determine their impact on the company's cost of capital.

A company's WACC should ultimately reflect the riskiness of the company's expected cash flow streams. Key factors that drive differences in WACC across companies include

- revenue, earnings, and cash flow volatility;
- asset nature and liquidity;
- financial strength, profitability, and leverage; and
- security features.

Revenue, Earnings and Cash Flow Volatility

Some companies, such as telecom companies and companies in the media streaming business, have subscription-based, recurring revenue that leads to fairly stable earnings and cash flow streams. A high proportion of recurring revenues for a company is generally viewed as a positive by investors because the company's revenue stream is likely to be more stable and predictable and less sensitive to the ups and downs of the macroeconomy. In contrast, companies in cyclical industries, such as those in the industrial equipment industry and companies with pay-per-use models, typically have more volatile revenues, earnings, and cash flow streams with greater sensitivity to the macroeconomic environment.

A company's business and financial risks affect the volatility of its revenues, earnings, and cash flow in that

- companies with greater **sales risk** (that is, uncertainty regarding the price and number of units sold) have greater potential revenue volatility;
- companies that generate a majority of their revenues from a few customers, and thus face **customer concentration risk**, also have higher sales risk; and
- companies with higher operating and **financial leverage** (or a higher proportion of fixed costs and debt burden) have greater earnings volatility.

For a given level of debt, a company with greater predictability and lower associated volatility in its revenues, earnings, and cash flow streams is likely to have a lower probability of default and a narrower credit spread, resulting in a lower cost of debt and equity capital.

Additionally, a company with higher environmental, social, and governance (ESG) risk is likely to have a higher cost of capital. Suppose a company is in an industry that has a significant carbon footprint, yet the company does not appear to be taking sufficient action to mitigate its environmental impact. Investors could demand a higher cost of capital for this company given the perceived financial risk from the externality, which might include mitigation costs, consumer preferences or boycotts that lower sales, and litigation costs.

Similarly, a company with known employee safety concerns is likely to be viewed as having a greater risk of lawsuits and negative customer perception, which would increase its associated risk and cost of capital demanded by investors. Companies with weak governance practices typically face higher costs of capital because of the inherent risks and costs associated with inadequate systems and poor oversight. For example, a company that has anti-takeover provisions might deter takeovers but increase management entrenchment. Rather than reflecting these ESG risks in the cost of capital, analysts can choose to adjust the future cash flow forecasts in their valuation models.

Exhibit 2 presents a summary of the relationships between business model characteristics and a company's cost of capital.

Exhibit 2: Revenues, Earnings, and Cash Flow Volatility and Cost of Capital

Revenue, Earnings, Cash Flow Volatility	Effect on Cost of Capital	
	Lower	Higher
Higher stability of revenues, earnings, and cash flows	✓	
Higher revenue concentration		✓
Higher earnings predictability	✓	
Higher operating leverage		✓
Higher financial leverage		✓
Higher ESG risks		✓

Asset Nature and Liquidity

The type and nature of a company's assets also determines its cost of capital. **Tangible assets** are physical assets such as property, plant and equipment, and inventory, whereas **intangible assets**, such as goodwill, patents, intellectual property rights, and an educated and stable employee workforce, do not exist in physical form. In general, companies with primarily tangible assets are likely to be able to access debt capital at lower cost than companies with a high proportion of intangible assets because they have the ability to pledge these assets as collateral.

Companies with primarily fungible, (i.e., interchangeable into other units of the same identity) and highly liquid assets, such as cash and marketable securities, are likely to have access to lower-cost capital than companies with mostly non-fungible, illiquid assets such as specialized property, plant, and equipment. Another factor to consider is whether the tangible assets are collateralized, supporting debt; this will have the effect of lowering the issuer's cost of debt but potentially increasing its cost of equity, given that creditors could have a prior claim on assets in the event of liquidation.

Exhibit 3 presents a summary of the relationships between a company's asset liquidity and its cost of capital.

Exhibit 3: Asset Type and Cost of Capital

Asset Type	Effect on Cost of Capital	
	Lower	Higher
Higher proportion of fungible, tangible assets	✓	
Higher proportion of liquid assets	✓	

Financial Strength, Profitability, and Financial Leverage

Another cost of capital determinant is the company's projected financial strength. Companies with weakening profitability, poor cash flow generation, low IC, or tight liquidity typically face higher costs of capital because their credit spreads widen and idiosyncratic ERPs increase to account for their deteriorating characteristics.

When a company elects to raise debt or equity capital, the cost of that capital is highly dependent on the company's existing debt level and capital structure. Holding business risk constant, companies with higher proportions of debt in their capital structure, typically measured by leverage ratios such as a higher total debt-to-EBITDA

IC = interest coverage

ratio, higher debt-to-equity (D/E) ratio, or a lower interest coverage (IC) ratio, could face higher costs of capital in the form of higher credit spreads and a higher probability of default arising from a reduced ability to service additional debt.

Exhibit 4: Financial Strength and Cost of Capital

Financial Strength	Effect on Cost of Capital	
	Lower	Higher
Higher profitability	✓	
Higher cash flow generation	✓	
Higher IC, liquidity	✓	
Higher leverage ratios		✓

Security Features

A company's cost of capital is also affected by the features embedded in the debt and equity securities it issues. An issuer's debt securities might have various features, such as a call, put, and convertible feature. These features can increase or decrease the cost of capital for an issuer depending on what benefits they offer to the investor or the company.

- *Callability.* Call features on debt provide a benefit to the corporate issuer. When interest rates fall, the issuer can issue new, lower-cost debt at the prevailing lower interest rates and use the proceeds to buy or "call" back the existing higher-cost debt from investors. Because investors are disadvantaged by the call feature, they demand a higher yield on a callable bond at issuance than they would on an otherwise similar option-free bond. Corporate issuers who issue callable bonds thus incur an initial higher cost or yield on debt capital than if they issued option-free bonds. However, this higher cost at issuance could be reduced in the future if interest rates fall and the issuer is able to issue new debt and call back the existing debt.

- *Putability.* In contrast, investors benefit from a put feature that grants them the option to sell or "put" the bond back to the issuer prior to maturity. When rates rise, this is a valuable option because investors holding the issuer's putable bond can sell the bond back to the issuer before maturity and reinvest the proceeds at the higher prevailing yields. By permitting investors to sell their bonds to the issuer before maturity, put features also allow investors to avoid the effects of company-related events, such as a leveraged buyout or an acquisition, that could increase the risk of the bond and negatively affect its price. In exchange for putability, investors accept a lower yield on a putable bond at issuance than they would receive on an otherwise similar option-free bond. However, this lower cost could increase in the future if interest rates rise and the issuer is forced to refinance at higher rates to buy back the bonds put back to the company.

- *Convertibility.* The conversion feature benefits investors by granting them the option to convert the bond into shares of the issuer's common stock at a specified ratio. Investors accept a lower rate of return on bonds with convertibility features than on option-free bonds.

Thus, corporate issuers who issue putable or convertible bonds will have a lower initial cost of debt capital than if they issued option-free bonds. It is important to note, however, that this lower cost at issuance can lead to higher costs later either in the form of having to issue higher-cost debt later if the bonds are put back to the issuer or, in the case of a convertible debt, in the form of equity dilution if investors ultimately convert the bonds into equity.

- *Cumulative versus Non-cumulative.* Preferred stock can differ with respect to the policy on missed dividends. **Cumulative preferred stock** requires that the company pay in full any missed dividends (that is, dividends promised but not paid) before paying dividends to common shareholders. In contrast, non-cumulative preferred stock does not require that missed dividends be paid before dividends are paid to common shareholders; the only requirement is that dividends to common shares cannot be reinstated unless preferred stock dividends are currently being paid. In a liquidation, preferred shareholders could have a claim for any unpaid dividends before distributions are made to common shareholders. Thus, investors accept a lower rate of return on cumulative preferred share compared to otherwise similar non-cumulative preferred shares.

- *Share Class.* Finally, some companies might issue different classes of common stock that provide different cash flow and voting rights. In general, an arrangement in which a company offers multiple classes of common stock (e.g., Class A and Class B) typically provides one class of shareholders with superior voting or cash flow rights, or both. The cost of common equity capital can be higher for shares with inferior cash flow or voting rights.

Exhibit 4 presents a summary of the relationships between the features of a corporate issuer's securities and the company's cost of capital.

Exhibit 5: Security Features and Cost of Capital			
		Effect on Cost of Capital	
	Feature	**Lower**	**Higher**
Debt			
	Callability		✓
	Putability	✓	
	Convertibility	✓	
Equity			
Preferred	Cumulative	✓	
Common	Inferior cash flow or voting rights		✓

EXAMPLE 2

Company-Specific Factors and Cost of Capital

GW next gathers the following common size balance sheet and other selected information on the two companies:

	Company 1	Company 2
Cash and equivalents	5%	10%
Marketable securities	15%	7%
Accounts receivable	12%	19%
Inventory	3%	2%
Other current assets	4%	4%
Property, plant, and equipment (net)	46%	29%
Intangible assets and goodwill	10%	24%
Other assets	5%	5%
Other Selected Information:		
Net debt/EBITDA	2.1	2.5
IC ratio	12.6	7.9
Operating leverage	Low	High
% Sales from top five customers	15%	27%
Features in existing debt securities	Put	Call

1. Which company is more likely to have a lower cost of capital? Justify your response.

   Solution

   Company 1 is likely to have a lower cost of capital. It has a larger percentage of cash and equivalents and marketable securities (20%) than Company 2 (17%). Company 1 also has a much lower percentage of intangible assets (10%) than Company 2 (24%). In general, companies with primarily tangible and liquid assets are likely to be able to access debt and equity capital at lower cost than companies with a high proportion of intangible assets. Company 1's higher proportion of tangible property, plant, and equipment (46%) might also allow the company to access debt capital at lower cost because of its ability to pledge these assets as collateral.

   Company 1 also operates with lower financial leverage, as indicated by a lower net debt-to-EBITDA ratio (2.1 versus 2.5) and a higher IC ratio (12.6 versus 7.9). Companies with lower levels of debt, typically measured by leverage ratios such as a lower net debt-to-EBITDA ratio or a higher IC ratio, will have lower capital costs. Company 1 also operates with lower operating leverage, reflecting a cost structure that includes a lower percentage of fixed costs and a more diversified customer base (top five customers accounting for 15% of total sales versus 27% for Company 2). Companies with lower operating leverage and lower customer concentration risk tend to have greater stability in their earnings and cash flow streams and thus are likely to have lower costs of capital than companies with high volatility in these streams.

   Finally, the existing debt securities of Company 1 have embedded put options that allow investors to sell the securities back to the company prior to maturity if interest rates rise. In contrast, the existing debt securities of Company 2 have embedded call options that allow the company to call the securities prior to maturity if interest rates rise. The put option is a benefit to investors, whereas the call feature is a benefit to the issuer, which leads

> to putable bonds having a lower cost or yield than otherwise comparable
> callable bonds.

Cost of Capital Factors Summary

- The costs of debt and equity capital are influenced by both top-down and bottom-up factors.

- Top-down factors include macroeconomic and political factors such as capital availability and market conditions (risk-free rates, credit spreads, and the ERP), legal and regulatory considerations such as the maturity of the regulatory environment in the country in which the company operates, and the company's tax jurisdiction.

- Key bottom-up factors include issuer-specific characteristics such as revenue and earnings volatility, the nature and liquidity of assets owned or used, financial leverage, and firm-specific risks.

- Features of debt securities, including callability, putability, and convertibility, affect the cost of debt. Features of equity securities, such as cumulative dividends, affect the costs of equity.

- Whether an analyst's approach to estimating WACC is top-down, bottom-up, or a combination, the analyst must make a number of assumptions and estimates to derive a company's WACC.

Exhibit 6 presents a summary of factors analysts should consider in determining WACC.

Exhibit 6: Analyst Checklist for WACC Determination

- **Top-down, external factors**
- Availability of debt and equity capital
- Debt market conditions (e.g., credit spreads)
- Equity market conditions (e.g., ERP)
- Business cycle (e.g., expansion versus recession)
- Legal and regulatory environment (e.g., country risk, common law versus civil law basis, maturity of regulatory environments)
- Tax jurisdiction

- **Bottom-up, company-specific factors**
- Sales risk
- Operating and financial leverage
- Debt features: type of interest, collateral, embedded options
- Equity features: seniority, voting rights
- ESG risks
- Asset tangibility and liquidity
- Tax deductibility of interest expense

KNOWLEDGE CHECK

---

1. Identify whether each of the following factors would positively or negatively affect an issuer's cost of capital. An issuer

   I. with a high degree of operating leverage.

   II. with relatively high earnings predictability.

   III. seeking capital in a m region with a high supply of available capital.

   IV. seeking capital in a region with weak legal and regulatory systems.

   Solution

   Factors I and IV would likely lead to an issuer having a higher cost of capital. Companies with higher operating leverage will experience greater earnings volatility for a given change in revenue than companies operating with lower operating leverage. Higher earnings volatility leads to lower earnings predictability which typically leads to a higher cost of capital. Further, issuers seeking capital in regions with weak legal and regulatory environments will face higher costs of capital to compensate investors for the weak investor protections.

   Factors II and III would likely lead to an issuer having a lower cost of capital. Higher earnings predictability typically leads to a lower cost of capital. Further, a high supply of capital available in a given market often leads to more favorable terms for corporate issuers, also resulting in a lower cost of capital.

---

2. Identify which issuer, based solely on its given business model characteristics, would likely have a lower cost of capital and be able to support a higher proportion of debt in its capital structure. Justify your selection.

Company 1	Company 2
Pay-per-use model	Subscription model
Asset base consists largely of intangible assets	Assets base consists largely of tangible assets
60% of revenues come from largest five customers	No more than 1% of revenues come from a single customer

   Solution

   Company 2 is correct. Companies with subscription-based business models are typically characterized by fairly predictable revenues and earnings than companies with pay-per-use models. Further, companies with asset bases consisting primarily of tangible assets are likely to access debt and equity capital at lower costs than companies with a high proportion of intangible assets because of the lower risk inherent in tangible assets. Finally, companies that generate their revenues from highly diversified customer bases (low customer concentration risk) are likely to have lower costs of capital than companies that generate a majority of their revenues from a very few customers.

3. Identify two market conditions that are most likely favorable for companies to issue debt securities. Justify your response.

Solution

A company's cost of debt is equal to a risk-free rate plus a credit spread specific to the company. Lower interest rates, for example arising from expansionary monetary policy, and tighter credit spreads, as during periods of economic expansion, would make borrowing less costly and debt financing relatively more attractive for companies.

In contrast, when interest rates are relatively high and or more restrictive monetary policy is expected, or when spreads are wider because of weak or worsening overall economic conditions, borrowing would be more expensive for companies.

4. Describe two embedded debt features that would most likely result in a lower cost of debt capital at issuance.

Solution

Bonds issued with either a put feature or a convertible feature offer a benefit to investors. Putable bonds offer investors the option to sell the bond back to the company prior to maturity when interest rates rise. Convertible bonds provide investors with the option of converting the bonds into shares of the issuer's common stock prior to maturity. Consequently, bonds with these features will typically be issued at a lower initial cost or yield relative to option-free bonds.

ESTIMATING THE COST OF DEBT

3

☐ | Compare methods used to estimate the cost of debt.

Analysts have several methods available to estimate the cost of debt, and the use of those methods depends on a number of factors, namely the following:

- *Type of debt*: Is the company's debt publicly traded? Non-traded or private? Bank debt? A lease?
- *Debt liquidity*: How liquid or marketable is the issued debt?
- *Credit rating*: Does the debt have a credit rating?
- *Debt currency*: In what currency is the debt denominated?

In the following sections, we examine these factors and the methods an analyst can use to estimate the cost of debt.

Traded Debt

If a company has publicly traded debt with no embedded options, otherwise known as **straight debt**, the yield to maturity (YTM) on the company's existing debt with the longest maturity could be a reasonable estimate of the company's cost of issuing straight debt. If the company has shorter-term bonds that are more liquid and trade more frequently than its longest dated bond, the YTM on the shorter-term debt might be a more reliable estimate of the company's cost of debt. Effectively, the YTM reflects the current market interest rate on the debt, which can be interpreted as the current cost of issuing new debt with similar features.

Non-Traded Debt

Most private companies, and some public companies, have non-traded or illiquid debt securities. In these cases, a quoted YTM either does not exist or is an unreliable estimate of the cost of debt because of the presence of a large liquidity premium embedded in the yield.

In such scenarios, an analyst can check whether credit ratings exist for the company's debt securities. If so, one approach to estimating a company's cost of debt is to use the yields to maturity of bonds of other companies with the same or similar maturities and credit ratings and apply matrix pricing to estimate a YTM for the subject company's bonds.

If no credit rating exists, an alternative is to use fundamental characteristics of the company, such as IC ratios or other financial leverage ratios, to deduce the likely bond rating, or a synthetic credit rating, of the company's outstanding debt. This approach requires a model that estimates a bond's rating class. Using proprietary information, bond ratings, features, and rating classes, it is possible to model the ratings classifications using statistical models.

Once a credit rating has been inferred, an analyst can use the YTM on bonds with a similar maturity and the inferred credit rating to estimate a cost of debt. Alternatively, the analyst can determine the current credit spread for that credit rating and maturity of the company's debt. This credit spread is then added to the benchmark risk-free rate to arrive at an estimate of the cost of debt for the subject company.

EXAMPLE 3

Synthetic Credit Ratings

After examining a large number of companies in the manufacturing industry with rated debt, analysts at the Brunswix Firm developed the likely range of ratios for each credit rating class, which are presented in Exhibit 7.

Exhibit 7: Rating Classes and Leverage Ratios

Rating class	IC (Int. Coverage)	D/E
AAA	IC > 10 times	D/E < 35%
AA	8 < IC < 10	35% < D/E < 40%
A	5 < IC < 8	40% < D/E < 42%
BBB	3 < IC < 5	42% < D/E < 44%
BB	2 < IC < 3	44% < D/E < 50%
B	1.4 < IC < 2.0	50% < D/E < 60%
CCC	1.0 < IC < 1.4	60% < D/E < 70%

Rating class	IC	D/E
CC	$0.6 < IC < 1.0$	$70\% < D/E < 80\%$
C	$0.3 < IC < 0.6$	$80\% < D/E < 100\%$
D	$IC < 0.3$	$D/E > 100\%$

A Lee, an analyst at the firm, would like to use this proprietary model to predict the debt rating for Gamma Company, a manufacturing company with non-traded debt. Gamma has an IC ratio of 1.5 and a D/E ratio of 43%.

1. What rating class should Lee assign to Gamma Company's debt and why?

   Solution

   Given a conflict in potential rating that exists for Gamma, it is not clear which rating class the company should be assigned. This is because even though Gamma's IC ratio indicates that the company aligns with a B rating, its D/E ratio indicates that a BBB rating is more appropriate.

2. What else should Lee do to estimate the synthetic rating?

   Solution

   Lee should attempt to look at these ratios historically for Gamma and examine whether trends appear in these ratios that might indicate future increases or decreases. For example, if the IC ratio has been trending upward, Lee might want to use personal judgement to suggest a BB rating for Gamma rather than the current synthetic B rating.

It should be noted that the issuer's overall credit rating might be different than the credit ratings on its issued securities. Further, some companies have different credit ratings for their own different outstanding debt issues, based on bond features. For instance, a company could have both AA- and A-rated debt, with the AA debt granting more protection to the investor through collateral, seniority, convertibility, or other features. The analyst's challenge is to estimate a cost of debt that best reflects the company's risk profile.

Bank Debt

In some countries, bank financing is a primary source of debt financing for companies and the primary source of funding for small businesses. Fixed-rate and floating-rate bank debt can be fully amortizing, partially amortizing, or non-amortizing. In general, amortizing loans typically have a lower cost of debt because of their lower default risk, given that some portion of principal is being repaid over the loan term. In contrast, non-amortizing loans, where the entire principal is repaid at maturity, similar to a bullet bond, typically have higher default risk and a higher cost of debt.

An analyst should attempt to determine the interest rate paid by the company on new bank debt financing to estimate the cost of bank debt. If a company has recently taken on new bank debt, the interest rate on that loan could be a good estimate of the company's cost of debt if the analyst believes the interest rate reflects current market conditions and the company's risk profile has not materially changed since issuance.

Again, it is important to note that an estimate of the cost of debt should be used with caution if there is any belief that market conditions or the company's risk profile has substantially changed since its issuance.

Leases

Some companies use lease financing to acquire assets such as property, aircraft, and other large-ticket capital assets. A **finance (or capital) lease** is an example of an amortized loan. In contrast, operating leases involve expenses, and the property is not capitalized on the lessee's financial statement. A finance lease has properties similar to the ownership of the leased asset: use of the asset, payment(s), and the lessee owns the asset at the end of the lease term or has an option for asset purchase. The interest rate or the implicit lease rate in a finance lease can be inferred from the lease payments and the fair value of the leased asset, considering the residual value of the asset and direct costs of the lessor. As a type of secured loan, leases often have lower associated borrowing costs for a company than if the company were to borrow in the capital markets on an unsecured basis to purchase the asset outright.

According to IFRS-16 and ASC-842, the interest rate, or the **rate implicit in the lease (RIIL)** is the discount rate that equates the sum of the present value of the lease payments and the present value of the residual value with the sum of the fair value of the leased asset and the lessor's direct costs (e.g., legal fees) such that:

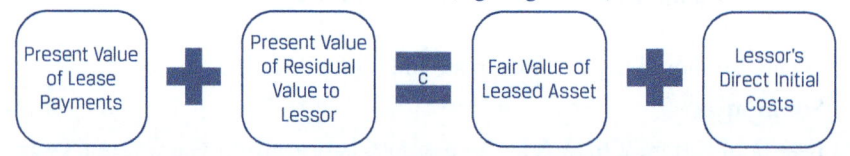

However, the present value of the residual value and the lessor's direct initial costs are often not known to the lessee (company) or analyst. If unknown, the **incremental borrowing rate (IBR)**, which is the rate of interest the company would pay to borrow using a collateralized loan over the same term, might be used. If this rate is not known, the analyst might use the non-traded debt estimation method. In most public company filings, however, lessees will disclose the interest rates for their lease liabilities.

Under some tax jurisdictions, a finance lease is considered a purchase (and therefore, a sale from the point of view of the lessor), and interest expense is tax deductible. In this case, an adjustment is made to the cost of debt to put it on an after-tax basis.

EXAMPLE 4

Leasing Costs

G&S Airlines is considering whether to borrow money or use cash on hand (equity) to purchase or lease a new aircraft needed for its business. The company's unsecured IBR is 6%, and its cost of equity is 11%.

The lease terms the company has negotiated are for a 15-year lease with annual payments (PMT) of EUR9.0 million at the end of each year. The leased asset has a fair value (FV) of EUR100 million. The lessor would incur a cost of €5 million at the time of the lease agreement. The residual value of the leased asset at the end of 15 years is EUR10 million.

1. What is the implied interest cost of this lease?

   Solution

   The cash flows associated with the lease are as follows:

	0	1	2	3	...	15
Lease PMT		€9.0	€9.0	€9.0		€9.0

	0	1	2	3	...	15
	|	|	|	|		|
Residual value						€10.0
FV of leased asset	−€100.0					
Lessor direct costs	−€5.0					
Net cash flows	−€105.0	€9.0	€9.0	€9.0		€19.0

Solving for the discount rate that equates the initial net cash outflow of €105.0 million to the present value (PV) of the net cash flows beyond the initial year results in a rate of 4.08%.

Using a calculator,

PMT = 9.0, PV = −105.0, N = 15, FV = 10.0

Using Microsoft Excel,

RATE(15,9.0,-105.0,10.0,0)

Using Python,

import numpy_financial as npf

r = npf(15,9.0,-105.0,10.0,0)

print(r)

Using R,

library(FinCal)

discount.rate(15,-105.0,10.0,9.0,0)

2. What factors should G&S consider in the decision to buy outright versus leasing?

Solution

At 4.08%, the leasing option is lower cost and lower risk than the company's unsecured IBR of 6%. It is also lower in cost than issuing equity, which would be dilutive. Leasing avoids the risks associated with ownership. However, G&S would have increased leverage as a result of the lease transaction.

International Considerations

When being estimated for international markets, the cost of debt should reflect the currency in which the company's cash flows occur. One approach to estimating the cost of debt for an entity in a less mature, foreign market is to add a country risk premium to the debt's yield. In this case, a **country risk rating (CRR)** can be used.

A CRR is a rating applied to a country based on the assessment of risk pertaining to that country, in areas such as

- economic conditions,
- political risk,
- exchange rate risk, and

- securities market development and regulation.

Risks are often assessed relative to a country's sovereign debt risk. Sovereign risk is a component of country risk and relates to a country's likelihood of defaulting on its debt obligations, whereas country risk includes the factors beyond the sovereign risk, such as political stability, economic competitiveness, and human development. This information is then used to adjust the cost of debt for a subject company. The ratings can be similar to credit ratings—that is, AAA, AA, and so on—or might have a numeric range (e.g., 0 to 10, 0 to 100) using a benchmark country. For each rating class or numeric score, the median interest rate can be calculated. By comparing the median interest rate with the benchmark country's rate, the country risk premium can be derived.

Consider the chart of rates and country risk premiums in Exhibit 8, using Country A as the benchmark (therefore, a 0% country risk premium). Country C has a risk rating of 2 and a median interest rate of 4.5%. Country C's country risk premium is therefore 0.5% (or 4.5% − 4.0%).

Exhibit 8: Country Risk Premiums

Country	Rating (1 = least risk, 10 = most risk)	Median interest rate	Country risk premium
A	1	4.0%	0.0%
B	5	7.0%	3.0%
C	2	4.5%	0.5%
D	8	15.5%	11.5%
E	7	9.5%	5.5%
F	6	7.5%	3.5%

EXAMPLE 5

Cost of Debt Summary

- The cost of debt is affected by the type of debt, the liquidity of the debt issue, the debt's credit rating, and the currency in which the debt is issued.

- Calculating the cost of traded debt is relatively uncomplicated, especially for straight debt, but determining the cost of non-traded debt requires using approaches such as a synthetic credit rating.

- Determining the cost of bank debt and leasing requires information for the calculation of the effective cost of this financing.

- The cost of debt in international markets can be estimated using CRRs that reflect economic, political, and exchange rate risk, as well as information about the financial markets and regulation.

1. An analyst is estimating the cost of debt for a company that leases its assets. What information does the analyst need to estimate the company's cost of debt?

   Solution

   To estimate the cost of debt, the analyst will need to know, or estimate

- lease payments,
- the residual value of the leased asset,
- the fair value of the leased asset,
- lessor direct costs, and
- the term of the lease.

2. If there is a limit on the monetary amount of the interest deduction for tax purposes, how would this affect a company's cost of debt?

Solution

If a company has already reached the limit on interest that might be tax deductible, the cost of debt is not adjusted for the tax rate. This is because the cost of debt is the cost of raising additional debt, and no further tax benefit can be realized by the company.

3. An analyst is estimating the cost of debt for a company with outstanding debt that is not traded. Which methods, if any, can be considered for estimating the company's cost of debt?

Solution

Potential methods include the following:
Matrix pricing – Identifying other debt that is publicly traded with similar features in maturity, features, and credit quality.
Synthetic rating – Using the companies' fundamentals, such as IC ratios and other leverage ratios, to estimate a credit rating class. Once a credit rating has been inferred, an analyst can simply use the YTM on bonds with a similar maturity and credit rating to estimate a cost of debt.

THE ERP

4

☐ explain historical and forward-looking approaches to estimating an equity risk premium

The ERP represents the expected incremental return that investors demand as compensation for holding risky equity securities rather than a risk-free asset. It is the difference between the expected return on equities and a benchmark risk-free rate.

Analysts estimate a company-specific ERP to calculate the company's cost of equity capital, or r_e, as

Company i $r_e = E(r_f) + $ (Systematic market ERP + Company i IRP)

$$= E(r_f) + (\text{ERP} + \text{IRP}). \tag{4}$$

The focus here is on estimating the size of the ERP rather than the IRP for the company. Even for long-established developed markets, estimating the size of the ERP is challenging and subject to estimation error, resulting in differing investment conclusions among analysts.

Two broad approaches used to estimate the ERP are

- the *historical approach (ex-post)*, which uses backward-looking historical data to estimate the ERP, and

- the *forward-looking approach (ex-ante)*, which uses forward-looking expectational data.

Given that both methods are used in practice, analysts should be aware of their limitations and how their conclusions can be affected by estimation error.

Historical Approach

A historical approach is often used when reliable long-term equity return data are available. A historical ERP estimate is typically calculated as the mean value of the difference between a broad-based equity market index return and a government debt return, as a proxy for the risk-free rate, over some sample period.

In using a historical estimate to represent the ERP going forward, the analyst is assuming that returns are stationary and that markets are relatively efficient, so over the long term, average returns should be an unbiased estimate of what investors expected to earn. An analyst therefore must assess whether historical returns in the market of interest provide useful information about future expectations before using the historical approach.

An analyst has four key decisions in the development of a historical ERP:

1. What equity index best represents equity market returns?
2. What time period is best to calculate the estimate?
3. What measure for mean returns should be used?
4. Which proxy for the risk-free rate is best?

Equity Index Selection

The analyst should select an equity index that accurately represents the typical returns earned by equity investors in the market. Broad-based, market-value-weighted indexes are typically chosen as representative. Examples include the S&P 500 Index, Russell 3000 Index, MSCI EAFE Index, Australia All Ordinaries, and the Shanghai Composite Index.

Time Period

Deciding on the best estimation time period will involve trade-offs. One method uses the longest reliable return series available, but this is problematic because the distant past might not be representative of the current market environment. In addition, research shows significant evidence of non-constant underlying return volatility in many equity markets. This fluctuating volatility has less of an effect on estimates from a long data series; however, this assumes the ERP has not experienced any permanent changes in its level.

Using a shorter data period avoids using less-representative periods contained in longer data series and makes it more likely that the ERP estimate is representative of the current market environment. The trade-off, however, is that using a shorter time period increases the likelihood of greater noise in the ERP estimate. More specifically, a shorter estimation period, such as one covering only a portion of a business cycle or a period of disruption such as the global financial crisis or the COVID-19 pandemic, might not be sufficiently robust to forecast future returns. In the case of the latter, a time period that does not include the market disruption is needed.

A similar issue arises when a series of strong market returns has increased historical mean ERP estimates, making it likely that the historical estimate could be overestimating the forward-looking ERP. In general, analysts tend to favor the use of a longer time period, given the reduction in the standard error of the ERP estimate that occurs as the estimation period lengthens.

Selection of the Mean Type

An analyst using the historical approach must also decide on the mean type to use in the estimation, the choices being to use either a geometric mean or an arithmetic mean in calculating the average difference between the equity market return and the benchmark risk-free rate. Exhibit 9 summarizes the advantages and disadvantages of each.

Exhibit 9: Arithmetic Mean Return versus Geometric Mean Return		
Mean Type	**Advantages**	**Disadvantages**
Arithmetic Mean	• Easy to calculate • Considers all observations in the time series	• Sensitive to extreme values • Overestimates the expected terminal value of wealth
Geometric Mean	• Considers all observations in the time series • Gives outliers less weight • Estimates the expected terminal value of wealth	

The arithmetic mean return as the average one-period return best represents the mean return in a single period. Popular models for estimating required return—the capital asset pricing model and multifactor models—are single-period models, so the arithmetic mean, with its focus on single-period returns, is a model-consistent choice.

The geometric mean return represents the compound rate of growth that equates the beginning value to the ending value of one unit of money initially invested in an asset.

The geometric mean is generally preferred because it is less sensitive to outliers and is also consistent with expected terminal wealth estimates. However, both mean types are used in practice.

Selection of the Risk-Free Rate Proxy

Lastly, the analyst must decide on a proxy for the risk-free return. Choices include a short-term government debt rate, such as a USD or EUR Treasury-bill rate, or the YTM on a long-term government bond. Given that they have less (near zero) default risk, government bonds are preferred over even the highest-rated corporate bonds. Exhibit 10 summarizes the advantages and disadvantages of using a short-term rather than long-term proxy.

Exhibit 10: Short- versus Long-Term Risk-Free Rate Proxy		
Risk-Free Proxy	**Advantages**	**Disadvantages**
Short-term government bill rate	• The rate is an exact estimate of the risk-free rate, assuming no default.	• The rate does not closely match the duration of an infinite-life equity security.

Risk-Free Proxy	Advantages	Disadvantages
Long-term government bond YTM	• The YTM more closely matches the duration of an infinite-life equity security.	• The YTM is not a completely risk-free return at the time of purchase because of unknown coupon reinvestment rates.

Some analysts prefer to use a very short-term government bond rate as a proxy, such as a three-month benchmark government bond rate, with the rationale being that a short-term government bond is typically a zero-coupon bond with a return known up front (at the time of purchase) that is not dependent on the reinvestment of coupons. The stated yield is truly the return received by the investor, assuming no default. The disadvantage of using the short-term government bond is that it does not closely match the duration of an infinite-life equity security or most investment horizons.

Industry practice has tended to favor the use of a long-term government bond yield as the risk-free rate proxy. The actual return an investor receives from owning the long-term government bond is not known up front at the time of purchase; the actual return depends, in part, on the rates of return earned from coupon reinvestment during the life of the bond. This is a disadvantage of using the YTM on a long-term government bond as a proxy: it is not a risk-free, known return at the time of purchase. Regardless, the current YTM on a long-term government bond is still used by analysts as an approximation for the bond's expected return.

Limitations of the Historical Approach

Although popular in practice, the historical approach is subject to several limitations, including the following:

- ERPs can vary over time. If the ERP has shifted to a permanently different level in recent years, estimates based on a long time series of historical data are not representative of the future ERP.
- **Survivorship bias** tends to inflate historical estimates of the ERP. This bias is present in equity market data when poorly performing or defunct companies are removed from index membership, so that only relative winners remain represented in index performance.

EXAMPLE 6

ERP Estimation Using the Historical Approach

1. Identify a reason why using a very short-term government bond rate to estimate a historical ERP might be justified. Explain its disadvantage.

Solution

The justification for using a very short-term government bond to estimate an ERP using the historical approach is that unlike a long-term government bond, a short-term government bond is typically a zero-coupon bond with a return known up front and is not dependent on the reinvestment of coupons. Thus, its stated yield is truly the return that the investor receives, assuming no default; this is not the case for the YTM on a long-term government bond. The disadvantage of using the short-term government bond is that it does not match the duration of an infinite-life equity security.

2. Describe a key assumption an analyst must make to justify the use of a historical ERP to estimate a required return using an asset pricing model.

   Solution

   An analyst who uses a historical ERP to estimate a required return using an asset pricing model is assuming that returns are stationary—that is, the parameters that describe the return-generating process are the same in the future as they were in the past.

3. Explain why using the geometric mean might be preferred over the arithmetic mean in the historical approach to estimating the ERP.

   Solution

   Estimated ERPs using geometric means are less sensitive to outliers than those using the arithmetic mean. Further, using the geometric mean to compound wealth forward estimates the expected terminal value of wealth.

D Smith and J Müller are equity analysts at Odyssey Investments. Smith and Müller estimate different ERPs using the following assumptions:

	Smith	**Müller**
Benchmark index	Russell 3000	S&P 500
Sample time period	35 years	65 years
Risk-free rate proxy	30-year Treasury bond	3-month Treasury bill
Mean measure used	Arithmetic	Geometric
Average benchmark index return	12.96%	11.23%
Average risk-free rate over sample period	6.25%	3.11%

1. Calculate two estimates of the ERP using both sets of assumptions.

   Solution

   The estimate of the ERP using Smith's assumptions is

   12.96% – 6.25% = 6.71%.

   The estimate of the ERP using Müller's assumptions is

   11.23% – 3.11% = 8.12%.

2. Explain why both estimates could be valid.

   Solution

   Even though the two estimates of the ERP are different, they might both be valid. The two analysts simply made different choices of the four key decisions in estimating the historical ERP to arrive at their different estimates. This example demonstrates that differences in underlying analyst assumptions can yield different ERP estimates with corresponding valuation implications.

Forward-Looking Approach

A forward-looking approach is consistent with the idea that the ERP depends strictly on future expectations, given that an investor's returns depend only on the investment's expected future cash flows. The ERP should therefore be based only on expectations for economic and financial variables that affect future cash flows. In a forward-looking approach, the ERP is estimated using current information and expectations concerning such variables. These estimates are often called **forward-looking estimates** or ex ante estimates. We provide an overview of three forward-looking estimation methods:

- Survey-based estimates
- Dividend discount models
- Macroeconomic modeling

Survey-Based Estimates

One forward-looking approach is to gauge expectations by asking people what they expect. Survey estimates of the ERP involve asking a sample of people—frequently, experts—about their expectations for the ERP, or for capital market expectations from which the ERP can be inferred. In general, such surveys reveal that the ERP is much higher in developing markets when compared to developed markets. One issue with using surveys to estimate the ERP is that these estimates tend to be sensitive to recent market returns.

Dividend Discount Model Estimates

The second approach involves use of a **dividend discount model (DDM)**, which expresses the value of a stock, V_0, as the present value of future expected dividends. A simplified form of a DDM used to estimate a forward-looking ERP is based on an expected constant earnings growth rate and known as the **Gordon growth model**:

$$V_o = \frac{D_1}{r_e - g}.$$

(5)

Solving for the required return on equity (r_e) yields

$$r_e = \frac{D_1}{V_0} + g,$$

(6)

where $\frac{D_1}{V_0}$ is an expected dividend yield, and g is the expected earnings growth rate.

Broad-based equity indexes typically have an associated dividend yield, and the year-ahead dividend (D_1) for the index might be fairly predictable. In addition, the expected earnings growth rate, g, can be inferred based on expectations such as consensus analyst expectations of the earnings growth rate for an equity market index. These expectations can be top-down or bottom-up generated forecasts.

Subtracting the current risk-free rate from this expected market equity return from Equation 6 yields a forward-looking ERP estimate:

$$\text{ERP} = E\left(\frac{D_1}{V_0}\right) + E(g) - r_f.$$

(7)

Note that an underlying assumption of the constant growth DDM is that earnings, dividends, and prices will grow at the same rate, resulting in a constant P/E. If, however, the analyst believes this is not likely to be the case going forward, an adjustment would be needed that reflects anticipated P/E multiple expansion or contraction. This is because from a given starting market level associated with a given level of earnings and P/E, the return from capital appreciation cannot be greater (or less than) than the earnings growth rate unless the P/E increases (or decreases). P/E increases (or decreases) can result from an increase (or decrease) in the earnings growth rate or a decrease (or increase) in risk. Some analysts also include the aggregate amount spent on buybacks by the index constituent companies in the dividend yield term to reflect total payout. When doing so, an analyst should also consider the degree to which buybacks might alter growth rates in earnings and dividends.

EXAMPLE 7

ERP Estimation Using the Constant Growth DDM

An analyst is estimating a forward-looking ERP for the UK market using the FTSE 100 Index. The analyst gathers the following information:

Market Index	FTSE 100 Index	Analyst Forecast Range
FTSE 100 Index forward dividend yield, $E\left(\dfrac{D_1}{V_0}\right)$	1.94%	1.5% to 3.5%
FTSE 100 Index expected long-term earnings growth rate, $E(g)$	5.0%	4.0% to 6.0%
Long-term Gilt bond yield, (r_f)	1.63%	1.5% to 2.5%

1. Calculate an estimate of the ERP using the constant growth DDM.

   Solution

   The UK ERP estimate is 5.31%, or

   ERP = 1.94% + 5.0% − 1.63% = 5.31%.

2. The analyst is developing a sensitivity analysis for the ERP. What is the effect of allowing for the variations in analyst forecasts in a simulation of the ERP?

   Solution

   At the forecast extremes, the ERP ranges from 1.5% + 4% − 2.5% = 3% to 3.5% + 6% − 1.5% = 8%. The analyst might want to simulate the dividend yield and the long-term bond yield based on this range, using information about distribution among the analysts as part of the simulation.

For rapidly growing economies, an analyst might assume multiple earnings growth stages. Applying the constant growth DDM in this situation, the analyst might forecast

1. a *fast growth stage* for the aggregate of companies included in the subject country equity index, followed by

2. a *transition growth stage* in which growth rates decline, and

3. a *mature growth stage* characterized by growth at a moderate, sustainable rate.

The required rate of return, r_e, is calculated as the rate that equates the sum of the present values for each stage to the equity index price, or

$$\text{Equity index price} = PV_{0,Stage1} + PV_{0,Stage2} + PV_{0,Stage3}, \tag{8}$$

where the $PV_{0,Stage1}$ is the value at time 0 (that is, today) of the Stage 1 dividends, and $PV_{0,Stage\,2}$ and $PV_{0,Stage\,3}$ are similarly for the other two stages. The calculation requires solving for the internal rate of return. Once we have this rate, the chosen proxy for the risk-free rate is then subtracted to arrive at the ERP.

Macroeconomic Modeling

ERP estimates derived from macroeconomic models rely on a number of forecasted economic variables such as inflation and expected growth in real earnings per share. Using relationships between macroeconomic and financial variables in equity valuation models, analysts can develop ERP estimates. These models might be more reliable when public equities represent a relatively large share of the economy, as in many developed markets.

One such model is the Grinold-Kroner (2001) decomposition of the return on equity:

$$ERP = [\text{Dividend yield} + \text{Expected capital gain}] - E(r_f)$$

or

$$ERP = [DY + \text{Expected repricing} + \text{Earnings growth per share}] - E(r_f). \tag{9}$$

Dividend yield, DY, reflects the expected income component of the equity investment. The expected repricing term relates to expected changes in P/E ratios within the market being evaluated. Earnings growth per share can be expressed as

Earnings growth per share

$$= \text{Expected inflation} + \text{Real economic growth} + \text{Change in shares outstanding}$$

$$= i + g + \Delta S. \tag{10}$$

Empirical studies suggest that ΔS, the change in shares outstanding or the dilution effect, varies significantly across countries for a variety of reasons. We assume that $\Delta S = 0$ here, but there is a further discussion in the economic growth module regarding ways to model this for a particular market.

$$ERP = [DY + \Delta(P/E) + i + g + \Delta S] - E(r_f). \tag{11}$$

The Grinold-Kroner model effectively builds the expected market equity return as a function of five factors. Note that this model explicitly considers expected changes in the P/E ratio of the market mentioned in our discussion of the DDM. The following table summarizes the factors, and their common proxies, in the Grinold-Kroner (2001) decomposition of the return on equity.

Factor	Symbol	Common Proxy
Expected income component	DY	Broad-based market index dividend yield
Expected growth rate in the P/E	ΔP/E	Analyst adjustment for market over or under valuation (commonly = 0)
Expected inflation	i	(nominal yield less real yield) for similar maturity security
Expected growth rate in real earnings per share	g	Real GDP growth
Expected change in shares outstanding	ΔS	Depends on market and time period

An analyst can compare the nominal and real yields for similar-maturity government benchmark bonds to estimate the expected inflation rate. For example, expected inflation can be estimated as the ratio of the yield on a US Treasury bond and a similar maturity Treasury Inflation-Protected Security (TIPS):

$$i = \frac{1 + YTM_{Treasury\ bond}}{1 + YTM_{TIPS}} - 1 \approx YTM_{Treasury\ bond} - YTM_{TIPS}. \tag{12}$$

[Handwritten margin notes:]
Grinold-Kroner model.
DY: dividend yield
$\Delta(P/E)$: expected repricing
i: expected inflation
g: real economic growth
ΔS: change in shares outstanding

EXAMPLE 8

ERP Estimation Using the Forward-Looking Approach

1. If the yield on a 10-year Treasury bond is 2.3% and the yield on a similar maturity, inflation-protected Treasury bond is 0.66%, what is the implied inflation rate?

Solution

$i = \frac{1.023}{1.0066} - 1 = 0.016$, or 1.6%.

An analyst is estimating a forward-looking ERP for a market based on the following information:

Input	Scenario 1	Scenario 2
r_f	2.5%	3%
i	1.6%	3%
g	3%	2%
Δ(P/E)	0	1%
DY	2.2%	2%
ΔS	−0.7%	0

1. Using the Grinold-Kroner model, calculate estimates of the ERP under Scenarios 1 and 2.

Solution

Using the Grinold-Kroner forward-looking approach, in Scenario 1, the ERP estimate is 3.6%, or

ERP = {2.2 + 0 +[1.6 + 3.0 + (− 0.7)] } − 2.5 = 3.6%.

Using the Grinold-Kroner model, the ERP estimate in Scenario 2 is 5.0%, or

ERP = {2.0 + 1.0 + [3.0 + 2.0 + 0.0)] } − 3.0 = 5.0%.

The premiums of 3.6% or 5.0%, respectively, compensate investors for average market risk, given expectations for inflation, real earnings growth, P/E growth, and anticipated income depending on the scenario.

2. How does the ERP change when expected inflation increases? When expected income declines?

Solution

Increases in the inflation rate increase the ERP because expectations are revised upward to compensate for the increased inflation. In contrast, decreases in the expected income decrease the ERP as expectations are adjusted downward given lower expected income.

3. Under what circumstances is it not appropriate to use the Grinold-Kroner model?

Solution

The model is not appropriate for estimating the ERP in a developing country where the stock market is not a sufficiently large portion of the economy.

Limitations of the Forward-Looking Approach

Relative to historical estimates, ex ante estimates are likely to be less subject to non-stationarity or data biases. Limitations of forward-looking approaches are listed in the following table:

Forward-Looking Approach	Limitation
Surveys	• Estimate data can be subject to sampling and response biases, and to behavioral biases such as **recency bias** (placing more relevance on recent events) and **confirmation bias** (paying more attention to information that supports one's opinions and ignoring the rest).
DDM	• Assumes constant P/E. where growth in earnings, dividends, and prices are different from one another; an adjustment is needed to reflect P/E multiple expansion or contraction.
Macroeconomic models	• Financial and economic models could have modeling errors or behavioral biases in forecasting.

EXAMPLE 9

ERP Summary

- The ERP represents the expected incremental return that investors demand as compensation for holding risky equity securities rather than a risk-free asset.
- Two broad approaches are used to estimate the ERP: the historical approach, which uses backward-looking historical data to estimate the ERP, and the forward-looking approach, which uses forward-looking, expectational data to estimate the ERP.
- When estimating the ERP using the historical approach, an analyst has four key decisions to make regarding the following choices: (1) equity index, (2) estimation time period, (3) mean measure, and (4) proxy for the risk-free rate.
- Care must be taken in using historical estimates because the ERP can vary over time, and there is a possibility of survivorship bias in the estimate.
- ERP using the forward-looking approach include (1) survey-based estimates, (2) DDM-based estimates, and (3) estimates derived from macroeconomic models.
- Limitations to using forward-looking approaches include sampling, response, and behavioral biases (recency and confirmation biases) associated with survey estimates, the assumption of a constant P/E in DDM estimates, and modeling errors and behavioral biases in macro-economic estimates.

1. Discuss the four key decisions that an analyst must make to estimate an ERP using the historical approach.

Solution

The four key decisions that an analyst must make to use the historical approach are as follows:

- Which equity index to use to represent equity market returns
- What time period to use for estimating the ERP

- Which mean measure to use
- What proxy to use for the risk-free return

2. Justify the use of a long-term government bond yield as a proxy for the risk-free rate in estimating an ERP using the historical approach.

Solution

Even though the YTM on a long-term government bond yield is not in fact risk free because of the coupon reinvestment risk over the life of the bond, the current YTM on a long-term government bond can still be used as an approximation for the expected return on the bond.

3. Calculate estimates of the ERP for a particular market using both the historical approach and the forward-looking approach using the following information:

Expected inflation	1.9%
Expected growth in the P/E	−1.2%
Expected income component	1.8%
Expected growth in real earnings per share	2.7%
Expected change in shares outstanding	0.0%
Current three-month government bond yield	0.96%
Long-term geometric average return of market equity index	9.96%
Long-term geometric average return of short-term government bond	3.15%

Solution

The ERP using the historical approach is calculated as the mean value of the difference between a broad-based equity market index return and a government debt return. Therefore, the ERP using the historical approach is calculated as 9.96% − 3.15% = 6.81%.

The ERP using the forward-looking approach is calculated as

$ERP = \{1.8 - 1.2 + (1.9 + 2.7 + 0.0)\} - 0.96$

$ERP = 5.20 - 0.96 = 4.24\%.$

4. Discuss limitations of using macroeconomic models to estimate a forward-looking ERP.

Solution

ERPs derived from macroeconomic models rely on a number of forecasts of economic variables such as inflation and expected growth in real earnings per share. These forecasts are often generated using financial and economic models that can be subject to potential modeling errors or behavioral biases in forecasting.

THE COST OF EQUITY (REQUIRED RETURN ON EQUITY)

5

☐ | compare methods used to estimate the required return on equity

Upon determining an ERP, analysts can then go on to estimate a company's required rate of return for use in a WACC calculation. To estimate the required rate of return on equity, analysts have a variety of methods available, which include

- DDMs,
- the bond yield plus risk premium build-up method, and
- risk-based models.

Estimating the required rate of return for private and international companies adds further complexity for an analyst.

DDMs

One method of estimating a company's required return on equity is to apply the constant growth DDM used earlier in estimating a forward-looking ERP. That is, we apply this model to a particular subject company given a forecast of its expected future dividend D_1, expected growth rate in dividends g, and current share price P_0, or

$$r_e = \frac{D_1}{P_0} + g. \tag{13}$$

For example, using the constant growth model and given the following inputs for Company X,

Company X	Definition	Value
Current share price	P_0	€40
Expected future dividend	D_1	€1.04
Expected (perpetual) growth rate in dividends	g	4%

the cost of equity estimate is 6.6%, or

$$r_e = \frac{€1.04}{€40.00} + 0.04 = 0.066.$$

Using a DDM for r_e estimation is straightforward and based on the logic that the share price of stock reflects the present value of future dividends and the relevant cash flow to equity holders is the dividend payment. However, it requires that the company's shares be publicly traded and that the company pays dividends that are stable and predictable.

In equity valuation, it is common to build a multiyear financial forecast inclusive of a forecasted share price at the end of the forecast period. Using the DDM, a company's required return on equity can also be estimated by solving the following equation for r_e:

$$P_0 = \left[\sum_{t=1}^{n} \frac{D_t}{(1+r_e)^t}\right] + \frac{P_n}{(1+r_e)^n}. \tag{14}$$

For example, suppose we have the following information:

Year	0	1	2	3	4
Dividend		$1.00	$1.25	$1.35	$1.50

Year	0	1	2	3	4
Stock price	$40.00				$45.00

Given a current share price of USD40, the required rate of equity can be solved for by using a calculator or software tools to arrive at a rate of 6.015%. This calculation incorporates not only the near-term dividend forecast but also the forecast of the share price at some period into the future (i.e., USD45).

TOOLKIT

Using Microsoft Excel,

```
=IRR({-40,1,1.25,1.35,46.5})
```

Using Python,

```
import numpy as np
irr = np.irr([-40,1,1.25,1.35,46.5])
```

Using R,

```
library(jrvFinance)
irr(c(-40,1,1.25,1.35,46.5))
```

Bond Yield Plus Risk Premium Approach

Recall that the **bond yield plus risk premium (BYPRP) approach** is another means of estimating the required return on equity for a company that has public debt. The BYPRP approach estimates a company's required return on equity as:

$$r_e = r_d + \text{RP},\tag{15}$$

where r_d is the company's cost of debt (typically proxied by the YTM on the company's long-term debt), and RP is a risk premium to compensate equity investors for additional risk relative to the risk of investing in the company's debt securities.

The challenge to the BYPRP approach is in estimating RP. One common approach to estimating this risk premium involves using the historical mean difference in returns between an equity market index and a corporate bond index, similar to the process of estimating a historical ERP estimate. This difference yields a historical estimate of the average extra return earned by equity investors relative to corporate bond investors.

Exhibit 11 summarizes key advantages and disadvantages of the BYPRP approach.

Exhibit 11: BYPRP Approach: Advantages and Disadvantages.

Advantages	Disadvantages
• Estimating a company's cost of debt provides a starting point estimate of the return demanded by that company's debt investors.	• Determination of RP is relatively arbitrary. • Approach requires company to have traded debt. • If the company has multiple traded debt securities, each with different features, there is no prescription regarding which bond yield to select. Common practice is to use the company's long-term bond YTM.

EXAMPLE 10

Cost of Equity Estimation using the BYPRP Approach

An analyst estimates a required return on equity for a company using the BYPRP approach. The analyst estimates the yield on the company's bonds as 4.3% and a historical risk premium of 6.1% earned by equity investors relative to long-term corporate bond yields.

1. Calculate an estimate of the required return on equity for the company using the BYPRP approach.

Solution

The required return on equity for the company using the BYPRP approach is estimated at 10.40%, calculated as $r_e = 0.043 + 0.061 = 0.1040$.

2. What are potential considerations associated with this method?

Solution

Considerations include the following:

- Using historical data might not be appropriate if the risk premiums are not stationary.
- The company might have no traded debt or might have multiple issues of traded debt with different yields.

Risk-Based Models

Risk-based models estimate the required return on equity as the sum of the compensation for the time value of money and compensation for bearing risk, or

$$r_e = \text{Compensation for the time value of money} + \text{Compensation for bearing risk.}$$

Several types of risk models are used to develop estimates for r_e, their primary difference being how they model compensation for bearing risk. One class of risk models is factor models, such as the **capital asset pricing model (CAPM)** and the Fama–French models we discuss here. Other factor models include theoretically derived models, statistical factor models, fundamental factor models, and macroeconomic factor models.

CAPM

Recalling the single-factor CAPM, given an estimate of a company's beta (β), the risk-free rate, and the ERP, a company's required return on equity can be estimated as

$$r_e = r_f + \hat{\beta}(\text{ERP}), \tag{16}$$

where $\hat{\beta}$ is a measure of the sensitivity of the company stock's returns to changes in the ERP.

The **market model**, which replaces expected returns on the company and market with their actual historic returns, is commonly used to estimate the company's beta, regressing the company i's equity excess returns, $r_{i,t}$, over the risk-free rate, $r_{f,t}$, against the excess returns of an equity market index, $r_{m,t}$:

$$(r_{i,t} - r_{f,t}) = b_0 + b_1(r_{m,t} - r_{f,t}) + \varepsilon_t. \tag{17}$$

The estimate of b_1, $\hat{b}_1$, is used as a proxy for β_i in Equation 17. A variation of the market model is to not subtract the risk-free rate from the stock's returns and the market returns.

Using this approach, the analyst should consider the following:

- What is the most appropriate equity market index?
- What period was used to estimate beta? As with choosing the time period when estimating a historical ERP, the analyst should seek a balance between sufficient data to develop a robust forecast and using data from too far back in time that might not be representative for the company's stock going forward.
- What proxy was used for the risk-free rate? In an environment of a normal upward-sloping yield curve, using the short-term benchmark government bill rate will yield a meaningfully lower cost of equity estimate than if the long-term government bond YTM is used, particularly if the yield curve is steep.

Even if a company is not publicly traded, it is still possible to estimate the cost of equity using CAPM. Recall that the beta of a comparable, publicly traded company with similar business risk can be estimated and then adjusted for the differing financial leverage of the company to arrive at a beta estimate for the subject company. This is done by "unlevering" the beta of the comparable company to arrive at a beta for a company with no debt in its capital structure and then "re-levering" it to adjust for the debt of the subject company. The estimated beta is then used in the CAPM to estimate a cost of equity for the subject company.

Fama–French Models

The **Fama–French models** are an alternative set of factor models to estimate a company's required return on equity. In the Fama–French three-factor model, in addition to the single market factor, equity returns can be explained by the size of the company—a size factor measured by market capitalization—and the relationship between the book value and equity value of a company's equity, termed the value factor. Using this three-factor model, a company's excess return on equity is calculated as

$$r_e = r_f + \beta_1 \text{ERP} + \beta_2 \text{SMB} + \beta_3 \text{HML}, \tag{18}$$

where SMB is the size premium, equal to the average difference in equity returns between companies with small and large capitalizations, and HML is the value premium, equal to the average difference in equity returns between companies with high and low book-to-market ratios.

The five-factor Fama–French model adds two other factors—a profitability factor (RMW) and an investment factor (CMA):

$$r_e = r_f + \beta_1 \text{ERP} + \beta_2 \text{SMB} + \beta_3 \text{HML} + \beta_4 \text{RMW} + \beta_5 \text{CMA}, \qquad (19)$$

where RMW is the profitability premium, equal to the average difference in equity returns between companies with robust and weak profitability, and CMA is the investment premium, equal to the average difference in equity returns between companies with conservative and aggressive investment portfolios.

In essence, the Fama–French models are an extension of the CAPM that add additional factors to explain excess returns. Like in the CAPM, the estimated slope coefficients in the Fama–French models represent the sensitivity of a stock's returns to the factors. Estimating the Fama–French models is similar to the CAPM: the company's excess equity returns are regressed on the factors to generate estimates of the three betas, referred to as **factor betas**. The required return on equity is then estimated using the factor betas and estimates of the **factor risk premiums**.

EXAMPLE 11

Cost of Equity Estimation using the Fama–French Five-Factor Model

An analyst estimates the required return on equity for a company using the Fama–French five-factor model. The analyst must estimate risk premiums for each factor and run a regression of the company's excess stock returns on the five factors to estimate the factor betas. The premiums and betas are presented in the following table:

Factor	Estimated Beta	Risk Premium
Market	1.2	6.5%
Size (SMB)	0.10	1.8%
Value (HML)	−0.20	4.0%
Profitability (RMW)	0.5	2.0%
Style (CMA)	0.2	1.0%

The risk-free rate is 3.82%.

---

1. Calculate an estimate of the required return on equity for the company using the Fama–French five-factor model.

   Solution

   Using the model, the required return on equity for the company is estimated at 12.2%, or

   $$r_e = 0.0382 + (1.2 \times 0.065) + (0.10 \times 0.018) + (-0.2 \times 0.04) + (0.5 \times 0.02) + (0.2 \times 0.01)$$

   $$r_e = 0.0382 + 0.078 + 0.0018 - 0.008 + 0.01 + 0.002 = 0.1220, \text{ or } 12.2\%$$

The use of these risk-based models is similar:

- Historical returns are used to estimate the relationship between a company's stock's excess returns and these factors.

- Slope coefficients from the estimated regression, along with expectations for the factor risk premiums and the risk-free rate, are used to calculate an estimate of the company's required return on equity.

However, analysts should be aware of the following:

- Estimates from the different risk factor models often yield different results.

- The beta coefficient on the market factor (ERP) normally differs between the single-factor CAPM and multifactor models such as the Fama–French models because of the presence of the additional factors in the models.

- Analysts often use a short-term risk-free rate when computing excess returns to estimate the factor betas in these risk-based models. In an environment with an upward-sloping yield curve, doing so can result in the understatement of the risk-free rate. However, this understatement can be remedied by using a different time series for the risk-free rate, properly adjusted for periodicity, when regressing historical stock returns against these different factors.

Estimating the Cost of Equity for Private Companies

Estimating the required return on equity for a privately held company is more challenging for analysts, given the following:

- Security prices and returns are not readily available for private companies, so risk factor models such as the CAPM and Fama–French models cannot be directly applied to privately held companies. However, these models can be adapted and applied indirectly to private companies.

- Unlike public companies, private companies might be smaller, earlier in the company life cycle, have owners as managers, and have ownership structures with greater concentration of control.

- Private companies are less liquid and might disclose less investor relevant information than public companies.

The required return on equity for private companies often includes

- a **size premium (SP)**,

- an **industry risk premium (IP)**, and

- a **specific-company risk premium (SCRP)**.

A smaller company size is typically associated with greater company risk which can arise from greater difficulty in securing capital, more uncertain growth prospects, and riskier business operations. Collectively, these can result in higher risk and required returns on equity for private companies. An IP can be added for private companies in relatively riskier industries.

The SCRP is a general risk premium that reflects factors such as geographic risk, key-person risk, or other firm-specific factors that might not be easy to diversify away. Another key risk factor inherent in private companies is their illiquidity. However, the higher illiquidity risk is typically not reflected in the required return as an additional risk premium but rather as a reduction in the estimated value for an equity interest, referred to as a discount for lack of marketability.

To estimate the required return on equity for a private company, analysts commonly have two choices, namely,

- the expanded CAPM and

- the build-up approach.

Expanded CAPM

To estimate r_e for non-publicly traded or private companies, analysts can use an adaptation of the CAPM called the expanded CAPM, which adds a premium for small company size and other company-specific risks. The expanded CAPM requires estimation of a beta from a peer group of publicly traded companies, with r_e calculated as

$$r_e = r_f + \beta_{peer}(\text{ERP}) + \text{SP} + \text{IP} + \text{SCRP}. \tag{20}$$

We use the following steps in the estimation:

1. Estimate an industry beta, β_{peer}, from a peer group of publicly traded companies in the same industry as the subject private company.

2. Given an estimate of the risk-free rate r_f and the ERP, compute a CAPM estimate for r_e.

3. Determine whether additional risk premia for company size and other company-specific risk factors are warranted.

4. If warranted, add relevant size and company-specific risk premia to arrive at a final estimate of r_e for the subject company.

Analysts typically add an SP to the required return on equity for smaller, privately held companies. The amount of the SP is often assumed to be inversely related to the size of the company being valued. When the SP estimate is appropriately based on the lowest market-cap decile of public companies—frequently the case because many private businesses are small relative to publicly traded companies—the result corresponds to the return on an average-systematic-risk micro-cap public equity issue.

An analyst should exercise caution when using historical measures of the SP. The population of small capitalization companies likely includes previously larger capitalization companies in financial distress. If this is the case, a historical risk premium estimate could require a downward adjustment for estimating the required return for a small, but financially healthy, private company.

The estimation of a company-specific risk premium is varied in practice and based on both qualitative and quantitative factors. These factors are summarized in Exhibit 12.

Exhibit 12: Company-Specific Premium: Qualitative versus Quantitative Factors

Qualitative Factors	Quantitative Factors
• The industry in which the business operates	• Financial and operational leverage
• Competitive position within the industry	• Volatility in cash flows and earnings
• Management's experience and expertise	• Earnings predictability
• Customer and supplier concentration	• Pricing power
• Geographic concentration of the business	
• Governance model of the company	
• Asset nature and type (tangible vs. intangible)	

These factors can be analyzed relative to those of a peer group of publicly traded or other privately held companies in the same industry. The larger the company-specific risks identified by the analyst, the larger the company-specific risk premium.

Build-Up Approach

A second approach analysts use for estimating a private company's r_e is the build-up approach. This approach involves "building up" the required return on equity, beginning with the risk-free rate, and then adding relevant risk premia to account for various risk considerations, or

$$r_e = r_f + \text{ERP} + \text{SP} + \text{SCRP}, \tag{21}$$

where SP is a size premium and SCRP is a specific-company risk premium.

The ERP is often estimated with reference to equity indexes of publicly traded companies and is not beta adjusted. The largest market-capitalization companies typically constitute a large fraction of these indexes' value. With a beta of 1.0 implicitly multiplying the ERP, the sum of the risk-free rate and the ERP is effectively the required return on equity for an average-systematic-risk large-cap public equity issue. The build-up approach starts with this and then adjusts for additional size and company specific premia as shown in Exhibit 13.

Exhibit 13: Build-Up Approach for Private Companies

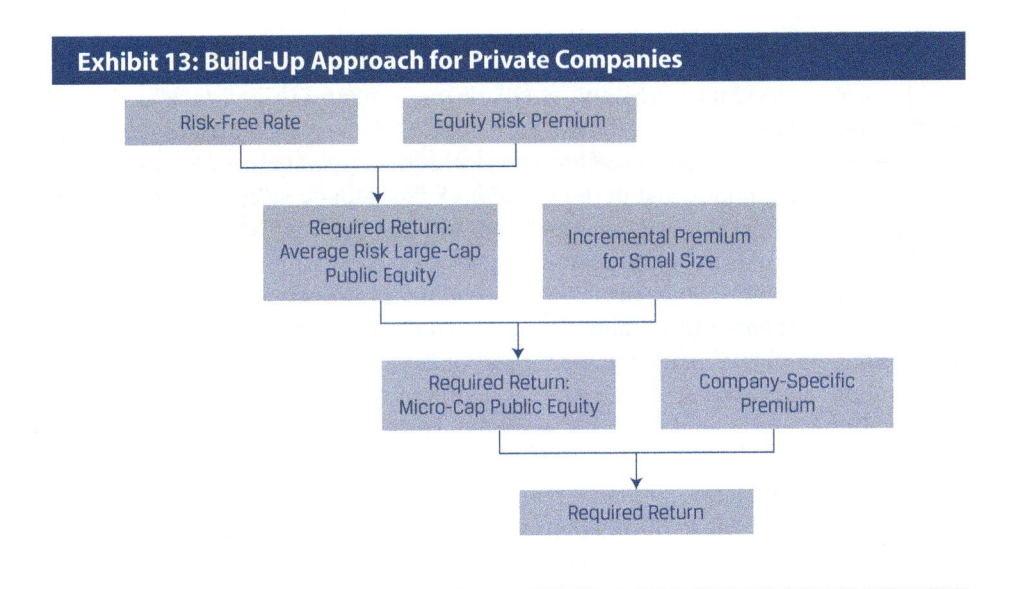

As with the extended CAPM method, analysts often add an SP to account for the smaller size of most privately held companies, again where the premium is typically after adjustment for the differences in the betas of small- and large-cap stocks to isolate the effect of size—a beta-adjusted SP.

Finally, an analysis of risk factors incremental to those captured by the previously included premia might lead the analyst to also add a specific-company premium to arrive at a final estimate of the subject company's required return on equity. The build-up approach might be appropriate when a set of comparable public companies are unavailable or of questionable comparability.

International Considerations

Exchange rates, inflation, data, and models in emerging markets are possible considerations for an analyst when estimating r_e for international companies. For example, factor models, such as the locally focused CAPM, might not work well for an emerging market.

Country Spread and Country Risk Rating Models

Risk premium estimation for emerging markets is particularly challenging. Of the numerous approaches that have been proposed to supplement or replace traditional historical and forward-looking methods, we look at two:

- the country spread model
- the country risk rating model

Using the country spread model for ERP estimation, an additional risk premium—the **country risk premium (CRP)** or country spread premium—is required by investors for the added risk of investing in another country, often referred to as the "local" country. The added risk could be due to economic conditions, risk of expropriation, political risk, or other risk.

For an emerging equity market, this model is

$$ERP = \frac{\text{ERP for a}}{\text{developed market}} + (\lambda \times \text{Country risk premium}), \tag{22}$$

where λ is the level of exposure of the company to the local country.

The CRP represents a premium associated with the anticipated greater risk of a market compared with the benchmark developed market. One method for calculating this premium is to use the **sovereign yield spread**, or a comparison of the yield on a local country, denominated in the benchmark developed country's currency, with the yield on a similar maturity sovereign bond in the developed country.

Typically, analysts hope that a sovereign bond yield spread is adequate for approximating this premium. Thus, the country premium is often estimated as the yield on emerging market bonds (denominated in the currency of the developed market) minus the yield on developed market government bonds.

Consider the sovereign risk ratings in Exhibit 14 and the corresponding CRPs. These CRPs are estimated using the sovereign yield spread relative to a benchmark country's yield.

The problem with this method is that we are using a bond yield spread to estimate a country's ERP. Because of differences in legal and market environments among countries, using the yield spread on sovereign bonds might not be appropriate for a cost of equity.

Exhibit 14: CRPs by Country Based on the Sovereign Yield Spread

Country	Sovereign Risk Rating (10 = Most risk)	CRP
A	6	3.90%
B	2	0.50%
C	5	2.75%
D	7	5.40%
E	4	1.75%
F	10	19.50%
G	9	14.50%
H	1	0.0%
I	3	1.0%

Country	Sovereign Risk Rating (10 = Most risk)	CRP
J	8	9.20%

Aswath Damodaran (2021) refined the CRP estimation by modifying the sovereign yield spread for the relative volatility between equity versus bond returns, where

$$\text{Country risk premium} = \text{Sovereign yield spread} \times \frac{\sigma_{Equity}}{\sigma_{Bond}}, \tag{23}$$

→ use this in equation (22)

where

σ_{Equity} is the volatility of the local country's equity market

σ_{Bond} is the volatility of the local country's bond market

This method, however, requires that the local country have both historical equity and bond returns.

Extended CAPM

In cases where there is exposure to a country's risk, a country risk adjustment should be made to r_e. Several approaches are used in estimating r_e for companies operating internationally. These include the following:

- global CAPM
- international CAPM
- country spread and risk rating models

In the **global CAPM (GCAPM)**, where a global market index is the single factor, there are no assumed significant risk differences across countries. The issue is that a likely result is a low, or even negative, slope coefficient because of the correlation between emerging and developed market returns being quite low in general. Expanding this model to include a second factor, such as domestic market index returns, mitigates this to a degree but depends on the availability of reliable financial data in the emerging market.

Another approach is the **international CAPM (ICAPM)**, where the returns on a stock in an emerging market are regressed against the risk premium of a global index (r_{gm}) in addition to that of wealth-weighted foreign currency index (r_c):

$$E(r_e) = r_f + \beta_G\big(E(r_{gm}) - r_f\big) + \beta_C\big(E(r_c) - r_f\big). \tag{24}$$

Proxies for the global index *(gm)* include the MSCI All Country World Index (MSCI ACWI) and the FTSE All-World Index. The foreign currency index, r_c, aggregates the return from investing in the foreign currency relative to the company's domestic currency using country relative wealth, not market capitalization, weightings. The return to each currency consists of the expected change in the exchange rate plus the risk-free return of that country.

The sensitivity to the global index, β_G, depends on the company's relationship with its local economy versus the global economy. Lower values of β_G are associated with companies that are less connected to the global economy. The sensitivity to the foreign currency index, β_C, depends on whether the company's cash flows are sensitive to exchange rates through its imports, exports, and investments.

Comparison of International Adjustment Methods

Analysts face challenges in estimating the cost of equity for cross-border valuations, given that there is no generally accepted methodology for estimating the CRP for companies with operations in a developing country.

- If the company's operations are global, but limited to developed countries, the GCAPM and ICAPM are reasonable methods to apply.

- If however, the company's operations extend to developing countries, the methodology is less clear. The estimation of the CRP using the sovereign yield approach might be appropriate, but these estimations are based on historical rates and might not reflect the risk premium going forward.

EXAMPLE 12

CRP

An analyst is estimating the CRP for the Makinassi Company headquartered in Country X that has 40% of its sales in Country Y. The analyst gathers the following information:

Country	Sovereign country yield spread	Standard deviation of equity returns	Standard deviation of bond returns
X (Headquarters)	1.5%	2.0%	1.0%
Y (Local)	3.2%	4.0%	2.5%

1. Using the Damodaran model, calculate the CRP that the analyst should use for the Makinassi Company.

Solution

From the perspective of a company operating in Country X, the relevant sovereign yield spread is 3.2% − 1.5% = 1.7%. Adjusting this spread for the relative volatility of the equity and bond returns in the local market, the premium is

$$CRP = 0.017 \times 0.04/0.025 = 0.0272$$

Adjusting this premium for the exposure that Makinassi has to Country Y,

$$Premium = 0.40 \times 0.0272 = 0.01088$$

Therefore, when the analyst calculates the cost of equity for Makinassi, he should add a CRP of 1.088% to the cost of equity for the company.

Required Return on Equity Summary

- Models used to estimate the cost of equity include (1) the DDM, (2) the BYPRP model, and (3) risk-based models.

- Risk-based models for estimating the cost of equity include the CAPM and factor models, such as the Fama–French models.

- Estimating the cost of equity for a private company using risk-based models requires adjusting the premiums for company size, the industry in which it operates, and any specific company premium. A method that can be used to estimate the cost of equity for private companies is the expanded CAPM.

- The build-up method for the cost of equity starts with the risk-free rate and the ERP, then adjusts this cost for any other premia.

- The cost of equity can be adjusted for additional risk related to international considerations using the CRP or the ICAPM.

KNOWLEDGE CHECK

1. What are the primary differences between the CAPM and the Fama–French models for estimating the cost of equity?

Solution

The CAPM is a one-factor model—the market factor, that is, the primary driver of security returns in the market. The Fama–French models allow for more factors to influence security returns beyond the market factor.

2. Classify each of the following elements of the DDM based on the effect on the cost of equity using the DDM.

Change, holding all other factors constant	Effect on Cost of Equity		
	No effect	Increase	Decrease
Increase in the current dividend			
Increase in the expected growth rate of dividends			
Increase in the share price			
Decrease in the current dividend			
Decrease in the expected growth rate of dividends			
Decrease in the share price			

Solution

Change, holding all other factors constant	No effect	Positive	Negative
Increase in the current dividend		✓	
Increase in the expected growth rate of dividends		✓	
Increase in the share price			✓
Decrease in the current dividend			✓
Decrease in the expected growth rate of dividends			✓
Decrease in the share price		✓	

3. An analyst is using a three-factor model with factors F1, F2, and F3 to estimate the risk premium for an individual stock. The results of the regression
   are

   $$r_i - r_f = 0.003 + 1.2\,F1 - 0.4\,F2 + 0.2\,F3.$$

   If the expected risk-free rate is 2%, and the three factor risk premiums are

   F1 = 0.05,
   F2 = 0.01, and
   F3 = 0.04,

   what is the expected cost of equity?

   Solution

   The required return on equity for the stock is

   $$r_e - r_f = 0.003 + (1.2 \times 0.05) - (0.4 \times 0.01) + (0.2 \times 0.04) = 0.067.$$
   The estimate of the cost of equity is $0.067 + 0.02 = 0.087$, or 8.7%.

4. Consider a company that currently pays a dividend of USD2.50. The current
   price of the stock is USD50, and the dividend is expected to grow at a rate of
   5% per year into perpetuity. Using the DDM, determine the following:

   What is the company's required rate of return on equity?

   Solution

   $$r_e = \frac{\$2.5(1 + 0.05)}{\$50} + 0.05 = \frac{\$2.625}{\$50} + 0.05 = 0.0525 + 0.05 = 0.1025, \text{ or } 10.25\%.$$

5. If the growth rate of dividends is revised upward, what effect does this have
   on the required rate of return on equity?

   Solution

   If the growth rate is revised upward, both the dividend yield (D_1/P_0) and the
   growth rate (g) increase, increasing the required rate of return on equity.

6. If the price of the stock declines, but expectations regarding dividends and
   dividend growth remain the same, what effect does this have on the required
   rate of return on equity?

   Solution

   If the stock price declines, the dividend yield (D_1/P_0) increases, resulting in
   the increased required rate of return on equity.

7. An analyst is estimating the required return on equity for a company and has
   gathered the following information:

Estimated risk-free rate (10-year government bond)	6%
Estimated equity market return	10%
Estimated ERP beta	0.8
Estimated SMB premium	5%
Estimated HML premium	2%
Fama–French three-factor regression estimation:	
Intercept	0.01
Coefficient on market factor	0.75

| Coefficient on SMB factor | 0.15 |
| Coefficient on HML factor | 0.05 |

The Fama–French three-factor model coefficients were estimated using the same risk-free rate that is used in the CAPM.

What is the required rate of return based on the CAPM?

Solution

$r_e = 0.06 + 0.8(0.10 - 0.06) = 0.092$, or 9.2%

8. What is the required rate of return based on the Fama–French model?

Solution

$r_e - 0.06 = 0.01 + [0.75(0.10 - 0.06)] + [0.15(0.05)] + [0.05(0.02)]$
$r_e - 0.06 = 0.0485$
$r_e = 0.1085$, or 10.85%

9. Why do these required rates of return on equity differ between these two models?

Solution

The Fama–French model allows more factors or drivers of returns, whereas the CAPM limits the factors to the single market factor. In this case, the SMB and HML factors increase the required return on equity by [0.15(0.05)] + [0.05(0.02)] = 0.0085, or 0.85%.

MINI-CASE 1

6

☐ | estimate the cost of debt or required return on equity for a public company and a private company

Gretna Engines

KM is a junior analyst at Atla Investments. KM meets with her manager to discuss a possible investment in Gretna Engines. KM's manager tasks her with estimating Gretna's cost of debt and equity as a starting point for determining Gretna's WACC and related valuation.

KM notes some of Gretna's key information:

Company: Gretna Engines	Small capitalization, publicly traded company
Business Model	Manufacturer of small engines for boats and recreational all-terrain vehicles (ATVs). Operates with a relatively high proportion of fixed costs in its cost structure.
Industry	Industrial equipment (cyclical)
Revenues, Earnings, Cash Flows	All have been trending upward in recent years but vary considerably over the business cycle.

Nature of Assets	Assets consist primarily of inventory and property, plant, and equipment representing its engine production facilities.

Gretna has recently been performing well in terms of sales and profitability. However, several years back, because of a significant decline in sales of boats and ATVs, the company found itself in a liquidity crisis. At that time, the company issued redeemable, preferred stock to improve its liquidity position, albeit at a rather high cost.

In recent financial filings, Gretna's management has indicated that given favorable market conditions, they are seeking to issue new, unsecured debt to retire the preferred shares at par value. Exhibit 15 presents Gretna's current capital structure and selected information about each capital type.

Exhibit 15: Gretna's Current Capital Structure and Related Information

Capital Type	Current Capital Structure	Selected Capital Type Information
Debt	20%	Single debt issue: 7% coupon rate; remaining maturity of seven years; semiannual payments. Straight unsecured debt; BBB credit rating; thinly traded issue—no reliable YTM available.
Preferred Equity	15%	Dividend rate of 7%, currently redeemable at par value of 1,000 per share Trades frequently; current share price is 980
Common Equity	65%	Actively traded

Next, KM gathers information on four liquid, semiannual-pay corporate bonds with the same BBB rating as Gretna, shown in Exhibit 16.

Exhibit 16: Selected Information on Liquid, BBB-Rated Bonds

	Coupon Rate	Remaining Maturity	Current Price (per 100 of par value)
Bond 1	5%	4 years	99.50
Bond 2	7%	4 years	106.46
Bond 3	6%	8 years	100
Bond 4	8%	8 years	112.42

Using the CAPM and the Fama–French five-factor (FF5) model, KM estimates Gretna's cost of equity by regressing Gretna's excess returns on the relevant risk factors using the most recent 60 months of returns. Factor betas from the CAPM and the FF5 model, along with her estimated factor risk premiums, are shown in Exhibit 17. She decides to use the 20-year government benchmark rate of 2.1% as the risk-free proxy.

Exhibit 17: CAPM and FF5 Factor Beta and Risk Premiums

Factor	Factor Beta	Risk Premium
A. CAPM Factor Beta and Risk Premium		
Market (ERP)	0.91	5.5%
B. FFM5 Factor Betas and Risk Premiums		
Market (ERP)	0.95	5.5%
Size (SMB)	0.45	1.8%
Value (HML)	0.14	3.9%
Profitability (RMW)	−0.19	3.1%
Investment (CMA)	0.30	3.7%

Finally, KM also estimates Gretna's cost of equity using the BYPRP approach. For this estimate, she assumes a historical risk premium of 6.2% earned by equity investors relative to long-term corporate bond yields.

KM reports back to her manager with her estimates of Gretna's costs of debt and equity. Her manager asks how she arrived at the ERP of 5.5% in her cost of equity estimates. KM tells her manager that she estimated it using the historical approach, electing to use the short-term government bill rate and an arithmetic mean in the estimation.

KNOWLEDGE CHECK

1. Identify two characteristics of Gretna's business model that might cause the firm to have a relatively higher cost of capital.

   Solution

   One characteristic would be relatively high volatility (less stability) in revenues and earnings, given the cyclical nature of the industry in which Gretna operates. Such firms are likely to face a higher cost of capital than firms with low volatility in revenues and earnings. Another factor could be the relative illiquidity of the firm's assets. All else equal, firms with asset bases comprising relatively low (high) proportions of liquid assets are more likely to have higher (lower) costs of capital. A third factor would be that Gretna currently operates with high operating leverage (a high proportion of fixed costs in its cost structure).

2. How might KM estimate a current cost of debt given Gretna's current capital structure? What is Gretna's current cost of debt?

   Solution

   In the absence of a reliable YTM, given the debt's illiquidity, KM could use matrix pricing to estimate Gretna's current cost of debt. The current market prices for each of the four similarly rated bonds in Exhibit 16 are presented in the following matrix:

Price Matrix: BBB-Rated Bonds				
Remaining Maturity	**5% Coupon**	**6% Coupon**	**7% Coupon**	**8% Coupon**
4 Years	99.5		106.46	
5 Years				

Remaining Maturity	5% Coupon	6% Coupon	7% Coupon	8% Coupon
6 Years				
7 years				
8 years		100		112.42

Step 1   Calculate the YTM for each bond based on its market price.

Bond 1 YTM: N = 8; PV= –99.5; PMT = 2.5; FV = 100; CPT I/Y
= 2.570% × 2 = <u>5.140%</u>

Bond 2 YTM: N = 8; PV= –106.46; PMT = 3.5; FV = 100; CPT I/Y
= 2.595% × 2 = <u>5.191%</u>

Bond 3 YTM: N = 16; PV= –100; PMT = 3; FV = 100; CPT I/Y
= 3.000% × 2 = <u>6.000%</u>

Bond 4 YTM: N = 16; PV= –112.42; PMT = 4; FV = 100; CPT I/Y
= 3.010% × 2 = <u>6.021%</u>

Step 2   Calculate the average YTM for each maturity (i.e., 4-year and 8-year). This can be done by placing the YTM and price for each bond into a similar matrix form.

Price and YTM Matrix: BBB-Rated Bonds					
Remaining Maturity	5% Coupon	6% Coupon	7% Coupon	8% Coupon	Average YTM
4 Years	99.5 (5.140%)		106.46 (5.191%)		5.165%
5 Years					
6 Years					
7 years					
8 years		100 (6.000%)		112.42 (6.021%)	6.010%

Average YTM (4-year maturity) = (5.140% + 5.191%)/2 = 5.166%
Average YTM (8-year maturity) = (6.000% + 6.021%)/2 = 6.011%

Step 1   Use linear interpolation to estimate the average YTMs for the 5-year, 6-year, and 7-year maturities by first computing the difference in YTMs between the 8-year average YTM and the 4-year average YTM (linear interpolation assumes that the yields between the two known yields are equal distance apart).

8-year average YTM – 4-year average YTM = 6.011% – 5.166% = 0.845%
Divide this difference by the difference in years between the known yields (in this case, 8 – 4 = 4): 0.845%/4 = 0.211%.
Use this 0.211% as the estimated annual incremental in average yield as the term to maturity increases after year 4:
Estimated average YTM for 5-year maturity =
4-year average YTM + 0.211% = 5.166% + 0.211% = 5.377%
Estimated average YTM for 6-year maturity =

5-year average YTM + 0.211% = 5.377% + 0.211% = 5.588%
Estimated average YTM for 7-year maturity =
6-year average YTM + 0.211% = 5.588% + 0.211% = 5.799%

Based on matrix pricing, Gretna's debt would likely have a YTM of approximately 5.799%, or 5.8%. However, given that this YTM was derived from more liquid bonds than Gretna's thinly traded bond, Gretna's debt would likely have a slightly higher YTM to compensate investors for liquidity risk.

3. What is Gretna's current cost of preferred equity?

Solution

Gretna's preferred equity is actively traded and is currently trading at a price of 980. Given its annual dividend rate of 7% and par value of 1,000, the annual dividend amount is 70. Therefore, the cost of the preferred issue can be estimated at 7.14%, calculated using the perpetuity formula (which is the DDM formula, solving for r_e, with a growth rate equal to 0):

Cost of preferred equity = 70/980 = 7.14%.

4. How might KM estimate Gretna's cost of debt should management execute its plan to redeem its preferred equity?

Solution

Currently, debt and preferred equity represent 35% of Gretna's capital structure. If Gretna's management follows through with its plan to issue new debt to redeem its preferred equity, the company's new capital structure would be 35% debt and 65% common equity. A starting point for KM to estimate a new cost of debt would be to look at the current estimated cost of debt of 5.8% and cost of preferred equity of 7.14%. Given that debtholders have a higher claim on assets than preferred shareholders, the additional debt would likely have a slightly higher cost than the current estimated cost of debt of 5.8% but lower cost than the current 7.14% cost of preferred equity.

5. Describe the market conditions that would lead Gretna's management team to reach its conclusion about the timing of issuing the new debt.

Solution

Favorable market conditions for issuing the new debt would be a relatively low risk-free rate and/or relatively tighter credit spreads. Such conditions would likely lead to a relatively lower cost of debt for Gretna. At the current price of 980, the preferred is trading at a slight discount to par. The fact that management believes current market conditions to issue the debt are favorable, even when the company would have to redeem the preferred equity at par value (a slight premium to the current price), suggests that the risk-free rate is relatively low and/or credit spreads are relatively tight.

6. What actions could Gretna's management team take to further lower the cost of issuing the new debt?

Solution

To further lower its debt cost at issuance, Gretna's management could consider (1) issuing secured debt, secured by some of its property, plant and equipment; (2) issuing the debt with a put option; or (3) issuing the debt with a conversion feature. First, issuing secured debt will typically be cheaper than issuing unsecured debt because the bondholder now has collateral to lessen the risk of loss given default. Second, issuing debt with a put or conversion feature provides investors with valuable rights that also serve to lower the initial yield on the new debt at issuance.

7. What is Gretna's cost of common equity using the (1) CAPM, (2) FF5 model, and (3) BYPRP model?

Solution

Gretna's estimated cost of common equity using the CAPM is 7.11%, calculated as

$$r_e = r_f + \beta(ERP)$$
$$r_e = 0.021 + 0.91(0.055) = 0.0711, \text{ or } 7.11\%.$$

Gretna's estimated cost of common equity using the FF5 model is 9.20%, calculated as

$$r_e = r_f + \beta_1(ERP) + \beta_2 SMB + \beta_3 HML + \beta_4 RMW + \beta_5 CMA$$
$$r_e = 0.021 + 0.95(0.055) + 0.45(0.018) + 0.14(0.0390) - 0.19(0.031) + 0.30(0.037)$$
$$= 0.0920, \text{ or } 9.20\%$$

Gretna's estimated cost of common equity using the BYPRP model can be calculated by adding the estimated cost of debt of 5.8% derived from matrix pricing and KM's estimated premium of 6.2% earned by equity investors relative to long-term corporate bond yields:

$$r_{e=}r_d + RP$$
$$r_e = 0.058 + 0.062 = 0.12, \text{ or } 12\%$$

8. Explain why, given the data from Panel A of Exhibit 17, the CAPM estimate of Gretna's cost of common equity might not be a reasonable estimate.

Solution

The three estimates of the cost of common equity, based on the information given, are as follows:

- CAPM: 7.11%
- FF5 model: 9.20%
- BYPRP estimate: 12.00%

The cost of preferred equity is 7.14%. Given that common shareholders have a residual claim on assets below that of preferred shareholders, they will demand a higher required return on equity. Thus, the CAPM estimate of 7.11% does not appear to be a realistic estimate, given the estimated cost of preferred shareholders of 7.14%.

9. Explain why KM's estimate of the ERP might be relatively high or low, given her two choices in the estimation.

Solution

Two of the four key assumptions an analyst must make in estimating the ERP using the historical approach are (1) which proxy to use for the risk-free return and (2) which mean measure to use. KM estimated the ERP using the short-term government bill rate and an arithmetic mean.
Assuming a typical normal yield curve for most of the estimation period where short-term government bond yields were lower than longer-term

government bond yields, the use of the short-term bill rate in the estimation would lead to a higher estimate of the ERP. Further, using an arithmetic mean rather than a geometric mean would very likely lead to a higher estimate of the ERP. Thus, KM's estimate of the ERP under her chosen assumptions is likely to be high relative to another estimate that uses other choices (long-term government bond YTM, geometric mean) for those two key assumptions.

MINI-CASE 2

7

☐ | evaluate a company's capital structure and cost of capital relative to peers

Precision Irrigation

LM is an analyst in the corporate development group at Hydrocrop Ltd, a company that manufactures and sells irrigation equipment. Management is considering the acquisition of Precision Irrigation, a private company that offers software solutions aimed at increasing irrigation efficiency. Precision is located in an emerging-market country with higher sovereign risk. LM has been tasked with estimating Precision's WACC.

LM gathers financial information on Precision and publicly traded software companies in the emerging country. The information is presented in Exhibit 18.

Exhibit 18: Selected Information for Precision and Peer Companies

	Precision Irrigation	Software Industry Average
A. Common-Sized Balance Sheet		
Cash and equivalents	9%	14%
Accounts receivable	10%	12%
Inventory	4%	3%
Other current assets	5%	4%
Property, plant, and equipment (net)	21%	30%
Intangible assets and goodwill	47%	32%
Other assets	4%	5%
B. Other Information		
Total debt (millions)	18.4	296.4
Total assets (millions)	105.2	1,276.2
EBITDA (millions)	12.2	177.4

	Precision Irrigation	Software Industry Average
Interest expense (millions)	1.6	23.5
Beta	N/A	1.25
Marginal tax rate	20%	25%

Other notes about Precision are as follows:

- The company's founder and CEO continues to be highly involved in all aspects of the company's operations, with no clear succession plan in place.
- Approximately 60% of the company's revenues come from software subscriptions, and 70% come from five major customers within close geographic proximity of each other.

LM estimates a cost of debt by estimating a synthetic bond yield on the company's 10-year non-traded bonds. He relies on an internally developed schedule of synthetic credit ratings driven by companies' leverage ratios. A portion of the schedule is presented in Exhibit 19.

Exhibit 19: Synthetic Credit Rating Schedule

Credit Rating	IC	D/E	Credit Spread
AAA	IC > 11 times	D/E < 15%	0.82%
AA	9 < IC < 11	15% < D/E < 20%	1.09%
A	7 < IC < 9	20% < D/E < 25%	1.46%
BBB	5 < IC < 7	25% < D/E < 30%	2.15%
BB	3 < IC < 1.4	30% < D/E < 40%	2.88%

The YTM on the emerging country's 10-year benchmark government bond is 5.41%. Interest expense is fully tax deductible.

LM also estimates a cost of equity for Precision using both the extended CAPM and the build-up approach. The corporate development team typically assigns an SP in the range of 3%–6% and an SCRP of 4%–8% for private companies, depending on company size and characteristics, respectively. After consulting with colleagues, LM assigns the relevant risk premiums presented in Exhibit 20.

Exhibit 20: Factor Risk Premiums

Factor	Risk Premium
Market (ERP)	6%
Size (SP)	5%
Industry (IP)	1%

Factor	Risk Premium
Specific-company (SCRP)	6%

In arriving at a final cost of debt and equity for Precision, LM believes a CRP of 2% is warranted to compensate for the higher sovereign risk. In estimating Precision's WACC, LM assumes that the company's current capital structure is its long-term, target capital structure.

PRACTICE PROBLEMS

An equity index is established in Year 1 for a country that has recently moved to a market economy. The index vendor constructed returns for the four years prior to Year 1 based on the initial group of companies constituting the index in Year 1. From Year 12 to Year 16, a series of military confrontations concerning a disputed border disrupted the economy and financial markets. The dispute is conclusively arbitrated at the end of Year 16. In total, 20 years of equity market return history is available. Other selected data are in the following tables.

Selected Data	
Geometric mean return relative to 10-year government bond returns (over a 20-year period)	2% per year
Arithmetic mean return relative to 10-year government bond returns (over a 20-year period)	2.3% per year
Index forward dividend yield	1%
Forecasted public company earnings growth	5% per year
Forecasted market P/E growth	1% per year
Forecasted real GDP growth rate (by Year 19)	4%
Current vs. long-term inflation forecast	6% vs. 4% per year
Current yield curve (inversion)	Short maturities: 9% 10-year maturities: 7%

1. The inclusion of index returns prior to Year 1 would be expected to:

   A. bias the historical ERP estimate upward.

   B. bias the historical ERP estimate downward.

   C. have no effect on the historical ERP estimate.

2. The events of 2012 to 2016 would be expected to:

   A. bias the historical ERP estimate upward.

   B. bias the historical ERP estimate downward.

   C. have no effect on the historical ERP estimate.

3. In the current interest rate environment, using a required return on equity estimate based on the short-term government bond rate and a historical ERP defined in terms of a short-term government bond rate would be expected to:

   A. bias long-term required return on equity estimates upward.

   B. bias long-term required return on equity estimates downward.

   C. have no effect on long-term required return on equity estimates.

4. An estimate of the ERP consistent with the Grinold-Kroner model is *closest* to:

    A. 2.7%.

    B. 3.0%.

    C. 4.3%.

5. Common stock issues in the aforementioned market with average systematic risk are *most likely* to have required rates of return of:

    A. between 2% and 7%.

    B. between 7% and 9%.

    C. 9% or greater.

SOLUTIONS

1. A is correct. The backfilling of index returns using companies that have survived to the index construction date is expected to introduce a positive survivorship bias into returns.

2. B is correct. The events of Year 12 through Year 16 depressed share returns but (1) are not a persistent feature of the stock market environment, (2) were not offset by other positive events within the historical record, and (3) have led to relatively low valuation levels, which are expected to rebound.

3. A is correct. The required return reflects the magnitude of the historical ERP, which is generally higher when based on a short-term interest rate (as a result of the normal upward-sloping yield curve), and the current value of the rate being used to represent the risk-free rate. The short-term rate is currently higher than the long-term rate, which will also increase the required return estimate. The short-term interest rate, however, overstates the long-term expected inflation rate. Using the short-term interest rate, estimates of the long-term required return on equity will be biased upward.

4. B is correct.

   i = 4% per year (long-term forecast of inflation)

   g = 4% per year (growth in real GDP)

   Δ (P/E0 = 1% per year (growth in market P/E)

   dy = 1% per year (dividend yield or the income portion)

   Risk-free return = r_f = 7% per year (for 10-year maturities)

   Using the Grinold-Kroner model, the ERP estimate is

   ERP = {1.0 + 1.0 +[4.0 + 4.0 + 0.0)] } − 7.0 = 3.0%.

   The premium of 3.0% compensates investors for average market risk, given expectations for inflation, real earnings growth, P/E growth, and anticipated income.

5. C is correct. Based on a long-term government bond yield of 7%, a beta of 1, and any of the risk premium estimates that can be calculated from the givens (e.g., a 2% historical risk premium estimate or 3.0% Grinold-Kroner ERP estimate), the required rate of return would be at least 9%. Based on using a short-term rate of 9%, C is the correct choice.

5

Corporate Restructuring

LEARNING OUTCOMES

Mastery	*The candidate should be able to:*
☐	explain types of corporate restructurings and issuers' motivations for pursuing them
☐	explain the initial evaluation of a corporate restructuring
☐	demonstrate valuation methods for, and interpret valuations of, companies involved in corporate restructurings
☐	demonstrate how corporate restructurings affect an issuer's EPS, net debt to EBITDA ratio, and weighted average cost of capital
☐	evaluate corporate investment actions, including equity investments, joint ventures, and acquisitions
☐	evaluate corporate divestment actions, including sales and spin offs
☐	evaluate cost and balance sheet restructurings

INTRODUCTION

1

Corporate issuers change over time. While many changes are evolutionary, such as launching new products and expanding capacity, others involve more revolutionary changes to the legal and accounting structure of the issuer. The most well-known among these structural changes is acquisitions, in which one company buys another. Other well-known changes include divestitures and spin offs, in which an issuer sells or separates a segment of its business. Common features among these changes are that they tend to attract significant press and analyst attention and their announcement is associated with increased securities trading volume.

In this reading, you will learn how to evaluate corporate restructurings from the perspective of an independent investment analyst. We begin our discussion in Section 2 with an overview of corporate restructurings, including putting these events in the context of the corporate life cycle, and corporate issuers' motivations for pursuing them. In Sections 3 and 4, we discuss a three-step process for evaluating corporate restructurings as an investment analyst. Sections 5–7 demonstrate the evaluation process with case studies for each major type of corporate restructuring. The reading concludes with a summary and practice problems.

2   CORPORATE EVOLUTION, ACTIONS, AND MOTIVATIONS

☐ | explain types of corporate restructurings and issuers' motivations for pursuing them

Corporate Life Cycle and Actions

Companies tend to follow a life cycle composed of four stages: start-up, growth, maturity, and decline. At each life-cycle stage, there is a corresponding revenue growth, profitability, and risk profile, which in turn generally determine the company's financing mix. A typical company's life cycle is illustrated in Exhibit 1.

Exhibit 1: Company Life Cycle

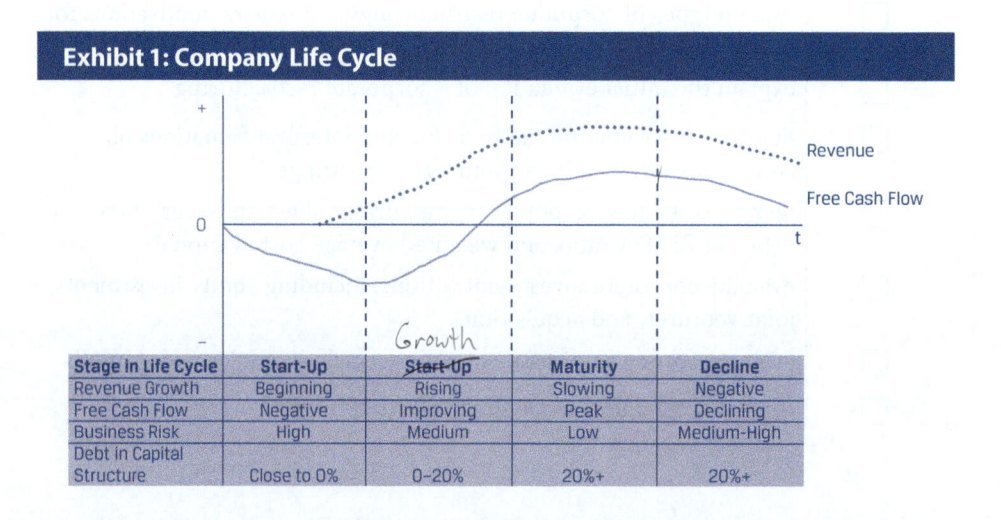

Stage in Life Cycle	Start-Up	Start-Up	Maturity	Decline
Revenue Growth	Beginning	Rising	Slowing	Negative
Free Cash Flow	Negative	Improving	Peak	Declining
Business Risk	High	Medium	Low	Medium-High
Debt in Capital Structure	Close to 0%	0–20%	20%+	20%+

While it may be in investors' best interest for maturing companies to simply operate the business for maximum cash flow until returns fall below investors' required rate of return and then liquidate the firm, most corporate managers and boards take actions to change their destiny. We can group the kinds of changes corporate managers can make into three general categories: investment, divestment, and restructuring.

- Investment involves actions that increase the size of the company or the scope of its operations, thereby increasing revenue and perhaps revenue growth. In this reading, we focus on external, or inorganic, growth through investment actions designed to increase revenues and improve margins. We do not look at investing in the existing business, or organic growth, through capital expenditures or research and development.

- Divestment involves actions that reduce a company's size or scope, typically by shedding slower-growing, lower-profitability, or higher-risk operations to improve the issuer's overall financial performance.

- Restructuring involves changes that do not alter the size or scope of the issuer but improve its cost and financing structure with the intention to increase growth, improve profitability, or reduce risks.

These three categories of changes, with an example of each, are shown in Exhibit 2.

Exhibit 2: Types of Corporate Structural Changes

Investment *Increase Size*	Divestment *Decrease Size*	Restructuring *Improve*
Example: Acquisition of Another Company	Example: Sale of a Business Segment for Cash	Example: Improve Productivity to Bring Profitability to Peer Levels

Most large corporate issuers are essentially portfolios of many diverse lines of business that often are in different stages of their life cycle and operate in different competitive environments. There are benefits to the individual business lines from common ownership and compatibility with other businesses, known as **synergies**. There can also be costs and inefficiencies, however, and some parts of the business might better fit in the hands of another corporate issuer or even operating as an independent company. Managers look to change the composition of the "corporate portfolio" in response to changing competitive conditions, limited synergies, poor profitability, or incompatibility with other businesses.

Motivations for Corporate Structural Change

An issuer's motivations to initiate a structural change can be issuer specific but can also be caused by broader macroeconomic or industry changes, known as top-down drivers, as shown in Exhibit 3.

Exhibit 3: Motivations for Corporate Structural Change

	Investment Actions	Divestment Actions	Restructuring Actions
Issuer-specific motivations	• Realize synergies • Increase growth • Improve capabilities or secure resources • Opportunity to acquire an undervalued target	• Focus operations and business lines • Valuation • Liquidity needs • Regulatory requirements	• Improve returns on capital • Financial challenges, including bankruptcy and liquidation
Top-down drivers	• High security prices • Industry shocks		

While issuer-specific motivations determine the type of action a corporate issuer may take, the response to top-down motivations span the three types of restructurings.

First, all types of changes have been found to be pro-cyclical, often coinciding with economic expansions and rising security prices and decreasing in recessions and when security prices are falling. From 2000 to 2019, the Boston Consulting Group (BCG) found that the correlation between the value of the MSCI World Index, a broad global equity market index, and the volume of corporate transactions was 0.80, as graphically shown in Exhibit 4 (Kengelbach, Gell, Keienburg, Degen, and Kim 2020).

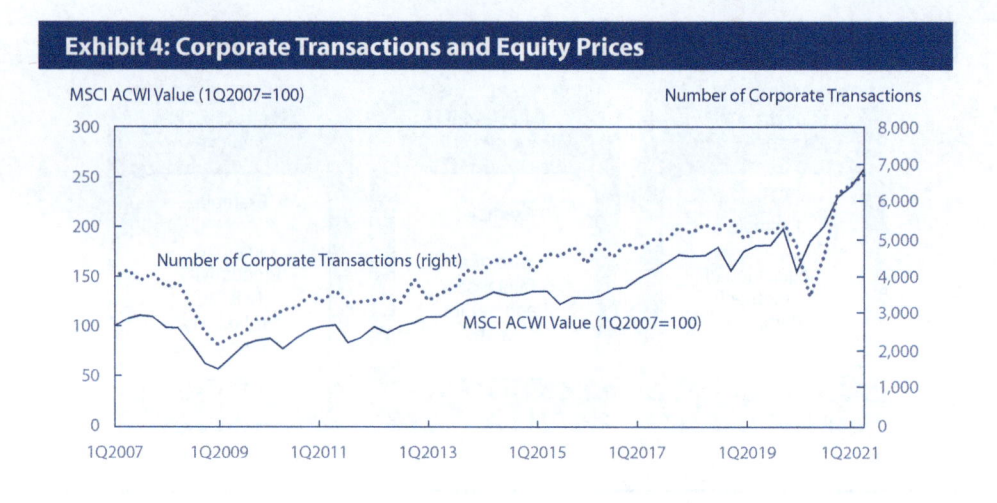

Exhibit 4: Corporate Transactions and Equity Prices

There are several possible explanations for the connection between asset prices and corporate transaction activity:

- *Greater CEO confidence.* High and rising security prices are associated with high and rising CEO confidence. While this explanation is controversial, it is likely true that CEOs take actions, especially large actions, only when they are confident about the future.

- *Lower cost of financing.* Lower interest rates (higher bond prices) and higher equity prices (lower equity risk premiums) result in lower interest expense and less dilution to existing shareholders from debt and equity-financed transactions, respectively.

- *Management and boards know that their stock is overvalued.* Higher equity valuations are beneficial for equity-financed acquisitions, sales, and spin offs. If a company believes its stock is overvalued, it can use these transactions to exchange overvalued stock and realize value.

While rarer, corporate transactions in periods of weak economic growth have been found to create more value, on average, than those in periods of strong economic growth. BCG found that "weak economy" deals are associated with a nearly 10% higher increase in shareholder return over three years than "strong economy" deals (Kengelbach, Keienburg, Gell, Nielsen, Bader, Degen, and Sievers 2019). In other words, in periods of economic stress and risk aversion, there are benefits to risk-taking.

Besides asset prices, empirical research also suggests that corporate restructuring activity tends to come in industry-specific waves during regulatory changes, technological changes, or changes in the growth rate of the industry, collectively known as **industry shocks**. Essentially, corporate issuers take action to adapt to disruptions in their competitive environment, which we will see through examples throughout this reading.

Types of Corporate Restructurings

Within the general categories of investment, divestment, and restructuring, most corporate restructurings can be classified as one of nine specific types, as shown in Exhibit 5. Leveraged buyouts (LBOs) are a special type of restructuring that combines elements of each category.

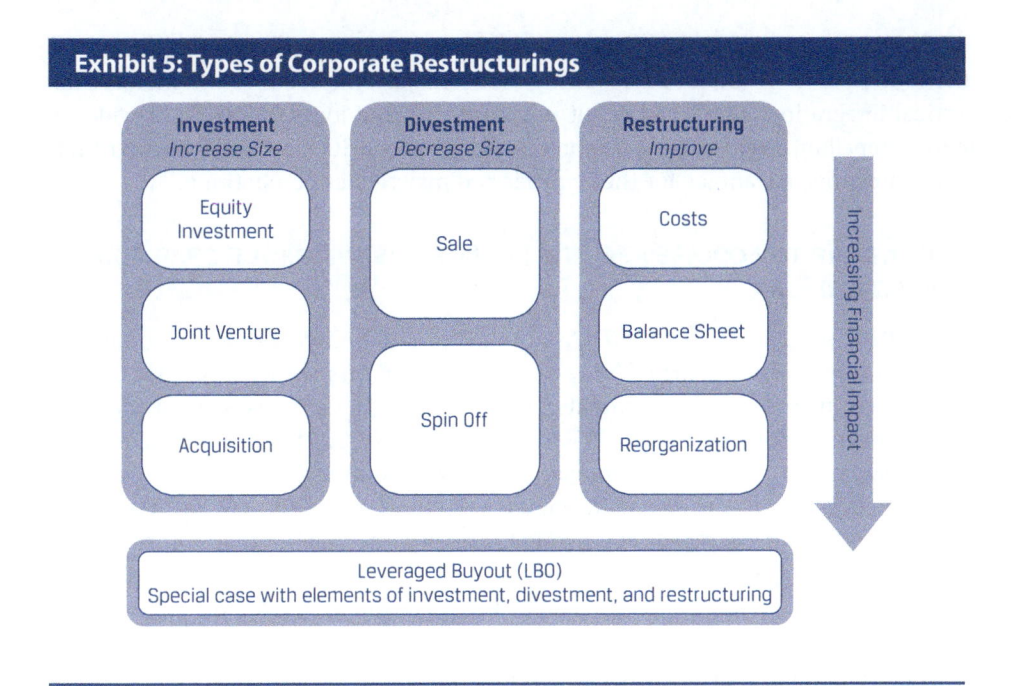

Exhibit 5: Types of Corporate Restructurings

Investment *Increase Size*	Divestment *Decrease Size*	Restructuring *Improve*
Equity Investment	Sale	Costs
Joint Venture		Balance Sheet
Acquisition	Spin Off	Reorganization

Increasing Financial Impact →

Leveraged Buyout (LBO)
Special case with elements of investment, divestment, and restructuring

Investment Actions: Equity Investments, Joint Ventures, and Acquisitions

There are several common issuer-specific motivations for investment actions, including creating synergies, increasing growth, improving capabilities and access to resources, and finding undervalued investment opportunities.

Synergies refer to the combination of two companies being more valuable than the sum of the parts. Generally, synergies take the form of lower costs ("cost synergies") or increased revenues ("revenue synergies") through combinations that generate lower costs or higher revenues, respectively, than the sum of the separate companies.

Synergies in general and administrative costs, manufacturing and distribution expenses, research and development spending, and sales and marketing costs are typically achieved through economies of scale. Synergies in general and administrative expenses arise from the consolidation of redundant functions; for example, a company needs only one headquarters, support department, and executive management team. Synergies can also be created in manufacturing and distribution by increasing capacity utilization and route density if an acquirer and target have comparable products and customers.

Revenue synergies are typically created through economies of scope, such as the cross-selling of products to increase market share, or by increasing bargaining power with customers from reduced competition. For example, a bank that acquires an insurance company may directly market its newly acquired insurance products to its existing banking customers. In some industries, customers tend to prefer buying several products from the same company because it is easier to manage fewer relationships.

The desires for growth and for improving unique capabilities or securing resources are closely related to synergies. For instance, acquiring or investing in an established but faster-growing company can increase consolidated revenue growth. Since the 1980s, cross-border acquisitions have been a popular strategy for companies seeking to extend their market reach because in many parts of the world, waves of deregulation and privatizations of state-owned enterprises provided opportunities to acquire new manufacturing facilities, to enter into new foreign markets, and to find new sources of talent and production resources.

Moreover, a corporation may be dependent on another company for inputs or for distribution of its products. By acquiring that company, the acquirer will increase its vertical integration, which can result in lower costs and lower risks and provides a more compelling proposition to customers and investors. Such acquisitions can result in a competitive advantage for the acquirer and may reduce competition.

NVIDIA CORP. TO ACQUIRE ARM LTD. FROM SOFTBANK GROUP CORP. FOR GBP30.2 BILLION

On 13 September 2020, NVIDIA announced a definitive agreement under which it will acquire Arm Limited from SoftBank, its owner. NVIDIA is a US-based manufacturer of computer graphics processors, chipsets, and related multimedia software. Arm, a UK-based subsidiary of SoftBank, is focused on standards-based Internet of Things (IoT) devices and offers a free operating system that consolidates the fundamental building blocks of the IoT. SoftBank is a Japanese holding company engaged in the management of its group companies across multiple sectors.

NVIDIA will pay to SoftBank a total of USD21.5 billion in NVIDIA common stock and USD12 billion in cash, which includes USD2 billion payable at signing. At closing, NVIDIA will issue 44.3 million new shares to SoftBank.

In its press release, NVIDIA emphasized that "the combination brings together NVIDIA's leading AI computing platform with Arm's vast ecosystem to create the premier computing company for the age of artificial intelligence, accelerating innovation while expanding into large, high-growth markets. SoftBank will remain committed to Arm's long-term success through its ownership stake in NVIDIA, expected to be under 10%."

The proposed transaction is subject to regulatory approvals from the United Kingdom, China, the European Union, and the United States due to the expected impact of the acquisition on competition in the industry.

There are three types of investment actions:

- An **equity investment** refers to a company purchasing a material stake in another company's equity but less than 50% of its shares. The two companies maintain their independence, but the investor company has investment exposure to the investee and, in some cases depending on the size of the investment, can have representation on the investee's board of directors to influence operations. Equity investments are often made for one of several reasons: establishing a strategic partnership between companies, taking an initial step towards an eventual acquisition, or investing by an investor company into a company it believes is undervalued.

- In a **joint venture**, two or more companies form and jointly control a new, separate company to achieve a business objective. Each participant contributes assets, employees, know-how, or other resources to the joint venture company. The participants maintain their independence otherwise and continue to do business apart from the joint venture but share in the joint venture's profits or losses. Joint ventures are technically a type of equity investment (in a newly formed company) but are often larger than equity investments in several respects: size, operational control over joint venture, and time spent by management. A common use of joint ventures is conducting business in new markets; a company with a product or service will form a joint venture with another company with local business knowledge in a different, often international, market.

- An **acquisition** is when one company, the acquirer, purchases most or all of another company's, the target, shares to gain control of either an entire company, a segment of the other company, or a specific group of assets, in exchange for cash, stock, or the assumption of liabilities, alone or in combination. Once an acquisition is complete, the target ceases to exist as an independent company and becomes a subsidiary of the acquirer, and the acquirer will report a single set of financial statements that include the results of the target. Depending on the acquirer's integration approach, the management, operations, and resources across the companies will be consolidated. Each line on the financial statements (e.g., revenue, expenses, cash, cash flows from operations) is an aggregation of all consolidated subsidiaries of the issuer.

Acquisitions are distinct from equity investments and joint ventures because the acquirer acquires full control over the target and consolidates the financial statements, reflecting control.

- Acquisitions require substantial greater capital investments than equity investments

Divestment Actions: Sales and Spin Offs

Motivations for divestment actions mirror those of investment actions because they represent a consolidation of the company's business. Common issuer-specific motivations to sell include focus, valuation, liquidity, and regulatory requirements.

Through either acquisitions or internal expansion over time, companies often operate across multiple different lines of business. Management may seek to improve performance by separating these businesses, either selling them to another company or spinning them off into independent companies. The source of performance improvement for the divested business may be increased management attention, focus, or effort and potential synergies with the acquirer.

Particularly in the case of spin offs, investors can be rewarded through increased stock prices that are tied directly to the performance of the specific business. Example 1 describes a divestment transaction intended to improve focus.

EXAMPLE 1

Daimler AG to Split into Daimler Truck and Mercedes-Benz

Until 2021, Daimler AG operated and reported in two business segments: Daimler Trucks & Buses and Mercedes-Benz Cars & Vans. In February 2021, Daimler AG announced that it will spin off Daimler Trucks & Buses into a separate Frankfurt-listed company and will rename itself (the remaining business segment) Mercedes-Benz, reflecting its focus on the car and van business that sells vehicles under that brand. The spin off will be effected by Daimler AG paying a stock dividend of newly created Daimler Trucks & Buses shares to Daimler AG shareholders, who will then own two separate types of shares: Daimler Trucks & Buses and Mercedes-Benz.

Ola Källenius, chairman of the Board of Management of Daimler AG, underlined that focus was the primary driver of the decision to split: "Mercedes-Benz Cars & Vans and Daimler Trucks & Buses are different businesses with specific customer groups, technology paths, and capital needs. Mercedes-Benz is the world's most valuable luxury car brand, offering the most desirable cars to discerning customers. Daimler Trucks & Buses supplies industry leading transportation solutions and services to customers. Both companies operate in industries that are facing major technological and structural changes. Given this context, we believe they will be able to operate most effectively as independent entities, equipped with strong net liquidity and free from the constraints of a conglomerate structure."

Conglomerate discount =
Total estimated enterprise value
from Sum-of-the-parts
evaluation

- Current Trading enterprise
value

While an undervalued target is a motivation for an investment action, an over-valued target—or at least one with a potentially higher valuation than the parent company—is a motivation for a divestment action. Many large corporate issuers own businesses that could be valued more highly by the capital markets if they were independent instead of inside the parent company. An issuer trading at a valuation lower than the sum of its parts is said to have a **conglomerate discount**, which is generally the result of diseconomies of scale or scope, owing to a deficit in focus, management effort, or investment; due to incompatible businesses; or because the capital markets have overlooked the business and its prospects. Example 2 describes a divestment transaction intended to reduce the conglomerate discount and realize that value for its stakeholders.

EXAMPLE 2

Novartis AG Divestments

Like other major pharmaceutical companies, Novartis AG had a sprawling port-folio of health care businesses. In the years since the appointment of a new CEO in 2013, Novartis has made several large divestments: It divested its vaccines and over-the-counter pharmaceutical business to rival GlaxoSmithKline, sold its animal pharmaceuticals business to Eli Lilly, another rival, and spun off Alcon, its eye care business, as an independent SIX-listed company.

Alcon was spun off, via a stock dividend payable to Novartis AG shareholders, on 9 April 2019. At the time of the spin off, Alcon equity was valued at over 30 times its EPS, while Novartis AG's price-to-earnings ratio (P/E) was half that amount. Two years after the spin off, Alcon shares had appreciated by over 35% while Novartis AG shares were roughly flat, demonstrating that Alcon was more valuable outside of its parent than inside. Alcon was the market leader in eye care devices and supplies, a growing market that does not face significant patent expirations like biopharmaceuticals and that requires less R&D.

The two remaining common issuer-specific motivations for divestment actions—liquidity and regulatory requirements—represent situations where external circum-stances force the issuer to act. Typically, unsustainable financial leverage prompts a corporate issuer to sell one or more of its businesses for cash and use these proceeds to reduce its leverage. Because these transactions are frequently made at compara-tively lower valuations, they are advantageous to the acquirer. The same may hold true for divestments required by regulators to avoid anti-competitive conduct and to safeguard against corporations building cartels and monopolies that would undermine competition. Regulators may force divestments as a requirement for their approval of a pending acquisition. Similarly, courts may impose divestiture as a remedy in an antitrust legal proceeding.

There are two main form of divestments:

- A sale, also known as a **divestiture**, is the other side of an acquisition; the seller sells a company, segment of a company, or group of assets to an acquirer. Once complete, control of the target is transferred to the acquirer. After a sale, the seller is no longer exposed to the divested business, because it has been exchanged for cash. The logic of the transaction is for capital to be reallocated to a better use (or returned to shareholders or creditors) and for the seller and acquirer to focus on their strengths.

- A **spin off** is when a company separates a distinct part of its business into a new, independent company. The term "spin off" is used to describe both the transaction and the separated component, while the company that conducts the transaction and formerly owned the spin off is known as the parent. The goal of a spin off is to increase management and employee focus by separating distinct businesses, awarding employees with stock-based compensation that is more directly tied to their efforts, and to remove any lack of compatibilities between the parent and the company that was spun off. Upon completion, the two companies will be independent, with their own debt and equity securities, financial reporting, management, and so on.

The choice between selling and spinning off a business involves many variables, but valuation is often among the most significant. A business of moderate size with many potentially interested acquirers will often receive a higher valuation. In a spin off, the investor receives the divested business's equity and must value it and make an investment decision; the parent receives less in proceeds. Spin offs may take several quarters to complete as independent business operations are created and new management teams and separate functions, such as legal and finance, are put in place. Because spin offs reduce, rather than increase, concentration of market power, they typically do not face strict regulatory scrutiny.

Restructuring Actions: Cost and Balance Sheet Restructuring and Reorganization

There are two general types of issuer-specific motivations for restructuring actions: opportunistic improvement and forced improvement. Opportunistic improvement includes actions that alter the business model, trim the cost structure, or modify the composition of the balance sheet—all with the intention to improve returns on capital. An example of opportunistic change to an existing business model is **franchising**, where an owner of an asset and associated intellectual property can divest the asset and license the intellectual property to a third-party operator. A well-known use of franchising is in restaurants, where a franchisor licenses intellectual property, including recipes, trademarks, and restaurant operating procedures, to third-party restaurant owner operators—franchisees—in exchange for royalties, typically in the mid-single digit range of percentage of restaurant sales. Franchisors, such as the restaurant chain McDonald's or the tutoring company Kumon, operate lean businesses with royalty income and a small, fixed cost base primarily composed of senior management, advertising, and product development. Franchisees operate the individual businesses independently under the franchisor's name and are subjected to meeting strict operational and business requirements under the franchisor's supervision and oversight. Because franchisors do not own stores or employ workers, they are shielded from store-level cost trends; franchising shifts away many business risks from the franchisors to the franchisees.

Forced improvements are actions taken to enhance returns on capital when profitability falls below investors' required rate of return. Several factors contribute to this happening, including insufficient effort by management, falling customer demand, a worsening competitive landscape, or increasing overcapacity. Three alternatives are available: cost restructuring, balance sheet restructuring, and reorganization.

- A **cost restructuring** refers to actions with the goal of reducing costs by improving operational efficiency and profitability, often to raise margins to a historical level or to those of comparable industry peers. Cost restructurings tend to follow periods of company underperformance and are often part of larger structural changes to focus the corporate issuer's operations, to realize synergies after an acquisition, or when there is a threat of activist investors or an unwelcome acquisition by another corporate issuer. Two common ways of reducing costs are **outsourcing** and **offshoring**.

  - A company outsourcing internal business services subcontracts specific, standardizable business processes, such as IT, call centers, HR, legal, and finance, to specialized third-party companies that can offer these services at lower costs through economies of scale from serving many clients. Manufacturing can also be outsourced; perhaps the best-known example is Apple outsourcing manufacturing of iPhones to Hon Hai Precision Ltd. Outsourcing reduces headcount, costs, and time spent on managerial oversight. Depending on what business processes are being outsourced, it can also free up expensive assets, such as office, manufacturing, and warehouse space, that can be disposed of or repurposed for alternative use. Apart from structural changes across the business, there are additional considerations, such as managing multiple contractual obligations with the outsourcing company that can introduce new risks in the decision to outsource.

- Offshoring refers to relocating operations from one country to another, mainly to reduce costs through lower labor costs or to achieve economies of scale through centralization, while still maintaining operations within the corporation. Offshoring may include starting up a new subsidiary in a foreign country or creating a multi-location business model. Global companies, such as Genpact, have created a multi-location model in which certain core business services are offshored and centralized to specific countries and managed by the company.

Outsourcing and offshoring are often combined, where not only does a company outsource operations to another company but it also does so with foreign partners.

- A **balance sheet restructuring** alters the composition of the balance sheet by either shifting the asset composition, changing the capital structure, or both. On the assets side, most forms of restructuring involve selling assets to third parties for cash and concurrently entering into contractual agreements for their continued use. The seller reduces the risks of asset ownership, such as maintenance or obsolescence, but assumes other risks, such as higher, variable, and less predictable operating costs and lower revenues. Two common balance sheet restructuring transactions are sale leasebacks and dividend recapitalization.

  - In a **sale leaseback**, an asset owner sells an asset to a lessor for cash and immediately signs a lease agreement for its use, typically for the asset's remaining economic life. The result is that the asset owner receives cash up front, no longer owns the asset, yet, as the lessee, retains the right for future use. Typically, the annual lease expense is higher than the annual depreciation and amortization expense would have been because the lessor earns interest income from the transaction. Sometimes, when lessors can secure capital at lower cost, they can offer the lessee more attractive financing terms than the lessee could have obtained. Sale leasebacks are commonly used to secure liquidity on relatively short notice. Airlines used sale leasebacks during the COVID-19 pandemic to raise cash as their operations were suspended.

  - In a **dividend recapitalization**, the corporate issuer restructures the mix of debt and equity, typically from equity to debt through debt-financed dividends or share repurchases. The objective is to reduce the issuer's weighted average cost of capital by replacing expensive equity with cheaper debt. Because this recapitalization reduces the number of outstanding shares and the value of the corporation does not change, these transactions can increase the value to shareholders. While the strategy can be beneficial if interest rates are low, it can increase financial leverage significantly and is thus often used only by issuers with revenue and operating cash flow stability.

- In a **reorganization**, a court-supervised restructuring process available in some jurisdictions for companies facing insolvency, a bankruptcy court assumes control of the company and oversees an orderly negotiation process between the company and its creditors for asset sales, conversion of debt to equity, refinancing, and so on. The company's business operations typically continue as normal, and existing management remains in place throughout the process. Once the company reaches an agreement with its creditors on a reorganization plan, it needs to receive an approval from the bankruptcy court to exit from the process and begin its operations with a lighter debt burden. Sometimes reorganization is a strategic measure to renegotiate contracts with unfavorable terms. While the process can take years, in some cases, companies reach an agreement with creditors prior to filing a formal petition for reorganization to the bankruptcy court and can seek approval from the court quickly. There have been cases of reorganizations lasting less than 24 hours.

The reorganization process is different from the liquidation process, which typically occurs when the reorganization process has failed to achieve its objectives and the company is still unable to pay its debts and meet its other contractual obligations. During the liquidation process, the bankruptcy court takes control of the corporation, divests these assets of the corporations, and then distributes proceeds to all creditors according to legal criteria.

EXAMPLE 3

Six Flags Inc. and Six Flags Entertainment Corp.

Six Flags Inc., an NYSE-listed owner and operator of amusement parks, began to struggle financially in 2006, as revenues stagnated and EBIT fell by 50% from 2005 because the company's operating expenses were primarily fixed. Its share price fell by almost 50%, closing in 2006 around USD5 per share.

Performance worsened in 2007, as revenues grew slightly but EBIT decreased by 34%, and the share price fell another 50%, closing around USD2.50. Standard & Poor's and Moody's downgraded the company's credit rating (though it was already speculative grade) because the company's net debt-to-EBITDA ratio increased to nearly 13× (see Exhibit 6). The United States, the company's primary operating region, entered a recession in late 2007, and credit markets seized, which was especially challenging for Six Flags because it was a highly levered company unable to refinance its debt and it faced a mandatory dividend payment on its preferred stock.

The company implemented an extensive cost restructuring program in 2008, which did improve profitability despite a 24% fall in revenue, but the company defaulted on its debt obligations by missing interest payments and preferred stock dividend payments. By early 2009, Six Flags shares had fallen below USD1.00, which triggered a delisting of its shares on the NYSE. Six Flags declared Chapter 11 (reorganization) bankruptcy on 13 June 2009, seeking an agreement with creditors to eliminate a significant amount of its debt, though its theme parks continued to operate.

Exhibit 6: Six Flags Inc. Net Debt and Net Debt to EBITDA, 2004–2008

A. Six Flags Inc.

Net Debt

2004: 2,082
2005: 2,162
2006: 2,217
2007: 2,229
2008: 2,156

B. Six Flags Inc.

Net Debt/EBITDA

2004: 8.2
2005: 7.8
2006: 12.1
2007: 12.7
2008: 7.6

In May 2010, Six Flags and its bondholders reached an agreement and received approval from the bankruptcy court on a reorganization. The company's bondholders invested USD725 million in equity to recapitalize and convert over USD1 billion in existing debt to equity in the company. As a result, the bondholders would own virtually all of the equity and the company would emerge with USD784 million in net debt, a ratio of less than 3.0× expected EBITDA for 2010. Prior equityholders had lost their entire investment.

In June 2010, Six Flags shares were relisted on the NYSE under the same symbol but with a new company name, Six Flags Entertainment Corp.

Leveraged Buyouts

A special case of corporate restructuring is a **leveraged buyout (LBO)**, a series of actions that include investment, divestment, and restructuring. In an LBO, an acquirer uses a significant amount of debt to finance the acquisition of a target and then pursues restructuring actions, with the goal of exiting the target with a sale or public listing.

The term is reserved for leveraged acquisitions by investment funds led by a private equity general partner, with additional capital from limited partners that are often institutional investors, rather than acquisitions made by other corporate issuers. Often, funds that conduct LBOs are "buyout funds" that specialize in these transactions, because both investment and operational expertise are required. If the target is a listed company, an LBO may also be referred to as a "take-private" transaction, because the issuer's equity shifts from the public to the private market. The general and limited partners' investment returns are primarily a function of four variables: the purchase price, the amount of leverage, free cash flow (FCF) generated during the ownership period—which is often augmented by cost and balance sheet restructurings and used to pay down debt—and the exit price. After the exit, the target typically has a substantially more leveraged capital structure than prior to the LBO, as in the case in Example 4.

LBO of Hilton Hotels Corporation by Blackstone Group

In 2007, funds managed by the Blackstone Group acquired Hilton Hotels Corporation, an NYSE-listed global hotel and hospitality company in a transaction valued at approximately USD26 billion, with the Blackstone funds acquiring all outstanding shares of Hilton for USD47.50 per share, approximately USD20 billion in total, and assuming USD6 billion in existing Hilton debt. The Blackstone funds financed the cash portion of the transaction by borrowing USD14.5 billion and using 5.5 billion of equity.

Upon closing the acquisition at the end of 2007, Blackstone replaced the management and implemented a growth strategy, primarily through franchising. It also made several divestitures of highly priced, flagship properties.

In 2013, Hilton re-listed on the NYSE via an initial public offering. The trajectory of Hilton's long-term debt shows the effect of the leveraged buyout; long-term debt increased by a factor of 3 once it was taken private (see Exhibit 7). Blackstone funds used cash flows from operations to reduce indebtedness while Hilton was private, but it still returned to the public markets with a different capital structure.

Exhibit 7: Hilton Hotels Debt Position through Its LBO

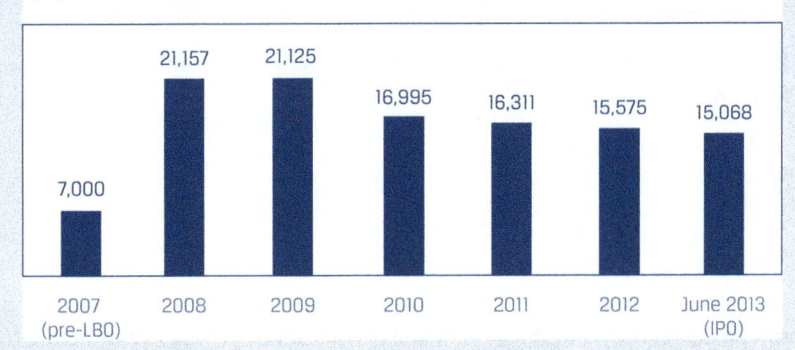

Long-Term Debt (USD, mins)

Year	Long-Term Debt
2007 (pre-LBO)	7,000
2008	21,157
2009	21,125
2010	16,995
2011	16,311
2012	15,575
June 2013 (IPO)	15,068

Blackstone funds did not sell any shares in the IPO; instead, Blackstone gradually sold its stake over 2013–2018, which resulted in significant gains as Hilton shares appreciated over that time. By 2018, 11 years after its initial investment, the funds had realized a cumulative net profit of over USD11 billion on the initial equity investment of USD5.5 billion.

EXAMPLE 5

Corporate Evolution and Actions

1. Explain what actions XYZ Ltd., a fictional company, might take in response to its declining revenue growth rates of 8%, 7%, 4%, 1%, and 1%, respectively, during the past five years.

   Solution

   XYZ Ltd. may make an investment in a faster-growing business, such as an acquisition, to accelerate its growth rate. If XYZ Ltd. operates multiple separable businesses with different growth rates, management may seek to divest those with growth rates below the consolidated rate to accelerate growth.

2. Instead of making an acquisition, a corporate issuer could invest internally via capital expenditures or R&D. Describe one possible advantage and one possible disadvantage of making an acquisition versus internal investment.

   Solution

   A potential advantage of an acquisition over internal investment is time to market for a new product. Internally developing and launching a new product, especially one with which the company lacks experience, may take significantly longer than acquiring a company already commercializing the product. A potential disadvantage of an acquisition is cost. Most companies are valued at prices greater than the replacement costs of their assets, and additionally, most acquisition values are greater than market valuations in the capital markets, reflecting a premium for control.

3. Identify which one of the following is *least likely* to be a motivation for divestment actions.

   A. Increase revenue

   B. Increase focus

   C. Increase return on invested capital

   Solution

   A is correct. Divestment actions, including sales and spin offs, reduce the size of a company and its revenues. B is incorrect because divestments, by shrinking the number or scope of businesses in the corporate issuer, do increase focus. C is incorrect because divestments are often motivated by the desire to reduce capital investment in areas of low returns.

4. Recommend a corporate restructuring action for each condition in the *Conditions* column by selecting one of the actions in the *Corporate Restructuring Action* column.

Conditions	Corporate Restructuring Action
1. As a result of a significant downturn in commodity prices, an oil and gas producer faces negative cash flows from operations. The company has interest payments and debt maturities in the next 6 months.	A. Balance sheet restructuring

Conditions	Corporate Restructuring Action
2. Slowing revenue growth, owing to its products reaching market share saturation in most markets	B. Reorganization
3. A company operates Segment A and Segment B. While Segment A is performing in line with expectations, Segment B revenue growth has declined, because of changes in its regulatory environment.	C. Acquisition
4. A company owns and operates 245 physiotherapy and sports medicine clinics. While the clinics are performing well, the business is capital and labor intensive because each clinic requires physical upkeep, capital equipment, and a skilled staff.	D. Spin off

Solution

B is correct. Reorganization is an appropriate action for companies facing significant debt levels that lack the financial wherewithal to service the debt. In reorganization, the company can negotiate adjusted debt payment plans with its creditors in an orderly fashion.

C is correct. An acquisition is a likely course of action for a company with slowing growth as it reaches maturity.

D is correct. Segments A and B have divergent performance and competitive landscapes. Unless there are significant synergies between the two, stakeholders may be better served if these businesses were separate rather than under the same ownership.

A is correct. The company should consider balance sheet restructuring, such as franchising the clinics to third-party owner operators—with the corporate entity retaining such functions as quality control, billing, marketing, and so on—or sale leasebacks of the fixed assets.

---

5. Identify the *most likely* reason for a corporate issuer to sell a segment of its business rather than spin it off.

   A. The issuer desires liquidity.

   B. The issuer operates capital-intensive, cyclical businesses.

   C. The issuer operates multiple businesses with varying revenue growth rates and risk profiles.

Solution

A is correct. A sale is the disposal of a segment in exchange for consideration, often cash consideration, while a spin off generally raises less liquidity because control is transferred to existing parent shareholders rather than sold. B is incorrect because capital intensity and cyclicality generally have no bearing on the choice of sale versus spin off. C is incorrect because this attribute is non-specific to sales or spin offs; it is an attribute that makes both options more logical.

6. What is the difference between a joint venture and an equity investment?

Solution

While the two share the same accounting treatment under IFRS and US GAAP, a joint venture is a specific type of equity investment, different from others in its formation, purpose, and governance.

	Joint venture	Equity investment
Formation	New legal entity formed when agreement is reached, and joint venture is financed	Investor acquires shares in existing investee company
Purpose	Specific—launch in new geography, new technology, etc.	General—investor company seeks exposure to investee
Governance	Controlled by participants by varying degrees	Investee maintains control over investee operations

7. Tyche, a fictional company, owns and operates 140 retail stores, including the real estate. As a result of a pandemic, Tyche's revenues and cash flows have declined severely, which may result in the inability to make interest and principal payments on its bonds and credit facility. Tyche management is considering selling the real estate for 40 of its stores to a commercial real estate investment fund and immediately leasing them (operating lease) for their remaining economic lives. Explain this type of action and its potential benefits and costs.

Solution

This is a balance sheet restructuring—more specifically, a sale-leaseback transaction. If completed, Tyche would receive cash from the sale and recognize a liability equal to the present value of future lease payments. Depreciation expense would be replaced with lease expense, which would include interest expense charged by the lessor. Potential benefits and costs of the sale leaseback versus asset ownership are as follows:

Benefits	Costs
Receive cash up front, to use for debt service	Lease expense includes interest expense, generally resulting in higher overall costs
Reduce costs of ownership, such as obsolescence and disposal	Increased indebtedness

8. Empirical research suggests that at least two-thirds of acquisitions fail to create meaningful value for acquirers. Explain why might this be the case.

Solution

The following are three common explanations for the failure of acquisitions to deliver meaningful value for acquirers:

1. Overpaying: While the target business and synergies associated with the acquisition may perform well, paying too great a price simply results in a negative net present value (NPV) transaction. In effect, value is transferred to the seller.

2. Under-realization of expected synergies: Acquisitions are often done with the assumption of greater revenue or greater profitability (lower costs) for the combined entity than for the two entities alone. Expected synergies are reflected, in part, in the acquisition price. These synergies can be overestimated, perhaps due to unrealistic assumptions.

3. Integration issues: Acquirers often change the business processes and resources of targets to match their existing processes. Additionally, target management is typically replaced. Such changes can result in the deterioration of the performance of the target.

AstraZeneca plc, an LSE-listed pharmaceutical company, announced its acquisition of Alexion Pharmaceuticals, a NASDAQ-listed biotechnology firm focused on therapeutics for rare diseases. AstraZeneca will pay USD60 in cash and 2.1243 AstraZeneca American Depositary Shares for each Alexion share, for a total consideration of USD39 billion, based on share prices just prior to the announcement.

AstraZeneca expects to realize annual recurring cost synergies of USD500 million (pre-tax), primarily from commercial and manufacturing efficiencies as well as savings in corporate costs. The achievement of the full USD500 million in synergies is expected by the end of the third year after the acquisition closes. AstraZeneca expects to incur cash costs in the first three years following the close of the transaction, reaching USD650 million in Year 3.

Prior to the acquisition announcement, expectations for revenues and total operating expenses for AstraZeneca and Alexion for the next three years are as shown in Exhibit 8.

Exhibit 8: AstraZeneca and Alexion Years 1–3 Figures, Prior to Acquisition (USD millions)

AstraZeneca	Year 1	Year 2	Year 3
Revenues	22,090	24,384	26,617
Operating expenses	16,418	17,948	19,277

Alexion	Year 1	Year 2	Year 3
Revenues	4,130	4,990	6,069
Operating expenses	1,952	2,201	2,646

1. Calculate the announced cost synergies as a percentage of Alexion's Year 3 standalone operating expenses.

Solution

By the end of the third year after the acquisition closes, AstraZeneca expects to realize USD500 million in synergies. As a standalone company, Alexion's total expected annual operating expenses are USD2,646 million. Therefore, cost synergies represent 500/2,646 = 19% of Alexion's standalone operating expenses.

2. Assuming synergies are realized in the amounts of USD166 million, USD333 million, and USD500 million in Years 1–3, respectively, and that cash costs of USD217 million, USD433 million, and USD650 million are incurred in

Years 1–3, respectively, calculate expected operating income in each of Years 1–3 for the combination of AstraZeneca and Alexion.

Solution

Given the information in Exhibit 6 and the assumptions for the pace of synergies and cash costs associated with the combination, the process for forecasting operating income is as follows in Exhibit 9.

Exhibit 9: Combined AstraZeneca and Alexion Operating Income for Years 1–3

AstraZeneca + Alexion	Year 1	Year 2	Year 3
AstraZeneca Revenues	22,090	24,384	26,617
Plus: Alexion Revenues	4,130	4,990	6,069
Combined Revenues	26,220	29,374	32,686
AstraZeneca OpEx	16,418	17,948	19,277
Plus: Alexion OpEx	1,952	2,201	2,646
Minus: Synergies	(166)	(333)	(500)
Plus: One-Time Costs	217	433	650
Combined OpEx	18,421	20,249	22,073
Operating Income (Revenue minus OpEx)	7,799	9,125	10,613

3. Explain the impact of the acquisition of Alexion on AstraZeneca's revenue growth in Years 2 and 3 and its operating margin in Years 1–3.

Solution

Exhibit 10 shows AstraZeneca's revenue growth rate and operating margin prior to the acquisition for Years 1–3.

Exhibit 10: AstraZeneca Prior to Acquisition of Alexion

AstraZeneca	Year 1	Year 2	Year 3
Revenues	22,090	24,384	26,617
Growth Rate		10%	9%
Operating Expenses	16,418	17,948	19,277
Operating Income	5,672	6,436	7,340
Operating Margin	26%	26%	28%

Exhibit 11 shows AstraZeneca's revenue growth rate and operating margin after the acquisition for Years 1–3.

Exhibit 11: AstraZeneca after the Acquisition of Alexion

AstraZeneca	Year 1	Year 2	Year 3
Revenues	26,220	29,374	32,686
Growth Rate		12%	11%
Operating Expenses	18,421	20,249	22,073

AstraZeneca	Year 1	Year 2	Year 3
Operating Income	7,799	9,125	10,613
Operating Margin	30%	31%	32%

As the exhibits show, the acquisition has positively impacted the revenue growth rate by approximately 200 bps in each of Years 2 and 3 and the operating margin by 400 bps–500 bps in Years 1–3. Even though cash costs associated with the acquisition exceeded the synergies, Alexion is a higher-margin, higher-growth business than AstraZeneca.

EVALUATING CORPORATE RESTRUCTURINGS

3

☐ explain the initial evaluation of a corporate restructuring

☐ demonstrate valuation methods for, and interpret valuations of, companies involved in corporate restructurings

Investment analysts evaluate corporate restructurings in a process composed of three general steps before updating their investment thesis for the corporate issuer in light of the restructuring, as shown in Exhibit 12.

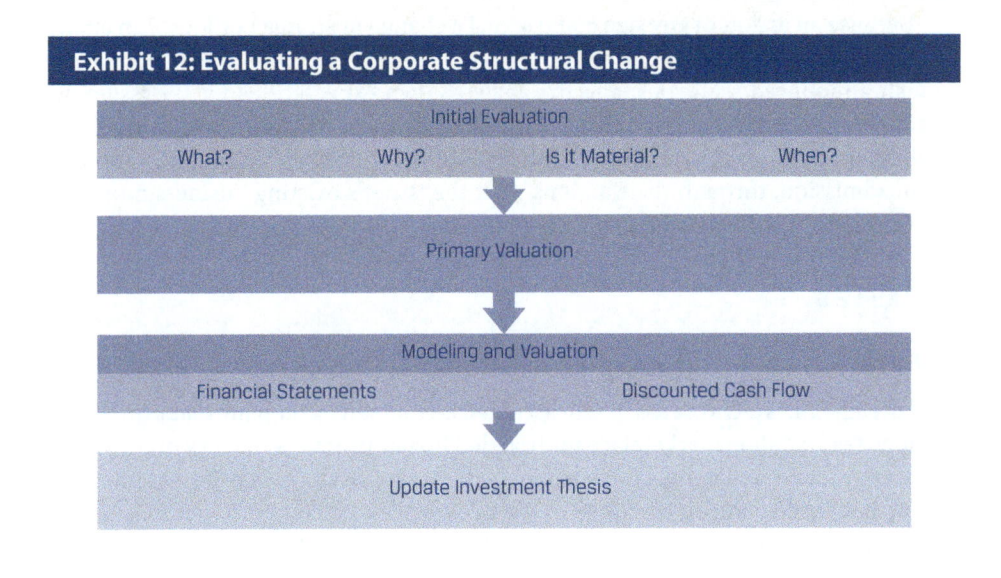

Exhibit 12: Evaluating a Corporate Structural Change

Initial Evaluation

An analyst's initial evaluation of a corporate restructuring involves answering four questions:

- What is happening?
- Why is it happening?

- Is it material?
- When is it happening?

Answering the first and second questions, covered in Section 2, typically involves reading the issuer's press release, securities filings, conference call transcripts, and relevant third-party research, if available. Once the relevant information is gathered, the analyst interprets the action and the issuer's motivations. Professional skepticism is required because management will virtually always frame restructuring positively.

The third question in the initial evaluation step is determining materiality. Analysts have finite time and must prioritize the most impactful announcements and focus on material changes. Materiality can be defined in this context along two dimensions: size and fit.

The larger a restructuring, the more likely it is to affect an issuer's future cash flows and financial position and thus its value. The size of a structural change can be measured in different ways for different types of restructurings. For restructuring involving a transaction, such as an acquisition, the value of the transaction (sum of cash paid, value of stock issued, and value of target's debt assumed) relative to the issuer's enterprise value (EV) is a good metric. For restructurings not involving a transaction, such as a cost restructuring, it is the scale of the intended action that is material—for instance, the announced cost reduction as a percentage of annual revenue or operating expenses. In any case, the size of the issuer matters: a EUR100 million acquisition may be large for one acquirer but small for another.

One rule of thumb for what constitutes a "large" acquisition is that the total transaction value exceeds 10% of the acquirer's enterprise value prior to the transaction. Most acquisitions (>95%) are under USD1 billion in value and over 80% of targets are private companies (source: Putz 2017). Therefore, for large-capitalization corporate issuers, most acquisitions are, in fact, immaterial.

Because an action of any size could signal a change in strategy or focus, an analyst should also assess how the current structural change fits in with earlier actions, previously announced strategies, and the analyst's own expectations for the issuer. For example, a company making a small acquisition of a company in a different industry or different business model could be interpreted as management changing its strategy or an admission, through their actions, that the issuer's existing business model has problems, as in the case in Example 6.

EXAMPLE 6

Farfetch Ltd. Acquires New Guards Groups

Farfetch Ltd. is a UK-based, publicly traded e-commerce company that primarily operates an online marketplace for branded luxury products. Luxury brands list their products and connect to consumers through Farfetch's website and mobile app but retain control over most of the sales process, such as product selection, pricing, promotions, and so on. Farfetch earns revenue through commissions on each sale.

In July 2019, Farfetch announced the acquisition of the privately held New Guards Groups, an apparel company that sells exclusively licensed luxury streetwear under the brand Off-White, for total consideration of USD704 million, which amounted to approximately 8% of Farfetch's total enterprise value just prior to the announcement.

Despite being relatively small financially, the acquisition was seen as a problem by investors, for two reasons: (1) It meant that Farfetch would start competing with sellers on its own platform by selling products itself, and (2) it represented a shift in business model away from an "asset-lite" online marketplace connecting third-party sellers to consumers towards an online retailer selling products under its own brands, with inventory risk and higher operating costs.

Farfetch shares, listed on the NYSE, fell 45% the day after the acquisition was announced.

A measure that is often used to judge all types of restructurings is the equity price returns on the day of the announcement; for a positive (negative) stock price reaction to the merger announcement on the day of the announcement, the merger is presumed to generate (decrease) value. However, research has cast doubt on the usefulness of this measure.

For instance, Rehm and West (2016) found no correlation between the announcement effects of a deal and its excess total return to shareholders two or more years later. More than half of the companies that initially saw negative price reactions were found to realize excess total shareholder returns over the longer term. Similarly, Ben-David, Bhattacharya, and Jacobsen (2020) reported that share price reaction on the announcement date has no correlation with transaction outcomes or future performance of an acquirer.

Finally, an important consideration in the initial evaluation is timing, because there is a substantial time delay, at least several quarters if not years, between the announcement of the transaction and its completion. The transaction is not reflected on the balance sheet of the acquirer until the date of closing, which is also when revenues, expenses, and cash flow effects are consolidated in the acquirer's financial statements. The length of the timeline is largely determined by the size and complexity of the transaction. For instance, a small-scale cost restructuring may take a matter of months to implement, and its effect would show up relatively quickly. But for a large acquisition or spin off, it may take over 12 months from announcement to the closing, on top of the time spent planning during the pre-announcement stage.

A key source of uncertainty in timing is the receipt of the required shareholder, creditor, and/or regulatory approvals. Depending on the corporate issuer's bylaws, shareholder approval may be required for a corporate transaction; typically, transactions large in scale and value must be approved by the shareholders. Additionally, most jurisdictions have antitrust laws and government authorities that enforce competition law. Approval from these authorities for acquisitions is typically a pre-requisite in all jurisdictions where the transacting entities conduct business. Transactions in some sectors tend to receive more scrutiny than others, particularly if they are perceived to affect geopolitical standing, industry competition, or employment levels.

Importantly, capital market participants discount the expected impact of a change (including the risk of it not closing) into security prices upon the announcement.

Preliminary Valuation

For restructurings that are material and involve transactions, an analyst will conduct a preliminary valuation of the target, typically using relative valuation methods to judge whether management uses stakeholder resources optimally to meet investors' required rate of return on capital. Three valuation methods analysts use in this step, often in combination, are comparable company analysis, comparable transaction analysis, and premium paid analysis. Discounted cash flow valuation will be discussed in the next step in the evaluation process with modeling.

Comparable Company Analysis

Comparable company analysis uses the valuation multiples of similar, listed companies to value a target. In this approach, the analyst first defines a set of other companies that are similar to the target under review.

Analysts often use a data aggregator, such as Bloomberg, FactSet, or Capital IQ, to create a set of comparable companies and transactions. The aggregator allows the user to specify time periods, the characteristics of the company, the involved parties, and the transaction (e.g., size, geography, form of payment). This set may include companies within the target's primary industry as well as companies in similar industries with similar financial characteristics, such as size, revenue growth rate, operating margin, and return on invested capital. The set should include as many similar companies as possible though not be diluted by dissimilar companies. A useful starting point for developing the comparable set is the company's peer group identified by management in its annual financial disclosures or provided by data aggregators.

Once a set of comparable companies is defined, the next step is to calculate valuation multiples and metrics based on the current market prices of the comparable companies. Common multiples used include enterprise value to EBITDA or sales, price to earnings, and, less commonly, enterprise value to free cash flow to the firm. Enterprise multiples are often used because they are less sensitive to differences in capital structure. An analyst may also use sector-specific valuation multiples, such as enterprise value to subscribers for technology companies, enterprise value to reserves for oil and gas companies, or enterprise value to funds from operations for real estate. Analysts typically then calculate the mean, median, and range for the chosen multiples and either compare those values for the target or apply the multiple to develop an estimated target value.

Comparable company analysis is more often employed for assessing the valuation of targets in spin offs than for acquisitions or sales because acquirers pay a premium for control; therefore, acquisition or sale multiples typically exceed trading multiples.

EXAMPLE 7

Spin Off Valuation

Wang, an analyst at Choice Fund covering the media and telecoms sector, has been asked to assess the valuation of a potential spin off by one of the companies owned by the fund.

The company operates and reports two segments: Connectivity and Media. Connectivity is a capital-intensive cable television and broadband distribution business, and Media produces and licenses television series, which are distributed to its Connectivity customers and other cable companies on traditional television, as well as to online video streaming companies. In the last 12 months, the company reported the following financial results.

Segment	Revenues (EUR mln)	EBITDA (EUR mln)
Connectivity	20,100	7,638
Media	8,000	2,000
Consolidated	28,100	9,638

The company is currently trading at an enterprise value of EUR96,380 million, or an EV/EBITDA multiple of 10.

A spin off of the Media segment has long been rumored, because it does not have material synergies with the Connectivity segment and has been under-invested in by the current management team, resulting in slower revenue growth than its peers.

1. If Wang finds that the median Connectivity and Media peers are trading at enterprise value-to-EBITDA multiples of 13 and 6, respectively, estimate whether a spin off of the Media segment has the potential to:

    A. decrease stakeholder value.

    B. increase stakeholder value.

    C. neither increase nor decrease stakeholder value.

    Solution

    B is correct. Multiplying the peer median EV/EBITDA multiples and last 12 months' segment EBITDA results in an estimated enterprise value of EUR111,294 million, which is more than 15% higher than the current enterprise value of EUR96,380 million. Based on this result, it seems that the market is undervaluing either the Connectivity segment, the Media segment, or both relative to peers. This may be justifiable, but we would need more information about peers and their prospects versus this company's prospects to evaluate it.

2. Explain why the Media segment might not be valued at the peer median multiple by market participants in a spin off.

    Solution

    Three general reasons for a different valuation from peers are differences in expected growth, differences in profitability, and differences in the risk profile. Relative to the median peer, the Media segment may differ on any or all these dimensions, particularly in profitability because the current management team has under-invested in the business; the period of under-investment may now necessitate a period of high investment, which would depress free cash flow.

3. The company incurs EUR250 million per year in corporate and headquarters operating costs. The company allocates the EUR250 million to the Connectivity and Media segments proportional to revenues. If the Media segment is spun off, estimate its annual EBITDA adjusted for the allocation of corporate and headquarters operating costs.

    Solution

    The Media segment accounted for 8,000/28,100 = 28.5% of the last 12 months' revenue. If the EUR250 million in corporate and headquarters operating costs are allocated based on its revenue contribution, then an allocation of 250 million × 28.5% = EUR71 million would be deducted from EBITDA, resulting in an adjusted figure of EUR2,000 million – EUR71 million = EUR1,929 million.

4. Wang's colleague suggests that a flaw in this analysis is that it fails to consider the capital structure of the Media segment if it's spun off; what if the

parent transfers a significant amount of debt to it? Interpret the colleague's concern and justify the analysis.

Solution

While the amount of debt transferred to it and its capital structure generally will impact the equity and debt valuations of the Media segment if it's spun off, Wang's analysis is not specific to any capital structure, because Wang is using enterprise value multiples. However, Wang's colleague could be correct if leverage, for example, is substantially higher for the Media segment spin off than for its peers, which could increase its cost of capital and thus its overall enterprise value.

Advantages of Using Comparable Company Analysis

- This method provides a reasonable approximation of a target company's value relative to similar companies in the market. It assumes that "like" assets should be valued on a similar basis in the market.
- With this method, most of the required data are readily available.
- The estimates of value are derived directly from the market. This approach is unlike the discounted cash flow method, in which the value is determined based on many assumptions and estimates.

Disadvantages of Using Comparable Company Analysis

- A comparable set of listed companies, especially in a larger number of potential comparables, can be difficult to find or may not exist. This is especially true for large, industry-leading corporations that have unique business models. For example, Alphabet Inc., the NASDAQ-listed technology company, owns and operates YouTube, a leading social video platform. In 2020, YouTube earned USD19.8 billion in advertising revenues, making it one of the largest digital advertising companies in the world. Given its size, unique business model, and revenue growth rate over 30%, a peer group for YouTube would be challenging to construct if Alphabet were to spin it off.
- The method is sensitive to market mispricing. Suppose that all the comparable companies are currently overvalued by the market. A valuation relative to those companies may suggest a value that is too high, should the values be revised downward upon a correction.
- This approach yields an estimated *fairtrading* price for the target company. To estimate a fair *takeover* price, analysts must add an estimated takeover premium.

Comparable Transaction Analysis

Comparable transaction analysis is closely related to comparable company analysis, except that the analyst uses valuation multiples from historical acquisitions of similar targets rather than trading multiples of similar listed companies. Similar to comparable company analysis, an analyst would look to descriptive statistics, such as the mean, median, and range of valuation multiples, and apply professional judgment to estimate or evaluate a target's value.

Unlike comparable company analysis, the valuation multiples in comparable transaction analysis include takeover premiums, because they reflect historical acquisitions (sales).

EXAMPLE 8

Comparable Transaction Analysis

Joel Hofer, an investment analyst, is evaluating the price General Health Company paid to acquire Medical Services, Inc., of USD55.00 per share. He has already taken the initial step and assembled a sample of comparable transactions, all of which closed within the last two years. Details on the acquisition prices and relevant variables are shown in the following table.

Valuation Variable (USD)	Acquired Company 1	Acquired Company 2	Acquired Company 3
Acquisition share price	35.00	16.50	87.00
Earnings per share	2.12	0.89	4.37
Cash flow per share	3.06	1.98	7.95
Book value per share	9.62	4.90	21.62
Sales per share	15.26	7.61	32.66

The next step in the process is for Hofer to calculate the multiples at which each company was acquired:

Relative Valuation Ratio	Acquired Company 1	Acquired Company 2	Acquired Company 3	Mean
P/E	16.5	18.5	19.9	18.3
P/CF	11.4	8.3	10.9	10.2
P/BV	3.6	3.4	4.0	3.7
P/S	2.3	2.2	2.7	2.4

After reviewing the distribution of the various values around their respective means, Hofer is confident about using the mean value for each ratio because the range in values above and below the mean is reasonably small. Based on his experience with this industry, Hofer believes that cash flows are a particularly important predictor of value for these types of companies. Consequently, instead of finding an equally weighted average, Hofer has decided to weight the P/CF multiple higher (40%) than the others (20% each) for calculating a weighted average estimated price.

Target Company Valuation Variables

	Target Company (a)	Comparable Companies' Valuation Multiples	Mean Multiple Paid for Comparable Companies (b)	Estimated Takeover Value Based on Comparables (c = a × b)	Weight (d)	Weighted Estimates (e = c × d)
Earnings per share	USD2.62	P/E	18.3	47.95	20%	USD9.59
Cash flow per share	USD4.33	P/CF	10.2	44.17	40%	USD17.67
Book value per share	USD12.65	P/BV	3.7	46.81	20%	USD9.36
Sales per share	USD22.98	P/S	2.4	55.15	20%	USD11.03
Weighted average estimate						**USD47.65**

> In sum, Hofer estimated a fair takeover value for Medical Services, Inc., of USD47.65 per share, which is 13% below the price at which General Health Company acquired it. Based on Hofer's analysis, General Health Company overpaid.

Advantages of Using Comparable Transaction Analysis

- The value estimates come from actual transaction prices for similar targets. This approach is unlike the discounted cash flow method, in which the value is determined based on many assumptions and estimates.

- It is not necessary to separately estimate a takeover premium. The takeover premium is embedded in the comparable transaction multiples.

Disadvantages of Using Comparable Transaction Analysis

- The market for corporate control is illiquid. There may be no or few comparable transactions. In these cases, analysts may try to use data from similar or related industries. These derived values may not be accurate for the specific industry and may have to be adjusted.

- Historical valuation multiples reflect not only historical industry conditions, such as the industry growth rate and regulatory environment, but also historical macroeconomic conditions, such as the business cycle, interest rates, equity price levels, and tax rates, that can significantly influence transaction multiples. The analyst may need to exclude transactions before a certain date (e.g., prior to 10 years ago) or make adjustments to reflect changes in these conditions.

- There is a risk that past acquirers over- or underpaid. Transactions where there were multiple competing offers typically rachet up the final transaction price. The analyst should investigate the comparable transactions to better reconcile these valuations.

Premium Paid Analysis

To estimate or judge a sale value or acquisition price for a listed issuer, an analyst could also calculate an estimated **takeover premium**. This premium is the amount by which the per-share takeover price exceeds the unaffected price expressed as a percentage of the unaffected price and reflects the price of control, or the control premium—the amount shareholders require to relinquish their control of the company to the acquirer. For historical transactions, the premium is calculated as follows:

$$PRM = \frac{(DP - SP)}{SP},$$

(1)

where

PRM = takeover premium (as a percentage of stock price)

DP = deal price per share of the target

SP = unaffected stock price of the target

The analyst must be careful to exclude any pre-announcement increase in the price that may have occurred because of rumors in the press or speculation. Common approaches to control for this include using a share price from one week prior to the announcement or sometimes even longer, particularly if there were persistent rumors preceding the transaction, or a trading volume–weighted average price over a week- or month-long period.

To estimate a sale price using the premium paid analysis, the analyst will compile takeover premiums paid for companies like the target and calculate descriptive statistics, such as the mean, median, and range, in a similar fashion to comparable company and transaction analyses. The premium paid will vary by the same factors responsible for variation in valuation multiples: the target's outlook and risk profile. The annual median share price premium paid for acquisitions announced from 1990 to 2018, based on the premium to share price from the week prior to deal announcement, has been just over 30%, with a range of 20%–40% (Exhibit 13).

Exhibit 13: Average Annual Acquisition Premium Paid, 1990–2018

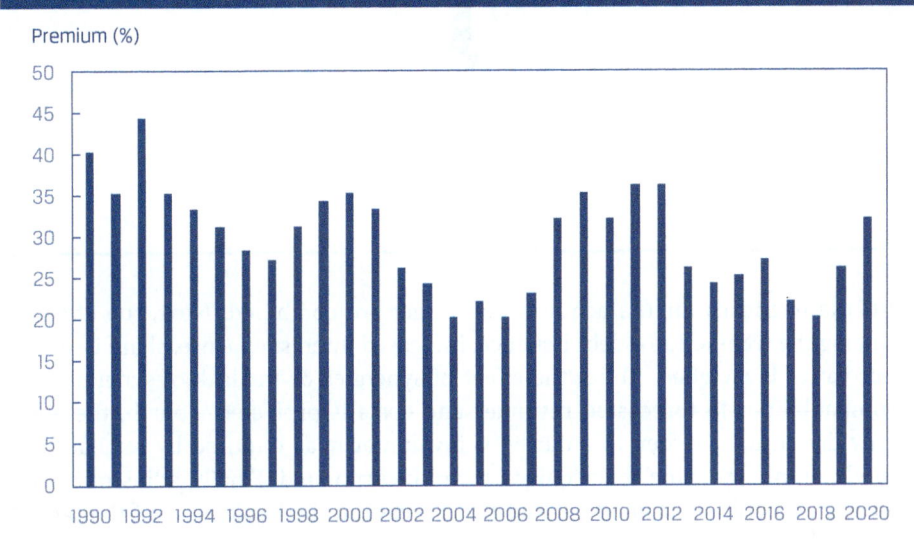

Source: Kengelbach, Keienburg, Gell, Nielsen, Bader, Degen, and Sievers 2019.

MODELING AND VALUATION

4

☐ | demonstrate how corporate restructurings affect an issuer's EPS, net debt to EBITDA ratio, and weighted average cost of capital

The next step of the evaluation process is estimating financial statements that include the effect of the restructuring, known as **pro forma financial statements**. Pro forma financial statements include important inputs for equity and credit evaluation, including revenue, EPS, the ratio of net debt to EBITDA, and free cash flow measures. The process for creating pro forma financial statements depends on the type of restructuring and situational specifics, which will be demonstrated in the case studies in Sections 4–6. As an initial example, the process for an acquisition is illustrated in the diagram in Exhibit 14.

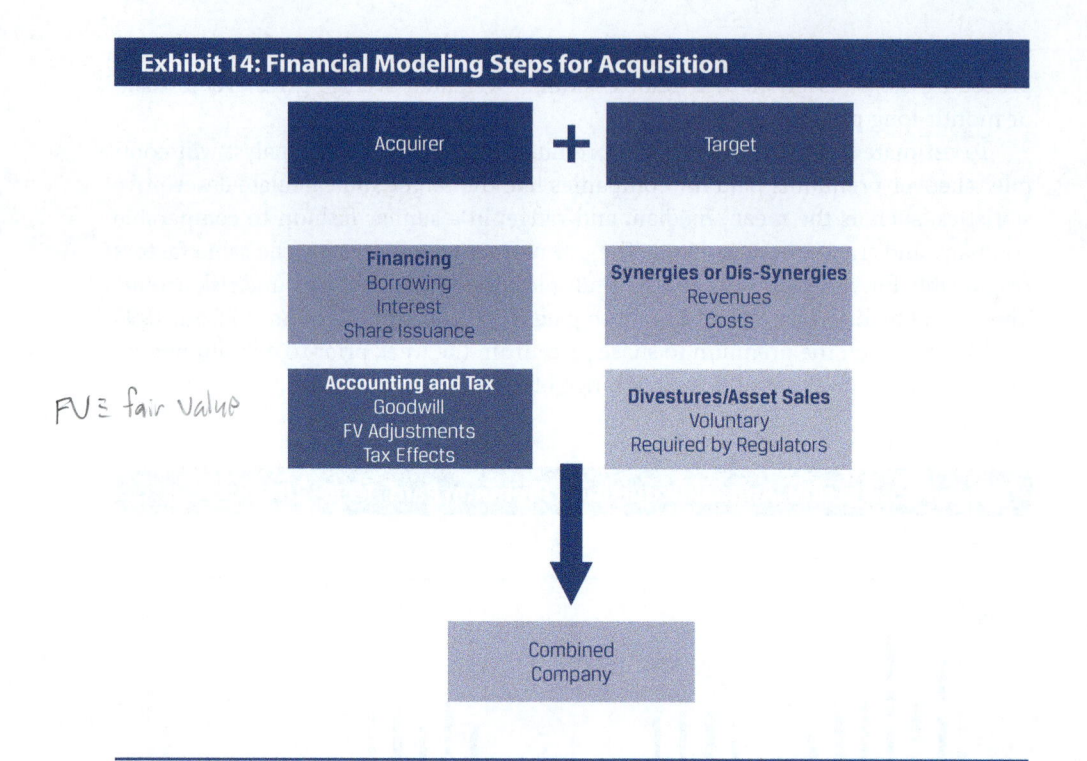

Exhibit 14: Financial Modeling Steps for Acquisition

FV = fair value

First, the financials for the acquirer and target are combined. Next, the effect of financing the transaction—debt issuance, increased interest expense, share issuance, lower cash—is included. Third, the effect of synergies or the lack of synergies and incompatibilities in forecasted revenues and costs is projected. Fourth, the effect of any divestitures, either voluntarily or involuntarily as required by regulators as a condition of approving the acquisition, are incorporated. Finally, adjustments are made for recognition of goodwill and the increase in the book value of the target's assets and liabilities to fair value.

An alternative presentation of these steps, in terms of how lines on the pro forma income statement (typically the first pro forma financial statement created) are estimated, is shown in Exhibit 15. After the pro forma financial statements are created, such ratios as EPS, net debt to EBITDA, and free cash flow are straightforward to calculate.

Exhibit 15: Pro Forma Income Statement (Acquisition) Modeling

Revenue	1. Combine acquirer and target revenues. 2. Add revenue synergies or subtract the cost of incompatible activities (dis-synergies).
Operating expenses	1. Combine acquirer and target operating expenses. 2. Subtract cost synergies or add the cost of incompatible activities (dis-synergies).
Depreciation and amortization	1. Combine acquirer and target depreciation and amortization. 2. Add amortization of acquired intangible assets.
Other expense or income	1. Combine acquirer and target other expense or income.
Interest expense	1. Start with current acquirer interest expense. 2. Add increased interest from new debt issuance and revised interest rate.

Income taxes	1. EBT-weighted average of tax rates of acquirer and target; estimate usually provided by issuers
Shares outstanding	1. Start with current acquirer shares outstanding
	2. Add shares from any share issuance

Pro Forma Weighted Average Cost of Capital

While the pro forma financial statements contain most of the inputs needed for a discounted cash flow valuation model (unlevered or levered free cash flow), a key variable is the required rate of return to discount the pro forma free cash flows. This is typically estimated using a weighted average cost of capital (WACC) approach. Like the financial statements, WACC must be adjusted to reflect the anticipated corporate restructuring.

Recall that an issuer's cost of capital is a market-value weighted average of its cost of debt, equity, and other capital, as shown in Exhibit 16.

Exhibit 16: Weighted Average Cost of Capital Components

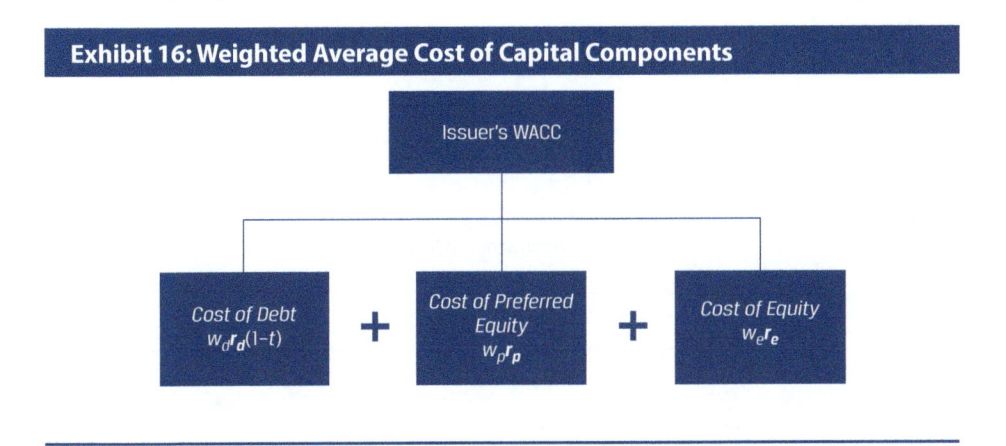

A restructuring can change both the weights of each type of capital (w_d, w_p, and w_e) in the capital structure and the costs of each type of capital (r_d, r_p, and r_e). The simplest example is an issuer acquiring a company for cash and financing it entirely with debt. If the equity price does not change materially, the capital structure will shift from equity to debt as debt increases (i.e., w_d increases and w_e decreases). Conversely, if an issuer sells a division for cash and uses that cash to retire debt, its capital structure will likely shift from debt to equity.

While changes in capital structure weights are straightforward, estimating the effect of a restructuring on the costs of debt and equity capital is more challenging. Recall that costs of capital are influenced by several factors and conditions both inside and outside the issuer, shown in Exhibit 17. Corporate restructurings change the costs of capital by changing these factors. For example, an acquisition that increases leverage and decreases profitability will generally result in an increase in the cost of capital.

Exhibit 17: Factors and Conditions Influencing Issuers' Costs of Capital

Factor/Condition	Primary measures
Profitability	EBITDA or EBIT to sales

Factor/Condition	Primary measures
Volatility	Standard deviation of revenues
	Standard deviation of EBITDA
Leverage	Debt to EBITDA
Assets that can serve as collateral	Asset specificity, liquidity, active market for the asset
Prevailing interest rates	Market reference rates
	Corporate credit spreads

For this reason, it is common to see investment-grade issuers structure transactions to maintain their investment-grade rating and minimize their weighted average cost of capital. Moving from an investment-grade to a speculative-grade credit rating is empirically associated with a several hundred basis point increase in WACC (see Exhibit 18).

Exhibit 18: Median US Large-Cap WACC for Each Credit Rating Notch

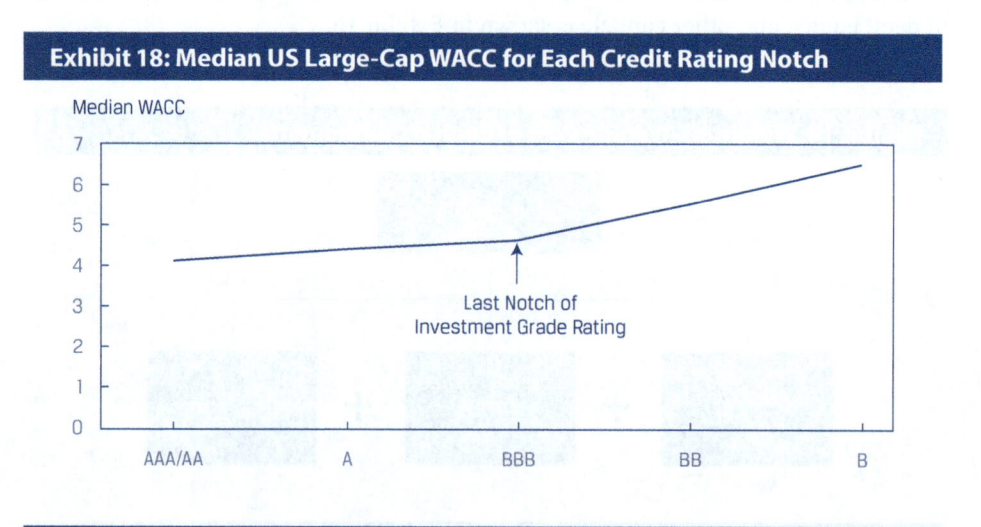

EXAMPLE 9

Competing Offers for Kansas City Southern

Kansas City Southern (KCS), an NYSE-listed railroad company, owns and operates railroads in the southern United States, northern Mexico, and Panama. In 2021, the company received acquisition offers from two Canada-based, TSX-listed railroad companies: Canadian Pacific Railway Limited (CP) and Canadian National Railway Company (CN). The table summarizes the terms of the two offers.

	CP	CN
Consideration:		
Offer price per KCS share, % premium	USD274 per share	USD325 per share
	23% premium	45% premium
Mix of consideration per KCS share	0.489 CP shares	1.129 CN shares
	USD90 in cash	USD200 in cash
Assumed KCS debt	USD3.8 billion	USD3.8 billion
Total consideration (enterprise value)	USD29 billion	USD33.6 billion

	CP	CN
Financing:*		
New borrowings	USD8.6 billion	USD19 billion
Share issuance	44.5 million CP shares	103 million CN shares
Post-acquisition debt to EBITDA	4.0×	4.6×
Current KCS shareholders ownership of combined company	25%	12.6%

*The balance of financing is funded with cash on hand.

Following the close, CP expects its outstanding debt will be approximately USD20.2 billion and stated that they "remain committed to maintaining an investment-grade credit rating." CN expects its outstanding debt would be approximately USD33 billion after its acquisition but also remains committed to maintaining an investment-grade credit rating.

1. If, prior to the acquisition, CN has 713 million shares outstanding trading at USD105 per share, estimate how the weights of debt and equity in its capital structure would change after the acquisition closes as a result of an acquisition of KCS under the proposed terms, assuming a constant share price and that the book value of debt equals its market value.

   Solution

   Following the close of the acquisition, CN expects its outstanding debt to total USD33 billion, after assuming USD3.8 billion in existing KCS debt and issuing USD19 billion itself. Therefore, prior to the acquisition, CN had approximately (33 − 3.8 − 19) = USD10.2 billion in debt and (713 million shares outstanding × USD105 per share) = USD74.9 billion in equity, resulting in a mix of debt and equity of 12% and 88%, respectively.
   After the acquisition, CN will have USD33 billion in debt and 816 (713 + 103) million shares outstanding, which, priced at USD105 per share, is USD85.7 billion in equity. The change in capital structure is shown in Exhibit 19.

Exhibit 19: CN Capital Structure before and after Proposed Acquisition of KCS

CN Capital Structure	Pre-Acquisition	Post-Acquisition
Debt %	12%	28%
Equity %	88%	72%

---

2. To increase the amount of the combined company that current KCS shareholders would own after the close, identify what change CN would have to make to the proportion of CN stock in its consideration.

   A. Increase

   B. Decrease

C. Keep the same

Solution

A is correct. By issuing more CN stock to existing KCS stockholders, KCS stockholders would own more CN stock after the acquisition and, thus, own more of the combined company.

3. Identify CN's primary means of financing a higher amount of cash in the consideration versus CP's offer. CN plans to:

A. offer a greater proportion of stock.

B. issue a greater amount of debt.

C. reduce operating expenses.

Solution

B is correct. By issuing a greater amount of debt and using the proceeds in its cash offer, CN's offer has a greater amount of cash in the consideration. A is incorrect because a greater proportion of stock would mean a lower proportion of cash in the consideration. C is incorrect because reducing operating expenses does not directly affect the mix of consideration offered.

4. Identify the *least* attractive element of CN's offer versus CP's offer, from the perspective of KCS shareholders.

A. Higher proportion of cash in the consideration

B. Higher total enterprise value

C. Higher leverage for the combined company

Solution

C is correct. The higher leverage (4.6 versus 4.0 debt-to-EBITDA ratio) for the combined company is less attractive because it introduces higher credit risk and magnifies any downside risks, such as less-than-expected synergies or integration problems. Accordingly, the higher leverage may result in investors having higher required rates of return (higher cost of capital for the issuer).

5. If credit rating agencies were to warn CN that its investment-grade credit rating were in jeopardy, identify a modification that CN could make to its consideration or financing to bolster its credit rating.

A. Borrow from credit facilities rather than issue bonds.

B. Use a greater proportion of cash on hand.

C. Use a greater proportion of stock.

Solution

C is correct. By using a greater proportion of stock in the consideration, less cash and therefore less debt issuance are needed to finance the acquisition. A is incorrect because the difference between bank debt and bond debt is immaterial to credit. B is incorrect because using cash on hand would have the same impact on net debt as borrowing.

You create a pro forma income statement for CN to evaluate the impact of its proposed acquisition of KCS. First, you compile forecasted income statements for the two companies on a standalone basis, shown in Exhibit 20 (see Example 9 worksheet in the downloadable Microsoft Excel workbook).

Exhibit 20: CN and KCS Standalone Historical and Forecasted Summary Income Statements

Canadian National	2019A	2020A	2021A	2022F	2023F	2024F
Revenue	14,917	13,819	15,063	15,966	16,765	17,603
Operating expenses	(7,762)	(7,453)	(7,833)	(8,303)	(8,718)	(9,154)
D&A	(1,562)	(1,589)	(1,614)	(1,765)	(1,916)	(2,016)
Other income	374	321	353	353	353	353
Interest expense	(538)	(554)	(604)	(640)	(672)	(706)
Income taxes	(1,213)	(982)	(1,180)	(1,235)	(1,279)	(1,338)
Net income	4,216	3,562	4,185	4,376	4,533	4,742
Shares outstanding	723	713	713	710	707	704
Diluted EPS	5.83	5.00	5.87	6.16	6.41	6.74
Kansas City Southern	**2019A**	**2020A**	**2021A**	**2022F**	**2023F**	**2024F**
Revenue	2,866	2,632	2,922	3,097	3,283	3,480
Operating expenses	(1,629)	(1,272)	(1,285)	(1,363)	(1,444)	(1,531)
D&A	(351)	(358	(380)	(403)	(427)	(452)
Other income	18	(29)	0	0	0	0
Interest expense	(116)	(151)	(154)	(163)	(161)	(165)
Income taxes	(248)	(204)	(276)	(292)	(313)	(333)
Net income	540	618	827	876	938	999
Shares outstanding	100	94	90	87	84	81
Diluted EPS	5.40	6.57	9.19	10.07	11.17	12.33

Based on the announcement and your own research, you make the following assumptions:

- The acquisition closes at the end of 2021, with 2022 a full year for the combined entity.
- CN announced that it expects to achieve annual cost synergies that reach USD1 billion by 2024; you assume that the synergies start at 1/3 of that in 2022, stepping up to 2/3 in 2023, and the full USD1 billion is achieved in 2024. There are no revenue synergies.
- The interest rate CN will pay on USD33 billion in outstanding debt—the amount it will have outstanding as of the acquisition closing—is 5.0%, and you assume CN's gross debt and interest rate remain constant to 2024.
- Amortization of acquired intangible assets is USD800 million per year from 2022 to 2024.
- Effective income tax rate is 22% from 2022 to 2024.

6. Given the information provided and the process outlined in Section 3, estimate a pro forma income statement, including diluted EPS, for CN.

Solution

Forecasted diluted EPS is USD5.24, USD5.89, and USD6.60 per share for fiscal years 2022, 2023, and 2024, respectively, as shown in Exhibit 21 (see Example 9 worksheet in the downloadable Microsoft Excel workbook).

Exhibit 21: CN Pro Forma Income Statement, 2022–2024F

CN + KCS = New CN	2022F	2023F	2024F
CN revenue	15,966	16,765	17,603
KCS revenue	3,097	3,283	3,480
New CN revenue	19,063	20,047	21,083
CN operating expenses	8,303	8,718	9,154
KCS operating expenses	1,363	1,444	1,531
Synergies	(333)	(667)	(1,000)
New CN operating expenses	9,332	9,495	9,685
CN D&A	1,765	1,916	2,016
KCS D&A	403	427	452
Amortization of acquired intangible assets	800	800	800
New CN D&A	2,968	3,143	3,268
CN other income	(353)	(353)	(353)
KCS other income	0	0	0
New CN other income	(353)	(353)	(353)
New CN interest expense	1,650	1,650	1,650
New CN income taxes	1,203	1,345	1,503
New CN net income	4,264	4,768	5,329
CN shares outstanding	710	707	704
CN shares issued	103	103	103
New CN shares outstanding	813	810	807
New CN diluted EPS	5.24	5.89	6.60

5   EVALUATING INVESTMENT ACTIONS

☐ | evaluate corporate investment actions, including equity investments, joint ventures, and acquisitions

This section and the two that follow are composed of case studies of corporate restructurings based on real-world events and demonstrate the evaluation process, discussed in prior sections, undertaken by analysts upon their announcement. The case studies, primarily selected based on their real-world prevalence, expand on and provide context for the concepts introduced earlier.

Equity Investment

Example 10 describes a large, mature company that faces growth and regulatory challenges. As is common in these situations, the company seeks to improve its prospects by making an investment in a fast-growing competitor.

Dilmun Inc. and Spina Ltd.

Dilmun Inc., a fictional company, makes and sells traditional combustible cigarettes and cigars. Over the last 10 years, its sales volumes have declined annually by a mid- to high-single-digit rate, as the number of smokers in its major markets has dwindled, but strong pricing power has enabled the company to maintain stable revenues. Dilmun is the market share leader in its geographies and remains highly profitable, with operating margins exceeding 35% and returns on invested capital exceeding 30%.

In recent years, two trends have emerged that have challenged Dilmun, beyond the impact of declining volumes:

1. Some lawmakers have advocated limiting nicotine in tobacco products to non-addictive levels and banning menthol and other flavorings.

2. The proliferation of ESG-focused strategies by asset managers has pressured Dilmun's share price because Dilmun's business model scores low on social metrics. Additionally, shareholders have engaged with the company's board and management to change its products or business model to better align with ESG goals.

At the end of 20X3, Dilmun made the following announcement by press release:

Dilmun Inc. today announces it signed and closed a USD1.2 billion investment in, and service agreements with, Spina Ltd., a market leader in e-vapor. The investment and service agreements will accelerate Spina's strategy to switch smokers of traditional cigarettes to e-vapor products. Dilmun's investment represents a 30% interest in Spina equity, valuing the company at USD4.0 billion on an enterprise value basis. Spina will remain fully independent.

As part of the service agreements, Spina will have access to Dilmun's sales and marketing infrastructure, including

- premium shelf and display space at over 225,000 retail locations worldwide, up from less than 75,000 today, and
- marketing material inside of Dilmun-branded cigarette packs and access to contact information from customer loyalty programs.

While public health authorities recommend against the use of e-vapor products or any tobacco product, they have acknowledged their increased safety over traditional cigarettes.

"We are taking significant action to prepare for a future where adult smokers choose non-combustible products over cigarettes by investing in Spina, a market leader," said Dilmun's chairman and chief executive officer. "Lower-risk products are a promising way forward for all stakeholders. Today, we are making a significant investment toward that goal."

Dilmun will finance the transaction with borrowings on its credit facility, which has an interest rate of 600 bps, and expects to maintain its investment-grade credit rating. Spina intends to use the investment proceeds to support product development and marketing. Spina does not intend to pay dividends for the foreseeable future.

Summary historical and forecasted financial data for Dilmun Inc. and Spina Ltd., prior to the transaction, are shown in Exhibit 22 and Exhibit 23, which are also provided in the Example 10 sheet in the downloadable Microsoft Excel workbook. Dilmun does not own any other equity method investments, and income (loss) from associates is reported as an operating item on its income statement. Dilmun expects amortization expense associated with the transaction, related to fair value adjustments of identifiable net assets, of USD10 million per year.

Exhibit 22: Dilmun Inc. Summary Financial Data (USD millions)

	20X1	20X2	20X3	20X4E
Net revenues	25,434	25,744	25,576	25,670
EBITDA	8,656	9,191	9,839	10,140
EBIT	8,406	8,941	9,589	9,890
Interest expense	(817)	(747)	(705)	(705)
Income tax expense	(1,594)	(1,721)	(1,866)	(1,929)
Net income	5,995	6,473	7,018	7,256
Diluted EPS	3.06	3.33	3.69	3.94
Diluted shares outstanding	1,960	1,943	1,901	1,840
Total debt	12,847	13,881	13,894	13,894
Cash and cash equivalents	4,878	4,569	1,253	2,000

Exhibit 23: Spina Ltd. Summary Financial Data (USD millions)

	20X1	20X2	20X3	20X4E
Net revenues	200	350	600	990
EBITDA	(300)	(400)	(400)	(350)
EBIT	(320)	(460)	(480)	(450)
Interest expense	0	0	0	0
Income tax expense	0	0	0	0
Net income (loss)	(320)	(460)	(480)	(450)
Diluted EPS	(0.37)	(0.53)	(0.56)	(0.52)
Diluted shares outstanding	860	860	860	860

1. Rather than this form of investment, identify other types of actions Dilmun could take with respect to Spina, and explain one advantage and one disadvantage of those alternatives, relative to the equity investment.

Solution

Two other types of actions Dilmun and Spina could have made to achieve similar objectives are acquisition and joint venture.

Alternative	Advantage vs. Equity Investment	Disadvantage vs. Equity Investment
Acquisition	• By acquiring control, Spina couldn't take actions that are against Dilmun's interest, such as sign other partnerships or reduce prices significantly.	• Substantially greater capital investment is required. If the target is risky, a smaller initial investment may be wise.
Joint Venture	• Dilmun and Spina would have governance representation, which reduces risks for Dilmun.	• A larger investment may be required, and Spina's independence may be an important element of its success to date.

2. Based on the information provided in the press release, explain both Dilmun's and Spina's motivations for this transaction.

Solution

Dilmun's motivations are investment exposure to a growing company and unique capabilities in the form of Spina's market-leading products. Dilmun is also seeking to diversify its business away from the declining (by volume) combustible cigarette market to an adjacent alternative that shares sales channels and customers.

Spina's motivations for entering the investment agreement are the synergies offered by the marketing agreement with Dilmun and the cash proceeds that enable it to increase investment to strengthen its position. The equity investment structure allows the current management and board to remain in control but benefit from the capabilities of a larger company.

3. Exhibit 24 shows current enterprise values and sales for the last 12 months for five listed companies comparable to Spina Ltd. Explain how the valuation multiple for Spina implied by the transaction differs from those for the comparable companies.

Exhibit 24: Comparable Company Analysis for Spina Ltd. (USD millions)

	Enterprise Value	Net Revenues (TTM)
Comparable A	1,211	269
Comparable B	821	82
Comparable C	973	191
Comparable D	768	157
Comparable E	1,346	224

Solution

The equity investment by Dilmun valued Spina Ltd. at USD4,000 billion, or an EV/Sales (trailing twelve months, or TTM) multiple of 6.7 (4,000/600 million in net revenues in 20X3). The EV/Sales (TTM) multiples of the comparables, including the median and average, are shown in Exhibit 25. The transaction multiple for Spina Ltd. was higher than both the peer median and average and is the second highest in the group, behind only Comparable B, valued at 10×.

Exhibit 25: EV/Sales Multiples of Comparables for Spina Ltd.

	Enterprise Value (USD mln)	Net Revenues (TTM)	EV/S
Comparable A	1,211	269	4.5
Comparable B	821	82	10.0
Comparable C	973	191	5.1
Comparable D	768	157	4.9
Comparable E	1,346	224	6.0
Median			5.1
Average			6.1

4. Discuss two potential reasons for the difference in valuation multiples for Spina Ltd. versus its comparables that should be investigated further.

Solution

Two potential reasons for the difference in valuation of Spina Ltd. versus its comparables that warrant further investigation are growth prospects and risk profile. On a standalone basis or by virtue of its partial ownership by and service agreement with Dilmun, Spina Ltd. may have faster revenue growth than its peers. Additionally, as a market leader with an established presence in the e-vapor category and the highest revenue, Spina likely has lower risk than its competitors, which may face significant problems as they scale.

5. Based on the information in the exhibits, estimate the effect of Dilmun's investment in Spina on Dilmun's debt-to-EBITDA ratio and its diluted EPS in 20X4E. Assume that Dilmun maintains its estimated effective tax rate.

Solution

As a result of the debt-financed investment in Spina, Dilmun's debt-to-EBITDA ratio in 20X4E will increase from 1.37 to 1.51 and its diluted EPS will decrease from USD3.94 to USD3.85 per share. Exhibit 26 shows the effect of the investment by reconciling the pre-investment to pro forma summary income statements. The investment reduces operating income by Dilmun's share of Spina's net loss ($0.3 \times 450 = 135$) plus the amortization (10) associated with the investment and increases interest expense by an amount equal to the 600 bps in interest expense multiplied by the increase in debt. The dilutive effect on EPS is partially offset by tax effects.

	Before Investment	Investment	After Investment
Exhibit 26: Estimated Effect of Spina Investment on Dilmun Inc.			
	20X4E	20X4E	20X4E
Net revenues	25,670	0	25,670
Income from associates		(145)	(145)
EBITDA	10,140	(145)	9,995
EBIT	9,890	(145)	9,745
Interest expense	(705)	(72)	(777)
Income tax expense	(1,929)	46	(1,883)
Net income	7,256	(171)	7,084
Diluted EPS	3.94	—	3.85
Diluted shares outstanding	1,840	—	1,840
Total debt	13,894	1,200	15,094
Cash and cash equivalents	2,000	0	2,000
Debt to EBITDA	1.37		1.51

Joint Venture

Example 11 shows a common joint venture arrangement: one company with a brand, technology, and know-how co-invests with a company in a foreign market that brings its established local market presence. This example also demonstrates an important step in the life cycle of many joint ventures: a partial buyout by one of the companies, which has significant financial statement impacts to both companies—particularly the acquirer, because the accounting model changes from the equity method to consolidation.

EXAMPLE 11

Opone-Hapalla Automotive Alliance SA

Opone SA, a fictional company headquartered in Brazil, designs, manufactures, and sells vehicles. While it sells some vehicles under its own brands, most of its business is a joint venture with Hapalla AG, named Opone-Hapalla Automotive Alliance SA (OHAA). OHAA was formed in 20X1 to make and sell Hapalla-branded vehicles in Latin America. Besides its participation in OHAA, Hapalla AG operates only in select European markets. OHAA has increased its annual vehicle sales volume from less than 10,000 in 20X1 to 1.5 million in 20X7. The joint venture has a contractually agreed-upon term of 25 years.

Opone SA and Hapalla AG disclose summary financial results and positions for OHAA in the notes to their financial statements and share equally in the joint venture's profit and loss, as well as any dividends paid. Exhibit 27 and Exhibit 28 (also in the Example 11 worksheet in the downloadable Microsoft Excel workbook) show summary financial data from Opone SA's 20X7 annual report and consensus forecast figures for 20X8E. OHAA is the only joint venture Opone SA has an investment in.

Exhibit 27: OHAA (Joint Venture) Summary Financial Data (BRL millions)

	20X5	20X6	20X7	20X8E
Net revenues	111,599	138,704	169,441	208,412
Profit after tax	10,476	12,491	15,267	18,757
Dividends paid	4,000	6,000	40,000	32,000
Cash and equivalents	60,418	62,537	32,461	12,653

Exhibit 28: Opone SA Summary Financial Data

	20X5	20X6	20X7	20X8E
Net revenues	5,305	4,377	3,862	3,910
Cost of sales	(5,119)	(4,091)	(3,788)	(3,793)
SG&A expense	(1,765)	(1,294)	(1,556)	(1,450)
Joint venture income	5,238	6,246	7,634	9,379
Interest expense	(138)	(114)	(95)	(95)
Income tax expense	(34)	(65)	(167)	(190)
Profit after tax	3,487	5,059	5,890	7,761
Cash flows from operations	(2,547)	(2,830)	(726)	(800)
Dividends received from joint venture	2,000	3,000	20,000	16,000
Capital expenditures	(624)	(461)	(795)	(560)
Free cash flow (non-IFRS measure)	(1,171)	(291)	18,479	14,640

1. Based on the information provided, explain how the OHAA joint venture is mutually beneficial for Opone SA and Hapalla AG.

   Solution

   The OHAA joint venture is clearly beneficial for Opone SA, because its income from the joint venture accounts for more than 100% of the company's net income; the company's other operations incur a net loss. The joint venture is beneficial for Hapalla AG because it enables the company to grow beyond its current markets and share the risks (and rewards) of international expansion with a partner that has an established presence in Latin America.

2. Exhibit 29 shows P/E and P/FCF valuation multiples for Opone SA and five listed comparable companies. Compare Opone SA's valuation to its comparables and explain why Opone SA's P/E differs significantly from its P/FCF multiple.

Exhibit 29: Comparable Company Analysis for Opone SA

	P/E (TTM)	P/FCF (TTM)
Comparable A	11	17
Comparable B	12	11
Comparable C	9	18
Comparable D	13	19
Comparable E	15	14
Opone SA	21	7

Solution

Exhibit 30 shows Opone SA's peer median and average P/E and P/FCF multiples. Opone SA is more expensive than peers in terms of P/E but far cheaper than peers on a P/FCF basis. The primary reason behind the difference in Opone SA's P/E and P/FCF multiples is that in 20X7, OHAA joint venture income recognized was less than 40% of dividends earned. Based on the financial data provided, it appears that OHAA has been reducing its cash balance through dividends that are well in excess of profits.

Exhibit 30: Comparable Company Analysis for Opone SA

	P/E (TTM)	P/FCF (TTM)
Comparable A	11	17
Comparable B	12	11
Comparable C	9	18
Comparable D	13	19
Comparable E	15	14
Median	12	17
Average	12	16
Opone SA	21	7

In the beginning of 20X8, Hapalla AG offered Opone SA BRL45 billion in cash to increase its stake in OHAA by 25% and replace the contractual term of 25 years with a perpetual agreement that Hapalla AG's interest in the joint venture would not exceed 75%.

3. If the OHAA joint venture has no debt, compare the valuation of OHAA implied by Hapalla AG's offer with those of comparable companies in Exhibit 29 on a P/E (TTM) basis.

Solution

Hapalla AG's offer of BRL45 billion to acquire a 25% interest in OHAA values OHAA at BRL180 billion (45/0.25) on an enterprise value basis, or BRL147,359 million in equity value after subtracting cash and cash equivalents at year-end 20X7. This equity value is 10.0× the joint venture's profit after tax in 20X7, which is 2.0 lower than the comparable company average and median of 12×.

4. If Opone SA were to accept Hapalla AG's offer at the beginning of 20X8, estimate the net effect of the transaction on Opone SA's 20X8 income statement based on Exhibit 28. Assume that Opone SA would account for its remaining interest in OHAA using the equity method, the carrying value of the OHAA joint venture interest on Opone SA's balance sheet as of 31 December 20X7 is BRL26 billion, and the effective tax rate is 10%.

Solution

The transaction would have two major effects. First, Opone SA would de-recognize half of its interest (BRL13 billion) from its balance sheet and recognize BRL45 billion in cash proceeds from the sale and a gain of (45 13 =) BRL32 billion. Second, the proportion of OHAA net income that Opone SA would recognize as joint venture income would fall from 50% to 25%. Exhibit 31 shows the effect of the transaction on the 20X8 income statement.

Exhibit 31: Pro Forma Opone SA Income Statement for Sale of Half of OHAA Joint Venture

	Before 20X8E	Transaction	After 20X8E
Net revenues	3,910	—	3,910
Cost of sales	(3,793)	—	(3,793)
SG&A expense	(1,450)	—	(1,450)
Joint venture income	9,379	(4,689)	4,689
Gain on sale	0	—	32,000
Interest expense	(95)	—	(95)
Income tax expense	(190)	—	(3,526)
Profit after tax	7,761		31,735

5. Describe the effect of the transaction on Hapalla AG's financial statements.

Solution

As of the date of the transaction close, Hapalla AG would change its accounting for OHAA from the equity method to consolidation and recognize a non-controlling interest that represents Opone SA's 25% interest. As a result, joint venture income will no longer be recognized while revenues, expenses, and other financial statement lines would, as of the close, reflect consolidated figures. On the balance sheet, Hapalla AG would de-recognize the joint venture investment and recognize OHAA's assets and liabilities, while reducing its cash balance for consideration transferred to Opone SA.

Acquisition

The next example illustrates an acquisition transaction, but unlike the prior Kansas City Southern example, the target is a segment of a company. While the financial statement impact is not categorically different for the acquirer, this type of transaction involves another party: a seller that continues to operate after the transaction. Example 12 is a common situation in which the seller is divesting a business segment to another company that is similar to the target but with much greater scale and focus. Additionally, the type of consideration transferred in this transaction results in the seller holding an equity investment in the acquirer.

EXAMPLE 12

Tulor to Acquire Retail Segment from Caracol Petroleum

Tulor Inc. is an Australian operator of convenience stores, including standalone corner shops, larger convenience stores, and stores with petroleum stations.

Caracol Petroleum is a global vertically integrated oil and gas company. Its Upstream operations focus on the exploration and production of oil and natural gas, its Downstream operations include several oil refineries, and its Retail business operates a large network of petroleum stations, all with convenience stores. As a result of a prolonged decline in oil prices and high financial leverage, Caracol Petroleum is seeking to improve its balance sheet and realize value for shareholders.

At the beginning of 20X2, Tulor and Caracol announced that the companies had reached an agreement in which Tulor would acquire the Retail segment of Caracol for AUD2 billion in cash and 80 million Tulor common shares for a total consideration of AUD3 billion, based on the unaffected share price prior to the announcement. Tulor and Caracol expect the transaction to close on 31 December 20X2.

Caracol will use the cash proceeds from the transaction to strengthen its balance sheet by retiring debt. Based on an effective tax rate of 18%, Caracol expects to receive after-tax cash proceeds of AUD1.6 billion, all of which will be used for debt retirement. In connection with the agreement, Caracol has agreed to not dispose of any Tulor shares for five years from the close of the acquisition.

Tulor intends to finance the cash portion of the consideration with cash on hand and by borrowing AUD1 billion from its credit facilities, which has already been committed by its lenders. Tulor intends to maintain an investment-grade credit rating.

Tulor expects to realize AUD125 million in EBITDA synergies by Year 3, primarily by expanding its private label products in the newly acquired stores, utilizing its scale in negotiating with suppliers, and closing unprofitable stores. Summary historical and consensus forecast financial data for Tulor and the Retail segment of Caracol are shown in Exhibit 32 and Exhibit 33, which are also included in the Example 12 worksheet in the downloadable Microsoft Excel workbook.

Exhibit 32: Tulor Summary Financial Data (Pre-Acquisition)

	20X1	20X2	20X3E
Net revenues	19,896	20,891	21,726
Cost of sales	(15,121)	(15,835)	(16,447)
Operating expense	(3,183)	(3,343)	(3,476)
EBITDA	1,592	1,713	1,803
D&A	(597)	(627)	(652)
EBIT	995	1,086	1,152
Interest income	22	24	24
Interest expense	(370)	(388)	(401)
Income tax expense	(129)	(144)	(155)

	20X1	20X2	20X3E
Net income	517	578	620
Diluted EPS	0.80	0.89	0.96
Diluted shares outstanding	648	648	648
Cash and equivalents	4,400	4,800	4,800
Total debt	5,692	5,969	6,169

Exhibit 33: Caracol Petroleum, Retail Segment (Pre-Acquisition) Summary Financial Data

	20X1	20X2	20X3E
Net revenues	4,974	5,223	5,432
Cost of sales	(4,004)	(4,204)	(4,372)
Operating expense	(796)	(836)	(869)
EBITDA	174	183	190
D&A	(99)	(104)	(109)
EBIT	75	78	81

1. Explain Tulor's and Caracol's motivations for pursuing this transaction.

Solution

Tulor's motivations are two-fold: synergies and growth. By utilizing its superior scale (Tulor had a store footprint six times the size of Caracol's) and scope, Tulor expects to significantly increase Caracol's stores' annual EBITDA by the end of the third year after closing. This also results in a >15% increase in Tulor's EBITDA prior to the acquisition in three years, which is likely a rare opportunity in a mature industry, such as convenience stores; Tulor's revenues are growing at a low-single-digit rate.

Caracol's motivations to sell are to strengthen its balance sheet by using the proceeds to retire debt and, likely, to sharpen its focus on its Upstream and Downstream segments. Based on the significant synergies announced by Tulor, it's likely that Caracol is not the best owner for the Retail segment.

2. Evaluate the valuation implied by the purchase price against comparable companies based on the selected financial data for companies in Exhibit 34. Explain two reasons why the transaction multiple paid by Tulor (based on 20X2 EBITDA) may differ from the median comparable.

Exhibit 34: Comparable Company Analysis for Caracol Petroleum, Retail Segment

	Enterprise Value	EBITDA (TTM)
Comparable A	2,422	295
Comparable B	1,642	287
Comparable C	1,946	163
Comparable D	1,536	201

	Enterprise Value	EBITDA (TTM)
Comparable E	2,692	264

Solution

Exhibit 35 shows the EV/EBITDA of the median comparable and the implied multiple for Tulor's acquisition of Caracol Petroleum's Retail segment. While the median comparable trades at 8× 20X2 EBITDA, the acquisition multiple was double that, at 16×. There are two likely reasons for the much higher valuation in the acquisition: control and synergies.

The acquisition multiple includes a control premium paid by Tulor, while the trading multiples in comparable company analysis reflect only prices for non-controlling stakes. Control allows a buyer to make operational decisions, which in this case enables Tulor to realize significant synergies through its existing business.

If synergies of AUD125 million (in Year 3) are included in the analysis, the acquisition multiple falls to 10×, which is within the peer range.

Exhibit 35: Comparable Company Analysis—Caracol Petroleum, Retail Segment

	Enterprise Value	EBITDA (TTM)	EV/EBITDA
Comparable A	2,422	295	8
Comparable B	1,642	287	6
Comparable C	1,946	163	12
Comparable D	1,536	201	8
Comparable E	2,692	264	10
Median			8
Caracol Petroleum Retail	3,000	183	16
Caracol Petroleum Retail + Synergies		308	10

3. Estimate the impact of the transaction on Tulor's debt-to-EBITDA ratio and diluted EPS in 20X3, assuming the following:

a. AUD42 million in cost synergies is realized,

b. incremental amortization expense associated with fair value adjustments of identifiable net assets acquired is AUD200 million per year,

c. Tulor earns 50 bps in annualized interest income on its cash and pays an interest rate of 650 bps on its debt, and

d. the effective tax rate is 20%.

Solution

Based on the information and assumptions provided, compared to 20X3E estimates prior to the acquisition, the acquisition results in Tulor's diluted EPS decreasing by AUD0.26 per share, to 0.70, and its debt-to-EBITDA ratio increasing by 0.1×, to 3.5× EBITDA. While the acquisition increases EBITDA, it results in a decrease in income before taxes because of the incremental amortization expense and interest expense. The increase in shares outstanding from the equity portion of the consideration is alone responsible for a loss of AUD0.26 per share in EPS. The full analysis is shown in Exhibit 36.

Exhibit 36: Pro Forma Tulor Summary Income Statement

	Before 20X3E	Acquisition	After 20X3E
Net revenues	21,726	5,432	27,158
Cost of sales	(16,447)	(4,372)	(20,819)
Operating expense	(3,476)	(869)	(4,345)
Cost synergies	—	42	42
EBITDA	1,803	232	2,035
D&A	(652)	(309)	(960)
EBIT	1,152	(77)	1,075
Interest income	24	(5)	19
Interest expense	(401)	(60)	(461)
Income tax expense	(155)		(127)
Net income	620		506
Diluted EPS	0.96		0.70
Diluted shares outstanding	648	80	728
Cash and equivalents	4,800	(1,000)	3,800
Total debt	6,169	1,000	7,169
Debt to EBITDA	3.4		3.5

6   EVALUATING DIVESTMENT ACTIONS

☐ | evaluate corporate divestment actions, including sales and spin offs

Either through acquisitions or internal expansion over time, companies often become engaged in multiple businesses. Management may seek to improve performance by separating these businesses, either selling them to another company or spinning them off as independent companies.

While investment analysts often cannot fully evaluate a corporate restructuring until details are announced, companies sometimes publicly announce "strategic reviews" or similarly titled initiatives regarding a part of their business or its entirety before a specific restructuring action is taken and announced. The outcome of the review can vary, so analysts must estimate the potential impact of different scenarios and judge their likelihood. Market participants will often price in risk-adjusted estimates of actions when the strategic review is announced, so an investment perspective at the time of the strategic review is necessary.

Example 13 describes a strategic review intended to evaluate the focus of a company, any conglomerate discount that may exist, and possible actions to realize value for its stakeholders.

EXAMPLE 13

Benefit Ltd. Strategic Review

Benefit Ltd., a fictional company headquartered in Johannesburg, South Africa, sells consulting services and subscription-based human capital management software called BenefitsExchange. The company operates and reports two segments: Consulting and BenefitsExchange. Summary financial data for Benefit Ltd. for the last 12 months (LTM) and the prior-year period are shown in Exhibit 37, Exhibit 38, and Exhibit 39 (see Example 13 worksheet in the downloadable Microsoft Excel workbook).

Exhibit 37: Benefit Ltd. Segment Data (ZAR millions)

Revenues	Prior-year period	Last 12 months (LTM)
BenefitsExchange	55	75
Consulting	402	404
Total revenues	457	479
Segment EBITDA	**Prior-year period**	**LTM**
BenefitsExchange	(10)	(5)
Consulting	83	84
Total segment EBITDA	73	79

Exhibit 38: Benefit Ltd. Reconciliation of Segment EBITDA to Consolidated Net Income and EPS

	Prior-year period	LTM
Total segment EBITDA	73	79
D&A	(19)	(20)
Corporate/unallocated cost	(4)	(4)
EBIT	50	55
Other expense (income)	0	0
Interest expense	8	9
Income taxes	10	11
Net income	32	35
Shares outstanding	1,454	1,454
Diluted EPS (cents)	2.20	2.41

Exhibit 39: Benefit Ltd. Balance Sheets, Most Recent Quarter (MRQ) and Prior Year

	Prior year	MRQ
Cash and equivalents	140	173
Other current assets	110	97
Total current assets	250	270
Non-current assets	540	590
Total assets	790	860
Current debt	20	20
Other current liabilities	110	120
Total current liabilities	130	140
Non-current debt	230	230
Other non-current liabilities	130	185
Total equity	300	305
Total liabilities and equity	790	860

While BenefitsExchange has grown at a rapid rate, Benefit Ltd. has significantly lagged its peers in share price performance over the last four years. Currently, the market values Benefit Ltd. at an enterprise value of ZAR1,437 million, or sales and EBITDA (last 12-month) multiples of 3 and 19, respectively.

Recently, an activist investor announced an 8% position in Benefit Ltd. equity and, in a public statement, expressed an interest in working with the company's management and board to improve stakeholder value. At the market close today, the company announced the following information in a press release.

> Benefit Ltd. (Benefit) announced that its board of directors has initiated a comprehensive review of strategic alternatives to maximize stakeholder value. The board has formed a Strategic Review Committee, which is chaired by the independent director and includes Benefit's CEO.
>
> "The board is committed to maximizing value and has initiated a comprehensive review of strategic alternatives, including selling or spinning off components of business, and a review of our strategic plans," said the independent director. "Benefit's management team and board have a strong track record of value creation."
>
> No assurances can be given regarding the outcome or timing of the review process. Benefit does not intend to make any further public comment regarding the review until it has been completed or the company determines that disclosure is required or beneficial.

You believe there are two actions that management might take in its strategic review:

A. Sell the Consulting segment.

B. Spin off the Consulting segment (which would split the Consulting and BenefitsExchange businesses into separate companies).

Data on relative valuation for both the Consulting and BenefitsExchange segments are shown in Exhibit 40–Exhibit 42.

Exhibit 40: Consulting Segment, Comparable Company Data

Comparable company	Market cap	Cash	Debt	EBITDA (LTM)
Comparable A	1,459	13	146	159
Comparable B	2,477	461	220	319
Comparable C	788	89	92	66
Comparable D	1,402	340	348	235
Comparable E	2,770	241	113	330
Comparable F	2,934	440	498	299

Exhibit 41: Consulting Segment, Comparable Transaction Data

Comparable transaction	Cash paid	Value of stock issued	Net debt (cash) assumed	Target EBITDA (LTM)
Comparable 1	791	0	118	101
Comparable 2	1,174	0	434	134
Comparable 3	578	84	(35)	87
Comparable 4	1,310	378	832	180

Exhibit 42: BenefitsExchange Segment, Comparable Company Analysis

Comparable company	EV/sales (LTM)	Sales growth rate (LTM)
Comparable A	20	55%
Comparable B	12	18%
Comparable C	11	22%
Comparable D	6	8%
Comparable E	15	35%

1. Based on Benefit Ltd.'s current valuation and that of its median peers, evaluate whether a conglomerate discount is present. Assume that corporate/unallocated costs are allocated to the Consulting segment.

Solution

Benefit Ltd.'s current enterprise value is ZAR1,437 million. To assess the conglomerate discount, we compare this valuation to a sum-of-the-parts valuation of its segments using comparable company analysis.

Comparable company analysis for the Consulting segment, shown in Exhibit 43, indicates that the median peer trades at an enterprise value-to-EBITDA multiple of 9.

Exhibit 43: Consulting Segment, Comparable Company Analysis

Comparable company	Market cap	Cash	Debt	EBITDA (LTM)	Enterprise value	EV/EBITDA
Comparable A	1,459	13	146	159	1,592	10
Comparable B	2,477	461	220	319	2,236	7
Comparable C	788	89	92	66	791	12
Comparable D	1,402	340	348	235	1,410	6
Comparable E	2,770	241	113	330	2,642	8
Comparable F	2,934	440	498	299	2,992	10
					Median	9

Comparable company analysis for the BenefitsExchange segment, shown in Exhibit 44, indicates that the median peer trades at an enterprise value-to-sales multiple of 12.

Exhibit 44: BenefitsExchange Segment, Comparable Company Analysis

Comparable company	EV/sales (LTM)
Comparable A	20
Comparable B	12
Comparable C	11
Comparable D	6
Comparable E	15
Median	12

Applying these peer valuation multiples to Benefit Ltd.'s segment EBITDA, less corporate costs, results in an enterprise value of ZAR1,621 million and an implied conglomerate discount of ZAR184 million, as shown in Exhibit 45.

Exhibit 45: Benefit Ltd. Sum-of-the-Parts Valuation I

Consulting segment EBITDA	84
Corporate/unallocated cost	(4)
Consulting segment EBITDA	80
Peer median EV/EBITDA multiple	9
Enterprise value	721
BenefitsExchange segment sales	75
Peer median EV/S multiple	12
Enterprise value	900
Total est. enterprise value	1,621
Current trading EV	1,437
Conglomerate discount	184

2. The market's valuations of BenefitsExchange's peers seem to be sensitive to companies' sales growth rates. If the valuation multiple of the company with the closest sales growth rate to BenefitsExchange is used in the analysis from Question 1, what is the estimated conglomerate discount?

Solution

The BenefitsExchange sales growth rate for the last 12 months was (75 – 55)/55 = 36.4%. The comparable company with the closest growth rate is Comparable E, which grew by 35% and trades at an enterprise value-to-sales multiple of 15. If this multiple is used in the sum-of-the-parts valuation of Benefit Ltd., the estimated conglomerate discount will increase from ZAR184 million to ZAR409 million, as shown in Exhibit 46.

Exhibit 46: Benefit Ltd. Sum-of-the-Parts Valuation II

Consulting segment EBITDA	84
Corporate/unallocated cost	(4)
Consulting segment EBITDA	80
Peer median EV/EBITDA multiple	9
Enterprise value	721
BenefitsExchange segment sales	75
EV/S multiple	15
Enterprise value	1,125
Total est. enterprise value	1,846
Current trading EV	1,437
Conglomerate discount	409

3. Benefit Ltd. receives only one bid from a competitor consulting company for its Consulting segment, for total consideration of ZAR800 million.

a. Compare the bid to comparable transactions. Ignore corporate/unallocated costs.

b. Compare the bid to the implied valuation of the Consulting segment in the current market value of Benefit Ltd., using the valuation of BenefitsExchange from Question 2.

Solution

a. This bid values the Consulting segment at an EV/EBITDA of approximately 10, while the median and average comparable stands at 11 (see Exhibit 47). Thus, the bid moderately undervalues the Consulting segment from this perspective.

Exhibit 47: Consulting Segment, Comparable Transaction Analysis					
	Cash paid	Value of stock issued	Net debt (cash) assumed	Target EBITDA (LTM)	EV/EBITDA
Comparable 1	791	0	118	101	9
Comparable 2	1,174	0	434	134	12
Comparable 3	578	84	(35)	87	7
Comparable 4	1,310	378	832	180	14
				Median	11
				Mean	11
Consulting segment bid	800			84	10

b. If the enterprise value of BenefitsExchange is assumed to be ZAR1,125 million and Benefit Ltd. currently trades at an enterprise value of ZAR1,437 million, then the implied valuation of the Consulting segment is ZAR312 million (see Exhibit 48). The bid of ZAR800 million values the segment substantially higher (488 million).

Exhibit 48: Consulting Segment Bid vs. Current Implied Segment Valuation	
Current Benefit Ltd. EV	1,437
BenefitsExchange segment sales	75
EV/S multiple	15
Est. enterprise value	1,125
Implied value of Consulting segment	312
Consulting segment bid	800
Premium to implied value	488

4. Assume Benefit Ltd. sells the Consulting segment for ZAR800 million in cash, transferring no cash or debt to the buyer, and reduces annualized corporate/unallocated operating costs by ZAR1 million and D&A expense by ZAR12 million. Additionally, assume Benefit Ltd., immediately upon receiving the proceeds, executes an accelerated share repurchase (ASR) for ZAR800 million, repurchasing 200 million shares.

Estimate the pro forma income statement for Benefit Ltd. for these transactions, using the LTM financial data provided. Assume a 0% effective tax rate.

Solution

As shown in Exhibit 49, the sale of the Consulting segment is dilutive to EPS, though the dilution is offset modestly by the using of the proceeds towards share repurchases.

Exhibit 49: Pro Forma Benefit Ltd. Income Statement	
	LTM
BenefitsExchange EBITDA	(5)
Corporate unallocated costs	(4)
Effect of Consulting disposal	1
D&A	(20)
Effect of Consulting disposal	12
Pro forma EBIT	(16)
Other expense (income)	0
Interest expense	9
Income taxes	0
Pro forma net income	(25)
Shares outstanding	1,454
Effect of ASR	(200)
Pro forma shares outstanding	1,254
Pro forma diluted EPS (cents)	(1.99)

5. If a spin off of the Consulting segment were to be valued at an EV/EBITDA multiple of 13, discuss whether Benefit Ltd. should sell the Consulting segment for ZAR800 million or spin it off?

Solution

If a spin off were to be valued at an EV/EBITDA multiple of 13, Benefit Ltd. should spin off the segment rather than sell it because the sale price of ZAR800 million values the company at 10× EV/EBITDA, or 3× lower. However, an advantage of a sale is that the valuation is definitive. If the spin off is valued lower or there is a capital market correction, then the sale may be a better option.

EVALUATING RESTRUCTURING ACTIONS

7

☐ | evaluate cost and balance sheet restructurings

Restructurings are challenging on many fronts, and so they are often prompted or forced on a company by external circumstances. The next example illustrates a cost restructuring that is prompted by two related external circumstances: (1) a rejected acquisition offer and (2) pressure from shareholders in response to that rejection. Example 14 also shows how there are multiple restructuring actions that can achieve the same objective: increased shareholder value.

EXAMPLE 14

Cyrene SARL Cost Restructuring

Cyrene SARL, a fictional European consumer goods company, received an unsolicited acquisition offer in 20X2 from a larger competitor that has a reputation for aggressive cost cutting. The offer valued Cyrene at a 20% premium, and Cyrene's share price appreciated 18% on the news. However, Cyrene's management and board flatly rejected the offer, releasing the following statement by press release: "This offer fundamentally undervalues Cyrene. We rejected the proposal because we see no merit for Cyrene's stakeholders. We do not see the basis for any further discussion." The competitor withdrew its bid, and Cyrene's share price fell by 3%.

Over the week following the bid and rejection, Cyrene management and board members held conversations with its large shareholders. Several large shareholders remarked that "for as long as you don't take actions to increase shareholder value, you are vulnerable to an acquirer who will."

Two weeks after the bid, Cyrene SARL announced the following by press release: "We are conducting a comprehensive review of our cost structure to accelerate delivery of shareholder value. Recent events have highlighted the need to quickly capture the value we see in the company. We expect the review to be completed in five weeks, after which time we will communicate further."

Summary financial data for the last 12 months for Cyrene and five other European consumer goods companies, including Competitor A, which made the initial offer to acquire Cyrene, are shown in Exhibit 50 (also in the Example 14 worksheet in the downloadable Microsoft Excel workbook).

Exhibit 50: Summary Financial Data, European Consumer Goods (LTM; EUR millions)

	Total Assets	Revenues	EBIT	Revenue Growth Rate*	Debt as % of Assets
Competitor A	236,648	56,444	16,933	1.50%	44%
Competitor B	86,381	35,410	8,782	−2.00%	45%
Competitor C	127,940	91,187	15,867	1.00%	29%
Competitor D	101,450	25,896	5,257	0.00%	29%
Competitor E	66,477	27,808	5,228	2.50%	29%
Cyrene SARL	23,738	18,990	2,659	4.00%	20%

*CAGR for last three years.

1. Explain Cyrene's motivations for conducting a review of its cost structure. What did the large shareholders mean by their remark?

Solution

The large shareholders meant that another company could acquire Cyrene and cut costs (equivalently, realize operating cost synergies) and earn an attractive rate of return on the acquisition. By having below-average profitability, Cyrene is a potentially inexpensive target, after synergies, for an acquirer. By improving its profitability on its own now, as a standalone business, it can improve shareholder value and fend off an acquirer.

2. If Cyrene were to restructure to reach its peer median EBIT margin, calculate how much in annual operating expenses, in euros and as a percentage of its TTM operating expenses, would have to be eliminated.

Solution

Based on the data in Exhibit 50, the peer median EBIT margin is 20%. In the last 12 months, Cyrene reported sales and EBIT of EUR18,990 million and EUR2,659 million, respectively, implying operating expenses of EUR16,331 million. To reach the peer median EBIT margin of 20%, Cyrene would have to reduce its operating expenses by EUR1,139 million, or 7%.

3. Past cost restructuring programs by consumer goods companies have taken four years, on average, to achieve target profitability. Assuming the following, estimate Cyrene's EBIT and EBIT margin next year:

a. Revenues grow by 3% annually.

b. Cyrene incurs one-time costs associated with the restructuring of EUR1,250 million.

c. EBIT margin increases towards the peer median, excluding the impact of one-time restructuring costs, in an even annual pace over four years.

Solution

Exhibit 51 shows the estimation of Cyrene's pro forma profitability for the restructuring plan, as outlined. If Cyrene's EBIT margin is to increase evenly over four years towards 20%, it will increase by $(20\% - 14\%)/4 = 6\%/4 = 1.5\%$ each year. Revenue growth and margin expansion are more than offset in the next 12 months by the one-time restructuring costs.

Exhibit 51: Cyrene Pro Forma Profitability, NTM (EUR millions)

	LTM	NTM
Revenues	18,990	19,560
EBIT ex. restructuring costs	2,659	3,032
Margin	14.0%	15.5%
Restructuring costs	—	1,250
Pro forma EBIT	—	1,782
Margin	—	9.1%

4. Explain two risks for Cyrene for pursuing a cost restructuring like the one modeled in Question 3.

Solution

The first risk is decelerating revenue growth. Over the last three years, Cyrene has grown materially faster than its five competitors. A major cost reduction may result in cutting spending responsible for that growth, which may erase any value creation associated with the restructuring.

A second risk is political. Cost restructurings typically result in layoffs and the closures of facilities, which may result in pressure from government officials and the public. Cyrene is a consumer-facing company and can lose business or be the target of regulatory pressure that preempts the cost restructuring or results in less value creation than anticipated.

5. Cyrene operates and reports results for three segments: Household Goods, Beauty & Personal Care, and Food. Summary segment financial data for the last 12 months are presented in Exhibit 52. Your colleague has advocated that as an alternative to a cost restructuring, Cyrene could sell or spin off its Household Goods segment to improve profitability. Evaluate your colleague's proposal, and identify other information you need to fully evaluate the proposal.

Exhibit 52: Cyrene Segment Results, LTM (EUR millions)

	Revenues	EBIT	Revenue Growth Rate*
Household Goods	5,507	496	7%
Beauty & Personal Care	8,166	1,960	3%
Food	5,317	583	2%
Corporate/unallocated	—	(380)	
Total	18,990	2,659	4.00%
Margin		14.0%	

Solution

As Exhibit 53 shows, selling or spinning off the Household Goods segment would result in a pro forma EBIT and EBIT margin of EUR2,163 million and 16%, respectively. While the margin is 2 percentage points higher, total EBIT is 19% lower in this scenario.

Exhibit 53: Cyrene Pro Forma Segment Results, LTM (EUR millions)

	Revenues	EBIT	Revenue Growth Rate*
Beauty & Personal Care	8,166	1,960	3%
Food	5,317	583	2%
Corporate/unallocated	—	(380)	
Total	13,483	2,163	
Margin		16%	

To fully evaluate a cost restructuring versus a sale or spin off of the Household Goods segment, several additional analyses are necessary, including the following:

- Estimated valuation of the Household Goods segment in a sale or spin off versus the value it has to the current Cyrene enterprise value
- Benefits or costs to the remaining Cyrene business segments as a result of a separation

- Amount, if any, of corporate/unallocated costs that could be reduced in the event of a sale or a spin off
- Additional details of the cost restructuring to compare to a sale or a spin off (it may be the case that both a cost restructuring and sale or spin off could be pursued)

Most corporate restructurings aim for strategic focus and operational simplification. Often corporate issuers find themselves owning business units that would be better served by a different ownership or operating model or governance structure. Ideally, restructurings work towards that objective.

This is true not only for businesses within a corporate issuer but also for the assets that underlie them. A common balance sheet restructuring is the sale and immediate leasing of real estate owned by issuers for which real estate is not their core business to a company that does focus on real estate investments. Example 15 demonstrates this situation with a retailer that owns valuable commercial real estate: its distribution centers.

EXAMPLE 15

Kosala Corp. Balance Sheet Restructuring

Kosala Corp. is a global omnichannel retailer with physical stores and e-commerce operations on its own and on third-party websites. While it leases most of its retail stores and its headquarters, Kosala owns the real estate (land and buildings) associated with several distribution centers the company built many years ago and expanded over time. Because e-commerce has continued to grow at a rapid rate and land use is highly regulated, distribution centers and associated real estate are valued at attractive cap rates. (The cap rate is net operating income expressed as a percentage of a property's value and is a reciprocal of a valuation multiple.)

— A lower cap rate is beneficial for the seller

On 1 June 20X2, Kosala Corp. made the following announcement by press release.

Kosala Corp. announced today that its board of directors approved a strategic real estate plan to pursue a separation of substantially all of its distribution centers and related real estate assets. The separation would be achieved through a series of sale-leaseback transactions with real estate investment companies that specialize in distribution center properties.

The company's board reached this decision after an extensive real estate evaluation process, along with the support of its legal and financial advisers. This evaluation included asset suitability screening, market rent analysis on a property-by-property basis, and prospective portfolio quality and diversification analysis.

"This strategic real estate plan is the result of a comprehensive review of alternatives to best take advantage of our real estate portfolio," said the chairman and CEO of Kosala. "We appreciate the valuation differential between retailers and real estate. Importantly, we expect this real estate plan to create minimal operational distraction."

Under the plan, Kosala will sell some of its distribution centers and related real estate and lease them for 15-year terms with the option to extend the term. The company expects to receive cash proceeds of approximately CHF425 million, which will be used to retire approximately CHF215 million of debt and the remaining proceeds to repurchase 10 million common shares.

Annual rent expense for the leased assets will total CHF19 million. Kosala will continue to be responsible for maintenance, property taxes, and utilities and will generally be able to make modifications to the properties as business needs arise. The transaction values the assets at an average capitalization rate of 4.5%.

The company believes the pro forma capital structure following the transaction will enable it to receive an investment-grade credit rating, which will offer more attractive financing terms from its current speculative-grade rating. However, the company's credit rating is the responsibility of credit rating agencies, and no assurances can be made as to any changes.

Kosala expects the transaction, including the retirement of debt and the share repurchase, to be completed by the end of 20X2. Additional financial details are as follows:

- Expect to recognize a gain on asset sales of CHF200 million, to be amortized over 15 years.
- Incremental occupancy expense is CHF19 million per year.
- Depreciation expense savings are CHF30 million per year.
- Interest savings from the retirement of debt are CHF15 million per year.
- Because management cannot make any assurance regarding a change in the company's credit rating, further interest savings from a decrease in the company's cost of debt cannot be quantified at this time.
- Expect to recognize operating lease right-of-use asset and lease liabilities of CHF198 million.

1. Explain Kosala's motivation for this action.

Solution

Kosala's motivations are two-fold: to unlock the value in its real estate assets, a non-core business for the company with attractive valuations, and to improve its balance sheet by retiring debt and improving its credit rating, which will likely decrease its costs of capital.

2. The 25th, 50th, and 75th percentile cap rates for transactions for similarly situated properties and similar lease terms in the last five years were 3.0%, 5.5%, and 8.0%, respectively. Based on these figures, evaluate the valuation on a preliminary basis and identify two characteristics that may influence the cap rate for these transactions.

Solution

For leases in which the tenant bears operating costs and taxes, net operating income is generally equal to rent. Because the cap rate is a reciprocal of a valuation multiple, a lower cap rate implies a higher valuation and vice versa. For a seller (and future tenant), such as Kosala, a lower cap rate is desirable. The 4.5% cap rate in this transaction compares favorably to the descriptive statistics provided, because it is 100 bps below the median. Two characteristics that may influence the cap rate for these transactions are the location of the property and its physical condition. Distribution centers near metropolitan centers are the most valuable, and one in good condition means that significant capital expenditures will not be required in the short run.

3. Based on the information provided and Exhibit 54, estimate Kosala's pro forma debt-to-EBITDA and interest coverage ratios for the announced transactions, assuming an effective tax rate of 25%.

Exhibit 54: Kosala Corp. Summary Financial Data (CHF millions)

	LTM (pre-transaction)
Net sales	5,323
Cost of sales	3,309
Gross margin	2,014
SG&A expenses	1,823
D&A expense	67
Operating profit	124
Interest expense	43
Income taxes	20
Net income	61
Diluted shares outstanding	97
Diluted EPS	0.63
Gross debt	615

Based on the information provided, Kosala's pro forma gross debt to EBITDA will decrease from 3.2 to 2.3 as a result of the transactions (see Exhibit 55; also in the Example 15 worksheet in the downloadable Microsoft Excel workbook). Note that while depreciation expense decreases, amortization expense increases from the annual amortization of the gain on sale of the assets. Interest coverage (EBIT to interest expense) increases from 2.9 to 4.3.

Exhibit 55: Kosala Corp. Pro Forma Debt-to-EBITDA Analysis (CHF millions)

	LTM (pre-transaction)	Transaction	LTM (pro forma)
Net sales	5,323		5,323
Cost of sales	3,309		3,309
Gross margin	2,014		2,014
SG&A expenses	1,823	19	1,842
D&A expense	67	(17)	50
Operating profit	124		122
Interest expense	43	(15)	28
Income taxes	20		23
Net income	61		70
Diluted shares outstanding	97	(10)	87
Diluted EPS	0.63		0.81
Gross debt	615	(215)	400
Debt to EBITDA	3.2		2.3

	LTM (pre-transaction)	Transaction	LTM (pro forma)
EBIT to interest	2.9		4.3

4. Assuming credit ratings are primarily determined by interest coverage and debt-to-EBITDA ratios, estimate pro forma interest expense for Kosala using Exhibit 56. Assume that the spot Treasury rate at a similar tenor to Kosala's remaining indebtedness is 125 bps.

Exhibit 56: Corporate Credit Ratings and Spreads to Fundamentals

	AAA/AA	A	BBB	BB	B
Debt to EBITDA	0–1.0	1.0–1.5	1.6–2.3	2.4–3.5	3.6–4.5
EBIT interest coverage	>12	11.0–8.0	7.9–4.0	3.5–1.6	1.5–0.5
Average spread over Treasury	125	232	450	575	731

Pro forma for the transactions, Kosala's estimated debt-to-EBITDA and interest coverage ratios are 2.3× and 4.3×, respectively. This puts Kosala in the BBB credit rating range, which has an average spread over Treasuries of 450 bps. Given the Treasury rate of 125 bps, the pro forma interest rate is 575 bps. On gross debt of CHF400 million, pro forma interest expense is CHF23 million, which is CHF5 million less than prior to its credit rating upgrade and reduction in cost of debt.

SUMMARY

- Corporate issuers seek to alter their destiny, as described by the corporate life cycle, by taking actions known as restructurings.

- Restructurings include investment actions that increase the size and scope of an issuer's business, divestment actions that decrease size or scope, and restructuring actions that do not affect scope but improve performance.

- Investment actions include equity investments, joint ventures, and acquisitions. Investment actions are often made by issuers seeking growth, synergies, or undervalued targets.

- Divestment actions include sales and spin offs and are made by issuers seeking to increase growth or profitability or reduce risk by shedding certain divisions and assets.

- Restructuring actions, including cost cutting, balance sheet restructurings, and reorganizations, do not change the size or scope of issuers but are aimed at improving returns on capital to historical or peer levels.

- The evaluation of a corporate restructuring is composed of four phases: initial evaluation, preliminary evaluation, modeling, and updating the investment thesis. The entire evaluation is generally done only for material restructurings.

- The initial evaluation of a corporate restructuring answers the following questions: What is happening? When is it happening? Is it material? And why is it happening?

- Materiality is defined by both size and fit. One rule of thumb for size is that large actions are those that are greater than 10% of an issuer's enterprise value (e.g., for an acquisition, consideration in excess of 10% of the acquirer's pre-announcement enterprise value). Fit refers to the alignment between the action and an analyst's expectations for the issuer.

- Three common valuation methods for companies involved in corporate restructurings, during the preliminary valuation phase of the evaluation, are comparable company, comparable transaction, and premium paid analysis.

- Corporate restructurings must be modeled on the financial statements based on the situational specifics. Estimated financial statements that include the effect of a restructuring are known as pro forma financial statements.

- The weighted average cost of capital for an issuer is determined by the weights of different capital types and the constituent costs of capital. The costs of capital are influenced by both bottom-up and top-down drivers. Bottom-up drivers include stability, profitability, leverage, and asset specificity. Corporate restructurings affect the cost of capital by affecting these drivers.

PRACTICE PROBLEMS

The following information relates to questions 1-5

Jane Chang is an analyst at Alpha Fund covering the real estate and energy sectors. She and her colleague are analyzing two companies that are currently held by the fund.

The first company is Jupiter Corp., a publicly traded, national retail grocery store chain that has 2,800 physical stores. Jupiter leases most of its grocery stores and all five of its office locations that help the company achieve its core business of operating 50,000 square foot stores in all markets of the United States. Jupiter also owns the real estate (land and building) associated with 100 physical store locations. Jupiter recently announced that its board of directors approved a strategic real estate plan to pursue a separation of all its owned assets. The company currently has a speculative-grade credit rating.

The separation would be achieved through a series of sale-leaseback transactions with real estate investment trusts (REITs) that specialize in owning retail properties. Under the plan, Jupiter will sell its 100 owned grocery stores and lease them for 15-year terms with a combined annual rent expense of USD40 million. Jupiter expects to receive cash proceeds of approximately USD800 million from the property sales, which will be used to retire approximately USD600 million of debt and repurchase 4 million common shares.

Jupiter believes the pro forma capital structure following the transactions will enable it to receive an investment-grade credit rating. The sale-leaseback transactions value the 100 assets at an average capitalization rate of 5.50%. Based on Chang's colleague's research, the 25th, 50th, and 75th percentile cap rates for sale transactions for similarly situated properties and similar lease terms in the last three years were 5.00%, 5.50%, and 6.00%, respectively.

The second company is Saturn Corp., a publicly traded US energy company. Chang has been asked to assess the valuation of a potential spin off for this company. Saturn operates and reports three segments: Upstream, Midstream, and Downstream. In the last 12 months, the company reported the financial results shown in Exhibit 1.

Exhibit 1	
Segment	**EBITDA (USD millions)**
Upstream	14,400
Midstream	5,760
Downstream	3,840
Consolidated	**24,000**

Saturn is currently trading at an enterprise value of USD408,000 million, or an EV/EBITDA multiple of 17. A spin off of the Downstream segment has long been rumored because it has been under-invested in by the current management team, resulting in slower revenue growth than its peers. Chang finds that the median Upstream, Midstream, and Downstream peers are trading at enterprise value-to-EBITDA multiples of 19, 17, and 13, respectively.

During an internal discussion, Chang's colleague makes the following three statements about the comparable company analysis method:

Statement 1: The method is not sensitive to market mispricing.

Statement 2: The estimates of value are derived directly from the market.

Statement 3: The method provides a reasonable approximation of a target company's value relative to similar transactions in the market.

1. Jupiter's strategic real estate plan would be best characterized as a:

    A. reorganization.

    B. cost restructuring.

    C. balance sheet restructuring.

2. Which of the following statements about Jupiter's motivations for the strategic real estate plan is incorrect?

    A. The transactions will enable Jupiter to sell a non-core business.

    B. The transactions will allow Jupiter to unlock the value of its real estate assets.

    C. The expected change in Jupiter's credit rating after the transactions will increase the firm's costs of capital.

3. Which of the following statements *best* describes Jupiter's average capitalization rate for the sale-leaseback transactions? Jupiter's average capitalization rate:

    A. is supported by the comparable transactions.

    B. compares favorably to the comparable transactions.

    C. compares unfavorably to the comparable transactions.

4. Based on Exhibit 1 and the peer median EV/EBITDA multiples, Saturn's estimated enterprise value is *closest* to:

    A. USD392,000 million.

    B. USD408,000 million.

    C. USD421,440 million.

5. Which of Chang's colleague's three statements is correct?

    A. Statement 1

    B. Statement 2

    C. Statement 3

The following information relates to questions 6-10

Elaine Lee is an analyst at an investment bank covering the energy sector. She and her junior analyst are analyzing Stratton Oil Corporation.

Stratton Oil Corporation is a publicly traded, US-based energy company that just announced its acquisition of Midwest Oil Corporation, a smaller US-based energy company. Stratton will pay USD55 in cash and 2.25 Stratton shares for each Midwest share, for a total consideration of USD40 billion based on share prices just prior to the announcement. Stratton's current trading enterprise value just prior to the announcement was USD170 billion. Lee concludes that the acquisition does not signal a change in strategy or focus for Stratton.

Stratton expects to realize annual recurring cost synergies of USD350 million (pre-tax), primarily from efficiencies in oil exploration and production activities and savings in corporate costs. The achievement of the full USD350 million in synergies is expected by the end of the third year after the acquisition closes. Synergies are realized in the amounts of USD117 million, USD233 million, and USD350 million in Years 1–3, respectively, and cash costs of USD175 million, USD280 million, and USD395 million are incurred in Years 1–3, respectively.

Expectations for revenues and total operating expenses for Stratton and Midwest for the next three years prior to the acquisition announcement are shown in Exhibit 1.

Exhibit 1: Stratton and Midwest Year 1–3 Figures, Prior to Acquisition (USD millions)

Stratton	Year 1	Year 2	Year 3
Revenues	21,325	22,391	23,511
Operating expenses	16,525	17,351	18,219
Midwest			
Revenues	5,350	5,618	5,898
Operating expenses	3,050	3,203	3,363

Lee's junior analyst makes the following comment during a conversation with Lee:

The acquisition is considered immaterial in the initial evaluation step for Stratton because it does not signal a change in strategy or focus.

Stratton's offer valued Midwest at an enterprise value of USD40.6 billion, including USD4.3 billion of existing Midwest debt. To finance the consideration of USD55 in cash and 2.25 Stratton shares for each Midwest share, Stratton will issue 104 million new shares and raise approximately USD26 billion in new debt and fund the remainder with cash on hand. Following the close, Stratton expects its outstanding debt will be approximately USD62 billion. Prior to the acquisition, Stratton has 1.096 billion shares outstanding trading at USD125 per share. Lee wants to determine how much the weights of debt and equity in Stratton's capital structure will change assuming a constant share price and that the book value of debt equals its market value.

During an internal meeting, Lee asks if Stratton could have achieved its same goals by undertaking an equity investment or joint venture. In response, Lee's junior analyst makes the following three statements.

Statement 1: Acquisitions require substantially greater capital investments than equity investments.

Statement 2: Acquisitions and equity investments are similar in that they both allow the acquirer to gain control of the target.

Statement 3: Relative to joint ventures, equity investments provide more equal governance representation and require larger investments.

Lee conducted a sum-of-the-parts valuation of Stratton's three segments and calculated an estimated enterprise value of USD187 billion just prior to the announcement.

6. Based on Exhibit 1, the forecasted operating income in Year 3 for the combined Stratton and Midwest is *closest* to:

    A. USD7,432.

    B. USD7,782.

    C. USD8,177.

7. Lee's junior analyst's comment about materiality is:

    A. correct.

    B. incorrect because the acquisition is considered a small acquisition.

    C. incorrect because the acquisition represents more than 10% of Stratton's enterprise value prior to the transaction.

8. The weight of equity in Stratton's capital structure as a result of the acquisition of Midwest assuming Lee's two assumptions is closest to:

    A. 29%.

    B. 71%.

    C. 81%.

9. Which of Lee's junior analyst's three statements is correct?

    A. Statement 1

    B. Statement 2

    C. Statement 3

10. Stratton's estimated conglomerate discount just prior to the announcement is:

    A. −USD17 billion.

    B. USD0.

    C. USD17 billion.

SOLUTIONS

1. C is correct. Jupiter is undertaking a sale-leaseback transaction, which is a type of balance sheet restructuring. Jupiter would receive cash from the property sales and recognize a liability equal to the present value of future lease payments. A is incorrect because a reorganization is a court-supervised restructuring process available in most jurisdictions for companies facing insolvency from burdensome debt levels and, sometimes, as a strategic measure to renegotiate contracts with unfavorable terms. B is incorrect because a cost restructuring refers to actions whose goal is to reduce costs by improving operational efficiency and profitability, often to bring margins to a historical level or to those of comparable industry peers.

2. C is correct. The sale leasebacks will improve Jupiter's balance sheet by retiring debt and likely improving its credit rating, which will decrease (not increase) its costs of capital. A is incorrect because real estate ownership represents a non-core business for Jupiter. Its core business is operating 50,000 square foot stores in all markets of the United States. B is incorrect because the sale leasebacks will allow Jupiter to unlock the value in its real estate assets. Jupiter would receive cash from the property sales and recognize a liability equal to the present value of future lease payments.

3. A is correct. Jupiter's average capitalization rate for the sale-leaseback transactions is 5.50%, which is supported by the median of the 25th, 50th, and 75th percentile cap rates for sale transactions for similarly situated properties with similar lease terms in the last three years (5.00%, 5.50%, and 6.00%). B and C are incorrect because Jupiter's average capitalization rate for the sale-leaseback transactions is 5.50%, which is supported by the median of the 25th, 50th, and 75th percentile cap rates for sale transactions for similarly situated properties with similar lease terms in the last three years (5.00%, 5.50%, and 6.00%).

4. C is correct. USD421,440 million is calculated as follows:

    Upstream: USD14,400 × 19 = USD273,600.

    Midstream: USD5,760 × 17 = USD97,920.

    Downstream: USD3,840 × 13 = USD49,920.

    Consolidated: USD421,440 million

    A is incorrect because USD392,000 million is incorrectly calculated by using the average of the peer segment multiples [(19 + 17 + 13)/3 = 16.33] to estimate the consolidated enterprise value.

    Upstream: USD14,400 × 16.33 = USD234,720.

    Midstream: USD5,760 × 16.33 = USD93.888.

    Downstream: USD3,840 × 16.33 = USD62,592.

    Consolidated: USD392,000 million

    B is incorrect because USD408,000 million is Saturn's current enterprise value, not the estimated enterprise value based on median peer multiples for all three segments.

5. B is correct. An advantage of the comparable company analysis method is that es-

timates of value are derived directly from the market. This approach is unlike the discounted cash flow method, in which the value is determined based on many assumptions and estimates. A is incorrect because the comparable company analysis method is sensitive to market mispricing. As an example, suppose that all the comparable companies are currently overvalued by the market. A valuation relative to those companies may suggest a value that is too high in the sense that values would be revised downward upon a correction. C is incorrect because the comparable company analysis method provides a reasonable approximation of a target company's value relative to similar companies (not transactions) in the market. It assumes that "like" assets should be valued on a similar basis in the market.

6. B is correct. The forecasted operating income in Year 3 is calculated as follows:

Combined Stratton and Midwest Oil: Year 1–3 Figures (USD millions)			
Revenues	**Year 1**	**Year 2**	**Year 3**
Stratton	21,325	22,391	23,511
Add: Midwest revenues	5,350	5,618	5,898
Combined revenues	**26,675**	**28,009**	**29,409**
Operating expenses			
Stratton	16,525	17,351	18,219
Add: Midwest	3,050	3,203	3,363
Subtract: synergies	(117)	(233)	(350)
Add: one-time costs	175	280	395
Combined operating expenses	**19,633**	**20,601**	**21,627**
Operating income (Rev-OpEx)	**7,042**	**7,408**	**7,782**

A is incorrect because it incorrectly excludes Year 3 synergies of USD350 million. C is incorrect because it incorrectly excludes Year 3 one-time costs of USD395 million.

7. C is correct. Materiality can be defined along two dimensions: size and fit. Although the acquisition does not signal a change in strategy or focus for Stratton, the transaction is considered large and material because it exceeds 10% of Stratton's enterprise value prior to the transaction. The total consideration is USD90 billion, based on share prices just prior to the announcement; thus, it represents 13.8% of Stratton's enterprise value just prior to the announcement of USD650 billion. A is incorrect because materiality can be defined along two dimensions: size and fit. Although the acquisition does not signal a change in strategy or focus for Stratton, the transaction is considered large and material because it exceeds 10% of Stratton's enterprise value prior to the transaction. B is incorrect because the transaction is considered large and material because it exceeds 10% of Stratton's enterprise value prior to the transaction.

8. B is correct. Following the close of the acquisition, Stratton expects its outstanding debt to total USD62 billion, after assuming USD4.3 billion in existing Midwest debt and issuing USD26 billion. Therefore, prior to the acquisition, Stratton

had approximately (62 – 4.3 – 26 =) USD31.7 billion in debt and (1.096 billion shares outstanding × USD125 per share =) USD137.0 billion in equity, resulting in a mix of debt and equity of 19% and 81%, respectively. After the acquisition, Stratton will have USD62 billion in debt and (1.096 billion + 104 million =) 1.2 billion shares outstanding, which, priced at USD125 per share, results in USD150 billion in equity, resulting in a mix of debt and equity of 29% and 71%, respectively. The change in capital structure is summarized below.

Stratton's Capital Structure before and after Acquisition of Midwest

Stratton Capital Structure	Pre-Acquisition	Post-Acquisition
Debt %	19%	29%
Equity %	81%	71%

A is incorrect because 29% represents the percentage of debt after acquisition. C is incorrect because 81% represents the percentage of equity prior to acquisition.

9. A is correct. Acquisitions require substantially greater capital investments than equity investments. Acquisitions—not equity investments—allow the acquirer to gain control of the target. Relative to equity investments, joint ventures provide more equal governance representation and require larger investments. B is incorrect because acquisitions (not equity investments) allow the acquirer to gain control of the target. C is incorrect because relative to equity investments, joint ventures provide more equal governance representation and require larger investments.

10. C is correct. The estimated conglomerate discount just prior to the announcement is calculated as follows: Total estimated enterprise value from sum-of-the-parts valuation – Current trading enterprise value = USD187 billion – USD170 billion = USD17 billion. A is incorrect because it incorrectly subtracts the estimated enterprise value from the current trading enterprise value. B is incorrect because the estimated and current trading enterprise values are not equal.

Equity Valuation

1

Equity Valuation: Applications and Processes

by Jerald E. Pinto, PhD, CFA, Elaine Henry, PhD, CFA, Thomas R. Robinson, PhD, CFA, CAIA, and John D. Stowe, PhD, CFA.

Jerald E. Pinto, PhD, CFA, is at CFA Institute (USA). Elaine Henry, PhD, CFA, is at Stevens Institute of Technology (USA). Thomas R. Robinson, PhD, CFA, CAIA, is at Robinson Global Investment Management LLC, (USA). John D. Stowe, PhD, CFA, is at Ohio University (USA).

LEARNING OUTCOMES

Mastery	The candidate should be able to:
☐	define valuation and intrinsic value and explain sources of perceived mispricing
☐	explain the going concern assumption and contrast a going concern value to a liquidation value
☐	describe definitions of value and justify which definition of value is most relevant to public company valuation
☐	describe applications of equity valuation
☐	describe questions that should be addressed in conducting an industry and competitive analysis
☐	contrast absolute and relative valuation models and describe examples of each type of model
☐	describe sum-of-the-parts valuation and conglomerate discounts
☐	explain broad criteria for choosing an appropriate approach for valuing a given company

1   INTRODUCTION

☐ define valuation and intrinsic value and explain sources of perceived mispricing

☐ explain the going concern assumption and contrast a going concern value to a liquidation value

☐ describe definitions of value and justify which definition of value is most relevant to public company valuation

Every day, thousands of participants in the investment profession—investors, portfolio managers, regulators, researchers—face a common and often perplexing question: What is the value of a particular asset? The answers to this question usually influence success or failure in achieving investment objectives. For one group of those participants—equity analysts—the question and its potential answers are particularly critical because determining the value of an ownership stake is at the heart of their professional activities and decisions. **Valuation** is the estimation of an asset's value based on variables perceived to be related to future investment returns, on comparisons with similar assets, or, when relevant, on estimates of immediate liquidation proceeds. Skill in valuation is a very important element of success in investing.

We address some basic questions: What is value? Who uses equity valuations? What is the importance of industry knowledge? How can the analyst effectively communicate his analysis? We answer these and other questions and lay a foundation for the topics that follow.

The following section defines value and describes the various uses of equity valuation. The subsequent sections examine the steps in the valuation process, including the analyst's role and responsibilities, and discuss how valuation results are communicated. They also provide some guidance on the content and format of an effective research report.

Value Definitions and Valuation Applications

Before summarizing the various applications of equity valuation tools, it is helpful to define what is meant by "value" and to understand that the meaning can vary in different contexts. The context of a valuation, including its objective, generally determines the appropriate definition of value and thus affects the analyst's selection of a valuation approach.

What Is Value?

Several perspectives on value serve as the foundation for the variety of valuation models available to the equity analyst. Intrinsic value is the necessary starting point, but other concepts of value—going-concern value, liquidation value, and fair value—are also important.

Intrinsic Value

A critical assumption in equity valuation, as applied to publicly traded securities, is that the market *price* of a security can differ from its intrinsic *value*. The **intrinsic value** of any asset is the value of the asset given a hypothetically complete understanding of the asset's investment characteristics. For any particular investor, an estimate of intrinsic value reflects his or her view of the "true" or "real" value of an asset. If one assumed that the market price of an equity security perfectly reflected its intrinsic value, "valuation" would simply require looking at the market price. Roughly, it is just such an assumption that underpins traditional efficient market theory, which suggests that an asset's market price is the best available estimate of its intrinsic value.

An important theoretical counter to the notion that market price and intrinsic value are identical can be found in the Grossman–Stiglitz paradox. If market prices, which are essentially freely obtainable, perfectly reflect a security's intrinsic value, then a rational investor would not incur the costs of obtaining and analyzing information to obtain a second estimate of the security's value. If no investor obtains and analyzes information about a security, however, then how can the market price reflect the security's intrinsic value? The **rational efficient markets formulation** (Grossman and Stiglitz 1980) recognizes that investors will not rationally incur the expenses of gathering information unless they expect to be rewarded by higher gross returns compared with the free alternative of accepting the market price. Furthermore, modern theorists recognize that when intrinsic value is difficult to determine, as is the case for common stock, and when trading costs exist, even further room exists for price to diverge from value (Lee, Myers, and Swaminathan 1999).

Thus, analysts often view market prices both with respect and with skepticism. They seek to identify mispricing, and at the same time, they often rely on price eventually converging to intrinsic value. They also recognize distinctions among the levels of **market efficiency** in different markets or tiers of markets (for example, stocks heavily followed by analysts and stocks neglected by analysts). Overall, equity valuation, when applied to market-traded securities, admits the possibility of mispricing. Throughout the discussion, then, we distinguish between the market price, P, and the intrinsic value ("value" for short), V.

For an active investment manager, valuation is an inherent part of the attempt to produce investment returns that exceed the returns commensurate with the investment's risk—that is, positive excess risk-adjusted returns. An excess risk-adjusted return is also called an **abnormal return** or **alpha**. (Return concepts will be more fully discussed later.) The active investment manager hopes to capture a positive alpha as a result of his or her efforts to estimate intrinsic value. Any departure of market price from the manager's estimate of intrinsic value is a perceived **mispricing** (i.e., a difference between the estimated intrinsic value and the market price of an asset).

These ideas can be illuminated through the following expression that identifies two possible sources of perceived mispricing:

$$V_E - P = (V - P) + (V_E - V),$$

where

V_E = estimated value

P = market price

V = intrinsic value

[Note: One can derive the above expression as $V_E - P = V_E - P + V - V = (V - P) + (V_E - V)$.]

This expression states that the difference between a valuation estimate and the prevailing market price is, by definition, equal to the sum of two components. The first component is the true mispricing—that is, the difference between the true but unobservable intrinsic value V and the observed market price P (this difference contributes to the abnormal return). The second component is the difference between the valuation estimate and the true but unobservable intrinsic value—that is, the error in the estimate of the intrinsic value.

— The difference between the true (real) but unobservable intrinsic value and the observed market price contributes to the abnormal return or alpha, which is the concern of active investment managers.

To obtain a useful estimate of intrinsic value, an analyst must combine accurate forecasts with an appropriate valuation model. The quality of the analyst's forecasts, in particular the expectational inputs used in valuation models, is a key element in determining investment success. For active security selection to be consistently successful, the manager's expectations must differ from consensus expectations and be, on average, correct as well.

Uncertainty is constantly present in equity valuation. Confidence in one's expectations is always realistically partial. In applying any valuation approach, analysts can never be sure that they have accounted for all the sources of risk reflected in an asset's price. Because competing equity risk models will always exist, there is no obvious final resolution to this dilemma. Even if an analyst makes adequate risk adjustments, develops accurate forecasts, and employs appropriate valuation models, success is not assured. Temporal market conditions may prevent the investor from capturing the benefits of any perceived mispricing. Convergence of the market price to perceived intrinsic value may not happen within the investor's investment horizon, if at all. So, besides evidence of mispricing, some active investors look for the presence of a particular market or corporate event (**catalyst**) that will cause the marketplace to re-evaluate a company's prospects.

Going-Concern Value and Liquidation Value

A company generally has one value if it is to be immediately dissolved and another value if it will continue in operation. In estimating value, a **going-concern assumption** is the assumption that the company will continue its business activities into the foreseeable future. In other words, the company will continue to produce and sell its goods and services, use its assets in a value-maximizing way for a relevant economic time frame, and access its optimal sources of financing. The **going-concern value** of a company is its value under a going-concern assumption. Models of going-concern value are our focus.

Nevertheless, a going-concern assumption may not be appropriate for a company in financial distress. An alternative to a company's going-concern value is its value if it were dissolved and its assets sold individually, known as its **liquidation value**. For many companies, the value added by assets working together and by human capital applied to managing those assets makes estimated going-concern value greater than liquidation value (although, a persistently unprofitable business may be worth more "dead" than "alive"). Beyond the value added by assets working together or by applying managerial skill to those assets, the value of a company's assets would likely differ depending on the time frame available for liquidating them. For example, the value of nonperishable inventory that had to be immediately liquidated would typically be lower than the value of inventory that could be sold during a longer period of time (i.e., in an "orderly" fashion). Thus, such concepts as **orderly liquidation value** are sometimes distinguished.

Fair Market Value and Investment Value

For an analyst valuing public equities, intrinsic value is typically the relevant concept of value. In other contexts, however, other definitions of value are relevant. For example, a buy–sell agreement among the owners of a private business—specifying how and when the owners (e.g., shareholders or partners) can sell their ownership interest and at what price—might be primarily concerned with equitable treatment of both sellers and buyers. In that context, the relevant definition of value would likely be fair market value. **Fair market value** is the price at which an asset (or liability) would change hands between a willing buyer and a willing seller when the former is not under any compulsion to buy and the latter is not under any compulsion to sell. Furthermore, the concept of fair market value generally includes an assumption that both buyer and seller are informed of all material aspects of the underlying investment. Fair market value has often been used in valuation related to assessing taxes. In a financial reporting context—for example, in valuing an asset for the purpose of impairment testing—financial reporting standards reference **fair value**, a related (but not identical) concept and provide a specific definition: "Fair value is the amount for which an asset could be exchanged, a liability settled, or an equity instrument granted could be exchanged between knowledgeable, willing parties in an arm's length transaction."

Assuming the marketplace has confidence that the company's management is acting in the owners' best interests, market prices should tend, in the long run, to reflect fair market value. In some situations, however, an asset is worth more to a particular buyer (e.g., because of potential operating synergies). The concept of value to a specific buyer taking account of potential synergies and based on the investor's requirements and expectations is called **investment value**.

Definitions of Value: Summary

Analysts valuing an asset need to be aware of the definition or definitions of value relevant to the assignment. For the valuation of public equities, an intrinsic value definition of values is generally relevant. Intrinsic value, estimated under a going-concern assumption, is the focus of these equity valuation sections.

APPLICATIONS OF EQUITY VALUATION

2

- [ ] describe applications of equity valuation

Investment analysts work in a wide variety of organizations and positions. As a result, they apply the tools of equity valuation to address a range of practical problems. In particular, analysts use valuation concepts and models to accomplish the following:

- *Selecting stocks.* Stock selection is the primary use of the tools presented here. Equity analysts continually address the same question for every common stock that is either a current or prospective portfolio holding or for every stock that he or she is responsible for covering: Is this security fairly priced, overpriced, or underpriced relative to its current estimated intrinsic value and relative to the prices of comparable securities?

- *Inferring (extracting) market expectations.* Market prices reflect the expectations of investors about the future performance of companies. Analysts may ask: What expectations about a company's future performance are consistent with the current market price for that company's stock? What assumptions about the company's fundamentals would justify the current price? (**Fundamentals** are characteristics of a company related to profitability, financial strength, or risk.) These questions may be relevant to the analyst for several reasons:

  - The analyst can evaluate the reasonableness of the expectations implied by the market price by comparing the market's implied expectations to his own expectations.

  - The market's expectations for a fundamental characteristic of one company may be useful as a benchmark or comparison value of the same characteristic for another company.

To extract or reverse-engineer a market expectation, the analyst selects a valuation model that relates value to expectations about fundamentals and is appropriate given the characteristics of the stock. Next, the analyst estimates values for all fundamentals in the model except the fundamental of interest. The analyst then solves for that value of the fundamental of interest that results in a model value equal to the current market price.

- *Evaluating corporate events.* Investment bankers, corporate analysts, and investment analysts use valuation tools to assess the impact of such corporate events as mergers, acquisitions, divestitures, spin-offs, and going-private transactions. Each of these events affects a company's future cash flows and thus the value of its equity. Furthermore, in mergers and acquisitions, the acquiring company's own common stock is often used as currency for the purchase. Investors then want to know whether the stock is fairly valued.

- *Rendering fairness opinions.* The parties to a merger may be required to seek a fairness opinion on the terms of the merger from a third party, such as an investment bank. Valuation is central to such opinions.

- *Evaluating business strategies and models.* Companies concerned with maximizing shareholder value evaluate the effect of alternative strategies on share value.

- *Communicating with analysts and shareholders.* Valuation concepts facilitate communication and discussion among company management, shareholders, and analysts on a range of corporate issues affecting company value.

- *Appraising private businesses.* Valuation of the equity of private businesses is important for transactional purposes (e.g., acquisitions of such companies or buy–sell agreements for the transfer of equity interests among owners when one of them dies or retires) and tax-reporting purposes (e.g., for the taxation of estates), among others. The absence of a market price imparts distinctive characteristics to such valuations, although the fundamental models are shared with public equity valuation. An analyst encounters these characteristics when evaluating initial public offerings, for example.

- *Share-based payment (compensation).* Share-based payments (e.g., restricted stock grants) are sometimes part of executive compensation. Estimation of their value frequently depends on using equity valuation tools.

INFERRING MARKET EXPECTATIONS

On 2 January 2019, Apple Inc. (AAPL) lowered its revenue guidance citing a variety of reasons, one of which was the weakening economies in some of its Asian markets. Apple's share price fell approximately 10%. When Biogen Inc. announced on 21 March 2019 that its experimental drug for Alzheimer's had failed in late-stage clinical trials, the company's share price dropped approximately 30%. What contributes to such large single-day price movements—changes in estimates of underlying intrinsic value, or market overreaction to negative news?

A rich stream of academic research probes overall market overreaction and underreaction based on large samples—for example, De Bondt and Thaler (1985), Abarbanell and Bernard (1992), and more recently, Bordalo et al. (2017) and Bouchaud et al. 2018). However, one classic research study addresses the topic with a case study of a single such dramatic price drop. This case study, shown in Exhibit 1, is useful for studying equity valuation.

Exhibit 1

Cornell's (2001) case study focuses on the 21 September 2000 press release by Intel Corporation containing information about its expected revenue growth for the third quarter of 2000. The announced growth fell short of the company's prior prediction by 2 to 4 percentage points and short of analysts' projections by 3 to 7 percentage points. In response to the announcement, Intel's stock price fell nearly 30% during the following five days—from $61.50 just prior to the press release to only $43.31 five days later.

To assess whether the information in Intel's announcement was sufficient to explain such a large loss of value, Cornell (2001) estimated the value of a company's equity as the present value of expected future cash flows from operations minus the expenditures needed to maintain the company's growth. (We will discuss such *free cash flow models* in detail at a later stage.)

Using a conservatively low discount rate, Cornell estimated that Intel's price before the announcement, $61.50, was consistent with a forecasted growth rate of 20% a year for the subsequent 10 years and then 6% per year thereafter. Intel's price after the announcement, $43.31, was consistent with a decline of the 10-year growth rate to well under 15% per year. In the final year of the forecast horizon (2009), projected revenues with the lower growth rate would be $50 billion below the projected revenues based on the pre-announcement price. Because the press release did not obviously point to any changes in Intel's fundamental long-run business conditions (Intel attributed the quarterly revenue growth shortfall to a cyclical slowing of demand in Europe), Cornell's detailed analysis left him skeptical that the stock market's reaction could be explained in terms of fundamentals.

Assuming Cornell's methodology was sound, one interpretation is that investors' reaction to the press release was irrational. An alternative interpretation is that Intel's stock was overvalued prior to the press release and that the press release was "a kind of catalyst that caused movement toward a more rational price, even though the release itself did not contain sufficient long-run valuation information to justify that movement" (Cornell 2001, p. 134).

EXAMPLE 1

1. Referring to Exhibit 1 on Cornell's study of the Intel stock price reaction, explain how an analyst could evaluate the two possible interpretations.

Solution:

To evaluate whether the market reaction to Intel's announcement was an irrational reaction or a rational reduction of a previously overvalued price, one could compare the expected 20% growth implicit in the pre-announcement stock price to some benchmark—for example, the company's actual recent revenue growth, the industry's recent growth, and/or forecasts for the growth of the industry or the economy. Finding the growth rate implied in the company's stock price is an example of using a valuation model and a company's actual stock price to infer market expectations. *Note*: Cornell (2001) observed that the 20% revenue growth rate implied by the pre-announcement stock price was much higher than Intel's average growth rate during the previous five years, which occurred when the company was much smaller. He concluded that Intel's stock was overvalued prior to the press release.

These examples illustrate the role of expectations in equity valuation and typical situations in which a given set of facts may be given various interpretations. These examples also illustrate that differences between market price and intrinsic value can occur suddenly, offering opportunities for astute investment managers to generate alpha.

3   UNDERSTANDING THE BUSINESS

☐ | describe questions that should be addressed in conducting an industry and competitive analysis

In general, the valuation process involves the following five steps:

1. *Understanding the business.* Industry and competitive analysis, together with an analysis of financial statements and other company disclosures, provides a basis for forecasting company performance.

2. *Forecasting company performance.* Forecasts of sales, earnings, dividends, and financial position (pro forma analysis) provide the inputs for most valuation models.

3. *Selecting the appropriate valuation model.* Depending on the characteristics of the company and the context of valuation, some valuation models may be more appropriate than others.

4. *Converting forecasts to a valuation.* Beyond mechanically obtaining the "output" of valuation models, estimating value involves judgment.

5. *Applying the valuation conclusions.* Depending on the purpose, an analyst may use the valuation conclusions to make an investment recommendation about a particular stock, provide an opinion about the price of a transaction, or evaluate the economic merits of a potential strategic investment.

Most of these steps are addressed in detail later. Here, we provide an overview of each.

Understanding the Business

To forecast a company's financial performance as a basis for determining the value of an investment in the company or its securities, it is helpful to understand the economic and industry contexts in which the company operates, the company's strategy, and the company's previous financial performance. Industry and competitive analysis, together with an analysis of the company's financial reports, provides a basis for forecasting performance.

Industry and Competitive Analysis

Because similar economic and technological factors typically affect all companies in an industry, industry knowledge helps analysts understand the basic characteristics of the markets served by a company and the economics of the company. An airline industry analyst will know that labor costs and jet fuel costs are the two largest expenses of airlines and that in many markets airlines have difficulty passing through higher fuel prices by raising ticket prices. Using this knowledge, the analyst may inquire about the degree to which different airlines hedge the commodity price risk inherent in jet

fuel costs. With such information in hand, the analyst is better able to evaluate risk and forecast future cash flows. In addition, the analyst would run sensitivity analyses to determine how different levels of fuel prices would affect valuation.

Various frameworks exist for industry and competitive analysis. The primary usefulness of such frameworks is that they can help ensure that an analysis gives appropriate attention to the most important economic drivers of a business. In other words, the objective is *not* to prepare some formal framework representing industry structure or corporate strategy, but rather to use a framework to organize thoughts about an industry and to better understand a company's prospects for success in competition with other companies in that industry. Further, although frameworks can provide a template, obviously the informational content added by an analyst makes the framework relevant to valuation. Ultimately, an industry and competitive analysis should highlight which aspects of a company's business present the greatest challenges and opportunities and should thus be the subject of further investigation and/or more extensive **sensitivity analysis** (an analysis to determine how changes in an assumed input would affect the outcome of an analysis). Frameworks may be useful as analysts focus on questions relevant to understanding a business.

- *How attractive are the industries in which the company operates in terms of offering prospects for sustained profitability?*

Inherent industry profitability is one important factor in determining a company's profitability. Analysts should try to understand **industry structure**—the industry's underlying economic and technical characteristics—and the trends affecting that structure. Basic economic factors—supply and demand—provide a fundamental framework for understanding an industry. Porter's (1985, 1998, 2008) five forces that characterize industry structure—explained in detail at a later stage and summarized in Exhibit 2— can help analysts assess industry profitability and prospects for companies.

Exhibit 2: Summary of Porter's Forces

Force	Features
Rivalry (intra-industry)	Lower rivalry, few competitors and/or good brand identification
Threat of new entrants	High costs to enter (& other barriers)
Threat of substitutes	Few substitutes exist, or cost to switch is high
Bargaining power of suppliers	Many suppliers exist
Bargaining power of buyers	Many customers for an industry's product exist

Analysts must also stay current on facts and news concerning all the industries in which the company operates, including recent developments (e.g., management, technological, or financial). Particularly important to valuation are any factors likely to affect the industry's longer term profitability and growth prospects, such as demographic trends.

- *What is the company's relative competitive position within its industry, and what is its competitive strategy?*

The level and trend of the company's market share indicate its relative competitive position within an industry. In general, a company's value is higher to the extent that it can create and sustain an advantage relative to its competition. Porter identifies several generic corporate strategies for achieving above-average performance:

i.   Cost leadership—being the lowest cost producer while offering products comparable to those of other companies so that products can be priced at or near the industry average

ii. Differentiation—offering unique products or services along some dimensions that are widely valued by buyers so that the company can command premium prices

iii. Focus—seeking a competitive advantage within a target segment or segments of the industry based on either cost leadership (cost focus) or differentiation (differentiation focus)

The term "business model" refers generally to how a company makes money: which customers it targets, what products or services it will sell to those customers, and how it delivers those products or services (including how it finances its activities). The term is broadly used and sometimes encompasses aspects of the generic strategies just described. For example, an airline with a generic cost leadership strategy might have a business model characterized as a low-cost carrier. Low-cost carriers offer a single class of service and use a single type of aircraft to minimize training costs and maintenance charges.

- *How well has the company executed its strategy, and what are its prospects for future execution?*

Competitive success requires both appropriate strategic choices and competent execution. Analyzing the company's financial reports provides a basis for evaluating a company's performance against its strategic objectives and for developing expectations about a company's likely future performance. A historical analysis means more than just reviewing, say, the 10-year historical record in the most recent annual report. It often means looking at the annual reports from 10 years prior, 5 years prior, and the most recent 2 years. Why? Because looking at annual reports from prior years often provides useful insights into how management has historically foreseen challenges and has adapted to changes in business conditions through time. (In general, the investor relations sections of most publicly traded companies' websites provide electronic copies of their annual reports from at least the most recent years.)

In examining financial and operational strategic execution, two caveats merit mention. First, the importance of qualitative—that is, non-numeric factors—must be considered. Such non-numeric factors include the company's ownership structure, its intellectual and physical property, the terms of its intangible assets (e.g., licenses and franchise agreements), and the potential consequences of legal disputes or other contingent liabilities. Second, it is important to avoid simply extrapolating past operating results when forecasting future performance. In general, economic and technological forces can contribute to the phenomenon of "regression toward the mean." Specifically, successful companies tend to draw more competitors into their industries and find that their ability to generate above-average profits comes under pressure. Conversely, poorly performing companies are often restructured in such a manner as to improve their long-term profitability. Thus, in many cases, analysts making long-term horizon growth forecasts for a company's earnings and profits (e.g., forecasts beyond the next 10 years) plausibly assume company convergence toward the forecasted average growth rate for the underlying economy.

ANALYSIS OF FINANCIAL REPORTS AND SOURCES OF INFORMATION

4

The aspects of a financial report that are most relevant for evaluating a company's success in implementing strategic choices vary across companies and industries. For established companies, financial ratio analysis is useful. Individual drivers of profitability for merchandising and manufacturing companies can be evaluated against the company's stated strategic objectives. For example, a manufacturing company aiming to create a sustainable competitive advantage by building strong brand recognition could be expected to have substantial expenditures for advertising but relatively higher prices for its goods. Compared with a company aiming to compete on cost, the branded company would be expected to have higher gross margins but also higher selling expenses as a percentage of sales.

EXAMPLE 2

Competitive Analysis

The following companies are among the largest publicly-traded providers of oilfield services, based on revenues in the most recent fiscal year:

- Schlumberger Ltd. (executive offices in Paris, Houston, London, and the Hague)
  - Revenue: $32.8 billion
  - Net income: $2.2 billion
- Halliburton (executive offices in Houston)
  - Revenue: $24.0 billion
  - Net income: $1.7 billion
- Baker Hughes, a GE Company (executive offices in Houston)
  - Revenue: $22.9 billion
  - Net income: $0.3 billion
- Saipem S.p.A. (executive offices in Milan)
  - Revenue (2017): €9.0 billion
  - Net income (loss) (2017): –€0.3 billion
- National Oilwell Varco Inc. (executive offices in Houston)
  - Revenue: $8.5 billion
  - Net income (loss): –$0.02 billion
- Weatherford International plc (executive offices in Baar, Switzerland)
  - Revenue: $5.7 billion
  - Net income (loss): –$2.8 billion

Note: Financial data are for fiscal 2018, except where noted.

Sources: Companies' 10-K, 20-F, or Investor Relations websites.

These companies provide tools and services—often of a very technical nature—to expedite the drilling activities of oil and gas producers and drilling companies.

1. Discuss the economic factors that may affect demand for the services provided by oilfield services companies, and explain a logical framework for analyzing and forecasting revenue for these companies.

Solution:

Because the products and services of these companies relate to oil and gas exploration and production, the levels of exploration and production activities by oil and gas producers are probably the major factors that determine the demand for their services. In turn, the prices of natural gas and crude oil are important in determining the level of exploration and production activities. Therefore, among other economic factors, an analyst should research those relating to supply and demand for natural gas and crude oil.

- Supply factors in natural gas, such as natural gas inventory levels.
- Demand factors in natural gas, including household and commercial use of natural gas and the amount of new power generation equipment being fired by natural gas.
- Supply factors in crude oil, including capacity constraints and production levels in OPEC and other oil-producing countries, as well as new discoveries of off-shore and land-based oil reserves.
- Demand factors in crude oil, such as household and commercial use of oil and the amount of new power generation equipment using oil products as its primary fuel.
- For both crude oil and natural gas, projected economic growth rates could be examined as a demand factor and depletion rates as a supply-side factor.

Note: Energy analysts should be familiar with sources for researching supply and demand information, such as the International Energy Agency (IEA), the European Petroleum Industry Association (EUROPIA), the Energy Information Administration (EIA), the American Gas Association (AGA), and the American Petroleum Institute (API).

2. Explain how comparing the level and trend in profit margin (net income/sales) and revenue per employee for the companies shown may help in evaluating whether one of these companies is the cost leader in the peer group.

Solution:

Profit margin reflects cost structure. In interpreting profit margin, however, analysts should evaluate any differences in companies' abilities to affect profit margin through power over price. A successfully executed cost leadership strategy will lower costs and raise profit margins. All else equal, we would also expect a cost leader to have relatively high sales per employee, reflecting efficient use of human resources.

With newer companies, or companies involved in creating new products or markets, nonfinancial measures may be critical to obtaining an accurate picture of corporate prospects. For example, a biotechnology company's clinical trial results or an internet company's unique visitors per day may provide information helpful for evaluating future revenue.

Sources of Information

Important perspectives on industry and competition are sometimes provided by companies themselves in regulator-mandated disclosures, regulatory filings, company press releases, investor relations materials, and contacts with analysts. Analysts can compare the information provided directly by companies to their own independent research.

Regulatory requirements concerning disclosures and filings vary internationally. In some markets, such as Canada and the United States, regulations require management to provide industry and competitive information and access to those filings is freely available (e.g., www.sedar.com for Canadian filings, www.sec.gov for US filings, and individual companies' Investor Relations websites). To take the case of the United States, in annual filings with the Securities and Exchange Commission made on Form 10-K for US companies and Form 20-F for non-US companies, companies provide industry and competitive information in the business description section and in the management discussion and analysis (MD&A). Interim filings (e.g., the quarterly SEC Form 10-Q for US companies and Form 6-K for non-US companies) provide interim financial statements but typically less-detailed coverage of industry and competition. In other jurisdictions, listed companies' financial disclosures can be found on individual companies' Investor Relations websites or centrally at government websites (e.g. Companies House in the UK at https://www.gov.uk/government/organisations/companies-house), stock exchange websites (e.g. Shenzhen Stock Exchange disclosures at http://www.szse.cn), or central banks' websites (e.g., National Bank of Belgium at https://www.nbb.be/en/central-balance-sheet-office). Required disclosures concerning industry and competitive information differ across jurisdictions.

So far as analyst–management contacts are concerned, analysts must be aware when regulations (e.g., Regulation FD in the United States) prohibit companies from disclosing material nonpublic information to analysts without also disseminating that information to the public. General management insights based on public information, however, can still be useful to analysts, and many analysts consider in-person meetings with a company's management essential to understanding a company.

The CFA Institute Code of Ethics and Standards of Professional Conduct prohibit use of material inside information, and Regulation FD (and similar regulations in other countries) is designed to prohibit companies from selectively offering such information. These ethical and legal requirements assist analysts by clarifying their main role and purpose.

Company-provided sources of information in addition to regulatory filings include press releases and investor relations materials. The press releases of most relevance to analysts are the press releases that companies issue to announce their periodic earnings. Companies typically issue these earnings press releases several weeks after the end of an accounting period and several weeks before they file their interim financial statements. Earnings press releases summarize the company's performance for the period and usually include explanations for the performance and financial statements (often abbreviated versions). Following their earnings press releases, many companies host conference calls in which they further elaborate on their reported performance and typically allocate some time to answer questions posed by analysts. On their corporate websites, many companies post audio downloads and transcripts of conference calls and presentations made in analyst conferences. The audio files and transcripts of conference calls and conference presentations provide access not only to the company's reports but also to analysts' questions and the company's answers to those questions.

Apart from company-provided sources of information, analysts also obtain information from third-party sources, such as industry organizations, regulatory agencies, and commercial providers of market intelligence.

SOURCES OF ESG INFORMATION: THE CASE OF THE US AUTO INDUSTRY

The evaluation of environmental, social, and governance (ESG) factors can help analysts identify potential business risks and practices that may produce long-term competitive advantages relative to peers. In the following example, we discuss the sources of ESG-related information that an analyst following US-domiciled automakers might consider.

The automotive industry is among the most resource-intensive manufacturing industries in the world. New vehicles are subject to multiple governmental standards concerning safety, fuel efficiency and emissions control, vehicle recycling, and theft prevention, among others. Manufacturing and assembly facilities must conform to strict standards for air emissions, water discharge, and hazardous waste management.

Because an auto company's manufacturing process and vehicles can significantly affect the environment, the industry is heavily regulated. The global nature of the automotive industry requires careful consideration of different regulatory environments within countries and regions. Regulatory bodies in the United States, such as the Environmental Protection Agency, as well as non-US regulatory bodies, such as the European Commission, the European Environment Agency, and the UK-based Environment Agency, help develop and track environmental standards and legislation.

The potential for serious injuries from manufacturing increases the importance of automobile worker safety. In addition, labor relations are also very important for US automakers because of the sizable representation of employees in labor unions. Avoiding costly lawsuits, lost production from work stoppages, and negative publicity are primary concerns for automakers.

Information relevant to analyzing ESG considerations for US automakers can be found in many sources that are common to most industries. These sources include corporate filings, press releases, investor calls and webcasts, and trade publications. Sustainability reports (often called corporate sustainability reports, or CSRs) are also relevant to analysts when examining ESG considerations. These reports address the economic, environmental, and social effects resulting from an organization's everyday activities and the organization's values and governance (see https://www.globalreporting.org/information/sustainability-reporting/Pages/default.aspx). Although there is no uniform standard for their issuance or disclosure by companies, sustainability reports can provide analysts with a better understanding of a company's sustainable business practices and whether a company's resource management supports an economically sustainable business model.

For more specific ESG-related information, analysts following US automakers may consult labor union boycott lists and disclosures from the Occupational Safety and Health Administration (OSHA) and the US Equal Employment Opportunity Commission (EEOC). As the federal agency responsible for overseeing working conditions for most private sector employers in the United States, OSHA can help analysts identify auto manufacturers that have demonstrated a history of safety violations or an improvement in workplace safety. The EEOC's litigation database helps in the investigation of any notable workplace discrimination issues that have affected individual automakers.

Several not-for-profit organizations can be valuable ESG resources to analysts of US automakers (or other industries, for that matter). The Sustainable Accounting Standards Board (SASB) sets industry-specific ESG standards and can help analysts identify ESG considerations that have a quantitative impact on companies' financial performance. The Carbon Disclosure Project collects and synthesizes self-reported environmental data that can provide for important information regarding automakers' exposure to climate change and water scarcity. Finally, Ceres, an organization committed to driving sustainability research and advocacy, can provide analysts with access to sustainability research reports for the auto industry.

CONSIDERATIONS IN USING ACCOUNTING INFORMATION

In evaluating a company's historical performance and developing forecasts of future performance, analysts typically rely heavily on companies' accounting information and financial disclosures. Companies' reported results vary in their persistence (i.e., sustainability). In addition, the information that companies disclose can vary substantially with respect to the *accuracy* of reported accounting results as reflections of economic performance and the *detail* in which results are disclosed.

The term **quality of earnings analysis** broadly includes the scrutiny of *all* financial statements, including the balance sheet, to evaluate both the sustainability of a company's performance and how accurately the reported information reflects economic reality. Equity analysts will generally develop better insights into a company and improve forecast accuracy by developing an ability to assess a company's quality of earnings. With regard to sustainability of performance, an analyst aims to identify aspects of reported performance that are less likely to recur. For example, earnings with significant components of nonrecurring events—such as positive litigation settlements, nonpermanent tax reductions, or gains on sales of nonoperating assets—are considered to be of lower quality than earnings derived mainly from the company's core business operations.

In addition to identifying nonrecurring events, an analyst aims to identify reporting decisions that may result in a level of reported earnings that is unlikely to continue. A good starting point for this type of quality of earnings analysis is a comparison of a company's net income with its operating cash flow. As a simple hypothetical example, consider a company that generates revenues and net income but no operating cash flow because it makes all sales on account and never collects its receivables. One systematic way to make the comparison is to decompose net income into a cash component (combining operating and investing cash flows) and an accrual component (defined as net income minus the cash component). Capital markets research shows that the cash component is more persistent than the accrual component of earnings, with the result that a company with a relatively higher amount of current accruals will have a relatively lower ROA in the future (Sloan 1996). Here, greater persistency means that compared to accruals in the current period, the cash component in the current period is more predictive of future net income. A relatively higher proportion of accruals can be interpreted as lower earnings quality.

A quality of earnings analysis for a particular company requires careful scrutiny of accounting statements, footnotes, and other relevant disclosures. Sources for studying quality of earnings analysis and accounting risk factors include Mulford and Comiskey (2005) and Schilit and Perler (2010). Examples of a few of the many available indicators of possible problems with a company's quality of earnings are provided in Exhibit 3.

Exhibit 3: Selected Quality of Earnings Indicators

Category	Observation	Potential Interpretation
Revenues and gains	Recognizing revenue early, for example: • bill-and-hold sales, and • recording sales of equipment or software prior to installation and acceptance by customer.	Acceleration in the recognition of revenue boosts reported income, masking a decline in operating performance.
	Classification of nonoperating income or gains as part of operations.	Income or gains may be nonrecurring and may not relate to true operating performance, possibly masking declines in operating performance.
Expenses and losses	Recognizing too much or too little reserves in the current year, such as: • restructuring reserves, • loan-loss or bad-debt reserves, and • valuation allowances against deferred tax assets.	May boost current income at the expense of future income, or alternatively, may decrease current year's earnings to boost future years' performance.
	Deferral of expenses by capitalizing expenditures as an asset, for example: • customer acquisition costs and • product development costs.	May boost current income at the expense of future income. May mask problems with underlying business performance.
	Use of aggressive estimates and assumptions, such as: • asset impairments, • long depreciable lives, • long periods of amortization, • high assumed discount rate for pension liabilities, • low assumed rate of compensation growth for pension liabilities, and • high expected return on assets for pension.	Aggressive estimates may indicate actions taken to boost current reported income. Changes in assumptions may indicate an attempt to mask problems with underlying performance in the current period.
Balance sheet issues (may also affect earnings)	Use of off-balance sheet financing (financing that does not appear on the balance sheet), such as securitizing receivables.	Assets and/or liabilities may not be properly reflected on the balance sheet.
Operating cash flow	Characterization of an increase in a bank overdraft as operating cash flow.	Operating cash flow may be artificially inflated.

The following example illustrates the importance of accounting practices in influencing reported financial results and the need for analysts to exercise judgment when using those results in any valuation model.

EXAMPLE 3

Historical Example

Quality of Earnings Warning Signs: Aggressive Estimates

In the section of his 2007 letter to the shareholders of Berkshire Hathaway titled "Fanciful Figures—How Public Companies Juice Earnings," Warren Buffett referred to the investment return assumption (the anticipated return on a defined benefit pension plan's current and future assets):

"Decades of option-accounting nonsense have now been put to rest, but other accounting choices remain—important among these [is] the investment-return assumption a company uses in calculating pension expense. It will come as no surprise that many companies continue to choose an assumption that allows them to report less-than-solid 'earnings.' For the 363 companies in the S&P that have pension plans, this assumption in 2006 averaged 8%."

(www.berkshirehathaway.com/letters/2007ltr.pdf. See pp.18–19.)

In his explanation, Buffett assumes a 5% return on cash and bonds, which averaged 28% of US pension fund assets. Therefore, this implies that the remaining 72% of pension fund assets—predominately invested in equities—must earn a return of 9.2%, after all fees, to achieve the 8% overall return on the pension fund assets. To illustrate one perspective on an average pension fund achieving that 9.2% return, he estimates that the Dow Jones Industrial Index would need to close at about 2,000,000 on 31 December 2099 (compared to a level under 13,000 at the time of his writing) for this century's returns on that US stock index to match just the 5.3% average annual compound return achieved in the 20th century.

1. How do aggressively optimistic estimates for returns on pension assets affect pension expense?

Solution:

The amount of "expected return on plan assets" associated with the return assumption is a deduction in calculating pension expense. An aggressively optimistic estimate for the rate of return that pension assets will earn means a larger-than-warranted deduction in calculating pension expense, and subtraction will lead to understating pension expense and overstating net income. In fact, pension expense could become pension income depending on the numbers involved.

2. Where can information about a company's assumed returns on its pension assets be found?

Solution:

Information about a company's assumed return on its pension assets can be found in the footnotes to the company's financial statements.

The next examples of poor earnings quality, in which management made choices going beyond making an aggressive estimate, are reminiscent of a humorous vignette from Benjamin Graham (1936) in which the chair of a company outlines plans for return to profitability, as follows: "Contrary to expectations, no changes will be made in the company's manufacturing or selling policies. Instead, the bookkeeping system is to be entirely revamped. By adopting and further improving a number of modern accounting and financial devices, the corporation's earning power will be amazingly transformed."

EXAMPLE 4

Quality of Earnings Warning Signs: Extreme Cases

CASE A.

In 2018, the Securities and Exchange Commission (SEC) charged Tangoe Inc., a formerly publicly-traded telecommunications expense management company, with fraudulent accounting practices that had allowed the company to improperly recognize revenues. Among the violations cited by the SEC were improperly recording revenue from customers who were unlikely to pay and understating the allowance for bad debts (*Sources:* US Securities and Exchange Commission press release 2018-175, issued 4 September 2018, and the related SEC complaint.)

1. Describe the financial statement impact of the accounting violations cited by the SEC.

Solution:

On the income statement, improperly recognizing revenue from customers unlikely to pay would inflate reported revenue and—all else equal—reported earnings. On the balance sheet, the improper practices would result in inflated receivables. On the statement of cash flows, if the amount of revenues included in net income exceeds the amount of cash collected from customers—all else equal—net income will exceed operating cash flow. (In actuality, this was not the case with Tangoe, where the company had other adjustments.)

2. How would a company's Accounts Receivable turnover (or days receivable) serve as an early warning sign of the revenue accounting violations cited by the SEC?

Solution:

Improperly recognizing revenue from customers who are unlikely to pay and understating the allowance for bad debts—all else equal—would result in a lower Accounts Receivable turnover (and higher days receivable).

Note: Analysis of Tangoe's last years of publicly-reported data actually shows the following (all $ in thousands):

- Revenues increased 12% from 2013 to 2014 (from $188,914 to $212,476), while average receivables increased by 32% (from $40,701 to $50,110).
- Accounts receivable turnover decreased from 4.6x (= $188,914/$40,701) to 4.2x (= $212,476/$50,110).
- Days receivable increased from 79 days (= 365/4.6) to 87 days (= 365/4.2)

The SEC also charged the company with other revenue recognition violations, including improperly recording a loan from a business partner as revenue, counting contingency-fee receipts as revenue, and recording customers' prepayments for future services as current revenue. Violations like these would result in understating such liabilities as loans payable and unearned revenue. The company, which paid penalties to settle the SEC's charges, was delisted from the NASDAQ stock exchange in 2017 and then was subsequently purchased by a private investment firm.

1. State the effect of Livent's accounting for preproduction costs on its reported earnings per share.

Solution:

Livent's accounting for preproduction costs immediately increased reported earnings per share because it deferred expenses.

2. State the effect of Livent's accounting for preproduction costs on its balance sheet.

Solution:

Instead of immediately expensing costs, Livent reported the amounts on its balance sheet as an asset. The warning signal—the deferral of expenses—can indicate aggressive accounting; preproduction costs should have been expensed immediately because of the tremendous uncertainty about revenues from theatrical productions. There was no assurance that there would be revenues against which expenses could be matched.

3. If an analyst calculated EBITDA/interest expense and debt/EBITDA based on Livent's accounting for preproduction costs without adjustment, how might the analyst be misled in assessing Livent's financial strength? (Recall that EBITDA is defined as earnings before interest, taxes, depreciation, and amortization. Such ratios as EBITDA/interest expense and debt/EBITDA indicate one aspect of a company's financial strength: debt-paying ability.)

Solution:

Livent did not deduct preproduction costs from earnings as expenses. If the amortization of capitalized preproduction costs were then added back to earnings, the EBITDA/interest and debt/EBITDA would not reflect in any way the cash outflows associated with such items as paying pre-opening salaries; but cash outflows reduce funds available to meet debt obligations. The analyst who mechanically added back amortization of preproduction costs to calculate EBITDA would be misled into overestimating Livent's financial strength. Based on a closer look at the company's accounting, the analyst would properly not add back amortization of preproduction expenses in computing EBITDA. If preproduction expenses are not added back, a very different picture of Livent's financial health would emerge.

Note: In 1996, Livent's reported debt/EBITDA was 1.7, but the ratio without adding back amortization for preproduction costs was 5.5. In 1997, debt/EBITDA was 3.7 based on a positive EBITDA of $58.3 million; however, EBITDA without the add-back was *negative* $52.6 million. In November 1998, Livent declared bankruptcy and is now defunct. The criminal trial, in Canada, concluded in 2009 with the conviction of Livent's co-founders on charges of fraud and forgery.

In general, growth in an asset account (such as accounts receivable in the Tangoe example and deferred costs in the Livent example) at a much faster rate than the growth rate of sales may indicate aggressive accounting.

Far more serious than aggressive accounting is the deliberate misstatement of financial reports (i.e., fraudulent financial reporting). In general, publicly-traded companies' annual financial statements are audited by certified, professional auditors. The official standards used by auditors can provide useful insights to analysts about a variety of risk factors that may signal possible future negative surprises. For example, both international auditing standards issued by the IAASB and US auditing standards issued by the PCAOB include examples of fraud risk indicators (IAASB 2018, PCAOB 2017). Fraud risk indicators are typically categorized as relating to incentives to commit fraud, opportunity to commit fraud, or attitude toward committing fraud. A working selection of risk factors for misreporting or misappropriation include the following:

- Excessive pressure on company personnel to make revenue or earnings targets, particularly when combined with a dominant, aggressive management team or individual.

- Management and/or directors' compensation tied to profitability or stock price (through ownership or compensation plans). Although such arrangements are usually desirable, they can be a risk factor for aggressive financial reporting.

- Economic, industry, or company-specific pressures on profitability, such as loss of market share or declining margins.

- Management pressure to meet debt covenants or earnings expectations, including "a practice by management of committing to analysts, creditors, and other third parties to achieve aggressive or unrealistic forecasts" (PCAOB, 2017).

- Existence of related-party transactions.

- Complex organizational structure, creating difficulty in determining who controls the company.

- High turnover—of management, directors, or legal counsel.

- Reported (through regulatory filings) disputes with and/or changes in auditors.

- A history of securities law violations, reporting violations, or persistent late filings.

6   SELECTING THE APPROPRIATE VALUATION METHOD

☐ | contrast absolute and relative valuation models and describe examples of each type of model

The second step in the valuation process—forecasting company performance—can be viewed from two perspectives: the economic environment in which the company operates and the company's own operating and financial characteristics.

Companies do business within larger contexts of particular industries, national economies, and world trade. Viewing a company within those larger contexts, a top-down forecasting approach moves from international and national macroeconomic forecasts to industry forecasts and then to individual company and asset forecasts. For example, a revenue forecast for a major home appliance manufacturer could start with industry unit sales forecasts that are, in turn, based on GDP forecasts. Forecasted company unit sales would equal forecasted industry unit sales multiplied by the appliance manufacturer's forecasted market share. A revenue projection would be based on forecasted company unit sales and sales prices.

Alternatively, a bottom-up forecasting approach aggregates forecasts at a micro level to larger scale forecasts, under specific assumptions. For example, a clothing retailer may have several stores in operation with two new stores about to open. Using information based on the sales per square meter of the existing stores (perhaps during their initial period of operation), the analyst could forecast sales per square meter of the new stores that, added to forecasts of a similar type for existing stores, would give a sales forecast for the company as a whole. In making such a bottom-up sales forecast, the analyst would be making assumptions about selling prices and merchandise costs. Forecasts for individual retailers could be aggregated into forecasts for the group, continuing in a bottom-up fashion.

In general, analysts integrate insights from industry and competitive analysis with financial statement analysis to formulate specific forecasts of such items as a company's sales, earnings, and cash flow. Analysts generally consider qualitative as well as quantitative factors in financial forecasting and valuation. For example, an analyst might modify his or her forecasts and valuation judgments based on qualitative factors, such as the analyst's opinion about the business acumen and integrity of management and/ or the transparency and quality of a company's accounting practices. Such qualitative factors are necessarily subjective.

Selecting the Appropriate Valuation Model

This section discusses the third step in the valuation process—selecting the appropriate model for the valuation task at hand. Detailed descriptions of the valuation models are presented later. Absolute valuation models and relative valuation models are the two broad types of valuation models that incorporate a going-concern assumption. Here, we describe absolute and relative valuation models in general terms and discuss a number of issues in model selection. In practice, analysts frequently use more than one approach to estimate the value of a company or its common stock (Pinto, Robinson, and Stowe 2019).

Absolute Valuation Models

An **absolute valuation model** is a model that specifies an asset's intrinsic value. Such models are used to produce an estimate of value that can be compared with the asset's market price. The most important type of absolute equity valuation models are present value models. In finance theory, present value models are considered the fundamental approach to equity valuation. The logic of such models is that the value of an asset to an investor must be related to the returns that investor expects to receive from holding that asset. Generally speaking, those returns can be referred to as the asset's cash flows, and present value models are also referred to as discounted cash flow models.

A **present value model** or **discounted cash flow model** applied to equity valuation derives the value of common stock as the present or discounted value of its expected future cash flows (such models are known as income models of valuation in private business appraisal). For common stock, one familiar type of cash flow is dividends, which are discretionary distributions to shareholders authorized by a corporation's board of directors. Dividends represent cash flows at the shareholder level in the sense that they are paid directly to shareholders. Present value models based on dividends are called **dividend discount models**. Rather than defining cash flows as dividends, analysts frequently define cash flows at the company level. Common shareholders in principle have an equity ownership claim on the balance of the cash flows generated by a company after payments have been made to claimants senior to common equity, such as bondholders and preferred stockholders (and the government as well, which takes taxes), whether such flows are distributed in the form of dividends.

The two main company-level definitions of cash flow in current use are free cash flow and residual income. Free cash flow is based on cash flow from operations but takes into account the reinvestment in fixed assets and working capital necessary for a going concern. The **free cash flow to equity model** defines cash flow net of payments to providers of debt, whereas the **free cash flow to the firm model** defines cash flows before those payments. We will define free cash flow and each model with more precision later. A residual income model is based on accrual accounting earnings in excess of the opportunity cost of generating those earnings.

Because the present value approach is the familiar technique for valuing bonds (here, the term "bonds" refers to all debt securities and loans), it is helpful to contrast the application of present value models to equity valuation with present value models as applied to bond valuation. The application of present value models to common stock typically involves greater uncertainty than is the case with bonds. That uncertainty centers on two critical inputs for present value models—the cash flows and the discount rate(s). Bond valuation discounts a stream of cash payments specified in a legal contract (the **bond indenture**). In contrast, in equity valuation an analyst must define the specific cash flow stream to be valued—dividends or free cash flow—and then forecast the amounts of those cash flows. Unlike bond valuation, no cash flow stream is contractually owed to common stockholders. Clearly, a company's total cash flows—and therefore the cash flows potentially available to common stockholders—will be affected by business, financial, technological, and other factors and are subject to greater variation than the contractual cash flow of a bond. Furthermore, the forecasts for common stock cash flows extend indefinitely into the future because common stock has no maturity date. In addition to the greater uncertainty involved in forecasting cash flows for equity valuation, significant uncertainty exists in estimating an appropriate rate at which to discount those cash flows. In contrast with bond valuation, in which a discount rate can usually be based on market interest rates and bond ratings, equity valuation typically involves a more subjective and uncertain assessment of the appropriate discount rate. Finally, in addition to the uncertainty associated with cash flows and discount rates, the equity analyst may need to address other issues, such as the value of corporate control or the value of unused assets.

The present value approach applied to stock valuation, therefore, presents a high order of complexity. Present value models are ambitious in what they attempt—an estimate of intrinsic value—and offer many challenges in application. Graham and Dodd (1934) suggested that the analyst consider stating a range of intrinsic values, and that suggestion remains valid. To that end, **sensitivity analysis** is an essential tool in applying discounted cash flow valuation. We discuss sensitivity analysis in more detail next.

Another type of absolute valuation is **asset-based valuation**, which values a company on the basis of the market value of the assets or resources it controls. For appropriate companies asset-based valuation can provide an independent estimate of value, and an analyst typically finds alternative, independent estimates of value to be useful. Exhibit 4 describes instances in which this approach to absolute valuation could be appropriate.

Exhibit 4: Asset-Based Valuation

Analysts often apply asset-based valuation to natural resource companies. For example, a crude oil producer, such as Petrobras, might be valued on the basis of the market value of its current proven reserves in barrels of oil, minus a discount for estimated extraction costs. A forest industry company, such as

Weyerhaeuser, might be valued on the basis of the board meters (or board feet) of timber it controls. Today, however, fewer companies than in the past are involved only in natural resources extraction or production. For example, Occidental Petroleum features petroleum in its name but also has substantial chemical manufacturing operations. For such cases, the total company might be valued as the sum of its divisions, with the natural resource division valued on the basis of its proven resources.

Relative Valuation Models

Relative valuation models constitute the second broad type of going-concern valuation models. A **relative valuation model** estimates an asset's value relative to that of another asset. The idea underlying relative valuation is that similar assets should sell at similar prices. Relative valuation is typically implemented using price multiples (ratios of stock price to a fundamental, such as cash flow per share) or enterprise multiples (ratios of the total value of common stock and debt net of cash and short-term investments to certain of a company's operating assets to a fundamental, such as operating earnings).

Perhaps the most familiar price multiple is the price-to-earnings ratio (P/E), which is the ratio of a stock's market price to the company's earnings per share. A stock selling at a P/E that is low relative to the P/E of another closely comparable stock (in terms of anticipated earnings growth rates and risk, for example) is *relatively undervalued* (a good buy) relative to the comparison stock. For brevity, an analyst might state simply *undervalued*, but the analyst must realize that if the comparison stock is overvalued (in an absolute sense, in relation to intrinsic value), so might be the stock being called undervalued. Therefore, it is useful to maintain the distinction between *undervalued* and *relatively undervalued*. Investing to exploit perceived mispricing in either case (absolute or relative mispricing) relies on a basis of differential expectations—that is, investor expectations that differ from and are more accurate than those reflected in market prices, as discussed earlier.

The more conservative investing strategies based on relative valuation involve over-weighting (underweighting) relatively undervalued (overvalued) assets, with reference to benchmark weights. The more aggressive strategies allow short selling of perceived overvalued assets. Such aggressive approaches are known as relative value investing (or relative spread investing, if using implied discount factors). A classic example is **pairs trading** that utilizes pairs of closely related stocks (e.g., two automotive stocks), buying the relatively undervalued stock and selling short the relatively overvalued stock. Regardless of which direction the overall stock market goes, the investor will be better off to the extent that the relatively undervalued stock ultimately rises more (falls less) than the relatively overvalued stock.

Frequently, relative valuation involves a group of comparison assets, such as an industry group, rather than a single comparison asset. The application of relative valuation to equity is often called the method of comparables (or just comparables) and is the subject of a later reading.

EXAMPLE 5

Relative Valuation Models

1. While researching Smithson Genomics, Inc., a (fictitious) healthcare information services company, you encounter a difference of opinions. One analyst's report claims that Smithson is at least 15% *overvalued*, based on a comparison of its P/E with the median P/E of peer companies in the health-care information services industry and taking account of company and peer

group fundamentals. A second analyst asserts that Smithson is *undervalued* by 10%, based on a comparison of Smithson's P/E with the median P/E of the Russell 3000 Index, a broad-based US equity index. Both analyses appear to be carefully executed and reported. Can both analysts be right?

Solution:

Yes. The assertions of both analysts concern *relative* valuations, and their benchmarks for comparisons differ. The first analyst compared Smithson to its peers in the healthcare information services industry and considers the company to be *relatively overvalued* compared to that group. The second analyst compared Smithson to the overall market as represented by the Russell 3000 and considers the company to be *relatively undervalued* compared to that group. If the entire healthcare information services industry is undervalued in relation to the Russell 3000, both analysts can be right because they are making relative valuations.

The investment implications of each analyst's valuation generally would depend on additional considerations, including whether the market price of the Russell 3000 fairly represents that index's intrinsic value and whether the market liquidity of an otherwise attractive investment would accommodate the intended position size. The analyst in many cases may want to supplement relative valuation with estimates of intrinsic value.

The method of comparables is characterized by a wide range of possible implementation choices; a later reading discusses various alternative price and enterprise multiples. Practitioners will often examine a number of price and enterprise multiples for the complementary information they can provide. In summary, the method of comparables does not specify intrinsic value without making the further assumption that the comparison asset is fairly valued. The method of comparables has the advantages of being simple, related to market prices, and grounded in a sound economic principle (that similar assets should sell at similar prices). Price and enterprise multiples are widely recognized by investors, so analysts can communicate the results of an absolute valuation in terms of a price or enterprise multiple.

7   ISSUES IN MODEL SELECTION AND INTERPRETATION

☐ describe sum-of-the-parts valuation and conglomerate discounts

☐ explain broad criteria for choosing an appropriate approach for valuing a given company

A variation to valuing a company as a single entity is to estimate its value as the sum of the estimated values of its various businesses considered as independent, going-concern entities. A valuation that sums the estimated values of each of the company's businesses as if each business were an independent going concern is known as a **sum-of-the-parts valuation**. (The value derived using a sum-of-the-parts valuation is sometimes called the **breakup value** or **private market value**.)

Sum-of-the-parts analysis is most useful when valuing a company with segments in different industries that have different valuation characteristics. Sum-of-the-parts analysis is also frequently used to evaluate the value that might be unlocked in a restructuring through a spin-off, split-off, tracking stock, or equity (IPO) carve-out.

Example 6 shows a case in which a sum-of-the-parts valuation could be used to gain insight into a company's future prospects. In practice, a detailed breakdown of each business segment's contribution to earnings, cash flow, and value would be needed.

EXAMPLE 6

Sum-of-the-Parts Valuation

Donaldson Company, Inc., is one of the largest and most successful filtration manufacturers in the world. Consistent with FASB guidance related to segment reporting, the company has identified two reportable segments: Engine Products and Industrial Products. Segment selection was based on the internal organizational structure, management of operations, and performance evaluation by management and the company's board of directors. 2018 10-K data (in millions of US dollars) for the segments appear in the following table.

Descriptions of the segments from the company's 2018 10-K are as follows:

The Engine Products segment sells to original equipment manufacturers (OEMs) in the construction, mining, agriculture, aerospace, defense, and truck markets and to independent distributors, OEM dealer networks, private label accounts, and large equipment fleets. Products include replacement filters for both air and liquid filtration applications, air filtration systems, liquid filtration systems for fuel, lube and hydraulic applications, and exhaust and emissions systems.

The Industrial Products segment sells to various industrial end-users, OEMs of gas-fired turbines, and OEMs and end-users requiring clean air. Products include dust, fume, and mist collectors; compressed air purification systems; gas and liquid filtration for food; beverage and industrial processes; air filtration systems for gas turbines; and specialized air and gas filtration systems for such applications as membrane-based products as well as specialized air and gas filtration systems for such applications as hard disk drives and semi-conductor manufacturing.

	Engine Products	Industrial Products	Total Company*
Fiscal 2018			
Net sales	$1,849.0	$885.2	$2,734.2
Earnings (loss) before income taxes	261.3	137.1	363.6
Assets	1,110.3	631.9	1,976.6
Capital expenditures	64.6	31.4	97.5
Fiscal 2017			
Net sales	$1,553.3	$818.6	$2,371.9
Earnings (loss) before income taxes	219.7	129.1	322.0
Assets	849.6	638.3	1,979.7
Capital expenditures	29.7	23.4	65.9
Fiscal 2016			
Net sales	$1,391.3	$829.0	$2,220.3
Earnings (loss) before income taxes	163.5	119.0	257.4
Assets	841.4	646.9	1,787.0
Capital expenditures	37.5	27.3	72.9

* Total company results differ from the sum of the two divisions by allocated corporate and unallocated amounts.

1. Why might an analyst use a sum-of-the-parts approach to value Donaldson?

Solution:

On the one hand, the Engine Products segment is already significantly larger than the Industrial Products segment and is growing at a much faster rate in terms of sales, income, assets, and capital expenditures. On the other hand, profit margins appear to be higher for Industrial Products. In 2018, the EBIT-to-sales ratio was 15.5% for the Industrial Products segment versus 14.1% for the Engine Products segment.

An investor presentation by Donaldson's management in May 2013 indicated that they expected Industrial Products to become 48% of the company's product portfolio by 2021. However, the recent results noted show that the Engine Products segment has become a larger and larger part of Donaldson's total business despite its lower margins. Whether or not the company will ultimately be successful in changing their product mix is fundamental to an analyst forming an opinion on Donaldson's share price.

2. How might an analyst use the provided information in an analysis and valuation?

Solution:

An analyst might use the information from Example 6 to develop separate valuations for each of the segments based on forecasts for each segment's sales and profitability. The value of the company in total would be the sum of the value of each of the segments, adjusted for corporate items—such as taxes, overhead expenses, and assets/liabilities not directly attributable to the separate operating systems.

The concept of a conglomerate discount often arises in connection with situations warranting a sum-of-the parts valuation. **Conglomerate discount** refers to the concept that the market applies a discount to the stock of a company operating in multiple, unrelated businesses compared to the stock of companies with narrower focuses. Alternative explanations for the conglomerate discount include 1) inefficiency of internal capital markets (i.e., companies' allocation of investment capital among divisions does not maximize overall shareholder value); 2) endogenous factors (i.e., poorly performing companies tend to expand by making acquisitions in unrelated businesses); and 3) research measurement errors (i.e., conglomerate discounts do not actually exist, and evidence suggesting that they do is a result of flawed measurement). Examples in which conglomerate discounts appear most observable occur when companies divest parts of the company that have limited synergies with their core businesses.

Note that a break-up value in excess of a company's unadjusted going-concern value may prompt strategic actions, such as a divestiture or spin-off.

Issues in Model Selection and Interpretation

How does one select a valuation model? The broad criteria for model selection are that the valuation model be:

- consistent with the characteristics of the company being valued;
- appropriate given the availability and quality of data; and
- consistent with the purpose of valuation, including the analyst's perspective.

Note that using more than one model can yield incremental insights.

Selection of a model consistent with the characteristics of the company being valued is facilitated by having a good understanding of the business, which is the first step in the valuation process. Part of understanding a company is understanding the nature of its assets and how it uses those assets to create value. For example, a bank is composed largely of marketable or potentially marketable assets and securities. Thus, for a bank, a relative valuation based on assets (as recognized in accounting) has more relevance than a similar exercise for a service company with few marketable assets.

In selecting a model, data availability and quality can be limiting factors. For example, a dividend discount model is the simplest discounted cash flow model; but if a company has never paid dividends and no other information exists to assess a company's future dividend policy, an analyst may have more confidence applying an apparently more complex present value model. Similar considerations also apply in selecting a specific relative valuation approach. For example, meaningful comparisons using P/Es may be hard to make for a company with highly volatile or persistently negative earnings.

Model selection can also be influenced by the purpose of the valuation or the perspective of the analyst. For example, an investor seeking a controlling equity position in a company may elect to value the company based on forecasted free cash flows rather than forecasted dividends because such flows might potentially be redirected by such an acquirer without affecting the value of the acquisition (this valuation approach will be discussed in detail in another reading). When an analyst reads valuations and research reports prepared by others, the analyst should consider how the writer's perspective (and potential biases) may have affected the choice of a particular valuation approach and/or valuation inputs. Specific guidance on model selection will be offered later when discussing present value models and price multiples.

As a final note to this introduction of model selection, it is important to emphasize that professionals frequently use multiple valuation models or factors in common stock selection. According to the *Merrill Lynch Institutional Factor Survey* (2018), respondent institutional investors report using an average of approximately 17 valuation factors in selecting stocks. (*Note:* In this report, the term "factor" covers market-based metrics, such as price multiples, as well as accounting-based metrics, such as return on equity.) There are a variety of ways in which multiple factors can be used in stock selection. One prominent way, stock screens, will be discussed in a later reading. As another example, analysts can rank each security in a given investment universe by relative attractiveness according to a particular valuation factor. The rankings for individual securities could be combined into a single composite ranking by assigning weights to the individual factors. Analysts may use a quantitative model to assign those weights.

THE ANALYST'S ROLE AND RESPONSIBILITIES | 8

Converting forecasts to valuation involves more than inputting the forecast amounts to a model to obtain an estimate of the value of a company or its securities. Two important aspects of converting forecasts to valuation are sensitivity analysis and situational adjustments.

Sensitivity analysis is an analysis to determine how changes in an assumed input would affect the outcome. Some sensitivity analyses are common to most valuations. For example, a sensitivity analysis can be used to assess how a change in assumptions about a company's future growth—for example, decomposed by sales growth forecasts and margin forecasts—and/or a change in discount rates would affect the estimated value. Other sensitivity analyses depend on the context. For example, assume an analyst is aware that a competitor to the target company plans to introduce a competing product. Given uncertainty about the target company's competitive response—whether it will lower prices to retain market share, offer discounts to its distributors, increase advertising, or change a product feature—the analyst could create a baseline forecast and then analyze how different competitive responses would affect the forecasted financials and, in turn, the estimated valuation.

Situational adjustments may be required to incorporate the valuation impact of specific issues. Three such issues that could affect value estimates are control premiums, lack of marketability discounts, and illiquidity discounts. A controlling ownership position in a company (e.g., more than 50% of outstanding shares, although a far smaller percentage often affords an investor the ability to significantly influence a company) carries with it control of the board of directors and the valuable options of redeploying the company's assets or changing the company's capital structure. The value of a stock investment that would give an investor a controlling position will generally reflect a **control premium**; that is, it will be higher than a valuation produced by a generic quantitative valuation expression that did not explicitly model such a premium. A second issue generally not explicitly modeled is that investors require an extra return to compensate for lack of a public market or lack of marketability. The value of non-publicly traded stocks generally reflects a **lack of marketability discount**. Among publicly traded (i.e., marketable) stocks, the prices of shares with less depth to their markets (less liquidity) often reflect an **illiquidity discount**. An illiquidity discount would also apply if an investor wishes to sell an amount of stock that is large relative to that stock's trading volume (assuming it is not large enough to constitute a controlling ownership). The price that could be realized for that block of shares would generally be lower than the market price for a smaller amount of stock, a so-called **blockage factor**.

Applying the Valuation Conclusion: The Analyst's Role and Responsibilities

As noted earlier, the purposes of valuation and the intended consumer of the valuation vary:

- Analysts associated with investment firms' brokerage operations are perhaps the most visible group of analysts offering valuation judgments. Their research reports are widely distributed to current and prospective retail and institutional brokerage clients. The term brokerage typically means the business of acting as agents for buyers and sellers. Analysts who work at brokerage firms are known as **sell-side analysts** because brokerage firms sell investments and services to such institutions as investment management firms.

- In investment management firms, trusts and bank trust departments, and similar institutions, an analyst may report valuation judgments to a portfolio manager or to an investment committee as input to an investment decision. Such analysts are widely known as **buy-side analysts**. The analyst's valuation expertise is important not only in investment disciplines involving security selection based on detailed company analysis but also in highly quantitative investment disciplines. Quantitative analysts work in developing, testing, and updating security selection methodologies. Ranking stocks by some measure(s) of relative attractiveness (subject to a risk control discipline), as we will discuss in more detail later, forms one key part of quantitative equity investment disciplines.

- More than 50% ownership is considered a controlling ownership position

- Analysts at corporations may perform some valuation tasks similar to those of analysts at money management firms (e.g., when the corporation manages in-house a sponsored pension plan). Both corporate analysts and investment bank analysts may also identify and value companies that could become acquisition targets.

- Analysts at independent vendors of financial information usually offer valuation information and opinions in publicly distributed research reports, although some focus solely on organizing and analyzing corporate information.

In conducting their valuation activities, investment analysts play a critical role in collecting, organizing, analyzing, and communicating corporate information, and in some contexts, recommending appropriate investment actions based on sound analysis. When they do those tasks well, analysts help their clients, the capital markets, and the suppliers of capital:

- Analysts help their clients achieve their investment objectives by enabling those clients to make better buy and sell decisions.

- Analysts contribute to the efficient functioning of capital markets by providing analysis that leads to informed buy and sell decisions and thus to asset prices that better reflect underlying values. When asset prices accurately reflect underlying values, capital flows more easily to its highest-value uses.

- Analysts benefit the suppliers of capital, including shareholders, when they are effective monitors of management's performance. This monitoring can serve to keep managers' actions more closely aligned with shareholders' best interests [see Jensen and Meckling (1976) for classic analysis of the costs of stockholder–manager conflicts].

WHAT ARE ANALYSTS EXPECTED TO DO?

When analysts at brokerage firms recommend a stock to the public that later performs very poorly, or when they fail to uncover negative corporate activities, they can sometimes come under public scrutiny. Industry leaders may then be asked to respond to such criticism and to comment on expectations about the role and responsibilities of analysts. One such instance occurred in the United States as a consequence of the late 2001 collapse of Enron Corporation, an energy, utility, trading, and telecommunication company. In testimony before the US Senate (excerpted below), the President and CEO of AIMR (predecessor organization of CFA Institute) offered a summary of the working conditions and responsibilities of brokerage analysts. In the following passage, **due diligence** refers to investigation and analysis in support of a recommendation; the failure to exercise due diligence may sometimes result in liability according to various securities laws. "Wall Street analysts" refers to analysts working in the US brokerage industry (sell-side analysts).

What are Wall Street analysts expected to do? These analysts are assigned companies and industries to follow, are expected to research fully these companies and the industries in which they operate, and to forecast their future prospects. Based on this analysis, and using appropriate valuation models, they must then determine an appropriate fair price for the company's securities. After comparing this fair price to the current market price, the analyst is able to make a recommendation. If the analyst's "fair price" is significantly above the current market price, it would be expected that the stock be rated a "buy" or "market outperform."

> How do Wall Street analysts get their information? Through hard work and due diligence. They must study and try to comprehend the information in numerous public disclosure documents, such as the annual report to shareholders and regulatory filings . . . and gather the necessary quantitative and qualitative inputs to their valuation models.
>
> This due diligence isn't simply reading and analyzing annual reports. It also involves talking to company management, other company employees, competitors, and others, to get answers to questions that arise from their review of public documents. Talking to management must go beyond participation in regular conference calls. Not all questions can be voiced in those calls because of time constraints, for example, and because analysts, like journalists, rightly might not wish to "show their cards," and reveal the insights they have gotten through their hard work, by asking a particularly probing question in the presence of their competitors.
>
> Wall Street analysts are also expected to understand the dynamics of the industry and general economic conditions before finalizing a research report and making a recommendation. Therefore, in order for their firm to justify their continued employment, Wall Street analysts must issue research reports on their assigned companies and must make recommendations based on their reports to clients who purchase their firm's research
>
> (*Source:* Thomas A. Bowman, CFA. Testimony to the Committee on Governmental Affairs (excerpted) US Senate, 27 February 2002).

From the beginnings of the movement to organize financial analysis as a profession rather than as a commercial trade, one guiding principle has been that the analyst must hold himself accountable to both standards of competence and standards of conduct. Competence in investment analysis requires a high degree of training, experience, and discipline (as reflected in the examination and work experience requirements that are prerequisites for obtaining the CFA designation). Additionally, the investment professional is in a position of trust, requiring ethical conduct toward the public, clients, prospects, employers, employees, and fellow analysts. For CFA Institute members, this position of trust is reflected in the Code of Ethics and Standards of Professional Conduct, as well as in the Professional Conduct Statement that they submit annually. The Code and Standards guide the analyst to independent, well-researched, and well-documented analysis and are described in the following sections.

9   COMMUNICATING VALUATION RESULTS

Writing is an important part of an analyst's job. Whether for review by an investment committee or a portfolio manager in an investment management firm or for distribution to the retail or institutional clients of a brokerage firm, research reports share several common elements. In this section, we briefly discuss the content and format of an effective research report and the analyst's responsibilities for preparing a report.

Contents of a Research Report

A primary determinant of a research report's contents is what the intended readers seek to gain from reading the report. From a sell-side analyst's report, an intended reader would be interested in the investment recommendation. In evaluating how much attention and weight to give to a recommendation, the reader will look for persuasive supporting arguments. A key element supporting any recommendation is the intrinsic value of the security.

Given the importance of the estimated intrinsic value of the security, most research reports provide the reader with information about the key assumptions and expectations underlying that estimated intrinsic value. The information typically includes an update on the company's financial and operating results, a description of relevant aspects of the current macroeconomic and industry context, and an analysis and forecast for the industry and company. Because some readers of research reports are interested in background information, some reports contain detailed historical descriptive statistics about the industry and company.

A report can include specific forecasts, key valuation inputs (e.g., the estimated cost of capital), a description of the valuation model, and a discussion of qualitative factors and other considerations that affect valuation. Superior research reports also objectively address the uncertainty associated with investing in the security and/or the valuation inputs involving the greatest amount of uncertainty. By converting forecasts into estimated intrinsic value, a comparison between intrinsic value and market price provides the basis for an investment recommendation. When a research report states a target price for a stock (based on its intrinsic value) in its investment recommendation, the report should clarify the basis for computing the target, a time frame for reaching the target, and information on the uncertainty of reaching the target. An investment recommendation may be accompanied by an explanation of the underlying rationale (i.e., investment thesis), which summarizes why a particular investment offer would provide a way to profit from the analyst's outlook.

Although a well-written report cannot compensate for a poor analysis, a poorly written report can detract from the credibility of an excellent analysis. Writing an effective research report is a challenging task. In summary, an effective research report:

- contains timely information;
- is written in clear, incisive language;
- is objective and well researched, with key assumptions clearly identified;
- distinguishes clearly between facts and opinions;
- contains analysis, forecasts, valuation, and a recommendation that are internally consistent;
- presents sufficient information to allow a reader to critique the valuation;
- states the key risk factors involved in an investment in the company; and
- discloses any potential conflicts of interests faced by the analyst.

Although these general characteristics are all desirable attributes of a useful and respected report, in some situations the requirements are more specific. For example, regulations governing disclosures of conflicts and potential conflicts of interest vary across countries, so an analyst must remain up-to-date on relevant disclosure requirements. In some situations, investment recommendations are affected by policies of the firm employing an analyst; for example, a policy might require that a security's price must be $X\%$ below its estimated intrinsic value to be considered a "buy." Even in the absence of such a policy, an analyst needs to maintain a conceptual distinction between a "good company" and a "good investment" because returns on a common stock investment always depend on the price paid for the stock, whether the business prospects of the issuing company are good, bad, or indifferent. Exhibit 5 provides a small sample of possible research report content.

Exhibit 5

Research Reports

The following two passages are closely based on the valuation discussions of actual companies in two actual short research notes. The dates and company names used in the passages, however, are fictional.

A. At a recent multiple of 6.5, our earnings per share multiple for 2020, the shares were at a discount to our projection of 14% growth for the period ... MXI has two operating segments ... In valuing the segments separately, employing relative acquisition multiples and peer mean values, we found fair value to be above recent market value. In addition, the shares trade at a discount to book value (0.76). Based on the value indicated by these two valuation metrics, we view the shares as worth holding. However, in light of a weaker economy over the near term, dampening demand for MXI's services, our enthusiasm is tempered. [*Elsewhere in the report, MXI is evaluated as being in the firm's top category of investment attractiveness.*]

B. Although TXI outperformed the overall stock market by 20% since the start of the year, it definitely looks undervalued, as shown by its low multiples ... [*the values of the P/E and another multiple are stated*]. According to our dividend discount model valuation, we get to a valuation of €3.08, implying an upside potential of 36.8% based on current prices. The market outperform recommendation is reiterated. [*In a parenthetical expression, the current dividend, assumed dividend growth rates, and their time horizons are given. The analyst also briefly explains and calculates the discount rate. Elsewhere in the report the current price of TXI is given as €2.25.*]

Although some of the concepts mentioned in the two passages may not yet be familiar, you can begin to assess the two reporting efforts.

Passage A communicates the analysis awkwardly. The meaning of "the shares were at a discount to our projection of 14% growth for the period" is not completely clear. Presumably, the analyst is projecting the earnings growth rate for 2020 and stating that the P/E is low in relation to that expected growth rate. The analyst next discusses valuing MXI as the sum of its divisions. In describing the method as "employing relative acquisition multiples and peer mean values," the analyst does not convey a clear picture of what was done. It is probable that companies similar to each of MXI's divisions were identified; then, the mean or average value of some unidentified multiple for those comparison companies was calculated and used as the basis for valuing MXI. The writer is vague, however, on the extent of MXI's undervaluation. The analyst states that MXI's price is below its book value (an accounting measure of shareholders' investment) but draws no comparison with the average price-to-book value ratio for stocks similar to MXI, for example. (The price-to-book ratio is discussed in a later reading.) Finally, the verbal summation is feeble and hedged. Although filled with technical verbiage, Passage A does not communicate a coherent valuation of MXI.

In the second sentence of Passage B, by contrast, the analyst gives an explicit valuation of TXI and the information needed to critique it. The reader can also see that €3.08, which is elsewhere stated in the research note as the target price for TXI, implies the stated price appreciation potential for TXI [(€3.08/€2.25) − 1, approximately 37%]. In the first sentence in Passage B, the analyst gives information that might support the conclusion that TXI is undervalued, although the statement lacks strength because the analyst does not explain why the P/E is "low." Nevertheless, the verbal summary is clear. Using less space than the analyst in Passage A, the analyst in Passage B has done a better job of communicating the results of his valuation.

Format of a Research Report

Equity research reports may be logically presented in several ways. The firm in which the analyst works sometimes specifies a fixed format for consistency and quality control purposes. Without claiming superiority to other ways to organize a report, we offer Exhibit 6 as an adaptable format by which the analyst can communicate research and valuation findings in detail. (Shorter research reports and research notes obviously may employ a more compact format.)

Exhibit 6: A Format for Research Reports

Section	Purpose	Content	Comments
Table of Contents	▪ Show report's organization	▪ Consistent with narrative in sequence and language	This is typically used only in very long research reports.
Summary and Investment Conclusion	▪ Communicate the large picture ▪ Communicate major specific conclusions of the analysis ▪ Recommend an investment course of action	▪ Capsule description of the company ▪ Major recent developments ▪ Earnings projections ▪ Other major conclusions ▪ Valuation summary ▪ Investment action	An executive summary; may be called simply "Summary."
Business Summary	▪ Present the company in more detail ▪ Communicate a detailed understanding of the company's economics and current situation ▪ Provide and explain specific forecasts[a]	▪ Company description to the divisional level ▪ Industry analysis ▪ Competitive analysis ▪ Historical performance ▪ Financial forecasts	Reflects the first and second steps of the valuation process. Financial forecasts should be explained adequately and reflect quality of earnings analysis.
Risks	▪ Alert readers to the risk factors in investing in the security	▪ Possible negative industry developments ▪ Possible negative regulatory and legal developments ▪ Possible negative company developments ▪ Risks in the forecasts ▪ Other risks	Readers should have enough information to determine how the analyst is defining and assessing the risks specific to investing in the security.
Valuation	▪ Communicate a clear and careful valuation	▪ Description of model(s) used ▪ Recapitulation of inputs ▪ Statement of conclusions	Readers should have enough information to critique the analysis.

Section	Purpose	Content	Comments
Historical and Pro Forma Tables	■ Organize and present data to support the analysis in the Business Summary		This is generally a separate section only in longer research reports. Many reports fold all or some of this information into the Business Summary section.

[a] *Actual outcomes can and generally will differ from forecasts. A discussion of key random factors and an examination of the sensitivity of outcomes to the outcomes of those factors are useful.*

Research Reporting Responsibilities

All analysts have an obligation to provide substantive and meaningful content in a clear and comprehensive report format. Analysts who are CFA Institute members, however, have an additional and overriding responsibility to adhere to the Code of Ethics and the Standards of Professional Conduct in all activities pertaining to their research reports. The CFA Institute Code of Ethics states:

> Members of CFA Institute must . . . use reasonable care and exercise independent professional judgment when conducting investment analysis, making investment recommendations, taking investment actions, and engaging in other professional activities.

Going beyond this general statement of responsibility, some specific Standards of Professional Conduct particularly relevant to an analyst writing a research report are shown in Exhibit 7.

Exhibit 7: Selected CFA Institute Standards of Professional Conduct Pertaining to Research Reports*

Standard of Professional Conduct	Responsibility
I(B)	Members and Candidates must use reasonable care and judgment to achieve and maintain independence and objectivity in their professional activities. Members and Candidates must not offer, solicit, or accept any gift, benefit, compensation, or consideration that reasonably could be expected to compromise their own or another's independence and objectivity.
I(C)	Members and Candidates must not knowingly make any misrepresentations relating to investment analysis, recommendations, actions, or other professional activities.
V(A)1	Members and Candidates must exercise diligence, independence, and thoroughness in analyzing investments, making investment recommendations, and taking investment actions.
V(A)2	Members and Candidates must have a reasonable and adequate basis, supported by appropriate research and investigation, for any investment analysis, recommendation, or action.
V(B)1	Members and Candidates must disclose to clients and prospective clients the basic format and general principles of the investment processes used to analyze investments, select securities, and construct portfolios and must promptly disclose any changes that might materially affect those processes.

Standard of Professional Conduct	Responsibility
V(B)2	Members and Candidates must disclose to clients and prospective clients significant limitations and risks associated with the investment process.
V(B)3	Members and Candidates must use reasonable judgment in identifying which factors are important to their investment analyses, recommendations, or actions and include those factors in communications with clients and prospective clients.
V(B)4	Members and Candidates must distinguish between fact and opinion in the presentation of investment analysis and recommendations.
V(C)	Members and Candidates must develop and maintain appropriate records to support their investment analysis, recommendations, actions, and other investment-related communications with clients and prospective clients.

* See the most recent edition of the CFA Institute Standards of Practice Handbook (www.cfainstitute.org).

SUMMARY

In this reading, we have discussed the scope of equity valuation, outlined the valuation process, introduced valuation concepts and models, discussed the analyst's role and responsibilities in conducting valuation, and described the elements of an effective research report in which analysts communicate their valuation analysis.

- Valuation is the estimation of an asset's value based on either variables perceived to be related to future investment returns or comparisons with closely similar assets.

- The intrinsic value of an asset is its value given a hypothetically complete understanding of the asset's investment characteristics.

- The assumption that the market price of a security can diverge from its intrinsic value—as suggested by the rational efficient markets formulation of efficient market theory—underpins active investing.

- Intrinsic value incorporates the going-concern assumption, that is, the assumption that a company will continue operating for the foreseeable future. In contrast, liquidation value is the company's value if it were dissolved and its assets sold individually.

- Fair value is the price at which an asset (or liability) would change hands if neither buyer nor seller were under compulsion to buy/sell and both were informed about material underlying facts.

- In addition to stock selection by active traders, valuation is also used for:

  - inferring (extracting) market expectations;

  - evaluating corporate events;

  - issuing fairness opinions;

  - evaluating business strategies and models; and

  - appraising private businesses.

- The valuation process has five steps:

1. Understanding the business.

2. Forecasting company performance.

3. Selecting the appropriate valuation model.

4. Converting forecasts to a valuation.

5. Applying the analytical results in the form of recommendations and conclusions.

- Understanding the business includes evaluating industry prospects, competitive position, and corporate strategies—all of which contribute to making more accurate forecasts. Understanding the business also involves analysis of financial reports, including evaluating the quality of a company's earnings.

- In forecasting company performance, a top-down forecasting approach moves from macroeconomic forecasts to industry forecasts and then to individual company and asset forecasts. A bottom-up forecasting approach aggregates individual company forecasts to industry forecasts, which in turn may be aggregated to macroeconomic forecasts.

- Selecting the appropriate valuation approach means choosing an approach that is:

  - consistent with the characteristics of the company being valued;

  - appropriate given the availability and quality of the data; and

  - consistent with the analyst's valuation purpose and perspective.

- Two broad categories of valuation models are absolute valuation models and relative valuation models.

  - Absolute valuation models specify an asset's intrinsic value, supplying a point estimate of value that can be compared with market price. Present value models of common stock (also called discounted cash flow models) are the most important type of absolute valuation model.

  - Relative valuation models specify an asset's value relative to the value of another asset. As applied to equity valuation, relative valuation is also known as the method of comparables, which involves comparison of a stock's price multiple to a benchmark price multiple. The benchmark price multiple can be based on a similar stock or on the average price multiple of some group of stocks.

- Two important aspects of converting forecasts to valuation are sensitivity analysis and situational adjustments.

  - Sensitivity analysis is an analysis to determine how changes in an assumed input would affect the outcome of an analysis.

  - Situational adjustments include control premiums (premiums for a controlling interest in the company), discounts for lack of marketability (discounts reflecting the lack of a public market for the company's shares), and illiquidity discounts (discounts reflecting the lack of a liquid market for the company's shares).

- Applying valuation conclusions depends on the purpose of the valuation.

- In performing valuations, analysts must hold themselves accountable to both standards of competence and standards of conduct.

- An effective research report:

  - contains timely information;

- is written in clear, incisive language;
- is objective and well researched, with key assumptions clearly identified;
- distinguishes clearly between facts and opinions;
- contains analysis, forecasts, valuation, and a recommendation that are internally consistent;
- presents sufficient information that the reader can critique the valuation;
- states the risk factors for an investment in the company; and
- discloses any potential conflicts of interest faced by the analyst.

- Analysts have an obligation to provide substantive and meaningful content. CFA Institute members have an additional overriding responsibility to adhere to the CFA Institute Code of Ethics and relevant specific Standards of Professional Conduct.

REFERENCES

Abarbanell, Jeffery S., Victor L. Bernard. 1992. "Tests of Analysts' Overreaction/Underreaction to Earnings Information as an Explanation for Anomalous Stock Price Behavior." Journal of Finance47 (3): 1181–207. 10.1111/j.1540-6261.1992.tb04010.x

Bordalo, Pedro, Nicola Gennaioli, Rafael La Porta, Andrei Shleifer. 2017. "Diagnostic Expectations and Stock Returns." NBER Working Paper 23863. 10.3386/w23863

Cornell, Bradford. 2001. "Is the Response of Analysts to Information Consistent with Fundamental Valuation? The Case of Intel." Financial Management30 (1): 113–36. 10.2307/3666393

De Bondt, Werner F.M., Richard Thaler. 1985. "Does the Stock Market Overreact?" Journal of Finance40 (3): 793–805. 10.1111/j.1540-6261.1985.tb05004.x

Graham, Benjamin. 1936. "U.S. Steel Announces Sweeping Modernization Scheme." Unpublished satire by Ben Graham, written in 1936 and given by the author to Warren Buffett in 1954. Presented in Warren Buffet's "Chairman's Letter to the Shareholders of Berkshire Hathaway Inc" (1 March 1991). www.berkshirehathaway.com/letters/1990.html.

Graham, Benjamin, David L. Dodd. 1934. Security Analysis. McGraw-Hill Professional Publishing.

Grossman, Sanford, Joseph Stiglitz. 1980. "On the Impossibility of Informationally Efficient Markets." American Economic Review70 (3): 393–408.

International Auditing and Assurance Standards Board (IAASB)2018. International Standard on Auditing (ISA) 240, The Auditor's Responsibility to Consider Fraud and Error in an Audit of Financial Statements. In *2018 Handbook of International Quality Control, Auditing, Review, Other Assurance, and Related Services Pronouncements*. https://www.iaasb.org/.

Jensen, Michael C., William H. Meckling. 1976. "Theory of the Firm: Managerial Behavior, Agency Costs and Ownership Structure." Journal of Financial Economics3 (4): 305–60. 10.1016/0304-405X(76)90026-X

Lee, Charles M.C., James Myers, Bhaskaran Swaminathan. 1999. "What Is the Intrinsic Value of the Dow?" Journal of Finance54 (5): 1693–741. 10.1111/0022-1082.00164

Mulford, Charles W., Eugene F. Comiskey. 2005. Creative Cash Flow Reporting: Uncovering Sustainable Financial Performance. Hoboken, NJ: John Wiley & Sons.

Pinto, Jerald E., Thomas R. Robinson, John D. Stowe. 2019. "Equity Valuation: A Survey of Professional Practice." Review of Financial Economics37 (2): 219–33. 10.1002/rfe.1040

Porter, Michael E. 1985. *The Competitive Advantage: Creating and Sustaining Superior Performance*. New York: Free Press. (Republished with new introduction in 1998.)

Porter, Michael E. 2008. "The Five Competitive Forces That Shape Strategy." Harvard Business Review86 (1): 78–93.

Public Company Accounting Oversight Board (PCAOB)2017. Auditing Standard (AS) 2401: Consideration of Fraud in a Financial Statement Audit. In *Auditing Standards of the Public Company Accounting Oversight Board* (15 December). www.pcaob.org.

Schilit, Howard, Jeremy Perler. 2010. Financial Shenanigans: How to Detect Accounting Gimmicks & Fraud in Financial Reports, 3rd edition. New York: McGraw-Hill.

Sloan, Richard G. 1996. "Do Stock Prices Fully Reflect Information in Accruals and Cash Flows about Future Earnings?" Accounting Review71 (3): 289–315.

PRACTICE PROBLEMS

The following information relates to questions 1-8

Global-Guardian Capital is a rapidly growing international investment firm. The firm's research team is responsible for identifying undervalued and overvalued publicly-traded equities that have a market capitalization greater than $500 million.

Due to the rapid growth of assets under management, Global-Guardian Capital recently hired a new analyst, Jack Richardson, to support the research process. At the new analyst orientation meeting, the director of research made the following statements about equity valuation at the firm:

Statement 1   "Analysts at Global-Guardian Capital seek to identify mispricing, relying on price eventually converging to intrinsic value. However, convergence of the market price to an analyst's estimate of intrinsic value may not happen within the portfolio manager's investment time horizon. So, besides evidence of mispricing, analysts should look for the presence of a particular market or corporate event—that is, a catalyst—that will cause the marketplace to re-evaluate the subject firm's prospects."

Statement 2   "An active investment manager attempts to capture positive alpha. But mispricing of assets is not directly observable. It is therefore important that you understand the possible sources of perceived mispricing."

Statement 3   "For its distressed securities fund, Global-Guardian Capital screens its investable universe of securities for companies in financial distress."

Statement 4   "For its core equity fund, Global-Guardian Capital selects financially sound companies that are expected to generate significant positive free cash flow from core business operations within a multiyear forecast horizon."

Statement 5   "Global-Guardian Capital's research process requires analysts to evaluate the reasonableness of the expectations implied by the market price by comparing the market's implied expectations to his or her own expectations."

After the orientation meeting, the director of research asks Richardson to evaluate three companies that are retailers of men's clothing: Diamond Co., Renaissance Clothing, and Deluxe Men's Wear.

Richardson starts his analysis by evaluating the characteristics of the men's retail clothing industry. He finds few barriers to new retail entrants, high intra-industry rivalry among retailers, low product substitution costs for customers, and a large number of wholesale clothing suppliers.

While conducting his analysis, Richardson discovers that Renaissance Clothing included three non-recurring items in their most recent earnings release: a positive litigation settlement, a one-time tax credit, and the gain on the sale of a non-operating asset.

To estimate each firm's intrinsic value, Richardson applies appropriate discount rates to each firm's estimated free cash flows over a ten-year time horizon and to the estimated value of the firm at the end of the ten-year horizon.

Michelle Lee, a junior technology analyst at Global-Guardian, asks the director of research for advice as to which valuation model to use for VEGA, a fast growing semiconductor company that is rapidly gaining market share.

The director of research states that "the valuation model selected must be consistent with the characteristics of the company being valued."

Lee tells the director of research that VEGA is not expected to be profitable for several more years. According to management guidance, when the company turns profitable, it will invest in new product development; as a result, it does not expect to initiate a dividend for an extended period of time. Lee also notes that she expects that certain larger competitors will become interested in acquiring VEGA because of its excellent growth prospects. The director of research advises Lee to consider that in her valuation.

1. Based on Statement 2, which of the following sources of perceived mispricing do active investment managers attempt to identify? The difference between:

    A. intrinsic value and market price.

    B. estimated intrinsic value and market price.

    C. intrinsic value and estimated intrinsic value.

2. With respect to Statements 3 and 4, which of the following measures of value would the distressed securities fund's analyst consider that a core equity fund analyst might ignore?

    A. Fair value

    B. Liquidation value

    C. Fair market value

3. With respect to Statement 4, which measure of value is *most* relevant for the analyst of the fund described?

    A. Liquidation value

    B. Investment value

    C. Going-concern value

4. According to Statement 5, analysts are expected to use valuation concepts and models to:

    A. value private businesses.

    B. render fairness opinions.

    C. extract market expectations.

5. Based on Richardson's industry analysis, which of the following characteristics of men's retail clothing retailing would *positively* affect its profitability? That

industry's:

A. entry costs.

B. substitution costs.

C. number of suppliers.

6. Which of the following statements about the reported earnings of Renaissance Clothing is *mostaccurate*? Relative to sustainable earnings, reported earnings are likely:

A. unbiased.

B. upward biased.

C. downward biased.

7. Which valuation model is Richardson applying in his analysis of the retailers?

A. Relative value

B. Absolute value

C. Sum-of-the-parts

8. Which valuation model would the director of research *most likely* recommend Lee use to estimate the value of VEGA?

A. Free cash flow

B. Dividend discount

C. P/E relative valuation

The following information relates to questions 9-12

Bruno Santos is an equity analyst with a regional investment bank. Santos reviews the growth prospects and quality of earnings for Phoenix Enterprises, one of the companies he follows. He has developed a stock valuation model for this firm based on its forecasted fundamentals. His revenue growth rate estimate is less than that implied by the market price.

Phoenix's financial statements over the past five years show strong performance, with above average growth. Santos has decided to use a lower forecasted growth rate in his models, reflecting the effect of "regression to the mean" over time. He notes two reasons for his lower growth rate forecast:

Reason 1	Successful companies tend to draw more competition, putting their high profits under pressure.
Reason 2	Phoenix's intellectual property and franchise agreements will be weakening over time.

Santos meets with Walter Hartmann, a newly hired associate in his department. In their conversation, Hartmann states, "Security analysts forecast company performance using both top-down and bottom-up analysis. I can think of three examples:

1. A restaurant chain forecasts its sales to be its market share times forecast industry sales.

2. An electric utility company forecasts that its sales will grow proportional to increases in GDP.

3. A retail furniture company forecasts next year's sales by assuming that the sales in its newly built stores will have similar sales per square meter to that of its existing stores."

Hartmann is reviewing some possible trades for three stocks in the health care industry based on a pairs-trading strategy. Hartmann's evaluations are as follows:

- HG Health is 15% overvalued.
- Corgent Cell Sciences is 10% overvalued.
- Johnson Labs is 15% undervalued.

9. Based on Santos's revenue growth rate estimate, the shares of Phoenix are *most likely*:

   A. undervalued.

   B. fairly valued.

   C. overvalued.

10. Which of the reasons given by Santos *most likely* justifies a reduction in Phoenix's forecasted growth rate?

    A. Reason 1 only

    B. Reason 2 only

    C. Both Reason 1 and Reason 2

11. Which of Hartmann's examples of company performance forecasting *best* describes an example of bottom-up forecasting?

    A. Restaurant chain

    B. Electric utility company

    C. Retail furniture company

12. Based on his trading strategy, which of the following should Hartmann recommend?

    A. Short HG Health and Corgent Cell Sciences

    B. Buy Johnson Labs and Corgent Cell Sciences

    C. Buy Johnson Labs and short Corgent Cell Sciences

The following information relates to questions 13-16

Abby Dormier is a sell-side analyst for a small Wall Street brokerage firm; she covers publicly and actively traded companies with listed equity shares. Dormier is responsible for issuing either a buy, hold, or sell rating for the shares of Company A and Company B. The appropriate valuation model for each company was chosen based on the following characteristics of each company:

Company A is an employment services firm with no debt and has fixed assets consisting primarily of computers, servers, and commercially available software. Many of the assets are intangible, including human capital. The company has a history of occasionally paying a special cash dividend.

Company B operates in three unrelated industries with differing rates of growth: tobacco (60% of earnings), shipbuilding (30% of earnings), and aerospace consulting (10% of earnings). The company pays a regular dividend that is solely derived from the earnings produced by the tobacco division.

Dormier considers the following development in making any necessary adjustments to the models before assigning ratings:

Company B has finalized the terms to acquire 70% of the outstanding shares of Company X, an actively traded tobacco company, in an all-stock deal.

Dormier assigns ratings to each of the companies and provides a rationale for each rating. The director of research asks Dormier: "How did you arrive at these recommendations? Describe how you used a top-down approach, which is the policy at our company."

Dormier replies, "I arrived at my recommendations through my due diligence process. I have studied all of the public disclosure documents; I have participated in the company conference calls, being careful with my questions in such a public forum; and I have studied the dynamics of the underlying industries. The valuation models are robust and use an extensive set of company-specific quantitative and qualitative inputs."

13. Based on Company A's characteristics, which of the following absolute valuation models is *most* appropriate for valuing that company?

   A. Asset based

   B. Dividend discount

   C. Free cash flow to the firm

14. Based on Company B's characteristics, which of the following valuation models is *most* appropriate for valuing that company?

   A. Asset based

   B. Sum of the parts

   C. Dividend discount

15. Which of the following is *most likely* to be appropriate to consider in Company B's valuation of Company X?

   A. Blockage factor

   B. Control premium

   C. Lack of marketability discount

16. Based on Dormier's response to the director of research, Dormier's process could have been more consistent with the firm's policy by:

    A. incorporating additional micro-level inputs into her valuation models.

    B. evaluating the impact of general economic conditions on each company.

    C. asking more probing questions during publicly available company conference calls.

SOLUTIONS

1. A is correct. The difference between the true (real) but unobservable intrinsic value and the observed market price contributes to the abnormal return or alpha, which is the concern of active investment managers.

2. B is correct. The measure of value the distressed securities fund's analyst would consider that the core equity fund analyst might ignore is liquidation value. The liquidation value of a company is its value if it were dissolved and its assets sold individually.

3. C is correct. For its core equity fund, Global-Guardian Capital screens its investable universe of securities for well-capitalized companies that are expected to generate significant future free cash flow from core business operations. The concern with future free cash flows implies that going-concern value is relevant.

4. C is correct. Market prices reflect the expectations of investors about the future performance of companies. The analyst can evaluate the reasonableness of the expectations implied by the market price by comparing the market's implied expectations to his own expectations. This process assumes a valuation model, as discussed in the text.

5. C is correct. The men's retail clothing industry is characterized by a large number of wholesale clothing suppliers. When many suppliers of the products needed by industry participants exist, competition among suppliers should limit their ability to raise input prices. Thus, the large number of suppliers is a factor that should positively affect industry profitability.

6. B is correct. The effects of favorable nonrecurring events in reported earnings would tend to bias reported earnings upward relative to sustainable earnings because non-recurring items are by definition not expected to repeat. Renaissance Clothing included three non-recurring items in their most recent earnings release that all led to higher earnings for the current period: a positive litigation settlement, a one-time tax credit, and the gain on the sale of a non-operating asset.

7. B is correct. An absolute valuation model is a model that specifies an asset's intrinsic value. The most important type of absolute equity valuation models are present value models (also referred to as discounted cash flow models), and the model described by Richardson is of that type.

8. A is correct. The broad criteria for model selection are that a valuation model be consistent with the characteristics of the company being valued—that it be appropriate given the availability and quality of the data and consistent with the purpose of the valuation. VEGA currently has negative earnings, making the use of P/E relative valuation difficult if not impossible. As VEGA does not pay a dividend and is not expected to for the foreseeable future, the application of a dividend discount model is problematic. However, the lack of a dividend would not be an obstacle to free cash flow valuation. Furthermore, the director of research has advised that the possibility that competitors may seek to acquire VEGA be taken in to account in valuing VEGA. The reading states that free cash flow valuation can be appropriate in such circumstances. Thus, the director of research would be most likely to recommend free cash flow valuation.

9. C is correct. If the revenue growth rate inferred by the market price exceeds the growth rate that the firm could reasonably expect, Santos should conclude that

the market price is too high and thus that the firm is overvalued.

10. C is correct. Increased competition for successful firms can cause a regression to the mean of a company's growth rate. Expiring and weakening intellectual property and franchise agreements can also reduce potential growth.

11. C is correct. The retail furniture company forecasting sales based on sales per square meter is an example of bottom-up forecasting because it aggregates forecasts at a micro level to larger-scale forecasts.

12. C is correct. Pairs trading involves buying an undervalued stock and shorting an overvalued stock in the same industry. Hartmann should buy Johnson Labs (15% undervalued) and short Corgent Cell Sciences (10% overvalued).

13. C is correct. The free cash flow to the firm model is the most appropriate of the choices because it can be used whether the company has significant marketable assets or consistently pays a cash dividend. Much of Company A's assets are intangible, and although the company has a history of paying a dividend, it has been only occasionally and in the form of a special dividend (i.e., not a consistent cash dividend).

14. B is correct. This valuation model would be consistent with the characteristics of the company. Company B is a conglomerate operating in three unrelated industries with significantly different expected revenue growth rates. The sum-of-the-parts valuation model sums the estimated values of each of the company's businesses as if each business were an independent going concern. Sum-of-the-parts analysis is most useful when valuing a company with segments in different industries that have different valuation characteristics.

15. B is correct. A control premium may be reflected in the value of a stock investment that would give an investor a controlling position. Company B acquired 70% of the outstanding stock of Company X; more than 50% is considered a controlling ownership position.

16. B is correct. A top-down forecasting approach moves from macroeconomic forecasts to industry forecasts and then to individual company and asset forecasts. Analysts are expected to understand the general economic conditions before finalizing a research report and making a recommendation. According to Dormier's response, she did not comment on the general economic conditions—although such considerations would be consistent with the firm's policy of using a top-down approach.

LEARNING MODULE

2

Discounted Dividend Valuation

by Jerald E. Pinto, PhD, CFA, Elaine Henry, PhD, CFA, Thomas R. Robinson, PhD, CFA, CAIA, and John D. Stowe, PhD, CFA.

Jerald E. Pinto, PhD, CFA, is at CFA Institute (USA). Elaine Henry, PhD, CFA, is at Stevens Institute of Technology (USA). Thomas R. Robinson, PhD, CFA, CAIA, is at Robinson Global Investment Management LLC, (USA). John D. Stowe, PhD, CFA, is at Ohio University (USA).

LEARNING OUTCOMES

Mastery	The candidate should be able to:
☐	compare dividends, free cash flow, and residual income as inputs to discounted cash flow models and identify investment situations for which each measure is suitable
☐	calculate and interpret the value of a common stock using the dividend discount model (DDM) for single and multiple holding periods
☐	calculate the value of a common stock using the Gordon growth model and explain the model's underlying assumptions
☐	calculate the value of non-callable fixed-rate perpetual preferred stock
☐	describe strengths and limitations of the Gordon growth model and justify its selection to value a company's common shares
☐	calculate and interpret the implied growth rate of dividends using the Gordon growth model and current stock price
☐	calculate and interpret the present value of growth opportunities (PVGO) and the component of the leading price-to-earnings ratio (P/E) related to PVGO
☐	calculate and interpret the justified leading and trailing P/Es using the Gordon growth model
☐	estimate a required return based on any DDM, including the Gordon growth model and the H-model
☐	evaluate whether a stock is overvalued, fairly valued, or undervalued by the market based on a DDM estimate of value
☐	explain the growth phase, transition phase, and maturity phase of a business
☐	explain the assumptions and justify the selection of the two-stage DDM, the H-model, the three-stage DDM, or spreadsheet modeling to value a company's common shares

LEARNING OUTCOMES

Mastery	The candidate should be able to:
☐	describe terminal value and explain alternative approaches to determining the terminal value in a DDM
☐	calculate and interpret the value of common shares using the two-stage DDM, the H-model, and the three-stage DDM
☐	explain the use of spreadsheet modeling to forecast dividends and to value common shares
☐	calculate and interpret the sustainable growth rate of a company and demonstrate the use of DuPont analysis to estimate a company's sustainable growth rate

1   INTRODUCTION

☐	compare dividends, free cash flow, and residual income as inputs to discounted cash flow models and identify investment situations for which each measure is suitable

Common stock represents an ownership interest in a business. A business in its operations generates a stream of cash flows, and as owners of the business, common stockholders have an equity ownership claim on those future cash flows. Beginning with John Burr Williams (1938), analysts have developed this insight into a group of valuation models known as discounted cash flow (DCF) valuation models. DCF models—which view the intrinsic value of common stock as the present value of its expected future cash flows—are a fundamental tool in both investment management and investment research.

Although the principles behind discounted cash flow valuation are simple, applying the theory to equity valuation can be challenging. Four broad steps in applying DCF analysis to equity valuation are:

- choosing the class of DCF model—equivalently, selecting a specific definition of cash flow;
- forecasting the cash flows;
- choosing a discount rate methodology; and
- estimating the discount rate.

In our coverage of this topic, we take the perspective that dividends—distributions to shareholders authorized by a company's board of directors—are an appropriate definition of cash flows. The class of models based on this idea is called dividend discount models, or DDMs. The basic objective of any DDM is to value a stock. The variety of implementations corresponds to different ways to model a company's future stream of dividend payments. The steps of choosing a discount rate methodology and estimating the discount rate involve the same considerations for all DCF models, so they have been presented separately in an earlier discussion.

The sections are organized as follows: We first provide an overview of present value models. We then provide a general statement of the dividend discount model. Forecasting dividends, individually and in detail, into the indefinite future is not generally practicable, so the dividend-forecasting problem is usually simplified. One approach is to assign dividends to a stylized growth pattern. In the subsequent section, we focus on the simplest pattern—dividends growing at a constant rate forever (the constant growth or "Gordon growth" model). We then explain that for some companies, it is more appropriate to view earnings and dividends as having multiple stages of growth. We present multistage dividend discount models along with spreadsheet modeling. We lay out the determinants of dividend growth rates in the last section and conclude with a summary.

Present Value Models

Present value models as a group constitute a demanding and rigorous approach for valuing assets. In this section, we discuss the economic rationale for valuing an asset as the present value of its expected future cash flows. We also discuss alternative definitions of cash flows and present the major alternative methods for estimating the discount rate.

Valuation Based on the Present Value of Future Cash Flows

The value of an asset must be related to the benefits or returns we expect to receive from holding it. Those returns are called the asset's future cash flows (we will define *cash flow* more concretely and technically later). We also need to recognize that a given amount of money received in the future is worth less than the same amount of money received today. Money received today gives us the option of immediately spending and consuming it, so money has a time value. Therefore, when valuing an asset, before adding up the estimated future cash flows, we must **discount** each cash flow back to the present: the cash flow's value is reduced with respect to how far away it is in time. The two elements of discounted cash flow valuation—estimating the cash flows and discounting the cash flows to account for the time value of money—provide the economic rationale for discounted cash flow valuation. In the simplest case, in which the timing and amounts of future cash flows are known with certainty, if we invest an amount equal to the present value of future cash flows at the given discount rate, that investment will replicate all of the asset's cash flows (with no money left over).

For some assets, such as government debt, cash flows may be essentially known with certainty—that is, they are default risk free. The appropriate discount rate for such a risk-free cash flow is a risk-free rate of interest. For example, if an asset has a single, certain cash flow of $100 to be received in two years, and the risk-free interest rate is 5% a year, the value of the asset is the present value of $100 discounted at the risk-free rate, $100/(1.05)^2 = 90.70.

In contrast to risk-free debt, future cash flows for equity investments are not known with certainty—they are risky. Introducing risk makes applying the present value approach much more challenging. The most common approach to dealing with risky cash flows involves two adjustments relative to the risk-free case. First, discount the *expected* value of the cash flows, viewing the cash flows as random variables (note that the expected value of a random quantity is the mean value of its possible outcomes, in which each outcome's weight in the average is its probability of occurrence). Second, adjust the discount rate to reflect the risk of the cash flows.

The following equation expresses the concept that an asset's value is the present value of its (expected) future cash flows:

$$V_0 = \sum_{t=1}^{n} \frac{CF_t}{(1+r)^t},$$

(1)

where

V_0 = the value of the asset at time $t = 0$ (today)

n = number of cash flows in the life of the asset (n is set equal to ∞ for equities)

CF_t = the cash flow (or the expected cash flow, for risky cash flows) at time t

r = the discount rate or required rate of return

For simplicity, the discount rate in Equation 1 is represented as the same for all periods (i.e., a flat term structure of discount rates is assumed). The analyst has the latitude in this model, however, to apply different discount rates to different cash flows. Such action could reflect different degrees of cash flow riskiness or different risk-free rates at different time horizons. Differences in cash flow riskiness may be caused by differences in business risk, operating risk (use of fixed assets in production), or financial risk or leverage (use of debt in the capital structure). The simple expression given, however, is adequate for this discussion.

Equation 1 gives an asset's value from the perspective of today ($t = 0$). Likewise, an asset's value at some point in the future equals the value of all subsequent cash flows discounted back to that point in time. Example 1 illustrates these points.

EXAMPLE 1

Value as the Present Value of Future Cash Flows

An asset is expected to generate cash flows of $100 in one year, $150 in two years, and $200 in three years. The value of this asset today, using a 10% discount rate, is

$$V_0 = \frac{100}{(1.10)^1} + \frac{150}{(1.10)^2} + \frac{200}{(1.10)^3}$$
$$= 90.909 + 123.967 + 150.263 = \$365.14$$

The value at $t = 0$ is $365.14. The same logic is used to value an asset at a future date. The value of the asset at $t = 1$ is the present value, discounted back to $t = 1$, of all cash flows after this point. This value, V_1, is

$$V_1 = \frac{150}{(1.10)^1} + \frac{200}{(1.10)^2}$$
$$= 136.364 + 165.289 = \$301.65$$

At any point in time, the asset's value is the value of future cash flows (CF) discounted back to that point. Because V_1 represents the value of CF_2 and CF_3 at $t = 1$, the value of the asset at $t = 0$ is also the present value of CF_1 and V_1:

$$V_0 = \frac{100}{(1.10)^1} + \frac{301.653}{(1.10)^1}$$
$$= 90.909 + 274.23 = \$365.14$$

Finding V_0 as the present value of CF_1, CF_2, and CF_3 is logically equivalent to finding V_0 as the present value of CF_1 and V_1.

In the next section, we present an overview of three alternative definitions of cash flow. The selected cash flow concept defines the type of DCF model we can use: the dividend discount model, the free cash flow model, or the residual income model. We also broadly characterize the types of valuation problems for which analysts often choose a particular model. (Further details are supplied when each model is discussed individually.)

Streams of Expected Cash Flows

In present value models of stock valuation, the three most widely used definitions of returns are dividends, free cash flow, and residual income. We discuss each definition in turn.

The dividend discount model defines cash flows as dividends. The basic argument for using this definition of cash flow is that an investor who buys and holds a share of stock generally receives cash returns only in the form of dividends. In practice, analysts usually view investment value as driven by earnings. Does the definition of cash flow as dividends ignore earnings not distributed to shareholders as dividends? Reinvested earnings should provide the basis for increased future dividends. Therefore, the DDM accounts for reinvested earnings when it takes all future dividends into account. Because dividends are less volatile than earnings and other return concepts, the relative stability of dividends may make DDM values less sensitive to short-run fluctuations in underlying value than alternative DCF models. Analysts often view DDM values as reflecting long-run intrinsic value.

A stock either pays dividends or does not pay dividends. A company might not pay dividends on its stock because the company is not profitable and has no cash to distribute. Also, a company might not pay dividends for the opposite reason: because it is very profitable. For example, a company may reinvest all earnings—paying no dividends—to take advantage of profitable growth opportunities. As the company matures and faces fewer attractive investment opportunities, it may initiate dividends. Generally, mature, profitable companies tend to pay dividends and are reluctant to reduce the level of dividends (Grullon, Paye, Underwood, and Weston 2011).

Dividend policy practices have international differences and change through time, even in one market. Typically, research has shown that a lower percentage of companies in US stock markets have paid dividends than have companies in most other markets (He, Ng, Zaiats, and Zhang 2017), although the US sample may have included a disproportionate number of smaller and younger companies, which are less likely to pay dividends (Denis and Osobov 2008). Research has also shown a decline over time in the fraction of companies paying cash dividends in most developed markets such as the United States, Canada, the European Union, the United Kingdom, and Japan (Fama and French 2001; von Eije and Megginson 2008). Although trends and determinants differ across markets, in general, the decline in the proportion of companies paying dividends has been attributed to some or all of the following: a growth in the number of smaller, publicly traded companies with low profitability and high growth potential; an overall reduced propensity to pay dividends (controlling for differences in profitability and growth opportunities); or the increase usage of share repurchases as an alternative way to distribute cash to shareholders (Fama and French 2001; von Eije and Megginson 2008; Julio and Ikenberry 2004).

Analysts will frequently need to value non-dividend-paying shares. Can the DDM be applied to non-dividend-paying shares? In theory it can, as is illustrated later, but in practice it generally is not.

Predicting the timing of dividend initiation and the magnitude of future dividends without any prior dividend data or specifics about dividend policy to guide the analysis is generally not practical. For a non-dividend-paying company, analysts usually prefer a model that defines returns at the company level (as free cash flow or residual income—these concepts are defined shortly) rather than at the stockholder level (as dividends). Another consideration in the choice of models relates to ownership perspective. An investor purchasing a small ownership share lacks the ability to meaningfully influence the timing or magnitude of the distribution of the company's cash to shareholders. That perspective is the one taken in applying a dividend discount model. The only access to the company's value is through the receipt of dividends, and dividend policy is taken as a given. If dividends do not bear an understandable relation to value creation in the company, applying the DDM to value the stock is prone to error.

Generally, the definition of returns as dividends, and the DDM, is most suitable when:

- the company is dividend-paying (i.e., the analyst has a dividend record to analyze);
- the board of directors has established a dividend policy that bears an understandable and consistent relationship to the company's profitability; and
- the investor takes a non-control perspective.

- A relatively consistent dividend payout ratio falls into this category

Often, companies with established dividends are seasoned companies, profitable but operating outside the economy's fastest-growing subsectors. Professional analysts often apply a dividend discount model to value the common stock of such companies.

EXAMPLE 2

AB InBev and Diageo plc: Is the DDM an Appropriate Choice?

As director of equity research at a brokerage firm, you have final responsibility in the choice of valuation models. An analyst covering consumer/non-cyclicals has approached you about the use of a dividend discount model for valuing the equity of two companies: Anheuser-Busch InBev SA/NV, referred to as "AB InBev" (Euronext: ABI, NYSE: BUD), and Diageo plc (LSE: DGE, NYSE: DEO). Exhibit 1 gives 15 years of data. (In the table, EPS is earnings per share, DPS is dividends per share, and the payout ratio is DPS divided by EPS.)

Exhibit 1: BUD and DEO: The Earnings and Dividends Record

	BUD			DEO		
Year	EPS ($)	DPS ($)	Payout Ratio (%)	EPS (pence)	DPS (pence)	Payout Ratio (%)
2018	2.17	2.05	94	121.1	65.3	54
2017	3.98	4.33	109	105.5	62.2	59
2016	0.71	3.85	542	89.1	59.2	66
2015	4.96	3.95	80	94.6	56.4	60
2014	5.54	3.52	64	89.3	51.7	58
2013	8.72	2.83	32	97.4	47.4	49
2012	4.40	2.24	51	75.8	43.5	57
2011	3.58	1.55	43	74.1	40.4	55
2010	2.50	1.07	43	64.3	38.1	59
2009	2.90	0.55	19	65.0	36.1	56
2008	1.93	0.35	18	58.9	34.4	58
2007	3.06	3.67	120	55.0	32.7	59
2006	1.81	0.95	52	66.9	31.1	46
2005	1.17	0.57	49	45.2	29.6	65
2004	NA	NA	–	48.2	27.6	57

Source: Companies' websites and filings on www.sec.gov.

Answer the following questions based on the information in Exhibit 1:

1. State whether a dividend discount model is an appropriate choice for valuing AB InBev. Explain your answer.

Solution:

Based only on the data given in Exhibit 1, a DDM does not appear to be an appropriate choice for valuing AB InBev. The company's dividends have ranged from $0.35 to $4.33 per share, and the annual payout ratio ranged from 18% to 542%, based on reported information. (The variation of earnings, dividends, and dividend payout reflects the company's history of growth through major mergers and acquisitions. ABInBev was formed when the US company Anheuser-Busch was acquired in 2008 by the Belgian company InBev. InBev itself was originally formed by a merger of the Belgian company Interbrew with the Brazilian company AmBev. Further, in 2016 AB InBev made another major acquisition, purchasing SABMiller.)

Based on the record presented and the company's profile, it is unlikely that there will be a consistent relationship between dividends and earnings. Because dividends are unlikely to adjust to reflect changes in profitability, applying a DDM to ABInBev is probably inappropriate. Valuing ABInBev on another basis, such as a company-level definition of cash flows, appears to be more appropriate.
Valuation is a forward-looking exercise. In practice, an analyst would check for public disclosures concerning changes in dividend policy going forward. In light of the increased debt from the 2016 purchase of SABMiller, ABInBev cut its dividend in 2018 and disclosed in its annual report that paying down its debt is a priority and could "restrict the amount of dividends" it is able to pay.

2. State whether a dividend discount model is an appropriate choice for valuing Diageo. Explain your answer.

Solution:

The historical earnings of Diageo show a relatively steady, long-term upward trend, and its dividends have generally followed its growth in earnings. Earnings per share and dividends per share grew at comparable compound annual growth rates of 6.8% and 6.3% during the entire period. In most years, the payout ratio ranged between 50% and 60%. In summary, because Diageo is dividend-paying and because dividends bear an understandable and consistent relationship to earnings, using a DDM to value Diageo is appropriate.

As noted earlier, valuation is a forward-looking exercise, and an analyst would check for public disclosures concerning changes in dividend policy going forward. In its 2018 annual report, Diageo disclosed that it continues to target dividend cover (defined as EPS/DPS) of between 1.8 times and 2.2 times, which implies a payout ratio of between 45% and 56%.

A second definition of returns is free cash flow. The term *cash flow* has been given many meanings in different contexts. Earlier in our coverage the term was used informally, referring to returns to ownership (equity). We now want to give it a more technical meaning, related to accounting usage. Over a given period, a company can add to cash (or use up cash) by selling goods and services. This money is cash flow from operations (for that period). Cash flow from operations is the critical cash flow concept addressing a business's underlying economics. Companies can also generate (or use up) cash in two other ways. First, a company affects cash through buying and selling assets, including investment and disinvestment in plant and equipment. Second, a company can add to or reduce cash through its financing activities. Financing includes debt and equity. For example, issuing bonds increases cash, and buying back stock decreases cash (all else equal).

> Internationally, accounting definitions may not be fully consistent with the presented concepts in distinguishing between types of sources and uses of cash. Although the implementation details are not the focus here, an example can be given. US generally accepted accounting principles include a financing item, net interest payments, in cash flow from operating activities. So, careful analysts working with US accounting data often add back after-tax net interest payments to cash flow from operating activities when calculating cash flow from operations. Under International Accounting Standards, companies may or may not include interest expense as an operating cash flow.

Assets supporting current sales may need replacement because of obsolescence or wear and tear, and the company may need new assets to take advantage of profitable growth opportunities. The concept of free cash flow responds to the reality that, for a going concern, some of the cash flow from operations is not "free" but rather needs to be committed to reinvestment and new investment in assets. **Free cash flow to the firm** (FCFF) is cash flow from operations minus capital expenditures. Capital expenditures—reinvestment in new assets, including working capital—are needed to maintain the company as a going concern, so only that part of cash flow from operations remaining after such reinvestment is "free." (This definition is conceptual; free cash flow concepts will be defined in detail later.) FCFF is the part of the cash flow generated by the company's operations that can be withdrawn by bondholders and stockholders without economically impairing the company. Conceptually, the value of common equity is the present value of expected future FCFF—the total value of the company—minus the market value of outstanding debt.

Another approach to valuing equity works with free cash flow to equity. **Free cash flow to equity** (FCFE) is cash flow from operations minus capital expenditures, or FCFF, from which we net all payments to debtholders (interest and principal repayments net of new debt issues). Debt has a claim on the cash of the company that must be satisfied before any money can be paid to stockholders, so money paid on debt is not available to common stockholders. Conceptually, common equity can be valued as the present value of expected FCFE. FCFF is a predebt free cash flow concept; FCFE is a postdebt free cash flow concept. The FCFE model is the baseline free cash flow valuation model for equity, but the FCFF model may be easier to apply in several cases, such as when the company's leverage (debt in its capital structure) is expected to change significantly over time.

Valuation using a free cash flow concept is popular in current investment practice. Free cash flow (FCFF or FCFE) can be calculated for any company. The record of free cash flows can also be examined even for a non-dividend-paying company. FCFE can be viewed as measuring what a company can afford to pay out in dividends. Even for dividend-paying companies, a free cash flow model valuation may be preferred when dividends exceed or fall short of FCFE by significant amounts. FCFE also represents cash flow that can be redeployed outside the company without affecting the company's capital investments. A controlling equity interest can bring about such redeployment. As a result, free cash flow valuation is appropriate for investors who want to take a control perspective. (Even a small shareholder may want to take such a perspective when potential exists for the company to be acquired, because the stock price should reflect the price an acquirer would pay.)

Just as there are cases in which an analyst would find it impractical to apply the DDM, applying the free cash flow approach is a problem in some cases. Some companies have intense capital demands and, as a result, have negative expected free cash flows far into the future. As one example, a retailer may be constantly constructing new outlets and be far from saturating even its domestic market. Even if the retailer is currently very profitable, free cash flow may be negative indefinitely because of the level of capital expenditures. The present value of a series of negative free cash flows is a negative number: The use of a free cash flow model may entail a long forecast horizon to capture the point at which expected free cash flow turns positive. The uncertainty associated with distant forecasts may be considerable. In such cases, the analyst may have more confidence using another approach, such as residual income valuation.

Generally, defining returns as free cash flow and using the FCFE (and FCFF) models are most suitable when:

- the company is not dividend-paying;
- the company is dividend-paying but dividends significantly exceed or fall short of free cash flow to equity;
- the company's free cash flows align with the company's profitability within a forecast horizon with which the analyst is comfortable; and
- the investor takes a control perspective.

The third and final definition of returns that we will discuss in this overview is residual income. Conceptually, **residual income** for a given period is the earnings for that period in excess of the investors' required return on beginning-of-period investment (common stockholders' equity). Suppose shareholders' initial investment is $200 million, and the required rate of return on the stock is 8%. The required rate of return is investors' **opportunity cost** for investing in the stock: the highest expected return available from other equally risky investments, which is the return that investors forgo when investing in the stock. The company earns $18 million in the course of a year. How much value has the company added for shareholders?

A return of 0.08 × $200 million = $16 million just meets the amount investors could have earned in an equivalent-risk investment (by the definition of opportunity cost). Only the residual or excess amount of $18 million – $16 million = $2 million represents value added, or an economic gain, to shareholders. So, $2 million is the company's residual income for the period. The residual income approach attempts to match profits to the period in which they are earned (but not necessarily realized as cash). In contrast to accounting net income (which has the same matching objective in principle), however, residual income attempts to measure the value added in excess of opportunity costs.

The residual income model states that a stock's value is book value per share plus the present value of expected future residual earnings. (**Book value per share** is common stockholders' equity divided by the number of common shares outstanding.) In contrast to the dividend and free cash flow models, the residual income model introduces a stock concept, book value per share, into the present value expression. Nevertheless, the residual income model can be viewed as a restatement of the dividend discount model, using a company-level return concept. Dividends are paid out of earnings and are related to earnings and book value (BV) through a simple expression:

BV of equity at t

= BV of equity at $(t-1)$ + Earnings for the period $(t-1)$ to t – Dividends paid at t

Please note that the foregoing expression is valid assuming that any items that go through the balance sheet (affecting book value) first go through the income statement (reflected in earnings), apart from ownership transactions.

The residual income model is a useful addition to an analyst's toolbox. Because the record of residual income can always be calculated, a residual income model can be used for both dividend-paying and non-dividend-paying stocks. Analysts may choose a residual income approach for companies with negative expected free cash flows within their comfortable forecast horizon. In such cases, a residual income valuation often brings the recognition of value closer to the present as compared with a free cash flow valuation, producing higher value estimates.

The residual income model has an attractive focus on profitability in relation to opportunity costs. Executive compensation schemes are sometimes based on a residual income concept. Knowledgeable application of the residual income model requires a detailed knowledge of accrual accounting; consequently, in cases for which the dividend discount model is suitable, analysts may prefer it as the simpler choice. Management sometimes exercises its discretion within allowable accounting practices to distort the accuracy of its financials as a reflection of economic performance. If the quality of accounting disclosure is good, the analyst may be able to calculate residual income by making appropriate adjustments (to reported net income and book value, in particular). In some cases, the degree of distortion and the quality of accounting disclosure can be such that the application of the residual income model is error-prone.

Generally, the definition of returns as residual income, and the residual income model, is most suitable when:

- the company is not paying dividends, as an alternative to a free cash flow model, or
- the company's expected free cash flows are negative within the analyst's comfortable forecast horizon.

In summary, the three most widely used definitions of returns to investors are dividends, free cash flow, and residual income. Although claims are often made that one cash flow definition is inherently superior to the rest—often following changing fashions in investment practice—a more flexible viewpoint is practical. The analyst may find that one model is more suitable to a particular valuation problem. The analyst may also develop more expertise in applying one type of model. In practice, skill in application—in particular, the quality of forecasts—is frequently decisive for the usefulness of the analyst's work.

In the next section, we present the general form of the dividend discount model as a prelude to discussing the particular implementations of the model that are suitable for different sets of attributes of the company being valued.

2   THE DIVIDEND DISCOUNT MODEL

☐ calculate and interpret the value of a common stock using the dividend discount model (DDM) for single and multiple holding periods

Investment analysts use a wide range of models and techniques to estimate the value of common stock, including present value models. In a survey of CFA Institute members with job responsibility for equity analysis, nearly 80% of respondents reported using a discounted cash flow approach (Stowe, Pinto, and Robinson 2018). Earlier we discussed three common definitions of cash flow for use in present value analysis: dividends, free cash flow, and residual income. In this section, we develop the most general form of the dividend discount model.

The DDM is the simplest and oldest present value approach to valuing stock. Recent survey data shows that among the analysts using a discounted cash flow approach to equity valuation, about 35.1% employ a dividend discount model (Stowe, Pinto, and Robinson 2018). Besides its continuing significant position in practice, the DDM has an important place in both academic and practitioner equity research. The DDM is, for these reasons, a basic tool in equity valuation.

The Expression for a Single Holding Period

From the perspective of a shareholder who buys and holds a share of stock, the cash flows he will obtain are the dividends paid on it and the market price of the share when he sells it. The future selling price should in turn reflect expectations about dividends subsequent to the sale. In this section, we will show how this argument leads to the most general form of the dividend discount model. In addition, the general expression developed for a finite holding period corresponds to one practical approach to DDM valuation. In that approach, the analyst forecasts dividends over a finite horizon, as well as the terminal sales price.

If an investor wishes to buy a share of stock and hold it for one year, the value of that share of stock today is the present value of the expected dividend to be received on the stock plus the present value of the expected selling price in one year:

$$V_0 = \frac{D_1}{(1+r)^1} + \frac{P_1}{(1+r)^1} = \frac{D_1 + P_1}{(1+r)^1} \tag{2}$$

where

V_0 = the value of a share of stock today, at $t = 0$

P_1 = the expected price per share at $t = 1$

D_1 = the expected dividend per share for Year 1, assumed to be paid at the end of the year at $t = 1$

r = the required rate of return on the stock

Equation 2 applies, to a single holding period, the principle that an asset's value is the present value of its future cash flows. In this case, the expected cash flows are the dividend in one year (for simplicity, assumed to be received as one payment at the end of the year) and the price of the stock in one year. Note that throughout the discussion of the DDM, we assume that dividends for a period are paid in one sum at the end of the period.

EXAMPLE 3

DDM Value with a Single Holding Period

Suppose that you expect Carrefour SA (CA: EN Paris) to pay a €0.46 dividend next year. You expect the price of Carrefour stock to be €23.00 in one year. The required rate of return for Carrefour stock is 8%. What is your estimate of the value of Carrefour stock?

Discounting the expected dividend of €0.46 and the expected sales price of €23.00 at the required return on equity of 8%, we obtain

$$V_0 = \frac{D_1 + P_1}{(1+r)^1} = \frac{0.46 + 23.00}{(1+0.08)^1} = \frac{23.46}{1.08} = 21.72.$$

The Expression for Multiple Holding Periods

If an investor plans to hold a stock for two years, the value of the stock is the present value of the expected dividend in Year 1, plus the present value of the expected dividend in Year 2, plus the present value of the expected selling price at the end of Year 2.

$$V_0 = \frac{D_1}{(1+r)^1} + \frac{D_2}{(1+r)^2} + \frac{P_2}{(1+r)^2} = \frac{D_1}{(1+r)^1} + \frac{D_2+P_2}{(1+r)^2} \tag{3}$$

The expression for the DDM value of a share of stock for any finite holding period is a straightforward extension of the expressions for one-year and two-year holding periods. For an n-period model, the value of a stock is the present value of the expected dividends for the n periods plus the present value of the expected price in n periods (at $t = n$).

$$V_0 = \frac{D_1}{(1+r)^1} + \cdots + \frac{D_n}{(1+r)^n} + \frac{P_n}{(1+r)^n} \tag{4}$$

If we use summation notation to represent the present value of the first n expected dividends, the general expression for an n-period holding period or investment horizon can be written as

$$V_0 = \sum_{t=1}^{n} \frac{D_t}{(1+r)^t} + \frac{P_n}{(1+r)^n}. \tag{5}$$

Equation 5 is significant in DDM application because analysts may make individual forecasts of dividends over some finite horizon (often two to five years) and then estimate the terminal price, P_n, based on one of a number of approaches. (We will discuss valuation using a finite forecasting horizon later.) Example 4 reviews the mechanics of this calculation.

EXAMPLE 4

Finding the Stock Price for a Five-Year Forecast Horizon

For the next five years, the annual dividends of a stock are expected to be $2.00, $2.10, $2.20, $3.50, and $3.75. In addition, the stock price is expected to be $40.00 in five years. If the required return on equity is 10%, what is the value of this stock?

The present values of the expected future cash flows can be written out as

$$V_0 = \frac{2.00}{(1.10)^1} + \frac{2.10}{(1.10)^2} + \frac{2.20}{(1.10)^3} + \frac{3.50}{(1.10)^4} + \frac{3.75}{(1.10)^5} + \frac{40.00}{(1.10)^5}.$$

Calculating and summing these present values gives a stock value of V_0 = 1.818 + 1.736 + 1.653 + 2.391 + 2.328 + 24.837 = $34.76.

The five dividends have a total present value of $9.926 and the terminal stock value has a present value of $24.837, for a total stock value of $34.76.

With a finite holding period, whether one, two, five, or some other number of years, the dividend discount model finds the value of stock as the sum of 1) the present values of the expected dividends during the holding period and 2) the present value of the expected stock price at the end of the holding period. As the holding period is increased by one year, we have an extra expected dividend term. In the limit (i.e., if the holding period extends into the indefinite future), the stock's value is the present value of all expected future dividends.

$$V_0 = \frac{D_1}{(1+r)^1} + \cdots + \frac{D_n}{(1+r)^n} + \cdots \tag{6}$$

This value can be expressed with summation notation as

$$V_0 = \sum_{t=1}^{\infty} \frac{D_t}{(1+r)^t}. \tag{7}$$

Equation 7 is the general form of the dividend discount model, first presented by John Burr Williams (1938). Even from the perspective of an investor with a finite investment horizon, the value of stock depends on all future dividends. For that investor, stock value today depends *directly* on the dividends the investor expects to receive before the stock is sold and *indirectly* on the expected dividends after the stock is sold, because those future dividends determine the expected selling price.

Equation 7, by expressing the value of stock as the present value of expected dividends into the indefinite future, presents a daunting forecasting challenge. In practice, of course, analysts cannot make detailed, individual forecasts of an infinite number of dividends. To use the DDM, the forecasting problem must be simplified. Two broad approaches exist, each of which has several variations:

1. Future dividends can be forecast by assigning the stream of future dividends to one of several stylized growth patterns. The most commonly used patterns are:

    -   constant growth forever (the Gordon growth model);
    -   two distinct stages of growth (the two-stage growth model and the H-model); and
    -   three distinct stages of growth (the three-stage growth model).

    The DDM value of the stock is then found by discounting the dividend streams back to the present. We present the Gordon growth model, the two-stage H-model, and three-stage growth models later.

2. A finite number of dividends can be forecast individually up to a terminal point, by using pro forma financial statement analysis, for example. Typically, such forecasts extend from 3 to 10 years into the future. Although some analysts apply the same horizon to all companies under analysis, the horizon selected often depends on the perceived predictability (sometimes called the **visibility**) of the company's earnings. We can then forecast either:

    -   the remaining dividends from the terminal point forward by assigning those dividends to a stylized growth pattern, or
    -   the share price at the terminal point of our dividend forecasts (**terminal share price**), by using some method (such as taking a multiple of forecasted book value or earnings per share as of that point, based on one of several methods for estimating such multiples).

    The stock's DDM value is then found by discounting the dividends (and forecasted price, if any) back to the present.

Spreadsheets are particularly convenient tools for implementing a DDM with individual dividend forecasts but are useful in all cases. We address spreadsheet modeling at a later stage.

Whether analysts are using dividends or some other definition of cash flow, they generally use one of the foregoing forecasting approaches when valuing stock. The challenge in practice is to choose an appropriate model for a stock's future dividends and to develop quality inputs to that model.

3   THE GORDON GROWTH MODEL

☐   calculate the value of a common stock using the Gordon growth model and explain the model's underlying assumptions

☐   calculate the value of non-callable fixed-rate perpetual preferred stock

☐   describe strengths and limitations of the Gordon growth model and justify its selection to value a company's common shares

The Gordon growth model, developed by Gordon and Shapiro (1956) and Gordon (1962), assumes that dividends grow indefinitely at a constant rate. This assumption, applied to the general dividend discount model (Equation 7), leads to a simple and elegant valuation formula that has been influential in investment practice. This section explores the development of the Gordon growth model and illustrates its uses.

The Gordon Growth Model Equation

The simplest pattern that can be assumed in forecasting future dividends is growth at a constant rate. In mathematical terms, this assumption can be stated as

$$D_t = D_{t-1}(1 + g),$$

where g is the expected constant growth rate in dividends and D_t is the expected dividend payable at time t. Suppose, for example, that the most recent dividend, D_0, was €10. Then, if a 5% dividend growth rate is forecast, the expected dividend at $t = 1$ is $D_1 = D_0(1 + g) = €10 \times 1.05 = €10.5$. For any time t, D_t also equals the $t = 0$ dividend, compounded at g for t periods:

$$D_t = D_0(1 + g)^t \tag{8}$$

To continue the example, at the end of five years the expected dividend is $D_5 = D_0(1 + g)^5 = €10 \times (1.05)^5 = €10 \times 1.276282 = €12.76$. If $D_0(1 + g)^t$ is substituted into Equation 7 for D_t, it gives the Gordon growth model. If all of the terms are written out, they are

$$V_0 = \frac{D_0(1 + g)}{(1 + r)} + \frac{D_0(1 + g)^2}{(1 + r)^2} + \dots + \frac{D_0(1 + g)^n}{(1 + r)^n} + \dots \tag{9}$$

Equation 9 is a geometric series; that is, each term in the expression is equal to the previous term times a constant, which in this case is $(1 + g)/(1 + r)$. This equation can be simplified algebraically into a much more compact equation:

Gordon Growth Model :

$$V_0 = \frac{D_0(1 + g)}{r - g}, \text{ or } V_0 = \frac{D_1}{r - g} \tag{10}$$

The simplification involves the expression for the sum of an infinite geometric progression with the first term equal to a and the growth factor equal to m with $|m| < 1$ [i.e., the sum of $a + am + am^2 + \dots$ is $a/(1 - m)$]. Setting $a = D_1/(1 + r)$ and $m = (1 + g)/(1 + r)$ gives the Gordon growth model.

Both equations are equivalent because $D_1 = D_0(1 + g)$. In Equation 10, it must be specified that the required return on equity must be greater than the expected growth rate: $r > g$. If $r = g$ or $r < g$, Equation 10 as a compact formula for value assuming constant growth is not valid. If $r = g$, dividends grow at the same rate at which they are discounted, so the value of the stock (as the undiscounted sum of all expected future dividends) is infinite. If $r < g$, dividends grow faster than they are discounted, so the value of the stock is infinite. Of course, infinite values do not make economic sense; so constant growth with $r = g$ or $r < g$ does not make sense.

To illustrate the calculation, suppose that an annual dividend of €5 has just been paid (D_0 = €5). The expected long-term growth rate is 5% and the required return on equity is 8%. The Gordon growth model value per share is $D_0(1 + g)/(r - g)$ = (€5 × 1.05)/(0.08 − 0.05) = €5.25/0.03 = €175. When calculating the model value, be careful to use D_1 and not D_0 in the numerator.

The Gordon growth model (Equation 10) is one of the most widely recognized equations in the field of security analysis. Because the model is based on indefinitely extending future dividends, the model's required rate of return and growth rate should reflect long-term expectations. Further, model values are very sensitive to both the required rate of return, r, and the expected dividend growth rate, g. In this model and other valuation models, it is helpful to perform a sensitivity analysis on the inputs, particularly when an analyst is not confident about the proper values.

Earlier we stated that analysts typically apply DDMs to dividend-paying stocks when dividends bear an understandable and consistent relation to the company's profitability. The same qualifications hold for the Gordon growth model. In addition, the Gordon growth model form of the DDM is most appropriate for companies with earnings expected to grow at a rate comparable to or lower than the economy's nominal growth rate. Businesses growing at much higher rates than the economy often grow at lower rates in maturity, and the horizon in using the Gordon growth model is the entire future stream of dividends.

To determine whether the company's growth rate qualifies it as a candidate for the Gordon growth model, an estimate of the economy's nominal growth rate is needed. This growth rate is usually measured by the growth in **gross domestic product**, a money measure of the goods and services produced within a country's borders. National government agencies as well as the World Bank (www.worldbank.org) publish GDP data, which are also available from several secondary sources. Exhibit 2 shows the real GDP growth record for a number of major developed markets.

Exhibit 2: Average Annual Real GDP Growth Rates: 1988–2017

Country	Period		
	1988–1997	1998–2007	2008–2017
Australia	3.2%	3.5%	2.6%
Canada	2.1	3.2	1.6
Denmark	2.0	2.0	0.8
France	2.2	2.4	0.8
Germany	2.6	1.7	1.3
Italy	1.9	1.5	-0.5
Japan	2.8	1.0	0.5
Netherlands	3.1	2.8	0.9
Sweden	1.4	3.5	1.6
Switzerland	1.5	2.4	1.4
United Kingdom	2.4	2.9	1.1
United States	3.1	3.1	1.5

Source: OECD.

Based on historical and/or forward-looking information, nominal GDP growth can be estimated as the sum of the estimated real growth rate in GDP plus the expected long-run inflation rate. For example, using 10 years of historical data through 2018, one estimate of the underlying real growth rate of the Canadian economy is 1.6%. Adjusting for the Bank of Canada's inflation target of 2% as the expected inflation rate gives an estimate of the Canadian economy's nominal annual growth rate of 1.6% + 2% = 3.6%. Publicly traded companies constitute varying amounts of the total corporate sector but always less than 100%. As a result, the overall growth rate of the public corporate sector can diverge from the nominal GDP growth rate during a long horizon; furthermore, within the public corporate sector, some subsectors may experience persistent growth rate differentials. Nevertheless, an earnings growth rate far above the nominal GDP growth rate is not sustainable in perpetuity.

When forecasting an earnings growth rate far above the economy's nominal growth rate, analysts should use a multistage DDM in which the final-stage growth rate reflects a growth rate that is more plausible relative to the economy's nominal growth rate, rather than using the Gordon growth model.

EXAMPLE 5

Valuation Using the Gordon Growth Model (1)

Joel Williams follows Sonoco Products Company (NYSE: SON), a manufacturer of paper and plastic packaging for both consumer and industrial use. Sonoco appears to have a dividend policy of recognizing sustainable increases in the level of earnings with increases in dividends, typically keeping the dividend payout ratio within a range of 40% to 60%. Williams also notes the following:

- Sonoco's most recent quarterly dividend, declared 13 February 2019, was $0.41, consistent with a current annual dividend of 4 × $0.41 = $1.64 per year.

- His forecasted dividend growth rate is 4.5% per year.

- With a beta (β_i) of 0.95, given an equity risk premium (expected excess return of equities over the risk-free rate, $E(R_M) - R_F$) of 4.5% and a risk-free rate (R_F) of 3%, Sonoco's required return on equity is $r = R_F + \beta_i[E(R_M) - R_F] = 3.0 + 0.95(4.5) = 7.3\%$, using the capital asset pricing model.

Williams believes the Gordon growth model may be an appropriate model for valuing Sonoco.

---

1. Calculate the Gordon growth model value for Sonoco stock.

Solution:

Using Equation 10,

$$V_0 = \frac{D_0(1+g)}{r-g} = \frac{\$1.64 \times 1.045}{0.073 - 0.045} = \frac{\$1.7138}{0.028} = \$61.21.$$

2. The current market price of Sonoco stock is $59.55. Using your answer to Question 1, judge whether Sonoco stock is fairly valued, undervalued, or overvalued.

Solution:

The market price of $59.55 is $1.66, or approximately 2.7% less than the Gordon growth model intrinsic value estimate of $61.21. Sonoco appears to be slightly undervalued based on the Gordon growth model estimate.

The next example illustrates a Gordon growth model valuation introducing some problems the analyst might face in practice. The example refers to adjusted beta; the most common calculation adjusts raw historical beta toward the overall mean value of one for beta.

EXAMPLE 6

Valuation Using the Gordon Growth Model (2)

As an analyst for a US domestic equity–income mutual fund, Robert Kim is evaluating Middlesex Water Company (NASDAQ: MSEX), a publicly traded water utility, for possible inclusion in the approved list of investments. Kim is conducting the analysis in early 2019.

Not all countries have traded water utility stocks. In the United States, most of the population gets its water from government entities; however, a group of investor-owned water utilities also supplies water to the public. With a market capitalization of about $880 million as of early 2019, MSEX is among the 10 largest publicly traded US water utilities. MSEX's historical base is the Middlesex System, serving residential, industrial, and commercial customers in a well-developed area of central New Jersey. Through various subsidiaries, MSEX also provides water and wastewater collection and treatment services to areas of southern New Jersey and Delaware.

MSEX's return on equity averaged 8.5% over the past 10 years with relatively little variation, and its profit margins are above industry averages. When MSEX's credit rating was upgraded in 2015, the reasons cited by Standard & Poor's included the company's "improving management of regulatory risk that is expected to result in less volatile profitability measures, moderately improved cash flow measures and the ability to consistently earn closer to its authorized returns" (according to MSEX's Form 8-K filed with the SEC on 24 August 2015). Because MSEX obtains most of its revenue from the regulated business of providing an important staple, water, to a relatively stable population, Kim feels confident in forecasting future earnings and dividend growth. MSEX appears to have a policy of maintaining an average dividend payout ratio between 60% and 70%. Other facts and forecasts include the following:

- MSEX's per-share dividends for 2018 (D_0) were $0.911.
- Kim forecasts a long-term earnings growth rate of 4.5% per year.
- MSEX's raw beta and adjusted beta are, respectively, 0.70 and 0.80 based on 60 monthly returns. The R^2 associated with beta, however, is under 20%.
- Kim estimates that MSEX's pretax cost of debt is 4.8% based on Standard & Poor's issuer rating of A for MSEX and on the current corporate yield curve.
- Kim's estimate of MSEX's required return on equity is 6.8%.

- MSEX's current market price is $43.20.

1. Calculate the Gordon growth model estimate of value for MSEX using Kim's required return on equity estimate.

Solution:

From Equation 10,

$$V_0 = \frac{D_0(1+g)}{r-g} = \frac{\$0.911(1.045)}{0.068-0.045} = \$41.39.$$

2. State whether MSEX appears to be overvalued, fairly valued, or undervalued based on the Gordon growth model estimate of value.

Solution:

Because the Gordon growth model estimate of $41.39 differs from the market price of $43.20 by a relatively small amount (less than 5%), MSEX appears to be fairly valued.

3. Justify the selection of the Gordon growth model for valuing MSEX.

Solution:

The Gordon growth model, which assumes that dividends grow at a stable rate in perpetuity, is a realistic model for MSEX for the following reasons:

- MSEX profitability is stable as reflected in its return on equity. This stability reflects predictable demand and regulated prices for its product, water.

- Dividends bear an understandable and consistent relationship to earnings, as evidenced by the company's policy of predictable dividend payout ratios.

- Although the company's earnings growth has been higher in recent years, the forecasted earnings growth rate of 4.5% a year seems both attainable and reasonable compared with the historical long-term nominal annual GDP growth for the United States (approximately 4.3% over the 20-year period 1998–2018, based on data from the US Bureau of Economic Analysis).

- The earnings growth forecast for the company does not include a period of forecasted very high or very low growth.

4. Calculate the CAPM estimate of the required return on equity for MSEX under the assumption that beta reverts to the mean. (Assume an equity risk premium of 4.5% and a risk-free rate of 3% as of the price quotation date.)

Solution:

The assumption of reversion to the mean is characteristic of adjusted historical beta. The required return on equity as given by the CAPM assuming a risk-free rate of 3% and an equity risk premium of 4.5% is given by the following: 3% + 0.80(4.5%) = 6.6% using adjusted beta, which assumes reversion to the mean of 1.0.

5. Calculate the Gordon growth estimate of value using A) the re-
    quired return on equity from your answer to Question 4, and B) a
    bond-yield-plus-risk-premium approach with a risk premium of 2.5%.

Solution:

A. The Gordon growth value of MSEX using a required return on equity
    of 6.6% is

$$V_0 = \frac{D_0(1+g)}{r-g} = \frac{\$0.911 \times 1.045}{0.066 - 0.045} = \$45.33.$$

$$V_0 = \frac{D_0(1+g)}{r-g} = \frac{\$0.911\,(1.045)}{0.066 - 0.045} = \$45.33$$

B. The bond-yield-plus-risk-premium estimate of the required return on
    equity is 4.8% + 2.5% = 7.3%. The Gordon growth value of MSEX using
    a required return on equity of 7.3% is

$$V_0 = \frac{D_0(1+g)}{r-g} = \frac{\$0.911\,(1.045)}{0.073 - 0.045} = \$34.00.$$

6. Evaluate the effect of uncertainty in MSEX's required return on equity on
    the valuation conclusion in Question 2.

Solution:

Using the CAPM estimate of the required return on equity (Question 5A),
MSEX appears to be fairly valued; although the estimated value of $45.33
exceeds the current market price, the difference is only around 5%. Further,
according to the facts given concerning R^2, beta explains less than 20% of
the variation in MSEX's returns. Using a bond-yield-plus-risk-premium
approach, MSEX appears to be significantly overvalued ($34.00 is more
than 20% lower than the market price of $43.20). No specific evidence,
however, supports the particular value of the risk premium selected in the
bond-yield-plus-risk-premium approach. In this case, because of the uncertainty in the required return on equity estimate, one has less confidence
that MSEX is overvalued. Given the results of the other two approaches, the
analyst may view MSEX as relatively fairly valued.

As mentioned earlier, an analyst needs to be aware that Gordon growth model values
can be very sensitive to small changes in the values of the required rate of return and
expected dividend growth rate. Example 7 illustrates a format for a sensitivity analysis.

EXAMPLE 7

Valuation Using the Gordon Growth Model (3)

In Example 6, the Gordon growth model value for MSEX was estimated as $41.39
based on a current dividend of $0.911, an expected dividend growth rate of 4.5%,
and a required return on equity of 6.8%. What if the estimates of r and g each
vary by 25 bps? How sensitive is the model value to changes in the estimates of
r and g? Exhibit 3 provides information on this sensitivity.

Exhibit 3: Estimated Price Given Uncertain Inputs			
	g = 4.25%	g = 4.50%	g = 4.75%
r = 6.55%	$41.29	$46.44	$53.02
r = 6.80%	$37.24	**$41.39**	$46.55
r = 7.05%	$33.92	$37.33	$41.49

A point of interest following from the mathematics of the Gordon growth model is that when the spread between r and g is the widest ($r = 7.05\%$ and $g = 4.25\%$), the Gordon growth model value is the smallest ($33.92), and when the spread is the narrowest ($r = 6.55\%$ and $g = 4.75\%$), the model value is the largest ($53.02). As the spread goes to zero, in fact, the model value increases without bound. The largest value in Exhibit 3, $53.02, is more than 55% larger than the smallest value, $33.92. Two-thirds of the values in Exhibit 3 are lower than MSEX's current market price of $43.20. All but two of the estimates, however, are within 10% of the current price, which supports the conclusion that MSEX is relatively fairly valued or slightly overvalued. In summary, the best estimate of the value of MSEX given the assumptions is $41.39, bolded in Exhibit 3, but the estimate is quite sensitive to rather small changes in inputs.

Example 6 and Example 7 illustrate the application of the Gordon growth model to a utility, a traditional source for such illustrations because of the stability afforded by providing an essential service in a regulated environment. Before applying any valuation model, however, analysts need to know much more about a company than industry membership. For example, if a utility company undertook an aggressive growth-by-acquisition strategy, then its expected growth in income and dividends could potentially diverge significantly from other companies in the industry. Furthermore, many utility holding companies in the United States have major, unregulated business subsidiaries so the traditional picture of steady and slow growth often does not hold.

In addition to individual stocks, analysts have often used the Gordon growth model to value broad equity market indexes, especially in developed markets. Because the value of publicly traded issues typically represents a large fraction of the overall corporate sector in developed markets, such indexes reflect average economic growth rates. Furthermore, in such economies, a sustainable trend value of growth may be identifiable.

The Gordon growth model can also be used to value the non-callable form of a traditional type of preferred stock, **fixed-rate perpetual preferred stock** (stock with a specified dividend rate that has a claim on earnings senior to the claim of common stock, and no maturity date). Perpetual preferred stock has been used particularly by financial institutions such as banks to obtain permanent equity capital while diluting the interests of common equity. Generally, such issues have been callable by the issuer after a certain period, so valuation must take account of the issuer's call option. Valuation of the non-callable form, however, is straightforward.

If the dividend on such preferred stock is D, because payments extend into the indefinite future a **perpetuity** (a stream of level payments extending to infinity) exists in the constant amount of D. With $g = 0$, which is true because dividends are fixed for such preferred stock, the Gordon growth model becomes

$$V_0 = \frac{D}{r}. \tag{11}$$

The discount rate, r, capitalizes the amount D, and for that reason is often called a **capitalization rate** in this expression and any other expression for the value of a perpetuity.

EXAMPLE 8

Valuing Noncallable Fixed-Rate Perpetual Preferred Stock

1. Kansas City Southern Preferred 4% (KSU-P), issued 2 January 1963, has a par value of $25 per share. Thus, a share pays 0.04($25) = $1.00 in annual dividends. The required return on this security is estimated at 5.5%. Estimate the value of this issue.

Solution:

According to the model in Equation 11, KSU-P preferred stock is worth D/r = 1.00/0.055 = $18.18.

A perpetual preferred stock has a level dividend, thus a dividend growth rate of zero. Another case is a declining dividend—a negative growth rate. The Gordon growth model also accommodates this possibility, as illustrated in Example 9.

EXAMPLE 9

Gordon Growth Model with Negative Growth

1. Afton Mines is a profitable company that is expected to pay a $4.25 dividend next year. Because it is depleting its mining properties, the best estimate is that dividends will decline forever at a rate of 4%. The required rate of return on Afton stock is 9%. What is the value of Afton shares?

Solution:

For Afton, the value of the stock is

$$V_0 = \frac{4.25}{[0.09 - (-0.04)]}$$
$$= \frac{4.25}{0.13} = \$32.69.$$

The negative growth results in a $32.69 valuation for the stock.

The Links among Dividend Growth, Earnings Growth, and Value Appreciation in the Gordon Growth Model

The Gordon growth model implies a set of relationships for the growth rates of dividends, earnings, and stock value. With dividends growing at a constant rate g, stock value also grows at g as well. The current stock value is $V_0 = D_1/(r - g)$. Multiplying both sides by $(1 + g)$ gives $V_0(1 + g) = D_1(1 + g)/(r - g)$, which is $V_1 = D_2/(r - g)$. So, both dividends and value have grown at a rate of g (holding r constant). Given a constant payout ratio—a constant, proportional relationship between earnings and dividends—dividends and earnings grow at g.

To summarize, g in the Gordon growth model is the rate of value or capital appreciation (sometimes also called the capital gains yield). Some textbooks state that g is the rate of price appreciation. If prices are efficient (price equals value), price is indeed expected to grow at a rate of g. If there is mispricing (price is different from value), however, the actual rate of capital appreciation depends on the nature of the mispricing and how fast it is corrected, if at all. This topic is discussed in the coverage of return concepts.

==Another characteristic of the constant growth model is that the components of total return (dividend yield and capital gains yield) will also stay constant through time, given that price tracks value exactly. The dividend yield, which is D_1/P_0 at $t = 0$, will stay unchanged because both the dividend and the price are expected to grow at the== same rate, leaving the dividend yield unchanged through time. For example, consider a stock selling for €50.00 with a **forward dividend yield** (a dividend yield based on the anticipated dividend during the next 12 months) of 2% based on an expected dividend of €1. The estimate of g is 5.50% per year. The dividend yield of 2%, the capital gains yield of 5.50%, and the total return of 7.50% are expected to be the same at $t = 0$ and at any future point in time.

4   SHARE REPURCHASES AND THE IMPLIED DIVIDEND GROWTH RATE

> ☐ calculate the value of a common stock using the Gordon growth model and explain the model's underlying assumptions
>
> ☐ calculate and interpret the implied growth rate of dividends using the Gordon growth model and current stock price

An issue of increasing importance in many developed markets is share repurchases. Companies can distribute free cash flow to shareholders in the form of share repurchases (also called buybacks) as well as dividends. In the United States, more than half of dividend-paying companies have also been making regular share repurchases (Skinner 2008). Clearly, analysts using DDMs need to understand share repurchases. Share repurchases and cash dividends have several distinctive features:

- Share repurchases involve a reduction in the number of shares outstanding, all else equal. Selling shareholders see their relative ownership position reduced compared with non-selling shareholders.

- Whereas many corporations with established cash dividends are reluctant to reduce or omit cash dividends, corporations generally do not view themselves as committed to maintaining share repurchases at any specified level.

- Cash dividends tend to be more predictable in money terms and more predictable as to timing (Wagner 2007). Although evidence from the United States suggests that, for companies with active repurchase programs, the amount of repurchases during two-year intervals bears a relationship to earnings, companies appear to be opportunistic in timing exactly when to repurchase (Skinner 2008). Thus, share repurchases are generally harder to forecast than the cash dividends of companies with an identifiable dividend policy.

- As a baseline case, share repurchases are neutral in their effect on the wealth of ongoing shareholders if the repurchases are accomplished at market prices.

The analyst could account for share repurchases directly by forecasting the total earnings, total distributions to shareholders (via either cash dividends or share repurchases), and shares outstanding. Experience and familiarity with such models is much less than for DDMs. ==Focusing on cash dividends, however, DDMs supply accurate valuations consistent with such an approach if the analyst takes account of the effect==

of expected repurchases on the per-share growth rates of dividends. Correctly applied, the DDM is a valid approach to common stock valuation even when the company being analyzed engages in share repurchases.

The Implied Dividend Growth Rate

Because the dividend growth rate affects the estimated value of a stock using the Gordon growth model, differences between estimated values of a stock and its actual market value might be explained by different growth rate assumptions. Given price, the expected next-period dividend, and an estimate of the required rate of return, the dividend growth rate reflected in price can be inferred assuming the Gordon growth model. (Actually, it is possible to infer the market-price-implied dividend growth based on other DDMs as well.) An analyst can then judge whether the implied dividend growth rate is reasonable, high, or low, based on what she knows about the company. In effect, the calculation of the implied dividend growth rate provides an alternative perspective on the stock's valuation (fairly valued, overvalued, or under-valued). Example 10 shows how the Gordon growth model can be used to infer the market's implied growth rate for a stock.

EXAMPLE 10

The Growth Rate Implied by the Current Stock Price

Suppose a company has a beta of 1.1. The risk-free rate is 5.6%, and the equity risk premium is 6%. The current dividend of $2.00 is expected to grow at 5% indefinitely. The price of the stock is $40.

1. Estimate the value of the company's stock.

Solution:

The required rate of return is 5.6% + 1.1(6%) = 12.2%. The value of one share, using the Gordon growth model, is

$$V_0 = \frac{D_0(1+g)}{r-g}$$
$$= \frac{2.00(1.05)}{0.122 - 0.05}$$
$$= \frac{2.10}{0.072} = \$29.17$$

2. Determine the constant dividend growth rate that would be required to justify the market price of $40.

Solution:

The valuation estimate of the model ($29.17) is less than the market value of $40.00, and thus the market price must be forecasting a growth rate above the assumed 5%. Assuming that the model and the required return assumption are appropriate, the growth rate in dividends required to justify the $40 stock price can be calculated by substituting all known values into the Gordon growth model equation except for g:

$$40 = \frac{2.00(1 + g)}{0.122 - g}$$

$$4.88 - 40g = 2 + 2g$$

$$42g = 2.88$$

$$g = 0.0686$$

An expected dividend growth rate of 6.86% is required for the stock price to be correctly valued at the market price of $40.

5 THE GORDON GROWTH MODEL: OTHER ISSUES

- ☐ calculate and interpret the present value of growth opportunities (PVGO) and the component of the leading price-to-earnings ratio (P/E) related to PVGO
- ☐ calculate and interpret the justified leading and trailing P/Es using the Gordon growth model
- ☐ describe strengths and limitations of the Gordon growth model and justify its selection to value a company's common shares
- ☐ estimate a required return based on any DDM, including the Gordon growth model and the H-model
- ☐ evaluate whether a stock is overvalued, fairly valued, or undervalued by the market based on a DDM estimate of value

The value of a stock can be analyzed as the sum of 1) the value of the company without earnings reinvestment and 2) the **present value of growth opportunities** (PVGO). PVGO, also known as the **value of growth**, sums the expected value today of opportunities to profitably reinvest future earnings. More technically, PVGO can be defined as the forecasted total net present value of future projects. In this section, we illustrate this decomposition and discuss how it may be interpreted to gain insight into the market's view of a company's business and prospects.

Earnings growth may increase, leave unchanged, or reduce shareholder wealth depending on whether the growth results from earning returns in excess of, equal to, or less than the opportunity cost of funds. Consider a company with a required return on equity of 10% that has earned €1 per share. The company is deciding whether to pay out current earnings as a dividend or to reinvest them at 10% and distribute the ending value as a dividend in one year. If it reinvests, the present value of investment is €1.10/1.10 = €1.00, equaling its cost, so the decision to reinvest has a net present value (NPV) of zero. If the company were able to earn more than 10% by exploiting a profitable growth opportunity, reinvesting would have a positive NPV, increasing shareholder wealth. Suppose the company could reinvest earnings at 25% for one year: The per-share NPV of the growth opportunity would be €1.25/1.10 − €1 ≈ €0.14. Note that any reinvestment at a positive rate below 10%, although increasing EPS, is not in shareholders' interests. Increases in shareholder wealth occur only when reinvested earnings earn more than the opportunity cost of funds—that is, when investments are in positive NPV projects (condition of profitability as return on equity [ROE] > r, with ROE calculated with the market value of equity rather than the book value of equity in the denominator). Thus, investors actively assess whether and to what degree companies will have opportunities to invest in profitable projects. In principle, companies without prospects for investing in positive NPV projects should distribute most or all earnings to shareholders as dividends so the shareholders can redirect capital to more attractive areas.

A company without positive expected NPV projects is defined as a **no-growth company** (a term for a company without opportunities for *profitable* growth). Such companies should distribute all their earnings in dividends because earnings cannot be reinvested profitably and will be flat in perpetuity, assuming a constant ROE. This flatness occurs because earnings equal ROE × Equity, and equity is constant because retained earnings are not added to it. If assets are in place to support the growth in earnings for the next year ($t = 1$) compared with the prior year ($t = 0$), E_1 is the appropriate measure of earnings to use in estimating the no-growth value per share. E_1 is $t = 1$ earnings, which is the constant level of earnings or the average earnings of a no-growth company if return on equity is viewed as varying about its average level. The **no-growth value per share** is defined as E_1/r, which is the present value of a perpetuity in the amount of E_1 where the capitalization rate, r, is the required rate of return on the company's equity. E_1/r can also be interpreted as the per-share value of assets in place because of the assumption that the company is making no new investments because none are profitable. For any company, the actual value per share is the sum of the no-growth value per share and the present value of growth opportunities:

$$V_0 = \frac{E_1}{r} + \text{PVGO} \tag{12}$$

If prices reflect value ($P_0 = V_0$), P_0 less E_1/r gives the market's estimate of the company's value of growth, PVGO. Referring back to Example 6, suppose that MSEX is expected to have average EPS of $1.52 if it distributed all earnings as dividends. Its required return of 6.8% and a current price of $43.20 gives

$43.20 = (\$1.52/0.068) + \text{PVGO}$

$= \$22.42 + \text{PVGO}$

and PVGO = $43.20 − $22.42 = $20.78. So, 48% ($20.78/$43.20 = 0.48) of the company's value, as reflected in the market price, is attributable to the value of growth.

Exhibit 4 presents selected data from early 2019 for three companies: Alphabet, Inc. (NASDAQ: GOOGL), McDonald's Corporation (NYSE: MCD), and Macy's, Inc. (NYSE: M). The data indicate that the value of growth represented about 53% of the market value of technology company Alphabet (the parent company of Google) and a much smaller percentage of McDonald's market value and Macy's market value. The negative value for Macy's PVGO could be explained in several ways: It could reflect the expected continued challenges that traditional retailers face from online competition, or it might indicate that the estimated no-growth value per share was too high because the earnings estimate was too high and/or the required return on equity estimate was too low.

Exhibit 4: Estimated PVGO as a Percentage of Price

Company	β	r	E_1	Price	E_1/r	PVGO	PVGO/Price
Alphabet, Inc.	1.16	8.2%	$47.49	$1,236.34	$579.14	$657.20	53.16%
McDonald's Corp	0.52	5.3%	$8.23	$194.12	$155.28	$38.84	20.01%
Macy's Inc.	0.45	5.0%	$3.09	$25.11	$61.80	($36.69)	n.m.

Source: NASDAQ for earnings estimate and S&P equity research for beta.

Note: The required rate of return is estimated using the CAPM with 3.0% for the risk-free rate of return and 4.5% for the equity risk premium.

What determines PVGO? One determinant is the value of a company's options to invest, captured by the word "opportunities." In addition, the flexibility to adapt investments to new circumstances and information is valuable. Thus, a second determinant of PVGO is the value of the company's options to time the start, adjust the scale, or even abandon future projects. This element is the value of the company's **real options** (options to modify projects, in this context). Companies that have good business opportunities and/or a high level of managerial flexibility in responding to changes in the marketplace should tend to have higher values of PVGO than companies that do not have such advantages. This perspective on what contributes to PVGO can provide additional understanding of the results in Exhibit 4.

As an additional aid to an analyst, Equation 12 can be restated in terms of the familiar P/E based on forecasted earnings:

$$\frac{V_0}{E_1} \text{ or } \frac{P_0}{E_1} \text{ or P/E} = \frac{1}{r} + \frac{PVGO}{E_1} \tag{13}$$

The first term, $1/r$, is the value of the P/E for a no-growth company. The second term is the component of the P/E value that relates to growth opportunities. For MSEX, the P/E is $43.20/$1.52 = 28.4. The no-growth P/E is 1/0.068 = 14.7 and is the multiple at which the company should sell if it has no growth opportunities. The growth component of $20.78/$1.52 = 13.67 reflects anticipated growth opportunities.

As analysts, the distinction between no-growth and growth values is of interest because the value of growth and the value of assets in place generally have different risk characteristics (as the interpretation of PVGO as incorporating the real options suggests).

Gordon Growth Model and the Price-to-Earnings Ratio

The price-to-earnings ratio is perhaps the most widely recognized valuation indicator, familiar to readers of newspaper financial tables and institutional research reports. Using the Gordon growth model, one can develop an expression for P/E in terms of the fundamentals. This expression has two uses:

- When used with forecasts of the inputs to the model, the analyst obtains a **justified (fundamental) P/E**—the P/E that is fair, warranted, or justified on the basis of fundamentals (given that the valuation model is appropriate). The analyst can then state his view of value in terms not of the Gordon growth model value but of the justified P/E. Because P/E is so widely recognized, this method may be an effective way to communicate the analysis.

- The analyst may also use the expression for P/E to weigh whether the forecasts of earnings growth built into the current stock price are reasonable. What expected earnings growth rate is implied by the actual market P/E? Is that growth rate plausible?

The expression for P/E can be stated in terms of the current (or trailing) P/E (today's market price per share divided by trailing 12 months' earnings per share) or in terms of the leading (or forward) P/E (today's market price per share divided by a forecast of the next 12 months' earnings per share, or sometimes the next fiscal year's earnings per share).

Leading and trailing justified P/E expressions can be developed from the Gordon growth model. Assuming that the model can be applied for a particular stock's valuation, the dividend payout ratio is considered fixed. Define b as the retention rate, the

---

[Handwritten marginal notes:]

growth component of leading PE: $\frac{P/E}{} = \frac{PVGO}{E_1}$

no-growth component of leading PE: $\frac{P}{} = \frac{1}{r}$

fraction of earnings reinvested in the company rather than paid out in dividends. The dividend payout ratio is then, by definition, $(1 - b) =$ Dividend per share/Earnings per share $= D_t/E_t$. If $P_0 = D_1/(r - g)$ is divided by next year's earnings per share, E_1, we have

$$\frac{P_0}{E_1} = \frac{D_1/E_1}{r - g} = \frac{1 - b}{r - g}. \tag{14}$$

This calculation represents a leading P/E, which is current price divided by next year's earnings. Alternatively, if $P_0 = D_0(1 + g)/(r - g)$ is divided by the current-year's earnings per share, E_0, the result is

$$\frac{P_0}{E_0} = \frac{D_0(1 + g)/E_0}{r - g} = \frac{(1 - b)(1 + g)}{r - g}. \tag{15}$$

This expression is for trailing P/E, which is current price divided by trailing (current year) earnings.

EXAMPLE 11

The Justified P/E Based on the Gordon Growth Model

Harry Trice wants to use the Gordon growth model to find a justified P/E for the French company L'Oréal SA (EN Paris: OR), a global cosmetics manufacturer. Trice has assembled the following information:

- Current stock price = €242.70.
- Trailing annual earnings per share = €7.08.
- Current level of annual dividends = €3.85.
- Dividend growth rate = 4.25%.
- Risk-free rate = 2.0%.
- Equity risk premium = 5.0%.
- Beta versus the CAC index = 0.72.

---

1. Calculate the justified trailing and leading P/Es based on the Gordon growth model.

Solution:

For L'Oréal, the required rate of return using the CAPM is

$r_i = 2.0\% + 0.72(5.0\%)$

$= 5.6\%$

The dividend payout ratio is

$(1 - b) = D_0/E_0$

$= 3.85/7.08$

$= 0.54$

The justified leading P/E (based on next year's earnings) is

$$\frac{P_0}{E_1} = \frac{1 - b}{r - g} = \frac{0.5438}{0.056 - 0.0425} = 40.28.$$

$$\frac{P_0}{E_1} = \frac{1 - b}{r - g} = \frac{0.5438}{0.056 - 0.0425} = 40.28$$

The justified trailing P/E (based on trailing earnings) is

[handwritten annotations:]

$D_1 = 3.85 \times 1.0425 = 4.01$

$E_1 = 7.08 \times 1.0425 = 7.38$

$\frac{D_1}{E_1} = \frac{4.01}{7.38} = 0.54$

$$\frac{P_0}{E_0} = \frac{(1-b)(1+g)}{r-g} = \frac{0.5438(1.0425)}{0.056-0.0425} = 42.00.$$

2. Based on the justified trailing P/E and the actual P/E, judge whether L'Oréal is fairly valued, overvalued, or undervalued.

Solution:

Based on a current price of €242.70 and trailing earnings of €7.08, the trailing P/E is €242.70/€7.08 = 34.3. Because the actual P/E of 34.3 is smaller than the justified trailing P/E of 42.0, the conclusion is that L'Oréal appears to be undervalued. The apparent mispricing can also be expressed in terms of price using the Gordon growth model. Using Trice's assumptions, the Gordon growth model assigns a value of 3.85(1.0425)/(0.05 − 0.0425) = €297.31, which is above the current market price of €242.70.

We will later present multistage DDMs. Expressions for the P/E can be developed in terms of the variables of multistage DDMs, but the usefulness of these expressions is not commensurate with their complexity. For multistage models, the simple way to calculate a justified leading P/E is to divide the model value directly by the first year's expected earnings. In all cases, the P/E is explained in terms of the required return on equity, expected dividend growth rate(s), and the dividend payout ratio(s). All else equal, higher prices are associated with higher anticipated dividend growth rates.

Estimating a Required Return Using the Gordon Growth Model

Under the assumption of efficient prices, the Gordon growth model has been used to estimate a stock's required rate of return, or equivalently, the market-price-implied expected return. The Gordon growth model solved for r is

$$r = \frac{D_0(1+g)}{P_0} + g = \frac{D_1}{P_0} + g. \tag{16}$$

As explained in the coverage of return concepts, r in Equation 16 is technically an internal rate of return (IRR). The rate r is composed of two parts: the dividend yield (D_1/P_0) and the capital gains (or appreciation) yield (g).

EXAMPLE 12

Finding the Expected Rate of Return with the Gordon Growth Model

Bob Inguigiatto, CFA, has been given the task of developing mean return estimates for a list of stocks as preparation for a portfolio optimization. On his list is NextEra Energy, Inc. (NYSE: NEE). On analysis, he decides that it is appropriate to model NextEra Energy using the Gordon growth model, and he takes prices as reflecting value. The company paid dividends of $4.44 in 2018 and in February 2019 announced an increase in quarterly dividends from $1.11 to $1.25, implying an annual dividend of $5.00. The current stock price is $169.83. The growth rate of dividends per share has averaged around 11.0% per year, based on the past five years. NextEra's recent earnings growth has been affected by non-recurring items, but based on his analysis, Inguigiatto has decided to use 5.50% as his best estimate of the long-term earnings and dividend growth rate. Next year's projected dividend, D_1, is $5.00(1.055) = $5.275. Using the Gordon growth model, NextEra Energy's expected rate of return is

$$r = \frac{D_1}{P_0} + g$$
$$= \frac{5.275}{169.83} + 0.055$$
$$= 0.0311 + 0.055$$
$$= 0.0860 = 8.60\%$$

The expected rate of return can be broken into two components: the dividend yield (D_1/P_0 = 3.11%) and the capital gains yield (g = 5.50%).

The Gordon Growth Model: Concluding Remarks

The Gordon growth model is the simplest practical implementation of discounted dividend valuation. The Gordon growth model is appropriate for valuing the equity of dividend-paying companies when its key assumption of a stable future dividend and earnings growth rate is expected to be satisfied. Broad equity market indexes of developed markets frequently satisfy the conditions of the model fairly well. As a result, analysts have used it to judge whether an equity market is fairly valued or not and for estimating the equity risk premium associated with the current market level. In the multistage models discussed in the next section, the Gordon growth model has often been used to model the last growth stage, when a previously high-growth company matures and the growth rate drops to a long-term sustainable level. In any case in which the model is applied, the analyst must be aware that the model's output is typically sensitive to small changes in the assumed growth rate and required rate of return.

The Gordon growth model is a single-stage DDM because all future periods are grouped into one stage characterized by a single growth rate. For many or even the majority of companies, however, future growth can be expected to consist of multiple stages. Multistage DDMs are the subject of the next section.

MULTISTAGE DIVIDEND DISCOUNT MODELS

6

☐ explain the growth phase, transition phase, and maturity phase of a business

☐ explain the assumptions and justify the selection of the two-stage DDM, the H-model, the three-stage DDM, or spreadsheet modeling to value a company's common shares

☐ describe terminal value and explain alternative approaches to determining the terminal value in a DDM

☐ calculate and interpret the value of common shares using the two-stage DDM, the H-model, and the three-stage DDM

☐ evaluate whether a stock is overvalued, fairly valued, or undervalued by the market based on a DDM estimate of value

Earlier we noted that the basic expression for the DDM (Equation 7) is too general for investment analysts to use in practice because one cannot forecast individually more than a relatively small number of dividends. The strongest simplifying assumption—a stable dividend growth rate from now into the indefinite future, leading to the Gordon growth model—is unrealistic for many or even most companies. For many publicly traded companies, practitioners have typically assumed that growth falls into three stages (see Sharpe, Alexander, and Bailey 1999):

- **Growth phase.** A company in its growth phase typically enjoys rapidly expanding markets, high profit margins, and an abnormally high growth rate in earnings per share (**supernormal growth**). Companies in this phase often have negative free cash flow to equity because the company invests heavily in expanding operations. Given high prospective returns on equity, the dividend payout ratios of growth-phase companies are often low or even zero. As the company's markets mature or as unusual growth opportunities attract competitors, earnings growth rates eventually decline.

- **Transition phase.** In this phase, which is a transition to maturity, earnings growth slows as competition puts pressure on prices and profit margins or as sales growth slows because of market saturation. In this phase, earnings growth rates may be above average but declining toward the growth rate for the overall economy. Capital requirements typically decline in this phase, often resulting in positive free cash flow and increasing dividend payout ratios (or the initiation of dividends).

- **Mature phase.** In maturity, the company reaches an equilibrium in which investment opportunities on average just earn their opportunity cost of capital. Return on equity approaches the required return on equity, and earnings growth, the dividend payout ratio, and the return on equity stabilize at levels that can be sustained long term. The dividend and earnings growth rate of this phase is called the **mature growth rate**. This phase, in fact, reflects the stage in which a company can properly be valued using the Gordon growth model, and that model is one tool for valuing this phase of a current high-growth company's future.

A company may attempt and succeed in restarting the growth phase by changing its strategic focuses and business mix. Technological advances may alter a company's growth prospects for better or worse with surprising rapidity. Nevertheless, this growth-phase picture of a company is a useful approximation. The growth-phase concept provides the intuition for multistage discounted cash flow (DCF) models of all types, including multistage dividend discount models. Multistage models are a staple valuation discipline of investment management firms using DCF valuation models.

A survey of CFA Institute members with job responsibility for equity analysis indicates that, among respondents using a dividend discount model, two-stage and multistage models are used more often than the single-stage model (Stowe, Pinto, and Robinson 2018). Among analysts using a dividend discount model, 55% use a two-stage model, 11% use an H-model (a type of two-stage model), and 50% use a model with more than two stages (Stowe, Pinto, and Robinson 2018). (Because analysts often use more than one model, the response percentages add up to more than 100%).

In the following sections, we present three popular multistage DDMs: the two-stage DDM, the H-model, and the three-stage DDM. Keep in mind that all these models represent stylized patterns of growth; they are attempting to identify the pattern that most accurately approximates an analyst's view of the company's future growth.

Two-Stage Dividend Discount Model

Two common versions of the two-stage DDM exist. Both versions assume constant growth at a mature growth rate (for example, 7%) in Stage 2. In the first version ("the general two-stage model"), the whole of Stage 1 represents a period of abnormal growth—for example, growth at 15%. The transition to mature growth in Stage 2 is generally abrupt.

In the second version, called the H-model, the dividend growth rate is assumed to decline from an abnormal rate to the mature growth rate during the course of Stage 1. For example, the growth rate could begin at 15% and decline continuously in Stage 1 until it reaches 7%. The second model will be presented after the general two-stage model.

The first two-stage DDM provides for a high growth rate for the initial period, followed by a sustainable and usually lower growth rate thereafter. The two-stage DDM is based on the multiple-period model

$$V_0 = \sum_{t=1}^{n} \frac{D_t}{(1+r)^t} + \frac{V_n}{(1+r)^n}, \tag{17}$$

where V_n is used as an estimate of P_n. The two-stage model assumes that the first n dividends grow at an extraordinary short-term rate, g_S:

$$D_t = D_0 \left(1 + g_S\right)^t$$

After time n, the annual dividend growth rate changes to a normal long-term rate, g_L. The dividend at time $n + 1$ is $D_{n+1} = D_n(1 + g_L) = D_0(1 + g_S)^n(1 + g_L)$, and this dividend continues to grow at g_L. Using D_{n+1}, an analyst can use the Gordon growth model to find V_n:

$$V_n = \frac{D_0 \left(1 + g_S\right)^n \left(1 + g_L\right)}{r - g_L} \tag{18}$$

To find the value at $t = 0$, V_0, simply find the present value of the first n dividends and the present value of the projected value at time n.

$$V_0 = \sum_{t=1}^{n} \frac{D_0 \left(1 + g_S\right)^t}{(1+r)^t} + \frac{D_0 \left(1 + g_S\right)^n \left(1 + g_L\right)}{(1+r)^n \left(r - g_L\right)} \tag{19}$$

EXAMPLE 13

Valuing a Stock Using the Two-Stage Dividend Discount Model

1. Carl Zeiss Meditec AG (AFX:GR), 65% owned by the Carl Zeiss Group, provides screening, diagnostic, and therapeutic systems for the treatment of ophthalmologic (vision) problems. Reviewing the issue as of early 2019, when it is trading for €80.55, Hans Mattern, a buy-side analyst covering Meditec, forecasts that the current dividend of €0.55 will grow by 9% per year during the next 10 years. Thereafter, Mattern believes that the growth rate will decline to 5% and remain at that level indefinitely.

   Mattern estimates Meditec's required return on equity as 5.88% based on a beta of 0.90 against the equity market benchmark DAX, a 1.2% risk-free rate, and his equity risk premium estimate of 5.2%.

Exhibit 5 shows the calculations of the first 10 dividends and their present values discounted at 5.88%. The terminal stock value at $t = 10$ is

$$V_{10} = \frac{D_0 \left(1 + g_S\right)^n \left(1 + g_L\right)}{r - g_L}$$

$$= \frac{0.55 \left(1.09\right)^{10} \left(1.05\right)}{0.0588 - 0.05}$$

$$= 155.358$$

The terminal stock value and its present value are also given.

Exhibit 5: Carl Zeiss Meditec AG

Time	Value	Calculation	D_t or V_t	Present Values $D_t/(1.0588)^t$ or $V_t/(1.0588)^t$
1	D_1	$= 0.55 \times (1 + 0.09)^1$	€0.600	€0.5662
2	D_2	$= 0.55 \times (1 + 0.09)^2$	0.653	0.5829
3	D_3	$= 0.55 \times (1 + 0.09)^3$	0.712	0.6001
4	D_4	$= 0.55 \times (1 + 0.09)^4$	0.776	0.6178
5	D_5	$= 0.55 \times (1 + 0.09)^5$	0.846	0.6360
6	D_6	$= 0.55 \times (1 + 0.09)^6$	0.922	0.6547
7	D_7	$= 0.55 \times (1 + 0.09)^7$	1.005	0.6740
8	D_8	$= 0.55 \times (1 + 0.09)^8$	1.096	0.6938
9	D_9	$= 0.55 \times (1 + 0.09)^9$	1.195	0.7143
10	D_{10}	$= 0.55 \times (1 + 0.09)^{10}$	1.302	0.7353
10	V_{10}	$= [0.55 \times (1 + 0.09)^{10} \times 1.05]/ (0.0588 - 0.05)$	155.358	87.7395
Total				€94.2145

In this two-stage model, the dividends are forecast during the first stage and then their present values are calculated. The Gordon growth model is used to derive the terminal value (the value of the dividends in the second stage as of the beginning of that stage). As shown in Exhibit 5, the terminal value is $V_{10} = D_{11}/(r - g_L)$. Ignoring rounding errors, the Period 11 dividend is €1.3671 (= $D_{10} \times 1.05$ = €1.302 × 1.05). By using the standard Gordon growth model, V_{10} = €155.36 = €1.3671/(0.0588 – 0.05). The present value of the terminal value is €87.74 = €155.36/1.0588^{10}. The total estimated value of Meditec is €94.21 using this model. Notice that approximately 93% of this value, €87.74, is the present value of V_{10}, and the balance, €94.21 – €87.74 = €6.47, is the present value of the first 10 dividends. If we recall the discussion of the sensitivity of the Gordon growth model to changes in the inputs, we can calculate an interval for the intrinsic value of Meditec by varying the mature growth rate through the range of plausible values.

The two-stage DDM is useful because many scenarios exist in which a company can achieve a supernormal growth rate for a few years, after which time the growth rate falls to a more sustainable level. For example, a company may achieve supernormal growth through possession of a patent, first-mover advantage, or another factor that provides a temporary lead in a specific marketplace. Subsequently, earnings will most likely descend to a level that is more consistent with competition and growth in the overall economy. Accordingly, that is why in the two-stage model, extraordinary growth is often forecast for a few years and normal growth is forecast thereafter. A possible limitation of the two-stage model is that the transition between the initial abnormal growth period and the final steady-state growth period is abrupt.

The accurate estimation of V_n, the **terminal value of the stock** (also known as its **continuing value**) is an important part of the correct use of DDMs. In practice, analysts estimate the terminal value either by applying a multiple to a projected terminal value of a fundamental, such as earnings per share or book value per share, or they estimate V_n using the Gordon growth model. In our coverage of market multiples, we will discuss using price–earnings multiples in this context.

[handwritten margin note: Terminal value is defined at period n, not period 0.]

In the examples, a single discount rate, r, is used for all phases, reflecting both a desire for simplicity and lack of a clear objective basis for adjusting the discount rate for different phases. Some analysts, however, use different discount rates for different growth phases.

The following example values P&G (Procter & Gamble Company) by combining the dividend discount model and a P/E valuation model.

EXAMPLE 14

Combining a DDM and P/E Model to Value a Stock

1. An analyst is reviewing the valuation of Procter & Gamble Company known as "P&G" (NYSE: PG) as of the beginning of 2019 when P&G was selling for $96.47. In the previous year, P&G paid a $2.79 dividend that the analyst expects to grow at a rate of 4% annually for the next four years. At the end of Year 4, the analyst expects the dividend to equal 60% of earnings per share and the trailing P/E for P&G to be 22. If the required return on P&G common stock is 6.5%, calculate the per-share value of P&G common stock.

   Exhibit 6 summarizes the relevant calculations. When the dividends are growing at 4%, the expected dividends and the present value of each (discounted at 6.5%) are shown. The terminal stock price, V_4, deserves some explanation. As shown in the table, the Year 4 dividend is $2.79(1.04)^4 = 3.2639. Because dividends at that time are assumed to be 60% of earnings, the EPS projection for Year 4 is $EPS_4 = D_4/0.60 = \$3.2639/0.60 = \$5.4398$. With a trailing P/E of 22.0, the value of P&G at the end of Year 4 would be $22.0(\$5.4398) = \$119.6765$. Discounted at 6.5% for four years, the present value of V_4 is $93.0273.

   Exhibit 6: Value of Procter & Gamble Common Stock

Time	Value	Calculation	D_t or V_t	Present Values $D_t/(1.065)^t$ or $V_t/(1.065)^t$
1	D_1	$2.79(1.04)^1$	$2.9016	$2.7245
2	D_2	$2.79\ (1.04)^2$	3.0177	2.6606
3	D_3	$2.79\ (1.04)^3$	3.1384	2.5981
4	D_4	$2.79\ (1.04)^4$	3.2639	2.5371
4	V_4	$22 \times [2.79\ (1.04)^4/0.60]$ $= 22 \times (3.2639/0.60)$ $= 22 \times 5.4398$	119.6765	93.0273
Total				$103.5476

The present values of the dividends for Years 1 through 4 sum to $10.52. The present value of the terminal value of $119.68 is $93.03. The estimated total value of P&G's common stock is the sum of these, or $103.55 per share.

Valuing a Non-Dividend-Paying Company

The fact that a stock is currently paying no dividends does not mean that the principles of the dividend discount model do not apply. Even though D_0 and/or D_1 may be zero, and the company may not begin paying dividends for some time, the present value of future dividends may still capture the value of the company. Of course, if a company pays no dividends and will never be able to distribute cash to shareholders, the stock is worthless.

To value a non-dividend-paying company using a DDM, generally an analyst can use a multistage DDM model in which the first-stage dividend equals zero. Example 15 illustrates the approach.

EXAMPLE 15

Valuing a Non-Dividend-Paying Stock

1. Assume that a company is currently paying no dividend and will not pay one for several years. If the company begins paying a dividend of $1.00 five years from now, and the dividend is expected to grow at 5% thereafter, this future dividend stream can be discounted back to find the value of the company. This company's required rate of return is 11%. Because the expression

$$V_n = \frac{D_{n+1}}{r - g}$$

values a stock at period n using the next period's dividend, the $t = 5$ dividend is used to find the value at $t = 4$:

$$V_4 = \frac{D_5}{r - g} = \frac{1.00}{0.11 - 0.05} = \$16.67$$

To find the value of the stock today, simply discount V_4 back for four years:

$$V_0 = \frac{V_4}{(1 + r)^4} = \frac{16.67}{(1.11)^4} = \$10.98$$

The value of this stock, even though it will not pay a dividend until Year 5, is $10.98.

If a company is not paying a dividend but is very profitable, an analyst might be willing to forecast its future dividends. Of course, for non-dividend-paying, unprofitable companies, such a forecast would be very difficult. Furthermore, as discussed previously, it is usually difficult for the analyst to estimate the timing of the initiation of dividends and the dividend policy that will then be established by the company. Thus, the analyst may prefer a free cash flow or residual income model for valuing such companies.

THE H-MODEL AND THREE-STAGE DIVIDEND DISCOUNT MODELS

7

- ☐ explain the assumptions and justify the selection of the two-stage DDM, the H-model, the three-stage DDM, or spreadsheet modeling to value a company's common shares
- ☐ describe terminal value and explain alternative approaches to determining the terminal value in a DDM
- ☐ calculate and interpret the value of common shares using the two-stage DDM, the H-model, and the three-stage DDM
- ☐ evaluate whether a stock is overvalued, fairly valued, or undervalued by the market based on a DDM estimate of value

The basic two-stage model assumes a constant, extraordinary rate for the supernormal growth period that is followed by a constant, normal growth rate thereafter. The difference in growth rates may be substantial. For instance, in Example 13, the assumed growth rate for Carl Zeiss Meditec was 9% annually for 10 years, followed by a drop to 5% growth in Year 11 and thereafter. In some cases, a smoother transition to the mature phase growth rate would be more realistic. Fuller and Hsia (1984) developed a variant of the two-stage model in which growth begins at a high rate and declines linearly throughout the supernormal growth period until it reaches a normal rate at the end. The value of the dividend stream in the H-model is

$$V_0 = \frac{D_0(1+g_L)}{r-g_L} + \frac{D_0 H(g_S-g_L)}{r-g_L} \tag{20}$$

or

$$V_0 = \frac{D_0(1+g_L) + D_0 H(g_S-g_L)}{r-g_L},$$

where

V_0 = value per share at $t = 0$

D_0 = current dividend

r = required rate of return on equity

H = half-life in years of the high-growth period (i.e., high-growth period = $2H$ years)

g_S = initial short-term dividend growth rate

g_L = normal long-term dividend growth rate after Year $2H$

The first term on the right-hand side of Equation 20 is the present value of the company's dividend stream if it were to grow at g_L forever. The second term is an approximation of the extra value (assuming $g_S > g_L$) accruing to the stock because of its supernormal growth for Years 1 through $2H$ (see Fuller and Hsia 1984 for technical details). Logically, the longer the supernormal growth period (i.e., the larger the value of H, which is one-half the length of the supernormal growth period) and the larger the extra growth rate in the supernormal growth period (measured by g_S minus g_L), the higher the share value, all else equal.

We can provide some intuition on the expression. On average, the expected excess growth rate in the supernormal period will be $(g_S - g_L)/2$. Through $2H$ periods, a total excess amount of dividends (compared with the level given g_L) of $2HD0(g_S - g_L)/2 = D0H(g_S - g_L)$ is expected. This term is the H-model upward adjustment to the first dividend term, reflecting the extra expected dividends as growth declines from g_S to g_L during the first period. Note, however, that the timing of the individual dividends in the first period is not reflected by individually discounting them; the expression is thus an approximation.

To illustrate the expression, if the analyst in Example 13 had forecast a linear decline of the growth rate from 9% to 5% over the next 10 years, his estimate of value of Meditec using the H-model would have been €78.13 (rather than €94.21 as in Example 13):

$$V_0 = \frac{D_0(1+g_L) + D_0H(g_S - g_L)}{r - g_L}$$
$$= \frac{55(1.05) + 55(5)(0.09 - 0.05)}{0.0588 - 0.05}$$
$$= 78.13$$

Note that an H of 5 corresponds to the 10-year high-growth period of Example 13. Example 16 provides another illustration of the H-model.

EXAMPLE 16

Valuing a Stock with the H-Model

An analyst has decided to use the H-model to estimate the value of a company and has gathered the following facts and forecasts:

- The share price is €41.70.
- The current dividend is €1.77.
- The initial dividend growth rate is 7%, declining linearly during a 10-year period to a final and perpetual growth rate of 4%.
- The analyst estimates the company's required rate of return on equity as 8.0%.

1. Using the H-model and the information given, estimate the company's per-share value.

Solution:

Using the H-model expression gives

$$V_0 = \frac{D_0(1+g_L) + D_0H(g_S - g_L)}{r - g_L}$$
$$= \frac{1.77(1.04) + 1.77(5)(0.07 - 0.04)}{0.08 - 0.04}$$
$$= \frac{1.84 + 0.27}{0.04}$$
$$= 52.75$$

2. Estimate the value of the company's shares if its normal growth period began immediately.

Solution:

If the company experienced normal growth starting now, its estimated value would be the first component of the H-model estimate, €46 (=1.84/0.04). The faster initial growth assumption adds €6.75 (=0.27/0.04) to its value, resulting in an estimated value of €52.75 per share.

3. Evaluate whether the company's shares appear to be fairly valued, overvalued, or undervalued.

Solution:

€52.75 is approximately 26% higher than the company's current market price of €41.70. Thus the company appears to be undervalued.

The H-model is an approximation model that estimates the valuation that would result from discounting all of the future dividends individually. In many circumstances, this approximation is very close. For a long extraordinary growth period (a high H) or for a large difference in growth rates (the difference between g_S and g_L), however, the analyst might abandon the approximation model for the more exact model. Fortunately, the many tedious calculations of the exact model are made fairly easy using a spreadsheet program.

Three-Stage Dividend Discount Models

There are two popular versions of the three-stage DDM, distinguished by the modeling of the second stage. In the first version ("the general three-stage model"), the company is assumed to have three distinct stages of growth and the growth rate of the second stage is typically constant. For example, Stage 1 could assume 20% growth for three years, Stage 2 could have 10% growth for four years, and Stage 3 could have 5% growth thereafter. In the second version, the growth rate in the middle (second) stage is assumed to decline linearly to the mature growth rate: essentially, the second and third stages are treated as an H-model.

The following example shows how the first type of the three-stage model can be used to value a stock.

EXAMPLE 17

The Three-Stage DDM with Three Distinct Stages

1. An analyst is analyzing a technology company and makes the following estimates:

   ▪ the current required return on equity for the company is 9%; and
   ▪ dividends will grow at 14% for the next two years, 12% for the following five years, and 6.75% thereafter.

   The company pays a dividend of $3.30 per year, and its stock currently trades at $194.98. Based only on the information given, estimate the value of the company's stock using a three-stage DDM approach.

Solution:

Exhibit 7 gives the calculations.

Exhibit 7: Estimated Value Using a Three-Stage DDM

Time	Value	Calculation	D_t or V_t	Present Values $D_t/(1.09)^t$ or $V_t/(1.09)^t$
1	D_1	$3.30(1.14)$	$3.7620	$3.4514
2	D_2	$3.30(1.14)^2$	4.2887	3.6097
3	D_3	$3.30(1.14)^2(1.12)$	4.8033	3.7090
4	D_4	$3.30(1.14)^2(1.12)^2$	5.3797	3.8111
5	D_5	$3.30(1.14)^2(1.12)^3$	6.0253	3.9160
6	D_6	$3.30(1.14)^2(1.12)^4$	6.7483	4.0238
7	D_7	$3.30(1.14)^2(1.12)^5$	7.5581	4.1346
7	V_7	$3.30(1.14)^2(1.12)^5(1.0675)/$ $(0.09 - 0.0675)$	$358.5908	196.161
Total				$222.8171

Given these assumptions, the three-stage model indicates that a fair price should be $222.82, more than 14% above the current market price. Characteristically, the present value of the terminal value of $196.16 constitutes the overwhelming portion (here, about 88%) of total estimated value.

A second version of the three-stage DDM has a middle stage similar to the first stage in the H-model. In the first stage, dividends grow at a high, constant (supernormal) rate for the whole period. In the second stage, dividends decline linearly as they do in the H-model. Finally, in Stage 3, dividends grow at a sustainable, constant growth rate. The process of using this model involves four steps:

- Gather the required inputs:

  - the current dividend;
  - estimates of the lengths of the first, second, and third stages and the expected growth rate during each stage; and
  - an estimate of the required return on equity.

- Compute the expected dividends in the first stage and find the sum of their present values.

- Apply the H-model expression to the second and third stages to obtain an estimate of their value as of the beginning of the second stage. Then find the present value of this H-value as of today ($t = 0$).

- Sum the values obtained in the second and third steps.

In the first step, analysts often investigate the company more deeply, making explicit, individual earnings and dividend forecasts for the near future (often 3, 5, or 10 years), rather than applying a growth rate to the current level of dividends.

EXAMPLE 18

The Three-Stage DDM with Declining Growth Rates in Stage 2

Elsie Bouvier is evaluating Rhinestone Energy (a hypothetical company) for possible inclusion in a small-cap, growth-oriented portfolio. The company is a diversified energy company involved in oil and gas exploration as well as natural gas distribution. In light of Rhinestone Energy's aggressive program of purchasing oil and gas producing properties, Bouvier expects above-average growth for the next five years. She establishes the following facts and forecasts:

- The current market price is $56.18.

- The current dividend is $0.56.

- Bouvier forecasts an initial five-year period of 11% per year earnings and dividend growth.

- Bouvier anticipates that Rhinestone Energy can grow 6.5% per year as a mature company and allows 10 years for the transition to the mature growth period.

- To estimate the required return on equity using the CAPM, Bouvier uses an adjusted beta of 1.2 based on two years of weekly observations, an estimated equity risk premium of 4.2%, and a risk-free rate based on long bond yields of 3%.

- Bouvier considers any security trading within a band of ±20% of her estimate of intrinsic value to be within a "fair value range."

1. Estimate the required return on Rhinestone Energy's equity using the CAPM. (Use only one decimal place in stating the result.)

Solution

The required return on equity is $r = 3\% + 1.2(4.2\%) = 8\%$.

2. Estimate the value of Rhinestone Energy's common stock using a three-stage dividend discount model with a linearly declining dividend growth rate in Stage 2.

Solution:

The first step is to compute the five dividends in Stage 1 and find their present values at 8%. The dividends in Stages 2 and 3 can be valued with the H-model, which estimates their value at the beginning of Stage 2. This value is then discounted back to find the dividends' present value at $t = 0$.

The calculation of the five dividends in Stage 1 and their present values are given in Exhibit 8. The H-model for calculating the value of the Stage 2 and Stage 3 dividends at the beginning of Stage 2 ($t = 5$) is

$$V_5 = \frac{D_5(1+g_L)}{r-g_L} + \frac{D_5 H(g_S - g_L)}{r-g_L},$$

where

$D_5 = D_0(1 + g_S)^5 = 0.56(1.11)^5 = \$0.9436$

$g_S = 11.0\%$

$g_L = 6.5\%$

$r = 8.0\%$

$H = 5$ (the second stage lasts $2H = 10$ years)

Substituting these values into the equation for the H-model gives V_5 as follows:

$$V_5 = \frac{0.9436(1.065)}{0.08 - 0.065} + \frac{0.9436(5)(0.11 - 0.065)}{0.08 - 0.065}$$
$$= 66.9979 + 14.1545$$
$$= \$81.1524$$

The present value of V_5 is $\$81.1524/(1.08)^5 = \$55.2310$.

Exhibit 8: Rhinestone Energy

Time	D_t or V_t	Explanation of D_t or V_t	Value of D_t or V_t	PV at 8%
1	D_1	$0.56(1.11)^1$	$0.6216	$0.5756
2	D_2	$0.56(1.11)^2$	0.6900	0.5915
3	D_3	$0.56(1.11)^3$	0.7659	0.6080
4	D_4	$0.56(1.11)^4$	0.8501	0.6249
5	D_5	$0.56(1.11)^5$	0.9436	0.6422
5	V_5	H-model explained earlier	$81.1524	55.2310
Total				$58.2731

According to the three-stage DDM model, the total value of Rhinestone Energy is $58.27.

3. Calculate the percentages of the total value represented by the first stage and by the second and third stages considered as one group.

Solution:

The sum of the first five present value amounts in the last column of Exhibit 8 is $3.0422. Thus, the first stage represents $3.0422/$58.2731 = 5.2% of total value. The second and third stages together represent 100% − 5.2% = 94.8% of total value (check: $55.2310/$58.2731 = 94.8%).

4. Judge whether Rhinestone Energy's stock is undervalued or overvalued according to Bouvier's perspective.

Solution:

The band Bouvier is looking at is $58.27 \pm 0.20(\$58.27)$, which runs from $58.27 + \$11.65 = \$69.92$ on the upside to $58.27 - \$11.65 = \$46.62$ on the downside. Because the current price of $56.18 is between $46.62 and $69.92, Bouvier would consider Rhinestone Energy to be fairly valued.

5. Some analysts are forecasting essentially flat EPS and dividends in the second year. Estimate the value of Rhinestone Energy's stock under the assumptions that EPS is flat in the second year and that 11% growth resumes in the third year.

Solution:

The estimated value becomes $52.56 with no growth in Year 2 as shown in Exhibit 9. The value of the second and third stages is given by

$$V_5 = \frac{0.8501(1.065)}{0.08 - 0.065} + \frac{0.8501(5)(0.11 - 0.065)}{0.08 - 0.065} = \$73.1103.$$

Exhibit 9: Rhinestone Energy with No Growth in Year 2

Time	D_t or V_t	Explanation of D_t or V_t	Value of D_t or V_t	PV at 8%
1	D_1	$0.56(1.11)^1$	$0.6216	$0.5756
2	D_2	No growth in Year 2	0.6216	0.5329
3	D_3	$0.56(1.11)^2$	0.6900	0.5477
4	D_4	$0.56(1.11)^3$	0.7659	0.5629
5	D_5	$0.56(1.11)^4$	0.8501	0.5786
5	V_5	H-model explained earlier	$73.1103	49.7576
Total				$52.5553

In Problem 5 of Example 18, the analyst examined the consequences of 11% growth in Year 1 and no growth in Year 2, with 11% growth resuming in Years 3, 4, and 5. In the first stage, analysts may forecast earnings and dividends individually for a certain number of years.

The three-stage DDM with declining growth in Stage 2 has been widely used among companies using a DDM approach to valuation. An example is the DDM adopted by Bloomberg L.P., a financial services company that provides "Bloomberg terminals" to professional investors and analysts. The Bloomberg DDM is a model that provides an estimated value for any stock that the user selects. The DDM is a three-stage model with declining growth in Stage 2. The model uses earnings estimates for assumed Stage 1 and the cost of capital for Stage 3 growth rates, and then it assumes that the Stage 2 rate is a linearly declining rate between the Stage 1 and Stage 3 rates. The model also makes estimates of the required rate of return and the lengths of the three stages, assigning higher-growth companies shorter growth periods (i.e., first stages) and longer transition periods, and slower-growth companies longer growth periods and shorter transition periods. Fixing the total length of the growth and transition phases together at 17 years, the growth stage/transition stage durations for Bloomberg's four growth classifications are 3 years/14 years for "explosive growth" equities, 5 years/12 years for "high growth" equities, 7 years/10 years for "average growth" equities, and 9 years/8 years for "slow/mature growth" equities. Analysts, by tailoring stage specifications to their understanding of the specific company being valued, should be able to improve on the accuracy of valuations compared with a fixed specification.

8

GENERAL MODELING AND ESTIMATING A REQUIRED RETURN USING ANY DDM

☐ explain the use of spreadsheet modeling to forecast dividends and to value common shares

☐ estimate a required return based on any DDM, including the Gordon growth model and the H-model

DDMs, such as the Gordon growth model and the multistage models presented earlier, assume stylized patterns of dividend growth. An analyst can use *any* assumed dividend pattern, however, to create a spreadsheet to value the stock and to test sensitivity of the value to growth and return assumptions. The following example presents the results of a valuation incorporating dividends that are estimated to change substantially over the forecast period.

EXAMPLE 19

Finding the Value of a Stock with Varying Dividend Assumptions

1. Yang Co. is expected to pay a $21.00 dividend next year. An analyst estimates that the dividend will decline by 10% annually for the following three years (i.e., the "growth rate" will equal –10%). In Year 5, Yang is expected to sell off assets worth $100 per share. The Year 5 dividend, which includes a distribution of some of the proceeds of the asset sale, is expected to be $60. In Year 6, the dividend is expected to decrease to $40 and to be maintained at $40 for one additional year. The dividend is then expected to grow by 5% annually thereafter. If the required rate of return is 12%, what is the value of one share of Yang?

Solution:

The value is shown in Exhibit 10. Each dividend, its present value discounted at 12%, and an explanation are included in the table. The final row treats the dividends from $t = 8$ forward as a Gordon growth model because after Year 7, the dividend grows at a constant 5% annually. V_7 is the value of these dividends at $t = 7$.

Exhibit 10: Value of Yang Co. Stock

Year	D_t or V_t	Value of D_t or V_t	Present Value at 12%	Explanation of D_t or V_t
1	D_1	$21.00	$18.75	Dividend set at $21

Year	D_t or V_t	Value of D_t or V_t	Present Value at 12%	Explanation of D_t or V_t
2	D_2	18.90	15.07	Previous dividend × 0.90
3	D_3	17.01	12.11	Previous dividend × 0.90
4	D_4	15.31	9.73	Previous dividend × 0.90
5	D_5	60.00	34.05	Set at $60
6	D_6	40.00	20.27	Set at $40
7	D_7	40.00	18.09	Set at $40
7	V_7	600.00	271.41	$V_7 = D_8/(r - g)$ $V_7 = (40.00 \times 1.05)/(0.12 - 0.05)$
Total			$399.48	

As the table in Example 19 shows, the total present value of Yang Co.'s dividends is $399.48. In this example, the terminal value of the company (V_n) at the end of the first stage is found using the Gordon growth model and a mature growth rate of 5%.

Several alternative approaches to estimating g are available in this context:

- Use the formula g = (b in the mature phase) × (ROE in the mature phase). We will discuss the expression $g = b \times ROE$ later. Analysts estimate mature-phase ROE in several ways, such as the following:

  - The DuPont decomposition of ROE based on forecasts for the components of the DuPont expression.
  - Setting ROE = r, the required rate of return on equity, based on the assumption that in the mature phase companies can do no more than earn investors' opportunity cost of capital.
  - Setting ROE in the mature phase equal to the median industry ROE.

- The analyst may estimate the growth rate, g, with other models by relating the mature growth rate to macroeconomic, including industry, growth projections.

When the analyst uses the sustainable growth expression, the earnings retention ratio, b, may be empirically based. For example, Bloomberg L.P.'s model has been assuming that b = 0.55 in the mature phase, equivalent to a dividend payout ratio of 45%, a long-run average payout ratio for mature dividend-paying companies in the United States. In addition, sometimes analysts project the dividend payout ratio for the company individually.

EXAMPLE 20

A Sustainable Growth Rate Calculation

1. An analyst is estimating the dividend growth rate of a company to incorporate in the final stage of a multistage dividend discount model. Assume the company's payout ratio is 25% and its ROE is equal to its estimated required return on equity of 9%. An estimate of the sustainable growth rate can be derived using the expression

   g = (b in the mature phase) × (ROE in the mature phase)

= 0.75(9%) = 6.75%.

The analyst's estimate of the company's sustainable dividend growth rate is 6.75%.

Estimating a Required Return Using Any DDM

We have focused on finding the value of a security using assumptions for dividends, required rates of return, and expected growth rates. Given current price and all inputs to a DDM except for the required return, an IRR can be calculated. Such an IRR has been used as a required return estimate (although reusing it in a DDM is not appropriate because it risks circularity). This IRR can also be interpreted as the expected return on the issue implied by the market price—essentially, an efficient market expected return. In the following discussion, keep in mind that if price does not equal intrinsic value, the expected return will need to be adjusted to reflect the additional component of return that accrues when the mispricing is corrected, as discussed earlier.

In some cases, finding the IRR is very easy. In the Gordon growth model, $r = D_1/P_0 + g$. The required return estimate is the dividend yield plus the expected dividend growth rate. For a security with a current price of $10, an expected dividend of $0.50, and expected growth of 8%, the required return estimate is 13%.

For the H-model, the expected rate of return can be derived as

$$r = \left(\frac{D_0}{P_0}\right) \left[(1 + g_L) + H (g_S - g_L) \right] + g_L. \tag{21}$$

When the short- and long-term growth rates are the same, this model reduces to the Gordon growth model. For a security with a current dividend of $1, a current price of $20, and an expected short-term growth rate of 10% declining over 10 years ($H = 5$) to 6%, the expected rate of return would be

$$r = \left(\frac{\$1}{\$20}\right) \left[(1 + 0.06) + 5 (0.10 - 0.06) \right] + 0.06 = 12.3\%.$$

For multistage models and spreadsheet models, finding a single equation for the rate of return can be more difficult. The process generally used is similar to that of finding the IRR for a series of varying cash flows. Using a computer or trial and error, the analyst must find the rate of return such that the present value of future expected dividends equals the current stock price.

EXAMPLE 21

Finding the Expected Rate of Return for Varying Expected Dividends

1. An analyst expects Johnson & Johnson's (NYSE: JNJ)) dividend of $3.60 for 2019 to grow by 7.0% for six years and then grow by 5% into perpetuity. A recent price for JNJ as of early 2019 is $136.61. What is the IRR on an investment in JNJ's stock?

In estimating the expected rate of return with a two-stage model, using trial and error is one approach. Having a good initial approximation is helpful. In this case, the expected rate of return formula from the Gordon growth model and JNJ's long-term growth rate can be used to find a first approximation: $r = (\$3.60 \times 1.07)/\$136.61 + 0.05 = 7.8\%$. Because the estimated growth rate for the first six years is higher than the long-term growth rate of 5%, the implied estimated rate of return must be above 7.8%. Exhibit 11 shows the value estimate of JNJ's shares for two discount rates, 8% and 8.5%.

Exhibit 11: Estimation of Required Return: Johnson & Johnson			
Time	D_t	Present Value of D_t and V_6 at $r = 8\%$	Present Value of D_t and V_6 at $r = 8.5\%$
1	$3.8520	$3.5667	$3.5502
2	$4.1216	$3.5336	$3.5011
3	$4.4101	$3.5009	$3.4527
4	$4.7188	$3.4685	$3.4050
5	$5.0491	$3.4363	$3.3579
6	$5.4025	$3.4045	$3.3114
7	$5.6726		
Subtotal 1	(t = 1 to 6)	$20.91	$20.58
Subtotal 2	(t = 7 to ∞)	$119.16	$99.34
Total		$140.07	$119.92
Market Price		$136.61	$136.61

In the exhibit, the amount labeled "Subtotal 1" is the present value of the expected dividends for Years 1 through 6. The amount labeled "Subtotal 2" is the present value of the terminal value, $V_6/(1 + r)^6 = [D_7/(r - g)]/(1 + r)^6$. For r = 8%, that present value is $[5.6726/(0.08 - 0.05)]/(1.08)^6 = \$119.16$. The present value for other values of r is found similarly.

Using 8.0% as the discount rate, the value estimate for JNJ is $140.07, which is about 2.5% larger than JNJ's market price of $136.61. This fact indicates that the IRR is greater than 8%. With an 8.5% discount rate, the present value of $119.92 is significantly less than the market price. Thus, the IRR is slightly more than 8%. The IRR can be determined to be 8.08% using a spreadsheet. For example, using the Goal Seek function of Excel: In the "set cell" parameter, enter the reference for the cell that contains the Total present value; in the "by changing" parameter, enter the current price as an amount; and in the "by changing cell" parameter, enter the reference for the cell that contains the discount rate.

Multistage DDM: Concluding Remarks

Multistage dividend discount models can accommodate a variety of patterns of future streams of expected dividends.

In general, multistage DDMs make stylized assumptions about growth based on a lifecycle view of business. The first stage of a multistage DDM frequently incorporates analysts' individual earnings and dividend forecasts for the next two to five years (sometimes longer). The final stage is often modeled using the Gordon growth model based on an assumption of the company's long-run sustainable growth rate. In the case of the H-model, the transition to the mature growth phase happens smoothly during the first stage. In the case of the standard two-stage model, the growth rate typically transitions immediately to mature growth rate in the second period. In three-stage models, the middle stage is a stage of transition. Using a spreadsheet, an analyst can model an almost limitless variety of cash flow patterns.

Multistage DDMs have several limitations. Often, the present value of the terminal stage represents more than three-quarters of the total value of shares. Terminal value can be very sensitive to the growth and required return assumptions. Furthermore, technological innovation can make the lifecycle model a crude representation.

9   THE FINANCIAL DETERMINANTS OF GROWTH RATES

☐ | calculate and interpret the sustainable growth rate of a company and demonstrate the use of DuPont analysis to estimate a company's sustainable growth rate

In a number of examples earlier, we have implicitly used the relationship that the dividend growth rate (*g*) equals the earning retention ratio (*b*) multiplied by the return on equity (ROE). In this section, we explain this relationship and show how it can be combined with a method of analyzing return on equity, called DuPont analysis, as a simple tool for forecasting dividend growth rates.

Sustainable Growth Rate

We define the **sustainable growth rate** as the rate of dividend (and earnings) growth that can be sustained for a given level of return on equity, assuming that the capital structure is constant through time and that additional common stock is not issued. The reason for studying this concept is that it can help in estimating either 1) the stable growth rate in a Gordon growth model valuation or 2) the mature growth rate in a multistage DDM in which the Gordon growth formula is used to find the terminal value of the stock.

The expression to calculate the sustainable growth rate is

$$g = b \times \text{ROE},\qquad(22)$$

where

g = dividend growth rate

b = earnings retention rate (1 − Dividend payout ratio)

ROE = return on equity

More precisely, in Equation 22 the retention rate should be multiplied by the rate of return expected to be earned on new investment. Analysts commonly assume that the rate of return is well approximated by the return on equity, as shown in Equation 22; however, whether that is actually the case should be investigated by the analyst on a case-by-case basis.

Example 22 illustrates the fact that growth in shareholders' equity is driven by reinvested earnings alone (no new issues of equity and debt growing at the rate *g*). Note that in scenarios in which debt is growing at *g*, the capital structure is constant. If the capital structure is not constant, ROE will not be constant in general because ROE depends on leverage.

EXAMPLE 22

Example Showing $g = b \times$ ROE

Suppose that a company's ROE is 25% and its retention rate is 60%. According to the expression for the sustainable growth rate, the dividends should grow at $g = b \times$ ROE $= 0.60 \times 25\% = 15\%$.

To demonstrate the working of the expression, suppose that, in the year just ended, a company began with shareholders' equity of $1,000,000, earned $250,000 net income, and paid dividends of $100,000. The company begins the next year with $1,000,000 + 0.60($250,000) = $1,000,000 + $150,000 = $1,150,000 of shareholders' equity. No additions to equity are made from the sale of additional shares.

If the company again earns 25% on equity, net income will be $0.25 \times \$1,150,000$ = $287,500, which is a $287,500 − $250,000 = $37,500 or a $37,500/$250,000 = 0.15% increase from the prior year level. The company retains 60% of earnings, 60% × $287,500 = $172,500, and pays out the other 40%, 40% × $287,500 = $115,000 as dividends. Dividends for the company grew from $100,000 to $115,000, which is exactly a 15% growth rate. With the company continuing to earn 25% each year on the 60% of earnings that is reinvested in the company, dividends would continue to grow at 15%.

Equation 22 implies that the higher the return on equity, the higher the dividend growth rate, all else constant. That relation appears to be reliable. Another implication of the expression is that the lower (higher) the earnings retention ratio, the lower (higher) the growth rate in dividends, holding all else constant; this relationship has been called *the dividend displacement of earnings*. Of course, all else may not be equal—the return on reinvested earnings may not be constant at different levels of investment, or companies with changing future growth prospects may change their dividend policy. Furthermore, research has shown that dividend-paying companies had higher future growth rates during the period studied, indicating that caution is appropriate in assuming that dividends displace earnings (Arnott and Asness 2003; ap Gwilym, Seaton, Suddason, and Thomas 2006; Zhou and Ruland 2006).

A practical logic for defining *sustainable* in terms of growth through internally generated funds (retained earnings) is that external equity (secondary issues of stock) is considerably more costly than internal equity (reinvested earnings), for several reasons including the investment banker fees associated with secondary equity issues. In general, continuous issuance of new stock is not a practical funding alternative for companies. Growth of capital through issuance of new debt, however, can sometimes be sustained for considerable periods. Further, if a company manages its capital structure to a target percentage of debt to total capital (debt and common stock), it will need to issue debt to maintain that percentage as equity grows through reinvested earnings. (This approach is one of a variety of observed capital structure policies.) In addition, the earnings retention ratio nearly always shows year-to-year variation in actual companies. For example, earnings may have transitory components that management does not want to reflect in dividends. The analyst may thus observe actual dividend growth rates straying from the growth rates predicted by Equation 22 because of these effects, even when her input estimates are unbiased. Nevertheless, the equation can be useful as a simple expression for approximating the average rate at which dividends can grow over a long horizon.

Dividend Growth Rate, Retention Rate, and ROE Analysis

Thus far we have seen that a company's sustainable growth, as defined earlier, is a function of its ability to generate return on equity (which depends on investment opportunities) and its retention rate. We now expand this model by examining what drives ROE. Remember that ROE is the return (net income) generated on the equity invested in the company:

$$\text{ROE} = \frac{\text{Net income}}{\text{Shareholders' equity}} \tag{23}$$

If a company has a ROE of 15%, it generates $15 of net income for every $100 invested in stockholders' equity. For purposes of analyzing ROE, it can be related to several other financial ratios. For example, ROE can be related to return on assets (ROA) and the extent of financial leverage (equity multiplier):

$$\text{ROE} = \frac{\text{Net income}}{\text{Total assets}} \times \frac{\text{Total assets}}{\text{Shareholders' equity}} \tag{24}$$

Therefore, a company can increase its ROE either by increasing ROA or through the use of leverage (assuming the company can borrow at a rate lower than it earns on its assets).

This model can be expanded further by breaking ROA into two components, profit margin and turnover (efficiency):

$$\text{ROE} = \frac{\text{Net income}}{\text{Sales}} \times \frac{\text{Sales}}{\text{Total assets}} \times \frac{\text{Total assets}}{\text{Shareholders' equity}} \tag{25}$$

The first term is the company's profit margin. A higher profit margin will result in a higher ROE. The second term measures total asset turnover, which is the company's efficiency. A turnover of one indicates that a company generates $1 in sales for every $1 invested in assets. A higher turnover will result in higher ROE. The last term is the equity multiplier, which measures the extent of leverage, as noted earlier. This relationship is widely known as the DuPont model or analysis of ROE. Although ROE can be analyzed further using a five-way analysis, the three-way analysis will provide insight into the determinants of ROE that are pertinent to our understanding of the growth rate. By combining Equation 22 and Equation 25, we can see that the dividend growth rate is equal to the retention rate multiplied by ROE:

$$g = \frac{\text{Net income} - \text{Dividends}}{\text{Net income}} \times \frac{\text{Net income}}{\text{Sales}} \\ \times \frac{\text{Sales}}{\text{Total assets}} \times \frac{\text{Total assets}}{\text{Shareholders' equity}} \tag{26}$$

This expansion of the sustainable growth expression has been called the PRAT model. Growth is a function of profit margin (P), retention rate (R), asset turnover (A), and financial leverage (T). The profit margin and asset turnover determine ROA. The other two factors, the retention rate and financial leverage, reflect the company's financial policies. So, the growth rate in dividends can be viewed as determined by the company's ROA and financial policies. Analysts may use Equation 26 to forecast a company's dividend growth rate in the mature growth phase.

Theoretically, the sustainable growth rate expression and this expansion of it based on the DuPont decomposition of ROE hold exactly only when ROE is calculated using beginning-of-period shareholders' equity, as illustrated in Example 22. Such calculation assumes that retained earnings are not available for reinvestment until the end of the period. Analysts and financial databases more frequently prefer to use average total assets in calculating ROE and, practically, DuPont analysis is frequently performed using that definition. The following example illustrates the logic behind this equation.

EXAMPLE 23

ROA, Financial Policies, and the Dividend Growth Rate

Baggai Enterprises (a fictional company) has an ROA of 10%, retains 30% of earnings, and has an equity multiplier of 1.25. Mondale Enterprises also has an ROA of 10%, but it retains two-thirds of earnings and has an equity multiplier of 2.00.

1. What are the sustainable dividend growth rates for (A) Baggai Enterprises and (B) Mondale Enterprises?

Solution:

   A. Baggai's dividend growth rate should be $g = 0.30 \times 10\% \times 1.25 = 3.75\%$.
   B. Mondale's dividend growth rate should be $g = (2/3) \times 10\% \times 2.00 = 13.33\%$.

2. Identify the drivers of the difference in the sustainable growth rates of Baggai Enterprises and Mondale Enterprises.

Solution:

Because Mondale has the higher retention rate and higher financial leverage, its dividend growth rate is much higher.

If growth is being forecast for the next five years, an analyst should use the expectations of the four factors driving growth during this five-year period. If growth is being forecast into perpetuity, an analyst should use very long-term forecasts for these variables.

To illustrate the calculation and implications of the sustainable growth rate using the expression for ROE given by the DuPont formula, assume the growth rate is $g = b \times \text{ROE} = 0.60 (15\%) = 9\%$. The ROE of 15% was based on a profit margin of 5%, an asset turnover of 2.0, and an equity multiplier of 1.5. Given fixed ratios of sales-to-assets and assets-to-equity, sales, assets, and debt will also be growing at 9%. Because dividends are fixed at 40% of income, dividends will grow at the same rate as income, or 9%. If the company increased dividends faster than 9%, this growth rate would not be sustainable using internally generated funds. Earning retentions would be reduced, and the company would be unable to finance the assets required for sales growth without external financing.

An analyst should be careful in projecting historical financial ratios into the future when using this analysis. Although a company may have grown at 25% a year for the last five years, this rate of growth is probably not sustainable indefinitely. Abnormally high ROEs, which may have driven that growth, are unlikely to persist indefinitely because of competitive forces and possibly other reasons, such as adverse changes in technology or demand. In the following example, an above-average terminal growth rate is plausibly forecasted because the company has positioned itself in businesses that may have relatively high margins on an ongoing basis.

EXAMPLE 24

Forecasting Growth with the PRAT Formula

1. An analyst is estimating a mature-phase growth rate for International Business Machines (NYSE: IBM) to use in her multistage dividend discount model. The company's ROE for 2018 was around 52%, and over the past 10

years, IBM's retention rate has averaged around 62%. Applying the formula for sustainable growth rate that was described previously [namely, $g = (b$ in the mature phase) $\times$ (ROE in the mature phase] would yield an unrealistic long-term growth rate, particularly given the decline in the company's sales and earnings over the past several years. Further, IBM's annual investment in property, plant, and equipment has also declined—from \$3.7 billion in 2014 to \$3.4 billion in 2018.

The analyst therefore decides to estimate the company's growth rate using the DuPont decomposition and PRAT formula. A decomposition of IBM's ROE for the past 10 years is shown in Exhibit 12. In addition, the exhibit shows a benchmark based on the median values of ROE components for a group of firms with the same two-digit SIC code as IBM.

Exhibit 12: ROE Decomposition for IBM

Year	ROE	Profit Margin	Asset Turnover	Financial Leverage
2018	52.0%	11.0%	0.65	7.35
2017	32.7%	7.3%	0.63	7.12
2016	65.1%	14.9%	0.68	6.44
2015	92.5%	16.1%	0.74	7.75
2014	101.3%	13.0%	0.79	9.90
2013	72.3%	16.5%	0.79	5.54
2012	88.0%	15.9%	0.88	6.32
2011	78.7%	14.8%	0.92	5.78
2010	64.4%	14.9%	0.88	4.92
2009	59.3%	14.0%	0.88	4.82

Benchmark Average

ROE	Profit Margin	Asset Turnover	Financial Leverage
13.5%	10.5%	0.62	2.07

IBM's ROE is much higher than the benchmark average, primarily because of much higher financial leverage. Its profit margin and asset turnover do not differ significantly from the benchmark average.

Suppose the analyst believes that IBM's profit margin and asset turnover will be roughly the same as the benchmark average. The analyst also believes that capital investment will continue to decline in IBM's maturity stage, and cash flow that was previously used for investment will be used to retire debt and pay dividends. The analyst forecasts a financial leverage ratio of 2.0, similar to the industry benchmark. The analyst also sees the dividend payout ratio continuing its recent rise and ultimately reaching a level of 50%.

Based on a profit margin of 10.5%, an asset turnover ratio of 0.62, and financial leverage of 2.0, a forecast of ROE in the maturity phase is (10.5%)(0.62)

(2.0) = 13.0%. Therefore, based on this analysis, the estimate of the sustainable growth rate for IBM would be $g = (0.50)(13.0\%) = 6.5\%$.

FINANCIAL MODELS AND DIVIDENDS   10

☐ | explain the use of spreadsheet modeling to forecast dividends and to value common shares

Analysts can also forecast dividends by building more-complex models of the company's total operating and financial environment. The company's ability to pay dividends in the future can be predicted using one of these models. The following example shows the dividends that a highly profitable and rapidly growing company can pay when its growth rates and profit margins decline because of increasing competition over time.

EXAMPLE 25

A Model for Forecasting Dividends Using More-Detailed Assumptions

1. An analyst is preparing a forecast of dividends for Hoshino Distributors (a fictional company) for the next five years. He uses a model with the following assumptions:

   - Sales are $100 million in Year 1. They grow by 20% in Year 2, 15% in Year 3, and 10% in Years 4 and 5.
   - Operating profits (earnings before interest and taxes, or EBIT) are 20% of sales in Years 1 and 2, 18% of sales in Year 3, and 16% of sales in Years 4 and 5.
   - Interest expenses are 10% of total debt for the current year.
   - The income tax rate is 40%.
   - Hoshino pays out 20% of earnings in dividends in Years 1 and 2, 30% in Year 3, 40% in Year 4, and 50% in Year 5.
   - Retained earnings are added to equity in the next year.
   - Total assets are 80% of the current year's sales in all years.
   - In Year 1, debt is $40 million and shareholders' equity is $40 million. Debt equals total assets minus shareholders' equity. Shareholders' equity will equal the previous year's shareholders' equity plus the addition to retained earnings from the previous year.
   - Hoshino has 4 million shares outstanding.
   - The required return on equity is 15%.
   - The value of the company at the end of Year 5 is expected to be 10.0 times earnings.

   The analyst wants to estimate the current value per share of Hoshino. Exhibit 13 adheres to the foregoing modeling assumptions. Total dividends and earnings are found at the bottom of the income statement.

Exhibit 13: Hoshino Distributors Pro Forma Financial Statements (in millions)

	Year 1	Year 2	Year 3	Year 4	Year 5
Income statement					
Sales	$100.00	$120.00	$138.00	$151.80	$166.98
EBIT	20.00	24.00	24.84	24.29	26.72
Interest	4.00	4.83	5.35	5.64	6.18
EBT	16.00	19.17	19.49	18.65	20.54
Taxes	6.40	7.67	7.80	7.46	8.22
Net income	9.60	11.50	11.69	11.19	12.32
Dividends	1.92	2.30	3.51	4.48	6.16
Balance sheet					
Total assets	$80.00	$96.00	$110.40	$121.44	$133.58
Total debt	40.00	48.32	53.52	56.38	61.81
Equity	40.00	47.68	56.88	65.06	71.77

Dividing the total dividends by the number of outstanding shares gives the dividend per share for each year shown in the following table. The present value of each dividend, discounted at 15%, is also shown.

	Year 1	Year 2	Year 3	Year 4	Year 5	Total
DPS	$0.480	$0.575	$0.877	$1.120	$1.540	$4.59
PV	0.417	0.435	0.577	0.640	0.766	2.84

The earnings per share in Year 5 are $12.32 million divided by 4 million shares, or $3.08 per share. Given a P/E of 10, the market price in Year 5 is predicted to be $30.80. Discounted at 15%, the required return on equity by assumption, the present value of this price is $15.31. Adding the present values of the five dividends, which sum to $2.84, gives a total stock value today of $18.15 per share.

SUMMARY

We have provided an overview of DCF models of valuation, discussed the estimation of a stock's required rate of return, and presented in detail the dividend discount model.

- In DCF models, the value of any asset is the present value of its (expected) future cash flows

$$V_0 = \sum_{t=1}^{n} \frac{CF_t}{(1 + r)^t},$$

  where V_0 is the value of the asset as of $t = 0$ (today), CF_t is the (expected) cash flow at time t, and r is the discount rate or required rate of return. For infinitely lived assets such as common stocks, n runs to infinity.

- Several alternative streams of expected cash flows can be used to value equities, including dividends, free cash flow, and residual income. A discounted dividend approach is most suitable for dividend-paying stocks in which the company has a discernible dividend policy that has an understandable relationship to the company's profitability and the investor has a non-control (minority ownership) perspective.

- The free cash flow approach (FCFF or FCFE) might be appropriate when the company does not pay dividends, dividends differ substantially from FCFE, free cash flows align with profitability, or the investor takes a control (majority ownership) perspective.

- The residual income approach can be useful when the company does not pay dividends (as an alternative to a FCF approach) or free cash flow is negative.

- The DDM with a single holding period gives stock value as

$$V_0 = \frac{D_1}{(1+r)^1} + \frac{P_1}{(1+r)^1} = \frac{D_1 + P_1}{(1+r)^1},$$

  where D_1 is the expected dividend at Time 1 and V_0 is the stock's (expected) value at Time 0. Assuming that V_0 is equal to today's market price, P_0, the expected holding-period return is

$$r = \frac{D_1 + P_1}{P_0} - 1 = \frac{D_1}{P_0} + \frac{P_1 - P_0}{P_0}.$$

- The expression for the DDM for any given finite holding period n and the general expression for the DDM are, respectively,

$$V_0 = \sum_{t=1}^{n} \frac{D_t}{(1+r)^t} + \frac{P_n}{(1+r)^n} \text{ and } V_0 = \sum_{t=1}^{\infty} \frac{D_t}{(1+r)^t}.$$

- There are two main approaches to the problem of forecasting dividends. First, an analyst can assign the entire stream of expected future dividends to one of several stylized growth patterns. Second, an analyst can forecast a finite number of dividends individually up to a terminal point and value the remaining dividends either by assigning them to a stylized growth pattern or by forecasting share price as of the terminal point of the dividend forecasts.

- The Gordon growth model assumes that dividends grow at a constant rate g forever, so that $D_t = D_{t-1}(1 + g)$. The dividend stream in the Gordon growth model has a value of

$$V_0 = \frac{D_0(1+g)}{r-g}, \text{ or } V_0 = \frac{D_1}{r-g} \text{ where } r > g.$$

- The value of non-callable fixed-rate perpetual preferred stock is $V_0 = D/r$, where D is the stock's (constant) annual dividend.

- Assuming that price equals value, the Gordon growth model estimate of a stock's expected rate of return is

$$r = \frac{D_0(1+g)}{P_0} + g = \frac{D_1}{P_0} + g.$$

- Given an estimate of the next-period dividend and the stock's required rate of return, the Gordon growth model can be used to estimate the dividend growth rate implied by the current market price (making a constant growth rate assumption).

- The present value of growth opportunities is the part of a stock's total value, V_0, that comes from profitable future growth opportunities in contrast to the value associated with assets already in place. The relationship is $V_0 = E_1/r + \text{PVGO}$, where E_1/r is defined as the no-growth value per share.

- The leading price-to-earnings ratio (P_0/E_1) and the trailing price-to-earnings ratio (P_0/E_0) can be expressed in terms of the Gordon growth model as, respectively,

$$\frac{P_0}{E_1} = \frac{D_1/E_1}{r-g} = \frac{1-b}{r-g} \text{ and } \frac{P_0}{E_0} = \frac{D_0(1+g)/E_0}{r-g} = \frac{(1-b)(1+g)}{r-g}.$$

  The foregoing expressions give a stock's justified price-to-earnings ratio based on forecasts of fundamentals (given that the Gordon growth model is appropriate).

- The Gordon growth model may be useful for valuing broad-based equity indexes and the stock of businesses with earnings that are expected to grow at a stable rate comparable to or lower than the economy's nominal growth rate.

- Gordon growth model values are very sensitive to the assumed growth rate and required rate of return.

- For many companies, growth falls into phases. In the growth phase, a company enjoys an abnormally high growth rate in earnings per share, called supernormal growth. In the transition phase, earnings growth slows. In the mature phase, the company reaches an equilibrium in which such factors as earnings growth and the return on equity stabilize at levels that can be sustained long term. Analysts often apply multistage DCF models to value the stock of a company with multistage growth prospects.

- The two-stage dividend discount model assumes different growth rates in Stage 1 and Stage 2:

$$V_0 = \sum_{t=1}^{n} \frac{D_0(1+g_S)^t}{(1+r)^t} + \frac{D_0(1+g_S)^n(1+g_L)}{(1+r)^n(r-g_L)},$$

  where g_S is the expected dividend growth rate in the first period and g_L is the expected growth rate in the second period.

- The terminal stock value, V_n, is sometimes found with the Gordon growth model or with some other method, such as applying a P/E multiplier to forecasted EPS as of the terminal date.

- The H-model assumes that the dividend growth rate declines linearly from a high supernormal rate to the normal growth rate during Stage 1 and then grows at a constant normal growth rate thereafter:

$$V_0 = \frac{D_0(1+g_L)}{r-g_L} + \frac{D_0 H(g_S-g_L)}{r-g_L} = \frac{D_0(1+g_L) + D_0 H(g_S-g_L)}{r-g_L}.$$

- There are two basic three-stage models. In one version, the growth rate in the middle stage is constant. In the second version, the growth rate declines linearly in Stage 2 and becomes constant and normal in Stage 3.

- In addition to valuing equities, the IRR of a DDM, assuming assets are correctly priced in the marketplace, has been used to estimate required returns. For simpler models (such as the one-period model, the Gordon growth model, and the H-model), well-known formulas may be used to calculate these rates of return. For many dividend streams, however, the rate of return must be found by trial and error, producing a discount rate that equates the present value of the forecasted dividend stream to the current market price.

- Multistage DDM models can accommodate a wide variety of patterns of expected dividends. Even though such models may use stylized assumptions about growth, they can provide useful approximations.

- Dividend growth rates can be obtained from analyst forecasts, statistical forecasting models, or company fundamentals. The sustainable growth rate depends on the ROE and the earnings retention rate, b: $g = b \times$ ROE. This expression can be expanded further, using the DuPont formula, as

$$g = \frac{\text{Net income} - \text{Dividends}}{\text{Net income}} \times \frac{\text{Net income}}{\text{Sales}}$$
$$\times \frac{\text{Sales}}{\text{Total assets}} \times \frac{\text{Total assets}}{\text{Shareholders' equity}}.$$

REFERENCES

ap Gwilym, Owain, James Seaton, Karina Suddason, Stephen Thomas. 2006. "International Evidence on the Payout Ratio, Earnings, Dividends, and Returns." Financial Analysts Journal62 (1): 36–53. 10.2469/faj.v62.n1.4057

Arnott, Robert D., Clifford S. Asness. 2003. "Surprise! Higher Dividends = Higher Earnings Growth." Financial Analysts Journal59 (1): 70–87. 10.2469/faj.v59.n1.2504

Denis, David J., Igor Osobov. 2008. "Why Do Firms Pay Dividends? International Evidence on the Determinants of Dividend Policy." Journal of Financial Economics89 (1): 62–82. 10.1016/j.jfineco.2007.06.006

Fama, Eugene F., Kenneth R. French. 2001. "Disappearing Dividends: Changing Firm Characteristics or Lower Propensity to Pay?" Journal of Financial Economics60 (1): 3–43. 10.1016/S0304-405X(01)00038-1

Fuller, Russell J., Chi-Cheng Hsia. 1984. "A Simplified Common Stock Valuation Model." Financial Analysts Journal40 (5): 49–56. 10.2469/faj.v40.n5.49

Gordon, Myron J. 1962. The Investment, Financing, and Valuation of the Corporation. Homeward, IL: Richard D. Irwin.

Gordon, Myron J., Eli Shapiro. 1956. "Capital Equipment Analysis: The Required Rate of Profit." Management Science3 (1): 102–10. 10.1287/mnsc.3.1.102

Grullon, Gustavo, Bradley Paye, Shane Underwood, James P. Weston. 2011. "Has the Propensity to Pay Out Declined?" Journal of Financial and Quantitative Analysis46 (1): 1–24. 10.1017/S0022109010000633

He, Wen, Lilian Ng, Nataliya Zaiats, Bohui Zhang. 2017. "Dividend Policy and Earnings Management across Countries." Journal of Corporate Finance42:267–86. 10.1016/j.jcorpfin.2016.11.014

Julio, Brandon, David L. Ikenberry. 2004. "Reappearing Dividends." Journal of Applied Corporate Finance16 (4): 89–100. 10.1111/j.1745-6622.2004.tb00676.x

Skinner, Douglas J. 2008. "The Evolving Relation between Earnings, Dividends, and Stock Repurchases." Journal of Financial Economics87 (3): 582–609. 10.1016/j.jfineco.2007.05.003

Stowe, J., J Pinto, T. Robinson. Equity Valuation: A Survey of Professional Practice", October 2018, Review of Financial Economics.

von Eije, J. Henk, William L. Megginson. 2008. "Dividends and Share Repurchases in the European Union." Journal of Financial Economics89:347–74. 10.1016/j.jfineco.2007.11.002

Williams, John Burr. 1938. The Theory of Investment Value. Cambridge, MA: Harvard University Press.

Zhou, Ping, William Ruland. 2006. "Dividend Payout and Future Earnings Growth." Financial Analysts Journal62 (3): 58–69. 10.2469/faj.v62.n3.4157

PRACTICE PROBLEMS

The following information relates to questions 1-6

Brian Dobson, an analyst at UK-based globally diversified equity mutual fund, has been assigned the task of estimating a fair value of the common stock of Charmed Energy. Dobson is aware of several approaches that could be used for this purpose. After carefully considering the characteristics of the company and its competitors, he believes Charmed will have extraordinary growth for the next few years and normal growth thereafter. So, he has concluded that a two-stage DDM is the most appropriate for valuing the stock.

Charmed pays semi-annual dividends. The total dividends during 2016, 2017, and 2018 have been C$0.114, C$0.15, and C$0.175, respectively. These imply a growth rate of 32% in 2017 and 17% in 2018. Dobson believes that the growth rate will be 14% in the next year. He has estimated that the first stage will include the next eight years.

Dobson is using the CAPM to estimate the required return on equity for Charmed. He has estimated that the company's beta, as measured against the S&P/TSX Composite Index (formerly TSE 300 Composite Index), is 0.84. The Canadian risk-free rate, as measured by the annual yield on the 10-year government bond, is 4.1%. The equity risk premium for the Canadian market is estimated at 5.5%. Based on these data, Dobson has estimated that the required return on Charmed Energy's stock is 0.041 + 0.84(0.055) = 0.0872, or 8.72%. Dobson is doing the analysis in January 2019, and the stock price at that time is C$17.

Dobson realizes that even within the two-stage DDM, there could be some variations in the approach. He would like to explore how these variations affect the stock's valuation. Specifically, he wants to estimate the value of the stock for each of the following approaches separately.

i.   The dividend growth rate will be 14% throughout the first stage of eight years. The dividend growth rate thereafter will be 7%.

ii.   Instead of using the estimated stable growth rate of 7% in the second stage, Dobson wants to use his estimate that eight years later, Charmed Energy's stock will be worth 17 times its earnings per share (trailing P/E of 17). He expects that the earnings retention ratio at that time will be 0.70.

iii. In contrast to the first approach, in which the growth rate declines abruptly from 14% in the eighth year to 7% in the ninth, the growth rate would decline linearly from 14% in the first year to 7% in the ninth.

1. What is the terminal value of the stock based on the first approach?

    A. C$17.65.

    B. C$31.06.

    C. C$33.09.

2. In the first approach, what proportion of the stock's total value is represented by

the value of second stage?

A. 0.10.

B. 0.52.

C. 0.90.

3. What is the stock's terminal value based on the second approach (earnings multiple)?

    A. C$12.12.

    B. C$28.29.

    C. C$33.09.

4. What is the stock's current value based on the second approach?

    A. C$16.24.

    B. C$17.65.

    C. C$28.29.

5. Based on the third approach (the H-model), the stock is:

    A. undervalued.

    B. fairly valued.

    C. overvalued.

6. Dobson is wondering what the consequences would be if the duration of the first stage was assumed to be 11 years instead of 8, with all the other assumptions and estimates remaining the same. Considering this change, which of the following is true?

    A. In the second approach, the proportion of the total value of the stock represented by the second stage would not change.

    B. The total value estimated using the third approach would increase.

    C. Using this new assumption and the first approach will lead Dobson to conclude that the stock is overvalued.

The following information relates to questions 7-15

Gianna Peters is an investment analyst who focuses on dividend-paying stocks. Peters uses a DCF approach to stock selection. She is meeting with her staff to evaluate portfolio holdings based on a bottom-up screening of stocks listed in the United States and Canada. Peters and her staff begin by reviewing the characteristics of the following portfolio candidates.

Company ABC

A Canadian company in the consumer staples sector with a required rate of return of 7.35%. Recent media reports suggest that ABC might be a takeover candidate. Peters and her team estimate that if the incumbent Canadian prime minister's party retains its power, the company's current annual dividend of C$0.65 per share will grow 12% a year for the next four years and then stabilize at a 3.5% growth rate a year indefinitely. If a new government takes office in Canada, however, then the team estimates that ABC will likely not experience the elevated 12% short-run growth because of new regulatory and tax changes, and instead it will grow by 3.5% indefinitely.

Company XYZ

A mid-sized US company in the utilities sector with a required rate of return of 10%. Peters and her team believe that because of a recent restructuring, the company is unlikely to pay dividends for the next three years. The team expects XYZ to pay an annual dividend of US$1.72 per share beginning four years from now, however. Thereafter, the dividend is expected to grow indefinitely at 4% even though the current price implies a growth rate of 6% during this same period.

Company JZY

A large US company in the telecom sector with a required rate of return of 8%. The stock is currently trading at US$32.76 per share with an implied earnings growth rate of 5.3%. Peters believes that because JZY is mature and has a stable capital structure, the company will grow at its sustainable growth rate. Over the past 10 years, the company's return on equity (ROE) has averaged 8.17% and its payout ratio has averaged 40%. Recently, the company paid an annual dividend of US$0.84 per share.

Peters asks a newly hired analyst, Kurt Thomas, to comment on the evaluation approach for these three stocks. Thomas makes the following statements:

1. A free cash flow valuation model would not be appropriate to evaluate Company ABC if the firm becomes a takeover candidate.

2. A dividend discount model cannot be applied to Company XYZ if dividends are suspended for a few years.

3. A dividend discount model is suitable for evaluating the stock of Company JZY because of the historically consistent payout ratio.

Peters then asks the team to examine the growth opportunities of three Canadian stocks currently held in the portfolio. These stocks are listed in Exhibit 1. Peters believes that the stocks are fairly valued.

Exhibit 1: Selected Stock Characteristics			
Stock	Required Rate of Return	Next Year's Forecasted EPS (C$)	Current Price per Share (C$)
ABTD	10.5%	7.30	80.00
BKKQ	8.0%	2.12	39.00
CPMN	12.0%	1.90	27.39

7. Which of the following statements made by Thomas is *correct*?

   A. Statement 1

   B. Statement 2

   C. Statement 3

8. Assuming the incumbent government retains office in Canada, Peters and her

team estimate that the current value of Company ABC stock would be *closest* to:

A. C$22.18.

B. C$23.60.

C. C$25.30.

9. Assuming a new government takes office in Canada, Peters and her team estimate that the current intrinsic value of Company ABC would be *closest* to:

A. C$9.15.

B. C$16.88.

C. C$17.47.

10. Assume that a new government takes office in Canada. If Peters and her team use the Gordon growth model and assume that Company ABC stock is fairly valued, then which of the following would *most likely* be true?

A. The total return of ABC stock will be 10.85%.

B. The dividend yield of ABC stock will be 3.85%.

C. The stock price of ABC will grow at 7.35% annually.

11. If the team uses the dividend discount model, the current intrinsic value of Company XYZ stock would be *closest to*:

A. US$19.58.

B. US$20.36.

C. US$21.54.

12. The dividend growth rate implied in the stock price of Company XYZ suggests that XYZ's stock price is *most likely*:

A. undervalued.

B. fairly valued.

C. overvalued.

13. Based on the relationship between the implied growth rate and the sustainable growth rate, Peters' team should conclude that Company JZY's stock price is *most likely*:

A. undervalued.

B. fairly valued.

C. overvalued.

14. Based on Exhibit 1, the stock with the largest present value of growth opportunities (PVGO) is:

A. ABTD.

B. BKKQ.

C. CPMN.

15. Based on Exhibit 1, the growth component of the leading P/E is largest for:

A. ABTD.

B. BKKQ.

C. CPMN.

The following information relates to questions 16-21

Jacob Daniel is the chief investment officer at a US pension fund sponsor, and Steven Rae is an analyst for the pension fund who follows consumer/non-cyclical stocks. At the beginning of 20X9, Daniel asks Rae to value the equity of Tasty Foods Company for its possible inclusion in the list of approved investments. Tasty Foods Company is involved in the production of frozen foods that are sold under its own brand name to retailers.

Rae is considering whether a dividend discount model would be appropriate for valuing Tasty Foods. He has compiled the information in the following table for the company's EPS and DPS during the last five years. The quarterly dividends paid by the company have been added to arrive at the annual dividends. Rae has also computed the dividend payout ratio for each year as DPS/EPS and the growth rates in EPS and DPS.

Year	EPS ($)	DPS ($)	Payout Ratio	Growth in EPS (%)	Growth in DPS (%)
20X8	2.12	0.59	0.278	2.9	3.5
20X7	2.06	0.57	0.277	2.5	5.6
20X6	2.01	0.54	0.269	6.3	5.9
20X5	1.89	0.51	0.270	6.2	6.3
20X4	1.78	0.48	0.270		

Rae notes that the company's EPS has been increasing at an average rate of 4.48% per year. The dividend payout ratio has remained fairly stable, and dividends have increased at an average rate of 5.30%. In view of a history of dividend payments by the company and the understandable relationship dividend policy bears to the company's earnings, Rae concludes that the DDM is appropriate to value the equity of Tasty Foods. Further, he expects the company's moderate growth rate to persist and decides to use the Gordon growth model.

Rae uses the CAPM to compute the return on equity. He uses the annual yield of 4% on the 10-year Treasury bond as the risk-free return. He estimates the expected US equity risk premium, with the S&P 500 Index used as a proxy for the market, to be 6.5% per year. The estimated beta of Tasty Foods against the S&P 500 Index is 1.10. Accordingly, Rae's estimate for the required return on equity for Tasty Foods is 0.04 + 1.10(0.065) = 0.1115, or 11.15%.

Using the past growth rate in dividends of 5.30% as his estimate of the future growth rate in dividends, Rae computes the value of Tasty Foods stock. He shows his analysis to Alex Renteria, his colleague at the pension fund who specializes in the frozen foods industry. Renteria concurs with the valuation approach used by Rae but disagrees with the future growth rate he used. Renteria believes that the stock's current price of $8.42 is the fair value of the stock.

16. Which of the following is *closest* to Rae's estimate of the stock's value?

    A. $10.08.

    B. $10.54.

    C. $10.62.

17. What is the stock's justified trailing P/E based on the stock's value estimated by Rae?

    A. 5.01.

    B. 5.24.

    C. 5.27.

18. Rae considers a security trading within a band of ±10% of his estimate of intrinsic value to be within a "fair value range." By that criterion, the stock of Tasty Foods is:

    A. undervalued.

    B. fairly valued.

    C. overvalued.

19. The beta of Tasty Foods stock of 1.10 that Rae used in computing the required return on equity was based on monthly returns for the last 10 years. If Rae uses daily returns for the last five years, the beta estimate is 1.25. If a beta of 1.25 is used, what would be Rae's estimate of the value of Tasty Foods stock?

    A. $8.64.

    B. $9.10.

    C. $20.13.

20. Renteria has suggested that the market price of Tasty Foods stock is its fair value. What is the implied growth rate of dividends given the stock's market price? Use the required return on equity based on a beta of 1.10.

    A. 3.87%.

    B. 5.30%.

    C. 12.1%.

21. If Renteria is correct that the current price of Tasty Foods stock is its fair value, what is the expected capital gains yield on the stock?

    A. 3.87%.

    B. 4.25%.

    C. 5.30%.

The following information relates to questions 22-28

BJL Financial provides clients with professional investment management services that are tailored to the specific needs of each client. The firm's portfolio manager, Angelique Kwaza, has called a meeting with the senior analyst, Samira Khan, to discuss the quarterly rebalancing of three client portfolios. The valuation model used in the analyses is the discounted dividend model.

- Client 1 has a portfolio with significant exposure to dividend-paying stocks.
- Client 2 is interested in including preferred stock in the portfolio.
- Client 3 has a growth-oriented equity-only portfolio.

Khan has identified two utilities (ABC and XYZ) for possible inclusion in Client 1's portfolio, as shown in Exhibit 1. She uses a discount rate of 7% for both common stocks.

Exhibit 1: Candidate Stocks for Client 1	
Stock	**Company Description**
ABC	▪ ABC is a publicly traded utility with an expected constant growth rate for earnings and dividends of 3.5%.
	▪ The most recent year's dividend payout is 70%. The expected dividend payout in future years is 60%.
	▪ The common stock price is $14.49 per share.
XYZ	▪ XYZ is a publicly traded utility with several unregulated business subsidiaries.
	▪ The company generates 3% growth in dividends and has an annual dividend payout of 80%. No changes in dividend growth or payout are expected.
	▪ The common stock price is $10 per share.
	▪ The current year earnings are $0.45 per share, and next year's earnings are expected to be $0.50 per share.

Kwaza asks Khan to investigate the most appropriate models for valuing utility companies. She tells Khan about the following points mentioned in various research reports on the utilities sector.

Report 1: A resurgence in domestic manufacturing activity will generate long-term growth in earnings and dividends that exceeds the cost of equity.

Report 2: Share repurchases are expected to increase. The report expresses confidence in the forecasts regarding the magnitude and timing of these repurchases.

Report 3: The report forecasts earnings growth of 4.5%. The key growth drivers are increases in population and business creation associated with stable GDP growth of 2.75%.

For Client 2's portfolio, Khan has identified the non-callable perpetual preferred stocks of Standard Company and Main Company.

- The Standard Company's preferred stock pays 2.75% on a par value of $100. Khan believes it to be fairly valued at a market price of $49.60.

- The perpetual preferred stock of Main Company has a par value of $50 per share and pays an annual dividend of 5.5%. Khan estimates a capitalization rate at 6%. The current market price of Main Company preferred stock is $42.

Finally, Khan has identified three stocks, shown in Exhibit 2, as likely candidates for Client 3's portfolio.

Exhibit 2: Candidate Stocks for Client 3	
Stock	**Company Description**
BIOK	- BIOK is a profitable biotech firm that currently pays an annual dividend of $1.20 per share.
	- The current annual dividend growth rate is 15%.
	- Patent protection runs out in eight years, after which dividend growth will likely decline at a steady rate over three years before stabilizing at a mature growth rate.
CCAX	- CCAX builds communication software for state and federal prisons and detention facilities.
	- The company is expected to hold its cash dividends steady at $0.56 per share for six years as it builds out facilities and acquires properties.
	- Dividends are expected to grow at the nominal GDP growth rate after the next six years.
HLTV	- HLTV is a health care equipment and services firm that is expected to maintain a stable dividend payout ratio.
	- Earnings are forecast to grow over the next two years by 27% annually.
	- After that, earnings will likely grow by 12% annually for another 10 years before stabilizing at a mature growth rate.

22. Based on the Gordon growth model, the justified leading P/E for ABC stock is *closest* to:

    A. 17.1.

    B. 17.7.

    C. 20.0.

23. Based on its justified leading P/E and the Gordon growth model, XYZ stock is:

    A. undervalued.

    B. fairly valued.

    C. overvalued.

24. Which sector report *best* describes a situation in which the Gordon growth model could be used to value utility stocks?

    A. Report 1

    B. Report 2

    C. Report 3

25. Based on Khan's estimate of the capitalization rate, Main Company's preferred stock is:

    A. undervalued.

    B. fairly valued.

    C. overvalued.

26. The capitalization rate of the preferred stock of Standard Company is *closest* to:

    A. 2.75%.

    B. 4.96%.

    C. 5.54%.

27. Based on Exhibit 2, which stock can most appropriately be valued using a three-stage DDM with the second and third stages being treated as an H-model?

    A. BIOK

    B. CCAX

    C. HLTV

28. Which of the following models is *most* appropriate for valuing HLTV?

    A. H-model

    B. Three-stage DDM

    C. Gordon growth model

The following information relates to questions 29-38

June Withers is analyzing four stocks in the processed food industry as of 31 December 2019. All stocks pay a dividend at the end of each year.

Ukon Corporation

Withers estimates a required rate of return for Ukon Corporation of 8% and notes that the dividend for 2019 was EUR 2.315 per share. Her first valuation approach is a basic two-stage DDM, with dividends growing at a rate of 5% from 2020 through 2023, after which time dividends will grow at a sustainable rate of 3%. Her second valuation approach is the H-model, assuming that dividend growth of 5% in 2020 declines linearly during the years 2021 through 2023 to the 3% growth rate after 2023. Exhibit 1 summarizes Withers's dividend growth assumptions.

Exhibit 1: Ukon Corporation Dividend Growth Assumptions, by Model

Model	Period	Rate
Two-stage DDM	2020 through 2023	5%
	Beginning 2024	3%
H-model	2020	5%
	2021 through 2023	Declining linearly to 3.5%
	Beginning 2024	3%

Venus Company

Withers has assembled the data on Venus Company in Exhibit 2. After analyzing competitive pressures and financial conditions in the industry, she predicts that Venus Company will lose market share because of new entrants but will stabilize within a few years. The required rate of return for Venus Company is 8%. Beginning with a per-share dividend of USD3.15 in 2019, she develops two scenarios regarding Venus Company's dividend growth. The scenarios, shown in Exhibit 2, are summarized as follows:

- In Scenario 1, the growth rate will fall in a linear manner over the years 2020 through 2023 from 8% to 4%. Using the H-model, Withers calculates a value of USD58.79 per share of Venus Company stock.
- In Scenario 2, the growth rate falls from 8% in 2019 to 6% in 2020 and 2021, to 5% in 2022 and 2023, and then to a sustainable rate of 3% for 2024 and beyond.

Exhibit 2: Venus Company Dividend Growth Scenarios

Scenario	Period	Rate
Scenario 1	2020 through 2023	Declining linearly to 4%
	Beginning 2024	Remaining stable at 4%
Scenario 2	2020 and 2021	6%
	2022 and 2023	5%
	Beginning 2024	Remaining stable at 3%

Wakuni Corporation

Withers evaluates Wakuni Corporation and uses recent financial data from Exhibit 3 to calculate a sustainable growth based on the DuPont model. In addition to this estimate, she performs a sensitivity analysis on the sustainable growth rate whereby the dividend payout ranges from 0% to 10% and the return on equity ranges from 8% to 12%.

Exhibit 3: Selected Data for Wakuni Corporation (JPY billions)

Net income	43,923
Sales	423,474

Total assets, average during year	486,203
Shareholders' equity, beginning of year	397,925
Dividends paid	1,518

Xavier Corporation

In her analysis of the stock of Xavier Corporation, Withers observes that it has a dividend of USD2 per share and a stock price of USD52. Two analyst interns have offered estimates of the company's required rate of return and dividend growth rate, as shown in Exhibit 4.

Exhibit 4: Xavier Corporation Required Rate of Return and Dividend Growth Rates (Estimates)

	Intern 1	Intern 2
Required rate of return	8.3%	7.8%
Growth rate, first four years	5.0%	4.8%
Growth rate, beyond first four years	3.6%	4.0%

29. Based on Exhibit 1, when Withers applies the first valuation approach to Ukon Corporation, the estimated value of the stock at the end of the first stage represents the:

    A. present value of the dividends beyond year 2023.

    B. present value of the dividends for years 2020 through 2023.

    C. sum of the present value of the dividends for 2020 through 2023 and the present value of dividends beyond year 2023.

30. Using her first valuation approach and Exhibit 1, Withers's forecast of the per share stock value of Ukon Corporation at the end of 2019 should be *closest to*:

    A. EUR48.

    B. EUR50.

    C. EUR51.

31. Using Withers's assumptions for the H-model and the basic two-stage dividend discount model, the forecasted Ukon stock price at the end of the year 2023 for the H-model should be:

    A. lower than the basic two-stage model.

    B. the same as the basic two-stage model.

    C. higher than the basic two-stage model.

32. Under her Scenario 1 and based on Exhibit 2, the required rate of return that Withers used for Venus Company stock valuation is *closest* to:

    A. 8.0%.

  B. 9.6%.

  C. 10.0%.

33. Under Scenario 2 and based on Exhibit 2, Withers estimates that the value of the Venus Company stock to be *closest* to:

  A. USD69.73.

  B. USD71.03.

  C. USD72.98.

34. Using the data in Exhibit 3, Withers can estimate the sustainable growth of the Wakuni Corporation as being *closest* to:

  A. 10.66%.

  B. 11.04%.

  C. 14.05%.

35. Withers's sensitivity analysis of Wakuni Corporation should produce a range of sustainable growth estimates between:

  A. 0.0% and 1.2%.

  B. 7.2% and 12.0%.

  C. 8.0% and 13.3%.

36. Based on Exhibit 4 and Intern 1's analysis, Xavier Corporation's sustainable dividend payout ratio is *closest* to:

  A. 43.4%.

  B. 44.6%.

  C. 56.6%.

37. Based on Exhibit 4, Intern 2 should conclude that the Xavier stock is:

  A. underpriced.

  B. fairly priced.

  C. overpriced.

38. Based on Exhibit 4 and Intern 1's estimate of the required rate of return and the dividend growth rate for the first four years, the growth rate beyond the first four years consistent with the current price of USD52 is *closest* to:

  A. 3.80%.

  B. 4.17%.

  C. 4.23%.

SOLUTIONS

1. B is correct. The following table provides the calculations needed to compute the value of the stock using the first approach, including the calculations for the terminal value V_8. As the table shows, the terminal value V_8 = C\$31.0550.

Time	Value	Calculation	D_t or V_t	Present Values $D_t/(1.0872)^t$ or $V_t/(1.0872)^t$
1	D_1	C\$0.175(1.14)	C\$0.1995	C\$0.1835
2	D_2	$0.175(1.14)^2$	0.2274	0.1924
3	D_3	$0.175(1.14)^3$	0.2593	0.2018
4	D_4	$0.175(1.14)^4$	0.2956	0.2116
5	D_5	$0.175(1.14)^5$	0.3369	0.2218
6	D_6	$0.175(1.14)^6$	0.3841	0.2326
7	D_7	$0.175(1.14)^7$	0.4379	0.2439
8	D_8	$0.175(1.14)^8$	0.4992	0.2557
8	V_8	$0.175(1.14)^8(1.07)/(0.0872 - 0.07)$	31.0550	15.9095
Total				C\$17.6528

2. C is correct. As shown in the foregoing table, the value of the second stage = PV of V_8 = C\$15.9095. The total value is C\$17.6528. As a proportion, the second stage represents $15.9095/17.6528 = 0.90$ of the total value.

3. B is correct.

$V_8/E_8 = 17$

$D_8/E_8 = 1 - 0.70 = 0.30$

From the table with the calculation details for the solution to Problem 22, $D_8 =$ C\$0.4992. So, $0.4992/E_8 = 0.30$, which means that $E_8 = 0.4992/0.30 = 1.6640$.

$V_8/E_8 = 17$ implies that $V_8/1.6640 = 17$, which gives $V_8 = 17(1.6640)$

  = C\$28.2880.

4. A is correct. As computed earlier, $V_8 = 17(1.6640) =$ C\$28.2880.

PV of $V_8 = 28.2880/1.0872^8 = 14.4919$

From the table with the calculation details for the solution to Problem 22,

Sum of PV of D_1 through $D_8 = 1.7433$

So, the value of stock $V_0 = 14.4919 + 1.7433 =$ C\$16.2352.

5. C is correct. Using the H-model,

$$V_0 = \frac{D_0(1+g_L) + D_0 H(g_S - g_L)}{r - g_L},$$

where

$D_0 = 0.175$

$r = 0.0872$

$H = 4$

$g_S = 0.14$

$g_L = 0.07$

$$V_0 = \frac{0.175(1.07) + 0.175(4)(0.14 - 0.07)}{0.0872 - 0.07} = 13.7355.$$

The market price is C$17, which is greater than C$13.7355. So, the stock is overvalued in the market.

6. B is correct. If the extraordinary growth rate of 14% is expected to continue for a longer duration, the stock's value would increase. Choice A is false because given that the first stage is longer (11 years instead of 8), the terminal value is being calculated at a later point in time. So, its present value would be smaller. Moreover, the first stage has more years and contributes more to the total value. Overall, the proportion contributed by the second stage would be smaller. Choice C is false because the intrinsic value of the stock would be higher and the appropriate conclusion would be that the stock would be undervalued to a greater extent based on the first approach.

7. C is correct. A dividend discount model is especially useful when dividend policy bears an understandable and consistent relationship to the company's profitability. The relatively consistent dividend payout ratio suggests Company JZY would be a suitable candidate for a dividend discount model.

8. B is correct. The value of ABC stock can be computed as follows:
Given: Dividend (D_0) = C$0.65, Return ($r$) = 7.35%, Short-term growth (g_S) = 12% for 4 years, Long-term growth (g_L) = 3.5% thereafter.
Then:

$D_1 = D_0(1 + g_S)^1 = 0.65(1.12) = $ C$0.7280

$D_2 = D_0(1 + g_S)^2 = 0.65(1.12)^2 = $ C$0.8154

$D_3 = D_0(1 + g_S)^3 = 0.65(1.12)^3 = $ C$0.9132

$D_4 = D_0(1 + g_S)^4 = 0.65(1.12)^4 = $ C$1.0228

$P_4 = [D_4(1 + g_L)]/(r - g_L) = [D_4(1.035)]/(0.0735 - 0.035) = $ C$27.4960.

$V_0 = D_1/(1 + r)^1 + \dots + D_4/(1 + r)^4 + P_4/(1 + r)^4.$

$V_0 = [0.7280/(1.0735)^1] + [0.8154/(1.0735)^2] + [0.9132/(1.0735)^3] + [1.0228/(1.0735)^4] + [27.4960/(1.0735)^4]$

$= $ C$23.5984 (rounded to C$23.60).

9. C is correct. The value of ABC would be calculated using the Gordon growth model as follows:

$V_0 = [D_0(1 + g)]/(r - g) = [0.65(1.035)]/(0.0735 - 0.035) = $ C$17.47.

10. B is correct. In the Gordon growth model, Total return = Dividend yield + Capital gains yield (i.e., constant growth rate). When a stock is fairly valued, the expected total return will equal the required return or discount rate (i.e., 7.35%). In the case of ABC, the total return is 7.35% and the capital gains yield is 3.5%. Therefore, the dividend yield is 7.35% − 3.5% = 3.85%.

11. C is correct. The current value of XYZ stock would be calculated as follows:

$V_0 = [P_3/(1 + r)^3]$, where $P_3 = D_4/(r - g)$.

Given $D_4 = 1.72$, $r = 10\%$, and $g = 4\%$,

$V_0 = [1.72/(0.10 - 0.04)]/(1.10)^3 = US\$21.54$.

12. C is correct. The dividend growth rate implied in the stock price of XYZ (i.e., 6%) is greater than the growth rate assumed by the analyst (i.e., 4%), suggesting that XYZ is overvalued.

13. C is correct. The sustainable growth rate of JZY stock = g = Retention ratio × ROE = $0.60 \times 0.0817 = 4.9\%$. JZY stock's implied growth rate of 5.3% is higher than the sustainable growth rate of 4.9%. Consequently, the stock is overvalued— that is, the intrinsic value of the stock will be less than its current market price. The current intrinsic value of JZY stock is as follows:

$V_0 = [D_0(1 + g)]/(r - g)$

$= [0.84 (1.0490)]/(0.08 - 0.0490)$

$= US\$28.42 < US\$32.76$

14. B is correct. BKKQ has the largest PVGO, calculated as follows:

PVGO (ABTD) = $P_0 - E_1/r = 80.00 - [7.30/0.105] = C\$10.48$

PVGO (BKKQ) = $P_0 - E_1/r = 39.00 - [2.12/0.08] = C\$12.50$

PVGO (CPMN) = $P_0 - E_1/r = 27.39 - [1.90/0.12] = C\$11.56$

where P_0 is the current price per share, E_1 is the forecasted earnings per share, and r is the required rate of return.

15. C is correct. The leading P/E is calculated as follows:

$P_0/E_1 = [1/r] + [PVGO/E_1]$,

where $1/r$ captures the no-growth component of P/E and $PVGO/E_1$ captures the growth component of the P/E.
PVGO is computed as follows:

PVGO (ABTD) = $P_0 - E_1/r = 80.00 - [7.30/0.105] = C\$10.48$

PVGO (BKKQ) = $P_0 - E_1/r = 39.00 - [2.12/0.08] = C\$12.50$

PVGO (CPMN) = $P_0 - E_1/r = 27.39 - [1.90/0.12] = C\$11.56$

where P_0 is the current price per share, E_1 is the forecasted earnings per share, and r is the required rate of return.
The growth component of the P/E for each stock $[PVGO/E_1]$ is as follows:

ABTD: $10.48/7.30 = 1.44\times$

BKKQ: $12.50/2.12 = 5.90\times$

CPMN: $11.56/1.90 = 6.08\times$

16. C is correct. Using the Gordon growth model,

$$V_0 = \frac{D_1}{r - g} = \frac{0.59(1 + 0.0530)}{0.1115 - 0.0530} = \$10.62.$$

17. A is correct. The justified trailing P/E or P_0/E_0 is V_0/E_0, where V_0 is the fair value based on the stock's fundamentals. The fair value V_0 computed earlier is \$10.62 and E_0 is \$2.12. So, the justified trailing P/E is $10.62/2.12 = 5.01$.

18. A is correct. Rae's estimate of the intrinsic value is \$10.62. So, the band Rae is looking at is $\$10.62 \pm 0.10(\$10.62)$, which runs from $\$10.62 + \$1.06 = \$11.68$ on the upside to $\$10.62 - \$1.06 = \$9.56$ on the downside. Because \$8.42 is less than \$9.56, Rae would consider Tasty Foods to be undervalued.

19. B is correct. Using a beta of 1.25, Rae's estimate for the required return on equity for Tasty Foods is $0.04 + 1.25(0.065) = 0.1213$, or 12.13%. The estimated value of the stock is

$$V_0 = \frac{D_1}{r - g} = \frac{0.59 \times (1 + 0.0530)}{0.1213 - 0.0530} = \$9.10.$$

20. A is correct. The price of the stock is \$8.42. If this price is also the fair value of the stock,

$$V_0 = 8.42 = \frac{D_1}{r - g} = \frac{0.59 \times (1 + g)}{0.1115 - g}$$

$$0.9388 - 8.42g = 0.59 + 0.59g$$

$$9.01g = 0.3488$$

$$g = 0.0387 \text{ or } 3.87 \text{ percent}$$

21. A is correct. If the stock is fairly priced in the market as per the Gordon growth model, the stock price is expected to increase at g, the expected growth rate in dividends. The implied growth rate in dividends, if price is the fair value, is 3.87%. Therefore, the expected capital gains yield is 3.87%.

22. A is correct. The justified leading P/E is calculated as

$$\frac{P_0}{E_1} = \frac{(1 - b)}{(r - g)},$$

where b is the retention ratio, $1 - b$ is the dividend payout ratio, r is the discount rate, and g is the long-term growth rate.

ABC's dividend payout rate, $1 - b$, is given as 0.60. For Company ABC, the justified leading P/E is

$$\frac{P_0}{E_1} = \frac{(1 - b)}{(r - g)} = \frac{(0.60)}{(0.07 - 0.035)} \approx 17.1.$$

23. B is correct. The justified leading P/E is calculated as

$$\frac{P_0}{E_1} = \frac{(1 - b)}{(r - g)},$$

where b is the retention ratio, $1 - b$ is the dividend payout ratio, r is the discount rate, and g is the long-term growth rate.

The justified leading P/E is

$$\frac{P_0}{E_1} = \frac{0.8}{(0.07 - 0.03)} = 20.$$

XYZ's actual leading P/E is

$$\frac{P_0}{E_1} = \frac{\$10}{\$0.50} = 20.$$

Because the justified leading P/E equals the actual leading P/E, the stock is fairly valued.

24. B is correct because the Gordon growth model can accurately value companies that are repurchasing shares when the analyst can appropriately adjust the dividend growth rate for the impact of share repurchases.

25. A is correct. The value of a share of Main Company's preferred stock is

$$V_0 = \frac{D}{r} = \frac{\$50 \times 0.055}{0.06} = \frac{\$2.75}{0.06} = \$45.83.$$

The current price of a share of Main Company's preferred stock is $42, so the stock is currently undervalued.

26. C is correct. The value of non-callable fixed-rate perpetual preferred stock is calculated as

$$V_0 = \frac{D}{r} \rightarrow r = \frac{D}{V_0},$$

where D is the constant dividend per share and r is the discount rate. The discount rate of a perpetuity is often called the capitalization rate.
For Standard Company, the dividend is $D = 2.75\% \times \$100 = \$2.75$.
Therefore,

$$r = \frac{\$2.75}{\$49.60} = 5.54\%.$$

27. A is correct because the dividend growth is declining linearly during the second stage of a three-stage DDM used to value BIOK. As noted in the text, a three-stage valuation clearly has an H-model process in the second and third stages. In contrast, abrupt—rather than linearly declining—dividend growth rates are implied for CCAX and HLTV.

28. B is correct because HLTV is forecast to have three growth stages: the growth phase (2 years at 27%), the transition phase (10 years at 12%), and the mature phase. Because the earnings growth has three stages and the dividend payout ratio is stable, a three-stage DDM is appropriate.

29. A is correct because the estimated value of the stock at the end of the first stage of a basic two-stage DDM (terminal value) is the present value of all dividends beyond the first stage. The first stage is 2020 through 2023, and the second stage begins in 2024, so the terminal value (that is, the value of the stock at the end of 2023) is the present value of future dividends beyond 2023.

30. C is correct based on Withers's assumptions applied to the dividend valuation model.
The stock value as of the end of 2019 equals the present value of all future dividends in 2020 through 2022 plus the present value of the terminal value at the end of 2022. The forecasted stock value equals EUR51.254:

Year	Dividend	Terminal Value	D_t or V_t	Present Value of D_t or V_t
2020	2.315(1.05) = 2.431		2.431	2.251
2021	2.431(1.05) = 2.553		2.553	2.189
2022	2.553(1.05) = 2.681		2.681	2.128
2023	2.681(1.05) = 2.815	57.980	60.795	44.686
2024	2.815(1.03) = 2.899			
Total				51.254

The terminal value at the end of 2023 is calculated using the dividend in the first year beyond the first stage, divided by the difference between the required rate of return and the growth rate in the second stage.

$$\text{Terminal value at end of 2023} = \frac{2.815\,(1.03)}{(0.08 - 0.03)} = 57.980$$

31. A is correct. During the first stage, the basic two-stage model has higher (i.e., 5%) growth than the H-model, in which growth is declining linearly from 5.0% to 3.5%. Higher growth rates result in higher forecasted dividends and stock prices at the beginning of the sustained growth phase. Because the long-term dividend growth rates are the same for both models, the difference in forecasted stock price arises from growth rate differences in the first stage.

    Therefore, the dividend at the end of the first stage will be lower for the H-model than for the basic two-stage DDM, and the terminal value will be lower in the H-model than in the two-stage model. Specifically, the 2023 dividends will be 2.734 (i.e., 2.315 × 1.05 × 1.045 × 1.04 × 1.035) for the H-model versus 2.815 [i.e., 2.315 × $(1.05)^4$] for the basic two-stage DDM.

32. C is correct, based on Exhibit 2 and the H-model.

    Estimate the required rate of return using Equation 21:

    $$r = \frac{D_0}{P_0}\left[\left(1 + g_L\right) + H\left(g_S - g_L\right)\right] + g_L$$

    Substitute the following:

    $D_0 = 3.15$

    $g_S = 8\%$

    $g_L = 4\%$

    $H = 4 \div 2 = 2$

    The model thus produces

    $$r = \frac{3.15}{58.79}\left[\left(1 + 0.04\right) + 2\left(0.08 - 0.04\right)\right] + 0.04$$

    $$= (0.053581 \times 1.12) + 0.04$$

    $$= 0.060010 + 0.04 = 0.10001 \approx 10\%.$$

33. B is correct based on the present value of forecasted dividends. The dividend at the end of 2019, based on case material, is USD3.15 per share.

Year	Dividend per Share, Prior Year	Growth Rate during Year	Dividend per Share, Current Year	Terminal Value	D_t or V_t	Present Value of D_t or V_t
2020	3.150	6%	3.339		3.339	3.092
2021	3.339	6%	3.539		3.539	3.034
2022	3.539	5%	3.716		3.716	2.950
2023	3.716	5%	3.902	80.381	84.283	61.951
					Total	71.027

Terminal value at the end of 2023 $= \dfrac{3.902\,(1.03)}{(0.08 - 0.03)} = 80.381$

34. A is correct, based on the use of average total assets and beginning-of-year shareholders' equity.

$$g = \frac{\text{Net income} - \text{Dividends}}{\text{Net income}} \times \frac{\text{Net income}}{\text{Sales}} \times \frac{\text{Sales}}{\text{Total assets}} \times \frac{\text{Total assets}}{\text{Shareholders' equity}}$$

To calculate sustainable growth,

$$g = \frac{43{,}923 - 1{,}518}{43{,}923} \times \frac{43{,}923}{423{,}474} \times \frac{423{,}474}{486{,}203} \times \frac{486{,}203}{397{,}925}$$

$$= 96.544\% \times 10.372\% \times 87.100\% \times 122.200\%$$

$$= 10.658\%$$

35. B is correct because the sustainable growth is the product of the return on equity and the retention ratio. If the payout ratio ranges from 0% to 10%, the percentage of earnings retained by the firm ranges from 100% to 90%.

Sensitivity: Sustainable Growth Rates		
Return on Equity	**Retention Ratio**	
	90%	100%
8%	7.2%	8.0%
12%	10.8%	12.0%

36. C is correct because it is based on the sustainable growth rate and the required rate of return:

Sustainable growth rate = (b in mature phase) × (Return on equity)

= (1 − Dividend payout) × (Return on equity)

0.036 = (1 − Dividend payout) × 0.083

Solving for the dividend payout ratio, the dividend payout = 56.627% ≈ 56.6%.

37. A is correct. Intern 2 values Xavier stock at USD56.372 per share, which is higher than the current price of USD52.

$D_1 = 2.000 \times (1.048)^1 = 2.096$

$D_2 = 2.000 \times (1.048)^2 = 2.197$

$$D_3 = 2.000 \times (1.048)^3 = 2.302$$

$$D_4 = 2.000 \times (1.048)^4 = 2.413$$

$$D_5 = 2.000 \times (1.048)^4 \times 1.04 = 2.510$$

$$\text{Value per share} = \frac{2.096}{(1+0.078)^1} + \frac{2.197}{(1+0.078)^2} + \frac{2.302}{(1+0.078)^3} + \frac{2.413 + \frac{2.510}{(0.078-0.04)}}{(1+0.078)^4}$$

$$= \text{USD56.372}$$

38. B is correct. The candidate can arrive at the answer one of two ways. The first way is to use Equation 19 and solve for g_L:

$$P_0 = \left[\sum_{t=1}^{n} \frac{D_0 (1+g_S)^t}{(1+r)^t} \right] + \left[\frac{D_0 (1+g_S)^n (1+g_L)}{(1+r)^n (r-g_L)} \right]$$

Insert the known values:

$$\text{USD52} = \sum_{t=1}^{4} \frac{2(1+0.05)^t}{(1+0.083)^t} + \frac{2(1+0.05)^4 (1+g_L)}{(1+0.083)^4 (0.083-g_L)}$$

$$= 7.4089 + \frac{2.431 (1+g_L)}{1.37567 (0.083-g_L)}$$

Solve for g_L:

$$g_L = 4.172\%.$$

Check:

$$7.4089 + \frac{2.431 (1+0.04127)}{1.3757 (0.083-0.04172)} = 7.4089 + 44.5830 \approx 52.00$$

The second way is to use Equation 19 and substitute the different choices to determine the value that produces a value of USD52 per share:

$$\text{USD52} = \sum_{t=1}^{4} \frac{2(1+0.05)^t}{(1+0.083)^t} + \frac{2(1+0.05)^4 (1+0.0417)}{(1+0.083)^4 (0.083-0.0417)}$$

Glossary

Abnormal earnings   See *residual income*.

Abnormal return   The amount by which a security's actual return differs from its expected return, given the security's risk and the market's return.

Absolute convergence   The idea that developing countries, regardless of their particular characteristics, will eventually catch up with the developed countries and match them in per capita output.

Absolute valuation model   A model that specifies an asset's intrinsic value.

Absolute version of PPP   An extension of the law of one price whereby the prices of goods and services will not differ internationally once exchange rates are considered.

Accounting estimates   Estimates used in calculating the value of assets or liabilities and in the amount of revenue and expense to allocate to a period. Examples of accounting estimates include, among others, the useful lives of depreciable assets, the salvage value of depreciable assets, product returns, warranty costs, and the amount of uncollectible receivables.

Accumulated benefit obligation   The actuarial present value of benefits (whether vested or non-vested) attributed, generally by the pension benefit formula, to employee service rendered before a specified date and based on employee service and compensation (if applicable) before that date. The accumulated benefit obligation differs from the projected benefit obligation in that it includes no assumption about future compensation levels.

Accuracy   The percentage of correctly predicted classes out of total predictions. It is an overall performance metric in classification problems.

Acquisition   When one company, the acquirer, purchases from the seller most or all of another company's (the target) shares to gain control of either an entire company, a segment of another company, or a specific group of assets in exchange for cash, stock, or the assumption of liabilities, alone or in combination. Once an acquisition is complete, the acquirer and target merge into a single entity and consolidate management, operations, and resources.

Activation function   A functional part of a neural network's node that transforms the total net input received into the final output of the node. The activation function operates like a light dimmer switch that decreases or increases the strength of the input.

Active factor risk   The contribution to active risk squared resulting from the portfolio's different-than-benchmark exposures relative to factors specified in the risk model.

Active return   The return on a portfolio minus the return on the portfolio's benchmark.

Active risk   The standard deviation of active returns.

Active risk squared   The variance of active returns; active risk raised to the second power.

Active share   A measure of how similar a portfolio is to its benchmark. A manager who precisely replicates the benchmark will have an active share of zero; a manager with no holdings in common with the benchmark will have an active share of one.

Active specific risk   The contribution to active risk squared resulting from the portfolio's active weights on individual assets as those weights interact with assets' residual risk.

Adjusted funds from operations (AFFO)   Funds from operations adjusted to remove any non-cash rent reported under straight-line rent accounting and to subtract maintenance-type capital expenditures and leasing costs, including leasing agents' commissions and tenants' improvement allowances.

Adjusted present value   As an approach to valuing a company, the sum of the value of the company, assuming no use of debt, and the net present value of any effects of debt on company value.

Adjusted R^2   Goodness-of-fit measure that adjusts the coefficient of determination, R^2, for the number of independent variables in the model.

Administrative regulations or administrative law   Rules issued by government agencies or other regulators.

Advanced set   An arrangement in which the reference interest rate is set at the time the money is deposited.

Advanced settled   An arrangement in which a forward rate agreement (FRA) expires and settles at the same time, at the FRA expiration date.

Agency issues   Conflicts of interest that arise when the agent in an agency relationship has goals and incentives that differ from the principal to whom the agent owes a fiduciary duty. Also called *agency problems* or *principal–agent problems*.

Agglomerative clustering   A bottom-up hierarchical clustering method that begins with each observation being treated as its own cluster. The algorithm finds the two closest clusters, based on some measure of distance (similarity), and combines them into one new larger cluster. This process is repeated iteratively until all observations are clumped into a single large cluster.

Akaike's information criterion (AIC)   A statistic used to compare sets of independent variables for explaining a dependent variable. It is preferred for finding the model that is best suited for prediction.

Allowance for loan losses   A balance sheet account; it is a contra asset account to loans.

Alpha   The return on an asset in excess of the asset's required rate of return; the risk-adjusted return.

American Depositary Receipt   A negotiable certificate issued by a depositary bank that represents ownership in a non-US company's deposited equity (i.e., equity held in custody by the depositary bank in the company's home market).

Analysis of variance (ANOVA)   The analysis that breaks the total variability of a dataset (such as observations on the dependent variable in a regression) into components representing different sources of variation.

Application programming interface (API)   A set of well-defined methods of communication between various software components and typically used for accessing external data.

Arbitrage   1) The simultaneous purchase of an undervalued asset or portfolio and sale of an overvalued but equivalent asset or portfolio, in order to obtain a riskless profit on the price differential. Taking advantage of a market inefficiency in a risk-free manner. 2) The condition in a financial market in which equivalent assets or combinations of assets sell for two different prices, creating an opportunity to profit at no risk with no commitment of money. In a well-functioning financial market, few arbitrage opportunities are possible. 3) A risk-free operation that earns an expected positive net profit but requires no net investment of money.

Arbitrage-free models Term structure models that project future interest rate paths that emanate from the existing term structure. Resulting prices are based on a no-arbitrage condition.

Arbitrage-free valuation An approach to valuation that determines security values consistent with the absence of any opportunity to earn riskless profits without any net investment of money.

Arbitrage opportunity An opportunity to conduct an arbitrage; an opportunity to earn an expected positive net profit without risk and with no net investment of money.

Arbitrage portfolio The portfolio that exploits an arbitrage opportunity.

Ask price The price at which a trader will sell a specified quantity of a security. Also called *ask*, *offer price*, or *offer*.

Asset-based approach Approach that values a private company based on the values of the underlying assets of the entity less the value of any related liabilities.

Asset-based valuation An approach to valuing natural resource companies that estimates company value on the basis of the market value of the natural resources the company controls.

At market contract When a forward contract is established, the forward price is negotiated so that the market value of the forward contract on the initiation date is zero.

Authorized participants (APs) A special group of institutional investors who are authorized by the ETF issuer to participate in the creation/redemption process. APs are large broker/dealers, often market makers.

Autocorrelations The correlations of a time series with its own past values.

Autoregressive model (AR) A time series regressed on its own past values in which the independent variable is a lagged value of the dependent variable.

Backtesting The process that approximates the real-life investment process, using historical data, to assess whether an investment strategy would have produced desirable results.

Backward propagation The process of adjusting weights in a neural network, to reduce total error of the network, by moving backward through the network's layers.

Backwardation A condition in the futures markets in which the spot price exceeds the futures price, the forward curve is downward sloping, and the convenience yield is high.

Bag-of-words (BOW) A collection of a distinct set of tokens from all the texts in a sample dataset. BOW does not capture the position or sequence of words present in the text.

Balance sheet restructuring Altering the composition of the balance sheet by either shifting the asset composition, changing the capital structure, or both.

Bankruptcy A declaration provided for by a country's laws that typically involves the establishment of a legal procedure that forces creditors to defer their claims.

Barbell portfolio Fixed-income portfolio that combines short and long maturities.

Base error Model error due to randomness in the data.

Basic earnings per share (EPS) Net earnings available to common shareholders (i.e., net income minus preferred dividends) divided by the weighted average number of common shares outstanding during the period.

Basis The difference between the spot price and the futures price. As the maturity date of the futures contract nears, the basis converges toward zero.

Basis trade A trade based on the pricing of credit in the bond market versus the price of the same credit in the CDS market. To execute a basis trade, go long the "underpriced" credit and short the "overpriced" credit. A profit is realized as the implied credit prices converge.

Bearish flattening Term structure shift in which short-term bond yields rise more than long-term bond yields, resulting in a flatter yield curve.

Benchmark value of the multiple In using the method of comparables, the value of a price multiple for the comparison asset; when we have comparison assets (a group), the mean or median value of the multiple for the group of assets.

Best ask The offer to sell with the lowest ask price. Also called *best offer* or *inside ask*.

Best bid The highest bid in the market.

Best offer The lowest offer (ask price) in the market.

Bias error Describes the degree to which a model fits the training data. Algorithms with erroneous assumptions produce high bias error with poor approximation, causing underfitting and high in-sample error.

Bid price In a price quotation, the price at which the party making the quotation is willing to buy a specified quantity of an asset or security.

Bid–ask spread The ask price minus the bid price.

Bill-and-hold basis Sales on a bill-and-hold basis involve selling products but not delivering those products until a later date.

Blockage factor An illiquidity discount that occurs when an investor sells a large amount of stock relative to its trading volume (assuming it is not large enough to constitute a controlling ownership).

Bond indenture A legal contract specifying the terms of a bond issue.

Bond risk premium The expected excess return of a default-free long-term bond less that of an equivalent short-term bond.

Bond yield plus risk premium (BYPRP) approach An estimate of the cost of common equity that is produced by summing the before-tax cost of debt and a risk premium that captures the additional yield on a company's stock relative to its bonds.

Bonus issue of shares A type of dividend in which a company distributes additional shares of its common stock to shareholders instead of cash.

Book value The net amount shown for an asset or liability on the balance sheet; book value may also refer to the company's excess of total assets over total liabilities. Also called *carrying value*.

Book value of equity Shareholders' equity (total assets minus total liabilities) minus the value of preferred stock; common shareholders' equity.

Book value per share The amount of book value (also called carrying value) of common equity per share of common stock, calculated by dividing the book value of shareholders' equity by the number of shares of common stock outstanding.

Bootstrap aggregating (or bagging) A technique whereby the original training dataset is used to generate n new training datasets or bags of data. Each new bag of data is generated by random sampling with replacement from the initial training set.

Bootstrapping The use of a forward substitution process to determine zero-coupon rates by using the par yields and solving for the zero-coupon rates one by one, from the shortest to longest maturities.

Bottom-up approach With respect to forecasting, an approach that usually begins at the level of the individual company or a unit within the company.

Breakup value The value derived using a sum-of-the-parts valuation.

Breusch–Godfrey (BG) test A test used to detect autocorrelated residuals up to a predesignated order of the lagged residuals.

Breusch–Pagan (BP) test A test for the presence of heteroskedasticity in a regression.

Bullet portfolio A fixed-income portfolio concentrated in a single maturity.

Bullish flattening Term structure change in which the yield curve flattens in response to a greater decline in long-term rates than short-term rates.

Bullish steepening Term structure change in which short-term rates fall by more than long-term yields, resulting in a steeper term structure.

Buy-side analysts Analysts who work for investment management firms, trusts, bank trust departments, and similar institutions.

Buyback A transaction in which a company buys back its own shares. Unlike stock dividends and stock splits, share repurchases use corporate cash.

CDS spread A periodic premium paid by the buyer to the seller that serves as a return over a market reference rate required to protect against credit risk.

Callable bond A bond containing an embedded call option that gives the issuer the right to buy the bond back from the investor at specified prices on pre-determined dates.

Canceled shares Shares that were issued, subsequently repurchased by the company, and then retired (cannot be reissued).

Capital asset pricing model (CAPM) A single factor model such that excess returns on a stock are a function of the returns on a market index.

Capital charge The company's total cost of capital in money terms.

Capital deepening An increase in the capital-to-labor ratio.

Capitalization of earnings method In the context of private company valuation, a valuation model based on an assumption of a constant growth rate of free cash flow to the firm or a constant growth rate of free cash flow to equity.

Capitalization rate The divisor in the expression for the value of perpetuity. In the context of real estate, it is the divisor in the direct capitalization method of estimating value. The cap rate equals net operating income divided by value.

Capitalized cash flow method In the context of private company valuation, a valuation model based on an assumption of a constant growth rate of free cash flow to the firm or a constant growth rate of free cash flow to equity. Also called *capitalized cash flow model*.

Capitalized income method In the context of private company valuation, a valuation model based on an assumption of a constant growth rate of free cash flow to the firm or a constant growth rate of free cash flow to equity.

Capped floater Floating-rate bond with a cap provision that prevents the coupon rate from increasing above a specified maximum rate. It protects the issuer against rising interest rates.

Carry arbitrage model A no-arbitrage approach in which the underlying instrument is either bought or sold along with an opposite position in a forward contract.

Carry benefits Benefits that arise from owning certain underlyings; for example, dividends, foreign interest, and bond coupon payments.

Carry costs Costs that arise from owning certain underlyings. They are generally a function of the physical characteristics of the underlying asset and also the interest forgone on the funds tied up in the asset.

Cash available for distribution See *adjusted funds from operations*.

Cash-generating unit The smallest identifiable group of assets that generates cash inflows that are largely independent of the cash inflows of other assets or groups of assets.

Cash settlement A procedure used in certain derivative transactions that specifies that the long and short parties settle the derivative's difference in value between them by making a cash payment.

Catalyst An event or piece of information that causes the marketplace to re-evaluate the prospects of a company.

Ceiling analysis A systematic process of evaluating different components in the pipeline of model building. It helps to understand what part of the pipeline can potentially improve in performance by further tuning.

Centroid The center of a cluster formed using the k-means clustering algorithm.

Chain rule of forecasting A forecasting process in which the next period's value as predicted by the forecasting equation is substituted into the right-hand side of the equation to give a predicted value two periods ahead.

Cheapest-to-deliver The debt instrument that can be purchased and delivered at the lowest cost yet has the same seniority as the reference obligation.

Classification and regression tree A supervised machine learning technique that can be applied to predict either a categorical target variable, producing a classification tree, or a continuous target variable, producing a regression tree. CART is commonly applied to binary classification or regression.

Clean surplus relation The relationship between earnings, dividends, and book value in which ending book value is equal to the beginning book value plus earnings less dividends, apart from ownership transactions.

Club convergence The idea that only rich and middle-income countries sharing a set of favorable attributes (i.e., are members of the "club") will converge to the income level of the richest countries.

Cluster A subset of observations from a dataset such that all the observations within the same cluster are deemed "similar."

Clustering The sorting of observations into groups (clusters) such that observations in the same cluster are more similar to each other than they are to observations in other clusters.

Cobb–Douglas production function A function of the form $Y = K^{\alpha} L^{1-\alpha}$ relating output (Y) to labor (L) and capital (K) inputs.

Coefficient of determination   The percentage of the variation of the dependent variable that is explained by the independent variables. Also referred to as the R-squared or R^2.

Cointegrated   Describes two time series that have a long-term financial or economic relationship such that they do not diverge from each other without bound in the long run.

Collateral return   The component of the total return on a commodity futures position attributable to the yield for the bonds or cash used to maintain the futures position. Also called *collateral yield*.

Collection frequency (CF)   The number of times a given word appears in the whole corpus (i.e., collection of sentences) divided by the total number of words in the corpus.

Commercial real estate properties   Income-producing real estate properties; properties purchased with the intent to let, lease, or rent (in other words, produce income).

Commodity swap   A type of swap involving the exchange of payments over multiple dates as determined by specified reference prices or indexes relating to commodities.

Company fundamental factors   Factors related to the company's internal performance, such as factors relating to earnings growth, earnings variability, earnings momentum, and financial leverage.

Company share-related factors   Valuation measures and other factors related to share price or the trading characteristics of the shares, such as earnings yield, dividend yield, and book-to-market value.

Comparables   Assets used as benchmarks when applying the method of comparables to value an asset. Also called *comps*, *guideline assets*, or *guideline companies*.

Compiled financial statements   Financial statements that are not accompanied by an auditor's opinion letter.

Complexity   A term referring to the number of features, parameters, or branches in a model and to whether the model is linear or non-linear (non-linear is more complex).

Composite variable   A variable that combines two or more variables that are statistically strongly related to each other.

Comprehensive income   All changes in equity other than contributions by, and distributions to, owners; income under clean surplus accounting; includes all changes in equity during a period except those resulting from investments by owners and distributions to owners. Comprehensive income equals net income plus other comprehensive income.

Comps   Assets used as benchmarks when applying the method of comparables to value an asset.

Concentrated ownership   Ownership structure consisting of an individual shareholder or a group (controlling shareholders) with the ability to exercise control over the corporation.

Conditional convergence   The idea that convergence of per capita income is conditional on the countries having the same savings rate, population growth rate, and production function.

Conditional heteroskedasticity   A condition in which the variance of residuals of a regression are correlated with the value of the independent variables.

Conditional VaR (CVaR)   The weighted average of all loss outcomes in the statistical (i.e., return) distribution that exceed the VaR loss. Thus, CVaR is a more comprehensive measure of tail loss than VaR is. Sometimes referred to as the *expected tail loss* or *expected shortfall*.

Confirmation bias   A belief perseverance bias in which people tend to look for and notice what confirms their beliefs, to ignore or undervalue what contradicts their beliefs, and to misinterpret information as support for their beliefs.

Confusion matrix   A grid used for error analysis in classification problems, it presents values for four evaluation metrics including true positive (TP), false positive (FP), true negative (TN), and false negative (FN).

Conglomerate discount   When an issuer is trading at a valuation lower than the sum of its parts, which is generally the result of diseconomies of scale or scope or the result of the capital markets having overlooked the business and its prospects.

Constant dividend payout ratio policy   A policy in which a constant percentage of net income is paid out in dividends.

Constant returns to scale   The condition that if all inputs into the production process are increased by a given percentage, then output rises by that same percentage.

Contango   A condition in the futures markets in which the spot price is lower than the futures price, the forward curve is upward sloping, and there is little or no convenience yield.

Contingent consideration   Potential future payments to the seller that are contingent on the achievement of certain agreed-on occurrences.

Continuing earnings   Earnings excluding nonrecurring components. Also referred to as *core earnings*, *persistent earnings*, or *underlying earnings*.

Continuing residual income   Residual income after the forecast horizon.

Continuing value   The analyst's estimate of a stock's value at a particular point in the future.

Control premium   An increment or premium to value associated with a controlling ownership interest in a company.

Convergence   The tendency for differences in output per capita across countries to diminish over time. In technical analysis, the term describes the case when an indicator moves in the same manner as the security being analyzed.

Conversion period   For a convertible bond, the period during which bondholders have the right to convert their bonds into shares.

Conversion price   For a convertible bond, the price per share at which the bond can be converted into shares.

Conversion rate (or ratio)   For a convertible bond, the number of shares of common stock that a bondholder receives from converting the bond into shares.

Conversion value   For a convertible bond, the value of the bond if it is converted at the market price of the shares. Also called *parity value*.

Convertible bond   Bond that gives the bondholder the right to exchange the bond for a specified number of common shares in the issuing company.

Convexity   A measure of how interest rate sensitivity changes with a change in interest rates.

Cook's distance   A metric for identifying influential data points. Also known as Cook's D (D_i).

Core earnings   Earnings excluding nonrecurring components. Also referred to as *continuing earnings*, *persistent earnings*, or *underlying earnings*.

Core real estate investment style   Investing in high-quality, well-leased, core property types with low leverage (no more than 30% of asset value) in the largest markets with strong, diversified economies. It is a conservative strategy designed to avoid real estate–specific risks, including leasing, development, and speculation in favor of steady returns. Hotel properties are excluded from the core categories because of the higher cash flow volatility resulting from single-night leases and the greater importance of property operations, brand, and marketing.

Corpus A collection of text data in any form, including list, matrix, or data table forms.

Cost approach An approach that values a private company based on the values of the underlying assets of the entity less the value of any related liabilities. In the context of real estate, this approach estimates the value of a property based on what it would cost to buy the land and construct a new property on the site that has the same utility or functionality as the property being appraised.

Cost of carry model A model that relates the forward price of an asset to the spot price by considering the cost of carry (also referred to as future-spot parity model).

Cost of debt The required return on debt financing to a company, such as when it issues a bond, takes out a bank loan, or leases an asset through a finance lease.

Cost of equity The return required by equity investors to compensate for both the time value of money and the risk. Also referred to as the required rate of return on common stock or the required return on equity.

Cost restructuring Actions to reduce costs by improving operational efficiency and profitability, often to raise margins to a historical level or to those of comparable industry peers.

Country risk premium (CRP) The additional return required by investors to compensate for the risk associated with investing in a foreign country relative to the investor's domestic market.

Country risk rating (CRR) The rating of a country based on many risk factors, including economic prosperity, political risk, and ESG risk.

Covariance stationary Describes a time series when its expected value and variance are constant and finite in all periods and when its covariance with itself for a fixed number of periods in the past or future is constant and finite in all periods.

Covered bonds A senior debt obligation of a financial institution that gives recourse to the originator/issuer and a predetermined underlying collateral pool.

Covered interest rate parity The relationship among the spot exchange rate, the forward exchange rate, and the interest rates in two currencies that ensures that the return on a hedged (i.e., covered) foreign risk-free investment is the same as the return on a domestic risk-free investment. Also called *interest rate parity*.

Cox-Ingersoll-Ross model A general equilibrium term structure model that assumes interest rates are mean reverting and interest rate volatility is directly related to the level of interest rates.

Creation basket The list of securities (and share amounts) the authorized participant (AP) must deliver to the ETF manager in exchange for ETF shares. The creation basket is published each business day.

Creation units Large blocks of ETF shares transacted between the authorized participant (AP) and the ETF manager that are usually but not always equal to 50,000 shares of the ETF.

Creation/redemption The process in which ETF shares are created or redeemed by authorized participants transacting with the ETF issuer.

Credit correlation The correlation of credit (or default) risks of the underlying single-name CDS contained in an index CDS.

Credit curve The credit spreads for a range of maturities of a company's debt.

Credit default swap A derivative contract between two parties in which the buyer makes a series of cash payments to the seller and receives a promise of compensation for credit losses resulting from the default.

Credit derivative A derivative instrument in which the underlying is a measure of the credit quality of a borrower.

Credit event An event that defines a payout in a credit derivative. Events are usually defined as bankruptcy, failure to pay an obligation, or an involuntary debt restructuring.

Credit protection buyer One party to a credit default swap; the buyer makes a series of cash payments to the seller and receives a promise of compensation for credit losses resulting from the default.

Credit protection seller One party to a credit default swap; the seller makes a promise to pay compensation for credit losses resulting from the default.

Credit risk The risk of loss caused by a counterparty's or debtor's failure to make a promised payment. Also called *default risk*.

Credit spread The compensation for the risk inherent in a company's debt security.

Credit valuation adjustment The value of the credit risk of a bond in present value terms.

Cross-validation A technique for estimating out-of-sample error directly by determining the error in validation samples.

Cumulative preferred stock Preferred stock that requires that the dividends be paid in full to preferred stock owners for any missed dividends prior to any payment of dividends to common stock owners.

Current exchange rate For accounting purposes, the spot exchange rate on the balance sheet date.

Current rate method Approach to translating foreign currency financial statements for consolidation in which all assets and liabilities are translated at the current exchange rate. The current rate method is the prevalent method of translation.

Curvature One of the three factors (the other two are level and steepness) that empirically explain most of the changes in the shape of the yield curve. A shock to the curvature factor affects mid-maturity interest rates, resulting in the term structure becoming either more or less hump-shaped.

Curve trade Buying a CDS of one maturity and selling a CDS on the same reference entity with a different maturity.

Customer concentration risk The risk associated with sales dependent on a few customers.

Cyclical businesses Businesses with high sensitivity to business- or industry-cycle influences.

Data preparation (cleansing) The process of examining, identifying, and mitigating (i.e., cleansing) errors in raw data.

Data snooping The practice of determining a model by extensive searching through a dataset for statistically significant patterns.

Data wrangling (preprocessing) This task performs transformations and critical processing steps on cleansed data to make the data ready for ML model training (i.e., preprocessing), and includes dealing with outliers, extracting useful variables from existing data points, and scaling the data.

Deep learning Machine learning using neural networks with many hidden layers.

Deep neural networks   Neural networks with many hidden layers—at least 2 but potentially more than 20—that have proven successful across a wide range of artificial intelligence applications.

Default risk   See *credit risk*.

Defined benefit pension plans   Plans in which the company promises to pay a certain annual amount (defined benefit) to the employee after retirement. The company bears the investment risk of the plan assets.

Defined contribution pension plans   Individual accounts to which an employee and typically the employer makes contributions during their working years and expect to draw on the accumulated funds at retirement. The employee bears the investment and inflation risk of the plan assets.

Delay costs   Implicit trading costs that arise from the inability to complete desired trades immediately. Also called *slippage*.

Delta   The relationship between the option price and the underlying price, which reflects the sensitivity of the price of the option to changes in the price of the underlying. Delta is a good approximation of how an option price will change for a small change in the stock.

Dendrogram   A type of tree diagram used for visualizing a hierarchical cluster analysis; it highlights the hierarchical relationships among the clusters.

Depository Trust and Clearinghouse Corporation   A US-headquartered entity providing post-trade clearing, settlement, and information services.

Diluted earnings per share   (Diluted EPS)Net income, minus preferred dividends, divided by the weighted average number of common shares outstanding considering all dilutive securities (e.g., convertible debt and options); the EPS that would result if all dilutive securities were converted into common shares.

Dilution   A reduction in proportional ownership interest as a result of the issuance of new shares.

Dimension reduction   A set of techniques for reducing the number of features in a dataset while retaining variation across observations to preserve the information contained in that variation.

Diminishing marginal productivity   When each additional unit of an input, keeping the other inputs unchanged, increases output by a smaller increment.

Direct capitalization method   In the context of real estate, this method estimates the value of an income-producing property based on the level and quality of its net operating income.

Discount   To reduce the value of a future payment in allowance for how far away it is in time; to calculate the present value of some future amount. Also, the amount by which an instrument is priced below its face value.

Discount factor   The price equivalent of a zero rate. Also may be stated as the present value of a currency unit on a future date.

Discount for lack of control   An amount or percentage deducted from the pro rata share of 100% of the value of an equity interest in a business to reflect the absence of some or all of the powers of control.

Discount for lack of marketability   An amount of percentage deducted from the value of an ownership interest to reflect the relative absence of marketability.

Discount function   Discount factors for the range of all possible maturities. The spot curve can be derived from the discount function and vice versa.

Discounted abnormal earnings model   A model of stock valuation that views intrinsic value of stock as the sum of book value per share plus the present value of the stock's expected future residual income per share.

Discounted cash flow (DCF) method   Income approach that values an asset based on estimates of future cash flows discounted to present value by using a discount rate reflective of the risks associated with the cash flows. In the context of real estate, this method estimates the value of an income-producing property based on discounting future projected cash flows.

Discounted cash flow method   Income approach that values an asset based on estimates of future cash flows discounted to present value by using a discount rate reflective of the risks associated with the cash flows. In the context of real estate, this method estimates the value of an income-producing property based on discounting future projected cash flows.

Discounted cash flow model   A model of intrinsic value that views the value of an asset as the present value of the asset's expected future cash flows.

Dispersed ownership   Ownership structure consisting of many shareholders, none of which has the ability to individually exercise control over the corporation.

Divestiture   When a seller sells a company, segment of a company, or group of assets to an acquirer. Once complete, control of the target is transferred to the acquirer.

Dividend   A distribution paid to shareholders based on the number of shares owned.

Dividend coverage ratio   The ratio of net income to dividends.

Dividend discount model   (DDM) A present value model of stock value that views the intrinsic value of a stock as present value of the stock's expected future dividends.

Dividend discount model (DDM)   The model of the value of stock that is the present value of all future dividends, discounted at the required return on equity.

Dividend displacement of earnings   The concept that dividends paid now displace earnings in all future periods.

Dividend imputation tax system   A taxation system that effectively assures corporate profits distributed as dividends are taxed just once and at the shareholder's tax rate.

Dividend index point   A measure of the quantity of dividends attributable to a particular index.

Dividend payout ratio   The ratio of cash dividends paid to earnings for a period.

Dividend policy   The strategy a company follows with regard to the amount and timing of dividend payments.

Dividend rate   The annualized amount of the most recent dividend.

Dividend recapitalization   Restructuring the mix of debt and equity, typically shifting the capital structure from equity to debt through debt-financed share repurchases. The objective is to reduce the issuer's weighted average cost of capital by replacing expensive equity with cheaper debt by purchasing equity from shareholders using newly issued debt.

Dividend yield   Annual dividends per share divided by share price.

Divisive clustering   A top-down hierarchical clustering method that starts with all observations belonging to a single large cluster. The observations are then divided into two clusters based on some measure of distance (similarity). The algorithm then progressively partitions the intermediate clusters into smaller ones until each cluster contains only one observation.

Document frequency (DF) The number of documents (texts) that contain a particular token divided by the total number of documents. It is the simplest feature selection method and often performs well when many thousands of tokens are present.

Document term matrix (DTM) A matrix where each row belongs to a document (or text file), and each column represents a token (or term). The number of rows is equal to the number of documents (or text files) in a sample text dataset. The number of columns is equal to the number of tokens from the BOW built using all the documents in the sample dataset. The cells typically contain the counts of the number of times a token is present in each document.

Dominance An arbitrage opportunity when a financial asset with a risk-free payoff in the future must have a positive price today.

Double taxation system Corporate earnings are taxed twice when paid out as dividends. First, corporate pretax earnings are taxed regardless of whether they will be distributed as dividends or retained at the corporate level. Second, dividends are taxed again at the individual shareholder level.

Downstream A transaction between two related companies, an investor company (or a parent company) and an associate company (or a subsidiary) such that the investor company records a profit on its income statement. An example is a sale of inventory by the investor company to the associate or by a parent to a subsidiary company.

Dual-class shares Shares that grant one share class superior or even sole voting rights, whereas the other share class has inferior or no voting rights.

Due diligence Investigation and analysis in support of an investment action, decision, or recommendation.

Dummy variable An independent variable that takes on a value of either 1 or 0, depending on a specified condition. Also known as an *indicator variable*.

Duration A measure of the approximate sensitivity of a security to a change in interest rates (i.e., a measure of interest rate risk).

Durbin–Watson (DW) test A test for the presence of first-order serial correlation.

Dutch disease A situation in which currency appreciation driven by strong export demand for resources makes other segments of the economy (particularly manufacturing) globally uncompetitive.

ESG integration An ESG investment approach that focuses on systematic consideration of material ESG factors in asset allocation, security selection, and portfolio construction decisions for the purpose of achieving the product's stated investment objectives. Used interchangeably with **ESG investing**.

Earnings surprise The portion of a company's earnings that is unanticipated by investors and, according to the efficient market hypothesis, merits a price adjustment.

Earnings yield EPS divided by price; the reciprocal of the P/E.

Economic profit Equal to accounting profit less the implicit opportunity costs not included in total accounting costs; the difference between total revenue (TR) and total cost (TC). Also called *abnormal profit* or *supernormal profit*.

Economic sectors Large industry groupings.

Economic value added (EVA*) A commercial implementation of the residual income concept; the computation of EVA* is the net operating profit after taxes minus the cost of capital, where these inputs are adjusted for a number of items.

Economies of scale A situation in which average costs per unit of good or service produced fall as volume rises. In reference to mergers, the savings achieved through the consolidation of operations and elimination of duplicate resources.

Edwards–Bell–Ohlson model A model of stock valuation that views intrinsic value of stock as the sum of book value per share plus the present value of the stock's expected future residual income per share.

Effective convexity A *curve convexity* statistic that measures the secondary effect of a change in a benchmark yield curve on a bond's price.

Effective duration Sensitivity of the bond's price to a 100 bps parallel shift of the benchmark yield curve, assuming no change in the bond's credit spread.

Effective spread Two times the difference between the execution price and the midpoint of the market quote at the time an order is entered.

Eigenvalue A measure that gives the proportion of total variance in the initial dataset that is explained by each eigenvector.

Eigenvector A vector that defines new mutually uncorrelated composite variables that are linear combinations of the original features.

Embedded options Contingency provisions found in a bond's indenture or offering circular representing rights that enable their holders to take advantage of interest rate movements. They can be exercised by the issuer, by the bondholder, or automatically depending on the course of interest rates.

Ensemble learning A technique of combining the predictions from a collection of models to achieve a more accurate prediction.

Ensemble method The method of combining multiple learning algorithms, as in ensemble learning.

Enterprise value Total company value (the market value of debt, common equity, and preferred equity) minus the value of cash and investments.

Enterprise value multiple A valuation multiple that relates the total market value of all sources of a company's capital (net of cash) to a measure of fundamental value for the entire company (such as a pre-interest earnings measure).

Equity charge The estimated cost of equity capital in money terms.

Equity investment A company purchasing another company's equity but less than 50% of its shares. The two companies maintain their independence, but the investor company has investment exposure to the investee and, in some cases depending on the size of the investment, can have representation on the investee's board of directors to influence operations.

Equity REITs REITs that own, operate, and/or selectively develop income-producing real estate.

Equity risk premium (ERP) Compensation for bearing market risk.

Equity swap A swap transaction in which at least one cash flow is tied to the return on an equity portfolio position, often an equity index.

Error autocorrelations The autocorrelations of the error term.

***Ex ante* tracking error** A measure of the degree to which the performance of a given investment portfolio might be expected to deviate from its benchmark; also known as *relative VaR*.

Ex ante version of PPP   The hypothesis that expected changes in the spot exchange rate are equal to expected differences in national inflation rates. An extension of relative purchasing power parity to expected future changes in the exchange rate.

Ex-dividend   Trading ex-dividend refers to shares that no longer carry the right to the next dividend payment.

Ex-dividend date   The first date that a share trades without (i.e., "ex") the right to receive the declared dividend for the period.

Excess earnings method   Income approach that estimates the value of all intangible assets of the business by capitalizing future earnings in excess of the estimated return requirements associated with working capital and fixed assets.

Exercise date   The date when employees actually exercise stock options and convert them to stock.

Exercise value   The value of an option if it were exercised. Also sometimes called *intrinsic value*.

Expanded CAPM   An adaptation of the CAPM that adds to the CAPM a premium for small size and company-specific risk.

Expectations approach   A procedure for obtaining the value of an option derived from discounting at the risk-free rate its expected future payoff based on risk neutral probabilities.

Expected exposure   The projected amount of money an investor could lose if an event of default occurs, before factoring in possible recovery.

Expected shortfall   The average loss conditional on exceeding the VaR cutoff; sometimes referred to as *conditional VaR* or *expected tail loss*.

Expected tail loss   See *expected shortfall*.

Exploratory data analysis (EDA)   The preliminary step in data exploration, where graphs, charts, and other visualizations (heat maps and word clouds) as well as quantitative methods (descriptive statistics and central tendency measures) are used to observe and summarize data.

Exposure to foreign exchange risk   The risk of a change in value of an asset or liability denominated in a foreign currency due to a change in exchange rates.

Extendible bond   Bond with an embedded option that gives the bondholder the right to keep the bond for a number of years after maturity, possibly with a different coupon.

Extra dividend   A dividend paid by a company that does not pay dividends on a regular schedule, or a dividend that supplements regular cash dividends with an extra payment.

F1 score   The harmonic mean of precision and recall. F1 score is a more appropriate overall performance metric (than accuracy) when there is unequal class distribution in the dataset and it is necessary to measure the equilibrium of precision and recall.

FX carry trade   An investment strategy that involves taking long positions in high-yield currencies and short positions in low-yield currencies.

Factor   A common or underlying element with which several variables are correlated.

Factor betas   An asset's sensitivity to a particular factor; a measure of the response of return to each unit of increase in a factor, holding all other factors constant.

Factor portfolio   See *pure factor portfolio*.

Factor price   The expected return in excess of the risk-free rate for a portfolio with a sensitivity of 1 to one factor and a sensitivity of 0 to all other factors.

Factor risk premium   The expected return in excess of the risk-free rate for a portfolio with a sensitivity of 1 to one factor and a sensitivity of 0 to all other factors. Also called *factor price*.

Factor risk premiums   The expected return in excess of the risk-free rate for a portfolio with a sensitivity of 1 to one factor and a sensitivity of 0 to all other factors. Also called factor price.

Failure to pay   When a borrower does not make a scheduled payment of principal or interest on any outstanding obligations after a grace period.

Fair market value   The price, expressed in terms of cash equivalents, at which a property (asset) would change hands between a hypothetical willing and able buyer and a hypothetical willing and able seller, acting at "arm's length" in an open and unrestricted market, when neither is under compulsion to buy or sell and when both have reasonable knowledge of the relevant facts. Fair market value is most often used in a tax reporting context in the United States.

Fair value   The amount at which an asset could be exchanged, or a liability settled, between knowledgeable, willing parties in an arm's-length transaction; the price that would be received to sell an asset or paid to transfer a liability in an orderly transaction between market participants.

Fama–French models   Factor models that explain the drivers of returns related to three, four, or five factors.

Feature engineering   A process of creating new features by changing or transforming existing features.

Feature selection   A process whereby only pertinent features from the dataset are selected for model training. Selecting fewer features decreases model complexity and training time.

Features   The independent variables (X's) in a labeled dataset.

Finance (or capital) lease   A lease that is viewed as a financing arrangement.

Financial contagion   A situation in which financial shocks spread from their place of origin to other locales. In essence, a faltering economy infects other, healthier economies.

Financial leverage   The use of fixed sources of capital, such as debt, relative to sources without fixed costs, such as equity.

Financial transaction   A purchase involving a buyer having essentially no material synergies with the target (e.g., the purchase of a private company by a company in an unrelated industry or by a private equity firm would typically be a financial transaction).

First-differencing   A transformation that subtracts the value of the time series in period $t - 1$ from its value in period t.

First-order serial correlation   The correlation of residuals with residuals adjacent in time.

Fitting curve   A curve which shows in- and out-of-sample error rates (E_{in} and E_{out}) on the y-axis plotted against model complexity on the x-axis.

Fixed price tender offer   Offer made by a company to repurchase a specific number of shares at a fixed price that is typically at a premium to the current market price.

Fixed-rate perpetual preferred stock   Nonconvertible, non-callable preferred stock that has a fixed dividend rate and no maturity date.

Flight to quality   During times of market stress, investors sell higher-risk asset classes such as stocks and commodities in favor of default-risk-free government bonds.

Float   Amounts collected as premium and not yet paid out as benefits.

Floored floater Floating-rate bond with a floor provision that prevents the coupon rate from decreasing below a specified minimum rate. It protects the investor against declining interest rates.

Flotation cost Fees charged to companies by investment bankers and other costs associated with raising new capital.

Forced conversion For a convertible bond, when the issuer calls the bond and forces bondholders to convert their bonds into shares, which typically happens when the underlying share price increases above the conversion price.

Foreign currency transactions Transactions that are denominated in a currency other than a company's functional currency.

Forward curve A series of forward rates, each having the same time frame.

Forward dividend yield A dividend yield based on the anticipated dividend during the next 12 months.

Forward-looking estimates Estimates based on current and expectations. Also referred to as ex ante estimates.

Forward P/E A P/E calculated on the basis of a forecast of EPS; a stock's current price divided by next year's expected earnings.

Forward price Represents the price agreed upon in a forward contract to be exchanged at the contract's maturity date, T. This price is shown in equations as $F_0(T)$.

Forward pricing model The model that describes the valuation of forward contracts.

Forward propagation The process of adjusting weights in a neural network, to reduce total error of the network, by moving forward through the network's layers.

Forward rate An interest rate determined today for a loan that will be initiated in a future period.

Forward rate agreement An over-the-counter forward contract in which the underlying is an interest rate on a deposit. A forward rate agreement (FRA) calls for one party to make a fixed interest payment and the other to make an interest payment at a rate to be determined at contract expiration.

Forward rate model The forward pricing model expressed in terms of spot and forward interest rates.

Forward rate parity The proposition that the forward exchange rate is an unbiased predictor of the future spot exchange rate.

Forward value The monetary value of an existing forward contract.

Franchising An owner of an asset and associated intellectual property divests the asset and licenses intellectual property to a third-party operator (franchisee) in exchange for royalties. Franchisees operate under the constraints of a franchise agreement.

Franking credit A tax credit received by shareholders for the taxes that a corporation paid on its distributed earnings.

Free cash flow method Income approach that values an asset based on estimates of future cash flows discounted to present value by using a discount rate reflective of the risks associated with the cash flows.

Free cash flow to equity The cash flow available to a company's common shareholders after all operating expenses, interest, and principal payments have been made and necessary investments in working and fixed capital have been made.

Free cash flow to equity model A model of stock valuation that views a stock's intrinsic value as the present value of expected future free cash flows to equity.

Free cash flow to the firm The cash flow available to the company's suppliers of capital after all operating expenses (including taxes) have been paid and necessary investments in working and fixed capital have been made.

Free cash flow to the firm model A model of stock valuation that views the value of a firm as the present value of expected future free cash flows to the firm.

Frequency analysis The process of quantifying how important tokens are in a sentence and in the corpus as a whole. It helps in filtering unnecessary tokens (or features).

Functional currency The currency of the primary economic environment in which an entity operates.

Fundamental factor models A multifactor model in which the factors are attributes of stocks or companies that are important in explaining cross-sectional differences in stock prices.

Fundamentals Economic characteristics of a business, such as profitability, financial strength, and risk.

Funds available for distribution (FAD) See *adjusted funds from operations.*

Funds from operations (FFO) Net income (computed in accordance with generally accepted accounting principles) *plus* (1) gains and losses from sales of properties and (2) depreciation and amortization.

Futures price The pre-agreed price at which a futures contract buyer (seller) agrees to pay (receive) for the underlying at the maturity date of the futures contract.

Futures value The monetary value of an existing futures contract.

Gamma A numerical measure of how sensitive an option's delta (the sensitivity of the derivative's price) is to a change in the value of the underlying.

General linear *F*-test A test statistic used to assess the goodness of fit for an entire regression model, so it tests all independent variables in the model.

Generalize When a model retains its explanatory power when predicting out-of-sample (i.e., using new data).

Global CAPM (GCAPM) A single-factor model with a global index representing the single factor.

Going-concern assumption The assumption that the business will maintain its business activities into the foreseeable future.

Going-concern value A business's value under a going-concern assumption.

Goodwill An intangible asset that represents the excess of the purchase price of an acquired company over the value of the net identifiable assets acquired.

Gordon growth model A DDM that assumes dividends grow at a constant rate into the future.

Grant date The day that stock options are granted to employees.

Green bond Bonds in which the proceeds are designated by issuers to fund a specific project or portfolio of projects that have environmental or climate benefits.

Greenmail The purchase of the accumulated shares of a hostile investor by a company that is targeted for takeover by that investor, usually at a substantial premium over market price.

Greenwashing The risk that a green bond's proceeds are not actually used for a beneficial environmental or climate-related project.

Grid search   A method of systematically training a model by using various combinations of hyperparameter values, cross validating each model, and determining which combination of hyperparameter values ensures the best model performance.

Gross domestic product   The market value of all final goods and services produced within the economy during a given period (output definition) or, equivalently, the aggregate income earned by all households, all companies, and the government within the economy during a given period (income definition).

Gross lease   A lease under which the tenant pays a gross rent to the landlord, who is responsible for all operating costs, utilities, maintenance expenses, and real estate taxes relating to the property.

Ground truth   The known outcome (i.e., target variable) of each observation in a labelled dataset.

Growth accounting equation   The production function written in the form of growth rates. For the basic Cobb–Douglas production function, it states that the growth rate of output equals the rate of technological change plus α multiplied by the growth rate of capital plus $(1 - \alpha)$ multiplied by the growth rate of labor.

Growth capital expenditures   Capital expenditures needed for expansion.

Guideline assets   Assets used as benchmarks when applying the method of comparables to value an asset.

Guideline companies   Assets used as benchmarks when applying the method of comparables to value an asset.

Guideline public companies   Public-company comparables for the company being valued.

Guideline public company method   A variation of the market approach; establishes a value estimate based on the observed multiples from trading activity in the shares of public companies viewed as reasonably comparable to the subject private company.

Guideline transactions method   A variation of the market approach; establishes a value estimate based on pricing multiples derived from the acquisition of control of entire public or private companies that were acquired.

Harmonic mean   A type of weighted mean computed as the reciprocal of the arithmetic average of the reciprocals.

Hazard rate   The probability that an event will occur, given that it has not already occurred.

Hedonic index   Unlike a repeat-sales index, a hedonic index does not require repeat sales of the same property. It requires only one sale. The way it controls for the fact that different properties are selling each quarter is to include variables in the regression that control for differences in the characteristics of the property, such as size, age, quality of construction, and location.

Heteroskedastic   When the variance of the residuals differs across observations in a regression.

Heteroskedasticity   The property of having a nonconstant variance; refers to an error term with the property that its variance differs across observations.

Hierarchical clustering   An iterative unsupervised learning procedure used for building a hierarchy of clusters.

High-leverage point   An observation of an independent variable that has an extreme value and is potentially influential.

Highest and best use   The concept that the best use of a vacant site is the use that would result in the highest value for the land. Presumably, the developer that could earn the highest risk-adjusted profit based on time, effort, construction and development cost, leasing, and exit value would be the one to pay the highest price for the land.

Historical exchange rates   For accounting purposes, the exchange rates that existed when the assets and liabilities were initially recorded.

Historical scenario analysis   A technique for exploring the performance and risk of investment strategies in different structural regimes.

Historical simulation   A simulation method that uses past return data and a random number generator that picks observations from the historical series to simulate an asset's future returns.

Historical simulation method   The application of historical price changes to the current portfolio.

Historical stress testing   The process that tests how investment strategies would perform under some of the most negative (i.e., adverse) combinations of events and scenarios.

Ho–Lee model   The first arbitrage-free term structure model. The model is calibrated to market data and uses a binomial lattice approach to generate a distribution of possible future interest rates.

Holdout samples   Data samples that are not used to train a model.

Homoskedasticity   The property of having a constant variance; refers to an error term that is constant across observations.

Horizontal ownership   Companies with mutual business interests (e.g., key customers or suppliers) that have cross-holding share arrangements with each other.

Human capital   An implied asset; the net present value of an investor's future expected labor income weighted by the probability of surviving to each future age. Also called *net employment capital*.

Hybrid approach   With respect to forecasting, an approach that combines elements of both top-down and bottom-up analyses.

Hyperparameter   A parameter whose value must be set by the researcher before learning begins.

iNAVs   "Indicated" net asset values are intraday "fair value" estimates of an ETF share based on its creation basket.

ISDA Master Agreement   A standard or "master" agreement published by the International Swaps and Derivatives Association. The master agreement establishes the terms for each party involved in the transaction.

I-spreads   Shortened form of "interpolated spreads" and a reference to a linearly interpolated yield.

Idiosyncratic risk premium (IRP)   The additional return required for bearing company-specific risks.

Illiquidity discount   A reduction or discount to value that reflects the lack of depth of trading or liquidity in that asset's market.

Impairment   Diminishment in value as a result of carrying (book) value exceeding fair value and/or recoverable value.

Impairment of capital rule   A legal restriction that dividends cannot exceed retained earnings.

Implementation shortfall   (IS) The difference between the return for a notional or paper portfolio, where all transactions are assumed to take place at the manager's decision price, and the portfolio's actual return, which reflects realized transactions, including all fees and costs.

Implied volatility   The standard deviation that causes an option pricing model to give the current option price.

In-sample forecast errors The residuals from a fitted time-series model within the sample period used to fit the model.

Income approach A valuation approach that values an asset as the present discounted value of the income expected from it. In the context of real estate, this approach estimates the value of a property based on an expected rate of return. The estimated value is the present value of the expected future income from the property, including proceeds from resale at the end of a typical investment holding period.

Incremental borrowing rate (IBR) The rate of interest that the lessee would have to pay to borrow using a collateralized loan over the same term as a lease.

Incremental VaR (IVaR) A measure of the incremental effect of an asset on the VaR of a portfolio by measuring the difference between the portfolio's VaR while including a specified asset and the portfolio's VaR with that asset eliminated.

Indenture A written contract between a lender and borrower that specifies the terms of the loan, such as interest rate, interest payment schedule, or maturity.

Independent board directors Directors with no material relationship with the company with regard to employment, ownership, or remuneration.

Independent regulators Regulators recognized and granted authority by a government body or agency. They are not government agencies per se and typically do not rely on government funding.

Index CDS A type of credit default swap that involves a combination of borrowers.

Industry risk premium (IP) The additional return that is required to bear industry-specific risk.

Industry shocks Unexpected changes to an industry from regulations or the legal environment, technology, or changes in the growth rate of the industry.

Industry structure An industry's underlying economic and technical characteristics.

Influence plot A visual that shows, for all observations, studentized residuals on the y-axis, leverage on the x-axis, and Cook's D as circles whose size is proportional to the degree of influence of the given observation.

Influential observation An observation in a statistical analysis whose inclusion may significantly alter regression results.

Information gain A metric which quantifies the amount of information that the feature holds about the response. Information gain can be regarded as a form of non-linear correlation between Y and X.

Information ratio (IR) Mean active return divided by active risk; or alpha divided by the standard deviation of diversifiable risk.

Informational frictions Forces that restrict availability, quality, and/or flow of information and its use.

Inside ask See *best ask*.

Inside bid See *best bid*.

Inside spread The spread between the best bid price and the best ask price. Also called the *market bid-ask spread, inside bid-ask spread*, or *market spread*.

Insiders Corporate managers and board directors who are also shareholders of a company.

Intangible assets Assets without a physical form, such as patents and trademarks.

Inter-temporal rate of substitution The ratio of the marginal utility of consumption s periods in the future (the numerator) to the marginal utility of consumption today (the denominator).

Interaction term A term that combines two or more variables and represents their joint influence on the dependent variable.

Intercept dummy An indicator variable that allows a single regression model to estimate two lines of best fit, each with differing intercepts, depending on whether the dummy takes a value of 1 or 0.

Interest rate risk The risk that interest rates will rise and therefore the market value of current portfolio holdings will fall so that their current yields to maturity then match comparable instruments in the marketplace.

Interlocking directorates Corporate structure in which individuals serve on the board of directors of multiple corporations.

International CAPM (ICAPM) A two-factor model with a global index and a wealth-weighted currency index.

International Fisher effect The proposition that nominal interest rate differentials across currencies are determined by expected inflation differentials.

Intrinsic value The amount gained (per unit) by an option buyer if an option is exercised at any given point in time. May be referred to as the exercise value of the option.

Inverse price ratio The reciprocal of a price multiple—for example, in the case of a P/E, the "earnings yield" E/P (where P is share price and E is earnings per share).

Investment value The value to a specific buyer, taking account of potential synergies based on the investor's requirements and expectations.

Joint test of hypotheses The test of hypotheses that specify values for two or more independent variables in the hypotheses.

Joint venture Two or more companies form and control a new, separate company to achieve a business objective. Each participant contributes assets, employees, know-how, or other resources to the joint venture company. The participants maintain their independence otherwise and continue to do business apart from the joint venture, but they share in the joint venture's profits or losses.

Judicial law Interpretations of courts.

Justified price multiple The estimated fair value of the price multiple, usually based on forecasted fundamentals or comparables.

Justified (fundamental) P/E The price-to-earnings ratio that is fair, warranted, or justified on the basis of forecasted fundamentals.

K-fold cross-validation A technique in which data (excluding test sample and fresh data) are shuffled randomly and then are divided into k equal sub-samples, with $k − 1$ samples used as training samples and one sample, the kth, used as a validation sample.

K-means A clustering algorithm that repeatedly partitions observations into a fixed number, k, of non-overlapping clusters.

K-nearest neighbor A supervised learning technique that classifies a new observation by finding similarities ("nearness") between this new observation and the existing data.

Kalotay–Williams–Fabozzi (KWF) model An arbitrage-free term structure model that describes the dynamics of the log of the short rate and assumes constant drift, no mean reversion, and constant volatility.

Key rate durations Sensitivity of a bond's price to changes in specific maturities on the benchmark yield curve. Also called *partial durations*.

kth-order autocorrelation   The correlation between observations in a time series separated by k periods.

LASSO   Least absolute shrinkage and selection operator is a type of penalized regression which involves minimizing the sum of the absolute values of the regression coefficients. LASSO can also be used for regularization in neural networks.

Labeled dataset   A dataset that contains matched sets of observed inputs or features (X's) and the associated output or target (Y).

Labor force   Everyone of working age (ages 16 to 64) who either is employed or is available for work but not working.

Labor force participation rate   The percentage of the working age population that is in the labor force.

Labor productivity   The quantity of goods and services (real GDP) that a worker can produce in one hour of work.

Labor productivity growth accounting equation   States that potential GDP growth equals the growth rate of the labor input plus the growth rate of labor productivity.

Lack of marketability discount   An extra return to investors to compensate for lack of a public market or lack of marketability.

Latency   The elapsed time between the occurrence of an event and a subsequent action that depends on that event.

Law of one price   A principle that states that if two investments have the same or equivalent future cash flows regardless of what will happen in the future, then these two investments should have the same current price.

Leading dividend yield   Forecasted dividends per share over the next year divided by current stock price.

Leading P/E   A P/E calculated on the basis of a forecast of EPS; a stock's current price divided by next year's expected earnings.

Learning curve   A curve that plots the accuracy rate (= 1 − error rate) in the validation or test samples (i.e., out-of-sample) against the amount of data in the training sample, which is thus useful for describing under- and overfitting as a function of bias and variance errors.

Learning rate   A parameter that affects the magnitude of adjustments in the weights in a neural network.

Level   One of the three factors (the other two are steepness and curvature) that empirically explain most yield curve shape changes. A shock to the level factor changes the yield for all maturities by an almost identical amount.

Leverage   A measure for identifying a potentially influential high-leverage point.

Leveraged buyout (LBO)   An acquirer (typically an investment fund specializing in LBOs) uses a significant amount of debt to finance the acquisition of a target and then pursues restructuring actions, with the goal of exiting the target with a sale or public listing.

Libor–OIS spread   The difference between Libor and the overnight indexed swap rate.

Likelihood ratio (LR) test   A method to assess the fit of logistic regression models and is based on the log-likelihood metric that describes the model's fit to the data.

Limit order book   The book or list of limit orders to buy and sell that pertains to a security.

Linear classifier   A binary classifier that makes its classification decision based on a linear combination of the features of each data point.

Linear trend   A trend in which the dependent variable changes at a constant rate with time.

Liquidating dividend   A dividend that is a return of capital rather than a distribution from earnings or retained earnings.

Liquidation value   The value of a company if the company were dissolved and its assets sold individually.

Liquidity preference theory   A term structure theory that asserts liquidity premiums exist to compensate investors for the added interest rate risk they face when lending long term.

Liquidity premium   An extra return that compensates investors for the risk of loss relative to an investment's fair value if the investment needs to be converted to cash quickly.

Local currency   The currency of the country where a company is located.

Local expectations theory   A term structure theory that contends the return for all bonds over short periods is the risk-free rate.

Log-linear model   With reference to time-series models, a model in which the growth rate of the time series as a function of time is constant.

Log odds   The natural log of the odds of an event or characteristic happening. Also known as the *logit function*.

Logistic regression (logit)   A regression in which the dependent variable uses a logistic transformation of the event probability.

Logistic transformation   The log of the probability of an occurrence of an event or characteristic divided by the probability of the event or characteristic not occurring.

Long/short credit trade   A credit protection seller with respect to one entity combined with a credit protection buyer with respect to another entity.

Look-ahead bias   A bias caused by using information that was unavailable on the test date.

Lookback period   The time period used to gather a historical data set.

Loss given default   The amount that will be lost if a default occurs.

Macroeconomic factor model   A multifactor model in which the factors are surprises in macroeconomic variables that significantly explain equity returns.

Macroeconomic factors   Factors related to the economy, such as the inflation rate, industrial production, or economic sector membership.

Maintenance capital expenditures   Capital expenditures needed to maintain operations at the current level.

Majority shareholders   Shareholders that own more than 50% of a corporation's shares.

Majority-vote classifier   A classifier that assigns to a new data point the predicted label with the most votes (i.e., occurrences).

Marginal VaR (MVaR)   A measure of the effect of a small change in a position size on portfolio VaR.

Market approach   Valuation approach that values an asset based on pricing multiples from sales of assets viewed as similar to the subject asset.

Market conditions   Interest rates, inflation rates, and other economic characteristics that comprise the macroeconomic environment.

Market conversion premium per share   For a convertible bond, the difference between the market conversion price and the underlying share price, which allows investors to identify the premium or discount payable when buying a convertible bond rather than the underlying common stock.

Market conversion premium ratio For a convertible bond, the market conversion premium per share expressed as a percentage of the current market price of the shares.

Market efficiency A finance perspective on capital markets that deals with the relationship of price to intrinsic value. The traditional efficient markets formulation asserts that an asset's price is the best available estimate of its intrinsic value. The rational efficient markets formulation asserts that investors should expect to be rewarded for the costs of information gathering and analysis by higher gross returns.

Market fragmentation Trading the same instrument in multiple venues.

Market impact The effect of the trade on transaction prices. Also called *price impact*.

Market model A regression model with the return on a stock as the dependent variable and the returns on a market index as the independent variable.

Market value of invested capital The market value of debt and equity.

Mature growth rate The earnings growth rate in a company's mature phase; an earnings growth rate that can be sustained long term.

Maximum drawdown The worst cumulative loss ever sustained by an asset or portfolio. More specifically, maximum drawdown is the difference between an asset's or a portfolio's maximum cumulative return and its subsequent lowest cumulative return.

Maximum likelihood estimation (MLE) A method that estimates values for the intercept and slope coefficients in a logistic regression that make the data in the regression sample most likely.

Mean reversion The tendency of a time series to fall when its level is above its mean and rise when its level is below its mean; a mean-reverting time series tends to return to its long-term mean.

Metadata Data that describes and gives information about other data.

Method based on forecasted fundamentals An approach to using price multiples that relates a price multiple to forecasts of fundamentals through a discounted cash flow model.

Method of comparables An approach to valuation that involves using a price multiple to evaluate whether an asset is relatively fairly valued, relatively undervalued, or relatively overvalued when compared to a benchmark value of the multiple.

Midquote price The average, or midpoint, of the prevailing bid and ask prices.

Minority interest The proportion of the ownership of a subsidiary not held by the parent (controlling) company.

Minority shareholders Particular shareholders or a block of shareholders holding a small proportion of a company's outstanding shares, resulting in a limited ability to exercise control in voting activities.

Mispricing Any departure of the market price of an asset from the asset's estimated intrinsic value.

Model specification The set of independent variables included in a model and the model's functional form.

Molodovsky effect The observation that P/Es tend to be high on depressed EPS at the bottom of a business cycle and tend to be low on unusually high EPS at the top of a business cycle.

Momentum indicators Valuation indicators that relate either price or a fundamental (such as earnings) to the time series of their own past values (or in some cases to their expected value).

Monetary assets and liabilities Assets and liabilities with value equal to the amount of currency contracted for, a fixed amount of currency. Examples are cash, accounts receivable, accounts payable, bonds payable, and mortgages payable. Inventory is not a monetary asset. Most liabilities are monetary.

Monetary/non-monetary method Approach to translating foreign currency financial statements for consolidation in which monetary assets and liabilities are translated at the current exchange rate. Non-monetary assets and liabilities are translated at historical exchange rates (the exchange rates that existed when the assets and liabilities were acquired).

Monetizing Unwinding a position to either capture a gain or realize a loss.

Monte Carlo simulation A technique that uses the inverse transformation method for converting a randomly generated uniformly distributed number into a simulated value of a random variable of a desired distribution. Each key decision variable in a Monte Carlo simulation requires an assumed statistical distribution; this assumption facilitates incorporating non-normality, fat tails, and tail dependence as well as solving high-dimensionality problems.

Mortgage A loan with real estate serving as collateral for the loan.

Multicollinearity When two or more independent variables are highly correlated with one another or are approximately linearly related.

Multiple linear regression Modeling and estimation method that uses two or more independent variables to describe the variation of the dependent variable. Also referred to as *multiple regression*.

Mutual information Measures how much information is contributed by a token to a class of texts. MI will be 0 if the token's distribution in all text classes is the same. MI approaches 1 as the token in any one class tends to occur more often in only that particular class of text.

N-grams A representation of word sequences. The length of a sequence varies from 1 to *n*. When one word is used, it is a unigram; a two-word sequence is a bigram; and a 3-word sequence is a trigram; and so on.

n-Period moving average The average of the current and immediately prior $n - 1$ values of a time series.

NTM P/E Next 12-month P/E: current market price divided by an estimated next 12-month EPS.

Naked credit default swap A position where the owner of the CDS does not have a position in the underlying credit.

Name entity recognition An algorithm that analyzes individual tokens and their surrounding semantics while referring to its dictionary to tag an object class to the token.

Negative serial correlation A situation in which residuals are negatively related to other residuals.

Nested models Models in which one regression model has a subset of the independent variables of another regression model.

Net asset balance sheet exposure When assets translated at the current exchange rate are greater in amount than liabilities translated at the current exchange rate. Assets exposed to translation gains or losses exceed the exposed liabilities.

Net asset value per share (NAVPS)   Net asset value divided by the number of shares outstanding.

Net lease   A lease under which the tenant pays a net rent to the landlord and an additional amount based on the tenant's pro rata share of the operating costs, utilities, maintenance expenses, and real estate taxes relating to the property.

Net liability balance sheet exposure   When liabilities translated at the current exchange rate are greater assets translated at the current exchange rate. Liabilities exposed to translation gains or losses exceed the exposed assets.

Net operating income (NOI)   Gross rental revenue minus operating costs but before deducting depreciation, corporate overhead, and interest expense. In the context of real estate, a measure of the income from the property after deducting operating expenses for such items as property taxes, insurance, maintenance, utilities, repairs, and insurance but before deducting any costs associated with financing and before deducting federal income taxes. It is similar to EBITDA in a financial reporting context.

Net regulatory burden   The private costs of regulation less the private benefits of regulation.

Network externalities   The impact that users of a good, a service, or a technology have on other users of that product; it can be positive (e.g., a critical mass of users makes a product more useful) or negative (e.g., congestion makes the product less useful).

Neural networks   Computer programs based on how our own brains learn and process information.

No-arbitrage approach   A procedure for obtaining the value of an option based on the creation of a portfolio that replicates the payoffs of the option and deriving the option value from the value of the replicating portfolio.

No-growth company   A company without positive expected net present value projects.

No-growth value per share   The value per share of a no-growth company, equal to the expected level amount of earnings divided by the stock's required rate of return.

Non-cash rent   An amount equal to the difference between the average contractual rent over a lease term (the straight-line rent) and the cash rent actually paid during a period. This figure is one of the deductions made from FFO to calculate AFFO.

Non-convergence trap   A situation in which a country remains relatively poor, or even falls further behind, because it fails to implement necessary institutional reforms and/or adopt leading technologies.

Non-monetary assets and liabilities   Assets and liabilities that are not monetary assets and liabilities. Non-monetary assets include inventory, fixed assets, and intangibles, and non-monetary liabilities include deferred revenue.

Non-renewable resources   Finite resources that are depleted once they are consumed; oil and coal are examples.

Non-residential properties   Commercial real estate properties other than multi-family properties, farmland, and timberland.

Nonearning assets   Cash and investments (specifically cash, cash equivalents, and short-term investments).

Normal EPS   The EPS that a business could achieve currently under mid-cyclical conditions. Also called *normalized EPS*.

Normal Q-Q plot   A visual used to compare the distribution of the residuals from a regression to a theoretical normal distribution.

Normalized EPS   The EPS that a business could achieve currently under mid-cyclical conditions. Also called *normal EPS*.

Normalized earnings   The expected level of mid-cycle earnings for a company in the absence of any unusual or temporary factors that affect profitability (either positively or negatively).

Normalized P/E   P/E based on normalized EPS data.

Notional amount   The amount of protection being purchased in a CDS.

Off-the-run   A series of securities or indexes that were issued/created prior to the most recently issued/created series.

Offshoring   Refers to relocating operations from one country to another, mainly to reduce costs through lower labor costs or to achieve economies of scale through centralization, but still maintaining operations within the corporation.

Omitted variable bias   Bias resulting from the omission of an important independent variable from a regression model.

On-the-run   The most recently issued and most actively traded sovereign securities.

One hot encoding   The process by which categorical variables are converted into binary form (0 or 1) for machine reading. It is one of the most common methods for handling categorical features in text data.

One-sided durations   Effective durations when interest rates go up or down, which are better at capturing the interest rate sensitivity of bonds with embedded options that do not react symmetrically to positive and negative changes in interest rates of the same magnitude.

One-tier board   Board structure consisting of a single board of directors, composed of executive (internal) and non-executive (external) directors.

Opportunity cost   Reflects the foregone opportunity of investing in a different asset. It is typically denoted by the risk-free rate of interest, r.

Option-adjusted spread   (OAS) Constant spread that, when added to all the one-period forward rates on the interest rate tree, makes the arbitrage-free value of the bond equal to its market price.

Orderly liquidation value   The estimated gross amount of money that could be realized from the liquidation sale of an asset or assets, given a reasonable amount of time to find a purchaser or purchasers.

Other comprehensive income   Items of comprehensive income that are not reported on the income statement; comprehensive income minus net income.

Other post-employment benefits   Promises by the company to pay benefits in the future, such as life insurance premiums and all or part of health care insurance for its retirees.

Out-of-sample forecast errors   The differences between actual and predicted values of time series outside the sample period used to fit the model.

Outlier   An observation that has an extreme value of the dependent variable and is potentially influential.

Outsourcing   Shifting internal business services to a subcontractor that can offer services at lower costs by scaling to serve many clients.

Overfitting   Situation in which the model has too many independent variables relative to the number of observations in the sample, such that the coefficients on the independent variables represent noise rather than relationships with the dependent variable.

Overnight indexed swap (OIS) rate An interest rate swap in which the periodic floating rate of the swap equals the geometric average of a daily unsecured overnight rate (or overnight index rate).

PEG ratio The P/E-to-growth ratio, calculated as the stock's P/E divided by the expected earnings growth rate.

Pairs trading An approach to trading that uses pairs of closely related stocks, buying the relatively undervalued stock and selling short the relatively overvalued stock.

Par curve A sequence of yields-to-maturity such that each bond is priced at par value. The bonds are assumed to have the same currency, credit risk, liquidity, tax status, and annual yields stated for the same periodicity.

Par swap A swap in which the fixed rate is set so that no money is exchanged at contract initiation.

Parametric method A method of estimating VaR that uses the historical mean, standard deviation, and correlation of security price movements to estimate the portfolio VaR. Generally assumes a normal distribution but can be adapted to non-normal distributions with the addition of skewness and kurtosis. Sometimes called the *variance–covariance method* or the *analytical method*.

Partial regression coefficient Coefficient that describes the effect of a one-unit change in the independent variable on the dependent variable, holding all other independent variables constant. Also known as *partial slope coefficient*.

Parts of speech An algorithm that uses language structure and dictionaries to tag every token in the text with a corresponding part of speech (i.e., noun, verb, adjective, proper noun, etc.).

Payout amount The loss given default times the notional.

Payout policy The principles by which a company distributes cash to common shareholders by means of cash dividends and/or share repurchases.

Payouts Cash dividends and the value of shares repurchased in any given year.

Penalized regression A regression that includes a constraint such that the regression coefficients are chosen to minimize the sum of squared residuals *plus* a penalty term that increases in size with the number of included features.

Pension obligation The present value of future benefits earned by employees for service provided to date.

Perfect capital markets Markets in which, by assumption, there are no taxes, transaction costs, or bankruptcy costs and in which all investors have equal ("symmetric") information.

Perpetuity A perpetual annuity, or a set of never-ending level sequential cash flows, with the first cash flow occurring one period from now.

Persistent earnings Earnings excluding nonrecurring components. Also referred to as *core earnings, continuing earnings,* or *underlying earnings*.

Physical settlement Involves actual delivery of the debt instrument in exchange for a payment by the credit protection seller of the notional amount of the contract.

Point-in-time data Data consisting of the exact information available to market participants as of a given point in time. Point-in-time data is used to address look-ahead bias.

Portfolio balance approach A theory of exchange rate determination that emphasizes the portfolio investment decisions of global investors and the requirement that global investors willingly hold all outstanding securities denominated in each currency at prevailing prices and exchange rates.

Positive serial correlation A situation in which residuals are positively related to other residuals.

Potential GDP The maximum amount of output an economy can sustainably produce without inducing an increase in the inflation rate. The output level that corresponds to full employment with consistent wage and price expectations.

Precision In error analysis for classification problems it is ratio of correctly predicted positive classes to all predicted positive classes. Precision is useful in situations where the cost of false positives (FP), or Type I error, is high.

Preferred habitat theory A term structure theory that contends that investors have maturity preferences and require yield incentives before they will buy bonds outside of their preferred maturities.

Premise of value The status of a company in the sense of whether it is assumed to be a going concern or not.

Premium leg The series of payments the credit protection buyer promises to make to the credit protection seller.

Premiums Amounts paid by the purchaser of insurance products.

Present value model A model of intrinsic value that views the value of an asset as the present value of the asset's expected future cash flows.

Present value of growth opportunities The difference between the actual value per share and the no-growth value per share. Also called *value of growth*.

Presentation currency The currency in which financial statement amounts are presented.

Price improvement When trade execution prices are better than quoted prices.

Price momentum A valuation indicator based on past price movement.

Price multiples The ratio of a stock's market price to some measure of value per share.

Price-to-earnings ratio (P/E) The ratio of share price to earnings per share.

Priced risk Risk for which investors demand compensation for bearing (e.g., equity risk, company-specific factors, macroeconomic factors).

Principal components analysis (PCA) An unsupervised ML technique used to transform highly correlated features of data into a few main, uncorrelated composite variables.

Principle of no arbitrage In well-functioning markets, prices will adjust until there are no arbitrage opportunities.

Prior transaction method A variation of the market approach; considers actual transactions in the stock of the subject private company.

Private market value The value derived using a sum-of-the-parts valuation.

Pro forma financial statements Financial statements that include the effect of a corporate restructuring.

Probability of default The likelihood that a borrower defaults or fails to meet its obligation to make full and timely payments of principal and interest.

Probability of survival The probability that a bond issuer will meet its contractual obligations on schedule.

Procedural law The body of law that focuses on the protection and enforcement of the substantive laws.

Projection error The vertical (perpendicular) distance between a data point and a given principal component.

Prospective P/E A P/E calculated on the basis of a forecast of EPS; a stock's current price divided by next year's expected earnings.

Protection leg The contingent payment that the credit protection seller may have to make to the credit protection buyer.

Protection period Period during which a bond's issuer cannot call the bond.

Provision for loan losses An income statement expense account that increases the amount of the allowance for loan losses.

Prudential supervision Regulation and monitoring of the safety and soundness of financial institutions to promote financial stability, reduce system-wide risks, and protect customers of financial institutions.

Pruning A regularization technique used in CART to reduce the size of the classification or regression tree—by pruning, or removing, sections of the tree that provide little classifying power.

Purchasing power gain A gain in value caused by changes in price levels. Monetary liabilities experience purchasing power gains during periods of inflation.

Purchasing power loss A loss in value caused by changes in price levels. Monetary assets experience purchasing power loss during periods of inflation.

Purchasing power parity (PPP) The idea that exchange rates move to equalize the purchasing power of different currencies.

Pure expectations theory A term structure theory that contends the forward rate is an unbiased predictor of the future spot rate. Also called the *unbiased expectations theory*.

Pure factor portfolio A portfolio with sensitivity of 1 to the factor in question and a sensitivity of 0 to all other factors.

Putable bond Bond that includes an embedded put option, which gives the bondholder the right to put back the bonds to the issuer prior to maturity, typically when interest rates have risen and higher-yielding bonds are available.

Qualitative dependent variable A dependent variable that is discrete (binary). Also known as a *categorical dependent variable*.

Quality of earnings analysis The investigation of issues relating to the accuracy of reported accounting results as reflections of economic performance. Quality of earnings analysis is broadly understood to include not only earnings management but also balance sheet management.

Random forest classifier A collection of a large number of decision trees trained via a bagging method.

Random walk A time series in which the value of the series in one period is the value of the series in the previous period plus an unpredictable random error.

Rate implicit in the lease (RIIL) The discount rate that equates the present value of the lease payment with the fair value of the leased asset, considering also the lessor's direct costs and the present value of the leased asset's residual value.

Rational efficient markets formulation See *market efficiency*.

Readme files Text files provided with raw data that contain information related to a data file. They are useful for understanding the data and how they can be interpreted correctly.

Real estate investment trusts (REITs) Tax-advantaged entities (companies or trusts) that own, operate, and—to a limited extent—develop income-producing real estate property.

Real estate operating companies (REOCs) Regular taxable real estate ownership companies that operate in the real estate industry in countries that do not have a tax-advantaged REIT regime in place or that are engage in real estate activities of a kind and to an extent that do not fit in their country's REIT framework.

Real interest rate parity The proposition that real interest rates will converge to the same level across different markets.

Real options Options that relate to investment decisions such as the option to time the start of a project, the option to adjust its scale, or the option to abandon a project that has begun.

Rebalance return A return from rebalancing the component weights of an index.

Recall Also known as *sensitivity*, in error analysis for classification problems it is the ratio of correctly predicted positive classes to all actual positive classes. Recall is useful in situations where the cost of false negatives (FN), or Type II error, is high.

Recency bias The behavioral tendency to place more relevance on recent events.

Reconstitution When dealers recombine appropriate individual zero-coupon securities and reproduce an underlying coupon Treasury.

Recovery rate The percentage of the loss recovered.

Redemption basket The list of securities (and share amounts) the authorized participant (AP) receives when it redeems ETF shares back to the ETF manager. The redemption basket is published each business day.

Reference entity The borrower (debt issuer) covered by a single-name CDS.

Reference obligation A particular debt instrument issued by the borrower that is the designated instrument being covered.

Regime With reference to a time series, the underlying model generating the times series.

Regular expression (regex) A series of texts that contains characters in a particular order. Regex is used to search for patterns of interest in a given text.

Regularization A term that describes methods for reducing statistical variability in high-dimensional data estimation problems.

Regulatory arbitrage Entities identify and use some aspect of regulations that allows them to exploit differences in economic substance and regulatory interpretation or in foreign and domestic regulatory regimes to their (the entities') advantage.

Regulatory burden The costs of regulation for the regulated entity.

Regulatory capture Theory that regulation often arises to enhance the interests of the regulated.

Regulatory competition Regulators may compete to provide a regulatory environment designed to attract certain entities.

Reinforcement learning Machine learning in which a computer learns from interacting with itself or data generated by the same algorithm.

Relative-strength indicators Valuation indicators that compare a stock's performance during a period either to its own past performance or to the performance of some group of stocks.

Relative VaR See *ex ante tracking error*.

Relative valuation models A model that specifies an asset's value relative to the value of another asset.

Relative version of PPP The hypothesis that changes in (nominal) exchange rates over time are equal to national inflation rate differentials.

Renewable resources Resources that can be replenished, such as a forest.

Rental price of capital The cost per unit of time to rent a unit of capital.

Reorganization A court-supervised restructuring process available in some jurisdictions for companies facing insolvency from burdensome debt levels. A bankruptcy court assumes control of the company and oversees an orderly negotiation process between the company and its creditors for asset sales, conversion of debt to equity, refinancing, and so on.

Repeat sales index As the name implies, this type of index relies on repeat sales of the same property. In general, the idea supporting this type of index is that because it is the same property that sold twice, the change in value between the two sale dates indicates how market conditions have changed over time.

Replacement cost In the context of real estate, the value of a building assuming it was built today using current construction costs and standards.

Reporting unit For financial reporting under US GAAP, an operating segment or one level below an operating segment (referred to as a component).

Required rate of return on equity The minimum rate of return required by an investor to invest in an asset, given the asset's riskiness. Also known as the required return on equity.

Residential properties Properties that provide housing for individuals or families. Single-family properties may be owner-occupied or rental properties, whereas multi-family properties are rental properties even if the owner or manager occupies one of the units.

Residual autocorrelations The sample autocorrelations of the residuals.

Residual income Earnings for a given period, minus a deduction for common shareholders' opportunity cost in generating the earnings. Also called *economic profit* or *abnormal earnings*.

Residual income method Income approach that estimates the value of all intangible assets of the business by capitalizing future earnings in excess of the estimated return requirements associated with working capital and fixed assets.

Residual income model (RIM) A model of stock valuation that views intrinsic value of stock as the sum of book value per share plus the present value of the stock's expected future residual income per share. Also called *discounted abnormal earnings model* or *Edwards–Bell–Ohlson model*.

Restricted model A regression model with a subset of the complete set of independent variables.

Restructuring Reorganizing the capital structure of a firm.

Return on invested capital A measure of the profitability of a company relative to the amount of capital invested by the equity- and debtholders.

Reverse carry arbitrage A strategy involving the short sale of the underlying and an offsetting opposite position in the derivative.

Reverse stock split A reduction in the number of shares outstanding with a corresponding increase in share price, but no change to the company's underlying fundamentals.

Reverse stress testing A risk management approach in which the user identifies key risk exposures in the portfolio and subjects those exposures to extreme market movements.

Reviewed financial statements A type of non-audited financial statements; typically provide an opinion letter with representations and assurances by the reviewing accountant that are less than those in audited financial statements.

Rho The change in a given derivative instrument for a given small change in the risk-free interest rate, holding everything else constant. Rho measures the sensitivity of the option to the risk-free interest rate.

Risk-based models Models of the return on equity that identify risk factors or drivers and sensitivities of the return to these factors.

Risk budgeting The establishment of objectives for individuals, groups, or divisions of an organization that takes into account the allocation of an acceptable level of risk.

Risk decomposition The process of converting a set of holdings in a portfolio into a set of exposures to risk factors.

Risk factors Variables or characteristics with which individual asset returns are correlated. Sometimes referred to simply as *factors*.

Risk-free rate The minimum rate of return expected on a security that has no default risk.

Risk parity A portfolio allocation scheme that weights stocks or factors based on an equal risk contribution.

Robust standard errors Method for correcting residuals for conditional heteroskedasticity. Also known as *heteroskedasticity-consistent standard errors* or *White-corrected standard errors*.

Roll When an investor moves its investment position from an older series to the most current series.

Roll return The component of the return on a commodity futures contract attributable to rolling long futures positions forward through time. Also called *roll yield*.

Rolling down the yield curve A maturity trading strategy that involves buying bonds with a maturity longer than the intended investment horizon. Also called *riding the yield curve*.

Rolling windows A backtesting method that uses a rolling-window (or walk-forward) framework, rebalances the portfolio after each period, and then tracks performance over time. As new information arrives each period, the investment manager optimizes (revises and tunes) the model and readjusts stock positions.

Root mean squared error (RMSE) The square root of the average squared forecast error; used to compare the out-of-sample forecasting performance of forecasting models.

Sale-leaseback A situation in which a company sells the building it owns and occupies to a real estate investor and the company then signs a long-term lease with the buyer to continue to occupy the building. At the end of the lease, use of the property reverts to the landlord.

Sales comparison approach In the context of real estate, this approach estimates value based on what similar or comparable properties (comparables) transacted for in the current market.

Sales risk The uncertainty regarding the price and number of units sold of a company's products.

Scaled earnings surprise Unexpected earnings divided by the standard deviation of analysts' earnings forecasts.

Scaling The process of adjusting the range of a feature by shifting and changing the scale of the data. Two of the most common ways of scaling are normalization and standardization.

Scatterplot matrix A visualization technique that shows the scatterplots between different sets of variables, often with the histogram for each variable on the diagonal. Also referred to as a *pairs plot*.

Scenario analysis   A technique for exploring the performance and risk of investment strategies in different structural regimes.

Schwarz's Bayesian information criterion (BIC or SBC)   A statistic used to compare sets of independent variables for explaining a dependent variable. It is preferred for finding the model with the best goodness of fit.

Scree plots   A plot that shows the proportion of total variance in the data explained by each principal component.

Screening   The application of a set of criteria to reduce a set of potential investments to a smaller set having certain desired characteristics.

Seasonality   A characteristic of a time series in which the data experience regular and predictable periodic changes; for example, fan sales are highest during the summer months.

Secured overnight financing rate (SOFR)   A daily volume-weighted index of rates on qualified cash borrowings collateralized by US Treasuries that is expected to replace Libor as a floating reference rate for swaps.

Security selection risk   See *active specific risk*.

Segmented markets theory   A term structure theory that contends yields are solely a function of the supply and demand for funds of a particular maturity.

Self-regulating organizations (SROs)   Self-regulating bodies that are given recognition and authority, including enforcement power, by a government body or agency.

Self-regulatory bodies   Private, non-governmental organizations that both represent and regulate their members. Some self-regulating organizations are also independent regulators.

Sell-side analysts   Analysts who work at brokerages.

Sensitivity analysis   Analysis that shows the range of possible outcomes as specific assumptions are changed.

Sentence length   The number of characters, including spaces, in a sentence.

Serial correlation   A condition found most often in time series in which residuals are correlated across observations. Also known as *autocorrelation*.

Serial-correlation consistent standard errors   Method for correcting serial correlation. Also known as *serial correlation and heteroskedasticity adjusted standard errors*, *Newey–West standard errors*, and *robust standard errors*.

Service period   For employee stock options, usually the period between the grant date and the vesting date.

Settled in arrears   An arrangement in which the interest payment is made (i.e., settlement occurs) at the maturity of the underlying instrument.

Settlement   The closing date at which the counterparties of a derivative contract exchange payment for the underlying as required by the contract.

Shadow banking   Lending by financial institutions that are not regulated as banks.

Shaping risk   The sensitivity of a bond's price to the changing shape of the yield curve.

Share repurchase   A transaction in which a company buys back its own shares. Unlike stock dividends and stock splits, share repurchases use corporate cash.

Shareholder activism   Strategies used by shareholders to attempt to compel a company to act in a desired manner.

Shareholders' equity   Total assets minus total liabilities.

Simulation   A technique for exploring how a target variable (e.g. portfolio returns) would perform in a hypothetical environment specified by the user, rather than a historical setting.

Single-name CDS   Credit default swap on one specific borrower.

Sinking fund bond   A bond that requires the issuer to set aside funds over time to retire the bond issue, thus reducing credit risk.

Size premium (SP)   Additional return compensation for bearing the additional risk associated with smaller companies.

Slope dummy   An indicator variable that allows a single regression model to estimate two lines of best fit, each with differing slopes, depending on whether the dummy takes a value of 1 or 0.

Soft margin classification   An adaptation in the support vector machine algorithm which adds a penalty to the objective function for observations in the training set that are misclassified.

Sovereign yield spread   The spread between the yield on a foreign country's sovereign bond and a similar-maturity domestic sovereign bond.

Special dividend   A dividend paid by a company that does not pay dividends on a regular schedule, or a dividend that supplements regular cash dividends with an extra payment.

Specific-company risk premium (SCRP)   Additional return required by investors for bearing non-diversifiable company-specific risk.

Spin off   When a company separates a distinct part of its business into a new, independent company. The term is used to describe both the transaction and the separated component, while the company that conducts the transaction and formerly owned the spin off is known as the parent.

Split-rate tax system   In reference to corporate taxes, a split-rate system taxes earnings to be distributed as dividends at a different rate than earnings to be retained. Corporate profits distributed as dividends are taxed at a lower rate than those retained in the business.

Spot curve   A sequence of yields-to-maturity on zero-coupon bonds. Sometimes called *zero* or *strip curve* (because coupon payments are "stripped" off the bonds).

Spot price   The current price of an asset or security. For commodities, the current price to deliver a physical commodity to a specific location or purchase and transport it away from a designated location.

Spot rate   The interest rate that is determined today for a risk-free, single-unit payment at a specified future date.

Spot yield curve   The term structure of spot rates for loans made today.

Stabilized NOI   In the context of real estate, the expected NOI when a renovation is complete.

Stable dividend policy   A policy in which regular dividends are paid that reflect long-run expected earnings. In contrast to a constant dividend payout ratio policy, a stable dividend policy does not reflect short-term volatility in earnings.

Standardized beta   With reference to fundamental factor models, the value of the attribute for an asset minus the average value of the attribute across all stocks, divided by the standard deviation of the attribute across all stocks.

Standardized unexpected earnings   Unexpected earnings per share divided by the standard deviation of unexpected earnings per share over a specified prior time period.

Statistical factor model   A multifactor model in which statistical methods are applied to a set of historical returns to determine portfolios that best explain either historical return covariances or variances.

Statutes   Laws enacted by legislative bodies.

Steady-state rate of growth The constant growth rate of output (or output per capita) that can or will be sustained indefinitely once it is reached. Key ratios, such as the capital–output ratio, are constant on the steady-state growth path.

Steepness The difference between long-term and short-term yields that constitutes one of the three factors (the other two are level and curvature) that empirically explain most of the changes in the shape of the yield curve.

Stock dividend A type of dividend in which a company distributes additional shares of its common stock to shareholders instead of cash.

Stop-loss limit Constraint used in risk management that requires a reduction in the size of a portfolio, or its complete liquidation, when a loss of a particular size occurs in a specified period.

Straight bond An underlying option-free bond with a specified issuer, issue date, maturity date, principal amount and repayment structure, coupon rate and payment structure, and currency denomination.

Straight debt Debt with no embedded options.

Straight-line rent The average annual rent under a multi-year lease agreement that contains contractual increases in rent during the life of the lease.

Straight-line rent adjustment See *non-cash rent*.

Straight voting A shareholder voting process in which shareholders receive one vote for each share owned.

Stranded assets Assets that are obsolete or not economically viable.

Strategic transaction A purchase involving a buyer that would benefit from certain synergies associated with owning the target firm.

Stress tests A risk management technique that assesses the portfolio's response to extreme market movements.

Stripping A dealer's ability to separate a bond's individual cash flows and trade them as zero-coupon securities.

Studentized residual A t-distributed statistic that is used to detect outliers.

Substantive law The body of law that focuses on the rights and responsibilities of entities and relationships among entities.

Succession event A change of corporate structure of the reference entity, such as through a merger, a divestiture, a spinoff, or any similar action, in which ultimate responsibility for the debt in question is unclear.

Sum-of-the-parts valuation A valuation that sums the estimated values of each of a company's businesses as if each business were an independent going concern.

Summation operator A functional part of a neural network's node that multiplies each input value received by a weight and sums the weighted values to form the total net input, which is then passed to the activation function.

Supernormal growth Above-average or abnormally high growth rate in earnings per share.

Supervised learning A machine learning approach that makes use of labeled training data.

Support vector machine A linear classifier that determines the hyperplane that optimally separates the observations into two sets of data points.

Survivorship bias The exclusion of poorly performing or defunct companies from an index or database, biasing the index or database toward financially healthy companies.

Sustainable growth rate The rate of dividend (and earnings) growth that can be sustained over time for a given level of return on equity, keeping the capital structure constant and without issuing additional common stock.

Swap curve The term structure of swap rates.

Swap rate The fixed rate to be paid by the fixed-rate payer specified in a swap contract.

Swap rate curve The term structure of swap rates.

Swap spread The difference between the fixed rate on an interest rate swap and the rate on a Treasury note with equivalent maturity; it reflects the general level of credit risk in the market.

Synergies The combination of two companies being more valuable than the sum of the parts. Generally, synergies take the form of lower costs ("cost synergies") or increased revenues ("revenue synergies") through combinations that generate lower costs or higher revenues, respectively.

Systematic risk Risk that affects the entire market or economy; it cannot be avoided and is inherent in the overall market. Systematic risk is also known as non-diversifiable or market risk.

Systemic risk Refers to risks supervisory authorities believe are likely to have broad impact across the financial market infrastructure and affect a wide swath of market participants.

TED spread A measure of perceived credit risk determined as the difference between Libor and the T-bill yield of matching maturity.

Tail risk The risk that losses in extreme events could be greater than would be expected for a portfolio of assets with a normal distribution.

Takeover premium The amount by which the per-share takeover price exceeds the unaffected price expressed as a percentage of the unaffected price. It reflects the amount shareholders require to relinquish their control of the company to the acquirer.

Tangible assets Identifiable, physical assets such as property, plant, and equipment.

Tangible book value per share Common shareholders' equity minus intangible assets reported on the balance sheet, divided by the number of shares outstanding.

Target In machine learning, the dependent variable (Y) in a labeled dataset; the company in a merger or acquisition that is being acquired.

Target capital structure A company's chosen proportions of debt and equity.

Target payout ratio A strategic corporate goal representing the long-term proportion of earnings that the company intends to distribute to shareholders as dividends.

Taxable REIT subsidiaries Subsidiaries that pay income taxes on earnings from non-REIT-qualifying activities like merchant development or third-party property management.

Technical indicators Momentum indicators based on price.

Temporal method A variation of the monetary/non-monetary translation method that requires not only monetary assets and liabilities, but also non-monetary assets and liabilities that are measured at their current value on the balance sheet date to be translated at the current exchange rate. Assets and liabilities are translated at rates consistent with the timing of their measurement value. This method is typically used when the functional currency is other than the local currency.

Term frequency (TF)   Ratio of the number of times a given token occurs in all the texts in the dataset to the total number of tokens in the dataset.

Term premium   The additional return required by lenders to invest in a bond to maturity net of the expected return from continually reinvesting at the short-term rate over that same time horizon.

Terminal price multiples   The price multiple for a stock assumed to hold at a stated future time.

Terminal share price   The share price at a particular point in the future.

Terminal value of the stock   The analyst's estimate of a stock's value at a particular point in the future. Also called *continuing value of the stock*.

Test sample   A data sample that is used to test a model's ability to predict well on new data.

Theta   The change in a derivative instrument for a given small change in calendar time, holding everything else constant. Specifically, the theta calculation assumes nothing changes except calendar time. Theta also reflects the rate at which an option's time value decays.

Time series   A set of observations on a variable's outcomes in different time periods.

Tobin's q   The ratio of the market value of debt and equity to the replacement cost of total assets.

Token   The equivalent of a word (or sometimes a character).

Tokenization   The process of representing ownership rights to physical assets on a blockchain or distributed ledger.

Top-down approach   With respect to forecasting, an approach that usually begins at the level of the overall economy. Forecasts are then made at more narrowly defined levels, such as sector, industry, and market for a specific product.

Total factor productivity (TFP)   A multiplicative scale factor that reflects the general level of productivity or technology in the economy. Changes in total factor productivity generate proportional changes in output for any input combination.

Total invested capital   The sum of market value of common equity, book value of preferred equity, and face value of debt.

Tracking error   The standard deviation of the differences between a portfolio's returns and its benchmark's returns; a synonym of *active risk*. Also called *tracking risk*.

Tracking risk   The standard deviation of the differences between a portfolio's returns and its benchmarks returns. Also called *tracking error*.

Trailing dividend yield   The reciprocal of current market price divided by the most recent annualized dividend.

Trailing P/E   A stock's current market price divided by the most recent four quarters of EPS (or the most recent two semi-annual periods for companies that report interim data semi-annually). Also called *current P/E*.

Training sample   A data sample that is used to train a model.

Tranche CDS   A type of credit default swap that covers a combination of borrowers but only up to pre-specified levels of losses.

Transaction exposure   The risk of a change in value between the transaction date and the settlement date of an asset of liability denominated in a foreign currency.

Treasury shares/stock   Shares that were issued and subsequently repurchased by the company.

Trend   A long-term pattern of movement in a particular direction.

Triangular arbitrage   An arbitrage transaction involving three currencies that attempts to exploit inconsistencies among pairwise exchange rates.

Trimming   Also called truncation, it is the process of removing extreme values and outliers from a dataset.

Triple-net leases   Leases that require each tenant to pay its share of the following three operating expenses: common area maintenance and repair expenses; property taxes; and building insurance costs. Also known as *NNN leases*.

Two-tier board   Board structure consisting of a supervisory board that oversees a management board.

Unbiased expectations theory   A term structure theory that contends the forward rate is an unbiased predictor of the future spot rate. Also called the *pure expectations theory*.

Unconditional heteroskedasticity   When heteroskedasticity of the error variance is not correlated with the regression's independent variables.

Uncovered interest rate parity   The proposition that the expected return on an uncovered (i.e., unhedged) foreign currency (risk-free) investment should equal the return on a comparable domestic currency investment.

Underlying earnings   Earnings excluding nonrecurring components. Also referred to as *continuing earnings*, *core earnings*, or *persistent earnings*.

Unexpected earnings   The difference between reported EPS and expected EPS. Also referred to as an *earnings surprise*.

Unit root   A time series that is not covariance stationary is said to have a unit root.

Unrestricted model   A regression model with the complete set of independent variables.

Unsupervised learning   A machine learning approach that does not make use of labeled training data.

Upfront payment   The difference between the credit spread and the standard rate paid by the protection buyer if the standard rate is insufficient to compensate the protection seller. Also called *upfront premium*.

Upfront premium   See *upfront payment*.

Upstream   A transaction between two related companies, an investor company (or a parent company) and an associate company (or a subsidiary company) such that the associate company records a profit on its income statement. An example is a sale of inventory by the associate to the investor company or by a subsidiary to a parent company.

Validation sample   A data sample that is used to validate and tune a model.

Valuation   The process of determining the value of an asset or service either on the basis of variables perceived to be related to future investment returns or on the basis of comparisons with closely similar assets.

Value additivity   An arbitrage opportunity when the value of the whole equals the sum of the values of the parts.

Value at risk (VaR)   The minimum loss that would be expected a certain percentage of the time over a certain period of time given the assumed market conditions.

Value of growth   The difference between the actual value per share and the no-growth value per share.

Variance error   Describes how much a model's results change in response to new data from validation and test samples. Unstable models pick up noise and produce high variance error, causing overfitting and high out-of-sample error.

Variance inflation factor (VIF)   A statistic that quantifies the degree of multicollinearity in a model.

Vasicek model   A partial equilibrium term structure model that assumes interest rates are mean reverting and interest rate volatility is constant.

Vega   The change in a given derivative instrument for a given small change in volatility, holding everything else constant. A sensitivity measure for options that reflects the effect of volatility.

Venture capital investors   Private equity investors in development-stage companies.

Vertical ownership   Ownership structure in which a company or group that has a controlling interest in two or more holding companies, which in turn have controlling interests in various operating companies.

Vested benefit obligation   The actuarial present value of vested benefits.

Vesting date   The date that employees can first exercise stock options.

Visibility   The extent to which a company's operations are predictable with substantial confidence.

Voting caps   Legal restrictions on the voting rights of large share positions.

Web spidering (scraping or crawling) programs   Programs that extract raw content from a source, typically web pages.

Weighted average cost of capital (WACC)   A weighted average of the after-tax required rates of return on a company's common stock, preferred stock, and long-term debt, where the weights are the fraction of each source of financing in the company's target capital structure.

Weighted harmonic mean   See *harmonic mean*.

Winsorization   The process of replacing extreme values and outliers in a dataset with the maximum (for large value outliers) and minimum (for small value outliers) values of data points that are not outliers.

Write-down   A reduction in the value of an asset as stated in the balance sheet.

Yield curve factor model   A model or a description of yield curve movements that can be considered realistic when compared with historical data.

Zero   A bond that does not pay a coupon but is priced at a discount and pays its full face value at maturity.

Zero-coupon bond   A bond that does not pay interest during its life. It is issued at a discount to par value and redeemed at par. Also called *pure discount bond*.